The Latin American Economies

The Latin American Economies

a study of their institutional evolution

WILLIAM P. GLADE

Professor of Business and Economics
The University of Wisconsin

AMERICAN BOOK Van Nostrand Reinhold

New York • Toronto • London • Melbourne

For Anita, Genie, Patton, and John, who confirmed my belief in the advantages of balanced growth, and for Marlene, whose long-term expectations for this project were always optimistic

Preface

It has been said that the process of invention consists essentially of the combination and recombination of existing culture traits; indeed, the general process of culture growth is not altogether dissimilar. Constructive synthesis, based upon internally accumulated traits and cultural borrowing, can be readily discerned in the historical evolution of social forms and patterns of organization down through the ages.

The development of knowledge seems no less governed by the principles of this larger social process. The extended essay which follows clearly builds upon the work of a long procession of scholars, government officials, and more casual but often quite prescient observers who have, since the beginning of the Latin American venture, recorded a vast amount of information relevant to any study of economic processes in the region. The mountain of reports and administrative instructions produced by the Iberian bureaucracy, the journals and memoirs of foreign travelers in the Americas, the published research of historians (both Latin American and foreign)—all these, and other sources of data as well, contain much from which new meaning and significance can be extracted by applying the insights of present-day economic understanding.

True enough, much of the material can hardly be said to have come from unbiased, objective sources. On reading it, one receives the distinct impression that, while the Crusades may have ended in the thirteenth century, the crusading spirit, attached to a variety of causes, has been a force of continuing importance in Western civilization—especially, perhaps, in Latin America. The Iberian commentators, for example, wrote as men who were *engagés* and proud of it. Later, when other foreigners descended upon the area, they likewise were unmistakably carriers of a point of view, as well as of notebooks and quill pens. Only in comparatively recent times have historical scholars, both from Latin America and from elsewhere, achieved a measure of emancipation from the thralldom of the *leyenda negra*.

All along, of course, still other problems were created for those who would now attempt to view the development process retrospectively. A good deal of the written material was preserved for purposes other than those of economic analysis, and, in consequence, the gaps in reliable economic information are frequently wide. One of the several unfortunate aspects of the nineteenth-century period of instability, for instance, was the breakdown in official coverage of economic trends. From then on, the generally qualitative or descriptive reports of the colonial period gave way to premature quantitative records. These must be used no less carefully than the former because of the propensity to employ statistics to document aspirations rather than reality. Even today, the amount of indisputably accurate information on the domestic economic arrangements of the Latin American republics is surprisingly small, although, naturally, the availability of reliable data varies from country to country and considerable progress has been made in economic reporting during the past decade or two. For this, the international agencies and an assortment of technical missions deserve much credit, as do individual investigators from a variety of social science fields.

Yet, as the Talmud notes, one can learn much even from inferior sources—especially from Menahem ben Solomon's advice to "study and retain the heart of the matter and forget the chaff." Plentiful though the chaff of bias has been in many of the foregoing sources, because the writers of the past lived in a simpler age when ethnocentricity was deemed a less reprehensible trait than it is today, their particular perspective was often far from subtle and can generally be detected, and allowed for, without difficulty. Of late, the preconceptions contained in the documentation of economic events, though more sophisticated, are scarcely less obvious. Where data are actually missing or, if available, of highly questionable validity, one may often reconstruct, inferentially, and therefore tentatively, that which has occurred by drawing upon the propositions of contemporary development analysis.

The present work is based upon study of the written material pertaining to Latin American development, direct observations made in the course of several stays in various parts of the region, and the many discussions which I have been privileged to have with a multitude of persons in Latin America and the United States, who are concerned and involved with contemporary Latin American problems. A great deal was gained from their helpful information, and from the opportunity to review with them unsettled matters of fact and the vexed quesions of interpretation which abound in the field of Latin American economic history.

In addition, no little credit is due the scores of students with whom it has been my pleasure to work during six years of courses and seminars on Latin American development at the University of Wisconsin. Their bright and critical intellects afforded an unparalleled opportunity to test the explanatory value of many of the notions herein presented, and for their constructive role in the dialogue of the university setting I am especially grateful. That this was, indeed, an integral part of the research process lies in the nature of the book, for it was not conceived as a panoramic view of Latin American economic history, much less as a country-by-country summary of the present state of affairs.

Rather, if a liberal use of terminology may be permitted, the intention was that of developing a sort of institutional geography which defines the organizational topography of the economic landscape in Latin America: i.e., the features of social organization which lie behind the growth models of economic theory and which give particular values to the elements of those models. More explicitly, by examining the institutions in which the various economic functions are lodged, it was hoped to trace the evolving pattern of relationships between the public and the private sectors and the implications of their interaction for the resource allocation process. For this, an historical approach seemed essential and fruitful inasmuch as, in Kroeber's words, "it is of the nature of culture to be heavily conditioned by its own cumulative past" wherein "it is the qualitative and the contextual associations of phenomena that are important." *

Yet, to place the emphasis on "recognition of quality and of organizing patterns" is not without risk. It was virtually imperative to be able to subject the integrative-contextual approach employed in this work to the critical scrutiny of many other sets of eyes and the many hours spent with students, both in and out of the classroom, in a joint exploration of the materials were immensely useful. A number of alternative explanations of the discrete patterns which at one time seemed promising were subsequently discarded; others were considerably modified. Hopefully, that which has remained from this continuing *choc des idées* will provide sufficient *lumière* to help point the way for further research in the field.

Obviously, from the nature of the case, a complete acknowledgment of all those who contributed to the content of this study would be so lengthy as to be impractical. A collective *abrazo* of appreciation must therefore substitute for a long listing of names in which unintended omissions would be almost certain to occur, to the never-ending chagrin of the author. I must, however, thank specifically Eastin Nelson and Charles W. Anderson, who read some of the early chapters of the manuscript, and especially Albert Lauterbach who, with unparalleled generosity, read virtually the entire work with painstaking care. Each made valuable suggestions for revisions, though, naturally, they are all exempted from any responsibility for its remaining imperfections. Among the several research assistants who had a hand in the project, Anne Ryder Zimmerman merits special recognition for her tireless efforts in collecting the material, while Mary E. Wilkie and Juan Viudez assisted greatly in preparing the final draft of the manuscript. My wife, Marlene Joseph Glade, and Rafael Valiente were enormously helpful in the laborious task of proofreading galleys.

As is, perhaps, appropriate for a study dealing with the material order, thanks for financial support should also be made specific. The General Research Board of the University of Maryland; the Graduate Research Committee, the Center for International Business Research, and the School of Business of the University of Wisconsin; and the Ford Foundation, through its Faculty Research Fellowship program and its grant to the

---

* A. L. Kroeber, *The Nature of Culture*, Chicago: The University of Chicago Press, 1952, p. 4.

Ibero-American Program of the University of Wisconsin—all were generous in alleviating the "dollar gap" in the author's personal balance of payments. It is hoped that the product will justify their classifying such aid as a long-term capital investment rather than an unrequited transfer payment. None of these institutions is, of course, in any way committed to the point of view expressed in this study. The University of Maryland and the University of Wisconsin were also helpful in granting the necessary leaves of absence for research and writing.

The warm personal encouragement given by my colleagues at the Universities of Maryland and Wisconsin was no less important as a support for the undertaking. Acknowledgment of appreciation is particularly in order for the following: Professor and Mrs. Dudley Dillard, Professor and Mrs. Charles Heye, David J. M. Hooson, Dean E. A. Gaumnitz, J. H. Herriott, and E. R. Mulvihill. From all of these, I have learned much about the great value of psychic income, a resource of lasting qualities to which Eastin Nelson, Robert H. Montgomery, Clarence E. Ayres, and the late Erich W. Zimmermann also contributed in a way which was central to this research.

Quite rightly, too, the typists, who deciphered pages of obscure handwriting and bibliographical citations in unfamiliar languages, deserve a commendation, since it is not within my power to award them a Purple Heart; especially Sue Kehoe and Mable Bauer.

Finally, an inexpressible debt of gratitude must be confessed to those who were the longest and, in many ways, the most involved in the study, my *familia,* for I would use deliberately, in this connection, the Spanish word with its especially meaningful and encompassing connotations.

W. P. G.

Madison, Wisconsin
October 1966

Contents

PART THREE

FROM INDEPENDENCE TO WORLD WAR I

PART FOUR

FROM 1914 TO THE PRESENT

Part One

Introduction

I

The Study of Latin American Economic Development

So kaleidoscopic is the Latin American scene that the utility of the very term Latin America can be questioned as anything other than a geographical designation for that portion of the Western Hemisphere lying south of the United States.

In size the nations range from the continental proportions of Brazil with its 3,295,000 square miles of national territory (almost half of the South American continent) to El Salvador with only 8,260 square miles (see Table I-1). To be sure, geographical size can be misleading, for not all of these national territories are to the same extent occupied. Portions of Brazil, Venezuela, Colombia, Ecuador, Peru, Bolivia, and Paraguay which lie toward the interior of the continent are largely outside the ecumene, whereas nearly all of El Salvador and Uruguay and much of Argentina have been taken up in one type of settlement or another. Other sizable patches of unused or still unusable territory are found in southern and northern Chile, southern Panama, eastern Honduras and Nicaragua, the Yucatán peninsula, and northern Mexico. Even allowing for varying patterns of effective territorial occupation, the differences in extent of national ecumenes are substantial. Although the spatial distribution of minerals, useful soils, and the like often bears little relation to the distribution of areas encompassed by national boundaries, it is scarcely surprising, with territorial differences of this magnitude, that the natural-resource endowments of the Latin American countries vary considerably. Thus, the general resource base, including industrially relevant raw materials, of the larger countries—Brazil, Mexico, Colombia, Venezuela, Peru—is more ample and diversified than that of, say, Ecuador or Panama. This is a factor of some significance for present-day economic development possibilities in the context of compartmentalized national economies. Even in Central America, which constitutes an area quite a bit smaller than any one of the seven largest countries, the range of the resource endowment is narrow. A recent United Nations study indicated, for instance, that local raw materials are not available for many of the industries being considered for development in that region.[1]

Population differences are also extreme, ranging from Brazil, with 80 million people, to Panama, with scarcely more than a million. But population differences alone fail to express the range of dissimilarity among Latin America's peoples. The ethnic composition of the populations varies almost

3

Table I-1. Latin American Countries; Area and Population

COUNTRY	AREA (SQUARE MILES)	1964 POPULATION
Brazil	3,294,600	79,830,000
Argentina	1,072,750	21,340,000
Mexico	761,601	39,500,000
Peru	496,222	11,050,000
Colombia	439,513	16,520,000
Bolivia	424,162	4,030,000
Venezuela	352,142	8,646,000
Chile	286,396	8,455,000
Paraguay	157,047	1,900,000
Ecuador	105,743	4,800,000
Uruguay	68,369	2,570,000
Nicaragua	57,143	1,590,000
Cuba	44,218	6,743,000[a]
Honduras	43,277	2,150,000
Guatemala	42,042	4,300,000
Panama	29,200	1,200,000
Costa Rica	19,695	1,402,000
Dominican Republic	18,682	3,440,000
Haiti	10,714	4,478,000
El Salvador	8,260	2,716,000

SOURCE: Inter-American Development Bank.
[a] 1960 estimate, U.N., *Monthly Bulletin of Statistics*, Vol. 15, No. 4.

as much, and it is an important factor in economic prospects, since culture traits can favor or impede modernization. Though it is difficult to arrive at an exact classification scheme and though census information is far from accurate, it can be said that, ethnically speaking, roughly 60 per cent of the population is Indian in Bolivia, Ecuador, Guatemala, and Paraguay, and some 40 per cent is Indian in Honduras. In Peru, the figure lies between 40 and 50 per cent, and in Mexico and El Salvador between 20 and 30 per cent. For all other countries the Indian population is substantially less or negligible.

Of the non-Indian portion of the Latin American population, some two-thirds of the people of Mexico, Colombia, Chile, Venezuela, and Nicaragua are designated as mestizo, that is, of mixed European and Indian ancestry. In Honduras, Costa Rica, and Panama about half the population is mestizo. In El Salvador, the figure is somewhat larger, but in Peru, Bolivia, Guatemala, Ecuador, and Paraguay, the mestizo portion is between 30 and 40 per cent. For Brazil and Cuba, mestizos constitute about a fifth of the total population. On the other hand, 90 per cent of Uruguayans and Argentines are of pure or nearly pure European origin, while for Costa Rica and Brazil the corresponding figures are 50 and 40 per cent respectively. In Colombia, Chile, and Cuba, the predominantly Caucasian group makes up between 20 and 30 per cent of the total. Almost all of the Haitians and four-fifths of the Dominicans are Negroid to one degree or another, as are nearly half of the Brazilians and Cubans and a third of the Panamanians. For the study of economic development, however, African ancestry can be regarded as of little consequence, except in Haiti, where political circumstances greatly retarded the assimilation of European culture traits. Elsewhere, the cultural significance of the Negroid elements appears largely limited to music, dance, dialectal speech variations, folklore, and some social practices whose economic bearing is remote. As a whole, assimilation of European cultural norms by the descendants of African slaves has been far greater than by some indigenous groups, probably because the sanctions of the original African cultures were weakened by the transatlantic move and subsequent mixing of different tribal groups. Among the Negroid population, socio-economic stratification is generally more important than ethnic differentiation.

Over the years, a vast amount of nonsense has been written concerning the implications of these racial differences for personality—e.g., the innate passivity of Indian blood, the psychogenetic conflicts of various racial mixtures—and by no means all of this fantasy has been turned out by pre-twentieth-century authors who knew no better. Even today the arguments in favor of immigration are sometimes couched in racist terms, though racism seems to be a relatively unimportant factor in Latin America in general. Yet there is another national differentiation, related to but not identical with racial origins, which is of greater economic relevance: the distinction between the ladino, or Europeanized, population (which includes some of those racially labeled as Indians) and the Indian population which is culturally identifiable as Indian. This distinction relates to linguistic differences and the consequent problems of communication and the transmission of skills and information, to differing patterns of taste and consumption, to variations in the structures of economic organization, and generally to the degree of participation in more modern forms of economic activity, especially the market economy. The persistence of indigenous subcultures in Peru, for example, is a factor behind a recent (June 1961) estimate by the economic research division of the Banco Continental that out of a total national population approaching 12 million, "the number of active consumers . . . is placed at no more than 3 million."

Size of national territories, size of national populations, and population composition are not the only distinguishing characteristics among Latin American countries, though they are interrelated with many of the other differences such as income levels and employment patterns. A common thread of poverty runs through all the countries, at least when they are viewed from the perspective of northwestern Europe, the United States, and Canada. But even this is a relative matter (see Table I-2). Though the per

Table I-2. Recent Aggregate and Per Capita Output Estimates: U.S. $ equivalents

COUNTRY	A (1961)		B (1961)		C (1956 EXCEPT WHERE NOTED)	
	GNP (MILLIONS $)	GNP PER CAPITA	GNP (MILLIONS $)	GNP PER CAPITA	NATIONAL INCOME (MILLIONS $)	INCOME PER CAPITA
Argentina	7,700	379	12,100	600 (1950$)	8,383	439
Bolivia	437	113	387	102 (1958$)	222	(1955) 70
Brazil	13,546	186	19,600	264 (1950$)	13,164	225
Chile	3,506	453	4,708	595 (1960$)	2,404	356
Colombia	4,300	283	4,810	334 (1950$)	4,283	338
Costa Rica	420	344			312	328
Dominican Republic	680	218	652	210 (1950$)	574	228
Ecuador	810	182	731	165 (1950$)	614	167
El Salvador	550	220	516	208 (1953$)	482	220
Guatemala	680	175	645	170 (1950$)	527	162
Haiti	300	71	311	74 (1955$)	230	(1955) 70
Honduras	395	207	340	172 (1950$)	283	170
Mexico	11,280	313	8,700	244 (1950$)	6,725	227
Nicaragua	325	213	350	223 (1958$)	(GNP) 146	(1950) 138
Panama	460	416	460		246	270
Paraguay	236	130	211	116 (1953$)	160	102
Peru	2,062	181	2,183	198 (1960$)	1,161	124
Uruguay	1,290	450			938	(1955) 359

Table I-2. (CONTINUED)

	A (1961)		B (1961)		C (1956 EXCEPT WHERE NOTED)	
	GNP (MILLIONS $)	GNP PER CAPITA	GNP (MILLIONS $)	GNP PER CAPITA	NATIONAL INCOME (MILLIONS $)	INCOME PER CAPITA
Venezuela	5,290	692	8,000	1,050 (1957$)	4,328	750

SOURCES: "A" columns: Statistics and Reports Division, Agency for International Development, estimates issued 30 April 1963. Estimates in national currencies were converted into current U.S. dollar equivalents by use of official exchange rates in most instances, or effective rates in some. They are unadjusted for disparities in the purchasing power of the dollar, though variations among countries in this respect do exist, even substantial variations.

"B" columns: Economic Development Division, Inter-American Development Bank. Dollar equivalents computed for value of dollar in year indicated. Estimates issued between 4 May 1962 and 10 April 1963. Exchange rate conversion ratios not indicated.

"C" columns: Institute of International Studies and Overseas Administration, University of Oregon, "Problems of Latin American Economic Development," Study No. 6 in *United States-Latin American Relations*, Compilation of Studies prepared under the direction of the Subcommittee on American Republics Affairs of the Committee on Foreign Relations of the United States Senate. Senate Document No. 125, 86th Congress, 2nd Session, Washington: 31 August 1960. In most cases the exchange rate chosen for conversion into current dollars was that applicable to the bulk of the imports.

NOTE: The disparities among the estimates reflect, among other things: differing base years of the dollar, differing exchange conversion rates (as between official and free rates and as among multiple rates of exchange), differing estimates of the GNP's in terms of local currencies, differing population estimates, etc. In addition, "C" columns were computed for earlier years and on a national income rather than GNP basis. Had, say, the estimates of national income (total and per capita) contained in the *Statistical Abstract of Latin America* (published by the University of California at Los Angeles) been cited, the result would have been a fourth listing of numbers displaying still other differences from the rest. In the 1961 edition, for example, the per capita incomes in Argentina, Brazil, and Peru were reported as being $296 (1959), $145 (1959), and $97 (1958) respectively.

It is obvious that in comparisons between countries all such statistical estimates should be used with caution and only to indicate general orders of magnitude, though even here, the reader will notice, the evidence tends to be confusing. The figures have been intentionally chosen to illustrate this major hazard in the field of Latin American economics.

capita income in Argentina is only about one-fifth that of the United States, the per capita income in Haiti is less than one-fifth that of Argentina and bears about a one-to-five relationship to the level of per capita income in such countries as Colombia, Chile, and Costa Rica. Comparing the per capita income data with the information on population composition, it will be seen that the former tend to reflect the low productivity and income levels associated with nonladino culture groups. The seven nations in which a substantial segment of the population retains more archaic cultural patterns (Bolivia, Ecuador, Guatemala, Haiti, Honduras, Paraguay, and Peru) are among the lowest per capita income countries of Latin America. Even in economically expanding Mexico, the incomplete assimilation of indigenous peoples partly explains the low per capita income figures in certain regions of the republic.

Population size and per capita income figures, with all that they imply with respect to population composition, contribute much to an understanding of present-day economic structures and employment patterns. Within the context of semiclosed national economies, i.e., economies somewhat insulated from each other and the rest of the outside world by trade restrictions and other barriers, industrialization has tended to be based upon the national market. This has limited the degree of industrialization which can be supported, for few of the newer nonextractive industries have thus far been established with an eye toward export markets. Of all the Latin American countries, only the Brazilian, Argentine, and Mexican markets might approximate (or perhaps in Brazil slightly exceed) the size of the market for industrial products in, say, Belgium or the Netherlands.

In the light of these considerations, it is no surprise that the seven largest countries in Latin American (Brazil, Mexico, Argentina, Colombia, Peru, Chile, Venezuela) are also, though not in quite the same order, the seven leading countries in aggregate value of manufacturing output (Brazil, Argentina, Mexico, Venezuela, Colombia, Chile, Peru). The difference in order of ranking corresponds roughly to the total purchasing power available within each national market, though it should be mentioned that Cuba is excluded for lack of comparable data. Brazil, Argentina, and Mexico account for two-thirds of the total Latin American manufacturing output. Many other conditions bear upon the extent of industrial development, among them the regional distribution of purchasing power, extent of urbanization, industrial resource availabilities, supply of entrepreneurial talent, national policy, and so on. For the moment, however, we are prescinding from these other considerations. Thus, despite their lower per capita income figures, both Brazil and Mexico stand high in manufacturing development— partly because of their large populations; even small per capita units of purchasing power, when added together in sufficient quantity, can create a significant market for certain kinds of manufactured goods. Both countries, moreover, have developed substantial industrial sectors even with 50 to 60 per cent of their labor forces employed in the agricultural sector.

The leading industrial positions held by Argentina and Chile relate closely to their population size, per capita income levels, and advanced degree of urbanization. In both countries, the agricultural labor force represents less than 30 per cent of total employment, a proportion matched only by much smaller Uruguay. Similarly, the ranking of Colombia follows closely its population and per capita income standing. The two other industrial leaders, Peru and Venezuela, demonstrate a special interplay of population and income factors. Peru, though relatively large in terms of total population, stands seventh in manufactures as a reflection of low per capita income levels. Venezuela, though smaller in total population, has been able to industrialize rapidly in recent years because of high urban income levels produced by the oil boom and a marked urbanization trend. Less than 35 per cent of the Venezuelan labor force is today employed in agriculture.

For the rest of the Latin American nations (excluding Uruguay, as mentioned above), employment patterns reflect the overwhelmingly agrarian nature of their economic structures and the narrow range of industrialization possibilities under prevailing circumstances. In Honduras, Haiti, Nicaragua, the Dominican Republic, and Guatemala, the portion of the labor force in agriculture is 70 per cent or more. In Bolivia, El Salvador, Paraguay, Panama, Costa Rica, Brazil, Peru, and Mexico, the portion ranges between a half and two-thirds. In Colombia the rural labor force is slightly under half of the total, owing to the large scale exodus induced, in part, by the widespread rural violence of recent years.

The foregoing relationships only suggest some of the differences among the Latin American economies. They merely hint at the nature of an accounting for these differences, but do not provide easy clues to understanding the Latin American economic scene today. A glance at Tables I-3, I-4, and I-5 is enough to bring an immediate appreciation of the varied economic experience of the Latin American nations in recent years.

To add to the complexity, singular economic disparities exist within individual countries. The cultural distance between Brazil's impoverished northeast and São Paulo, one of the most diversified industrial complexes of the world, is as great as the geographical distance between the two areas. The Federal District is the hub of Mexico's modern industrial structure, but less than half a day's drive to the north lies the hopeless destitution of the Mesquital Valley. Contrasts of this nature abound throughout Latin America. Peru, for example, is generally considered to be one of the most tradition-clad nations of Latin America, and its low per capita income rank would seem to place it unequivocally in the more backward group. In the jungles of eastern Peru live tribes who have hardly caught up with the iron age. Yet the sugar estates of the Peruvian coast are among the most productive and efficient in the world, while high in the sierra the organization of production and distribution has remained in many places as primitive as it was centuries earlier. It is commonly supposed that in countries like Peru the domestic supply of the spirit of enterprise and initiative constitutes a

Table I-3. Indexes of Total Gross National Product (in 1960 Prices), Selected Countries 1950–1961: 1950 = 100

	1950	1951	1952	1953	1954	1955	1956	1957	1958	1959	1960	1961	ANNUAL GROWTH RATE[a]		
													Total GNP	Population	Per Capita GNP
Argentina	100	103	96	101	105	110	109	113	116	111	115	121	1.8	2.0	-0.3
Brazil	100	107	111	114	123	128	132	142	152	160	170	178	5.4	2.4	2.9
Chile	100	99	107	116	121	126	119	124	129	131	134	137	2.9	2.3	0.6
Colombia	100	103	110	117	125	130	135	137	140	149	152	157	4.1	2.8	1.3
Costa Rica	100	101	113	127	134	143	148	155	161	167	175	178	5.4	3.9	1.4
Cuba	100	107	113	103	106	111	115	131	122	120	–	–	–	2.1	–
Ecuador	100	104	113	117	127	130	134	141	145	151	160	163	4.5	3.3	1.3
Guatemala	100	98	105	107	103	119	129	134	142	152	157	161	4.4	2.9	1.4
Honduras	100	107	113	121	122	126	130	145	147	153	160	167	4.8	3.2	1.6
Mexico	100	107	108	107	115	127	135	140	146	152	161	169	4.9	3.0	1.8
Nicaragua	100	107	126	125	142	155	157	170	175	172	181	187	5.9	3.4	2.4
Panama	100	104	112	120	120	130	132	148	151	160	167	178	5.4	2.8	2.5
Peru	100	106	112	120	116	127	132	133	135	128	135	139	3.0	2.5	0.5
Venezuela	100	107	116	126	138	150	166	185	187	202	205	206	6.8	3.1	3.6
TOTALS[b]															
GNP, Total	100.0	104.7	107.5	111.2	117.8	124.9	129.2	136.9	141.5	145.3	151.5	156.9	4.1	–	–
Population	100.0	102.2	104.7	107.3	109.9	112.6	115.5	118.4	121.4	124.5	127.9	131.3	–	2.5	–
Per Capita GNP	100.0	102.8	102.8	103.6	107.2	111.2	112.0	115.7	116.9	116.9	118.9	119.7	–	–	1.6

[a]Compound rates 1950-1961.

[b]Twenty republics. For earlier years (generally 1950-1958), trends for the six republics not shown (Bolivia, Dominican Republic, El Salvador, Haiti, Paraguay, and Uruguay) were based on the combined total of the fourteen republics shown above. These fourteen countries accounted for 95 percent of estimated total GNP for the twenty republics in 1960.

SOURCE: U.S. Agency for International Development, Statistics and Reports Division, *Latin America, Trends in Production, 1950-1961*, Washington: July, 1962.

Table I-4. *Manufacturing Indexes, Eight Latin American Republics: 1950 = 100*

	1950	1951	1952	1953	1954	1955
Argentina	100	103	94	93	100	109
Brazil	100	106	111	122	133	148
Chile	100	119	133	143	149	143
Colombia	100	104	116	132	136	139
Guatemala	100	99	104	103	104	109
Mexico	100	106	104	104	114	126
Peru	100	118	122	135	146	154
Venezuela	100	121	137	159	187	216

	1956	1957	1958	1959	1960	1961
Argentina	108	112	117	102	104	116
Brazil	157	166	194	218	241	261
Chile	153	149	153	174	170	180
Colombia	154	157	158	171	178	183
Guatemala	119	132	144	153	153	161
Mexico	139	147	154	166	180	189
Peru	164	178	177	182	192	197
Venezuela	233	265	287	337	332	349

SOURCE: U.S. Agency for International Development, Statistics and Reports Division, *Latin America, Trends in Production, 1950—1961,* Washington: July 1962.

Table I-5. *Agricultural Production Indexes by Country: 1950 = 100*

	1950	1951	1952	1953	1954	1955	1956	1957	1958	1959	1960	1961
Argentina	100	78	108	107	112	111	120	122	121	111	103	111
Bolivia	100	109	108	109	108	95	91	98	106	110	111	113
Brazil	100	99	103	109	112	118	120	127	137	154	151	162
Chile	100	105	107	115	114	124	121	126	139	144	141	140
Colombia	100	113	116	120	125	134	137	143	151	159	163	167
Costa Rica	100	105	142	129	140	118	132	147	162	160	181	178
Cuba	100	121	95	97	88	93	111	113	114	114	122	109
Dominican Rep.	100	104	104	108	111	123	127	135	143	134	170	173
Ecuador	100	95	117	117	129	137	159	157	169	186	198	199
El Salvador	100	106	120	110	137	140	152	157	163	157	171	191
Guatemala	100	101	111	120	127	131	132	148	149	149	161	175
Haiti	100	96	104	109	99	116	96	104	97	114	102	121
Honduras	100	98	107	107	103	105	129	129	136	132	133	143
Mexico	100	103	108	112	130	141	145	157	171	167	172	179
Nicaragua	100	113	176	213	276	247	278	282	287	242	282	313
Panama	100	95	119	135	135	142	142	144	155	161	160	165
Paraguay	100	100	108	111	111	107	108	118	119	119	113	120
Peru	100	108	117	118	125	124	113	118	124	133	130	134
Uruguay	100	100	102	120	116	109	100	110	93	82	106	104
Venezuela	100	108	115	109	129	127	134	140	145	154	167	174
20 REPUBLICS												
Total	100	98	107	110	114	118	123	129	134	137	137	144
Per Capita	100	96	102	102	104	104	107	109	110	110	107	107

SOURCE: U.S. Agency for International Development, Statistics and Reports Division, *Latin America, Trends in Production, 1950–1961,* Washington: July 1962.

critical deficiency in the economic setting. But the meteoric rise of Peru to a position of preeminence in the world's fishing industry attests to the capacity of Peruvian entrepreneurs, drawn largely from the small urban sector, to seize lucrative opportunities and turn them to account—with practically no assistance, it might be added, from governmental *fomento* or promotion agencies.

From a sectoral perspective, internal contrasts are also evident, with modern enterprises such as the Colombian textile mills and the Venezuelan petroleum firms playing a striking counterpoint to the backward hoe-agriculture which, with its slash-and-burn techniques of land clearing, can still be found in both countries, and in almost every other Latin American economy as well. For the region as a whole, the 1 per cent of the labor force which is in mining produces 5 per cent of the gross domestic product, while the 14.6 per cent of the labor force which is employed in manufacturing accounts for approximately 22 per cent of the gross domestic product. In contrast, the 47 per cent of the labor force which is in agriculture generates only 22 per cent of the gross domestic product. Even this figure, low as it is, overstates the productivity of agricultural labor, for included in the gross measure are the comparatively efficient firms of the agricultural export sector and the productive farm units of the Platine republics. Were it possible to subtract these elements, the residual level of productivity in agriculture would be lower still.

Apart from the overall problem of underdevelopment in Latin America as reflected in per capita income figures and other indices, there exists, therefore, considerable unevenness in national development. Side by side with modern sectors which make substantial contributions to national economic strength are found backward sectors and conditions which not only weaken the economy but also inhibit the capacity of the leading sectors to develop further. So prevalent and pronounced is this debilitating unevenness of development, in fact, that it may constitute something of a general characteristic in Latin America. Only Argentina and Uruguay are partial exceptions.

Two primary objectives of a study of the Latin American economic setting are to account (1) for the marked differential development which is discernible among the several national economies of the area and (2) for the enormous intersectoral development disparities, for these often contribute tellingly to regional and national variations. By approaching the subject in this fashion rather than as a blanket case of underdevelopment, one is in a position to state the nature of the task which confronts Latin America today: it is that of locating the weak or backward segments of economic life, determining their dimensions and ramifications, and settling upon reasonably appropriate remedies to reduce their detrimental impact on the national economy without impairing the islands of strength which have been built up thus far. However, for reasons that will become evident during this study, the way ahead to sustained economic advance is far from easy.

GEOGRAPHY AND RESOURCES IN LATIN AMERICAN DEVELOPMENT

The roots of this complex diversity lie in the historical interaction of cultural and geographical factors in Latin America. While this study focuses on the institutional side of the process, geography has also functioned as a limiting and forwarding agent in Latin American economic development; it is difficult, in fact, to overemphasize the importance of geographical factors in an area in which geography presents itself in such a dramatic manner. Furthermore, geography's economic significance has been modified only in a limited way by the overlay and interplay of social phenomena.

Perhaps the bearing of geography on Latin American economic development can best be illustrated in terms of the resource concept. This is the meeting point of geographical, technological, and institutional data and is fundamental to the analysis of this book. Inasmuch as the economic concept of resources has a dual aspect, referring to things which are both useful and usable, it is clear that more is involved than just the things themselves. In other words, the term is conceptually more extensive than the data presented by geography and geology alone.

Whether a particular item of the landscape is a resource or not is a function of three mutually conditioning elements: the interaction between natural (i.e., nonhuman) factors and cultural factors along a continuum of time. Natural factors are such elements as soils, climates, minerals, and location, which in conventional usage are called natural resources. These elements are not, however, resources if the other two components of the resource concept are lacking, and for this reason mere inventories of these items are not the same as resource inventories, properly speaking. The cultural factors in the resource equation are the complex of technological and institutional conditions which give rise to uses for the raw ingredients of nature and make possible their appropriation and utilization for those ends.

Usefulness, a notion inherent in the resource concept, comprehends all the elements which make up market demand, domestic and foreign—institutional elements such as wants, scales of preferences, and the social distribution of economic power, technological elements such as input requirements implied by the technical coefficients of production, and elements such as the level of income which are inseparably institutional and technological in character. *Usability,* on the other hand, depends upon such elements as the stock of scientific and engineering knowledge, the technical skills of management and labor, capital equipment, and the organization of production and marketing. While conceptually it is possible to dichotomize technological and institutional elements, reality admits of no such clear-cut distinction. Technological considerations influence the institutional structure, which in turn conditions the size, character, and utilization of the technological endowment. Finally, as technology is cumulative in character and as institutional structure changes with time, the concept of resources is necessarily imbued with a temporal dimension. Actual resources are, therefore, largely a function of past resource availabilities and resource use.

Thus, "resources" is not a static concept but a dynamic one in that economic resources are functionally related to a complex of variables. It is this characteristic which renders so many descriptions of Latin American resources unhelpful. In historical writing the resource availabilities and potentialities of an earlier era have often been looked at, invalidly, in the light of latter-day resource patterns. One need only refer to the conventional historic treatment of the colonial era in the La Plata region to illustrate this point. Repeatedly the position has been taken that Spanish colonial administration grossly neglected the alleged resource wealth of the Argentine. It is true that at the end of the colonial era, the Argentine pampa was still largely unexploited and that late in the nineteenth century it became one of the most richly productive regions of the entire Latin American area. The inference, however, that with less myopic policies the pampa might have become an important center of development at an earlier time is altogether misleading. It became a rich resource area in the nineteenth century only because of trends and forces which were historically inoperative earlier.

Indeed, the resource base of modern Latin America differs considerably from that of both the nineteenth century and the long colonial period. Though development is resource-using, it is also resource-creating. The Cerro Bolívar iron ore deposits in eastern Venezuela, for example, had no resource value up until quite recent times; under prevailing conditions they were not economically exploitable. Known for decades, the deposits became valuable resources as fuller geological exploration by U.S. companies revealed the dimensions of the mineralized area, as the Venezuelan government adopted legislation favorable to foreign mining investments, as the exhaustion of certain U.S. iron ore reserves in the 1940's forced iron and steel producers to look abroad for raw materials and to shift production facilities to the eastern seaboard, as advances in maritime shipping technology made long-distance iron-ore shipments more economical, and as abundant supplies of low-cost capital were available for investment in expensive river-dredging operations, the construction of new rail and port facilities, and the application of mass-mining techniques.

Failure to distinguish between resources and natural elements, as well as ignorance and wishful thinking, lies behind the El Dorado myth which has long colored discussion of Latin American resources. Time and again, various regions in Latin America have been described in figures of speech similar to "a beggar seated on a bench of gold." [2] While real El Dorados have been found which paid off handsomely, often much more was needed than mere perception of the landscape to translate geographical realities into resources.

The land problem is a case in which confusion of geographical data with resources has led to unfortunate policy failure in a number of countries. Alongside recognition of the obvious problems of overcrowding on uneconomically small plots (*minifundismo*) and the concentration of large landholdings in a few ownership units (*latifundismo*), reference is often made to extensive unoccupied areas in which the soil is reasonably fertile and the climatic conditions benign. For some, mainly the large landholders, settlement of these empty lands has appeared as the deus ex machina for resolving agrarian problems. But whether these unoccupied lands have an actual resource value and, hence, much relevance to the discussion of agrarian policy depends not only upon their natural characteristics but also upon their accessibility to consuming centers and the availability of capital for land clearing, land drainage, and the like. It is not at all certain that, under current conditions, many of these areas are significant resources. Frequently they have remained unoccupied or sparsely settled for very good economic reasons, and to the extent this is the case policy deliberations have been predicated on a sort of myth of open spaces.[3]

Thus, any extended examination of Latin American resources is plainly interwoven with the general economic evolution of the region and must be deferred to later chapters in which it can be taken up in the appropriate context. Suffice it to state at this point that geography has been one of the chief bases for differentiation in development, especially in the external sectors of the Latin American economies. Argentina and Uruguay, for example, are mainly exporters of temperate-zone agricultural products: grains, wool, and meat. Chile, Venezuela, and Bolivia are primarily suppliers of minerals to the world market, exporting copper, petroleum, and tin respectively. Except for Mexico and Peru, which enjoy the advantages of a diversified export pattern, the other countries are mainly exporters of tropical-zone agricultural commodities: coffee is the chief export of Brazil, Colombia, Costa Rica, El Salvador, Guatemala, and Haiti; bananas are the main export of Ecuador, Honduras, and Panama; and sugar is the principal export of Cuba and the Dominican Republic. The major export of Nicaragua is cotton, followed by coffee. Coffee is also the second export of Ecuador and Honduras, while bananas are the second export of Costa Rica and Guatemala. Timber and cotton are the main Paraguayan exports, though livestock products are also gaining in importance, as they are in Nicaragua.

Notwithstanding the diversity of total exports and the variety of national resource patterns, the composition of Latin American exports reveals a certain uniformity. By and large, Latin American exports move abroad as raw or semiprocessed commodities—a feature which indicates that in all Latin American countries, irrespective of different levels of economic attainment, the structure of comparative advantage is still close to nature and only moderately influenced by technological advances and the higher skills of organization and production know-how. For this, geographical factors are themselves partly responsible, as can be illustrated by a brief look at two aspects, topography and vegetation, and a few observations on soils and climate.

In Middle America, the term ordinarily used to designate Mexico and Central America, the rugged terrain which characterizes much of Latin America is a dominant geographical feature. The extensive central Mexican plateau occupies most of the territory from the northern border to south of Mexico City. Broken here and there by mountains, especially in the southern portion, the plateau is bounded by ranges which separate the highlands from the *tierras calientes* of the coastal plains. Toward the center of the Republic the ranges converge and, with a few exceptions, the terrain south to the low-lying Isthmus of Tehuantepec is dominated by verticality. Beyond the Isthmus rise the Chiapas highlands which merge, to the south, with the volcanic ranges that cover the major portion of the land area of Guatemala, Honduras, El Salvador, and Nicaragua. In this region, the Yucatán peninsula affords the greatest expanse of low elevation territory. A break in the mountains in southern Nicaragua provided an overland route for the "forty-niners" and has given rise to intermittent speculation and study concerning its feasibility as the location for an east-west canal. In northern Costa Rica, however, the mountains reappear, running down through that country and Panama to terminate in the Serranía de Baudó of the Colombian Pacific coast.

In South America the formidable Andean chain—the world's longest continuous mountain range—commences along Venezuela's Caribbean coast and, with various subdivisions, extends down through the populous central portions of Colombia, Ecuador, Peru, and Bolivia. Below Bolivia, it forms the border between Chile and Argentina all the way to the southernmost extremity of the hemisphere. The triangular shape of the South American continent is determined not only by the Andean cordilleras of the west coast but also, on the east, by the Patagonian plateau of southern Argentina, the Guiana highland block with its scarplike edge in the Amazonian interior, and, between them, the long Brazilian escarpment which fronts closely upon the south Atlantic. Behind the last-mentioned of these lie the hilly uplands, the low mountains, and the *planalto central* of the Brazilian interior.

Thus, along virtually the entire west coast of Latin America and much of the east coast as well, high elevations are found close to the sea. Only in three or four places do navigable rivers of any importance offer an easy penetration of the hinterland. Of these, the Paraná-Paraguay system of the River Plate region has had the most long-standing value, while the Orinoco of Venezuela, broken by rapids 600 miles upstream, has acquired importance only with the dredging carried on in connection with resource developments of the past two decades. The Amazon, navigable by ocean-going vessels for a greater distance than any other river in the world, serves, unfortunately, a vast territory which has historically been of little consequence except for the brief but spectacular rubber boom around the turn of this century. In Colombia, the Magdalena River valley has had historical importance as a trade route from the Caribbean into the interior, but the river, because of numerous rapids along its course, leaves a great deal to be desired as an easily navigable artery. For the most part, therefore, Latin America has been denied the substantial advantages of cheap fluvial transport afforded by the river systems in both the United States and Europe—river systems which represented important substitutes for investment in transport capital in the early stages of development.

The broken topography of South America has presented obstacles to interregional communications and transmontane economic interchange, particularly in the West of South America where the passes across the Andes are few and far between and at high elevations. Thus, commercial intercourse between areas lying on the coastal side of the range and the interior has been held to a minimum by this wall, as has traffic within the populous mountain region itself. Both the construction and maintenance of transport facilities in such difficult terrain are extremely costly; grading, bridging, and tunneling requirements are high, and landslides, rockslides, and washouts occur with frequency. On occasion, some of the higher Andean passes are also blocked by snow. Consequently, transport charges have always restricted the region's capacity for economic performance. Productive capacity is also impaired by steep slopes which subtract large amounts of acreage from the land available for cultivation without initial investment in terracing, retaining walls, and the like.

As assets, on the other hand, the mountains contain highly mineralized regions and provide Latin America with an estimated 11 per cent of the world's hydroelectric power potential.[4] This compensates somewhat, in the present era though not previously, for the region's generally deficient supply of coal, which amounts to less than 1 per cent of the world's known reserves.[5] By varying the effect of latitude with altitudinal controls, the mountains also provide temperate regions even in the tropics. The milder climates of the *tierras templadas* of the Mexican *mesa central*, the Central American highlands, and the scattered intermontane valleys of the Andean region supplement the more extensive temperate-zone lands of Chile, Argentina, Uruguay, and southern Brazil and permit the cultivation of a variety of crops which do not ordinarily prosper in tropical latitudes. While these temperate areas are often small and widely scattered, they contribute possibilities for some diversification of agricultural production in a majority of the countries—subject to limits imposed by locational factors or economic distance.

Over much of Latin America, climate, elevation, and latitude combine to support a luxuriant growth of vegetation. A variety of tropical climates tending to be warm and wet (relieved, in some areas, by dry seasons) extend, at lower elevations, from central Mexico down over most of South America to below the Tropic of Capricorn. A dense *selva,* or jungle, lies over the huge Amazonian region, and tropical scrub woodlands, montane rain forests, and tropical semideciduous forests occupy most of the rest of this climatic area. The arid and semiarid area north of the twenty-second degree of latitude in Mexico, the Pacific coastal desert which runs the length of Peru and northern Chile, the central Chilean valley, the semiarid Patagonian plateau, the pampas, the savannas and *caatinga* of Brazil, and the *llanos* or grasslands of Venezuela and Colombia constitute the chief exceptions to the assortment of forest coverings—along with some of the intermontane valleys, the higher elevations of the mountains, and the semibarren altiplano of Peru and Bolivia. Altogether approximately 40 per cent of Latin America is forested.

Though the region contains nearly a quarter of the total forests of the world, it does not possess anywhere near a quarter of the world's forest resources. Most of the tropical woods are hardwoods, often extremely hard. These require heavy and costly equipment for extraction, processing, and transport and are less serviceable for most purposes than softer temperate-zone woods. Selective logging is usually unfeasible because the composition of the dense tropical forest stands tends to be much variegated, with as many as eighty-five species from several tree families within a single square kilometer, all with widely differing physical and chemical properties. Some varieties are difficult to bark, others cannot be chipped, others may not burn because of their high density and silica content, and many are so heavy and dense that they do not even float, thereby ruling out a cheap means of transport. Heavy underbrush also makes timber extraction difficult, especially of the larger trees which abound in tropical jungles. Yet fairly quick removal, processing, and shipment is often essential because of the difficulty or impossibility of longer-term storage; bacterial, fungoid, and insect attack make for rapid decay after felling. In addition, much of the forested region is simply inaccessible, lying far overland from the consuming centers and often separated from them by a formidable twin barricade of mountains and the forest itself.[6] The expenses of clearing, of constructing adequate roadbeds, and of maintaining these in the face of washouts lead to a double cost burden: the expense of bringing supplies into the area (hence raising regional costs of production) and the cost of moving the regional product out to extraregional markets. Small wonder, then, that José Eustacio Rivera wrote in *La Vorágine* of the "inhuman" jungle with its malaria, its "tangled misanthropic undergrowth, the stagnant backwaters and swamps." In his graphic portrayal of the effects of the jungle on the human senses, he was also making a telling commentary on Latin American resources.

The vast tropical wilderness and the mountains have rendered much of the region inaccessible, or accessible only on costly terms, and have made a substantial portion of the Latin American land area unsuitable for lumbering, agriculture, or other types of productive activities. Even were the expense of land clearing to be assumed, the climatic and soil conditions—heavy rainfall, thin topsoil, and poor soil structure—would produce a rapid leaching out of the few nutrients present, and in a number of areas, would lead to the formation of a subsurface hardpan inhibiting the practice of agriculture. In fact, the crude slash-and-burn techniques of clearing and shifting cultivation have, for all their low productivity, long represented the chief feasible method of deriving even a bare subsistence from the area.[7] Even where the forest cover is less dense, as in the Chaco region of Argentina, Paraguay, and Bolivia and the northeastern Brazilian backlands (or *sertões*), and where the forest is virtually absent, as in the *llanos* of Colombia and Venezuela, the economic prospects are only slightly more favorable. In both cases, the seasonal distribution of rainfall is such that periods of flooding alternate with periods of extreme aridity. In the *sertões* there is the additional complication that the region is afflicted with irregularly recurring intervals of severe drought. Thus, as Pierre Gourou has pointed out in his important work, *The Tropical World,* the agricultural potentialities of tropical regions are quite limited despite the technology and science now available, and as a result, less than 5 per cent of the Latin American land area is considered to have actual or potential value for agricultural use.

The forests, rough terrain, arid stretches, and the lack of inland water transport combine to give Latin America one of its pronounced characteristics: a marked geographical fragmentation which applies both to the region as a whole and to most of the individual countries within it. In a way, this fragmentation (only Uruguay, Argentina, Paraguay, and possibly Chile are partial exceptions) is one of the uniform features of Latin America; it provides a physical basis for strong tendencies toward economic localism, social parochialism, and political regionalism. In South America fragmentation is compounded by distance. Not only does the continent lie somewhat off the world's main lanes of commerce; it also has great overland distances from one side of the continent to the other. Chile's length, for example, is greater than the width of the United States, and Brazil, by itself, is larger than the continental United States. The economic distances are even greater and have given rise to a pattern of settlement which has had important consequences for the economics of transport.

In Middle America the pockets of settlement and economic significance tend to be interspersed among the interior highlands, hampered by the terrain in their communication with each other and with the outside world. On the South American continent, the heartland can be classified as almost an economic void; the clusters of population and productive activity are widely scattered around the coastal periphery and along the Andes south through Bolivia. It has been said that Latin America is more an archipelago than a continent, and indeed since the early nineteenth century this fringe pattern of settlement has been reinforced by the increasing importance of foreign trade, which subjected the location of economic activities to the pull of low maritime shipping costs. From the beginning, Latin America has had an especially severe handicap in the internal movement of goods. Facilities for handling the transport and communications functions have historically been expensive to construct and maintain, thereby boosting both production costs and delivery prices to relatively high levels and limiting the size of the marketable surplus produced in many of the individually small regions of settlement. In addition, little traffic has been generated en route in long transport intervals over sparsely settled or unoccupied territory, and this reduced volume of traffic has led to exceptionally high per-unit costs of use, to the detriment of local economic specialization and development.

Consumers and producers alike have suffered from substantial inter-regional transport charges: the former from the higher prices they must pay, the latter from the lower net returns on sales in output markets. Furthermore, given the small scale of marketable regional surpluses and the generally low density of development in interregional transport and communications networks, the opportunities afforded marketing intermediaries for monopsonistic-monopolistic (or oligopsonistic-oligopolistic) advantages have been immeasurably enhanced. As the net resources available to a society condition the degree of feasible institutional elaboration, it appears that this situation has also been a major impediment to Latin America's evolving the highly developed, complex forms of economic activity which a richer resource base and a less fragmented geography would have permitted. Latin America's natural disadvantages stand out sharply when its chief geographical features are contrasted with those of Europe and North America. In each of the latter, there is an overall geographical unity based upon a complementarity of resources in adjacent and easily linked regions, and in neither have settlements around the continental margins had to function as a narrow fringe encompassing a central wasteland.

THE INTERLOCKING NATURE OF LATIN AMERICAN ECONOMIC PROBLEMS

The economic problems of Latin America are scarcely unique; most of them are encountered in other underdeveloped regions of the globe and a good many have their counterparts in the experience of developed regions as well. Few if any of these problems lie altogether beyond the boundaries of conventional economic analysis, however much certain Latin Americans have on occasion argued against the relevancy of the received body of economic doctrine. Hence the conceptual tools of conventional microeconomic and macroeconomic theory are invaluable for illuminating the facets and consequences of particular problems and for indicating the general direction that policies to resolve these problems should take, although such an analysis must take account of the influence of noneconomic factors. Still, as will be seen in a moment, there is a germ of truth in the antipathetic stance of some Latin American vis-à-vis what is represented as economic orthodoxy, though the point at issue may well be the insufficiency rather than the invalidity of the latter.

For example, much of price behavior in Latin America, particularly the recent accelerated increases, is readily explained as the conventional repercussions of inflationary fiscal policy in an environment in which supply inelasticities and other imperfections exist in both final output and factor markets. Though there is little overall correlation in Latin America between growth rates and inflation rates, this in no way negates the customary economic indictment of inflation (much less does it support the occasional contention that inflation is a necessary instrument or at least accompaniment of growth), for no economist has ever claimed that monetary policy is the sole determinant of growth. The dissociation between national capital formation rates and national growth rates in Latin America also constitutes no perplexity for routine economic analysis, for it has often been pointed out that the direction of investment is at least as important as the amount of investment in determining the growth rate of aggregate output. Moreover, few economists would maintain that, given the institutional deficits which exist in Latin America, there is anything automatic about transforming financial resources into output-increasing investment. Consequently, while traditional savings-centered development theory (and the theory of the so-called low-level equilibrium trap) does seem to suggest that the lack of sufficient domestic savings constitutes a major scarcity barrier to development, it has been widely recognized that it would be normatively misleading to assume as a constant the past statistical relationships between savings and growth in output. Since Keynes' day it has been common to assume that, as John P. Lewis has put it, the savings rate itself is a symptom of economic performance and this performance is determined by many variables; the individual propensity to save is only one of the lesser.

Nevertheless, a great deal of other information is necessary if one is to comprehend the dynamics of economic life in Latin America, for economic action takes place in a larger cultural environment which conditions the motivation of economic actors, their perception of economic opportunities, the distribution and strength of incentives, and access to the opportunity structure. In principle, the desirability of probing into the political, sociological, and psychological aspects of human behavior and of incorporating these, insofar as they are relevant, into economic analysis has gained widespread acceptance in recent times. With the increasing sophistication developed during postwar study of the problems of backward regions, economic development has been seen quite clearly as an indissociable aspect of a larger social or cultural process. Perhaps in fact, it is most accurately conceived as a matter of total systemic adjustment, for economic development involves both economic growth, in the sense of an increasing output, and economic change, in the sense of changes in the composition of output, in the composition of factor inputs, and in the whole social organization of production and distribution. To explain adequately the widening range of production functions and production alternatives which is the essence of development, one must necessarily inquire rather extensively into the character of the social complex which serves as a matrix to economic development. So close, in fact, is the connection between the narrower process and its larger setting that S. Frankel has argued that possibly "technological change as a social consequence" is a more fitting description of the relation than the conventional phrase, "the social consequences of technological change."

Individual economic problems, therefore, originate in a particular social setting, a setting which strongly affects the over-all *Gestalt* of economic problems which must be coped with, the ways in which the several problems bear upon one another, and, finally, the attainment of a solution in fact rather than in theory—giving rise to a design of interaction between objective and subjective reality which W. W. Rostow has aptly called an "economic style." One suspects that an insufficient feeling for this total environment within which economic development takes place has led to the air of unreality which pervades some of the economic prescriptions made for Latin America, just as it may also account for the multitude of development studies and plans which so regularly have been consigned to dusty archives, unimplemented.

A second glance at a few of the economic problems of Latin America is sufficient to indicate the complex phenomena which are intimately associated with economic diagnosis. For example, the quite widespread pattern of investor preference for urban real estate is far from being just a traditional deflection of funds away from more socially productive employment. Investment in urban construction provides a suitable and fairly effortless hedge against inflation, and in more than one Latin American country the hedge is made more attractive still by the preferential tax treatment of income derived from real property as compared with income derived from industrial and mercantile enterprises. Even in the absence of tax preferences and in a context of noninflationary economic expansion, urban real estate development remains an attractive investment. In accordance with the Engel-Schwabe law, the level of income in Latin America is such that a major portion of disposable income is directed into a demand for housing rather than for comparatively less essential goods. The production and sale of shelter is, therefore, less risky than the production and sale of many other goods for which there is a much more restricted market demand. The production of rental units, in particular, has been lucrative because a sizable segment of the growing urban population cannot get long-term credit for financing home ownership and must therefore pay rent to the comparative few who can obtain loans for residential construction. Housing demand is also strongly affected by the population explosion and the rural-urban migration, the latter reflecting the substantial disparities between the countryside and the central cities in levels of culture and the supply of economic opportunities. Bad as conditions in the urban slums may be, rural conditions are often judged to be so irredeemably hopeless that the inhabitants of these "belts of misery" can nevertheless conclude that in the cities "la vida es más alegre." In turn, an inquiry into such factors as the tax structure, the construction finance system, and the marked rural-urban disparities leads to an examination of the power structure and other features of the social context of development.

Similarly, the pricing policies of many Latin American business firms—a high mark-up on a low volume of sales—need not be attributed to some atavistic Iberian mercantile mentality unexposed to the wisdom of Henry Ford. These policies may represent a rational adaptation to the shape of the market demand curve presented by the concentrated pattern of income distribution, which reduces the number of middle-income consumers who might be reached with lower prices. With purchasing power concentrated in the upper income groups, moderate price reductions reflecting lower unit profits would not, for a number of goods, increase market demand sufficiently to offset the loss of earnings per unit of sales. Really substantial price cuts would be necessary to reach the more elastic portion of the aggregate demand schedule represented by the numerous low-income consumers. Pricing policies are probably also influenced by the behavior characteristic of oligopolistic markets. Both the pattern of income distribution and the oligopolistic structure of markets relate directly to the distribution of wealth and, once again, to the social power structure, the opportunity structure, and so forth. To the extent that high mark-ups or high unit profits are a function of a foreshortened time horizon produced by political instability, which makes longer-term market development risky, the explanation of business behavior further extends the compass of analysis.

In yet another area of economic life, a common feature of twentieth-century labor policy in much of Latin America has been the degree to which a variety of fringe benefits—worker housing, medical and dental care, schools, etc.—have been incorporated into the labor bill by legal requirements that such services, financed through payroll charges, be provided directly by employers to their workers. Where labor codes have not so stipulated, collective agreements have often aimed at obtaining these objectives, with the result that the provision of social services has been related rather more to the size of the work force of a firm than to its taxable net income. This practice influences the choice of production functions in capital-intensive and labor-saving directions which are not altogether consistent with the comparative factor endowments of the firms' operating environments. While a certain element of macroeconomic irrationality appears to be involved in such policies, they nonetheless are rational to the employed labor force. With public, tax-supported social services deficient on a number of counts, direct provision of such services by employers acquires an understandable appeal for the workers. Another appeal is that these fringe benefits substitute real payments for money payments, and the workers thus acquire a partial hedge against inflationary erosion of their total (i.e., direct and indirect) wage receipts.

Inflationary pressures have been mentioned in two of the foregoing Latin American problems. The analysis of inflation begins by studying the elements summarized by $MV = PT$, but a complete comprehension of the process rests upon an analysis of relevant sociological and political changes and the power struggle which ensues from these changes quite as much as it springs from an exploration of fiscal and monetary policies and inelasticities of supply. Indeed, the fiscal and monetary policies which contribute to inflation cannot be fully understood without a look at the prevailing power structure of Latin American society as it relates to the formation of policy in government and banking institutions. David Felix was not being facetious when he suggested, a few years ago, that advice on curtailment of the money supply should be accompanied by an estimate of "the number of machine guns needed at the presidential palace to enforce the curtailment." As Felix observed, rioting bank clerks and school teachers are not Walter Mittyish daydreams but real phenomena in Latin America.

Three characteristics stand out from this brief overview of certain Latin American problems. One is that the word "problem" is too simplistic to designate accurately the subject matter under discussion. "Problem complex" is a better term, a more adequate expression of the multiplicity and intricacy of the elements involved. In this study, accordingly, the word "problem" is usually a shorthand way of saying "problem complex." Second, a dominant attribute of the problem complexes discussed is their interrelatedness. This characteristic stems partly from the interrelations which exist among the different aspects of the economic process and partly from the third salient characteristic: the common connection with or grounding in a basic institutional structure from which each problem complex receives its essential nature and its fullest dimensions. Thus, each problem complex not only constitutes part of the total pattern of activity and contributes its measure to the overall characteristics of the Latin American economies, but each is also influenced—through interaction with the other parts—by that total pattern. To an important degree, the characteristics of the parts derive from the larger scheme of economic dynamics. While this makes analysis more difficult, it also implies a certain degree of complementarity in solutions, i.e., measures which are taken to resolve problems in one area of the economy produce side effects that may contribute to relief of other problem complexes.

A COMMENT ON METHODOLOGY:
THE HISTORICO-INSTITUTIONAL APPROACH

Just as microeconomic analysis is valuable in understanding atomistic economic behavior and macroeconomic theory has furnished great insight into aggregative relations within a national economy, so institutionalism is the branch of economics concerned with the forces and factors involved in the evolution of economic systems—without, it might be added, the rather forced, teleological rigidity of Marxian analysis, which has a similar general focus. It is peculiarly appropriate to the present investigation, in which the concepts employed are those that have been fashioned over the years by such scholars as Thorstein Veblen, John R. Commons, Clarence Ayres, Erich Zimmermann, and Gunnar Myrdal. To a greater or lesser extent, the conceptual structure of institutionalism has been employed by most students of development today, albeit frequently more implicitly than explicitly. The validity of the approach seems confirmed by the fact that so many contemporary economists working with the problems of underdeveloped regions have come to utilize institutionalist concepts—often, apparently, quite independently of their development in institutionalism.

It is important, however to stress the indispensable role of microeconomic and macroeconomic theory, if only because some expositors of the institutionalist point of view have appeared to deprecate their value. While institutionalism transcends the limits of these other branches of economic analysis, it is not a substitute for them, for one must utilize analytical tools from these latter fields both to identify the portions of the larger institutional structure which are relevant to the problems at hand and to chart the economic repercussions of various institutional phenomena. That which institutionalism contributes is a view of the economic system as a going concern, its special objective being an interpretation of the factors which may either produce a transformation of that going concern or impede such a technological and organizational metastasis.

In the process of exploring the social conditions of production in Latin America, it is evident that we shall perforce be examining a wide and varying range of phenomena in the institutional order, phenomena which it is more appropriate to classify as "more economically relevant" and "less economically relevant" than "economic" and "noneconomic." As an eminent scholar of economic growth, Moses Abramovitz, has observed, the study of the secular expansion of output leads inevitably into areas of psychology, sociology, and institutions. Because it comprehends analytically the total pattern of social relations insofar as they impinge on the economic process, the cultural or holistic approach of institutionalism is essential to the aim of the present study. Beyond this, however, one must probe the institutional circumambience of the economy in order to get at the heart of Latin America's current difficulties; the problem of backwardness inheres in the institutional structure itself and the patterns of development which are compatible with or permitted by that structure. While geography and the other conditions laid down by nature contribute to this problem, the human significance of geography resides in the concept of resources, a functional relationship in which institutional phenomena play a critical role. One notes, for example, that a monocultural pattern of exports is typical of most of the Latin American economies and that all of them depend mainly upon the export of crude raw materials, or, at most, semi-processed materials. This is largely because none of the economies has developed its social overhead capital enough to generate new science-based comparative advantages; the dominant characteristic of modern industrial complexes is that comparative advantage in these fields is not "given" by natural endowments, but is acquired institutionally by building up the knowledge and specialized human resources inputs of these complexes. Since most, if not all, of Latin America's economic problems can be traced to failures in institutional development, it seems logical to conclude that what is needed is not so much a further study of economic processes as such but rather a study of the institutions which incorporate these processes into their functioning, for better or for worse.

There is, finally, one more reason for employing the cultural approach: the problem of accounting satisfactorily for the area's diversity while discerning at least the minimal elements of uniformity which allow one to treat the region *tout ensemble*. While national size, population composition, geography, and other factors are all interlaced in the diversity of Latin America, the necessary lowest common denominator is found in the institutional order. As the designation "Latin" suggests, it is really only in this aspect that one finds a basis for the concept of Latin America. The unifying element is the common source of the basic institutional heritage of all but one of the Latin American nations; it is from this source that they have taken their separate paths into the modern age.

Language, religion, architectural forms, are merely the outward manifestations of this essential Iberian bond. The value systems and modalities of behavior described by Gillin and other anthropologists, the Latin philosophical bent and Weltanschauung celebrated by José Enrique Rodó, and the social structures of the several Latin American countries are all imbued with a style derived from the underpinnings of Iberian culture. Given this derivation, the term neo-Iberian seems an appropriate characterization of the culture and institutional arrangements of the region. Though there is cultural heterogeneity (Wagley and Harris, for example, have described nine subcultures [8]), one can nevertheless speak of the larger cultural matrix in terms of which these variants are defined as subtypes.

The institutionalist analysis of economic change and development is also historical in approach, as the subtitle of this section suggests, since the institutional order is the net result of historical evolution and a sequence of cumulative change which continuously shapes and reshapes the resource base. The reasons why the Latin American economies function the way they do today lie in the way they functioned yesterday and the day before. As Joseph Schumpeter once commented, of all the dimensions of economic problems, the historical dimension is the most important.

On this account, the following chapters are grouped into three chronological eras. At the appropriate points in time are introduced, when they first appear, the factors and trends which have worked subsequently in the direction of cumulative expansion as well as the impediments, the drag effect of which is carried over to depress the level of economic performance throughout later periods. In this manner, it is hoped to emphasize the cumulative costs of inheritance, which are as much a part of economic reality as the positive role of compound interest.

The point of the historico-institutional approach becomes clear when one notes that at the 1960 Inter-American Economic Conference in Bogotá the intellectually perceptive president of Colombia, Lleras Camargo, spoke of Latin America as being on the verge of a crisis unprecedented in all its history. Few could doubt the accuracy of his statement, for by all indications, Latin America is an area in the midst of fundamental changes in the social, political, and economic orders. At first glance, the reasons for such critical circumstances in the middle of the twentieth century are not obvious, since the region was the first important overseas offshoot of European civilization. It is, therefore, strange that four and a half centuries later this branch of the most dynamic and economically progressive civilization in the world should still be so underdeveloped and still have such a large balance in the "cultural change receivables" ledger. It is also strange that as a sharer in a civilization in which change has been the central feature for centuries, the Latin American transplant finds in contemporary change the threat of widespread social breakdown. That the neo-Iberian institutional order demonstrates such a low level of tolerance of social change may be not unrelated to the difficulty the Latin American countries have had in crossing the threshold of sustained economic growth, for, as the following chapters will indicate, the Latin American variant of Western civilization has actually had little more than a century of experience with the forms of modern economic life—a short period, indeed, in which to develop the vast array of institutions and practices which underlie the operations of contemporary industrial society.

Part Two

Institutional Foundations of
Latin American Economic Growth

Part Two

Institutional Foundations of
Latin American Economic Growth

II

Origins of The Neo-Iberian Institutional Framework

ONE of Brazil's leading social historians, Pedro Calmon, has described his country's culture as an example of the "superimposition of epochs"—a sequence of cultural formation in which the evolutionary processes of innovation, modification, and adaptation are incomplete in their compass. Because the sweep of change has affected less than the total way of life of the people concerned, the cultural residue of earlier periods is more conspicuous in later periods than it is in societies where greater amalgamation has been accomplished in consecutive historical eras. The difference in the extent of overall cultural integration in the two cases is, of course, one of degree rather than kind, for by its very nature any society is part of a double continuum of time and space. There is never, socially speaking, a tabula rasa on which new cultural specifications are inscribed, nor is there an eraser, even in revolutionary situations, that can obliterate all past institutional instructions as a prelude to reformulating them anew.

Calmon's phrase suggests that antecedents of Brazilian culture are especially discernible in the current set of economic and social arrangements. But with possibly even greater accuracy, Calmon's description applies to other Latin American countries.

In Brazil the superimposition of epochs is most clearly manifested in the form of regional disparities which were created by the shifting geographical incidence of export booms. From these came a marked spatial discontinuity in the sequence of cultural changes. To some extent the regions of the nation are like museum exhibits, each displaying devitalized forms left over from an earlier age. Superimposition is even more striking in the smaller countries of Spanish America where the events of successive epochs have occurred in close geographical proximity. In Mexico City it is possible to dine on frozen foods (the product of twentieth-century national industry) in a restaurant owned by foreign capital (which did so much to set off the nineteenth century from the centuries preceding) and located in a famous colonial palace, while a few blocks away excavations are revealing the impressive character of the pre-Columbian Aztec capital of Tenochtitlán. Indeed, some of the excavators may well have grown up in nearby villages where Nahuatl, the Aztec tongue, is still the *lingua populi*. In a Guatemala torn with the dissension of cold war politics, the writer once visited a backlands Indian market which displayed handicraft products developed before the coming of the Spaniards. From a vendor to whom Spanish was a foreign language (despite his attire in elements of medieval Spanish costume), he bought a canteen-shaped clay vessel which, to the detriment of authenticity but to the greater glory of acculturation, bore the unmistakable imprints of the Ford V-8 hubcaps which had served as a mould. In such circumstances, the superimposition of epochs is indeed the dominant feature of life.

The Colombian Alvaro Gómez Hurtado has suggested that it is more helpful to liken the cultural evolution of a number of Latin American countries to an H than to a Y (Fig. II-1).[1] The point is well taken, for an H is a better diagram of the asynchronous development to which Calmon was referring. In this plural culture complex, parallel strands of cultural tradition persist as discrete phenomena rather than as the components of a fusion—even though some measure of interpenetration has taken place over the centuries and the separate strands are currently converging. Actually, a slightly more complex diagram (Fig. II-2) would serve better than Gómez Hurtado's to illustrate the nature of Latin American cultural evolution, for since shortly before the close of the eighteenth century a third distinctive element has been added to the scene in gradually increasing proportions, particularly during the past fifty years. The cultural setting of today's Latin America, therefore, consists of three major traditions which coexist in unstable association. In this, the Iberian elements may, for most purposes, be taken as the major tradition, for though it was preceded by the indigenous cultures which form the bedrock of this superimposition of epochs, it has set the dominant tone in the region since the sixteenth century. Since the conquest, the indigenous tradition has been subject to a sometimes rapid, sometimes gradual, displacement by norms and forms of European origin. It seems safe to assume, therefore, that aboriginal ways will continue to count for progressively less in the overall picture, though they still present difficulties (as well as touristic assets) for certain Middle American and Andean regions. The principal problems of intercultural adjustment in contemporary development lie rather in the processes through which the basic Iberian heritage assimilates the traits of North Atlantic industrial society. This much said, however, one must

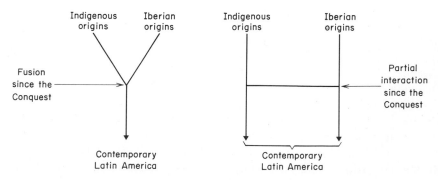

Fig. II-1

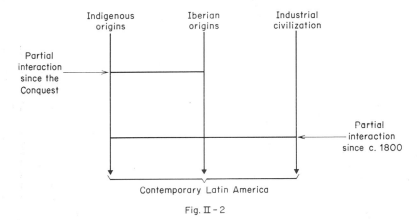

Fig. II - 2

recognize that Iberian culture is itself a complex of subcultures. The Lusitanian variant differs from the Hispanic variant in a number of respects, and the latter comprises several distinctive regional subcultures. In this and the following two chapters, the focus is upon the Hispanic variant; in Chapter V the Luzo-Brazilian variant will be considered.

THE CHARACTER OF IBERIAN CULTURE:
SOURCES OF CONTEMPORARY DYSFUNCTIONALITY

The colonial era—a span of approximately three centuries in which the neo-Iberian culture was formed—constitutes the most important unifying bond of Latin America. From this shared background of vital historical experiences have come the central value system, basic patterns of behavior and social interaction, and forms of government, law, property and other organizational structures which control economic processes—in short, the underlying common-sense tradition of the neo-Iberian peoples.[2] Crucial to a comprehension of this tradition are three considerations: the timing of the transatlantic leap, the character of the culture which was brought to the Americas, and the nature of the geographical and cultural environments encountered there by the Iberians.

As part of Western civilization, Iberian and neo-Iberian cultures are not entirely alien to our own cultural tradition. Their constituent elements, in fact, display a much closer degree of kinship with our own social arrangements than is the case in any other less developed region of the world, and from this association stem expectations—not always valid in the social, political, and economic realms—that like causes produce like results. Yet there are significant differences between these two streams of cultural tradition within Western civilization: the North Atlantic continuum of northwest Europe and North America on the one hand and the Mediterranean–Iberian–neo-Iberian continuum on the other. Disregard of these differences has led to many of the mistaken expectations in political and economic policy areas.

That Iberian culture does have certain peculiar properties has long been recognized. The European adage, "Africa starts at the Pyrenees," may be overdrawn, but it illustrates that the differences of Spain have not gone unnoticed. Most economic histories of the Western world, for example, evince some difficulty in fitting Spain and Latin America into the mainstream of discussion and analysis and customarily treat these areas as a special case.[3] Moreover, the distinctive qualities of the Iberian scheme of use and wont appear to transcend the bounds of the economic order; they have also been remarked in such fields as religion and dramatic criticism. The distinguishing attributes of Spanish Catholicism have often been the object of despair for coreligionists from other countries.[4] And some years ago the critic John Crosby, reviewing Lorca's *The House of Bernarda Alba*, observed that the value system incorporated in Spanish drama is far more exotic to the North American audience than, say, that of the French or Scandinavian theater. The difference is well exemplified in the *corrida de toros*, the symbol par excellence of the Hispanic ethos which, Hemingway notwithstanding, ordinarily strikes the non-Spaniard as a rather mixed package. The source of this ambivalent or even negative reaction comes from the mistaken view of bullfighting as an athletic event when it is really an ancient drama, one in which the element of sacrifice is a key component, as it is in most primitive theatrical experience and religious expression. The customary allusions to Roman circuses made by detractors of the *corrida* describe with some accuracy the close ancestry of the neo-Iberian tradition and also say something about the temper of mind which sets that tradition apart from its North Atlantic parallel. With his usual perspicacity in such matters, Veblen once attributed the peculiar character of Iberian culture to its possession of a certain archaic quality.[5] The point was apposite, as we shall see.

Yet, if there does exist a special ethos in Iberian institutions, the questions remain, just what this orientation may be and what its bearing on economic life has been. By way of examining these questions, it may be helpful briefly to view Iberian historical experience in the light of four concepts which have been used to interpret Latin American underdevelopment and from the vantage point of a fifth concept which might seem to be relevant but which has been rather seldom utilized in most of the writing on the subject.

1. The first concept is an old *leyenda negra* cliché: the Puritans came to America for God while the Spaniards came for gold. The implication is that, in contrast to the sober (and economically useful) Puritan virtues, the Spanish venture had about it something of the atmosphere of mining-camp life or a plundering expedition.[6] In this view, the chief aim of Spanish colonization was essentially exploitive, a feverish search for gold and silver to the neglect of more solid and steady sources of economic prosperity. When stated in this simplistic form, the concept is obviously untenable, although

much of nineteenth-century Latin American historiography was scarcely more refined in its approach to the subject. But a rough equivalent often lingers on in attenuated form, as anyone who has read much in the Latin American field will readily recognize.[7]

The treasure-oriented search of the conquistadores did occur in the early years of the conquest, but this hardly explains the total pattern of colonial organization, much less its enduring contribution to neo-Iberian institutional life. Only a small minority of the colonists were either directly or indirectly involved in the conduct of mining activity. Agriculture, not mining, generated the major portion of gross colonial product. Further, as Lewis Hanke and other historians have indicated, the Spanish venture was by no means devoid of exemplary humanitarian personages and policies.[8] Contrasted with the treatment that other colonial powers meted out to subjugated peoples, e.g., the slavery and Indian-extermination policies of the Anglo-Americans and the harsh Belgian policies in the Congo, the Spanish regime emerges as one tempered at least as much as any other by welfare considerations of a civilized nature. Mining was prominent in the life of colonial Mexico, Peru, and Bolivia, but this was because the Spaniards were luckier than other Europeans in laying claim to territories which contained a great deal of silver and gold. By developing their strong comparative international advantage in mining, the Spaniards were able to obtain directly that which rival European powers had to seek by piracy, smuggling, and other ungodly means. Obsession with material gain was, moreover, not a characteristic exclusive to Spaniards and could be viewed as part of the rising commercial spirit of the times. The colonizing motivation, therefore, is clearly insufficient as an explanation of the properties of the institutional structure which in later years has appeared to be so resistant to the forces of economic progress.

2. A concept, which continues to pass as sound currency even where the *leyenda negra* is repudiated as counterfeit, is the attribution of Latin America's arrested development to the onerous burden of Spanish mercantilism and thus to the presumed deficiencies of the mercantilist doctrines which were long ago discredited by Hume and Smith.

Yet other western European countries pursued mercantilist practices with rather different results. Indeed, in the judgment of many scholars, the historic role of mercantilism in these other countries was that of effecting the transition from feudalism to capitalism, in which capacity it functioned as an agency of early capitalist development.[9] One must, therefore, question what mercantilism was and whether Spanish practices could really be labeled mercantilist without stretching the term so far as to empty it of any historically specific content.[10] Further, an examination of the writings of the Spanish mercantilists suggests that their economic doctrines were far more sophisticated than the policies actually pursued for most of the period.[11] Indeed, when a variety of mercantilism was eventually introduced by the

Bourbon monarchy in the eighteenth century, it came as a liberating and progressive influence in the life of Spain's overseas dominions.

3. A third concept points to the supposed Spanish legacy of feudalism. In fact it would be difficult to find any adjective which has appeared with greater frequency than "feudal" in combination with the nouns, Spain and Latin America. The feudal theme is usually proposed as a supplementary rather than alternative explanation of the institutional deficiencies of Iberian and neo-Iberian countries, a fact which leads to some arresting possibilites. One infers, therefore, that mercantilistic feudalism or a feudalistic mercantilism must lie at the roots of Latin America's difficulties.

Leaving aside the quite radical conflict between feudalism and mercantilism observed in other European countries, one must recall that feudalism was, after all, the seedbed for the development of modern European civilization. At the least, then, the quality of Spanish feudalism must be investigated to determine what set it so much apart from the feudalism of other European countries. The facile use of the feudalism concept is further discouraged by Ortega y Gasset's intriguing contention that the trouble with Spain was not that it was feudal, but that it was not feudal enough.[12] There are, it should be noted, sufficient restrictions placed on the application of the term "feudal" to Spanish conditions by serious investigators of Iberian history to suggest that this contention was not merely a paradox like other paradoxes with which Spaniards are thought to decorate their writings.[13] Just as one comes to suspect that the concept of mercantilism gets expanded to comprehend any sort of interventionist policy, so one is inclined to wonder if feudal is not being equated with any nonegalitarian social structure. In both cases, given the historical prevalence of interventionism and socio-economic inequality, the concepts appear to lose their usefulness when employed generically rather than specifically.

4. A fourth questionable concept relates to the social organization of the colonial undertaking and is stated by Clarence Haring in his outstanding study, *The Spanish Empire in America*. He describes the "discovery, conquest, and settlement of Spanish America" as being "from the time of Christopher Columbus on preeminently the achievement of private enterprise." [14] Underscoring the point, he quotes J. M. Ots Capdequí to the effect that "in nearly every instance it [the occupation of Spanish America] reflected private initiative and effort, rather than official action by the state." [15] Nor are Haring and Ots Capdequí alone in this stand. The Argentine historian, Sergio Bagú, has viewed the conquest of the New World in much the same perspective,[16] while the distinguished Colombian writer German Arciniegas has gone so far as to call the Spanish empire a capitalistic enterprise—in fact, "the first great enterprise of capitalism in the world." [17] In this fashion, the Spanish expansion has been associated with the rise of modern individualism, and numerous psycho-cultural analyses appear to con-

firm this with their stress on an almost anarchic individualism as a central trait of the Spanish personality.

Cortés, Pizarro, Balboa, and the other conquistadores were without doubt "individuals" both in the sense that everyone is an individual and in that they stood out prominently among other individuals. It is true, too, that at the outset the impecunious Spanish monarchs had to resort to the coffers of their wealthier subjects to finance the New World expeditions. But to refer to the Spanish conquest and settlement as the work of individuals and private enterprise might be construed to mean that it was a part of the same Western cultural package as the private colonizing companies and trading enterprises of, say, England and Holland. As such, Spanish colonization would seem to be related to the early stages of economic individualism and capitalism—particularly when the characterization is combined, as it is in one of the works cited above, with a reference to the Welsers as an example of the impresarios engaged in this massive private endeavor.[18]

For reasons which will be developed later, the emphasis of these and similar remarks seems misleading.[19] A conspicuous failure in Latin America has been its inability, in an era of emergent capitalism, to evolve a system of individual initiative and private enterprise which could lead to economic expansion such as the system achieved elsewhere. If the Spanish venture had been a culturally authentic case of private initiative and private enterprise, at least as those terms are commonly understood, this failure would be especially remarkable, for Spain, rather than other countries, might have been expected to preempt the lead in the modern era of economic institutional renovation on the basis of its new-found assets and commercial opportunities. While most authors qualify the implications of their statements, the qualifications are so decisive that it seems reasonable to argue that the concepts need never have been introduced in the first place.

5. As a fifth concept, the gradual "pacification" of the New World suggests that the Turner frontier hypothesis might have at least some explanatory utility for this experience.[20] The Latin American case would seem, in fact, to offer a suitable "laboratory" for testing the hypothesis for its cross-cultural applicability.

The fact that so few of the cultural characteristics that Frederick Jackson Turner ascribed to the North American frontier emerged as significant products of the Latin American frontier appears to support the critics who have offered the germ hypothesis as a competing explanation for the origins of a free society.[21] To some extent, however, the Iberian and neo-Iberian continuum of cultural development appears to support both Turner and his critics: the latter in the short run or Western Hemisphere setting, the former in the long run which includes the European antecedents of developments in the Western Hemisphere.

In employing these concepts to illuminate the formative economic stage of neo-Iberian culture, a brief schematization of the two streams of Western cultural evolution should be of benefit. This is not to bring into question the general merits of the Iberian way of life but to make the contrasts stand out by providing a point of reference which may be especially relevant to detecting the cultural factors which bear on secular economic performance. Thanks to its great material success and by virtue of its long exposure to technological change, the North Atlantic institutional framework may be said to represent adjustment to the exigencies of material growth and appears suitable as the basis for a comparative look at the economic processes of other societies.

In drawing this comparison, one is struck, first of all, by the fact that when Spain acquired its extensive overseas possessions at the close of the fifteenth century, the Iberian peoples had already been exposed to a series of events which had differentiated them from the inhabitants of northwestern Europe and shaped the distinctive dominating insight of Iberian institutions. Important as were the differences between the two regions by the close of the fifteenth century, the prevailing perspectives of the two cultures were to diverge still more markedly during the three centuries which followed. The sixteenth and seventeenth centuries were to work profound changes in the temper and tone of European life, and it was within a cultural pattern transmuted by the impact of these changes that the English, the Dutch, and the French launched their major colonization efforts during the seventeenth and eighteenth centuries.

THE NORTH ATLANTIC CULTURAL CONTINUUM

By 1500—and certainly by 1600 or 1700—northwest Europe was uniquely a society-in-transit.[22] Relative to other contemporary and to earlier social systems, it was an open society, receptive to innovation and novelty. For this reason, it was and has been ever since imbued with a special dynamic quality which sets it off from the traditional societies which have predominated in the world's cultural arrangements. Long before the idea of progress was explicit in Western thinking, it was implicit in the objective order of reality. Change—technological, social, economic, philosophical, and political—had become an integral, if not consciously articulated, part of the experience of the northwestern European peoples. While the fortuitous historical circumstances that brought forth this special capacity are not a proper subject for detailed exposition in this book, they can be limned out in a summary way.

Compared with the Mediterranean civilizations, northwest Europe was long an underdeveloped area inhabited by barbarian tribes. Somewhat remote, with respect to the Mediterranean world, it was not so isolated as to remain unexposed to influences emanating from that emergent center of cultural development. Yet even with the territorial expansion of the Roman empire, it remained a frontier region and represented the point of contact between the bearers of the civilizational heritage of antiquity and the cruder peoples drifting in from beyond the borders of the empire. While assimilating much of the skills and material artifacts brought by the Romans from the Mediterranean cultural storehouse, the primitive population of northwestern Europe adopted less thoroughly the other institutional accoutrements of ancient civilization: the elaborate ceremonial traditions, the weighty legal structure, the highly developed machinery of government. In an environment much like Turner's frontier, a considerable cultural distance separated the rustic life of northwestern Europe from the complex institutional forms developed around the shores of the Mediterranean.

As time went on, the tenure of Roman authority grew less and less secure. Waves of barbarian tribes moved in on the empire, picked up the cultural traits that attracted them, and then moved farther on into the interior of the empire, displaced by the tribes pressing in after them. In the process, there was a steady attenuation of the Roman inheritance, for when the political framework of the empire was finally ruptured, few of the old Roman institutions appear to have endured in the outlying regions inhabited by the less acculturated latecomers. In England, for example, Roman law disappeared almost completely, allowing for the evolution of the common-law tradition which, as John R. Commons has indicated, carried important implications for the much later evolution of capitalism.[23] Not until centuries afterwards did the English monarchy attempt a revival of Roman law to support its claims to an expanded royal power, and on that occasion the attempted resurrection was largely unsuccessful.[24]

Henri Pirenne has shown that the basic economic unity of the empire persisted long after the region's political fragmentation.[25] But the rapid sweep of Islam through the Mediterranean world into Spain eventually reduced the mainstay of this unity—the exchange of products between western Europe and the eastern Mediterranean region—to a fraction of its former proportions. With less access to this important trade, the economic order of antiquity disintegrated as had the political order before it. The urban centers established by Roman administration declined, and northwestern Europe lapsed further and further into the atomistic manorial feudalism of the Middle Ages.[26]

Yet the Middle Ages were far from having the stable, extremely rigid institutional order which the conventional characterization of those times long depicted. Compared with the more direct lineal descendant of the Roman world, the Byzantine empire, medieval Europe was notable for institutional fluidity,[27] as revisionary efforts of modern research have established. In fact, it is now possible for a serious article, "Did the Dark Ages Exist?," to appear [28] without the reader's assuming that the question is purely rhetorical. Trade, on a reduced scale, continued and cross-cultural contacts and cultural borrowing slowly enriched the material inheritance received from Rome, little of which was ever really lost, popular notions to the contrary notwithstanding. Impressive technological advances were developed locally as well, often by the members of an ecclesiastical system which in contrast to the eastern branch of Christianity was more this-worldly in orientation and more involved in mundane matters. The fragmented, decentralized society of feudalism contrasted institutionally with the monolithic, centralized Roman empire which had preceded it in that it was a polycentric order—a society with multiple loci of power and discretionary authority.[29]

Under the aegis of feudal constitutionalism, the notion of subsidiarity developed to support a certain measure of diffused autonomy, i.e., a limited scope for independent roles and action by the several constituent parts of the feudal structure. The lords of the manors had their fiefs, the towns and guilds had their charters, and even the serfs were legally quite distinct from the old Roman slaves. In this decentralized constitutionalism the principle of order was thought to devolve from a preestablished harmony of interests which sprang, in the teachings of the church, from the nature of society as ordained by the Creator.[30] As an organic theory of society, which Tawney has studied so revealingly, the larger pattern of social integration was achieved from the grass roots up by virtue of each segment's (artisan guilds, feudal lords, and the like) performing its allotted social role. From this conception to the social contract and the automatic self-regulating market of later days there was no great leap, for the essence of the changes of the eighteenth century was merely, in Carl Becker's choice phrasing, a "denaturing of God and a deification of nature." The modern English democratic tradition owes much, for instance, to the autonomous rights of the feudal barons who asserted these rights with sufficient vigor to extract the Magna Carta from King John, establishing thereby that the king also was subject to law. The subsequent expansion of these rights of medieval constitutionalism, with the "inevitability of gradualness," was abetted by the simple expedient of redrawing the ambiguous boundaries between the provinces of divine law and natural law.[31]

Loose as this system was, there were forces at work which served to loosen it further and to elicit the growth of new activities with their associated social roles and classes amid the interstices of feudal society. The crusades and plagues provided the solvents for some of the feudal bonds, and in their wake came the Renaissance and a notable revival of trade and urban life. The commercial revolution was on. In the assorted undertakings of the Italian city states, the Hanseatic League, and the Flemish Hanse, in the far-flung operations of the Lombardian papal bankers, the Cahorsins, and the Fuggers, the pattern of economic life was reorganized and oriented toward the quest for wealth through pecuniary and commercial transactions. Mercantilism was almost an inevitable outgrowth of these trends, and under the joint auspices of merchants, financiers, and kings, Europe was prepared for the age of industrial capitalism. The Reformation put an end to the one remaining inherited element of institutional unity in northwestern Europe, and the Enlightenment confirmed the central role of wide-ranging inquiry in the new scheme of things.

A skeptical and mercantile man—somewhat amoral and pragmatic, as Eli Heckscher has shown—represented the new cultural order being built on the debris of the old. And it was he who played a leading role in the colonial extensions of northwestern European countries, imparting to these undertakings a certain commercial basis and orientation and integrating them with the flowering of private enterprise. As the medieval cities had earlier been populated in part by the *déracinés,* people culturally and physically uprooted from the feudal life of the countryside, the settlers who emigrated to the new transoceanic possessions were also in a sense *déracinés.* Many were also dissenters from the social arrangements of the homeland and predisposed to engage in experimental restructuring to build a partially new order abroad.[32] It was not altogether unfortunate that the colonies were often made a convenient dumping ground for the malcontents of the motherland. The practice only continued the cultural and social *démarrage* which had been going on for centuries.[33]

THE IBERIAN CONTINUUM

In the Iberian continuum of cultural development, the record of decisive events during this period of history reads otherwise. When Christopher Columbus set sail for the Indies, he embarked from a land which had remained much closer to its ancient cultural antecedents. In a book published in 1891 the North American historian Blackmar noted the strong similarity between Spanish colonial institutions and the organizational patterns devised by the Romans during the apogee of their imperial expansion.[34] More recently, Clarence Haring stated:

> It has been remarked that more than all the other peoples of the modern world the Spaniards of the sixteenth century displayed the characteristics of the ancient Romans. They revealed in the conquest and settlement of America the same courage and enterprise, the same military qualities, the same patience under hardship, that distinguished Roman soldiers and colonists in the times of Scipio Africanus and Julius Caesar. And like the Romans they were preeminently creators of laws and builders of institutions. Of all the colonizing peoples of modern times, the Spaniards were the most legal-minded. They speedily developed in the new empire a meticulously organized administrative system such as the world had rarely seen.[35]

That the Spaniards should have resembled their Roman forebearers so closely is not mere happenstance. Occupied for seven centuries with the reconquest of the Iberian peninsula and absorbed for three centuries more in empire building in the New World, the Spanish people participated only marginally in the trends recounted earlier in this chapter. For almost a thousand years, they were at least partially insulated from the culture-changing impact of the barbarian intrusions, the reorientation of trade, the spread of the feudal order, the crusades, the Renaissance, and the new commercial revolution.[36] Owing to the conditioning of the circumstances in which they found themselves during these years, their reaction to these movements, when exposed to them, took a distinctive form. Towards the end of the period in question, this becomes especially clear.

The response to the Reformation is a case in point. In place of an Erasman Christian humanism, the Spanish reaction to religious and philosophical changes was a reinforcement (but not an introduction) of a politically inspired militant orthodoxy, though in justice it must be said that the Spanish Inquisition was perhaps no worse in its strictly religious dealings than the inquisition of Bavaria, nor was it, possibly, as brutal as the French version.[37] Despite the enormous overseas trade which poured through Spain with the opening up of the Americas, one looks almost in vain for Spanish counterparts to the Ravensburg company, the great trading houses of Nuremberg and Augsburg, the Medici or the Bardi, Jacques Coeur, or the famous joint-stock companies, banks, and bourses of England, France, and the Low Countries.[38] True, the Genoese merchant colony in Seville participated lucratively in this expansion,[39] as did for a while the Welsers and the Fuggers; but the wealth and proliferation of commercial opportunities that were the seeds of a capitalistic economic order in northwestern Europe fell on a less fertile institutional soil in the Iberian world.[40] While mercantilistic state-building policies were hastening the transformation of feudal society north of Spain, the dynastic objectives of Spanish commercial policy brought repercussions which were quite dissimilar. In Spain the stimuli to systemic change filtered through a different perception of reality and a different social structure, and commercial policy was assessed in the light of Iberian notions of what was right and proper in regard to both goals and procedures.

The institutional resiliency of northwestern European society and hence its susceptibility to adaptation and innovation were, as summarized above, the product of historical circumstances. By the same token, the ethos of Hispanic culture is also traceable to a particular series of occurrences: the Romanization of the Iberian peninsula, the Visigothic invasion, the Moslem occupation of Spain, and the Reconquest. The net impact of these events was to sustain and reaffirm the old Roman norms. These norms guided the Spaniards in their construction of an empire and gave a distinctive cast to the way of life fashioned in the New World.

Historians generally agree that the Iberian peninsula was among the most Romanized provinces under the Roman rule.[41] Therefore the character of the Roman culture implanted and maintained there is important in the later development of Iberian structures. Essentially, this imprint was from the Roman culture of the late empire, in which the imperial structure of Rome had become increasingly monolithic. One state reigned supreme. One law, with the juridical and political norms embedded therein, prevailed. And with the establishment of Christianity as a state church, religious uniformity was added as well.[42] Beginning with the reign of Theodosius the Great (346-395), efforts to achieve imperial unity were generally combined with those enforcing religious harmony.

The political and social structure of the Late Empire moved away from the republicanism of early Rome [43] and there appears to have been an increasing absorption of the norms of autocratic government from the Hellenistic East—from Syria, Persia, and Egypt [44]—particularly in the Byzantine stage of the empire, which was decisive in the formulation of Roman law. The office of the emperor moved far toward unlimited absolutism, and the political order became the dominant aspect of life to which the other areas of social existence were more and more subordinated.[45]

Two features of the Late Roman Empire are particularly germane to later developments.[46] (1) Power became centralized in the person of the emperor and the palatine office, which, like the king's council of later Spain, combined legislative and juridical functions with those of an executive, advisory, and administrative nature. (2) A vast, complex, and professionalized civil bureaucracy grew up, separate from the military orders, which the palatine office completely controlled. From the administrative center, proconsuls or governors were sent out to exercise authority over the empire's territorial dependencies. In the regions subject to their jurisdiction the proconsuls (corresponding to the latter-day Spanish viceroys) had wide powers, subject only to the control and instructions of higher officials and to the surveillance exercised by secret agents sent from the imperial capital. During the Byzantine era, a dual bureaucratic system evolved and ecclesiastical personnel served as a further source of scrutiny over civil functionaries. The scope of authority which municipalities had once enjoyed under the Roman system eroded as the inhabitants of towns and countryside fell more and more under the dominance of the bureaucracy.

The theory of colonial organization was affected by these trends.[47] The territories colonized or conquered became integral parts of the empire, directly subject to central authority. In time they tended to be treated as the patrimony of the emperor rather than of the Roman community as a whole. Whereas Grecian colonies were culturally linked to the motherland but politically autonomous, and whereas centuries later the English colonies often resembled commercial enterprises, the Roman colonies represented primarily an extension of government power.

After the conquest of a territory, the emperor customarily appropriated all the royal domains and often a part of the common lands as well. Roman officials were sent out to preside over the parceling out of lands to settlers, often as payments to the Roman soldiery, and from these land payments emerged the latifundia which played an important role in eventually eliminating the previously more egalitarian structure of Roman society. The concept of *regalías,* the rights and privileges of the crown, also developed during the period of imperial aggrandizement, especially in the Byzantine phase. Under this concept all mines, lands, woodlands, waters, and the like and certain industrial activities belonged to or were preempted by the emperor, except those which were specifically granted by the sovereign to the inhabitants.

The establishment of municipalities (the *civitas*) was evolved as a technique for colonizing and administering new lands and possessions; and, established primarily for military and administrative functions, towns functioned as the lowest administrative unit in the structure of imperial rule. Central authorities provided the municipal laws and administrative procedures. Thus the towns developed not so much in response to local ends-in-view as to serve the larger goals of the empire. The commerce conducted within their confines derived largely from the handling of tribute and from the provisioning and consumptive needs of the empire. Essentially creatures of the political order rather than of the economic order, they were not like the more "capitalistic" cities of late medieval and more modern times which, like Topsy, "just grew" along the natural lanes of commerce and trade.

The most enduring contribution of the Roman empire to the development of civilization lay in the fields of law and administration, the two being inextricably linked.[48] Although tribal and local practices initially contributed to Roman law, in the course of imperial development Roman law tended to originate in one primary source: the decrees of the emperor together with the subsidiary decrees of the palatine office and lower administrative units. In contrast to legislatively derived laws and the common-law tradition, Roman law was preeminently administrative and executive in character, sanctioned less by custom and convention than by the coercive force of the state.

From time to time the flow of decree laws was systematically organized into codes by jurists who, as Paul Collinet has remarked, most often received their juridical training in the law centers of the eastern Mediterranean.[49] The codes were designed to provide a semblance of logical symmetry to the main body of law and to permit deduction from this structure of abstract legal principles, but they also incorporated a theory of authentication of imperial power and established clearly the division between private law and public law, the latter representing the body of special rules and principles applicable to the activities of the emperor and the state.[50] Permeating all was a strong tradition of legalism: a legal place for everything and everything in its place. Thereby, there came to be incorporated into the basic institutional structure a strong emphasis on order, stability, control and hierarchy—the static, conservative values commonly associated with an inflexible institutional fabric.

With the establishment of Christianity as the official Roman religion, the notion of a universal church was attached to that of a universal monarchy.[51]

This close affiliation of the sacral with the secular orders led to a species of caesaro-papism in which the emperor exercised rights of patronage in ecclesiastical appointments and exerted a certain measure of temporal authority over the regulation of spiritual matters. The high degree of unity of church and state achieved in Byzantium has perhaps been approximated only twice in the West.[52] Temporary union developed in the Carolingian empire, but there the civil authority lacked the bureaucracy necessary for subordinating the church to the state to the degree of the late Roman empire. The other instance of such an intimate union was found in Spain. While the establishment of various official Protestant churches after the Reformation might seem to be additional examples of this blending, spiritual authority was on the wane at that time and no longer represented such a powerful adjunct of royal authority.

Amid these social arrangements there seems to have been no real conception of the economic order as a sphere of activity separate and distinct from the political order. From the time of Diocletian, there was a growing body of detailed regulation applied by the state to all aspects of economic life: production, trade, the ownership of assets, and so forth.[53] Unlike postmedieval mercantilism, this regulation was not directed towards increasing production so much as it was towards control of the provisioning of various parts of the empire and the collection of revenues for the imperial treasury. It was, in other words, a centrally guided interventionist economy in which commercial considerations played a secondary role. As Polanyi and others have demonstrated, there was no real concept of a market institution for the very simple reason that the market institution, at least as we understand it today, did not exist in this kind of environment.[54] Both the market institution and its conceptualization presuppose a degree of emancipation in the conduct of economic activity from other, noneconomic considerations. Yet, in the Roman period, these other considerations were the overriding ones.[55] In such a setting, there was only a very limited scope for experience with the functioning of the market mechanism as an instrument for achieving economic goals because these goals were achieved through direct order, regulation, and control. So obvious must this relationship have been that it can be said to constitute the common-sense tradition of the ancient Mediterranean world with regard to economic life.[56]

In the highly organized life of the later Roman empire, the social power structure was formally defined in the civil, religious, and military constitutional hierarchies, of which the civil was usually preeminent. By all accounts, during this period of development increasing emphasis was placed on ceremoniousness, considerations of status, and authority resting on precedence and ideology. Economic reward was part of this pattern but, along with prestige and power, it followed hierarchical ranking and hierarchical advance, rather than vice versa. And given the transactional framework of the hierarchically organized imperial society, rank in the power structure was ordinarily attained by means other than economic activity.

POST-ROMAN DEVELOPMENTS: TRUNCATED FEUDALISM

The Iberian Peninsula also experienced the Gothic invasions which reduced Roman control over the outlying territories, although for a time in the sixth century portions of southern Spain were ruled directly from Constantinople. The Visigoths settled in the northern parts of the peninsula and left behind the residue of feudalism which Spain was to inherit from this period. In the Germanic kingdoms which displaced Roman rule, the Visigothic nobility acquired the hallmarks of feudalism—rural estates and the special charters of privilege which in Spain went by the name *fueros*.[57] Though the basis for a full development of feudalism was thereby provided, tendencies toward feudalism were held in check by a combination of factors.

Throughout the Visigothic occupation of Spain, urban life continued largely uninterrupted, functioning as the repository of Roman culture and traditions.[58] The urban centers even enjoyed a revived importance, for in feudal fashion the municipalities were granted *fueros* which accorded them a greater measure of independence than they had under imperial Rome.[59] Significantly for the contrasting implications of feudal and Roman institutional life, the municipal *fueros* laid the basis for the outstanding municipal democracy which flourished in Spain around the tenth, eleventh, and twelfth centuries, while the *fueros* of both the nobility and the towns were the predecessors of the later Cortés, the Spanish equivalent of parliamentary democracy.

In the main, it appears that the underlying Iberian population, especially in the towns, continued the practices of Roman culture while the Germanic elements of law applied primarily to the Gothic ruling class. Even among the latter, however, there was more than a passing acquaintance with the Roman scheme of life; historians report that the Visigoths, at least by the time they arrived in Spain, were the most Romanized of all the Germanic tribes which settled in the empire.[60] The nature of the dual society which existed during this period is exemplified in the Fuero Juzgo, which contained elements of Gothic feudalism and Roman centralism,[61] the latter being largely attributable to the influence of ecclesiastical jurists who upheld the tradition of the Roman law which informed canon law.

The legally recognized cultural separation of the ruling Germanic class from the underlying Iberian population was also reinforced by a religious conflict which aligned Catholic Iberians against Arian Goths. During the reign of the Arian king Leovigild (568-586), for example, the conflict erupted, in Andalucía, in outright religious warfare. Creedal adherence also became a bond of ethnic cohesion which had political overtones; while the Iberians could rise within the ecclesiastical bureaucracy, the upper ranks of government were reserved for the Gothic nobility. Under the circumstances, the majority of the peninsula's inhabitants came to identify closely with the church, the leading exponent of Roman norms and the major carrier of the Roman cultural tradition under the Visigothic domination. Because of this and the special charters conceded to the municipalities, the Gothic nobility, which was chiefly rural, never succeeded in dominating the life of the Iberian population in the Catholic Roman towns.

The power of feudalism was weakened further in the struggle that occurred between the kings and the nobility.[62] When, in 586 the Gothic king Recared declared himself a Catholic, he swung to the support of the monarchy the church, the towns, and the general population. Thus, the monarchy joined with ecclesiastical power rather than submit to the claims of the feudal elements of society, and in so doing reinstituted the close Byzantine relationship between the state and sacerdotal authority. During the reign of Recared, religious unity became a Spanish political principle, and the Third Synod of Toledo (in 589) revived the old Theodosian restrictions on minority groups. Aided by its clerical advisers and jurisconsults, the crown was thereafter able to give even greater weight to the Roman norms which suited its pretensions to power.[63]

During the conflict between Catholic Iberians and Arian Germanic nobility, the first forces of Moorish power were invited into the peninsula (711); but as has happened at other times and places, the invited guests stayed longer than expected. They took up what seemed to be a permanent residence in Spain, the beginning of the Moslem occupation which was not terminated until approximately seven centuries later. For most of their stay, the Islamic intruders seem to have been, for that day and age, especially tolerant and capable rulers. Under their direction, Spanish civilization contrasted sharply with that of the rest of the European continent, for the Moslem overlords assiduously cultivated the arts and sciences, fostered crafts and improved agricultural practices, and brought to the universities the lore which they had acquired in the eastern Mediterranean and developed further on their own. As a reflection of their leniency, the subjugated Christian population was generally permitted to follow its accustomed Roman pattern of life, while the Jewish minority was accorded a tolerance (not duplicated until centuries later in mercantilistic Holland) thanks to which it developed a flourishing economic and intellectual life.

The material basis for the perpetuation of this life was found in the continued prosperity of the Iberian towns.[64] Unlike cities north of the Pyrenees, the Spanish cities were directly linked with the ancient Levantine trade routes which had supported urban life during the Roman empire, for the Moslem occupation maintained this important link with the now Islamic East. Indeed, under the benevolent tutelage of the Moors, the Spanish municipalities flourished as never before. Unquestionably, the sustained vigor of urban activity, both in occupied and unoccupied Spain, throughout this long period was an important factor in preventing the emergence of full-blown feudalism in the Iberian peninsula. In contrast to the urban remnants of northwestern Europe which were "isolated in a sea of feudal agrarianism," Spanish towns and cities carried on an active economic exchange both with the surrounding countryside and with foreign regions. A vigorous municipal democracy developed which was probably unequaled elsewhere in Europe for many years. During the Reconquest, after several centuries of such vitality, these municipalities were utilized by the Spanish crown as a counterpoise to the claims of the nobility, much as they had served the Gothic kings in their earlier struggle with the Visigothic nobility.[65]

In the long, intermittent struggle of the Reconquest, which culminated with the fall of Granada in 1492, the preestablished cultural tendencies of the Iberian peoples were substantially reconfirmed. The Spanish religious commitment deepened and became further bound up in the preservation of ethnic identity and in political objectives as crown and church faced a common adversary.[66] Orthodoxy and Spanish nationalism became practically synonymous. Intolerance replaced on both sides the previous atmosphere of relative religious toleration and made for a militant zeal bordering on fanaticism, the more so as the contest for supremacy in the peninsula was sharpened by the successful expansion of the Spanish and the defensive posture of the retreating Moors.

Old concepts of Caesarism and centralism were validated anew by the exigencies of military organization, and the pressures exerted on society by the reconquest effort reenforced the arguments for increased social control.[67] Alongside the fight to expel the Moslems there was reenacted the old struggle between feudalism and monarchical power. From around 800 on, a centralizing trend was observable in the royal position, especially in Castile and Leon, where feudal elements seem originally to have been somewhat weaker than elsewhere in Spain.[68] While nobles were rewarded with grants of land in reacquired territory, the monarchs frequently retained control of justice and government administration. Similarly, grants of various rights and lands were awarded the towns for their contributions to the Reconquest, a policy which in time enabled the monarchs to enhance their position in the struggles of the municipalities with the nobility.[69] By the time of the compilation and formulation of the Siete Partidas (c. 1300), which followed upon the strong reception of Roman law in Spain during the twelfth century, the *fueros* were still recognized, but as concessions rather than autonomously derived rights, and Roman norms of law were dominant, particularly the exaggerated Roman concept of imperial power.[70] The fact that central authority was strongest and that feudal power was correspondingly weakest in Castile and Leon is of interest, for Castile was the core of the royal authority which eventually asserted itself over all of Spain and the modalities of Castilian life predominated in the organization of the New World.[71]

The nobility was absorbed into the expanding civil bureaucracy of the crown, where its rights and perquisites derived from royal appointment rather than from an independent power base of a feudal nature, and it grew to be more and more a nobility of office in the machinery of administration. As the municipalities, too, were gradually subordinated to the sovereignty of the king, the chief power structure again rested, as it had under Byzantium, in the scepter-and-cross alliance and in the growing numbers of career administrators, legists known as *letrados* who were employed by the monarchs to staff the bureaucracy and who were trained in the monarchical principles of Byzantine law.[72]

One of the most important features of the period after the mid-thirteenth century was this development of a monarchical bureaucracy which administered the newly acquired territories. Alfonso X, especially, had worked hard in this direction. And while public administration had at first drawn heavily upon participation by nobles, in the thirteenth century and thereafter the nobles themselves were to some extent displaced by a professional bureaucracy of trained lawyers of both secular and ecclesiastical backgrounds. For more than three centuries of Islamic retreat, this governmental apparatus accumulated experience in the business of reoccupying and administering territory.

All the while, economic life was characterized by a growing interventionism.[73] This had been a Roman tradition, and it was an Islamic policy as well. In Spain, as in the rest of Europe, church doctrine provided an additional rationale for the propriety of regulating the conduct of business. Guilds performed their conventional role as agencies of control, but in many towns they were regulated by municipal authorities. With the gradual eclipse of quasi-independent municipal institutions, the royal bureaucracy supplanted lower-level governments in exercising the major direction over economic activity.[74] And given the overriding political and dynastic objectives of the crown, economic processes continued to play a subordinate role to social ends in the tradition of Mediterranean antiquity: the provisioning of the population under a system of regulation designed to insure orderliness and to extract for the royal purse the revenue necessary to finance the operations of a garrison state. The structure of economic relationships was still, in Polanyi's useful term, embedded in institutions which were essentially non-economic in character. Priorities of resource appropriation and allocation and the larger pattern of social dynamics responded primarily to claims other than the exigencies of material advance. Comparatively few resources were allocated to technological development, and the economic mechanism was not highly sensitive to the possibility of technical change. Indeed, in such a milieu, technical efficiency in economic activity was less relevant a concept than what might be called social efficiency, a matter of systems maintenance; in this perspective, the sacrifice of economic benefits was justifiable on the grounds of meeting certain social ideals.

Unlike northwestern Europe which had been repeatedly cut adrift from its ancient institutional moorings, the historical experiences of Spain had produced, by the end of the fifteenth century, a faithful reproduction of the monolithic prototype, the Roman-Byzantine pattern of social organization.[75] Perhaps it was inevitable that a certain siege mentality, crystallizing in a vigorous spirit of dogmatic hyperorthodoxy, should have developed as a consequence of the more than a millennium of struggle to maintain ethnic identity in the confrontation with alien cultures. By the time of Ferdinand and Isabella the institutions of a closed but self-confident society were firmly radicated in Hispanic culture, a feature which helped to insulate it from the potentially disruptive forces in the more fluid cultural milieu to the north. The requisite authentication of social arrangements was provided in the ideological basis of monarchical absolutism: one faith, one nationalism, and one political authority firmly grounded in Roman law. This was soon buttressed by the doctrines of clerical scholars of legal philosophy like Vitoria and Suárez regarding the nature of social order and the concept of the state.[76]

In practice, the consequences of this orientation were several. It implied a policy of uniformity imposed from the top but willingly accepted by the people as the common-sense mode of operation. It also involved the suppression of dissent as an intolerable menace to the integrity of the social order and the national political fabric, a view which led ultimately to the expulsion of Jews and Moors and to a relentless search for those suspected of heterodox or heretical leanings.[77] As the modern Spanish novelist José María Gironella has noted, the Spaniards had acquired a deeply held belief that religious faith was the very foundation of their national unity.[78] The monastic inquisition was established in Aragon after the middle of the thirteenth century and was extended to Castile under Ferdinand and Isabella in 1480.[79] Operating under royal rather than episcopal or papal control, it became an arm of the government and a weapon of total royal control.

Not only did the Inquisition promote political despotism and intellectual stagnation during the latter half of the fifteenth century, but it also severely impaired the capacity of Spain to realize maximum benefit from the commercial opportunities presented with the discovery of America. Considerable harm, for example, issued from the destruction of the 250 or so Jewish communities in Spain whose members were sent into exile in 1492.[80] Among the deportees (whose numbers ran possibly as high as 200,000) were entrepreneurs and others who had played active roles in the critical fields of public and private finance as well as in the learned professions, although formal Jewish leadership in other fields, such as textile manufacturing in Barcelona, had already been weakened after the thirteenth century. Similarly damaging, especially to Spanish artisan industries, was the expulsion of the Moors. Still more detrimental was the uncertainty which jeopardized the functioning of a goodly portion of the surviving business enterprises, for many were owned by the *conversos* (converts from Judaism) and, to a lesser extent, by the Moriscos (converts from Islam) against whom the Spanish Inquisition was primarily directed in the late fifteenth and sixteenth centuries.[81] While in its totality the thesis of Werner Sombart concerning the role of Jews in modern capitalism is difficult to accept, it seems nevertheless reasonable to assign a strongly contraproductive effect to the repressive Spanish measures which weighed particularly heavily upon precisely those ethnic groups which had been so instrumental in trade, finance, and industry. Religious persecution was, therefore, very nearly tantamount to persecution of the business community; it deprived the Spanish economy of scarce managerial talent and disrupted business organization at just that point in history when both were required for using the catalyst of the American trade to initiate a process of economic growth and transformation.[82] The opportunity was present, but the capacity to respond to it had been undermined, though Christian merchants, including nobility as well as commoners, did become active in the American trade.[83]

The possible contributions of feudal decentralization and constitutionalism were also largely forfeited by the course of Spanish evolution, though some vestiges remained in northern and northeastern Spain and in the *consulados* (merchant guilds) of certain coastal cities.[84] It is suggestive that these originally more feudalized regions have since displayed a temper and habit more attuned to the commercial age and have taken a leading role in the subsequent economic development of Spain while chafing at the national political hegemony of Castile. Similarly, it was through the *consulado*, particularly the one at Seville which worked closely with the official regulatory trade agency (the Casa de Contratación), that private enterprise mainly participated in the development of the American dominions, although the quasi-public functions of the Sevillian merchant guild converted it, to some extent, into an instrument of monopoly power and, indirectly, of state regulation of economic life through officially sanctioned corporate groupings.[85] However, the Roman doctrines elaborated by Vitoria and Suárez generally prevailed. The authority of the state (the crown) was construed as deriving from natural law and divine sanction rather than from any delegated consent of the governed. And this authority was charged with the main business of regulating the subsidiary social components to insure their orderly articulation, each with the others, and to impose on them the direction it determined to be in the common good. In pursuit of this function, the state was accorded a wide latitude of action.

What emerged, in short, was a concept of order and administration which flowed from the top down. An ideological basis was developed which legitimized the directive role of the state and rationalized the downgrading of alternative clusters of institutionally organized social interaction and initiative. It was not, however, an ideology built of pure cerebration, for the de facto situation involved a skewed sort of institutional development in which the central public institutions had amplified their structure and operations to an accentuated degree while all subsidiary institutions played a diminished social role.[86] In such a system, in contrast to feudalism, there was scant room for the development of the concept of the "community" as a society of voluntary associations of individuals intervening in logic (as well as practice) between the person and the state. Neither was there much doubt as to which institutionally defined considerations would be decisive in the marshaling and deployment of the system's economic resources.

Again in contrast to the ethos of northwestern Europe, the ethos of Spanish culture remained essentially precommercial, and in that sense, archaic. That the Spaniards sought material wealth such as gold or land did not necessarily make them commercially minded. A quest for material gain has been evident since the time of the early Mesopotamian river civilizations, but this scarcely justifies labeling all these societies as commercial or capitalistic. Neither does the transoceanic exchange of goods with the New World suffice to designate Spain a full-fledged member of the commercial revolution. There was also a substantial movement and exchange of goods in the earlier Mediterranean world, but, with some exceptions such as the Phoenicians, this could not be linked to commercialism in any historically meaningful way.

The point at issue in this question of ethos relates, therefore, more to methods than to goals. In an historically specific sense commercialism implies the conduct of production and trade for market sale (in a market as defined by economic theory today), with the principal objective of making profits (rather than mere provisioning), and with predominantly private organization of the activity on a basis of the pecuniary calculus. To a greater or lesser degree, it may also be supposed that in a regime of commercialism the social distribution of rewards follows commercial success. In Spain, few of these attributes of commercialism were present, and the distribution of rewards and prerogatives was primarily related to the apparatus of state, which preempted the free play of market forces in setting the chief parameters of business and economic decisions. Practically all wealth-producing activity was, directly or indirectly, subject to state control.[87]

Yet, though the history of Spain may not have prepared the country to cash in on the major institutional changes of the times, though its background may have oriented it primarily in the direction of consolidating and preserving a received cultural inheritance, and though the very integration of the Spanish social order may have closed out many possibilities for experimentation and innovation, the same historical sequence prepared Spain admirably, in other ways, for the important task just at hand. Though the Spanish state often seemed inept in the matter of economic development, as, indeed, the eighteenth-century Spanish economists repeatedly pointed out, it was enormously skilled in the arts and techniques of governing. By

1492 the Iberians had evolved a stabilized social-political-economic order which was ready for export and implantation in the New World—complete with a comprehensive theoretical authentication of this order, should any questions be asked.[88] The replication of that order in the American kingdoms was to provide the guiding principle for resource organization during the next three centuries.

III

The Organization and Management of the Public Sector: Colonial Spanish America

WITHIN a few decades after Cortés landed in Mexico, the outlines of Spanish American institutional life began to take shape, extending through space and time the socio-economic system that had evolved in the Iberian peninsula.[1] Of the important structural features of the system, only the regime of the hacienda and its institutional symbiont, peonage, remained to be developed at a later time. This is not to say that the quality of Spanish life had been permanently fixed by the close of the fifteenth century. Under eighteenth-century Bourbon rule, for example, a certain belated accommodation to European trends was effected: government administration was reorganized, economic policy was revamped, and the Enlightenment was ushered in, cautiously. Meanwhile, the Spanish system underwent further modification in its American setting. The crucial question, however, is whether this New World adjustment moved, on balance, in the direction of relative economic modernity.

Some historical interpretations suggest that it did, such as the contention by Germán Arciniegas, and others, that the Spanish brought capitalism to the New World.[2] Indeed, the writing which purports to describe a Spanish mercantilism implicitly links the colonial policies of the empire with a movement which historically functioned as an engine of incipient capitalistic development. So interpreted, however, the colonial period would be assessed primarily for its effect on the indigenous peoples. In their case, the coming of the Spaniards unquestionably pulled the organization of economic life closer to that of fifteenth-century Europe, even if it did so at heavy cost to the aboriginal population and their pre-Columbian cultural existence. From the beginning, the ties established with Spain functioned as a bridge with European civilization over which intangible and material culture traits were imported and diffused among the inhabitants of the New World.

New crops and crop technologies, medieval European mining techniques, new arts and crafts, wheeled vehicles, livestock and draught animals—all these were brought in by the Iberians and increased the potential economic capacity of the Western Hemisphere.[3] Postconquest organization of economic and general social activity also marked an advance over most preexisting tribal patterns, though the Mexican Indians had evolved an extensive network of market exchange centers, and the Incaic welfare system surpassed that introduced by the Spaniards in several respects.[4] But the termination of human sacrifices (a prominent feature of the Aztec civilization) and intertribal warfare, with its conspicuous consumption of human resources, must both be counted as steps in a desirable direction.[5] Moreover, the imperial system of Spain did provide a connection of sorts with external economic centers, however much influences from these centers were diminished by filtering through that system.

This is not to denigrate the technological accomplishments of the higher Indian civilizations nor the particularly remarkable social organizational advances which distinguished, say, the Inca empire (though neither of these deserve to be romanticized as they have been by some Hispanophobic writers). It is, rather, to record that the American technological base was broadened by the addition of the Mediterranean heritage and that the political unification of Spanish America was more favorable for productivity than the antecedent complex of smaller-scale, often belligerent tribal groupings. That the consequent increase in the per capita productive capacity of the New World was not, for a couple of centuries, reflected in a larger population enjoying a higher standard of living is attributable to an unexpected (and unintentional) collateral consequence of culture contact. During the sixteenth and seventeenth centuries there was a dramatic decline in the indigenous population when the Indians fell prey to European diseases carried in by the Iberians.[6] So great was the decline that gross American output must have fallen steeply for a considerable period, notwithstanding the per capita increases in productivity resulting from Spanish-sponsored innovations.

Throughout the period, however, the numbers of criollos (American-born persons of pure European descent), mestizos (persons of mixed European and Indian ancestry), and *gauchupines* or *peninsulares* (immigrants from Spain) rose as did their average standard of living, and long before the close of the colonial age, the region's product permitted a generous measure of both private and civic ostentation, as numerous contemporary observers recorded. Concerning the material existence of the dwindling Indian population, however, the evidence is far from clear. In the mission territories, Paraguay and California, for example, the aboriginals undoubtedly attained a higher level of output and consumption. But balancing this, the inhabitants of the Inca empire almost certainly suffered a severe retrogression in real per capita income and welfare levels.[7] Elsewhere, it is difficult to say whether the surviving Indians fared less well under the Spanish regime than under the exploitive arrangements of most pre-Columbian societies. Those who lived in some of the *congregaciones* (special native communities or reservations), on the church's rural estates, and in the crown *encomiendas* (native communities placed in trust under the monarch) may have lived about the same as previously, except that the labor draft for work in mines and on public works often reduced the time available for the practice of agriculture for self-sustenance. On the other hand, the living conditions and security levels of many aboriginals deteriorated with the disruption of autochthonous community organization, the harsh conditions of employment in the mines and *obrajes* (manufacturing workshops), and the gradual displacement of indigenous peoples from their original lands and settled community life to more marginal or submarginal lands or debt peonage. Even where indigenous productivity was raised by Spanish technological innovations, the relations of production were such that most of the increased per capita output was probably reflected in the rising per capita income of the ladinos and in the revenues of crown and church.

Despite this mixed record of actual benefits, it does appear that the colonial regime generally represented a noticeable economic updating of the pre-Columbian economies of the Americas. It is much less certain that the same was true for Iberian institutions. Because of the organization and aims of the Spanish empire and the geographical and social conditions surrounding the effort to implant Iberian institutions in the New World, these may well have moved away from instead of towards capitalistic forms and modalities, at least until the last half of the eighteenth century, when mercantilistic writers gained a certain influence in the determination of Spanish policies. As long as governmental guidance was the chief force of economic life, however, the state was neither conspicuous for its economic sagacity nor fully attuned to the drift of events elsewhere in the Western world. From this deviation from the mainstream of Western evolution sprang the problems of development and systemic adjustment encountered during the nineteenth and twentieth centuries.

THE ORGANIZATION OF THE EMPIRE

The preceding chapter examined the cumulative sequence of events which produced in Spain a quasi-Byzantine structure of archaic Mediterranean character. The structure so described possessed even greater validity as a projection of Iberian cultural ideals, for everyday Spanish reality was cluttered with the residue of centrifugal regional differences, attenuated feudalistic elements, and the like. In a very meaningful way, the construction of the New World empire was an effort by the Spanish crown, stunning in the magnitude of its conception, to reproduce abroad a pattern of society which resembled more closely the Iberian ideal of a managed society than did life in the Iberian peninsula itself [8]—hence the necessity of examining the operations of the public sector and the influence of the state's policies on private economic organization. Since the Spanish system represented the most complete union of church and state in the history of the Roman Catholic Church, the public sector should be defined as comprehending the assets managed by both civil and sacerdotal bureaucracies.[9] Without exaggeration, then, one may view the colonial arrangements of Spain as a sort of latter-day Byzantium—a conceptualization which is perhaps closer than the labels "capitalism," "private enterprise," "individualism," and "mercantilism" to discerning the central rationale of the empire and its internal dynamics, economic and otherwise.[10]

After a few years of tentative experimentation, the intentions of the crown with respect to New World organization became clear. Having struggled long to quash the political pretensions of the Spanish nobility, the rulers of Spain were loath to permit the development in the overseas territories of any groups possessing an autonomous power that could challenge monarchical absolutism. Accordingly, the organization of the colonial regime was entrusted neither to private monopolists and privileged or chartered companies nor to recipients of feudalistic fiefs.[11] The only, and temporary, exceptions occurred in areas of only marginal importance in the colonial system, such as Venezuela and Campeche. Because of Hapsburg financial obligations, a Welser company was briefly active in Venezuela during the early days of settlement; there also the Caracas company, a Basque enterprise, operated for several decades in the eighteenth century.[12] The principal exception to the proscription of feudal grants was the large estate awarded Cortés in the valley of Oaxaca. During the first three decades of the Conquest, when the royal treasury was at a low ebb, there were also private impresarios, the *adelantados,* who conceived and directed expeditions of exploration and settlement, usually under official authorization. Financed by individual investors, the *adelantados* usually sought mining wealth in new areas, over which they frequently received appointment as governors. Occasionally they discovered the objects of their quest, delivering, in accordance with the law, a portion of their gains to the crown as royalty payment. At other times they were granted land and other privileges in compensation for their efforts. But they were generally accompanied by representatives of the church and the government to insure the articulation of these ventures with the larger institutional fabric of the empire, as Paul Horgan depicted in his *The Centuries of Santa Fe.* Apparently, too, the monarchs soon had second thoughts about the prudence of conferring special rights on private individuals, for in subsequent years the crown moved to circumscribe and revoke the privileges granted earlier. Thereafter, these would-be entrepreneurs were deposed by the official bureaucracy, and government jurisdiction, at least in theory and formal organization, was supreme.

After the early years, therefore, the pacification of the Americas was mainly a controlled and directed colonization incorporating preexisting norms—an ordered, preplanned settlement conducted under a highly centralized administration after the Roman fashion.[13] In fact, the New World territories were not legally colonies, in the sense of collective undertakings of the Spanish nation, but were organized as kingdoms or direct dependencies of the crown and were always referred to officially as *estos reinos, esos reinos* (these, those kingdoms).[14] Furthermore, the new lands were regarded, in the Roman tradition, as the patrimony of the monarch, who might, at his discretion, grant a portion of it to others to achieve royal objectives. Thus, in the concept of the *real hacienda,* the New World became the private estate of the crown in which private ownership was impossible without special dispensation. Even when the royal patrimony was alienated, the disposition of property rights seems not to have been absolute. Original title to minerals remained vested in the crown, as the royalty payments demanded of mine operators indicated.[15] Property use was almost always legally subject to public regulation, and intermittent decrees suggest that, in theory at least, even land grants were conditional, and private property rights were contingent upon the crown's satisfaction that they were serving a public function.[16] In a number of instances, for example, official reports indicated that where the original grantees of land had failed to cultivate their properties, these lands were legally eligible for reassignment to others.[17] From this conditional character of property assignment, and the Catholic teaching with which it was in full accord, there developed the Iberian institutional precedent for the twentieth-century Latin American doctrine of the social function of property.[18] Indeed, during the colonial era the public utility concept extended beyond property rights to include labor power as well, which was often treated as a resource vested with a public interest and hence subject to public disposition and regulation.[19]

As in Spain, the crown, personifying the state, was the agency which both defined and achieved the common good; in the Iberian frame of reference the concept of the common good as something that might be approximated through decentralized interaction was exotic.[20] In accordance with conventional Iberian practice, the common good was achieved through a complex bureaucratic apparatus that administered the ever-growing body of decrees and juridical directives, which both legitimized the administrative machinery and laid down its course of action. Thus, monarchic and bureaucratic centralism, rather than feudal subsidiarity or spontaneous private interaction, was the prevailing technique of colonial organization.[21] In this structure—weighted heavily in favor of administrative and public law— there were few decision makers, and major decisions were made not so much with local ends in view as for the larger goals of the empire.[22]

"The soldier, the legist, and the priest"—these, in Haring's incisive comment, were the characteristic figures of the Spanish colonial scene. There is a pointed contrast here with North America of the colonial period, where the predominating settlers were farmers, planters, merchants, trappers, traders, and, less numerous, artisans, not a few of whom were also nonconformists of one stripe or another. Most were free-floating individuals, generally functioning tangentially to the main lines of traditional institutional structure and engaged in pragmatic activity for commercial gain. To a significant degree, the guiding rules of conduct were formulated empirically on the basis of an ad hoc style of adaptation. Confronted with a small, nomadic native population, most of the settlers were forced to work in order to make their way. Insofar as a principle of integration was involved, it was, aside from the general transactional environment associated with a particular sovereignty, a market mechanism of one sort or another. Significantly too, the economic attributes of these typical roles were precisely the basis for their identification—a feature which suggests a certain measure of autonomy in the economy, as related to other orders of societal organization.

Radically different was the trinity of soldier, legist, and priest, in its bearing on the etiology of Latin American social organization. While these, like the North American categories, were obviously composed of individuals, they were identified with social roles which were defined by well-established, complex, hierarchically organized institutions. The soldier, legist, and priest came primarily as carriers of institutional power and traits, serving institutionally defined ends which were larger than the individual actors themselves: the subjugation of a large, sedentary native population and the systematic transplantation of the cultural and political forms of sixteenth-century Spain. Each group had a body of doctrine and theory which both authenticated the institutional role and laid down formal rules for its conduct. Questions of procedure were resolved by rules, weighted more heavily by considerations of ceremonial adequacy and legitimacy than by purely instrumental efficacy, while the chief institutional focus was other than economic. Individualism there was, but it worked within the confines of highly structured and stable institutions of venerable vintage, all of which responded, *au fond,* to the sentential voice of the crown.

Equally significant, throughout most of the colonial period, emigration to the new kingdoms was generally allowed only to persons thoroughly institutionalized or imbued with Spanish Catholic norms—a policy which was fundamentally at variance with that practiced in North America, where dissenters were sent to the colonies.[23] Thus, the whole panoply of Spanish institutional life and power—its law, its government, and its religion—was implanted in the urban settlements at the very margins of the empire as a formal enterprise directed by the royal bureaucracy.

As a consequence of this approach, the kind of frontier which Turner described in North America simply did not exist in Spanish America as a significant conditioning factor in social experience. Indeed, the very solidity of the Spanish social edifice in the New World indicates that the aim was not a quest for a new type of social order. Octavio Paz, a Mexican intellectual of our day, summarized the ethos of the colonial venture well when he observed: "La sociedad colonial es un orden hecho para durar . . . una sociedad regida conforme a principios jurídicos, económicos, y religiosos plenamente coherentes entre sí y que establecían una relación viva y armónica entre las partes y el todo." [24]

In North America, vacant areas were taken up by a rural drift of persons from a hodgepodge of cultural backgrounds, and the amalgamation of cultures which resulted from interaction among heterogeneous ethnic groups weakened the cultural sanctions of all the contributing traditions. The process of institutional attenuation was hastened when the settlers were dissidents and hence only marginally institutionalized carriers of their old cultural orientation to begin with. Furthermore, as Denis Brogan has observed, the machinery of central government was weak; frontier communities and areas were thrown largely on their own in devising an adaptation of civic forms, law, and economic and social life to the exigencies of frontier conditions.[25] In all of this, the settlers were reenacting the basic historical experience of the North Atlantic cultural continuum, and from it emerged the distinctive features which have since captivated the imagination of social historians: the informality of life on the frontier, the fluidity of its social arrangements, and the pragmatic, experimental vigor which was expressed in a spirit of improvisation and modification. The "law west of the Pecos," developed by Judge Roy Bean and other less publicized magistrates, evolved in the common-law manner, because of the modest inheritance of specific legal directives, just as the weakness of central government led to a greater measure of self-government based on local initiative and control in dealing with local problems.[26]

Turner's North American case was, therefore, a dual sort of frontier. First, it was a geographical frontier which enjoyed a certain latitude of regional autonomy because of difficulties that communications and transport problems raised for effective exercise of central authority. Second and more important, it was an institutional frontier—the latter-day transoceanic extension of a cultural region which had long been a frontier in this institutional sense. Among its features was the absence of a geographically and socially comprehensive system of regulation, and thus a considerable portion of economic life was left, by default, to be determined by the interplay of market forces.

The Spanish American frontier, on the other hand, was primarily a geographical frontier and was not a frontier in the institutional sense at all. Individuals came to improve their lot within the limits set by the existing social order, not to devise new and variegated social forms. Their movement was not a disorganized rural drift; by and large, they moved from town to new town, being amply supplied ab initio in each transposition by laws, notaries, administrators, and clergy.[27] They did not need to devise a "law west of the Pecos" because they had already the law from Castile— indeed, a superabundance of it, together with the organizational mechanisms for its implementation.[28] Neither did they need to do much on their own to develop the other institutional aspects of collective existence in a new region. Like the Roman colonies, towns and cities in the Spanish New World developed chiefly as units of colonial administration and defense rather than as by-product social organizations which sprang up astride the lanes of regional and interregional trade.[29] Often, even the physical arrangements of town life and town sites conformed to the Procrustean bed of the planning decrees in which the early construction of churches and government buildings on the central plaza symbolized the order of priorities in the institutional sphere as well.[30]

Although Salvador de Madariaga has cited the colonial municipal government, the town councils or *cabildos,* as an example of democratic local organization in the Spanish New World, the general case for this interpretation is not altogether convincing.[31] At first the *cabildos* may have operated as genuine instruments of local government, but their functional significance gradually changed. In some instances, the crown, or its administrators, appointed a portion of the *cabildo* members (*regidores* or councilmen and *alcaldes* or magistrates),[32] while later, the crown, desperate for revenue, often declared the posts hereditary and sold them to the highest bidders. Over the years the *cabildo* offices came to be dominated by the wealthier colonists, especially those with large landholdings.

The practical import of the municipal councils was twofold. First, the councils often transferred to their members indigenous properties and valuable community lands (the *baldíos* and *ejidos* which were originally to be kept public in perpetuity with only the temporary usufruct of the land being leased out for public revenue).[33] In addition, the *cabildos* often distributed the lands of the *municipio* in parcels larger than those favored by the crown.[34] By these means of dubious legality, the municipal *cabildos* contributed to the formation of a landed criollo oligarchy which, with independence, became the residuary legatees of Spanish authority. Because of this development, municipal governments were seldom able to emerge as citadels of urban economic interest groups, as they had become in Europe. Rather, dominated by landed interests, they were often zealous in applying their authority to supervise and regulate markets in such a fashion as to circumscribe rather narrowly the ambit of trade and manufacturing activities.[35]

Second, the criollo group which eventually inherited the mantle of government did not gain significant experience in the responsible exercise of public authority, for over the same period the actual governmental functions of the councils often passed into the hands of a royal bureaucracy, cautious about intrusions on its political prerogatives. Furthermore, like all units of colonial administration, the *cabildos* had to work within the framework of the detailed legislation received from above, and *cabildo* acts required approval or confirmation from those higher up in the administrative hierarchy. Very often, *cabildo* membership became a ceremonial office; and wealthy members of the town councils occupied themselves largely with providing a seemly display on festive occasions—and mismanaging town finances.[36] Since *cabildo* officials had little direct participation in the business of government, no significant experiential basis was laid for enabling local community structures to function conjunctively, when independence came, with any national system.

Considering their conception and organization, the overseas Spanish dominions bore little resemblance to the economic enterprise which mercantilism held to be the chief function of colonization. For the latter, overseas territories were viewed chiefly as assets which could function as a springboard for commercial and industrial development in the metropolitan economy. Spanish aims were much less specific and, not infrequently, contradictory. This is not surprising since Spanish colonization was essentially an undertaking in civilization building in which the guiding directives and basic orientation related mainly to geographical extension of the government and the official religion, and to consolidation of political dominion both in the New World and on the European continent. As creatures of the central political organization, the New World kingdoms were, as Roscher observed, administered primarily for the benefit of the royal treasury, the administrative system, and the clergy.[37] Only secondarily were they employed to promote industry and commerce at home. In practice, given the overriding weight of dynastic political and military objectives, the secondary objectives were scarcely realized at all. By virtue of the rich gold and silver mines which Spain acquired in its territories, the royal purse was well supplied with disposable income directly and there was little pressure to obtain these metals via foreign trade balances on the basis of aggressive national development policies. If anything, the colonial expansion, with the inflation its bullion exports unleashed, may have actually hastened the economic decay of the motherland.[38]

With business and financial organization disrupted, with agriculture declining, and with an economic life saddled by a growing volume of rigid controls, Spain had embarked upon its American venture in a context of inelastic and eventually diminishing domestic supplies. To the New World it sent many of its more enterprising subjects, along with considerable numbers of what must surely have been a scarce commodity in that day and age, talented and trained administrators. Neither of these exports left the domestic economy the better for their departure. Of the rapid increase in bullion imports which followed occupation of the American mainland, a substantial portion was channeled by the apparatus of colonial administration into the coffers of profligate monarchs and, to a lesser extent, the treasury of the Spanish church.[39] Indeed, the bureaucracy itself absorbed a considerable portion of the revenue.[40] Relatively little flowed into the debilitated private sector of the economy under conditions which might have served the process of capital formation and expansion of peninsular output. The consequence was a severe and protracted price inflation which was aggravated even more by intermittent efforts to stem the flow of specie out of the realm.[41] Thus, inflation was added to all the other contraproductive factors present in the Spanish milieu, and the Spanish economy faltered and stagnated.

Altogether, the organizational basis of the empire was such that if mercantilism is appropriate at all as a description, it should be used only with drastic qualification.[42] For over two centuries, Spain's so-called mercantilism was not much more than a policy of imperial expansion combined with a crude sort of bullionism which, in J. W. Horrocks' evaluation, "failed to produce anything other than an artificial appearance of wealth and power." [43] Late in the colonial period, Spanish policy did move in the direction of a more authentic, Colbertian style mercantilism—thanks to the French influence introduced by a change of dynasties, and to the policies propounded by such Spanish mercantilists as Gerónimo de Uztáriz, Bernardo de Ulloa, Bernardo Ward, and Pedro Campomanes.[44] By that time, however, so many exogenous forces were operative that it is almost impossible to gauge the real impact of mercantilism proper on the colonial economy, though it produced, tardily, a marginal organizational modernization.[45] For the most part, the relation of the Spanish system to mercantilism has been best summarized by Eli F. Heckscher in his classic study, *Mercantilism*. Noting that the mercantilist "political writers of every country were preoccupied with the economic policy of Spain," Heckscher goes on to observe that "in these discussions, Spain was held up as a deterrent example." [46]

The subordination of the commercial spirit and private economic enterprise to empire building had decisive consequences for the course of American development: a large share of the exportable surplus of Spanish America was devoted to the royal ceremonial concerns or absorbed by the administrative bureaucracy. The amount available for public sector (and private sector) capital formation was correspondingly reduced, and the exportable surplus itself was kept small by the lack of a long-term growth-optimizing allocation of resources conducted in a framework of calculated inputs and outputs. Had the latter criteria prevailed, it is likely that the geographical focus of colonization efforts would have been much less diffused and the overall organization of the enterprise different. As it was, there were significant costs of system maintenance, for the territory claimed was far vaster than the territory effectively occupied. The economic life of the settled regions was thus subject to charges for the defense and administration of the larger area, and to the cost of maintaining some semblance of political and economic integration among the widely dispersed settlements.[47]

Unlike the North American colonists who settled in the temperate zone, the Spanish moved into an inhospitable part of the world. Much of the area had few attractive features for people accustomed to life in the temperate zone, and the coastal areas in particular were uninviting. The enormous distances and imposing terrain, the deficiency of river highways to the more habitable interior highlands, and the lack of economic value in a large part of the region led to widely scattered settlements located principally in the more favorable highland regions of Middle and South America: the Mexican *mesa central*, the dispersed *tierras templadas* of Central America, the *cordillera* valleys of Venezuela, Colombia, Ecuador, Peru, and Bolivia. Settlements of secondary consequence were also established in the northwestern portion of Argentina and central Chile, but the areas of major colonial importance were the Mexican and Peruvian viceroyalties, the latter including also the territory of upper Peru or Charcas (Bolivia). Some towns were established on the coast to service the populations of the interior: Veracruz, Acapulco, Porto Bello, Cartagena, Guayaquil, and Callao. Others, like Buenos Aires, were primarily defense outposts. But with the chief exceptions of the Peruvian coast and central Chile, the major Spanish settlements were found inland.

Under the circumstances, communications and transport were exceptionally difficult and absorbed a substantial amount of resources: labor and pack animals, and the land necessary for supporting both. Even in the case of the famous Inca road network, the fact that it had been designed mainly for use by a light volume of foot traffic and llama trains rendered it either unsuitable for post-Conquest uses or subject to rapid deterioration under the heavier volume of traffic moving by wheeled vehicles and burro, horse, and mule trains. Even late in the colonial period, the viceroy of Mexico could still lament that the vastness of the territory and the sparsity of the population made the execution of public works exceedingly difficult.[48]

To the exterior, these conditions reinforced the politically imposed isolation of the empire; internally, the high costs of long-distance trade greatly impeded the development of specialization in local production based upon a growing volume of economic intercourse among regions.[49] Only a small category of high-unit-value and more durable goods could absorb the costs and survive the rough conditions of transport: luxury and semiluxury goods of a specialty nature, textiles, gold and silver bullion, and livestock products (meat, hides, and wool) which could move to market by hoof.[50] Consequently, each local area tended to develop a diversified pattern of small-scale production for the limited local market demand, with productive efficiency conditioned adversely by the system of local economic controls, and the lack of competition caused by the transport situation and the numerous trade taxes and regulations.[51] Cottage industries abounded, especially around the viceregal capitals and major mining centers, but with few possibilities for advance to more sophisticated techniques and character of organization.[52] Given the similarity in regional products and production cost differences which were less than transport costs (not to mention transport costs plus trade taxes), only a limited volume of intercolonial trade was feasible. The fact that cottage industries operated under constant or increasing cost conditions served to restrict further the possibilities for interregional exchanges. Similarly, the opportunities for commercial agricultural development were limited by the transport problems, except for ranching, raising a few specialty export crops, and farming in the areas around the fringes of the larger population centers.[53]

Both the pattern of settlement and the intervening terrain, therefore, interacted with the prevailing level of technology and other factors to hold down the economic surplus of the American kingdoms. But the magnitude of the challenge of reproducing Spain overseas and adding to the glory of the crown—a much broader and more resource-consuming objective than mere "economic development"—required that no small part of this meager surplus be expended in pushing forward the frontier, in financing the ponderous organization of government, in establishing even minimal transport and communications facilities, and in furnishing the colonial elite with the physical and institutional appurtenances of Iberian civilization. Nowhere else did American life approximate the pomp and splendor which Genaro Estrada has described for colonial Mexico City in his *Visionario de la Nueva España* and which Raúl Porras Barrenechea has depicted for colonial Lima in his *Pequeña Antología*.[54] Yet, in a multitude of other places—in Puebla and Guanajuato (Mexico), Antigua (Guatemala), Cartagena and Bogotá (Colombia), Cuzco (Peru), to cite only a few—the evidence remains to this day that life in the New World, notwithstanding the low general level of productivity, was not mean for all concerned. Indeed, when Francisco de Miranda, a hero of Venezuelan independence, toured the newly established United States of America, he could remark with some surprise the rather crude aspect presented by the less elegant cities of the northern republic.[55] Since the external capital received initially by Spanish America was modest and since the area was exporting bullion throughout most of the colonial era, virtually all of the capital formation which occurred in the New World was generated out of the operations of the colonial economy itself, and because of the fiscal system, the region was exporting substantial amounts of capital as well.

If the consequences of this pattern of resource use were less than optimal from the perspective of ordinary economic criteria, the durability of neo-Iberian civilization suggests that nevertheless a certain maximizing of the relevant political and cultural values was achieved. In the face of a declining metropolitan economy, the destruction of Spanish sea power in 1588, the aggressive strength of rival European states, and the seeming unsusceptibility of the New World territory (with its geographical obstacles and large indigenous population) to easy external control, the Spanish empire did after all hang together for over three centuries. An astonishing degree of social and political stability was, in fact, one of its chief characteristics.

In this system, economic relationships, processes, and decisions were largely meshed with those that accompanied the functioning of institutions which were based on political, religious, or other noneconomic criteria. The mundane business of making a living was a major absorber of human energies, but it did not set the pace for other social relationships so much as take its cues from them. Production and distribution occurred as adjuncts of the behavior of larger social complexes, and the operations of the economy were influenced less by the decentralized decisions of the market than by governmental guidance. Market forces were only operative in an exceedingly imperfect manner, mainly around the margins of the major institutions which sat in control of the economic process at its key points.

The civil government controlled much of the economic environment, either directly or indirectly, and allocated resources essentially according to its own conception of the criteria of systems maintenance—i.e., fostering of intra-empire integration, affording protection from externally induced subversion, enhancing centralized control, and deterring coalitions among its subordinated subjects. Reinforcing state control over the status differentiation system and the distribution of valuable resources was the state's control of access to commercial or trading opportunities. Even in the private sector, as in the case of the artisan guilds, the *obrajes*, and the *consulados*, it was often hard to distinguish between the private and public aspects of the dominant institutions.[56]

The church—with its estates, workshops, missions, revenues, and accumulated funds—presided over other extensive portions of economic and social life, at times overlapping the realm of civil government. Through it the state controlled the process of forming a value consensus, by means of which particularistic values were used to create a common unity and legitimate the basic authority structure of the empire. But in addition to forming the normative orientations which facilitated general social control, public investment in religious institutions enhanced the value of the special item (access to salvation) which those institutions were in a position to confer or withhold. As a result, public authority was able to employ spiritual as well as mundane sanctions to enforce its will.

The indigenous *congregaciones, resguardos,* or *reducciones* (institutions somewhat like the Indian reservations of today) represented a third distinct area of economic organization, albeit with important links to civil government and the church.[57] In general, however, the resources available to the Indian communities gradually diminished so that, except as a residual category of resource organization, their determinative role in the development process was largely conditioned by the behavior of the other principal institutions.

Of far greater consequence was the hacienda, which modern research has revealed to be much more comprehensive in aim and scope than a mere organizational focus for economic activity. From the seventeenth century on, the hacienda emerged as a fourth significant nucleus of social interaction. It gained resources at the expense of the indigenous communities, absorbed the usufruct of financial and real resources held by the church, and eventually contested the state itself for de facto control of political power.

The balance of this chapter will be concerned with the state and the church which functioned as the public sector and had major resources at their command. Though they did not always employ the resources of the society in an entrepreneurial fashion to a degree commensurate with their primordial control, they were nevertheless the chief sources of initiative in the colonial order. Among the decision makers of these directing institutions there was little belief in the efficacy of a market system as a major allocator of resources. Thus, for three hundred years the market mechanism functioned under all manner of restraint and modification, including its outright suspension over significant areas of resource organization, and this has led to many of the current economic idiosyncrasies in Spanish America.

THE COMPLEXITY OF PUBLIC SECTOR ORGANIZATION

Underpinning the enduring social and political stability of the empire was a web of four interrelated and overlapping bureaucracies. The monarch was the pivot point of this complicated network, aided by his exchequer and the Council of the Indies (the Real y Supremo Consejo de las Indias), the jurisdiction of which was supreme in the all-encompassing framework of colonial administration.[58] Legislative, executive and administrative, judicial, and military functions were all combined in the Council, along with extensive powers of regulation over financial, commercial, and ecclesiastical affairs. Working closely with the Council and the royal exchequer, the Trade House or Casa de Contratación trained pilots and navigators, operated a cartographic office, assembled geographical information and resource surveys, controlled transatlantic commerce, and supervised the trade fleets and the important trade fairs in the New World, thereby subjecting the most important segment of wholesale exchanges to royal direction.[59]

It is neither necessary nor possible to trace out here the exact outlines of this complicated hierarchical system, allowing for all the regional variations therein and the changes introduced from time to time in the course of three centuries. The most important changes occurred in the last half of the eighteenth century, at which time the administrative organization was modernized, the *intendiente* system introduced, the fiscal system simplified, and the control of foreign trade liberalized.[60] Concurrently, the state made strenuous efforts to revitalize the colonial economy.[61] For our purposes, it is sufficient to observe the general character of this system and its implications for the pattern of social and economic dynamics. As will be seen, through the manifold functions of the four bureaucratic hierarchies, the government became for all intents and purposes the agent responsible for the entire state of society and the chief source of economic initiative.[62]

The first structure may be defined as the group of offices designated by the titles viceroy, captain-general (a military office), governor, and *cor-*

regidor (a local or provincial governor). In the offices of viceroy and governor there was reproduced on a lower level and to a more limited degree the multiplicity of functions held by the Council of the Indies. Both civil authority and control of the secular aspects of ecclesiastical government fell within their scope of action, as did, frequently, military command since these officials were often also captains-general.[63] The functional jurisdiction of the *corregidores* was more restricted, but nevertheless still quite extensive in economic matters.[64]

The second structure included the judges and other officials associated with the royal tribunals known as *audiencias*, which were, below the Council of the Indies, the highest courts of appeal in the districts of their jurisdiction. Beyond their judicial functions, however, the *audiencias* served in an advisory capacity as councils of state to the viceroys and governors and also possessed certain legislative powers. In various areas they held important administrative powers as well and thus were characterized by the conglomeration of functions found elsewhere in the Spanish system.[65]

The third bureaucracy consisted of the royal-exchequer officials who were charged with administering royal revenue and held financial authority coordinate with that of the viceroy.[66] The fourth bureaucracy was the ecclesiastical hierarchy, which was multiple in character as it included the bishops and diocesan clergy on the one hand and the various religious orders on the other.

Nominally, the viceroys were the coordinators of these several hierarchies. Just as the king was the chief patron of the church, intervening between the Vatican and the clergy of the Spanish possessions, so the viceroy was the vice-patron of the church in his jurisdiction. As such, he presided over administration of the system of ecclesiastical taxation and the nomination of persons to most ecclesiastical posts down to the parish level. As president of the royal exchequer office, the Junta Superior de la Real Hacienda, he was affiliated with the fiscal apparatus; and as presiding officer or president of the *audiencias* in the districts directly subject to his authority, he played a role in that bureaucracy too.

The intricacies of the system, however, are by no means adequately described in the foregoing sketch. There was no clear-cut division of functions among the various bureaucracies and offices, but rather a situation of overlapping jurisdictions. Different offices exercised similar functional roles, and the functions of one bureaucracy were sometimes exercised by members of another hierarchy, as, for example, when prelates were appointed as viceroys. In some *audiencia* districts the viceroy was president of the *audiencia* tribunal and acted as governor and captain-general as well. In others the *audiencias* had their own presidents, in some of which the powers of governor were retained by the viceroy and in others of which the *audiencia* president was at the same time governor and captain-general. Still other variations were found in the system.

Moreover, despite the apparent centrality of the viceregal position, the crown, as a technique of control, retained a close relationship with the various hierarchies independently of the viceroys. Exchequer officials, *audiencia* judges, high churchmen, and even many of the viceregal subordinates such as the governors were appointed by the crown and reported directly to the Council of the Indies. Functionaries of the church maintained a continuing scrutiny of the civil bureaucrats, and the latter in turn reported on the activities of clerics. Lower-echelon officials, *consulados*, *cabildos*, and at least the wealthier colonial subjects were also on occasion moved to write directly to the Council in Spain to seek favorable treatment.[67] In addition, the municipalities were empowered to send to the crown special representatives known as *procuradores* to plead their interests on particular matters, although occasionally the viceroys were able to block such appeals.

To minimize the intrusion of local interests into public administration, virtually all positions in which sizable executive, legislative, and judicial authority was vested were reserved for *peninsulares* or *gauchupines*. Rotation of appointments was the rule, and a variety of decrees were issued to keep colonial civil servants detached from local interests of a familial or economic nature, although this intent was not always successfully realized. Not only was it hoped thereby to minimize conflicts of interest in the performance of public function, but also the system was designed to hold in rein the inherent centrifugal tendencies which might arise in the overseas kingdoms and to insure some measure of bureaucratic loyalty to the crown.[68]

Other channels of central surveillance over the bureaucracies were the *memorias* or reports which the viceroys issued at the expiration of their terms of office and the *instrucciones* or instructions they left for their successors. But the chief formal checks were provided by two institutions, the *residencia* and the *visita*. The former was a public court of inquiry presided over by a judge, the *juez de residencia*, which reviewed the terms of office of all important officials except those of the church. It investigated the possibilities of malfeasance and heard complaints together with the defense of the official under scrutiny. The judgments of the *residencia* were, however, apparently subject to appeal to Spain, so that a friend at court could sometimes aid in reversing an unfavorable review. The *visita* was a secret inquiry, conducted by a *visitador* or inspector-general during a term of office, not so much to detect malfeasance (though it did this incidentally to its main business) as to stimulate more efficient action by the bureaucracies.[69] Apart from the *residencia* and the *visita*, there were also specially commissioned judges known as *pesquisidores* or *jueces de comisión* who were dispatched by the *audiencias* from time to time to examine the conduct of *cabildo* affairs. The *audiencias* could also pass upon policies set forth by other colonial administrative units such as the governors.[70] Special roving investigators were also sent over from time to time to tour the American possessions and to report back to the crown the deficiencies observed on these travels.[71]

Finally, the scope of all action, laws, and decrees promulgated by authorities in the New World was subject to constraints imposed by the voluminous stream of decrees or *cédulas* which poured forth continually from the king and the council.[72] These decree-laws not only set forth basic directives but also regulated in quite specific detail almost all aspects of colonial life and administration, combining both public and private law. As the source of the strong tradition of administrative law in Latin America, the proliferation of *cédulas* eventually assumed such proportions that a minimum attempt at systematization was necessary, and various compilations or Recopilaciones were made.[73] Comprehensive as they were, however, the Recopilaciones give only a glimpse of the welter of legislation. For example, the first, published in 1681, contains some 6,400 laws which were distilled from an earlier attempt in 1624-1635 to reduce approximately 400,000 *cédulas* to about 11,000 decrees. And, of course, the stream of new decrees continued even as each Recopilación was being published.

STATE INTERVENTIONISM: FORMS AND OBJECTIVES

The host of imperial administrative agencies functioned also as organs of economic intervention, and from these agencies and such quasi-public bodies as the *consulados,* mining tribunals, and guilds, there emanated an extensive and complex regulation of production, distribution, and consumption in the New World. Corresponding to the prevailing bias of *étatisme,* the lower level entities were largely subordinated to the authority of the higher level official regulatory agencies.[74] The array of economic policies which are documented in the records of legislation and other sources of information on colonial life reveals a variety of objectives, and these were not always consistent with one another. All attest, however, to the comprehensive role of the state in the economies of the overseas dominions.

Settlement and Provisioning

Many of the measures implemented by the crown, or its subsidiary organs, were employed primarily to encourage the settlement of outlying territories and to insure a basic provisioning of the various parts of the empire. To these ends, the government made direct allocations of land and on many occasions specifically prescribed the use of the land so granted.[75] Probably with a view to avoiding the unsettling effects of a floating population, crown officials sometimes utilized vagabonds in the founding of these new settlements, and by making land grants conditional upon land use (as well as by prohibiting unauthorized settler movements), expressed the hope of fixing the settlers to their new locations. Additional developmental subsidy was supplied by viceregal loans and grants of funds, together with public grants of seeds, livestock, food provisions, and agricultural implements.[76] Both civil and ecclesiastical officials were active in fostering the propagation of new crops and livestock, and where special skills were required, as in viniculture, sericulture, and sugar production, the state also provided technical advice and trained artisans.[77] Still other provisioning efforts of the government led to the opening up of copper, tin, and iron mines, as local sources of supply for metal fabricating shops, although the quality of the known deposits together with the level of transport and other costs generally resulted in a small and sporadic output of these metals (mainly when European imports were not available) and the bulk of colonial requirements was imported in crude form for local fabrication.[78] More important, however, was the patronage of the state and the church which encouraged the establishment of the many artisan industries needed to support an Hispanic life style in the New World. Decrees of the crown urged the instruction of the natives and imported Negro slaves in mechanical arts, and similar efforts were undertaken by the religious orders at the urging of the clerical hierarchy. Schools were established to provide training in such crafts as carpentry, blacksmithing, weaving, tailoring, cobbling, and the like, and the immigration of skilled craftsmen to the Americas was encouraged. Significantly, the general prohibitions against foreigners in Spanish America did not apply to those who were mechanics or artisans. Public and ecclesiastical expenditures paid the wages of many skilled craftsmen, and even some of the *obrajes* were administered directly by public officials, on crown account, or by the clergy as part of the operations of religious institutions. Besides the foregoing, the government—with the collaboration of the church and the *consulados* in many instances—was the primary organizer of a variety of public works activities such as schools, hospitals, roads and bridges, drainage and flood control projects, water supply systems, inns, and the construction of public and church buildings.[79]

To reinforce these general promotional and provisioning goals, state influence in the labor market extended well beyond the supply of skilled labor. Formal enslavement of the indigenous population, permitted in the early days of the Conquest, was reduced substantially by legislation in the 1530's and 1540's; thereafter Indian slavery was generally prohibited except for captives taken from tribes which carried on continuous warfare with the Spaniards. As a substitute for enslavement of the Indians, the state introduced two other techniques of labor mobilization. Slave labor was imported from Africa for use on the plantations of the Antilles and the mainland coasts, and a regime of conscript labor was imposed on the Indian population.[80] On the basis of a legal concept similar to the law of public purpose, the native communities were obligated to participate in a *corvée* system to supply manpower for purposes determined by public authorities. Under the *mita*, the *repartimiento*, the *cuatequil*, or the *mandamiento*, as the system was known in different regions, the state determined the man-power-supply quotas for the villages, allocated these labor supplies among alternative uses, and set quotas of labor and scales of payment for the various employments [81]—although the legal stipulations regarding minimum wages and maximum hours were by no means always conscientiously ob-served. Of the labor force so recruited, some were assigned to public works: the construction of roads, drainage systems, and buildings, the maintenance of inns and resting stations (*tambos*) for travelers, and the like. In these instances, the *mita* became a technique for converting labor power into compulsory capital formation, and throughout most of the colonial period public construction was at least partially dependent upon forced labor. Other Indians, particularly in times of food shortages, were assigned to private employers for the care of livestock, the planting and harvesting of crops deemed essential to community welfare, and as field hands on the sugar plantations (though not as mill workers). Even late in the colonial period, when the *mita* system had been replaced by debt peonage in agri-culture, the regime of conscript labor was occasionally revived to mobilize labor for particular crops.[82] In Peru, at least, *mitayos* (Indians in the *mita*) were also employed in *obrajes*. Quite apart, however, from direct allocation of labor, the colonial administration intervened extensively to regulate the use of labor in various fields.[83]

With a more-or-less chronic situation of short supplies prevailing, un-regulated monopoly was an ever present danger. Throughout the empire, therefore, the provisioning of centers of settlement was also attended to by deliberate control of retail transactions in local markets, especially trans-actions involving basic necessities.[84] At the same time, however, the state, by manipulating the structure of the market, was also intervening to help set the equilibrium among the various social classes; from the evidence available it would appear that interventionary controls were applied less frequently to horizontal or intra-class transactions than to vertical or inter-class transactions. In particular, regulations tended to be strict on the supply of food staples, artisan products, and the like to the upper classes.

Public market places were established with the requirement that economic exchanges be made in designated areas under official scrutiny. In addition, public warehouses and storage facilities were built, from which, to regulate supplies and prices, the crown sold produce collected from the taxes in kind paid by Indians and other agricultural producers. In times of particularly acute food shortages, the government went so far as to ration certain staples, to expropriate the tribute grain of the *encomenderos*, to set production quotas and stipulate agricultural land use, to require compulsory deliveries of food-stuffs at fixed prices, and to prohibit regional exports.[85] On occasion, ecclesiastical sanctions were added to those imposed by the civil govern-ment, and the marketing of food surpluses from the church's estates was occasionally used to gain additional leverage over retail transactions in

staples. Even nonstaple items came in for some attention; at various times
and places sumptuary laws were in force, covering such matters as buttons,
the permissible adornment of clothing, and the details of funeral corteges.[86]
An interesting example of compulsory economic transactions is that Indians
subject to the supervision of the *corregidores* were, at least on occasion,
required to make purchases at fixed prices of a variety of fabricated goods.[87]

Intercity and interregional trade in less essential goods was dominated
by the larger mercantile houses and the *consulados,* which exercised quasi-
official regulatory powers over certain aspects of the marketing process.
In this interdistrict trade, merchants operated as intermediaries between the
guild and *obraje* producers on the one hand and distant markets on the
other, and while this traffic was conducted with somewhat greater freedom
for the merchants, it was not entirely outside the purview of official supervision. For some of this trade, licenses were required, and depending upon
circumstances public authorities were empowered to withhold permission
to move goods between local markets.[88] Nevertheless, since these transactions were carried on across municipal jurisdictions, regulation was more
difficult, especially in the outlying areas where close scrutiny by public
officials was less likely. In this traffic, merchant capitalists were sometimes
able to realize large gains from their transactions, and towards the end of
the colonial period the effective control of production occasionally passed
into the hands of these mercantile intermediaries.[89]

The bulk of production and exchange in colonial Spanish America, however, took place on a purely local basis under such extensive regulation
that one may conclude that the major portion of the nonsubsistence sector
of the economy was subjected to some system of control. Besides the regulation of retail prices, there were also numerous regulations of the quantities
and quality of the goods produced as well as production costs such as wages
and hours of labor. The viceroys, *audiencias, corregidores,* and *cabildos*
were all active in promulgating ordinances relating to such matters.[90] Accordingly, the output of both the artisan guilds, which seem seldom to have
had much real autonomy, and the licensed *obrajes* or manufacturing workshops was subject to the control of public authority.[91] The guilds, in fact,
functioned primarily as local agencies of control subordinated to the larger
structure of interventionist mechanisms, and presented substantial obstacles
to the free movement of labor and entrepreneurship in manufacturing.[92] In
other words, imperfections in both factor and output markets were built-in
features of the colonial secondary activity sector. Moreover, although to
some extent the guilds permitted, or even in certain instances fostered, improved production techniques in such fields as ironworking, woodworking,
and ceramics, the advances along this line were not impressive as a whole.[93]
Generally speaking, the degree of intervention applied to manufacturing
discouraged initiative, enterprise, and technological progress. Similarly, the
close regulation of costs and prices precluded the manufacturing sector

from becoming an important source of capital accumulation in the colonial system. For both the guilds and the *obrajes,* the possibilities for material gain depended less upon production and marketing efficiency than on the exercise of political influence to obtain more favorable regulatory treatment. Thus, however comprehensible the system of regulation was from the standpoint of short-term consumer welfare, the controls applied to production and marketing were ultimately detrimental to the attainment of longer-term provisioning objectives.[94]

Export Development and Industrial Modernization

Beyond securing an economic base for the American dominions, governmental direction also sought to develop specialty export products. Sugar was one of these of early importance, although most of the sugar output was destined for colonial consumption, while later on other products such as cochineal and cacao were objects of special attention from public authorities. During the eighteenth century, in particular, bureaucratic entrepreneuring was utilized more forcefully to expand the export base of the overseas possessions. When, for example, vanilla became an important export from Mexico and Central America, governmental officials began to regulate the cutting of pods to maintain a higher quality in the beans entering commercial channels.[95] During approximately the same period, the *audiencia* in Guatemala encouraged the cultivation of indigo by establishing collection centers, setting price schedules, and creating a revolving fund—financed by a grant from the treasury and by an assignment of certain export taxes—for making low-interest loans (4 per cent) to finance crop production.[96] When growing export competition from Asian indigo threatened the Guatemalan producers, who also suffered a chronic labor shortage, the state issued a directive in 1784 which resumed the earlier system of conscripting native workers. One-fourth of the able-bodied Indians in each village were placed on the labor rolls for assignment by public authority to the growers, with governmental regulation of wage rates, conditions of work, and the like.

For most of the colonial period, though, export diversification took second place to the government's program of basic provisioning intervention. This was the case largely because Spain, being able to obtain bullion from its American mines, was under reduced pressure to promote a pattern of production development which, when combined with appropriate trade policies, would bring in bullion through an active external trade balance. The mining industry itself, however, was from the earliest times the focus of a whole series of developmental measures, both because it produced the major export and because of its key role in increasing the flow of royal revenues.[97] Salt and mercury mines, a few silver mines, and some of the more important copper mines were administered on government account.[98]

In Colombia, the platinum mines were also eventually taken over by the government.[99] Most of the industry, however, was operated by private individuals (albeit under close governmental supervision), and state encouragement of mining expansion consisted mainly of policies designed to support private endeavors. Accordingly, to stimulate the growth of mining, the state supplied tools and implements, technicians, loans, grants of funds and usufructuary titles to mining properties. Additional inducements were held out to mine operators in the form of grants of aristocratic status, exemption from imprisonment for debt, limitations on the sequestration of mining properties, preferential treatment of miners' offspring in appointments to royal service, tax and royalty reductions, and differential supply prices on the government-controlled basic mining inputs of gunpowder and mercury.[100] On occasion, as at Potosí in the latter half of the 1500's, elaborate public works projects were launched to facilitate the adoption of improved mining technology.[101] From taxes collected in kind, foodstuffs were made available through government commissaries in the mining centers to supply the labor force.[102]

Long after compulsory labor assignments had fallen into disuse for agriculture, the practice was continued in the mining industry which had the most notorious and extensive use of the *mita* device in the entire colonial economy. It lingered on longer in South America than in Mexico, where it was of little importance by the mid-eighteenth century.[103] While forced labor was never the exclusive source of manpower for the mines,[104] it did represent a substantial subsidy, for the evidence indicates that there was a considerable discrepancy between the wages paid the *mitayos* and those paid free labor. In a report on his visit to the Potosí mining center in the second decade of the seventeenth century, for example, Antonio Vásquez de Espinosa noted that the 13,300 *mitayos* assigned to the mines and smelters of the region each received an average payment of four reales a day while the 4,000 *mingados* or free laborers earned from twelve to sixteen reales (and in some cases up to 24 reales) a day.[105] Paradoxically, although the use of coerced labor to promote mining development had been justified on a public purpose basis, in the long run the practice actually worked against the public interest. The availability of an unfree labor force, paid lower than its marginal productivity, diminished the incentive to employ labor-saving capital and introduce newer techniques of production. Consequently, part of the gross technological backwardness which eventually characterized colonial mining was due to the chief policy instruments that had been intended to foster its development.

Coercive labor policies, however, were not the only problem in the mining industry. The deficiencies of private organization appear to have been even more of a liability than the influence of government. Unsound business practices—including the corruption of public officials, promotional hoaxes, and rashly conceived projects—seem to have been prevalent among the mine operators, and poor financial and managerial organization was common.[106] Violations of technically oriented mining ordinances contributed to the disorderly operation of the mines, while the vulnerability of irregularly established mining claims to protracted litigation constituted still another obstacle to the progress of the industry. Moreover, mining profits seem generally to have been dissipated in conspicuous consumption, leaving the improvident miners little capital for routine reinvestment purposes or for investment in new technologies and the development of new areas.[107] Indeed, despite the long period of experience which had been built up in mining activities (or perhaps, because of the character of that experience), the chronic shortage of capital and of suitable private financing institutions was a serious problem to the rehabilitation of the industry even in the late eighteenth century.[108] Yet, by that period, because of the exhaustion of the richer and more accessible veins, the increasing depth of operations, water encroachment, and cave-ins, extensive rehabilitation was absolutely essential. Worse still, private management was so technologically conservative that it strongly resisted the government's belated attempts to renovate the industry in the late 1700's. The effort to restore output levels at the vital Huancavelica mercury mine in Peru, for example, met with adamant and successful opposition.[109] The crown also sent over a number of European mining experts to upgrade the level of technical practices—e.g., the Elhuyar, del Río, and Sonneschmidt missions to Mexico, and the Elhuyar, Ulloa, and Nordenflicht missions to Peru and Bolivia—but their efforts encountered not only apathy but also active hostility from the mine operators they were trying to help.

Yet, even though efforts to rehabilitate the colonial mining industry were not well received, the situation illustrates the important role played in the economic system by state initiative. Given the attitudes which prevailed in the private sector, the administrative bureaucracy was, with all its deficiencies, a major source of constructive programs of economic action. In both Mexico and South America it was the government rather than private enterprise which took the main responsibility for trying to improve and modernize the mining industry. In Mexico, for example, the state opened a mining school to augment the supply of trained technicians, set up a special mining development bank with government funds to alleviate (by means of what today would be called supervised credit) the shortage of private capital, and reorganized the industry under a new mining tribunal which also received government financing. At first designed to operate as an industry-elected board, the tribunal was, in effect, nationalized after about a decade of operations since the mining industry had proved incapable of improving itself.[110] Thereafter, government operation of both the tribunal and the *avío* or development bank placed the program on a far more responsible basis. During the same period, to increase the supply of capital to the South American mining sector, governmental mining banks (known as *bancos de rescate*) were established on the basis of assignments of special taxes to operate in Peru, Bolivia, and Chile. In both Peru and Mexico, the state launched a search for new sources of mercury to assure a more reliable supply of that essential ingredient in silver refining, while at Colima in Mexico a government-backed iron works was established to produce mining implements and tools.[111]

To be sure, some of these measures, such as the search for new mercury mines, were unsuccessful, and all of them came too late to have lasting effects, since the modernization program was terminated by the wars for independence. But they reveal much which is important about the initiative structure of the colonial system—and help to explain why the new republics which replaced the empire and which attempted to operate their economies by quite different rules, were generally unsuccessful in developing viable domestically-controlled export industries in the minerals field despite their strong natural comparative advantages in that line.

Retrospectively, the history of colonial mining affords a convenient base from which to diagnose the economic shortcomings of the Spanish system. Contrary to what many interpretations of the era have asserted, the preoccupation with mining was not objectionable in an economic development perspective, since minerals represented one of the chief comparative international advantages of the area. Instead, it was the mode of mining development which was inadequate. Apart from the fact that it imposed deplorable conditions upon the native population (though these must be viewed in the light of the notoriously poor working conditions in mining which prevailed in other countries in pre-twentieth-century times), the social organization surrounding the industry was conducive to technological backwardness and severely inhibited the evolution of the supportive ancillary institutions on which modern economic development is based. Finally, the social use of the surplus generated by the industry, whether one considers that portion appropriated privately or the part appropriated by the state over most of the period, departed substantially from the canons of self-sustaining economic growth, for the windfall gains of mining strikes flowed primarily into public and private consumption rather than into capital accumulation.

Imperial Integration

Internal economic integration in the empire was maintained through policies which controlled interregional competition in various market areas.[112] In particular, controls were often imposed on activities in one part of the empire which jeopardized the economic well-being of another portion of the domain.[113] For example, restrictions were placed on the export of Peruvian wines to Central American and Mexican markets in the interests of reserving the latter for Spanish producers. Restraint of trade, however, was not designed solely to benefit Spanish peninsular interests. Free admission of colonial sugar into Spain, for instance, undercut peninsular sugar production, and the silk industry in Spain encountered competition from the state-backed industry in the New World.[114] Intercolony trade was also controlled. Mexican and Peruvian sugar exports, for example, were limited in order to protect the position of the Antillean economies, which, it was alleged, had few or no production alternatives.[115] In like manner, restrictions were placed on the exportation of Ecuadoran cacao to Mexico to protect the market outlets of Venezuelan growers of the commodity.[116] Again, the argument advanced by the Venezuelan interests was that, in the absence of preferential treatment in the Mexican market, unemployment would result for lack of suitable alternative production possibilities. This case also is instructive in that the victory of the provincial Venezuelan producers and merchants over both Spanish shippers and the Lima *consulado* indicates that protection was not automatically accorded to the most prestigious groups.[117] On still another occasion, restrictions were laid on the exportation of Chilean wheat to Peru as part of a government program to revive wheat cultivation in Peru.[118]

Of its nature, therefore, the regulated imperial economy was not so much a common market as a politically integrated trading area. Although, at the time, the logic of this system of administered integration must have seemed convincing and while it did result in a greater volume of intra-Latin American trade (relative to total Latin American trade) than has been realized at any time since the colonial period, the cumulative costs of such arrangements were probably substantial over three centuries. Development of regions along the lines of their comparative advantages was distorted, marketing imperfections were structured into the system, entrepreneurial conditions were given a political bias, and a general atmosphere of economic conservatism was reinforced. Only in a limited way were Spanish American producers prepared to meet the performance tests they encountered once independence thrust them into the much less protected world market of the nineteenth century.

Fiscal Objectives

The most compelling motive of all for intervention was probably that of safeguarding the solvency of the crown. Many, if not most, of the previously cited instances of state regulation were related to efforts to enhance the efficiency of the fiscal system as a provider of revenue. When regulatory objectives were in conflict, the fiscal aim ordinarily took precedence. So urgent was the royal need for revenue that measures increasing the short-run tax proceeds were often resorted to at the expense of policies which would have been more fruitful over the longer run—as the eighteenth-century Spanish economists pointed out. The list of interventionary revenue-oriented measures is extremely lengthy and extended even to the auctioning of minor public offices and the declaration that the proceeds from vacant benefices were to accrue to the civil government. Of particular significance, however, was the regulation of mining and transoceanic trade.

Given the special importance of mining as the mainstay of public finance, it is scarcely surprising that the industry was closely supervised from several vantage points.[119] Elaborate mining ordinances laid down regulations governing wages, hours of work, the provisioning of workers, and the disposal of output.[120] Enforcement, such as it was, was in the hands of official inspectors and was supplemented by state control of certain basic mining inputs and market outlets. On the input side, the royal monopolies of gunpowder and mercury (from the two principal sources of quicksilver, the Almadén mines in Spain and the Huancavelica mine in Peru) gave the state a twofold leverage over the industry: (1) sales of these basic supplies provided a technique for estimating the probable output of processed and hence taxable ores [121] and (2) the supply price of these ingredients constituted a method of extracting from the mining sector revenues over and beyond those accruing from the ordinary production taxes, royalties, and brassage and seigniorage charges. On the output side, functionaries of the royal exchequer were stationed at the assaying offices, smelters, and mints to preside over collection of the payments due the crown.[122]

Of equal importance as a source of revenue was the heavily taxed trading system, especially that transoceanic portion which moved through the publicly controlled and organized system of semistate shipping and trade fairs.[123] While there was a fair amount of intracolonial maritime traffic, especially in the Caribbean region, and transpacific trade between the Americas and the Philippines (long officially confined to the "Manila galleon" which sailed between Acapulco and Manila),[124] the most important oceanic trade was the transatlantic commerce. This bullion-extracting traffic was the funnel through which revenues gathered in the overseas territories were remitted to the exchequer in Spain. In view of its strategic role, therefore, this trade was closely scrutinized to stem the leakage of bullion out of the empire before it reached the treasury.

To reduce the evasion of taxes, private participation in the transatlantic traffic required a license and was subject to strict controls and detailed regulations promulgated by the Casa de Contratación. In 1526, owing to the threat of pirates and other interlopers, the sailing of single vessels was prohibited, and about a decade later the royal armada was organized as a further defensive measure. From the 1560's, with occasional interruptions because of war, up to the trade liberalization of the eighteenth century, the bulk of the legal transoceanic exchange was confined to the intermittent sailing of the two trade fleets which set forth from Spain with naval protection and sailed part of the way across the ocean together. One fleet, know as the *flota*, served the northern Caribbean and Mexico; the other, the *galeones,* landed at Cartagena in Colombia and Porto Bello in Panama. Included in it were armed trading ships belonging to the state, which carried both official and private cargoes, and the privately owned trading vessels licensed by the Casa de Contratación. Besides these, the ships of the slave trading *asiento* engaged in some supplementary legal trade (and a great deal of illegal trade).[125] A further supplement to the fleet system was provided by occasional sailings of specially licensed or registered ships (*navios de registro*). In addition, trade with neutrals was permitted during periods of war when Spanish ships had difficulty reaching the New World. Throughout most of the colonial period, though, the ports of the empire were formally closed to foreign ships, or, when later concessions were made, to all unauthorized foreign vessels, and only a limited number of ports in Spain and the New World were ordinarily permitted to participate in the commerce.

For two centuries, the wholesale level of exchange in this traffic was restricted to a few entrepôts such as Seville and Cádiz in Spain and Cartagena, Porto Bello, and Veracruz-Jalapa in the New World. Participants in the fairs held at these sites were required to be licensed; and before the opening of each fair, royal officials, in consultation with deputies of the merchants from both sides of the Atlantic, listed the supplies of goods and drew up price schedules.[126] Thereafter, the exchanges of goods were supervised to insure their conformity to the set prices, although there are indications that prices were occasionally allowed to fluctuate.[127] The fair at Porto Bello lasted from two weeks to forty days, and if a schedule of prices could not be agreed upon in that time, the Spanish merchants were authorized to send their goods on to Peru for sale. Normally, however, Peruvian traders were not permitted to bypass the fair by sending gold and silver to Spain to buy goods directly nor were Spanish merchants ordinarily allowed to make any sales beyond Porto Bello.

The fairs exemplify the weakness of the price mechanism in the market structure of the Spanish colonial system. At times, for instance, the length of the fair had to be extended, owing to the difficulty of selling all the goods brought over from Europe at the established price schedule. On other occasions, the galleons returned to Spain with many of the goods they had carried over, there having been insufficient transactions at the set prices to dispose of the goods; the consequent assumption of a double burden of shipping costs affords at least a minimum indication of the inflexibility of the price structure. On yet other occasions, the sailing of the trade fleet was delayed, once for about five years, because goods were still unsold from previous sailings.[128] Whatever the cost to the economy, however, the system nevertheless had distinct advantages in facilitating the collection of trade taxes and channeling colonial treasure back to Spain.

Sedulous fiscal attention was also devoted to regional and local traffic. The closure of the port of Buenos Aires and the confinement of La Plata

trade to the long overland route to Lima, for instance, revealed an awareness that nearby Brazil offered opportunities for illicit trade in silver produced in the mines of upper Peru or Bolivia. Undoubtedly the late sixteenth-
century embargo on trade between Mexico and Peru, during the boom period
of South American silver mining, was similarly inspired as was the restriction
of the Acapulco-Manila trade through which American treasure, including
Peruvian output, was being drained to the Orient.[129] In the former, the
Pacific coast trade routes were less susceptible to fiscal supervision than the
closely guarded chief Lima–Porto Bello–Seville route, and trade between
the viceroyalty of Peru and the then somewhat more developed viceroyalty
of Mexico (or New Spain, as it was called) would surely have retained
more of the treasure of Potosí on the western side of the Atlantic, even
when it did not move on to the Orient. Some of the economic integration
measures also had fiscal aspects. While the Spanish wine growers, for
example, had reason to complain about the competition of Peruvian wines
in Middle American markets, the crown had an even greater interest in
closing a channel of exchange through which South American silver might
bypass the collection centers the exchequer had established at the nodal
points of trade and communications.

In like manner, the temporary suspension of overland trade between
Colombia and Peru during the Cartagena and Porto Bello fairs may well
have been instigated to secure the markets of Peru for the politically
influential distributors of Lima. But the trade focused through Lima was
also subject to closer supervision by the exchequer bureaucracy than the
Colombian-Peruvian inland traffic. At the lowest level in the system, the
requirement that local retail transactions take place in designated areas
appears to have served the end of tax collecting as well as the objective
cited earlier. From the highest to the lowest level of the economy, therefore, efforts were made to confine production and trade to regulated routes
where the exchequer could more readily extract trade and production taxes.

Employing the Roman concept of *regalía*, the state often intervened still
more directly in the economic life of the empire to increase its revenue.
Royal monopolies, sometimes leased out on a concessionary basis, were
established for salt, tobacco, playing cards, snow, gunpowder, and quicksilver.[130] Indian villages were placed in *encomienda* to the sovereign, and
even some of the *obrajes* and mines were operated for the account of the
crown. In the eighteenth century the expropriation of certain clerical
properties further increased the earning assets operated directly by the
state.

Additional exemplification of the pressing need for money is contained
in many of the *cédulas* which at first glance appear to have been blanket
prohibitions of certain types of activity. Examination of the records, however, reveals that some of these decrees were left unenforced by colonial
administrators while many others were actually injunctions against un-

licensed economic activity.[131] Their apparent design was to protect the revenue system by restricting economic activity to authorized enterprises presumably more subject to royal legislation. Proscriptions of vineyards and olive groves, for example, were sometimes followed by published descriptions by viceroys and other officials of flourishing enterprises in these fields, even in the environs of the viceregal capitals.[132] In other instances, injunctions against *obrajes* and similar activities were followed by promulgation of ordinances regulating the supposedly prohibited undertaking.[133] While some of the decrees were intended to suppress certain forms of production, it seems probable that a large part of them simply underscored the salient feature of the Spanish economy. With some exceptions, mostly in agriculture, the *right* to trade and to participate in economic enterprise simply did not exist but was a privilege conferred by the crown to enter a controlled economic environment on regulated terms. It was this feature, then, rather than any notion of systematically suppressing colonial industry, which accounts for the main body of industrial legislation.[134]

The foregoing description of intervention is not an assertion that economic life was in fact always effectively regimented. There is abundant evidence that clandestine transactions occurred both in intra-American trade and in international traffic throughout the colonial period.[135] Around the Caribbean, the number of unauthorized foreign ships putting in at Spanish American ports was probably quite large, for the English and Dutch islands were centers of wholesale smuggling activity. Brazil also was a major channel for contraband goods. Indeed, despite the care exercised in regulating immigration and supervising government functionaries, it was known that the colonists connived in the illicit trade and that it was even conducted, on occasion, with the tacit complicity of the officials charged with preventing it. In spite of the ensemble of regulatory devices, there were also reported regional variations and changes in price levels, particularly grain prices in times of crop failure.[136] There was, therefore, a certain amount of "free trade" and market-directed economy, the formal design of the system notwithstanding. The long-run import of this free market activity, however, was negligible. Representing an outlaw phenomenon and occurring in a highly unstable transactional framework, its conduct could never become institutionalized as a meaningful part of the economic system.

THE DEVELOPMENTAL IMPACT OF INTERVENTIONISM

Clearly, economic controls abounded in the overall organization of the Spanish system, and few features of colonial arrangements have been the object of such impassioned animadversions since the late eighteenth century, by both Latin Americans and others. Yet, whatever else it may have represented, the colonial system does not appear to have been an open-and-shut case of mere exploitation of America by Spain. The degree to which colonial industry was discouraged as a matter of official policy has often been grossly exaggerated. Unquestionably the bulk of the fabricated goods consumed in the New World were also produced there, as the research of Bourne, Cappa, and others has demonstrated, and an official veto was by no means applied uniformly even to colonial industries which were similar to those in the mother country. By and large, the policy was to permit the establishment of colonial manufacturers so long as they were licensed by the appropriate officials.[137] A variety of luxury and semiluxury specialty goods was imported by the colonies, but this was mainly due to the comparative advantage of technically superior European artisanship rather than to any mercantilistic penchant of the Spanish rulers.[138] Most manufactured imports did not come from Spain, peninsular industry having been ruined by the inflation produced from squandering the New World treasure. Instead, through covermen or dummy partners in Spanish ports (especially Cádiz) as well as through the credit financing of Spanish merchant houses, non-Spanish European producers garnered the lion's share of colonial expenditures for imports.

Moreover, it is not clear that the fiscal system weighed any more heavily upon the economy of the American kingdoms than it did upon that of the Iberian Peninsula. On both sides of the Atlantic, commerce and industry operated under a burden of taxation and in an environment of stultifying regulations;[139] the two regions appear to have been about equally afflicted by the self-regarding policies of the crown.[140] While some writers have described the American price of imported European goods as being extortionately high and have seen in this prima facie evidence of exploitation, a close scrutiny of the record does not altogether substantiate the charge. Considering the high costs of oceanic transshipment, including the substantial risk premiums which had to be calculated for the hazardous voyage, the generous markups normally placed on luxury and semiluxury goods (which many of the items of trade were), and the many trade taxes, the prices do not appear as artificially high as an uncritical examination of the evidence would suggest.

The exclusive commercial regime of Spain has also been indicted for having constricted American export possibilities. In the late eighteenth century, commercial policy regarding the overseas territories was liberalized, and in the same period the records reveal striking increases in the volume and value of Spanish American exports. On the basis of a *post hoc ergo propter hoc* type of reasoning, this trade expansion has sometimes been taken to reflect the degree of constriction posed by preliberalization policies. Yet, in the late eighteenth century the volume of international trade was, for all of the major areas of the world linked with northwestern Europe, undergoing a similar sharp expansion, even in those areas which had nothing whatever to do with Spanish colonial policy. Therefore, though it might be conceded that the liberalization of Spanish commercial policy enabled Latin American regions to participate more extensively in this growth, the general expansion itself had other, more complicated, roots.

In accounting for the lower levels of foreign trade in the earlier colonial period, Spanish policy was probably less decisive than other matters, including shipping costs and the resource endowment of the Latin American area. Further, because of the mercantilist policies of the major trading nations of the world, the opportunities for shipping significant amounts of commodities to non-Spanish markets were rather limited anyway. France, England, and the Netherlands, for example, had their own colonial sources of supply for a number of the goods the Spanish colonies were then able to furnish. What these countries lacked in their possessions, what they were primarily interested in extracting from the Spanish colonies, and, for that matter, what they were already obtaining via Spain from the colonies, was gold and silver. In other words, the Spanish colonies were deprived of alternative market outlets as much by the policies of the other European powers as by Spanish trade policy. For most of the colonial era, therefore, it is doubtful whether the Spanish transatlantic trade controls had an important impact on the volume and composition of Latin American exports. More likely their chief effect was on the terms of trade, and this impact was felt primarily by the wealthy criollo elite who had to pay higher prices on goods required for emulating an European life style. The largest part of the American population participated either not at all or quite marginally in the consumption of international goods. The system did penalize the small, and lower income, colonial bourgeoisie; it was, however, not the only factor to impair the development of a class whose social function was critical in the rise of modern economic systems.

Although the fiscal levies undoubtedly hindered economic intercourse, particularly long-distance exchanges in which goods passed through several tax jurisdictions, they, along with the many restrictions which protected vested economic interests, merely accentuated more fundamental impediments. Costly and defective transport conditions and deficient market information systems held interregional exchanges to relatively low levels independently of the other trade barriers. And only a restricted category of items could economically bear the sundry charges involved in long distance haulage—hence the proliferation of small-scale industries chiefly serving local markets. Furthermore, the concentration of money income (which, as will be seen, was more concentrated than real income) created a pattern of market demand which favored the specialized quality consumer goods produced in Europe. It is a moot point, therefore, just how contraproductive the fiscal system and trade restrictions per se were, for in part they merely substituted higher levels of government spending (in Spain and in the colonies) for higher levels of private conspicuous consumption (of imported items). The system did transfer a substantial amount of income from the Americas to Spain, in a form, moreover, which might properly be labeled "unrequited transfer payments." But given the spending patterns of those who possessed the bulk of private discretionary income in the Americas, it does not follow that their retention of a larger portion of the total income would have contributed much to the process of economic development. In short, the burden of the tax and trade system was onerous and contributed to arresting the institutional evolution of the empire; but it was not one of the most fundamental defects in the socio-economic structure.

A second criticism which often has been raised regarding the Spanish system, one which crudely paraphrases in a general way the Weber and Tawney theses concerning religion and development, attributes many of the system's shortcomings to the official religion. The particular bearing of Catholicism as a state religion on the economic development of the region will be taken up later in this chapter; for the present one may consider three points which favor a cautious use of religious commitment as an explanatory factor of economic retardation. In the first place, it is evident that many of the moral and ethical precepts common to Catholicism and other Western religions were widely disregarded; thus there is a certain difficulty in explaining prevailing behavior by reference to nonobserved rules of conduct. Second, the spread of secularization in nineteenth-century Latin America did little to lay down a more propitious environment for growth. Third, a number of regions in Europe which shared the Catholic religion with Spanish America made significantly greater headway than did the Spanish possessions in constructing a productive and modern economic system.

The third common criticism of the Spanish system involves the presence of conspicuous consumption. That the colonial elite groups indulged their considerable appetite for luxuries can hardly be denied, and the economic development contribution of many public and private expenditures was clearly negative. Yet for all the elegance of, say, the Torre Tagle Palace of Lima or the equivalent residences in Mexico City, even the most ostentatious showpieces of Spanish America rank far behind the "achievements" of western Europe in this respect.

Having placed in perspective some of the more familiar criticisms of the colonial regime, one may go on to public policy features which were of greater consequence for the secular growth process in the region. Taken in the totality, it is clear that the rationale of the concatenation of interventionist policies was not tied to revamping the institutional order in a manner conducive to capitalistic development. Still less did it aim at that "total transformation of society and its organization, as well as of the state and its institutions" which Gustav Schmoller saw as the essence of the mercantile system.[141] On the contrary, the interventionist policies came close to stifling capitalistic development in both Latin America and the Iberian peninsula. That they did so derived from the basic intention of the policies: that of systems maintenance. Essentially, the neo-Byzantine Spanish regime—with all the ancient expedients it comprehended—was based upon the conservative goals of consolidating the existing social order, of integrating (through administrative direction) the component territories of the empire, and of insulating imperial territory from corrosive contacts with the outside world. These were the values to be optimized, rather than expansion of aggregate output or development of a system open to technological and institutional changes. Thus, the American possessions were controlled by the western European power which most embodied the forces of institutional conservatism and which, accordingly, was one of the least promising sources of the host of factors making for change.

There was, indeed, a material cost associated with the regime: the continuing sacrifice of economic output induced by the system's pattern of allocating resources. With the maze of regulatory encumbrances applied to every sector of Iberian economic life and with decisions being made, by and large, on the basis of the political power structure rather than on the basis of forces of the market place, the automatic discipline of the market place was absent, and the opportunities for exercising market-guided initiative, unavailable. If, in some sense, resources were "economized" in their allocation among alternative political ends, the same cannot be said for their allocation among alternative uses associated in the economic order with the growth of material output. After the initial introduction and diffusion of medieval Spanish techniques of production, neither technological progress nor capital accumulation received any consistent support from public policy. And although in the artisan sector certain labor skills were fostered, the improvement of private entrepreneurial resources was relegated to a secondary level if not actually frustrated by the system of controls and constrictions on the diffusion of economic information. Thus, the long-run consequence was a reduced level of productivity and a smaller economic surplus out of which all relevant objectives might have been met in varying degree.[142]

The origins of this material sacrifice—a sacrifice which, incidentally, persisted long after the colonies dispensed with Spanish rule—are found in the pattern of economic relationships established by the Hispanic institutions which public policy upheld in both Spain and America. In other words, the material costs were a function of certain defects in social structure which were felt in all its operations—e.g., the inhibition of factor mobility by rigidities of social organization, the disincentive effects of class stratification (as well as of public policy), and so on. So fundamental were these defects that they not only lowered the output of the colonial era but also contributed to the economic imbalance of the post-colonial experience of Spanish America.

The material costs of the Spanish regime were, therefore, a reflection of social organizational costs: the complex conditions which blocked the way to institutional renovation and modernization. A summation of such costs indicates the extent to which the institutional prerequisites of capitalistic evolution went unattained. These costs included (1) fragmentation of commodity and product markets by taxes, restrictions on trade, regulations placed on producers, and transport costs, (2) the numerous imperfections in the market information system, (3) the practical absence of money and capital markets of an early modern type, and (4) the various obstructions to the development of a market in land. Besides these, the institution of compulsory labor early in the colonial period was also an important block to development of a free labor market. Though it was argued that the natives would not respond to money wage incentives and that, therefore, force was necessary to mobilize labor power, the observed wage differentials between voluntary and coerced labor lead one to suspect that a good part of the difficulty lay in the wages the Spaniards were offering.[143] Moreover, though the conscription of Indian labor was at its peak between 1580 and 1650, the era of the most acute labor shortage because of indigenous demographic trends, it began to decline later in the colonial era, being confined in the main to public works and mining. By the time that this occurred, legally sanctioned debt peonage had arisen to replace it, especially in agriculture, as a system of involuntary servitude.[144] Most of the work-incentive arrangements of the age (slavery, *mitas*, and peonage) inhibited initiative, the acquisition of skills, and the assumption of responsibility—and possibly productive exertion as well. For the Indians, the unrewarding employment forced upon them by ladino policies undoubtedly figured in inculcating a deep suspicion of intercultural contacts and was therefore one of several factors which both impeded the process of acculturation over the centuries and frustrated development of a positive commitment of the labor force to work. Such policies also depressed the labor market and operated as a direct deterrent to the immigration of yeoman farmers and artisans, as was, in fact, recognized as early as the eighteenth century.

It is from the standpoint of social organizational atrophy that the Spanish policies towards trade with the colonies had the most lasting significance. These policies weakened private individual and group initiative so much that the subsidiary social organizations which were prominent elsewhere in the rise of capitalistic enterprise had only a limited opportunity to develop. This was particularly evident in the system of semistate trading and controlled private participation which was applied to the most important commercial traffic of the age, the transoceanic trade.

It has long been recognized that foreign trade played a critically important role in the early development of capitalism during the period known as the commercial revolution. Even while the predominant portion of economic activity was still enmeshed in medieval regulation, it was in the foreign-trade field that commercial activity was able to transcend the confines of municipal exclusiveness. In part, this stemmed from the fact that the exotic products traded could be obtained from foreign sources rather than from the traditional and regulated local supply sources. And in part it was because the products marketed were often not those which conventionally had been traded and which were, therefore, subject to the established regulatory system. Even where both supply sources and market outlets were locally regulated, the interurban structure of foreign trade opened up the possibilities of a selection among both alternative supply sources and alternative market outlets. Therefore, the whole marketing process could be conducted more freely and more capitalistically, i.e., with a greater responsiveness to market demand and supply conditions. Moreover, the existence of competition in this area, as contrasted with purely local traffic, exerted a pressure for efficiency, while the intersticial nature of the activity placed it somewhat outside the established organs of control and thereby gave rise to the possibilities of more flexible business organization and greater capital accumulation opportunities on the basis of mercantile and financial skill.

In the Spanish case, however, the chief trade channel was, institutionally speaking, an internal one, controlled at all points by the all-embracing imperial apparatus. The bulk of the traffic consisted of gold, silver, and other goods for which there was ample precedent in the customary system of regulation. A substantial amount of the proceeds of this trade was diverted, by charges exacted for the royal exchequer, from the Iberian business enterprise sector and from the accumulation possibilities therein. The Spanish monarchy used this treasure to hire European mercenary armies for its territorial designs on the continent and to finance the colonial imports which the decrepit Spanish economy could not itself supply.[145] Therefore, insofar as capitalistic business organization was served by the Spanish colonial trade, it was largely the non-Spanish European capitalists who benefited, for the institutional flexibility required for advantageous participation in the trade flow was enjoyed mainly by the parties which could operate entirely or partially outside of the Spanish regime of controls.[146] In consequence, until late in the eighteenth century, Spanish business organization, including that of the Americas, remained relatively primitive and based predominantly upon small trading companies which consisted of individual proprietorships and partnerships adopted from late medieval Italian practice, rather than the chartered company and joint-stock techniques of English and other early capitalisms. Dominated by government and the quasi-official *consulados*, it was incapable of contributing significantly to the transformation of the overall system.[147]

Given the degree to which the foregoing social organizational costs were built into the basic structure of the Spanish system, it is more accurate to view the policies of the crown as constituting the directives of a regulated imperial economy in the archaic Mediterranean tradition rather than as an expression of the embryonic capitalism of mercantilism proper. Indeed, as Heckscher has put it, "the Spanish . . . methods of solving their new problems had . . . [no] influences on the development in those countries

which were the true protagonists of mercantilism." [148] Essentially precapitalistic in nature, the social order of priorities of the Spanish regime had a
profound impact in Latin America upon the quality of social leadership, the
differentiated distribution of access to resources and economic opportunities,
and the character of the predominating experience in economic activity.

THE CHURCH AND THE COLONIAL ECONOMY

As a major institutional prop of the Iberian system with which it was
coetaneous, the Spanish church in the New World was deeply involved in the
economic order. But so extensive was its activity and so entwined were the
spiritual and the temporal in its functioning that it is extremely difficult
to arrive at a *jugement d'ensemble* concerning its true economic role, especially if one dissociates the influences particular to the church from those
deriving from the general social structure, for the church was greatly affected
by the operations of the latter. It is the failure to make this distinction which
(along with bigotry) accounts for the prejudicial assessment reached by
exponents of the *leyenda negra* tradition in which the ecclesiastical institution represented, next to the crown, the chief scapegoat of the age. Their
simplistic excesses, while containing a measure of truth, unfortunately served
more to obscure the actual role of the church than to define its economic
relevance in a manner germane to the analysis of development.

Raynal's *Histoire philosophique et politique . . . des Indes*, from which
much of this literature seems to have taken its inspiration, was not entirely
beside the mark, but one can wonder that events of the post colonial period
did not sooner lead to critical reevaluation of this point of view. The diminishing role of the church which began with the crown's expulsion of the
Jesuits and its confiscation of religious trust funds, and which continued in
the independence period did not appear to advance appreciably the prospects
for a sounder social and economic development, except insofar as it was
accompanied by other institutional changes of greater economic consequence. In other words, reduction of nonreligious ecclesiastical activity was
growth-conducive in that it left areas of economic interaction open for reorganization under alternative institutional forms more befitting a modern
society, but this is not the same as saying that dissolution of ecclesiastical
organization was, in fact, always accompanied by changes of this nature.
Often, indeed, it was not; and where the superseding arrangements merely
reflected the received secular features of colonial society, it is not easy to
argue that change was improvement.

In order to understand the complicated relationships between religion
and material growth in the colonial system, it is useful to examine four
categories of church operations: the role of the institution as a mechanism
of social integration, its functions in the provision of social overhead capital,
the implications of church holdings of real assets, and the position of the

church in the flow of money income. In each, one finds a commingling of positive and negative elements.

THE CHURCH AS AN INSTRUMENT OF SOCIAL INTEGRATION

The church served as the main ideological buttress of the social order, and the whole structure of law and government was grounded in postulates of a theological character concerning the public order, the state, and property.[149] For example, the exercise of authority by the crown was legitimized by churchmen in a rationale which, by according a certain position of primacy to the values of stability and security, helped to create a Spanish integralist tradition that was generally unreceptive to innovation. But apart from the adminicular arguments supplied by theological reasoning, a greater immediacy was lent the church's teaching in support of temporal authority by the *patronato real*, which, in the tradition of Constantine, made the king both a sacred and secular person.[150] Ecclesiastical appointments were made by the civil power, and clerics were employed by the crown as legal theoreticians, as advisers, and occasionally as officeholders in the regular structure of colonial administration. Moreover, the prelates, priests, and missionaries functioned as an intelligence-gathering agency to influence the formulation and implementation of imperial policies. Insofar as any general consensus can be discerned in colonial times, it rested upon a widespread assent to the doctrines propounded by the church on behalf of the state, so that within the closed society of the empire—afflicted as it was by a tremendous diversity of internal conditions and by latent centrifugal forces—religion provided a basis of social cohesion.

That in America the altar and the throne again reaffirmed their common interests in safeguarding religious and political orthodoxy was attributable to the external situation of the empire. Maintaining the unity of the political and ideological system was an act of mutual defense designed to shield the peoples of the empire from alien influences. Rival nation states were appearing with new strength on the European scene. While contesting Spain for continental supremacy, they were also assessing with ill-disguised avarice the flow of treasure pouring out of the New World. Much of the treasure had filtered out of Spain, but this was not sufficient to stifle European speculation about the advantages of going more directly to the mother lodes.

Privateers, buccaneers, and an assortment of freebooters were encouraged to prey upon the Spanish trade fleets, and pirates even invaded important coastal settlements in the Spanish realm. More substantial incursions were also supported, as in the French and Dutch occupations of Brazil and the British occupation of portions of the Caribbean area. Over the centuries, various Antillean islands, the Guianas, and the Louisiana Territory were carved off the Spanish empire. These became bases for still another avenue of infiltration, contraband trade. Some of the rival powers were plainly pursuing economic and commercial penetration of the empire as a prelude to political encroachment. During the same period of history the Reformation gained strength, and doctrinal differences merged with political ambition. Papal authority in theological matters having been rejected, the Vatican's grand gift of the New World to Spain and Portugal was viewed with similar scepticism.

For both external and internal reasons, therefore, a coincidence of interests united the church with the state, and accordingly, by thoughts, words, and deeds the minions of Melchizedek acted in an adjuvant capacity to the secular authority to stabilize, defend, and administer the social order of the empire. Giving the situation its most charitable interpretation, the role of the church was critical to insuring the degree of social and political stability necessary to erect the colonial economy and to enable it to operate as a going concern. Without the work of religion as an integrating mechanism, the various stresses and strains might well have produced a chaos inimical to even the limited development which was achieved; and undoubtedly it was the centrality of this social function of the church which enabled it to exercise such a strong influence in the economic arrangements of the day, notwithstanding the chariness with which the crown often regarded its operations in that field. From its investments in support of the ecclesiastical structure, therefore, the state realized a fairly high return in the form of social control.

Particularly important in this connection was the question of the Indian population. In incorporating the natives into the social order established by the Spanish, the church played a vital role. As Octavio Paz has put it, "Gracias a la religión el orden colonial no es una mera superposición de nuevas formas históricas, sino un organismo viviente." [151] The general social structure appeared to be incapable of assimilating the Indians through agencies other than religious ones, since it failed to provide significant opportunities for upward social and economic mobility as an inducement for assimilation. Be that as it may, however, ecclesiastical and regal interests were sufficiently near to each other that the two were able to work closely in building the structure of the empire, especially in the early days when the church gave much help in the pacification of the New World.

Unlike the situation encountered in the North American colonies and the Brazilian settlements, the Spanish did not move in upon a sparsely inhabited region in which their way of life could simply displace that of the primitive occupants of the premises. In important parts of both Middle and South America they came upon large sedentary indigenous populations possessing many structural features of higher civilization: an urban-rural division, fairly complicated and large political units of a centralized character, a comparatively advanced division of labor in rural and urban crafts, a society with sharp class distinctions, and a tremendous concentration of wealth and power in the noble class. In both the Aztec and Incan empires, military aggression had long been employed to extend the rule of the emperors to considerable numbers of conquered peoples, and the overwhelming majority of the native population was relegated to a status of servile obediency.

Somehow these people had to be permanently subjugated and incorporated into the Spanish system by a small stream of European immigrants. Not only was this prerequisite to exercising full political dominion over the new kingdoms; it was also essential to convert the native population into a labor supply that could be put to work in pursuit of the imperial objectives. Though assimilation remained an unresolved problem throughout the colonial period, except as cultural assimilation followed biological assimilation (a technique pursued with spirited, if not spiritual, dedication by both Spanish and Portuguese immigrants), these objectives, political dominion and labor mobilization, were attained in remarkably short order. The Spaniards were assisted enormously by the nature of the Indian civilizations they subdued, in which the whole superstructure of culture rested upon an axis of polytheistic religious beliefs, expressed in complex rituals, and a ruling class which centered in the person of semidivine monarchs. In the course of the Spanish conquest, the governing and ceremonial cities—centers of wealth, power, and culture—were captured and mostly demolished, often with the help of native allies. The ruling nobility was destroyed as a class, through battles, disease, and deprivation of property and position, and partially absorbed through intermarriage and concubinage. Similarly the religious basis of pre-Columbian social arrangements was eliminated as temples and idols were razed and the native priesthood wiped out. In short, the entire sociopolitical system of indigenous life was thrown off balance with the destruction of its core of cities, religious specialists, and ruling classes. The aftermath of this triple decapitation was a radical change in the Indian societies; only isolated backwoods vestiges of the culture survived. The subordinated Indian masses that remained were those least capable of carrying on the essential characteristics and functions of the vanquished higher civilizations.

Armed with a pantheon of saints to replace the Indian deities and with new rituals for the old, Spanish religion facilitated the transfer of aboriginals from submission to the old priestly hierarchy to the new; and while elements of the preconquest paganism have endured to present times, the broader social organizational implications of the native belief system were redirected to the new Spanish authority. Following an initial period of debate and indecision, the arguments of humanitarian churchmen bore fruit and resulted in the declaration that the indigenous population was not subject to enslavement. Church doctrine also propounded the ideal of racial, though not cultural, equality. With this background, there followed a series of promulgations which, in effect, constituted a body of welfare and protective legislation for the preservation of native peoples and groups.[152] This was probably the most creditable single achievement of the Spanish church and state alliance.

Since neither church nor state could permit the continuation of non-Christian, non-Spanish indigenous life on an autonomous, independent basis, many of the rulings of this Indian legislation looked toward the eventual incorporation of the natives into Iberian society, but with an awareness of the difficulties of acculturation and of the need for special treatment of the Indian population. This meant a recognition of the temporary validity of indigenous cultural patterns pending completion of the task of hispanization.[153] For example, native property claims and conventions were accorded legal recognition, while being reconciled to some extent with the quite different modalities of Iberian jurisprudence. The cacique (native chieftain) structure of local rule was also perpetuated in Indian communities, subject to certain modifications such as the subordination of the caciques to civil and clerical administration. In addition, for more effective administration and to facilitate religious and secular instruction, the dispersed population of the countryside was brought together and concentrated in the special Indian communities known as *reducciones* or *congregaciones*.[154]

Except for the functions assigned the *encomenderos* during the early stage of settlement, the church was charged with the primary responsibility for inducting the natives into Spanish ways of life. On the frontiers, the missionary vanguard assisted in the pacification of the various tribes, and throughout the area of Spanish rule dedicated missionaries, especially Jesuits and Franciscans, contributed to raised economic productivity by upgrading and diversifying the Indian supply of artisan skills and disseminating new crops and methods of production.[155] Every mission was partly an agricultural and industrial school; and other vocational schools prepared native students in the manual and fine arts required for public construction, ceremonial activities, and private employment.[156]

Besides the fostering of assimilation, a protective purpose was also embodied in the decrees on Indian affairs, undoubtedly because the early Antillean experience had made both crown and churchmen aware of the exploitative intentions of Spanish settlers and the depopulating consequences of these intentions when left uncontrolled. Initially, some of the Indians had been placed in trust (in *encomienda*) to private citizens to whom the state was indebted.[157] In exchange for supervising in several respects the Indians entrusted to their charge, the *encomenderos* (i.e., recipients of *encomienda* grants) collected the capitation tax from the Indians, retaining part of the proceeds of the tax as a pension for their services to the crown. At the outset some labor services had been allowed on a legally limited basis, but as time went on these were gradually eliminated by law. That the system of *encomienda* grants was susceptible of glaring abuses was brought to the attention of the crown, and the system was abandoned as an instrument of policy. *Corregidores*, who were crown officials, replaced the *encomenderos* as administrators of the Indians. At clerical instigation, numerous decrees were issued to protect the natives from the settlers, and a degree of segregation was fostered as a necessary bulwark against the rapacity of the colonists. Cognizant of the vulnerability of the Indians to exploitation in the new institutional framework, the crown assigned to the church a major role as protector of Indian rights and designated clerical lawyers, together with the *fiscal* of each *audiencia,* as the guardians of native interests to represent the Indians in the courts.   Apropos of this protective role, it has been argued that in actuality the church stood in the way of assimilation, contributing to a cultural dualism which has plagued the efforts for social and economic integration ever since.   The motives—whether humanitarian (to protect the Indians), selfish (to keep them more subject to ecclesiastical control),[158] or a mixture of the two, need not concern us; the fact is that the church did to some extent promote a type of *apartheid* by somewhat isolating Indians from direct contact with and involvement in the life of the ladino population. But is must also be observed that cultural assimilation beneficial to the Indians did not always result even in the absence of this wall of separation. In the mission territory in Paraguay, for example, the clerically enforced isolation of the Indians was removed; elsewhere, it was often circumvented or never effectively installed in the first place.   Yet in almost all these cases, the social and economic position of the native inhabitants either remained unchanged in any significant respect or deteriorated when they were placed into closer contact with the colonists.

The deplorable aftermath of the Paraguayan *reducciones* is a telling commentary on the sort of social system to which the Indians were exposed when ecclesiastical exclusivism and paternalism were absent or removed.   Apart from the clergy and some of the more farsighted royal administrators, most Spanish settlers were not interested in developing the potentialities of the natives in mental and higher labor skills; much less was there any discernible concern with providing a social environment in which such a development would have been rewarding and meaningful to the possessors of such skills. On the contrary, the interest of most of the settlers seems to have been primarily that of obtaining the Indian's lands and placing the natives in some form of servitude to exploit their physical energy.

While humane considerations may have dictated a protective segregation for the Indians, it must be conceded that there were other advantages to the crown in such a system.   For one thing, neither church nor state deemed it desirable to permit the Indian population to fall under extra-official control (though ultimately this came about in spite of their wishes in the matter).[159] Accordingly, the Indian statutes of the Laws of the Indies looked toward the absorption of native peoples into a subordinate position in the central hierarchic structures.   By maintaining a dependency relationship between the Indians and the machinery of state, the crown undoubtedly hoped to avert the rise of competing power centers in its overseas possessions.[160]   Moreover, if the acculturation and protection objectives of the law registered an explicit public responsibility for the welfare of those newly brought under Spanish government, this was also joined, under the law, with a reciprocal obligation;

namely, the role of the native population as valuable public assets. Capitation taxes (*tributo*) and production taxes (tithes) were levied on the Indians for support of civil and ecclesiastical administration,[161] and labor was conscripted for works of public utility. By reserving the indigenous manpower pool under government jurisdiction, the Indian laws, together with the doctrine of the *real hacienda,* helped to maintain the preeminent position of the state in colonial economic life; through them the state claimed the two chief assets of the region: labor and land. Given the usefulness of the natives to the public authorities, some interpreters have even suggested that the main motivation behind the segregation and protective legislation might well have been the desire to forestall the conversion of public assets into private assets.

Valuable as was the role of the church in social integration, there were certain adverse consequences for long-term social and economic development; the desire of the state and the church to retain direct control of the natives (even for commendable reasons) was a factor in perpetuating cultural dualism in Spanish America. While in theory the objective was that of implementing a process of guided acculturation behind the shield of the protective legislation, in practice the results turned out rather differently.

The state, for its part, received the revenues accruing to vacant benefices, and as the crown grew more desperate for funds, it felt no strong sense of urgency in filling posts, which, presumably, were key positions in the process of directed hispanization. For the same reason, the sale of ostensibly public land came to be conducted with such single-minded concern for fiscal considerations that a growing number of the native communities fell under the thralldom of the private latifundia, where the interest in promoting acculturation was, to state it charitably, minimal. The confiscation of the well-managed Jesuit properties in the 1700's provided further relief for the royal purse but seriously undermined the work of education and assimilation, while near the close of the colonial age the expropriation of the so-called pious funds (trust funds used for financing religious undertakings) dealt another blow to the system. In addition, the *patronato real* impeded the application in the Americas of newer missionary methods and constricted the emergence of a native American clergy which might have been more effective in working among the Indians.

For its part, the church seems to have suffered a certain failure of spirit as the colonial age wore on. To borrow the apposite phrase of Roger Vekemans, a Belgian sociologist who has studied Latin American religious development, a vigorous "incarnational Christianity" was a feature chiefly of the earlier colonial period. The missionaries in the outlying regions continued to transmit skills to their Indian charges, but in general the church developed a far more extramundane orientation—where its personnel did not succumb altogether to the temptings of earthly pleasures. Mysticism became more prominent, the contemplative orders increased, and ceremonalism became richer and more central to the institutional life of the church. Meanwhile, the loss of humanitarian zeal reduced interest in the task of acculturating the Indians; nearly all of the creative experiments launched by churchmen to benefit the natives date from the earlier part of the era. As the main bridge between the coexisting culture groups in the New World, the church, therefore, fell short of its original ideals.

As time passed, there was also less of the notable concern which early church leaders had demonstrated for protecting the Indians from ladino abuse. In the later days of the empire, reform-minded clerics such as Bishop Abad y Queipo and Fathers Hidalgo and Morelos seem to have been exceptional; and in the so-called Catholic culture of Spanish America, there was a remarkably high level of indifference to social injustice and an easy acceptance of exploitation. While the close association of the church with the Spanish monarchy had the merits of reinforcing social stability and political continuity, it appears that the role of the church as an independent arbiter of social relationships was compromised by its subordination to the state, particularly in the attitudes and actions of the higher clergy. Furthermore, as the religious orientation shifted in the direction of ceremonial formalism and an emotional mysticism, the moral and ethical content of the religious commitment suffered deemphasis; the behavioral implications of the dominating type of religious experience, which was highly individualized in character and nonsocial in orientation, might be described as a species of antinomianism. Thus, despite the heavy infusion of religiosity in Hispanic culture and the prestigious public position accorded the church, individual behavior and social goals seem often to have been quite amoral, especially as regards respect for law and the treatment meted out to the aboriginals, and religion was scarcely any more effective as a source of internalized social controls than it was elsewhere in the contemporary Western world.

Finally, the significance of the investment in the church as an instrument of social integration must also be assessed in terms of two other facets of institutional behavior which negatively affected later developments in Spanish America. First, the institutional commitment to a dogmatic orthodoxy, in which contingent secular arrangements were not always clearly distinguished from theological verities, was not conducive to development of capability in the management of differences: i.e., the mutual accommodation of divergent interests through compromise. So comprehensive, in other words, was the church's integrating role that religious belief, political loyalty, and social structural relationships all became blended in an amalgam, in much the way that this total cultural package had been prefigured in Byzantium and in Spain of the Reconquest. With such a background, the eventual introduction of novelty, pluralism, and diversity was certain to be socially disruptive. Indeed, the long conditioning of social experience had engendered an accustomed mental bent which affected even the expression of dissent; both Hispanic orthodoxy and the later reaction to it by criollo nationalists of a liberal stripe displayed a dogmatic total commitment, an "all or none" attitude. Thus the aftermath of the rejection of old conservative dogmas was often merely the substitution of a new libertarian dogmatism rather than a turn to a nondogmatic, empirically oriented liberalism. The effect on political stability and the continuity of national policy was devastating, and the possibilities of economic development suffered accordingly. In fusing its identity with that of the crown, the church unwittingly insured that, when the late eighteenth and nineteenth centuries brought a reaction to traditional civil authority, the criollo insurgents would also often repudiate the traditional religious authority. With that repudiation came a breakdown in the important social and economic functions performed by the church in Spanish America.

In the second place, given the church's organizational structure and the crown's policy on personnel appointments under the *patronato real,* the Americans—whether criollos, mestizos, or Indians—could only relate to the institution in the way that they did to the state, i.e., as subjects rather than as participants. Thus, church life offered no alternative social experience to the prevailing authoritarian centralism of the state; in both explicit teaching and organizational behavior religion reinforced hierarchical assumptions concerning the nature of political authority and social structure. Despite its vast and resource-consuming structure, the church provided the Americans with little institutionalized experience in group relationships of a community or participative character; and for all the extensiveness of the ecclesiastical span of control, the church afforded minimal opportunities for the Americans to acquire the administrative experience which they were denied by the forms of civil government.

THE CHURCH AS A SUPPLIER OF SOCIAL OVERHEAD CAPITAL

During the colonial age, the church had a further importance as the chief provider and manager of much of Spanish America's social overhead capital, a factor which must be kept in mind when evaluating the social implications of the church's holdings of real estate and its large share in the colonial income stream. Bishops contributed financial support for various works of public construction,[162] and most public welfare services were supplied by the church, either directly or through various religious foundations and *cofradías* (lay religious confraternities that combined ceremonial duties with charitable activities and social security systems for their members). Church personnel staffed such programs, while financial support often came from ecclesiastically managed endowment or trust funds or from revenues received from the church's urban and rural properties. In addition, public relief—for the indigent on a continuing basis and for the general populace in times of food crises—originated in part from the tithes-in-kind gathered by ecclesiastical authority and from the produce of church-owned rural estates.[163] The postcolonial disruption of ecclesiastical organization left a serious deficit in this area, for it impaired the conventional social-security mechanisms at a time when alternative secular arrangements could not, for a long period, be installed in their stead. In this respect the consequences of independence were quite similar to the undermining of the church as an agency of cultural assimilation, for when the church was largely shorn of this function, no adequate institutional replacement was available— or even, in many instances, considered—to continue the work of reducing the barriers posed by cultural dualism for social integration.

Most public educational facilities in the colonial period had also been initiated and organized by the church.[164] While the *cabildos* were obliged by law to set up educational facilities, they were often slow to discharge this responsibility, and the major responsibility for developing a colonial education system fell to the church. By 1560, several universities had already been established under clerical auspices. Patterned after the University of Salamanca in Spain, they functioned as autonomous state institutions and enjoyed many privileges and official patronage. Below the institutions of higher learning were the primary and secondary schools, of which the most important were probably the *colegios* operated by the various religious orders and the elementary parochial schools attached to local churches. In addition, there were a fair number of vocational and mission schools for the native population and instruction in practical arts was also offered in many of the orphanages and asylums. Of the several orders engaged in educational work, the Jesuits attained a particular distinction for excellence, although the Franciscans were also notable in the field of mission schools. Among the American kingdoms, it was Mexico which made the greatest headway in education,[165] but Lima, too, was graced with a number of important schools, among them the University of San Marcos. Indeed, both the crown and the church were solicitous in developing education in the colonies and "provision was made for its promotion on a far greater scale than was possible or even attempted in the English colonies."[166] The same might also be said in contrasting Spanish America with Brazil.

Spanish colonial education fell far short of what are understood today to be the training requirements of development, but it is open to question if it was much less adequate than that generally found elsewhere in the contemporary Western world. Its defects, in other words, were largely the defects of the age.

While some element of income redistribution may have been implied by the educational system, as in the mission schools and the schools established for *mestizo* children, education was primarily the perquisite of the elite. Linguistic barriers, cultural attitudes, the financing of the *colegios*, and so on, all tended to favor the criollos, and, chiefly excepting the mission schools, most institutions of education were located in urban areas, whereas most of the population was rural. The scattering of the population over large areas of difficult terrain increased the difficulty of bringing education to large numbers of people, especially when there was a shortage of trained, multi-lingual priest-teachers to begin with. Viceroys, bishops, and others, for example, were continuously writing to the king to complain of shortages, which were especially acute in outlying districts where some towns did not have a single priest. In addition, since the priests who were available had also to attend to routine pastoral duties, make conversions, combat residual paganism, and give basic catechetical instruction, all of which were quite time-consuming because of distances and bad transport, the supply of teaching manpower for popular instruction in secular subjects was extremely limited.

Moreover, the differential access of ladinos and natives to the social opportunity structure doubtless led to differing subcultural assessments of the worthwhileness of educational exposure, while, in turn, disparities in educational preparation fed back to distort the distribution of access to the opportunity structure. Thus, notwithstanding the educational aims of the state and the church and despite the fact that school attendance (at least at the elementary level) was often possible on low-fee or feeless basis, a number of conditions combined to make substantial exposure to education the prerogative of the privileged classes.

While the educational system must be viewed in the context of the society it served, the substantive content of much of colonial education left much to be desired from the point of view of economic development. The problem of the educational system was not that it actually worked in dispraise of economic virtues and technical competence but that these were deemed largely irrelevant by the segments of society most closely associated with education. Disregarding the labors of the vocational schools, the content of the education dealt largely with upper class concerns, confirming the cultural assumption of inequality and the differing social worth of individuals. Throughout the sixteenth and seventeenth centuries, for example, the dominating influence in intellectual life was a sort of baroque scholasticism which rested upon Aristotelian methods, the primacy of revealed doctrine, and the appeal to received authority.[167] Rhetoric, speculative philosophy, law, literature, the arts, and moral and dogmatic theology appear to have occupied most of the curriculum, along with the study of religious histories and administrative literature.[168] In approach, therefore, the intellectual training of the day, particularly that provided for the classes whence social leadership came, was literary, formalistic, legalistic, and speculative, oriented toward the mastery of ideas rather than of techniques and especially suited to developing the skills of rhetoric and verbal expression and manipulation.

Within these general intellectual boundaries, a certain freedom of thought did prevail in the universities, as Luis Alberto Sanchez has pointed out.[169] But to the degree that colonial education was undiluted by later developments, it may be said to have perpetuated an archaic and romantic world view, in which a concern for style and an emphasis on a learning process that was based upon dictation and memorization afforded little opportunity for developing empirical procedures related to practical questions.[170] The whole mental bent of colonial education was antithetical to the conditions of material progress, and the values postulated were at variance with the mechanical discipline imposed by scientific research and technological development.[171]

Yet, certain developments occurred, principally in the eighteenth century, which helped to improve the colonial education system. The Holy Office of the Inquisition, for example, was far less severe in the colonies as a censor of intellectual life than it was in Spain and was never very successful in preventing the infiltration of ideas then circulating in Europe.[172] Influential members of both the secular and ecclesiastical bureaucracy occasionally opposed the operations of the Inquisition, and many clerical authorities appear to have been fairly tolerant of divergent points of view when they did not directly attack the doctrinal foundations of Spanish religion. From the late seventeenth century on, when university professorships were becoming ever more secularized, the system of higher education also benefited from the growing influence of Jesuit humanism; members of the Society, recruited from all over Europe, came to America and brought with them their interests as geographers and naturalists.[173] As early as 1736 the Jesuits in Quito were teaching the ideas of Descartes, Newton, and Leibniz, and later, during the 1700's, additional contact with contemporary ideas came from the European scientists who traveled in the Americas, frequently on missions for the crown.[174] In Spain itself, during the 1770's and 1780's, the universities were modernizing their curricula to incorporate ideas from Bacon, Locke, and others, while the works of the *encyclopédistes* were popularized by the efforts of Fr. Benito Feijoo. Books by these and other European intellectuals were brought to the colonies, often in the libraries of clerics and university teachers.[175] Churchmen and others in the colonies inveighed against the sterility of old modes of thinking, and here and there natural history, natural law, and natural philosophy courses were instituted in American universities. Thus, by the late colonial period, higher education in the overseas kingdoms was by no means exclusively a celebration of the transcendental and the archaic.

These developments did not suffice, however, to transform the intellectual and educational scene in the colonies, even though after 1750, scholasticism was in retreat and Cartesianism was on the rise. The new trends were not without their detractors; the influence of scholasticism lingered on; and as late as the close of the eighteenth century the apostles of change could still complain about the time wasted in universities on speculative philosophy in preference to the useful and exact sciences. The lack of adequate libraries and equipment for the study of scientific subjects was also a problem. Meanwhile, the crown's expulsion of the Jesuits from the New World in 1767 dealt a severe setback to some of the most progressive and higher-quality institutions in the American educational system.[176] The portion of the total American population exposed to the new trends in the universities was exceedingly small to begin with, and though the predominantly criollo faculties and students avidly adopted the new philosophical ammunition provided to sustain their claim to political equality, their interest in the more economically-relevant scientific side of the Enlightenment was notably less. Neither before independence nor afterwards did anything even remotely resembling a scientific and technological renaissance develop in Spanish American society. Thus, though the political and religious repercussions of the Enlightenment and independence were momentous, their implications for a technological revolution originating in, or at least sustained by, the cultural milieu of Latin America were so slight as to be practically inconsequential. For a long while, the old *patio* process in metallurgy, developed in sixteenth century Mexico, was virtually the sole credit entry in the Latin American ledger of original productive innovation.

What Independence brought was in fact a further weakening of the educational system, particularly at the pre-university level. The forced loans exacted by the revolutionary governments from ecclesiastical coffers, the confiscation of church properties inspired by anticlerical elements in the new governments, and depletion of the ranks of the clergy because of the exile of Spanish clerics and quarrels between the new regimes and the Holy See [177] over patronage rights—all this impaired severely the inherited educational structure at a time when most of the new republican governments were incapable of devising a viable secularized alternative. Meanwhile, the basic social structure of Spanish America, which was not much changed by the break with Spain, continued to be mostly unconducive to cultivating the intellectual and educational underpinnings of the "progress of opulence," to borrow Adam Smith's choice phrase. This, rather than the colonial connection of education with religion, appears to have been the most fundamental obstruction to Latin America's ability to invest in an adequate educational program in order to harvest the resources created by the exponential advance of science.[178]

THE CHURCH AS AN OWNER OF REAL ASSETS

After the crown, the church was the largest single owner of real property in the American kingdoms.[179] Through mortmain and other bequests, dowries of the religious, donations made in quest of salvation or in pursuit of good works, and its own investments, the church acquired title to extensive tracts of agricultural land and blocs of urban real estate. Endowments for the support of parishes, chaplaincies, convents, schools, and eleemosynary institutions augmented its holdings further. Other properties it acquired, at least in formal title, through its mortgage lending activity; and still others were nominally deeded to it as various persons sought, by transfer of title to an institution with immunity from juridical scrutiny, to conceal from the crown the dubious methods by which they had acquired real property. Moreover, the corporate nature of the church, with its indefinite life span as a legal person, meant that unlike private individual owners it could amass such holdings in a cumulative fashion for the entire three centuries of colonial rule.

It is impossible to define the exact extent of ecclesiastical ownership because reliable empirical evidence is lacking, and many statements on the subject, even in contemporary accounts, are clearly conjectural and based on hearsay.[180] Moreover, since lending against real estate collateral was the chief form of finance in colonial times and since the church was the major lending institution, a good many of the properties which were identified as belonging to the church were probably those which it held on a contingent mortgagor's claim rather than on a fee simple basis. Where church landholding arose out of endowment grants which were specifically tied to, say, the support of orphanages, schools, or hospitals, or where land grants were made for the restricted purposes of mission enterprises, full discretionary title to property was not acquired by the church, and this, too, must be taken into consideration. Nevertheless, with due allowance for these and other conceptual problems, it is incontrovertible that ecclesiastical latifundism became a major feature of the system and that the value of church assets was enhanced further as population growth and general economic development gradually gave rise to windfall gains in the values of the centrally located properties the church had acquired in earlier colonial times.

The process did not go unnoticed. At an early period the crown had expressed its concern, and both viceroys and lay settlers often anticipated later criticisms of the supposed evils of clerical ownership. The showdown in the 1760's with the Society of Jesus sharply interrupted the progressive growth of ecclesiastical land ownership, but generally speaking, the intermittent efforts made to divest the church of its holdings and to arrest the growth of clerical land acquisitions were unavailing.[181] The institution was simply too powerful to be effectively countermanded for long, for it was continually omnipresent in the colonial scene and able, therefore, to resume the process whenever conditions permitted.

It is necessary, however, to exercise considerable care in arriving at conclusions as to the economic significance of church land ownership, for the actual manner of land utilization varied considerably. Certainly most of the land was not completely unproductive as contemporary lay allegations of the evils of "dead hand" ownership might imply. Some of the properties— probably a minority of the total holdings—were operated directly by various religious bodies, and in some such cases the level of productive technique was in all likelihood the highest achieved in the entire colonial agricultural sector.[182] Generally, however, the lands were not employed with maximum efficiency. Though some tracts were left idle, this was not the usual case and the frequency of such misuse was mentioned as having been much less than in Spain.[183] Others were given over to cultivation by Indian tenants of varying degrees of agricultural skill, in which instances the lax regime of metayage served at least to preserve a means of livelihood for some of the aboriginal inhabitants and safeguarded them from more exploitive treatment by private employers.

For the most part, the practical usufruct of the land remained with private persons under a variety of arrangements in which the exactions of the ecclesiastical landlord were customarily rather light. For example, as Abad y Queipo observed, the church was a lenient creditor and often did not demand repayment of the principal, even after the maturity of the loans, so long as the rather moderate interest payments continued to be met.[184] Consequently, the church seldom foreclosed on its mortgages, and much of the land to which it held mortgage title was operated for generations by the individuals and their descendants who had only to pay what amounted to a low quitrent for use of the property against which they had borrowed. Where title had been conveyed to the church to conceal illegitimate private acquisitions, the former private owners were not actually parting with their land in an effort to assuage their consciences. Rather, the assignment of ownership to an owner immune to juridical scrutiny was a mere artifice to permit continued private use of the land, by means of low-cost leasing agreements, with security against interruption of control. Even where the church lands had not been obtained in this manner, the practice was frequently employed of leasing them out to *hacendados,* who were far from conspicuous for their productive acumen.[185] The bulk of the church's properties, in fact, were probably rented to private individuals.[186] It should be observed that the leasing terms were ordinarily so lenient that there was little pressure on renters to work the land effectively.[187] Consequently, the low rents, like the low interest and lax amortization policies, were permissive factors in land mismanagement by private operators.

The practical import, therefore, of placing discretionary control of extensive landholdings in a non-profit-oriented institution was that a substantial portion of the colonial society's resources fell under the control of a management which felt little need to foster technological advance or to promote good land management and raise agricultural productivity. A chronic misallocation of land resources was thus a basic feature of the Spanish American colonial economy. Furthermore, both the extensiveness of church holdings of land (which were hardly ever sold) and its lenient mortgage lending practices (which facilitated the growth of poorly managed private latifundia) frustrated the development of an active market in land whence a remedy for the uneconomic situation might have come.

But while the church was partially culpable as a permissive factor, it was not fundamentally responsible for the consequent sacrifice of material output. Since such a large portion of the church's real estate was put out on lease, the way was potentially open to a reasonably economic utilization of these assets by the leaseholders. That this more satisfactory employment of land resources did not materialize pushes the search for contraproductive constraints to another quarter. Further, it was not on church-owned lands alone that productive organization was so antieconomic. As the nineteenth century was to make clear, in most areas the realistic alternative to large-scale ecclesiastical ownership was private latifundism—the private haciendas to which many of the ecclesiastically held properties were already attached (through leases) for all practical purposes. And there is no evidence whatever that privately owned haciendas were any more efficiently operated than the clerically owned latifundia. Thus much of the nineteenth-century criticism of the "dead hand" of the church appears, in retrospect, to have been based on an uncritical assumption that the "dead hand" of private haciendas was somehow preferable. Given the prevailing power structure, one sees the significance of church landholdings and the corresponding misuse of land resources as merely an alternative to direct private misuse of the same resources—and generally a harsher treatment of the natives in addition. Indeed, when liberal reforms were ushered in during the republican era and church holdings were reduced, the change was, from the point of view of economic development, largely an exchange of Tweedledee for Tweedledum. In the overall view, such developments were more a matter of the redistribution of asset ownership than a social increase in asset value.

THE CHURCH AS A FINANCIER

Over the decades, a stream of tithes,[188] bequests, grants and gifts, alms, conventual endowments and dowries, the establishment of "pious funds" or charitable foundations and annuity endowment trusts, and revenues from ecclesiastical *encomiendas* and the church's income-producing assets intimately linked the service of God with the business of this world.[189] In the spending pattern of the colonial economy, the church was, along with the state, the largest single component of market demand. Inasmuch as a large portion of the total colonial economy was conducted on a nonmonetized basis, the impact of this clerical disposition of money income acquires an even greater proportional significance, for the church's share in the money income stream was substantially higher than its share in the real income stream. It is essential, therefore, to take into account the nature of the church's demand pattern, and, accordingly, the impact of its spending on the direction of resource use.

The inquiry is not a difficult one to make, for apart from the ample documentation supplied by colonial sources, the evidence of the predominating pattern of clerical expenditures is readily visible in Latin America today. Magnificent edifices were constructed and maintained with retinues of servants. The fine arts—sculpture, painting, and music—were encouraged, and often the labor skills brought over by immigrants and those painstakingly taught to the Indians were devoted to the production of works of art and religious adornment. Church spending, in fact, must have constituted a major agency of nonagricultural employment and to this extent was a salient factor in supporting the colonial development of a variety of artisan skills. The chronicles of the time are replete with evidence that still more resources were consumed in a similar nonutilitarian fashion in frequent pageants and festivities staged in connection with the use of the durable ceremonial goods. At the same time, however, it must in justice be recalled that a great deal of the church's capital and current account spending went into the social overhead functions discussed previously.

Yet, so far as concerns the nonproductive expenditures of the church, it is not possible, considering the probable alternative uses of money in that system, to infer that the church was anything more than one agent among several which were responsible for allocating resources in a manner antithetical to long-term growth. The major contending claimants for shares in the income stream were, after all, the state and the private plutocracy. From the viewpoint of long-run economic expansion, therefore, it made little difference whether the resources were expended on religious buildings, ceremonial observances, and support of the clergy and its entourage or on private palaces, the Spanish court, secular celebrations, the household retinues of the colonial aristocracy, or, for that matter, the armies of Spain in Europe. In other words, any judgment on the influence of ecclesiastical spending must be stated in the context of the institutionally defined practical alternatives.

Important as was the direction of resource use signaled by clerical expenditures, there was another aspect to the church's commanding position in the income stream which was of still greater long-run consequence. Indeed, the most significant role of colonial religious institutions in the process of economic development follows from the fact that the religious establishment was the most important single accumulator of liquid capital and the chief source of loanable funds. In addition to being a major spender, a director of schools and charities, and a *latifundista* par excellence, the church was thus the colonial equivalent of a capital and money market. A great deal of the long-term capital financing in agriculture, for example, was provided through mortgage loans by convents, confraternities, religious trust funds, and the like. Sandoval even reports that an important lender to the Mexican sugar industry was the treasury of the Inquisition.[190] To some extent, apparently, long-term loans in the mining industry also came from ecclesiastical institutions, as did the shorter-term financing used for providing working capital.[191] Much of the short-term *avío* and intermediate-term *refaccionario* loans for financing production and investment in agriculture and manufacturing came out of the sums held by religious organizations, while commercial credit for financing the conduct of trade was also provided by these sources. For example, much of the Philippines trade was financed by loans from the charitable foundations.[192]

But as a capital and money market, the church left much to be desired. In the first place, the "market" was quite imperfectly organized in that the accumulation of funds in various administrative subdivisions of the church segmented the financial holdings to a degree which impeded their ready transfer among alternative uses. That this structural rigidity obtained was, of course, a reflection of the simple fact that the institution had not been designed with its financing function in mind in the first place. The imperfection of financial market organization was, in other words, a cost of institutional improvisation and insufficient functional specialization, for prelates and monks were, after all, financiers *malgré eux* and their chief occupational training was hardly that of managing the loanable funds of the economy in an efficacious manner. Moreover, since it operated within the context of a comparatively long time horizon with the comfortable knowledge that it could afford to wait to get its capital back, the church seems, from all accounts, to have been distinguished by a very low liquidity preference. The substantial funds at clerical disposition were therefore lent out on exceptionally easy terms, at low interest rates and for long amortization periods—not only to larger borrowers but to smaller ones as well.[193]

In this ready availability of church funds for loans on lenient terms may be discerned the most contraproductive impact of the intrusion of the religious institution into the economic order. While the church was, in a sense, the prime saver as well as the chief lender, and was thus one of the chief institutions capable of assemblying sufficient resources to impel economic change, it is also true that savings formation alone does not necessarily result in economic progress. For this to occur, the assembled savings must be properly channeled to productive activities, and it was precisely here that the process of savings mobilization and allocation went awry.

For one thing, the church was an indulgent creditor and could well afford to be. Because of its noneconomic orientation, the church was under no pressure to amortize its investments in a short period and thereby maximize its returns from lendings. The loan process, in effect, transmitted this noneconomic orientation to the operations of the economy at large, for the easy loan and collection policies meant, in turn, that borrowers did not have to attain higher productivity levels in the use of capital and cooperant resources in order to cover interest charges, nor were they regularly faced with foreclosure and eviction if they failed to repay the loan principal on schedule. In the case of mortgage loans, they could sometimes go on for years just by meeting the relatively moderate interest payments of around 6 per cent.[194] For mortgage loans, therefore, the interest payments became, for all practical purposes, a sort of quitrent having only a loose relation to the marginal efficiency of capital, and there is some evidence that hypothecated properties were on occasion rehypothecated when additional spendable sums of cash were desired by the borrowers. Even multiple rehypothecation was not unknown.

Lending leniency, therefore, did not encourage or press users of borrowed capital to try to maximize returns from the funds obtained on loan, and very likely a significant portion of loan capital—particularly that taken up by the landowning classes—was dissipated into consumption rather than channeled into real investment.[195] Loans negotiated with religious institutions were also not uncommonly used to expand the size of landholdings; thus mortgage loans of indefinite duration indirectly facilitated the growth of latifundism.[196] Further, the ready availability of loanable funds from the church undoubtedly encouraged firms to rely more upon continuous borrowing than on accumulating capital internally through a more productive use of the resources at their disposition. Over the long run, then, these various uneconomic ways of using the accumulated capital of the church occasioned a serious misallocation of the scarce capital resources of the period and held the economic surplus to a level lower than would have been realized had the church's stock of capital been utilized more efficiently.

If capital misallocation represented the material costs of ecclesiastical financing, there was also an important institutional cost. Church institutions preempted the control of a large portion of the available liquid capital in the New World, at least a large portion of that which was not siphoned back to Spain through the fiscal system and trade arrangements; and church-provided financing was, therefore, by far the most important single component of the colonial credit activity. Moreover, the fact that, unlike the case in western Europe, the management of church funds was not given over to private firms such as the Lombardian papal bankers further emphasized the prominence of ecclesiastical finance. Under the circumstances, it was especially difficult for competing private financial institutions to gain much of a foothold in the colonial economic order—particularly since in various lines of economic endeavor resources were often either allocated directly by the state (as in the labor corvées) or mobilized through grants and loans from the royal exchequer.

Private bankers or, more accurately, money lenders there were, especially among the wealthier merchants associated with the *consulados,* but they were few and were engaged in financing of mining and trade activity. The arrangements, however, were insufficient to meet the needs of the mining industry,[197] and even in commercial credit, the quasi-monopolistic nature of trade channels did not afford much room for more modern banking practices to develop. The strategic transatlantic trade was financed by the larger mercantile establishments of Seville and Cádiz which dealt principally with their appointed correspondents and agents in the New World. Within the American trade area, the wholesale merchant importers and distributors of the *consulados* provided some financing for provincial purchasers with whom they enjoyed longstanding customary relationships, sometimes drawing upon the credit which they in turn received from Spanish firms.[198] But in both the maritime and internal commercial traffic, free play in transactions was reduced to a minimum by the official regulatory system and the prerogatives held by the semi-official *consulado* associations. Under such conditions, therefore, the financing of commerce more nearly approximated the internal finance of a firm rather than financial transactions taking place at arm's length between independent firms, and the possibilities for evolving specialized, private financial intermediary institutions were quite limited.

The limited demand for financial services also limited the evolution of modern capital and money market institutions. Throughout much of the colonial economy productive activity was conducted in a context in which credit requirements were relatively modest. Artisan manufacturing, for example, was not highly capitalized.[199] In agriculture, subsistence farming accounted for much of the total output, but even in the case of production for market sale there was little need for money financing. The production functions characteristic of the hacienda system did not call for much in the way of capital inputs, and land parcels were often allotted to the hacienda workers for subsistence farming in lieu of money wages. Thus, where Indians were available for impressment into involuntary servitude, the necessary labor force could be acquired with scarcely any initial money outlay.

The organizational structure of the colonial economic system thus precluded development in Spanish America of private ancillary financial institutions—banks, bourses, and the like—which were indispensable social instruments for mobilizing capital and cooperant resources for development. The progressive evolution of financial organization in Europe—from, say, the eleventh-century Pierleoni banking house down through the early Genoese and Florentine bankers, the Medici and Fuggers, to the Bank of Amsterdam (established 1609) and the Bank of England (established 1694)—had virtually no counterpart in Spain's overseas dominions. Consequently, the inhabitants of the colonial realm entered the modern age in the 1800's with an extremely limited experience in organizing and dealing with a commercially oriented system of banking and finance.[200] The closest approach to a more modern type of lending activity was not instigated until 1782, when the crown set up the Bank of San Carlos to provide general banking services throughout the empire and, in connection with its efforts to revivify the mining sector, established the *rescate* banks of South America and the *avio* mining bank in Mexico. But this new system, along with the economy it served, soon collapsed in the turbulence and dislocation of the early-nineteenth-century period.

Dismantled, with the end of Spanish rule, was the elaborate fiscal system contrived by the crown. Gone, too, were a goodly number of the merchant houses and moneylenders who had previously provided a limited range of financial services, for with independence many of the Spaniards involved in these activities decamped, taking their liquid assets with them.[201] Even the once-powerful *consulados* were reduced to penury by the forced loans extracted from them by new governments desperate for revenues.[202] Meanwhile the ecclesiastical bulwark of the colonial financial structure was plundered and virtually destroyed, for as the wealth of the church had increased, it became an ever more attractive prize for those interested in putting that wealth to alternative, though not necessarily more economic, uses. In the late eighteenth century, the crown used its control of church administration to appropriate considerable portions of this wealth, thereby extracting and dissipating a large share of the accumulated colonial capital. During the struggle for independence in the nineteenth century, the new national governments of Latin America were disposed to do likewise, utilizing the claim that the *patronato real* had passed to the new regimes. Thereupon, a combination of forced loans, expropriations, and other exactions rapidly depleted church coffers, while administrative disorganization in the church, the termination of ecclesiastical taxation, the confiscation of church properties, and widespread disregard of mortgage and other loan obligations made it impossible to replenish them. As it turned out, the ecclesiastical revenue-gathering system had suffered irreparable damage, and the days of the church as financier were over.

By the early 1800's, when the Spanish American countries embarked on a development stage in which economic performance presupposed an increasingly intricate and comprehensive supporting network of financial institutions, there existed in most of Latin America only the most rudimentary banking services and, properly speaking, no banking and financial system at all. Moreover, while the traditional financial props that had sustained if not nourished economic life were gone, the conditions then prevailing were inauspicious for devising newer, more effective replacements. If the consequences for continuity in the material processes of production were ruinous, there was another implication which was of at least equal import. For a lengthy period of time and during a crucial era, Spanish America was deprived of the institutional instruments which, elsewhere, had historically facilitated the shift of social and economic power from archaic elites to the entrepreneurs of the modern age.

IV

The Colonial Private Sector and Economic Growth

LATIN American geographical and cultural conditions produced key operational changes in the Spanish monarchy's comprehensive design for settlement and governing. Practically speaking, resolute assertion of the power of the central government was much tempered by conflicting policy aims and by the actual capabilities of policy implementation. And one of the chief defects of Spanish administration was its insufficient regard for the old Iberian proverb: "Del dicho al hecho hay mucho trecho"—which means, freely translated, that there's a long hard road between stating a principle and putting it into practice.

The geographical conditions which made for high transport costs weighed heavily also upon the conduct of public administration and the efficiency of law enforcement. If, between the formulation and implementation of colonial policies, there were often discrepancies, the situation was largely attributable to the geographical separation from the mother country and to the strong incentives for colonists to take advantage of opportune conditions for violating the law. Some legislation was disregarded, and the crown was forced to allow even some laws which were crucial to its general policy design to fall into desuetude. Above all, the crown was nearly powerless to curb the growth of latifundism, which, while neither deliberately introduced nor, for that matter, especially desired by Spanish authority, eventually assumed such proportions that ultimately the crown had to recognize it as a *fait accompli*.

The significance of latifundism can hardly be overrated, whether for understanding the colonial economic system or for interpreting the development patterns of postcolonial times. Directly and indirectly, it came to determine the chief modes and relations of production in agriculture. And, because of the importance of the agricultural sector, the characteristics of latifundism played a major role in influencing the conditions of life for most of the Latin American populace: by affecting prevailing forms of social organization, by influencing levels of productivity and income (and the distribution of the latter) and by determining to an important extent the degree of development possible for a large bloc of the area's human resources.[1] The ramifications of agrarian structure have historically affected the nonagricultural sectors as well by fixing the major market and resource constraints on the development possibilities of the nonagricultural portions

110

of the economy.[2] An abundance of studies give testimony to the persisting backward state of agricultural organization in virtually every Latin American country, and to the adverse developmental repercussions thereof. By examining the colonial foundations of the land tenure system, it is possible to distinguish the various elements bound up in this problem complex and to trace their influence on patterns of resource control and use.[3]

LATIFUNDISM AS A BASIC ELEMENT IN ECONOMIC ORGANIZATION

The lands and Indians which were so valuable to the royal patrimony were also potentially valuable assets to the Spanish settlers, who by one means or another sought to appropriate them. Indeed, land ownership was for most of the settlers the chief basis of social prestige and preferential status and was thus a principal objective of the upwardly mobile immigrants who came to the New World in search of *hidalguismo* or gentility. It was so, partly because of the status that European countries conferred on owners of property and partly because of the circumstances of life in the New World, particularly the dearth of alternative sources of high status.

In general, criollos were denied access to the more important positions in colonial government because of the royal practice of reserving these for peninsular Spaniards. The *encomienda* pensions, which initially conferred a measure of prestige upon their recipients, became less valuable with the decline of the indigenous population and were seldom awarded after the crown became aware of the manifold abuses associated with the institution. For most American-born settlers, the possibilities of attaining high status through manufacturing or commercial enterprise were limited, partly because of the arrested development of these lines of activity and partly because peninsular Spaniards, aided by the regulatory apparatus and personal contacts in Spain, were generally able to maintain an upper hand in the most rewarding branch of trade, the maritime commerce. Mining was an obvious opportunity for advancement, but there were only a limited number of mines adequate to propel their operators to positions of invidious distinction. Patents of nobility constituted still another source of high status, but these were not available in quantity sufficient to meet the demand, even though the crown eventually came to recognize the lucrative possibilities of creating titles and decorations and selling them to those who had grown wealthy in colonial mining, commerce, or agriculture.[4]

What remained, then, as more widely distributed status-conferring appropriable assets were land and Indians, particularly as the growth of urban settlements gave rise to a limited but increasing demand for the output of rural property holdings. Even in the absence of markets for the sale of estate production, however, the resources of the rural sector could, if commandeered on an ample enough scale, be exploited to provide the owner directly with a respectable standard of living. Thus, for both criollos and those *peninsulares* who decided to settle permanently in the American kingdoms, the acquisition of real estate—whether by purchase, governmental grants, marriage, or chicane—constituted the major avenue to social prestige. Even those whose wealth derived from mining or trade often found it expedient to provide themselves with land as insurance against the vagaries of trade and the playing out of mining ores. A not altogether different view of the insurance function of investment in real property remains widely characteristic even today in Latin America.

The incentives were provided, therefore, for an irresistible development of latifundism as the distinctive product of New World conditions of social organization. Much of the area's history can be described as a dialectical competition between Iberian centralism and the centrifugal forces of American latifundism. Being a local product, the latifundism was so deeply rooted in the conditions of American life that it survived intact during the nineteenth-century period of political disorder when the crown was overthrown and the church greatly weakened. In fact, during the postcolonial era latifundism was even strengthened and for over a century enjoyed an uncontested role as the determinative institution in Latin American society. The establishment of national governments removed the restraints imposed by imperial rule which, at most, begrudgingly ratified the land-hogging efforts of the settlers; and to the privileges already held by the colonial landowning elite, the achievement of independence added that which was previously denied them: control of the political processes.

LATIFUNDISM VS. FEUDALISM IN SPANISH AMERICAN SOCIAL ORGANIZATION

During the colonial period the structure of power rested upon what was in effect a system of shared authority. The state was ostensibly the authoritative institution, but whereas in Spain land concentration was combined with a partial political sterilization of the landowning nobility, the distances and communications problems of the overseas kingdoms made it much more difficult to divorce landownership from effective local power of a political and economic nature. In spite of the official rationale of colonial organization, therefore, the latifundia became the main system of local government in many rural regions and the arbiter of other social relationships as well.

Since the population was overwhelmingly rural, the growth of this quasi-governmental power center was especially important. It meant that the quotidian encounter of a large portion of the monarchs' rural subjects with the exercise of authority was with the private governments represented by the *grandes terratenientes* or large landholders, not with the formal administrative machinery of the state. However, in both areas of organization—the official public organization and the extraofficial private governments—the asymmetrical distribution of power tended to be exercised autocratically so that most individuals were related to social authority as subjects rather than as participants, with limited opportunities and resource support for the exercise of initiative and enterprise. Consequently, the predominating social interaction patterns involved a nonparticipative subordination to a dominant decision maker, not experience in voluntaristic, collaborative associations operating for mutual interests. In addition, the latifundia, like virtually all colonial institutional structures, were functionally diffuse and governed a variety of social relationships.[5]

Yet, there were differences between the control patterns of the government and the latifundia, and these took on added significance when independence removed the crown's loose checks against a fuller development of the informal power structure of the latifundia. In the first place, the public organization, for all its autocratic features, possessed its own inner system of checks and controls. The *residencias,* the *visitas,* and the custom of corresponding directly with the power center in Spain provided an institutionalized feedback mechanism of sorts between the decision-making authority and the field. While the last-mentioned of these devices involved colonial subjects in an essentially petitionary relationship with the state, the others at least approximated the regularized procedures and relationships of a comprehensive system of law. In the second place, the rules of procedure, appointment practices, and administrative organization in general were sufficiently developed that, in accordance with the Weberian conceptualization, the system can be described as a protobureaucratic if not a fully bureaucratic administration.

In contrast, the internal organization of the latifundia was almost a pure case of patrimonial administration, for which reason, among others, latifundism has often been equated with feudalism. Moreover, as in the conditions which generated feudalism in Europe, American latifundism was a function of operational limitations on the exercise of central authority and of the high degree of local self-sufficiency in an economic regime based primarily on agriculture. In this regard, it tended, by blocking the routes of cultural diffusion and restricting networks of contacts, to foster cultural separation and parochialism, thereby maintaining regional and class differences in psychological set, life style, and even language. Once central authority was weakened by the break with Spain, it was also feudal in that it inhibited the gathering of loyalties and consensus at a national level. The causal relationship between the latifundia and concentrated control over rural wealth and income, as well as social stratification and inequality, also resembled feudalism; for historically the latifundian system played a major role in setting the social distance between the various segments of society and thereby fostered the high degree of discreteness which pervades Latin American social structure.

Yet, to identify feudalism with all manifestations of social inequality or even with any regime of large landholdings is to deprive the term of historic specificity; both were features of, say, the late Roman empire and Byzantine life, and, and, before that, the civilizations of ancient Egypt and Mesopotamia. The definitive aspect of feudalism was the historic combination of these ingredients with a type of medieval constitutionalism that recognized a multiplicity of quasi-autonomous corporate entities and was based on a plurality of power structures and loci of decision-making activity. In all of these elements, a concept of community was, at least in theory, central; underpinning the whole system were the requirements of mutual defense and security and a politico-religious ideology which focused upon reciprocity in rights and obligations. From this came the grounds for a general consensus. This is not to claim that in actuality feudalism always operated, as the theory and logic of feudalism supposed, in the common good. Nor is it to deny that the reciprocal claims of feudalism may not often, in practice, have been honored more in the breach than in the observance. It is, however, to recognize that the social structural relationships of western European feudalism were articulated in both an expressed rationale and in customary rules, claims, and counterclaims which had something of the force of common law, so that the whole formed an integrated pattern of organization and cultural outlook.

The Spanish American latifundian system was a bastard sort of feudalism, for it lacked the legitimacy of medieval feudal arrangements and many of its redeeming merits. Extralegal and even illegal in origins and development, the latifundian system forfeited the persuasive sanctions of legitimacy and consensus. Instead, it rested upon trickery, fraud, and the unilateral exercise of power—at best accompanied by a thin veil of legality which came from outmaneuvering the native population on complex institutional grounds which to them were unfamiliar. Since it long remained at or beyond the margins of the law, it could not evolve into a constitutional system. There was, correspondingly, little possibility for integrating it with the prevailing law and philosophy of the land, except on a de facto recognition basis. Nor could the interpersonal relations obtaining within its confines be institutionalized into a conventional system of reciprocal rights and obligations authenticated by social, political, and juridical theory. Practically speaking, the latifundia were off-limits to the magistrates of the crown, though intermittently the crown and its appointed defenders of indigenous rights took legal action to halt the encroachment of the latifundia upon native lands.[6] Spurred on by ecclesiastical and other lawyers, some Indians developed what contemporary observers described as a veritable mania for litigation—a situation which reveals the high incidence of hacienda expansion on Indian properties and the frequency of resort to the crown's protective legislation.[7] But if the frequency of recourse to courts of law was "manic," the outcome was, over the long run, "depressive," for crown, church, and Indians all seem to have been engaged in what was at best a delaying action.[8] In contradistinction to European feudalism, which, however tenuously, was related to a rule by law, latifundism was a social system pinned essentially to rule by personal force and personal authority, and to jockeying for differential advantage in the nether regions of legality and political influence. It was tempered only by such paternalism as was voluntarily conceded by the *grandes terratenientes* in response to the promptings of conscience.

Within this system, in which a quasi-governmental power flowed from the top downwards, economic and other relationships had a conspicuously one-sided character. Furthermore, interpersonal relations between laborers and employers were determined, in the last analysis, by a political sort of power which was only slightly diluted by public responsibility. The essentially outlaw nature of the latifundian phenomenon insured that only a very anemic set of informal, common law norms could develop to govern these relationships in substitute for either market forces or direct public regulation. Thus, American latifundism represented a regime of personal rule in direct contravention of the rule of law. Accordingly, for much of the population in colonial agriculture, the transactional framework had a petitionary rather than a bargaining character, and the security of expectations was highly unstable, unpredictable, and unsatisfactory.

That the longstanding conflict between royal government and private latifundian government was ultimately resolved in favor of the latter is attributable to certain other institutional features of the colonial system. In late medieval Europe, while feudalism still dominated the countryside, the important towns and cities grew up, as Pirenne put it, in the crevices of the feudal order and lay, in a sense, outside the main control patterns of the prevailing manorial agrarianism. Such was not the case in Spanish American experience. At first, most of the small villages in which the rural native population resided were simply the lowest level control units of the administrative hierarchies, but as time went on the relative portion of villages in this status was progressively reduced. In the backwash of a spreading wave of hacienda expansion, the villages increasingly lost their character as civic centers and remained merely as housing for the labor force employed on the large estates.[9] Most of the towns and cities—which in Europe played such an important role in the development of mercantilism's urban self-consciousness—were also affected by the rural overlords. Among the perquisites of property ownership was qualification for the status of *vecino*, a citizen with full political rights within the *municipio*: the right to vote for elective positions and eligibility to hold the increasingly honorific membership in the *cabildos* or town councils. Since the wealthy landed gentry were absentee owners and generally resided in the towns, it was they who ordinarily came to occupy the *cabildo* offices—especially after these offices were put up for sale. So long as the Spanish empire remained intact, the administrative bureaucracy existed as a counterpoise to the urban expression of rural latifundian interests. When the royal bureaucracy was removed and when the *cabildo* offices were no longer relegated to a largely ceremonial role, becoming instead the stepping stones to national offices, the *grandes terratenientes* emerged as the controlling group in the urban and national scene as well as in the rural areas. Thereupon, the patrimonial administration of latifundism was extended to society at large. As it increasingly influenced the official public organization, there occurred, in Weberian terms, what was essentially a retrogressive social development from the protobureaucratic colonial administration.

Spanish American towns did not, therefore, enjoy the special institutional dispensation which proved so vital to the development of modern European society. Though in both nineteenth-century western Europe and Spanish America, national politics were largely urban politics, in the former they were bourgeois-dominated and in the latter, rural-dominated. Thus, the relations of production obtaining in agriculture were the socially decisive relations of production in Spanish American organization as a whole and played the major role in the national policies which governed the social utilization of resources during the republican period. When rapid commercial expansion and, later, industrialization made their appearance on the scene, they did so within the structural constraints laid down by this set of land-based relationships and, in the short term, reinforced the fundamental features of the established order with its segmented social system. Consequently, for most of the region, a radical change in the agricultural sector was very nearly prerequisite to modernization of the national patterns of social, political, and economic relationships.

THE GENESIS OF LATIFUNDISM [10]

The problem of latifundism did not have its origins in the *encomienda*, which, in actuality, was essentially a curious technique of public finance, a sort of public pension which pledged a share in future capitation tax revenues in return for the expenditure of private venture capital and effort, though the *encomienda* was conceived initially also as a means of organizing settlement and establishing public order. Neither was the progenitor of the latifundium contained in feudal fiefs established by Spain in America, for the vast estate granted Hernán Cortés, the Marquesado del Valle de Oaxaca, was the sole grant which, in the feudal manner, explicitly conceded political rights in combination with the grant of land and labor. Though the settlers themselves may have wished to transpose feudalism from Europe, the crown had no such similar desire.

The initial settlement pattern placed the Spanish immigrants mainly in or near the areas of densest Indian occupancy. Consequently, *ex initio* there were thrown together in continuing proximity two groups whose quite disparate legal and general cultural traditions were bound to give rise to conflicts of interest, particularly as the regions most naturally productive and favorable for habitation were, with some exceptions, roughly coextensive with the spread of the great sedentary Indian civilizations of pre-Columbian times. In the *tierras templadas* of central and southern Mexico, those of Central America, and in the Andean highlands from roughly the Sabana de Bogotá and Cauca valley regions on south through Peru, the new arrivals from Europe encountered reasonably fertile patches of land which were suited to the practice of the European agricultural heritage they brought with them.[11] Because of their natural advantages, however, many of these lands had already been taken up by the native populations: the assorted Mexican tribes, the declining remnants of Mayan tribes in Central America, the Chibchas in Colombia, and the various groups enthralled under Inca suzerainty in Ecuador, Peru, and Bolivia. It was mainly in the colonial fringe areas that reasonably good but sparsely settled farming lands were found: the highlands of Venezuela and northern Colombia, Costa Rica, central Chile, and northwestern Argentina. And in some of these, such as Chile, the native population, while sparse, was quite bellicose.

Apart from the attraction of good land, a significant amount of Spanish colonization was also based on the mining industry. Silver, gold, and precious stones were especially sought. Mercury was mined for the processing of silver ores and such metals as tin, lead, zinc, iron, and copper were also exploited on a small-scale basis.[12] Eventually the development of mining justified the extension of Spanish settlement into northern Mexico, central Chile, and parts of Central America, which had previously not been thickly populated by indigenous folk, and thus acted as a catalyst for the agricultural development of outlying territories. These cases aside, the principal centers of minerals exploitation for most of the colonial period were: the rich silver deposits developed in central Mexico (e.g., Zacatecas, Guanajuato, Pachuca), the silver mining which centered around Potosí in Bolivia, and the various vein and placer deposits of silver in Peru, where mercury was also important. Colombia was the chief source of gold, emeralds, and platinum, though individually its mines tended to be smaller in scale than those of the major silver areas, and some smaller mines were worked in the Ecuadoran highlands. Most of the major mining centers were located, as were the principal agriculturally based settlements, in or close to the chief regions of indigenous population from which they could draw both food supplies and manpower.

Some of the secondary centers of settlement depended upon their role as supply sources for the primary colonization areas. For example, Chile exported (in addition to some minerals) a variety of temperate-zone agricultural products to Peruvian and Bolivian markets, the Ecuadoran port of Guayaquil became a shipbuilding center for the growing Pacific Coast trade, and northwest Argentina supplied carts and wagons, foodstuffs (including *xarqui* or dried beef), leather goods, and pack animals for the Peruvian viceroyalty. In many of these peripheral regions, settlement was tied to the development of extensive ranching for which large spreads of land (*estancias*) were necessary; as the labor requirements were low, the industry provided several salable products (hides, meat, tallow, draught animals, etc.) which could furnish their own transportation to distant markets by moving on the hoof. Other secondary settlement regions were based upon special imperial functions. For example, Buenos Aires was a defense outpost and Cartagena an entrepôt for European goods moving to interior markets. Still other secondary settlements depended upon the export of specialty agricultural products to both colonial and European markets. Coffee was grown in some locations by the late colonial period. But sugar, cultivated mainly on plantations using African slave labor, had a longer history of development in such areas as the Antilles, along the Caribbean, Gulf of Mexico, and Pacific coasts, and some of the subtropical lands at higher elevations. Similar settlement cases were the cochineal and indigo plantations of Middle America, the tobacco-growing areas of Colombia and Venezuela, and the cacao plantations of Ecuador, Venezuela, and Guatemala. The opportunities for expanding output, however, were limited by the small size of the colonial market and by the fact that after the first half of the seventeenth century Spanish American producers faced export competition from French, English, Dutch, and Portuguese colonies which, under the mercantilist regimes, were accorded a preferential place in the main European markets.[13]

Except for the secondary centers of settlement, colonization brought the majority of both Spanish settlers and Indians into a competitive confrontation on the most preferred land resources, a limited portion of the total region. From the Spanish point of view, the fact that the more valuable lands and the bulk of the native people were found together was a positive factor, in spite of the conflicts it created. While the natives were rival claimants to land use, they were also considered important as labor resources, particularly in the light of the comparatively small stream of immigration. Increased mining activity called for a lavish expenditure of manpower for mineral extraction, processing, and transportation. The extensive program of urban construction undertaken by the Spaniards and the labor-intensive character of agriculture also made Indian labor an extremely valuable asset, particularly as the growth of colonial towns increased the demand for rural sector output. A certain ethnic division of labor arose out of the production coefficients of mining and farming, as well as out of the requirements of commerce and urban settlement. The European immigrants preempted many of the urban occupations in which they had superior training advantages and organized the mining industry and general commercial traffic. The relatively more abundant native labor supply was mobilized primarily for minerals extraction, construction, and farming.

From the beginning of Spanish settlement a further complicating factor created intense new pressures for radical changes in land use patterns: the introduction of domesticated livestock into the New World. Not only did this innovation relate to the Spanish-introduced demand for leather, tallow,[14] and sheep's wool, but also with the growth of the ladino population there came a rising demand for meat as a dietary staple. Even more significant was the fact that the introduction of livestock also ushered in a technological revolution in American transport. After the Conquest the human carrier was increasingly displaced by animal-drawn vehicles and pack animals as a means of handling cargo and passenger traffic, and with the rapid expansion of minerals exports and the general colonial trade the need for transport services mounted sharply. Accordingly, a great deal of acreage was redirected into stock raising, under the management of the Spaniards who were more versed in animal husbandry than were the natives. Thus, the critics who lamented the change of land use from crop cultivation to pasturage were often overlooking the changes in the means of transport and market demand which brought this about. The supply of livestock and livestock products could only be partially met from the outlying regions. Within the areas of densest Spanish and Indian settlement, where the demand for these products was concentrated, the pressure for reallocating land resources became acute, particularly since stock raising was, in that age, organized on an extensive land use basis.

Even with Solomonic wisdom, it would have been difficult for the crown to reconcile all these competing pressures in defining the ownership claims to be allowed as concessions from the *real hacienda*. Yet governmental allocation was the crux of the system, since private access to the basic land resources depended essentially upon the relationship worked out between the private claimants and the state apparatus which dispensed the privilege of access. In subsequent years, the fortunes of the groups contending for control over land were therefore largely conditioned by their relative access to the machinery of state rather than by their relative economic capabilities (in an instrumental sense) or business transactions within the context of a land market.

Once it had been decided that the aboriginals were not to be viewed as chattels, the monarch's policy was that of confirming the natives' rights to the lands they had customarily used—with due regard, of course, for the needs of the system to mobilize Indian labor and for the necessity of permitting the new stock raising industry to develop. In some instances the estates of the pre-Columbian nobility were validated by the crown, for there are reports that Spaniards occasionally acquired large properties through marriage with the offspring of the Indian caciques.[15] In most cases, the confirmation of Indian claims implied the recognition of communal holdings.[16] This, however, soon led to problems, for, owing to the entirely different property concepts prevailing in indigenous culture, these communal claims were, from a Spanish point of view, quite imprecise in nature and vague as to their delimitations. Compounding the trouble and making Indian claims still more difficult to determine was the fact that the *reducciones* or *congrega-*

ciones policy disrupted the original organization of native communities and left vacant tracts in the wake of the population shifts occasioned by the policy. Other quite extensive tracts of native land became unoccupied as the indigenous people succumbed to the epidemics of European diseases, which often wiped out entire villages, or fled before the advance of the Spanish settlers.[17] These factors greatly complicated the processes of adjudication whenever native land titles were called into question by the courts —as they often were throughout the period, especially later when the native population was on the rise.[18] Lawsuits over land titles, between Spaniards and native communities and among the native communities themselves, became a constant feature of the colonial legal system, constituting a heavy drain on the small sums of funds accumulated by the Indians and providing a continuous threat to the security of property holdings.[19]

The crown had also to reward the conquistadores and their heirs. Desiring to establish the colonists where they could begin to produce tax revenue, it made grants of land in fee simple ownership (*gracias de tierra*) to most of the Spaniards who came in the earlier days of the empire. Most grants were of modest size, varying between the *peonías*, the parcels distributed as payment to foot soldiers, and the *caballerías*, the more generous allotments given to horsemen.[20] Leaders of expeditions and other notables, however, were granted substantially larger tracts, ranging, at least in outlying parts, up to one hundred square leagues.[21] In addition, *ejidos* (common lands around the towns) and *baldíos* (pasture lands originally intended to be kept public for all to use) were set aside for the new settlements. The balance of the vast territory remained part of the public domain (*realengas*).

Immediately problems began to arise. Not only were there the difficulties with native properties, but also land grants were made without benefit of cadastral surveys and often the limits of the grants were not clearly defined. The ambiguity of the situation led to overlapping claims as well as to the existence of unassigned tracts between and among the deeded parcels.[22] Under the circumstances, it was difficult to protect the *realengas* from unauthorized seizures, since it was hard to decide just where the boundaries of the public domain lay. The integrity of the native properties was also difficult to defend, particularly when the epidemics had carried off so many of the claimants. The situation was ready-made, therefore, for the plethora of lawsuits which occurred and which, among other consequences, affected the occupational structure by enhancing the attraction of the legal profession.

As properties became increasingly valuable, especially riparian acreage, valley lands, and lands nearer to the urban centers, the foregoing conditions operated almost irresistibly to concentrate the ownership of land. In some instances, grantees who lacked the capital and/or inclination to work their parcels sold out to those who had the means to do so. In time, marriage and inheritance led to the consolidation of other land tracts. The need for food supplies also played a part. When, for example, the demand for food on the part of the ladino population was rising (while the native labor force was diminishing), the consequent urban food crisis even erupted into riots, compelling the state to take a lenient view of whatever measures would alleviate the situation and increase the food supply. Hacienda encroachment upon lands belonging to the depopulated native communities was one such measure. It permitted an expansion of the ranching industry, which had lower labor-input requirements than crop production, and also enabled the Spaniards to capture, by control of the means of production, a portion of the remaining indigenous manpower to compel them to deliver a larger share of their output to the urban markets.[23] Increased coercion of the Indians was, after all, a cheaper means of relieving the labor shortage than purchasing slaves imported from Africa.

Ignoring the laws which proscribed sales of native properties, the Spanish settlers bought such properties anyhow or by force and fraud simply seized them outright.[24] Control of scarce water resources provided another means of forcing the less favored landowners, natives and other Spaniards alike, to part with their properties.[25] Disregarding laws forbidding them from acquiring lands from the natives placed in their charge, the *encomenderos* took advantage of their positions to appropriate the properties of those they were supposed to protect.[26] Illegal land seizures from the *realengas* also abounded. Gradually, too, the *municipios* redefined the concept of the *baldíos*, and to raise funds for their treasuries and increase food production, began to award *asientos*, or leasing contracts ("sin propiedad y señoría"), for the usufruct of the lands.[27] But as the *asiento* grantees generally controlled the municipal councils, often the leased lands were ultimately taken over in fee simple ownership. Unable effectively to revoke such assignments, the viceroys recognized the practical situation and, as in the case of viceroy Velasco, merely tried to limit the size of the properties and keep them a safe distance from Indian villages.

The complexities of land-title determination and the processes of adjudication furnished still another important avenue for property enlargement, that of gaining differential advantage in legal maneuver. In the courts, Spaniards and criollos enjoyed the upper hand over Indians, who were less familiar with the alien legal system, while the wealthier and more influential colonists could better afford costly court battles and legal appeals than the less affluent settlers.[28] Continued and protracted litigation appears to have been frequent [29]—so frequent that contemporary reporters concluded it was allowed for as a regular item in hacienda expenditures budgets.

Eventually the state acquiesced in the growth of latifundism as the crown sought to raise funds from all available sources. Indeed, nothing shows more clearly than the evolution of public land policy that economic and social policy was continually prompted by the fiscal need to incorporate a variety of opportunistic expedients; as a result, imperial rule came to have less and less coherence as a definite system of policy. Although the new measures might have had some value as a means of clearing the courts of the growing burden of land-title litigation, fiscal considerations were prominent in the process of *composición* which the government instituted at the close of the sixteenth century.[30] Under this process, in exchange for the payment of fees and the registration of property claims, the crown confirmed the title to the land so registered. Since by this time some criollo settlers were prosperous enough to "buy legality" through this means, much land appears to have been sold in the recurrent *composiciones*, including lands previously usurped by various methods. As if to pressage the more lavish nineteenth-century giveaways, the public domain was alienated progressively into private hands. Moreover, a good deal of the land registered in the *composiciones* was inscribed unbeknown to the actual occupants,[31] for the safeguards provided against abuse of the *composición* were rather weak.[32] Despite the stated intention to protect native properties from encroachment in the *composiciones*, abuse of the process was probably encouraged by the fact that the payment for validation of title brought exemption from possible future reviews of earlier irregularities.

Progressive expansion of the latifundia was also greatly assisted by the access large landowners enjoyed to hypothecation financing from clerical money lenders, for existing properties could be mortgaged (and even rehypothecated) to obtain funds for acquiring additional lands—whether through conventional purchases, *composición*, or successful defense of land claims in the courts. The additional lands could then be pledged as collateral for further loans to repeat the cycle again. On some of the estates, the crown conferred the additional advantage of the *mayorazgo*, a type of primogenitary entail.

The growth of latifundian firms was so extensive that it debarred the development of an active market in land, though it is plain that this growth depended not so much upon these firms' demonstrated economic performance in efficiency of resource use as upon their differential access to mortgage financing, adroit juridical actions, influence with the land granting agencies, and success in the *composición* processes. By roughly similar methods, latifundian growth was accelerated during postcolonial times. Even so, while the latifundium had acquired a preponderant position at the end of the colonial regime, it was not the exclusive form of land tenure. Not all haciendas were entailed; some were subdivided among heirs, sold, and reconsolidated along different boundaries throughout the centuries of Spanish rule. Small and medium-sized settler landholdings survived, too, though in some areas—particularly in the zones of secondary settlement— their survival chances were better than elsewhere. Costa Rica and the Antioquian region of Colombia, for example, are two cases in which the growth of latifundism was relatively contained by the economics of labor scarcity and transport. Further, even though the balance of institutional advantage was against them and though the force of circumstances operated strongly against their preservation, some of the indigenous communal properties managed to persist to the end of the colonial dispensation, albeit usually in reduced size. The free villages—i.e., those placed in *encomiendas* and *corregimientos* directly under the crown—endured throughout the colonial era, though even they were impaired somewhat by the exactions of forced labor under the *mita* system and were, in many cases, exploited by the caciques and *corregidores* who governed them. Brand's Quiroga study, for example, indicates that certain lands maintained by the Indians in central Mexico were not lost until after the Ley Lerdo of 1856.[33]

SELF-SUSTAINING FEATURES IN LATIFUNDIAN GROWTH: LAND AND LABOR MARKETS

Once the latifundian movement acquired momentum, it generally commanded a sufficiently dominant position to preempt the resources necessary for its survival—and not only because of the cumulative advantages of political influence and mortgage borrowing, though certainly these were central to its self-perpetuation. Since, for example, the latifundia often appropriated the better lands, the growth of population gave rise to windfall gains in land value appreciation, and this, together with other power components of the hacienda, made these properties preferred risks in the distribution of loanable funds, quite apart from the preferential access that large landholders had with the major lenders by virtue of their personal connections. So long as the colonial period lasted, at least some of the owners of smaller and medium-sized parcels could borrow funds on reasonable terms, but with the onset of the republican era, the latifundia were generally the only agricultural firms which enjoyed the privilege of access to the formal institutions of credit. Similarly, the strong political influence wielded by the *hacendados* became even greater with the inauguration of the national period, which increased the value of the hacienda as an entrée to the ascriptive system of national leadership recruitment and allowed the large landowners an almost uncontested hand in shaping national land policies, public spending, and taxation. Land taxes, for example, were seldom employed, and in some countries the landowner-controlled national governments specifically enjoined local governments from using the device to raise revenues for local needs.

More immediately decisive, however, was the relationship which developed between the haciendas and the supply of labor factors. When the native demographic resurgence began during the last half of the colonial age, the latifundian movement was already well under way. Consequently, the remaining communal lands of the natives were able to absorb, with progressive crowding, only a fraction of the growing rural labor force. Cultural differences, reinforced by deficiencies in social investment and prevailing policies, precluded many of the Indians' being pulled upward into the narrow nonagricultural opportunity structure of commerce, mining, the civil service, and the professions. To the extent that nonagricultural job opportunities were presented, the Indians sought them or were forced to seek them—even appearing as voluntary labor to work in the mines. But the total socio-economic context of the colonial age constricted the expansion of the economy and, hence, amplification of the employment structure, especially in the urban centers. Meanwhile, defective transport and communications systems and the high risk of insecurity assumed by Indian migrants leaving their own villages for distant points hindered the geographical mobility of labor, just as the former set of conditions worked against the intersectoral mobility of labor. *Nolens volens,* therefore, the majority of those who could not be absorbed by the native communities were thrown back upon the limited job options in the more immediate rural proximity.

Self-employment on small individually owned properties was seldom possible, partly because the Laws of the Indies did not make adequate provision for natives to obtain, as individuals, secure title to the *realengas.* Accordingly, when the Indians moved onto these, their occupancy status was simply that of squatters. At the same time, there was no market in private land at a level which was meaningful to the impoverished natives, or for that matter, to the more impecunious Spanish settlers. Part of the area was taken up in entail and another part was irretrievably incorporated into the patrimony of the church. Of the remainder, a substantial portion was held by the haciendas and ordinarily changed hands in connection with inheritance or marriage, or was disposed of in units so large and at such inflated prices as to be beyond the buying capacity of the Indians. The inherent income stability of the large estates and their usefulness as a basis for mortgage borrowing meant, on the one hand, that their owners were only infrequently forced to sell. On the other hand, this very economic security was a factor in the computation of land values. As a prestige source which opened the door to a variety of the ancillary benefits of status, the latifundium commanded still another premium that elevated its price above the capitalized value of its yields of agricultural output. In addition, the large estate conferred upon its owner a further "economy of scale" which was not so readily available to the small holder: an advantageous monopsonistic position in the hiring of labor. Consequently, the existence of these several supplemental values in the large holdings reduced the amount of private land available for sale and bid up the supply price of this land to levels higher than its real economic productivity alone would justify.

Transport and market conditions, particularly the demand for livestock, also favored the large estate over the smaller holdings. Though in the rural districts immediately surrounding the capital cities and mining centers a fairly well developed and diversified agriculture emerged, the land-extensive plantation crops and ranching activities were ordinarily the most feasible commercial types of land use in regions more removed. Exploited labor was used to supply grain to the urban markets, while the size of the urban populace and the low income levels of most of that populace depressed the demand for other agricultural items. The more diversified food requirements of the wealthier urban consumers was ordinarily met directly from the produce of the estates they possessed in the adjacent countryside, and the majority of the population was not a factor at all in the food market, since it produced for its own meager demand in the subsistence sector. As a result, the commercial production possibilities of smaller-scale crop farming were rather limited. Often, therefore, there existed a situation in which, to obtain land for crop cultivation, small-scale tenants (or small purchasers) were unable to pay a rent (or a price) which was equal to what the land yielded the *hacendados* in its uncultivated state as pasturage. Thus, as Thomas Malthus long ago observed, "lands which might be capable of supporting thousands of people may be left to support a few hundreds of cattle." [34]

For a variety of reasons, then, natives not absorbed on the lands of Indian communities often had little choice other than to seek employment on the large estates; and when the native population began to increase, the supply of agricultural labor tended to exceed demand, depressing the level of labor remuneration. The bargaining position of the workers was rendered more unfavorable still by geographical and intersectoral immobility. Consequently, within the noninteracting regional labor markets, the latifundia were frequently, by their preemption of land resources, in the position of monopsonistic (or, at most, oligopsonistic) purchasers of labor power. With employers able to lay down the terms on which labor was hired, wages not only were reduced to the subsistence level, but also were pushed out of the area of money payment altogether. The characteristic mode of labor remuneration in agriculture became, accordingly, the permission to cultivate on a subsistence basis a small parcel of land in exchange for whatever need the estate might have for the worker's services (or for the services of the rest of his household).

Hacienda labor was one of bondage, primarily because the worker was "bound by lack of [employment] alternatives rather than by slavery." [35] De facto serfdom, however, was also converted into something approaching de jure serfdom since, in conformity with the customs of the age, hereditary debt was recognized in the Spanish courts. [36] As most of the rural population lived on the edge of dire necessity, it was not very difficult for landowners to lure them into debt and to hold them in thralldom by means of the *tienda de raya,* or company store. [37] By the close of the seventeenth century debt peonage was well established in New Spain.

In the eighteenth century, the practice was widespread in Spanish South America as well.

From the *hacendado's* point of view, the peonage system had much to recommend it, quite apart from the leverage it provided for reducing the factor returns to labor. The character of market demand confined agricultural activity to a very limited number of production alternatives. The institutional environment which governed factor availability favored selection from among a quite constricted range of production functions, so that capital was used sparingly while land and labor were used extensively. Even where agricultural capital was employed, much of it took the form of irrigation systems and the like which could be constructed on site with local labor power employed on a nonwage basis. Given the low levels of capitalization, the potentially significant items of cost were, therefore, land and labor.

For the most part, land acquisition costs were not very great. Debt peonage, the use of subsistence plots (on marginal lands) in lieu of money wages, and the resort to sharecropping arrangements (in which the advantage is setting shares lay with the landlord) held the hacienda's real costs of production to low levels, and the out-of-pocket money costs for labor were even lower than the real labor costs. The cost situation, hence, was favorable to the hacienda owner, and the tiny share of the total represented by monetized costs made the picture more favorable still. With cash expenditures on production so minimal, the hacienda could easily absorb even considerable fluctuations in the amount of money income realized from the sale of output. Whatever the impact of changes in harvest yields and price levels on aggregate money intake, only a small subtraction was generally necessary to cover money outlays and, consequently, to derive the net money income which accrued to the landowner. Thus, from the cushion provided by nonmonetized labor costs, the hacienda derived a special resiliency which at once enabled it to weather changing economic conditions and made it so attractive as an asset.

The systems of latifundism and peonage were mutually reinforcing. And just as control of land had created monopsonistic and oligopsonistic power in the appropriation of labor, latifundian control of both land and labor resources afforded a basis for monopolistic and oligopolistic positions in the supply of goods to local and regional markets; this was reinforced by the rudimentary state of transport and communications development. To be sure, during the colonial era the output markets were largely regulated, but the regulatory system was one in which, at the municipal level, the landowners had influence by virtue of their domination of municipal councils. Since the haciendas usually sold goods for which the demand was fairly inelastic with respect to both decreases in income and increases in price, it was possible for the haciendas to exploit an advantageous market position in output as well as factor markets; this gave these firms pecuniary economies of scale not realizable by smaller, competing enterprises. Both of these market advantages were heightened when political independence led to a breakdown of the traditional colonial system of market controls and to enhanced possibilities of market manipulation. For economic reasons no less than for political and social considerations, large-scale landownership was viewed as a uniquely desirable investment.

The effects of latifundism on institutional evolution were anything but favorable. After the outright enslavement of Africans and the *repartimiento* or *mita* allocations, the spreading regime of debt peonage came as a coup de grace to development of a free labor market,[38] especially since Indians living in the *congregaciones* and on the church's estates and missions were also rather isolated from contact with employment markets organized on the basis of a cash nexus between employers and workers. As in the case of land, private control over labor resources flowed less from bargaining within a market context than from a political relationship: one derived from the state's role in furthering the monopolization of land, its sanctioning of slavery and compulsory labor assignments, and its endorsement of hereditary debt peonage. With so much of the rural labor force enmeshed in precapitalistic regimes of labor organization, a high degree of labor immobility was structured into the fabric of Spanish American economic organization. This was the human factor counterpart to the immobility of land use. And again as in the case of land resources, the volume of labor resources which could be commanded by the latifundian firms was related much less to efficiency in resource use than to management of other variables in the environment.

LATIFUNDISM AND THE EFFICIENCY OF RESOURCE USE

A major institutional block to the evolution of land and labor markets in Spanish America, latifundism was also negative in its effects on the efficiency with which these basic resources were used. In this respect the contraproductive impact of latifundism has in many places continued down to the present day.[39] For analytical purposes, these effects may be discussed under three heads: the quality of resource management, the utilization of land, and the utilization of labor. In each of these, as will be evident, there was both a material cost (in the sense of a sacrifice of output) and an institutional cost (in the sense of arrested institutional development).

Latifundism was historically associated with a managerial orientation which, from a developmental perspective, was singularly unenterprising in increasing the output from the available resources. This was even more the case insofar as the culture valued conspicuous leisure over conspicuous consumption, at least after a conventionally suitable level of material consumption had been attained. Moreover, two of the prime forms of elite-status consumption—the construction of urban residences and country houses, and the lavish consumption of personal services—could generally be met by requisitioning labor from the ample reserve present on the elite's rural holdings. Foodstuffs, except for imported delicacies, could be similarly garnered directly from the rural estates. Since many of the household furnishings could also be turned out by hacienda workers, the money income required to sustain a respectably high standard of living was not nearly so great as it would have been under altered circumstances. Whenever an exceptional cash outlay was contemplated, there was always the possibility of mortgaging some more of the property.

The consumption preferences and the secure income base possessed by the major controllers of Spanish America's agricultural resources largely exempted these aristocrats from the necessity of direct managerial involvement in the processes of agricultural production. The virtual absence of competition in either factor or output markets reinforced this dispensation. Except for ranching activity and some of the colonial plantations, the unitary large-scale ownership which was represented by the hacienda did not imply that the institution was also a large-scale producing unit. Instead, from a production organization standpoint, it was more commonly a conglomeration of small-scale producing units. Actual crop production was generally handled by tenants and sharecroppers, under terms which reflected the strong bargaining position of the landowner. Few, if any, real economies of scale, in either technological or organizational efficiency, were therefore generated by the hacienda mode of crop farming, and the type of management provided by the landowner was scarcely more than that of the passive rentier. Extensive ranching activity was still less troublesome as a source of income.

Given both the size and character of the income which accrued to the *hacendado* households and given the high cultural value placed on avoidance of gainful employment in the ordinary sense of that term, the marginal disutility of additional effort (in managerial activity) tended generally to exceed the marginal utility of the additional income that effort might produce. Furthermore, the cultivation of useful personal contacts among the clergy and other public officials and the hiring of lawyers constituted a more lucrative mode of effort for most hacienda owners than did direct participation in production management, for it was through these that the major gains in the system were to be had. Thus, while the hacienda institution possessed the sole discretionary authority over much of the land and labor resources in the rural sector, the quality of resource management provided by the absentee owners was so poor as to render the term "management" almost inapplicable. The managerial function, if such it was, was only remotely oriented towards technological efficiency, since there was little pressure exerted by the environment to stimulate more efficient resource employment.

Yet, if hacienda owners were inefficient in a technological sense, they could very easily afford to be; neither market nor political sanctions compelled them to be otherwise. And anyway, by fundamentally noneconomic means, they had already arrived at the top of the social structure, while the limited horizons of their day tended to dampen ambition to seek still greater material gain. Ceremonial honorifics, cultivation of the social amenities, and, later, the capture of full political power were the relevant goals for a class which was, assuredly, not achievement oriented.[40]

Hacienda management was also noninnovative in character. Stable and limited markets, deficient transport systems, the virtual absence of competition in input and output markets, the assured income and status position of the large landowners, and their ignorance of, and indifference to, production processes were all forces which favored continuation of traditional and backward methods of organization and productive technique. Thus, agricultural production took place in a static environment which was hardly conducive to the technical and organizational innovation that would have increased productivity. Furthermore, the social and economic position of the latifundian owners was such that the exercise of power of a quasi-political nature—e.g., the "capture" of more land for the practice of extensive agriculture and the increase in exactions from the tenant farmers and hacienda laborers—could substitute in large measure for increases in production and marketing efficiency. More extensive exploitation of land plus more intensive exploitation of the captive labor force, in other words, were practical alternatives to a rise in technical productivity through greater investment and organizational efficiency and were, in addition, alternatives generally more readily realizable in the conventional scheme of action. Since the predominant wage system consisted of allowing hacienda workers to farm a parcel of land which was marginal or unsuitable from the *hacendado's* point of view, the opportunity cost of labor to the employer was generally close to zero. Consequently, with labor functioning virtually as a free resource for the latifundia owners, the utilization of labor inputs up to the point where their marginal cost (to the employer) was equal to their marginal value output resulted in farm operations based on labor-intensive production functions. Because of the established regime of labor organization, it was therefore "uneconomic" (given the prevailing institutional structure) to shift to newer production coefficients in which capital inputs would play a larger relative role. That additional disposable income could be raised by mortgage financing and by such opportunities for monopolistic sales practices as circumstances afforded reduced still more the incentive to introduce improved technology. Consequently, the whole latifundian system not only resulted in a lax management of existing resources, but also perpetuated a backward technological and organizational condition in agricultural production.[41] Moreover, since such a large portion of the available agricultural resources was preempted by this institution, there were few opportunities for developing a more progressive system of farm management on other types of rural firms.

Given the character of the management, it is not surprising that the pattern and intensity of land and labor use failed to correspond to the social requisites of development even though they were functional in terms of the existing institutional arrangements. Side by side with widespread destitution, there often existed, within the confines of the large estates, lands which were left idle because the landowner lacked the inclination or ability (or both) to use them. Besides this quantitative underemployment of the land resources, however, there was also a serious problem of qualitative underemployment, for frequently some of the best acreage was devoted to low-intensity uses such as grazing while food crop production (for the maintenance of the labor force) was relegated to lands which, for one reason or another, were less productive.[42] While such practices were a rational adaptation to the social conditions of the time, they nevertheless indicate, from a developmental perspective, the essential irrationality of the institutions which dictated such patterns of land use.

Quantitative underemployment of labor resources was also inherent in the system. Even allowing for the reduced work capacity of rural laborers due to malnutrition and poor health, there was a degree of involuntary leisure or idleness which can by no means be accounted for simply by the seasonality of agricultural production cycles.[43] The explanation lies instead in the limited resource combinations permitted by the latifundian regime and by the influence of latifundism on the general economic environment. Idle land of some fertility existed because it was not required to support the income position of the owner of land. Idle labor was largely a function of the same circumstance insofar as the laborers were underemployed for want of access to the existing land resources and because cooperant capital factors were not available, given the landowners' disposition of the investible surplus. Other circumstances were also operative: the limited access to markets and the weakness and narrow shape of market demand. These, however, were related to the pattern of wealth control for the former was partly due to the insufficiency of investment in overhead capital while the latter was related to the prevailing pattern of income distribution.

There was also a parallel qualitative underemployment of rural human resources. Cut off from attainment of European culture elements by the superimposed power structure of the hacienda, rural people were severely limited in their capacity to become incorporated into the emerging sociocultural system. Large landowners did not, for example, support formal education, with its teaching of skills and its general fostering of cultural assimilation, as part of the operations of their estates.[44] And latifundian control of rural resources and the decision-making process appears generally to have been exercised in such a manner as to preclude rural communities from undertaking and supporting such social overhead activities on their own. Indeed, under the patrimonial regime of the haciendas, native community organization was generally discouraged except for the most innocuous and ceremonial forms. Neither, for that matter, could informal educational processes develop as an effective surrogate for the missing system of formal education. Owing to the latifundia's unilateral control of productive assets and to the conservative technological and organizational bias of latifundian management, the rural population was largely denied the opportunity to develop the exercise of initiative, to acquire managerial and other skills through active participation in the decision-making processes, and to work with improved agricultural practices. Thus, the subservient rural labor force was only passively involved in production and auxiliary economic activities. Deployed on a crudely undifferentiated basis as, essentially, so many units of unskilled (or at best, semiskilled) draught animals, the labor resources of the haciendas had therefore practically no opportunity to develop the higher mental skills and abilities which account for the uniquely productive contribution of the human agents of production.

The rural populace dwelt in a cultural and linguistic isolation, which, combined with the geographical problems of transport and communications, served to prolong cultural dualism. Only slightly modified were the traditional thought-world and the customary primitive technologies of prehispanic days. Indeed, it is probable that the regime even accentuated a type of cultural conservatism among the rural population since the experience of most of the natives with change was largely negative. The nonwage method of payment, the high rents and low real wages, the inability of the haciendas' native workers and tenants to transmit the fruits of their labors to oncoming generations, the insecurity of expectations, and the utter lack of producer autonomy and safeguards against the exercise of asymmetrically distributed power—all these conspired to establish a situation in which, for the majority, meaningful incentives were almost inoperative. It would, in fact, be difficult to imagine a system so thoroughly devoid of built-in incentives for individual and collective improvement, or one which was so generous in its supply of disincentives. Furthermore, even had incentives somehow arisen, the native work force was generally denied the resource support for acting upon them.[45]

LATIFUNDISM AND MINIFUNDISM

Side by side with the growth of the latifundia, there emerged another land tenure phenomenon which was a by-product of the same convergence of demographic and other trends.[46] The principal locus of this phenomenon, minifundism (the fragmentation of land into uneconomically small plots), was the Indian community. It appeared as a problem functionally related to the encroachment of the haciendas upon native properties. As the native population began to recover in numbers, there occurred both a progressive subdivision of the indigenous property holdings which remained intact and an increased offering of labor to the latifundia. The main alternative, which was utilized increasingly as the native population continued to grow, was the migration of considerable numbers of people who became squatters on public lands more remotely situated. Latifundism and minifundism, therefore, developed in tandem.

To be exact, there were two sets of subsistence farming plots or mini-fundia: the parcels used for labor remuneration within but on the fringes of the hacienda holdings, and the parcels which were crowded onto the more marginal lands that had thus far remained outside the boundaries of the larger properties. In both cases, primitive techniques of slash-and-burn land clearing, planting, and harvesting were applied to poor lands to eke out a bare subsistence for the cultivator and his family. On both, economic pressure combined with tradition (e.g., customary dietary preferences) and producer ignorance to restrict output to relatively few crops, particularly staples such as maize, beans, and potatoes whose comparatively high natural yields per acre could in some measure compensate for the unfavorable quality and the limited quantity of the land used. Precariously exposed, because of their slim margin of production, to the impact of pests, blights, and weather, the minifundia could seldom generate a surplus sufficient for reinvestment in raising labor productivity or expansion of the unit size. Not always, for that matter, could the minifundia's highly variable yields even provide a subsistence. When occasional market-able surpluses were produced, the lack of storage facilities and financial reserves generally forced the independent minifundia operators to sell these surpluses on terms which left them pretty much at the mercy of the buyers. Frequently, the minifundia farmers who worked on the haciendas were obliged to sell their output directly to the hacienda owner who, exploiting his monopsonistic advantage, paid correspondingly reduced prices.

Credit was rarely obtainable, because of the economic instability of the minifundia units and because they often lacked title (or, at least, secure title) to the land. When credit was extended, however, it was usually for emergency subsistence consumption and came either from *hacendados* interested in adding to their captive labor pool by debt peonage arrangements or from merchant moneylenders to whom the cultivators were obliged to sell their small crops in advance, at substantial discount, as surety. Through neither internal capital accumulation nor borrowing, then, was it possible for minifundia operators to better their lot.

With barely enough space to cultivate staples for family consumption, the farmers would customarily (and necessarily) plant the same lands with the same crops year after year; crop rotation was seldom practiced. The cost of field rotation (i.e., letting fields lie fallow periodically) was so high in the short run, because of the scarcity of land for minifundia operators, that it was only feasible where there was sufficient remaining land to maintain a subsistence level of output. On the fringes of settlement, some relief was available in the form of shifting cultivation as the overworked lands wore out. But this, too, had its disadvantages in that each move tended to increase the distance of the cultivators from possible markets for their occasional meager surpluses, raising transport costs, and increasing the losses in transit and the wastes of spoilage so that the returns from small-scale marketing tended to decline sharply.[47] The long-term social costs were also heavy; impoverishment of the soil and gradual diminution of yields were the usual results of the system—along with deforestation and erosion, since often the minifundia parcels were situated on mountainsides which were ill suited to crop farming.[48] Later on, the same slopes, the small size of the holdings, and the remoteness of location were to militate against introduction of mechanized agricultural practices to lift per-worker output, while the inadequacy of the water supplies available to minifundia operators prevented the introduction of simple irrigation systems to increase production and reduce the need for shifting cultivation. In general, tenure insecurity strongly discouraged the minifundia farmers from making simple improvements on the land—particularly in dependent minifundia (i.e., those on the haciendas), but also, in many instances, in independent minifundia.

On the independent minifundia, the poverty and insecurity of the cultivators left them in much the same circumstances as the landless *peones* of the estates, and both were equally victims of latifundism. The insufficiency of the basic land assets available to minifundia farmers, for example, must be viewed in the light of land tenure arrangements which resulted in the latifundian withdrawal of so much of the productive acreage from cultivation and higher intensity use. The shortage of the other cooperant factor, capital, must likewise be considered in conjunction with the surplus extracted by landlords from agriculture and dissipated elsewhere in the system.

Where the haciendas' wage and rent system isolated the landless laborer from participation in the money economy, the minuscule economic base of the minifundia natives accomplished much the same effect. Where the haciendas fostered low productivity and primitive technology, so also did the minifundia. Neither set of arrangements was conducive to the exercise of popular initiative, and both contained a minimum of incentives and substantial barriers to acting effectively on any incentives that might appear. Qualitatively speaking, the human agents connected with minifundia operation remained as low grade and underdeveloped as those of the haciendas. In both portions of the agricultural sector, therefore, lie the historical origins of the neglect of human resources and the backward organization and technology which have persistently vitiated the most elemental development strategies down through the years.

In one respect, some of the minifundia outside the hacienda boundaries differed from their counterparts within. When the core of minifundia operations was a *congregacion* village, there remained at least the rudiments of communal organization. Yet even here, the *congregaciones* were often largely subordinated to representatives of the central authority and had little scope to develop as more autonomous local organizations. Commonly, the oversight of the communities was vested in caciques retained by the crown as local functionaries, clergymen, and *corregidores,* and, accordingly, the effectiveness of the *congregaciones* as nuclei of collaborative action depended mainly on the caliber of the administrative direction supplied from above. When this supervision was not actually exercised in an abusive fashion, as was often the case, it was generally so desultory in its attention to such matters as education, acculturation, and community organization (outside of religious fiesta structures and the like) that little of lasting consequence came out of the system from the standpoint of community development. In time, mounting economic pressures occasioned by population growth and land scarcity appear to have undermined even further the integrative elements of community organization, leaving them operationally useless as a source of effective collective action.[49]

THE CONSTRAINTS ON NONAGRICULTURAL DEVELOPMENT

Just about every nonagricultural activity was influenced by the agrarian regime. Even the colonial export industries were not impervious to the influences of latifundism and suffered liabilities which in the long run impaired their ability to perform effectively. The relations of production in Spanish American agriculture in general, for example, had a strong bearing on the conditions of labor supply in both export agriculture and mining, the staples of the colonial export trade. And by holding the opportunity costs of labor at a very low level for both the plantations and the mines, the latifundia-minifundia complex (reinforced by slavery and *mita* labor recruitment) operated to reduce considerably the incentive to modernize the technology and organization of the export industries. Reciprocally, the traditional organization of export agriculture and mining was such that they contributed little to the development of the domestically oriented portions of the colonial economy.

The latifundia-minifundia complex was not the sole dominating institutional influence on the development possibilities of the private sector, for the environment was also influenced by pervasive bureaucratic intervention and state-church control of productive assets. Both sorts of institutional parameters set constraints on private sector growth.

DISTRIBUTION OF INCOME AND WEALTH IN THE PRIVATE SECTOR

The most pronounced feature of the colonial socio-economic system was the high degree of concentration of income and ownership of wealth in the hands of elite households or other social units such as government and religious institutions. On the one hand, the fiscal system and the *real hacienda* concept together with the complicated system of ecclesiastical finance and religious support served to channel a large portion of the wealth and income into the public sector. On the other hand, the fortuitous occurrence of rich mining strikes, the extent of monopolization in commercial intercourse, and the latifundian land tenure system served to concentrate the remaining wealth and income among a relatively reduced number of units in the private sector. Excepting chiefly the miners and the merchants, the system placed a substantial portion of the society's wealth and income in the hands of holders who were not very involved in the actual business of production.

While the foregoing describes the state of affairs prevailing in respect of real wealth and real income, it must be remembered that a large amount of economic activity, especially in the agricultural sector, was conducted outside the compass of the money economy. Independent minifundia farmers, for example, were (at least when fortunate) able to earn a subsistence-level real income, but they received very little money income at all. Similarly, workers on the private haciendas and church estates commonly received a low level of real wages from their subsistence plots; but their actual money wages were negligible. Even in mining, at least a portion of the wages paid out came in real form from the state-operated system of commissaries. Thus, in consequence of the nonmonetized internal resource organization of the latifundia, the *hacendados* not only received a considerable amount of real income in kind (e.g., foodstuffs, labor services, and the like), but they were also in a position to claim virtually the whole of the money income generated by the estate. Therefore, skewed as was the distribution of real income in the agricultural sector, the concentration of money income (and liquid wealth) was greater still.

Geographically and in a sense, sectorally, the same concentrated pattern of income and wealth distribution prevailed. Just as the fiscal system functioned to gather resources from the economy at large and to channel them into the principal colonial capitals, so also the regime of privileged positions in trade operated to siphon mercantile profits out of the provinces into the few urban centers which were the focus of both administrative and marketing activities. To these more favored sites the wealthier miners also gravitated, at least for occasional residence, while the institution of absentee ownership in agriculture meant that the enormous disparity in economic power present in the rural sector would be evidenced as well in the urban sector. In other words, the aristocratic landowners, by their custom of maintaining permanent residences in the central cities (the viceregal capitals in the case of the wealthier and more influential *hacendados*, the provincial capitals in the case of the lesser landed gentry), not only appropriated almost the entire amount of the disposable money income generated in agriculture but also funnelled its flow into the major cities. Often, the operations of the ecclesiastical sector served to transfer liquid wealth and income in exactly the same direction.

Few countervailing forces were present to offset the trend towards concentration. The economic relationships of the latifundia-minifundia complex condemmed a large segment of the rural populace to perpetual involvement in subsistence units of production with little or no possibility for material improvement. Simultaneously, the isolation this system imposed on the natives, together with the inadequate performance of the formal agencies of acculturation, preserved a system of cultural dualism which effectively cut off a huge portion of the population in rural areas from access to the opportunity structure of the age. The regulated system of artisan production set upper limits on economic mobility for many of those who dwelt in the towns and cities as did the strong vested interest of the merchants associated with the privileged *consulados*. More generally, the extremely limited development of private agencies of accumulation such as joint-stock companies and banks, and the absence of security markets, simply reinforced the existing system of social stratification and economic differentiation; the lack of the institutions which elsewhere constituted the financial seedbed of capitalistic endeavor implied that such capital and money market functions as were performed were handled by the imperfect substitute mechanisms of primitive money lending and transactions within the extended family networks of the moneyed elite. To these, the agencies of ecclesiastical finance provided an equally imperfect supplement. The ability to mobilize resources was, in general, closely related to familial and class affiliation; correspondingly, ascriptive and particularistic criteria generally prevailed in determining economic as well as social leadership.[50] Given, then, the persistence of particularistic considerations and the institutional barriers to universalistic economic decisions based on rationalistic merit, the possibilities for recruiting lower-class members into the upper class, thereby broadening the distribution of income and wealth, were infrequent.

The political system did little to change the distribution of economic power and generally worked to reinforce the pattern already outlined through the awarding of lucrative privileges and the tolerance of latifundian growth. Moreover, neither on the latifundia nor outside of them did the colonial system permit much development of authentic rural communities (as contrasted with mere residential agglomerations) such as might have evolved as social mechanisms for harnessing local resources to serve local ends-in-view.[51] Consequently, the neglect of local social investment and rural infrastructure helped to perpetuate the lopsided distribution of wealth and income. Meanwhile the structuring of governmental decision processes and the concentration of resource control also debarred the evolution of local community organizations which could function significantly as bargaining units vis-à-vis the principal power centers (e.g., the central government and the latifundian "governments") on behalf of the underlying population. Thus, when those at the top of the social hierarchy did not provide, things were not provided.[52]

THE CONSTRICTION OF SECONDARY AND TERTIARY SECTOR DEVELOPMENT

Although some nonagricultural and nonmining activity did develop within the imperial realm, this was not sufficient to change the basic economic character of the region, which, even by the close of the nineteenth century, remained firmly wedded to primary sector economic pursuits. In this, geographical factors played a role, as did the burden of the fiscal system and the inhibitory consequences of marketing and production regulation. Yet, even before the colonial period ended, it was recognized that institutional considerations relating to the distribution of resource control and income were major barriers to a sounder development of the economic system.[53] The concentrated pattern of wealth and income was also perpetuated by its own constricting effects on the evolution of the colonial economic structure.

The arrested development of private financial intermediary institutions has already been mentioned as one by-product of the regime of ecclesiastical finance, the largely nonmonetized organization of agricultural production, and the restricted and monopolized channels of marketing. But apart from its effects on financial evolution, the constricted flow of goods to and from an agrarian system which was organized by means other than monetary transactions also prevented the elaboration of more versatile and modern structures in such important ancillary fields as marketing and transport services—areas of enterprise and organization which were crucial, historically, to successful commercialization of agriculture and to economic development generally. Much of the haciendas' output was transported and marketed locally by the haciendas' own rudimentary organization, while the marketable surpluses produced sporadically by the minifundia tended to dribble into the market in quite small units. Neither situation was very conducive to the development of a comprehensive and modern type of marketing apparatus.[54] For that matter, linguistic barriers seriously impeded the dissemination of market information in rural areas, just as they blocked the dissemination of technical information relevant to production. Guild regulations, market controls, and entrenched mercantile privileges proved similarly detrimental to progress in the marketing organization of urban sector output. Finally, the development of marketing structures and of the firms producing the goods marketed could not advance further than they did because of the weakness of market demand. The condition affected both sides of the reciprocal demand relationship which existed between the urban sector and the rural sector.

For agriculture, the concentration of income in the hands of the urban upper classes depressed the volume of rural deliveries to urban consumers and, at the same time, reduced the variety of goods supplied. The majority of town dwellers, in other words, had only a limited purchasing power, and this was generally spent for only the dietary staples. Consequently, the pull towards commercialization of agriculture was weakened, and the possibilities for developing a more diversified pattern of land use in farming —permitting a more selective and efficient adaptation of crops to soils and climates—were diminished. Only in a few places, chiefly around the viceregal capitals and the mining centers of Mexico,[55] was urban demand sufficient to support more productive patterns of farming.

On the reverse side of the intersectoral exchange, the haciendas' workers, who participated little in the market either as sellers of goods or of labor power, were also only tenuously related to the market as consumers inasmuch as the relations of production on the latifundia served to transfer out of agriculture most of the money income generated therefrom, leaving little or nothing with which to supply the rural labor force with consumer and incentive goods. The simple poverty of the independent minifundia farmers sufficed to accomplish the same exclusion from the market for much of the balance of the rural populace. Thus lacking rural markets, in a society in which the population was overwhelming rural, and with urban markets narrowly circumscribed by income patterns, taxes, transport costs, and local market regulations, only a limited number of nonagricultural enterprises could flourish—and these on a not very large scale. Both manufacturing enterprises and the majority of mercantile enterprises were constricted by these circumstances. Since the pattern of market demand did not register the full social array of wants, the kinds of urban enterprises which did develop were often those which catered to the consumption preferences of the wealthy few.

Thus, the phenomenon of concentrated landownership not only restricted directly the number of agricultural firms but also restricted indirectly the number and type of nonagricultural business enterprises. This led to a narrow occupational structure which provided few rungs (with not much room on each) to support gradual upward mobility along the occupational-status ladder.[56] Because of the weak development of institutional bridges (such as educational institutions and financial agencies) to support individual betterment and because of the paucity of opportunities for advance in a class and occupational structure characterized by discontinuities, an inflexible and stratified social structure was virtually assured.

There were geographical variances in this pattern. Most towns, for example, were residential centers for government personnel and the landowning gentry; others, which were located along commercial trading routes, became regional distribution centers with a middle class of some size made up of merchants, artisans, mule drivers, and the like.[57] But, in the main, development of a colonial middle class in the secondary and tertiary sectors was restricted and it was only in Lima and Mexico City that the economic and administrative structure supported a middle class of substantial proportions.[58] There was hardly a rural middle class at all. Furthermore, while the arrested development of secondary population centers stemmed from the lack of purchasing power in the surrounding rural districts, it also was a major factor in retarding the commercialization and modernization of agriculture: both because of the limited urban demand for the rural products of the environs and because of the inability of such centers to serve as adequate links between urban and rural society.[59] There were, finally, a few fringe areas such as Costa Rica or Antioquia (in Colombia) which were anomalous in that latifundism had not taken root, there were few Indians, and the criollo settlers were generally neither very rich nor very poor.

CAPITAL ACCUMULATION IN THE PRIVATE SECTOR

Despite the presence of acute income inequality, the system did not do much to foster savings and capital accumulation either in or outside of the agricultural sector. On the one hand, latifundism and absentee ownership served mainly to transfer money income out of the agricultural sector on an unrequited basis. Thus, little of the money income originating in agriculture was returned to that sector to finance a counterflow of consumption goods to the rural populace, for supporting social overhead facilities to upgrade the quality of rural human resources, or for equipping agricultural workers with investment goods procured from the nonagricultural sector. Though expenditures were made to finance land acquisitions through the *composición* process or through protracted litigation in courts of law, the conditions of agrarian production were such that there was little inducement for large landowners to reinvest their money earnings in agricultural capital formation.

On the other hand, the landowners' security of income expectations, their protected production and marketing position, and the shortage of nonagricultural investment opportunities permitted them to devote a relatively high percentage of their disposable income to consumption rather than capital accumulation. Social approbation did not necessarily follow material gain; but to the extent that higher status (with its privileged access to the opportunity structure) was gained by observance of the proprieties and proper ceremonial display, it could be said that upward social mobility depended more on the willingness to spend than on the willingness to save. Thus, of the income extracted from agriculture by the relations of production in that sector, little appears to have been saved and channeled into real investment anywhere in the system. Most went, instead, for the purchase of heavily taxed imported luxuries, into contributions to religious institutions, for personal services, and for furnishing urban residential centers with the assortment of public and private amenities—e.g., promenades, mansions, parks, fountains, and festivities—which made up the colonial equivalent of gracious living. Invidious distinction rather than the growth of productive capacity was the principle applied to the utilization of land-owner income. This being the case, latifundian control over resource use in the private sector often channeled these resources in as nonutilitarian a direction as did the operations of the state and the church in the public sector—a matter to be kept in mind when considering the postcolonial transfers of income and wealth from church and crown to the criollo benefi-ciaries of independence.

As for the less affluent colonial subjects, it seems that when small sums of money were occasionally accumulated they were more likely to be spent on fiestas and in other ways which facilitated advancement in village politico-religious structures than on means of improving economic perform-ance.[60] Indeed, for most groups, the balance of preferences was structured in a way which scarcely encouraged capital accumulation as a customary and meaningful habit of behavior. The constrictions on general develop-ment depressed the inducement to save and invest, limited the number of capital-requiring enterprises, and reduced the number of capital-accumulat-ing firms. The high average propensity to consume, in other words, was partly a function of the absence of attractive investment opportunities which might have served to elicit a higher rate of savings and investment on the part of the few holders of the economic surplus as well as a result of non-economic considerations. Therefore, the consequent social deficit of acquired skills and experience in working with capitalistic monetary arrange-ments was considerable.

Given the limited growth possibilities for capital placed in the secondary and tertiary sectors, the continued prime importance of real property ownership was assured. And with latifundian landownership as the major attraction for investment, the structural equilibrium of the system was reinforced once again, for this was a channel which largely resulted in a transfer of savings out of the private sector to the bureaucracy and the state and which primarily affected the social distribution of asset ownership rather than the real value of total assets. Those who might conceivably have seen some logic in savings-investment acts of a productive character lacked, by and large, the wherewithall to do so; those who had the wherewithall to promote real capital formation were often situated in a decision environment, that of the latifundia, in which the logic of such behavior was much less apparent. As with the pattern and intensity of resource use in agriculture, the disposition of the economic surplus was dictated not by the social req-uisites for development but by the situation of the controlling decision-makers. Consequently, while the operating efficiency of the system was such that there was not an especially large potential investible surplus to begin with, little of what was generated actually was reinvested to expand aggregate output. Neither the public sector not the private sector performed very efficiently as an agency of capital formation.

THE TRANSACTIONAL ENVIRONMENT AND PRIVATE ENTREPRENEURSHIP

The colonial system was poorly structured for fostering the growth of private entrepreneurial capacity. The concentration of authority and control over resource use sharply limited participation in economic decision-making processes and restricted considerably the acquisition of managerial experience. Concomitantly, material advance was difficult, if only because so few controlled so many of the assets which might have been used by ambitious aspirants in gaining access to higher status positions. Indeed, the objective conditions of life for a large percentage of the colonial population simply confirmed the prevailing subjective outlook or cultural assumption which Rostow has described as one of long-term fatalism: "the assumption that the range of possibilities open to one's grandchildren would be just about what it had been for one's grandparents." For the majority, then, a strong dependency syndrome and an attitude of fatalism rather than ambition were the only possible responses which were suitable for the environment.

The incentive structure in agriculture was another obstacle not readily overcome; the lack of correspondence between effort expended and income received was so great as to amount to a complete divorce between the two, if not a negative correlation. The return to the *hacendado* was mostly free income arising out of ownership alone; seldom was it a reward for successful managerial involvement in production and marketing. The major income rewards, therefore, accrued to those whose contribution to production was minimal; instead of financing a supply of incentive goods to the rural work force, the income provided the absentee owners with leisure and the means of gaining access to an opportunity structure from which those actually engaged in production were excluded.

Outside of agriculture, the controls which reduced producer autonomy, the administered price inflexibilities, high transport costs, the embryonic state of factor markets and factor immobility, and the low and fairly stable level of market demand [61] sustained a rather indifferent sort of resource management and discouraged entrepreneurial development by limiting the range of production and marketing alternatives. Educational conditions weakened seriously the organizational supports of the scientific and technological development which was needed to nourish the process of innovation, and little encouragement was provided in the general social structure for scientific and mechanical endeavor.[62] Although the crown was favorably disposed towards the immigration of technicians and artisans, the economically advantageous accessory effects of immigration were realized only slightly. Spain did not really have, by the seventeenth and eighteenth centuries, very large numbers of artisans and adepts in business enterprise to send to the New World, and the exploitive labor conditions existing in the Americas were not attractive to skilled craftsmen who might have brought with them the technical qualifications for innovation.[63]

Besides the foregoing deterrents, there was still another which thwarted entrepreneurial evolution in the Schumpeterian sense and which was particularly inimical to the growth of large-scale, impersonal types of organization of a modern character—especially, perhaps, in marketing and finance. John R. Commons, in his *Legal Foundations of Capitalism*, pointed out the crucial role of the Law Merchant and the common law tradition as contributory factors in the rise of the modern economy. Thanks to the feature of judicial precedent and to the gradualistic and evolutionary character of the legal system which grew up in adaptive response to the exigencies of economic (and sociopolitical) change, the transactional framework of business in the English-speaking countries established an impersonal rule of law under the jurisdiction of which the participants in the market system could engage in impersonal market-centered relations with a certain basic reliability of expectations. The comparative short-term stability of the transactional framework facilitated the reduction of uncertainties to calculable risks and, by holding noneconomic considerations relatively constant, permitted attention to be devoted increasingly to the management of economic variables. The transactional environment of the Spanish dominions, however, was quite different. For all its legalism, it contained substantial areas of ambiguity which resulted in a system of shifting decision parameters. Interjected exogenous variables of major import produced a legal milieu of a rather capricious character, and within the framework of law and regulation there was ample scope for the exercise of power of an arbitrary nature. Thus, the expectational aspect of business transactions was often unreliable, and it was difficult for enterprises to operate along conventionally economic norms.

Three features of colonial organization affected this state of affairs: (1) the detailed complexity of administrative law with its mass of sometimes conflicting decrees, (2) the overlapping bureaucracies invested with the task of interpreting and implementing this legislation, and (3) the wide and ambiguous latitude for intervention.[64] To these must be added a characteristic stemming from the Roman law tradition: the absence of the doctrine of stare decisis or judicial precedent.[65]

A virtually inevitable outcome of these organizational conditions was the continuous and frequently acrimonious jurisdictional clashes between the several hierarchies of administration and a transactional environment which, for all its heavy burden of legalism, operated on the basis of standards both complex and ambiguous. Because of the snares and entrapments of the complicated Iberian legal system, litigation, appeals, and the practical settling of policy could drift on inconclusively for years with the final outcome in doubt.

The very source of all this law posed an additional problem, for the Council of the Indies was too far from the area of policy application to appreciate actual conditions in the New World. In the interests of standardization, the decrees of the Council tended to treat all areas alike and disregarded regional variations. Accordingly, in many cases the detailed instructions transmittèd from Spain were not realistically attuned to the practical exigencies of life in the overseas territories and were impracticable if not impossible to enforce. Paralleling the tradition of legalism, there developed, consequently, an institutionalized pattern of behavior which amounted to virtual disregard of the law.

In the famous *obedezco pero no cumplo* formula, the administrative personnel formally "obeyed" the decree sent from Spain and thereby gave ceremonial recognition to the sovereign power of the crown, but they did not execute the order or "comply" with it. In theory, execution of the directive was merely suspended or deferred on grounds that its enforcement would, for example, be unjust or unwise, that it would aggravate an economic crisis or accentuate social conflict. The leniency with which criollo usurpation of Indian lands and labor power was viewed in seventeenth-century Mexico was undoubtedly conditioned by the imperative of overcoming urban food shortages; the lingering life of *encomiendas* after the New Laws were promulgated to extinguish them stemmed from the quite rebellious reception accorded their initial proclamation in the colonies. Presumably, during the interim of delay in these *obedezco pero no cumplo* cases, the orders, together with reasons for their postponed implementation, were sent back to Spain for reconsideration and possible modification or rescission.

When used with discretion, suspended application of directives did not involve penalty. But the range of discretionary authority was by no means clear or invariable. Some officials did not exceed the margins and continued to govern with impunity; others transgressed the bounds and were called back to Spain in disgrace. Frequently, it was difficult to determine which of several conflicting decrees might be applicable to a particular case; previous court decisions provided no assured guide to the matter as prior rulings were not necessarily binding on later cases. To a large extent it appears that in cases of selective law enforcement, jurisdictional disputes, policy clarification, and the litigation of claims, an influential friend at court was a distinct asset. In any event, the personal temper, views, aims, and dispositions of administrative superiors, peers, and subordinates (all of whom might be reporting directly to higher bureaucratic echelons in the New World and in Spain) became important factors in the decision-making process—the more so as so many of the critical economic relationships were at least potentially subject to administrative determination in the Iberian system of comprehensive governmental responsibility.

The practical ambiguity of law and policy and the necessity of anticipating the balance of reactions created a situation which greatly hindered development of an objectively reliable, impersonal system of law and which placed a high premium on direct, personalistic interrelationships. As there was the ever-present possibility of arbitrary rulings and interpretations, the transactional framework tended to be unstable and imbued with a radical element of incalculability, with uncertainty levels higher still for decisions lying farther in the future. Moreover, the stability of expectations in interpersonal relations, especially those of an impersonal character, was low, again with a further discount for futurity. Both aspects constricted considerably the possibilities for effecting mutually satisfactory economic transactions on an impersonal basis among a wide range of coparticipants and on a geographically widespread basis. Both internal and external transactions of firms were subject to expectational diseconomies of scale: i.e., a risk that relationships of an impersonal character would be translated into real costs. Security could be sought either through situations which permitted the unilateral imposition of power or in the degree of influence which could be exercised and the amount of insight obtained through affective personal connections such as friendship, family ties, ritual kinship obligations, and the like. In other words, the socially available security guarantees stemmed more from *personalismo* than from law and generally accepted conventions.[66]

Family affiliation, especially, was a source of security.[67] It was also one of the chief means of assigning economic roles and of helping the individual achieve prominence or otherwise attain his goals. This strongly circumscribed the extent of participation in key enterprises and the recruitment of economic leadership, but was practically unavoidable since extrafamilial relationships were assessed so negatively.[68] Furthermore, given the desirability of relating to the decision-making structure at the highest, and consequently the most influential, level possible, status was also an invaluable asset which could be exploited for differential gain. The structure of the central government, in other words, placed the political center of gravity at a high level, beyond practical access by the majority; yet access to this machinery was of vital importance since governmental paternalism was a fundamental principle of colonial economic life and the royal government played the role of the chief patron in society. In provincial regions, for example, it was only the upper stratum of the elite which was apt to have the useful translocal connections which could be turned to material advantage. High status, therefore, gave privileged access to the opportunity structure, while differential access was the source of the requisite status expenditures for supporting social acceptance and prestige. This relationship was decisive in distributing economic leadership roles, although there was no necessary correspondence between the social distribution of status and the social distribution of objective economic capabilities. For those whose social station was lowly and more vulnerable, personal affiliation with a more powerful patron, with whom loyalty and service might be exchanged for protection and favors, became essential both for security and, in view of the limited opportunities for advancement, for access to the positions of employment controlled by the holders of wealth.[69] For all, the personal tie was a functional necessity, both for the emotional leverage it provided in lieu of reliable impersonal mutual expectations and for the possibilities afforded therein for reciprocity in favors to substitute for stable contractual relationships.

This personalistic precondition for effecting transactions was deeply embedded in the whole web of social relationships and behavior. The social environment, including the obvious differential enforcement of laws, fostered a personality trait which has been frequently noted as characteristic of the ladino population: a proclivity for noncompliance with the law when opportunities for individually useful evasion should arise. Thus centuries of experience with either unenforceable or differentially enforced legislation—with frequent occasions for realizing individual advantage from legal ambiguities and evasion—contributed heavily towards a negative popular evaluation of legality and a basic cynicism regarding the impersonal rule of law, both of which operated to ratify the expectations of unreliability in interpersonal activities.

Under the circumstances, the modal experience with interpersonal behavior not only restricted the range of organizational and transactional alternatives but also adversely conditioned entrepreneurial formation. Because the social setting tended to isolate individuals from each other by engendering attitudes of mutual mistrust and suspicion,[70] the lack of significant experience in technological teamwork was a fundamental lacuna in the business milieu.[71] As population growth intensified the competition for the limited benefits available in the slowly expanding opportunity structure, the level of interpersonal confidence was undermined further by chronic dissension, and aggressive rivalries which grew increasingly acute. The evidence, moreover, seems unmistakable that astute trickery, guile, and shrewdness in manipulating or outwitting others came to be valued as the chief means of turning situations to individual advantage.

The last-mentioned behavioral valuations lead, finally, to the question of entrepreneurial motivation or, more broadly stated, to the action alternatives presented and rewarded by the social system and to the bearing of these on the motivational patterns of the dominant groups in the decision-making hierarchy. Repeatedly, the spirit of private economic initiative and the elements of entrepreneurship, business acumen, and economic creativity have been remarked as missing from the Spanish American scene, at least until quite recent years. This ostensible absence of a vital domestic tradition of business enterprise has been cited both as a contributing factor in the growth of foreign dominated enclave sectors during the nineteenth century and as part of the rationale for direct governmental economic action in the present century. As modern techniques of psychological investigation have been brought into use, the evidence appears to indicate that, except for a few rather anomalous cases such as that of the *antioqueños* of Colombia, achievement motivation is generally rather weak.[72]

At the same time, however, Latin America has not lacked persons of ambition nor has it been devoid of creative talent and skills, using these terms in a generic, not a specifically economic, sense. Notwithstanding the high cultural valuation of leisure, there is no denying the ladino's capacity for expending prodigious amounts of energy, as in the arduous business of the conquest or the turbulence of postcolonial times. Furthermore, the Spanish immigrants who came to grapple with conditions of life in the New World were not, for the most part, of aristocratic origin but were an upwardly mobile group driven by ambition to get ahead. The available studies of neo-Iberian personality types indicate that, while achievement needs are low, a pronounced need for power is the cultural drive which characteristically actuates the behavior of ladino individuals. For the ladino, routine is intensely disagreeable and manual work, even of a skilled sort, distasteful; gratification is ordinarily sought in "managerial" roles which permit the strong power drive to be expressed in domination of others.[73] Even so, it is clear that ambition, skill, and accomplishment figure in some sense in the motivational patterns of the area. The crux of the issue, therefore, is the social manifestation, under particular historical circumstances, of these general motives and propensities insofar as this manifestation was translated into a set of psychocultural dynamics which affected the economic process.

To understand the socially sanctioned modes of realizing ambition, the transactional environment just described must be set against the regime of *estadismo* and *dirigismo* considered in the previous chapter. The scope of state interventionary powers, the complex structure of bureaucratic centralism, and the luxuriant exfoliation of administrative law all testified to the preeminence of imperial political authority in the scheme of social organization. Autocratic control of administration and planning produced a continuing dependence on state initiative; many of the directive economic decisions were made in the labyrinthine channels of the governing bureaucracy. Like the political order, the economic order was, in essence, imposed from above rather than emergent from the nature of, and the interrelations among, the economic activities themselves. The dynamic or guiding force in economic life was, correspondingly, an external one, not one which grew out of its own operations. In Hobbesian fashion, the public economic interest was largely identified with the private interest of the monarch, and the public shared in this interest through favors dispensed by the crown. The comprehensive regulatory system which expressed the paramount royal interest and registered its allocation of favors strongly conditioned, where it did not actually determine, many of the relevant parameters of economic decisions.

Given this *déformation institutionelle*, the quest for economic advantage often had more of the character of petitionary activity before the favor-dispensing bureaucracy than that of bargaining activity by autonomous producers in a market, and political sanctions of deprivation and reward were frequently of much greater importance than market sanctions. Indeed, the relation of the individual to the machinery of state was the critical variable in establishing his relation to productive assets. Thus, superimposed upon the "objective" structure of economic opportunities was a politico-legal environment which governed both access to those opportunities and the operating conditions under which opportunity appropriation could be turned to account.

While the formal structure of political control was centralized and monolithic, the actual structure was more amorphous. Between the individual and the state there was an intermediate zone of indeterminancy, created by complexities and inconsistencies in laws, overlapping bureaucratic jurisdictions, difficulties of enforcement, and so on. Consequently, it was in this realm, as well as in the direct appeal for state favors, that there existed an ample area for maneuver and the exercise of initiative.[74] Enterprise and initiative were not, therefore, absent from Spanish America, but the enterprise and initiative which were relevant to and rewarded by the context often involved action along legal and political lines. The dominant transactions, in other words, related to a political rather than a cash or market nexus; and the manipulation of political variables for institutional advantage was the preferred route to increases in income and wealth, not technical proficiency in production, marketing, and finance.

This exploitation of institutional advantages through politico-legal maneuver illuminates the underlying basis of the prevalent pattern of "entrepreneurial" motivation and the value of alternative skills, for competence and efficiency in the manipulation of power variables was a more decisive factor in success than economic efficiency or technical competence. Consequently, differential gain from the available array of economic opportunities stood some distance removed from instrumental economic ability; and given sufficient influence and skill in the area of social behavior which really counted, in the kind of enterprise and skill that mattered, the former had no necessary correspondence at all to the latter. This was accentuated by the highly stratified social structure, in which the disproportions of power and status among the various social classes and the impediments to social mobility provided great leverage in the exercise of influence and the quest for differential institutional advantage. Thus the observed cultural passion for status and power was quite explicable and rational inasmuch as the exercise of the power which followed status was highly rewarding. If people were little motivated toward economic achievement, it was because the Iberian institutional framework was unable to insure that such effort would bring reward on a reasonably predictable basis. Power-oriented conduct, not achievement-oriented conduct, was the pattern of behavior validated by the social order. As usual, the people themselves had a phrase for it: "He who works has no time for making money." [75]

THE COLONIAL ECONOMY AND GROWTH: A SUMMARY VIEW

By the time independence from the yoke of the Spanish was gained, the Hispanic American institutional structure differed considerably from that of the countries in the North Atlantic cultural continuum. Medieval practices and institutional relics from earlier Mediterranean social organization continued to play a strong role in economic life and were only partly ameliorated by influences emanating from the European commercial revolution and mercantilism. In agriculture, the dominant institutional forms were of more antique vintage than those which prevailed in nonagricultural sectors, but throughout the economy the systemic organization was essentially precapitalistic in character. When the attempt was made, in the nineteenth century, to usher in a full-fledged capitalism, the pattern of capitalistic dynamics purportedly described by the marginalism of Marshallian economics applied to only a very small portion of the economy; the social order which prevailed in Spanish America had become increasingly anachronistic when compared with the culture centers with which the area would primarily interact when the era of republican government replaced the imperial system of Spain.

During the three centuries of colonial rule in Spanish America, the micro- and macro-economic organization of western Europe and the United States was sweeping towards the nineteenth-century apogee of capitalism, and under the chieftainship of Schumpeterian entrepreneurs a new social class was assuming control of the economic process. Almost stealthily during the late Middle Ages and the early commercial revolution, the cumulative processes of scientific and technological development were gaining momentum; by the latter half of the eighteenth century the age of industrialization was well under way. Meanwhile, locked in the routine of age-old practices, Spanish American society and economy were left ill prepared to absorb the vast social changes associated with industrialism, since many of the cultural changes antecedent to the industrial order had not yet been effectively received in the region. For the emancipated colonies the nineteenth century, therefore, represented a delayed adjustment to a large group of changes, and this was accompanied by an extraordinary amount of dislocation and conflict. As a result, most of Spanish America fell far behind the rest of the Western world as it began to pay off the accumulated deferred charges of institutional atrophy. Although it is manifestly impossible to estimate the material penalty incurred in the form of forfeited aggregate output, modern growth theory—as developed by such specialists as Abramovitz, Kuznets, Cairncross, Kendrick, and Fabricant—does provide a basis for specifying the major shortcomings of the colonial system.

Regarding the simple increases in factor inputs which help to account for secular economic growth, colonial Spanish America performed poorly indeed in terms of capital formation. Though it accomplished somewhat more through additions to the labor supply (at least after 1650-1700) and increases in land inputs, both of these factors were often underemployed because of the structure in which they functioned. As growth theory has pointed out, however, a great deal of secular economic growth is attributable not to quantitative factor changes, but to qualitative changes such as technological progress, improvements in organization, and improvements in human capital. Under the colonial dispensation, these were precisely the areas of greatest neglect.

From the nature of the system, science and technology were relegated to a position of distinct marginality inasmuch as they were largely irrelevant to the main orientation of social interaction. With few exceptions, the only technological advance worth noting came at the outset of the colonial era when the medieval European heritage was brought to the New World. Following that, the state of the technical arts fell progressively behind the level of technology being utilized in the North Atlantic culture area. As for organization, the dominant features of the Hispanic institutional framework were its inflexibility and inability to foster the growth of the new, functionally specific forms of social and economic organization which played such a crucial role in economic evolution elsewhere. Neither markets nor market-related institutions had as yet exuviated the shell of traditional economic policy expedients except in a quite limited way. If Marshall was correct in asserting that "the most valuable of all capital is that invested in human beings," then it was here that Spanish America fell furthest behind in meeting the requisites of secular material expansion. Most of the area's human resources were deployed in a manner which did little or nothing to develop and utilize effectively the innate capacities of the people. Of the rest, to put it most charitably, a goodly portion appears to have been "employed" largely for their decorative value so far as concerns their contribution to production.

V

Distinctive Elements in the
Formation of Brazil

IN one region or another, Brazil displays socio-economic traits which are typical of other countries in Latin America. Disparities in the distribution of income and wealth, sharply differentiated regional and sectoral growth patterns, and the underdeveloped state of its human resources have been as much a part of the Brazilian scene as of the Hispanic American environment. From its very inception as a center of overseas European settlement, however, Brazil began to diverge in certain important respects from its cultural kin in the Americas.

Its very name, taken from the wood which was the region's first important export, was not the "New Portugal" equivalent of Nueva España, Nueva Andalucía, Nueva Granada, or Hispaniola; the seafaring Portuguese did not arrive on Brazilian shores inspired by a grand design for replicating a civilization. In contrast to Spanish America, Brazil had no seminary until 1687, no printing presses operating regularly until 1809, and no universities until early in the nineteenth century.[1]

THE PENINSULAR BACKGROUND

The different conceptions of colonial development suggested by these points of contrast grew out of antecedent variations in the cultural evolution of the mother countries of which the New World societies were the offspring. Though Portugal and Spain had shared various historical experiences under Romans, Visigoths, and Moslems, long before the sixteenth century Portugal had begun to develop as a unique culture area in the Iberian peninsula. Stanislawski observes, for example, that even during the period in which barbarian invaders were inundating the ordered life of the Roman empire, certain distinctions emerged. In northern Portugal, where Swabian influence was much stronger than that of the Visigoths who dominated central Spain, vestigial evidences of early differentiation remain visible today. The numerous, dispersed small holdings of individual proprietors, reminiscent of the Germanic patterns of use observed by Tacitus, contrast with both the Roman urban settlement model and the large Roman and Visigothic rural estates, though Swabians, too, took over some of the large Roman estates and created new ones of their own alongside the small farms.[2] Later, Moslem power intruded into western Iberia as it did elsewhere on the penin-

sula, but in northern Portugal the Moorish influence was much less pronounced and even middle Portugal was something of a transition zone in
this regard. Finally, the Portuguese struggle for independence was—in
contrast to that of the Spanish kingdoms—successfully completed long before the Portuguese began their overseas expansion. During the middle and
latter half of the twelfth century, most of the Lusitanian area had been regained from the Moors, and by 1250 the present outlines of Portuguese
boundaries were virtually complete. For much of the Iberian reconquest
period, therefore, Portugal was relatively unaffected by events taking place
on the rest of the peninsula. Thanks also to the offside geographical position which enabled the country to avoid involvement in the continuing
political struggles of the Spanish people, the Portuguese kingdom enjoyed
important locational advantages which it was not long in turning to account.

With political consolidation achieved and not seriously threatened for
many years,[3] the Portuguese kings devoted their attention to national development. Industry, fishing, and mining were encouraged, and the monarchs
particularly fostered the rise of a comparatively prosperous agriculture. On
the one hand, the nobility were encouraged to become actively involved in
agricultural progress. On the other, the crown worked toward creation of a
settled peasantry by ceding unoccupied lands to families and redistributing
uncultivated land which, by law, had reverted to the crown. From this
agrarian base, the government went on to promote the development of commercial fairs. It was not, however, only domestic trade which was being
encouraged. Perhaps stimulated by the opportunities for provisioning passing fleets of English crusaders—who helped, incidentally, in the capture of
Lisbon in 1147 and in expelling the Moors from central and southern Portugal—the Portuguese began fairly early to turn their attention to the possibilities of international trade. The fact that Lisbon, the capital, was situated
on a great natural harbor was probably also instrumental in developing this
orientation.

The first commercial treaty, made with England in 1294, was the start of
a long-standing commercial tie of considerable significance for future development alternatives, and in 1381 this commercial connection evolved into a
political-military alliance with England which thereafter helped to preserve
national independence from Spain.[4] Linked through commerce with the
British Isles, Portugal and its later colonial dependencies were thereby
linked with one of the chief northwestern European centers of economic
expansion during the centuries that lay ahead. Exports of fruits and wines
constituted the mainstay of this trade by the early fourteenth century, and
olive oil was added towards the end of the same century. African and Asiatic
goods entered into the trade stream in the following century. To consolidate
this tie, the Treaty of Windsor in 1386, which guaranteed safe-conduct to
Portuguese merchants in England and to English merchants in Portugal,
provided for certain reciprocal commercial privileges; and by 1450 the

English had been granted the right to hold hearings on all Portuguese-English commercial cases before a special judge. Two years later, in marked contrast to the growing exclusionist tendencies in Spain, the Portuguese crown conferred on Englishmen the right to live and move about freely within the kingdom of Portugal.[5] Some two hundred years afterwards, three Portuguese-British treaties, drafted in 1642, 1654, and 1661 and based originally on Britain's assistance in ending the period of Spanish rule, laid the final basis for English supremacy in Portuguese commerce.[6] From then on, as Manchester has put it, "British merchants and shipping interests made of Portugal practically an English commercial vassal." [7] For example, following the treaty of 1654, English merchants enjoyed access to the trade with Brazil and Portuguese West Africa on terms of equality with Portuguese subjects and were even given a say in the determination of the Portuguese customs duties which were levied on this trade. With the Methuen Treaty of 1703, Anglo-Portuguese relations were cemented further by concessions which gave certain Portuguese exports a preferred position over competing French products in the English market and which expanded British exports to Portugal.[8]

Against a background of expanding external trade, the Portuguese embarked upon their "age of discoveries." In the early fifteenth century Madeira and the Azores were settled. Exploratory expeditions pushed down along the Atlantic coast of Africa, establishing trading centers at a number of points. Soon afterwards, the Cape of Good Hope was circumnavigated, and with that there lay ahead the passage to India and the other treasure troves of Asia. Meanwhile, around 1420 the Portuguese brought the cultivation of sugar cane to Madeira from Sicily, and around 1493 they did the same for the island of São Thomé. On both, sugar developed rapidly as a cash export crop and soon enabled the Portuguese to acquire a major position in the small but growing European trade in this commodity. The spice trade also linked Portugal with the important entrepôt traffic of the Low Countries, which were then a principal center of capitalistic development and capital accumulation in Europe. By virtue of these growing international commercial relations, the Portuguese were placed in contact with the chief contemporary sources of investment and working capital while, simultaneously, they were building up a distributional system to connect their colonies with export market outlets.

Private companies representing a fairly advanced type of trading association were formed to exploit the opportunities of the island and African trade, as well as the mainland export trade. And although the lucrative Indian commerce was, until 1577, organized as a state trading enterprise conducted on royal ships for the account of the monarchs, in some instances private merchants were licensed to participate in the state trade fleets, especially for business at the African ports of call. On an unlicensed, extralegal or illegal basis, both shipping officials and members of the crews used the royal vessels to bring back a considerable volume of cargo on their personal account.

This was the central experience of the Portuguese during the long formative period which antedated their arrival in the New World. They were not, as were the Spanish, an embattled people with a certain siege mentality acquired from long combat to maintain and assert their ethnic identity. On the contrary, the "thalassic Portuguese," as W. L. Schurz has aptly called them, had grown increasingly cosmopolitan and adaptable in outlook, attuned to the potentialities of the new opportunities their enterprising explorers were creating. Moreover, for at least two centuries prior to the establishment of Brazil, the relative weight and attraction of mercantile activity was becoming steadily greater as a result of explorations and the growth of trade. Thus, the limited, land-based feudal aristocracy of the country was no longer unchallenged as a ruling class, and, indeed, persons connected with the new mercantile interests intermarried with the older aristocracy as they moved up the social ladder on the basis of newly acquired commercial wealth. Consequently, the established elite began to acquire more of a mercantile mentality and national policy was increasingly influenced by commercial considerations. Therefore, fifteenth-century Portugal was, for the time, an open and expanding society. The range of opportunity was widening, incentive rewards were provided for the expression of economic initiative, and, at least to a limited extent, upward mobility in status accompanied success in business enterprise.

It is perhaps indicative of the temper of Portuguese life that, while religious hostility and harassment occurred occasionally, Portuguese Catholicism generally lacked the rigorous militancy of the Spanish church. In its rather tolerant and lenient spirit, it resembled somewhat the lyrical, warmly mystical, and even softening influence which students of Brazilian culture have noted as a characteristic of religion in that country.[9] The high social and economic position of the Sephardim, for example, endured in Portugal up until around 1500. Thus, long after religious persecution had weakened and disorganized the community life of Spanish Jewry, Portuguese Jews continued to be prominent in public and private finance, royal administration, the learned professions, and trade. Sephardic and convert entrepreneurs played a vital role in the technical and organizational development of the export sugar industry of the islands, and marriages between wealthy Jewish families and the Gentile nobility occurred on more than a few occasions.[10] Significantly, a good many of the religious refugees from the Spanish expulsion of 1492 fled across the border to Portugal. This added to the country's supply of entrepreneurial capability and provided additional ties, through family connections with Sephardic exiles in the Low Countries, with the emergent network of international trade and finance.

While, unfortunately, the comparative religious tolerance of Portugal did not last long after 1492, the subsequent expulsion of Jews from the Lusitanian kingdom was largely nominal. As Cecil Roth has pointed out, the Portuguese king soon succumbed to pressure from Spain to enforce religious uniformity. But though expulsion was decreed, the monarch, mindful of the economically disruptive consequences of such action, also decreed compulsory conversion on an unprecedentedly comprehensive scale. Some lost their lives resisting the enforcement of the decree. Others managed to flee—to other European countries or to the Portuguese colonies where the religious climate was less hostile. The overwhelming majority of the Sephardic population, however, was forced to stay on as *cristãos novos* or "New Christians," in which guise they continued through the sixteenth century to play a singularly prominent role in commerce and the export trade, in setting up banking houses, in the faculty at the university at Coimbra, and so on.[11] Although an inquisition along Spanish lines was set up in Portugal in 1547, it was not given full powers, including the especially important one of property confiscation, until 1579. During the "Spanish captivity" of 1580-1640, inquisitorial activities produced some enormities of persecution, but following restoration of Portuguese independence in 1640, the Inquisition's severity abated somewhat.

On the whole, the commercial ethos of Portuguese life had come to be a much more significant factor in setting the course of social development than in Spain; the organization of Portuguese business enterprise and the private sector was also less affected by the disruptive intrusion of noneconomic considerations. Royal promotion in 1649 of the first major privileged commercial company for Brazil made this practical turn of mind abundantly plain. To raise capital for the Companhia Geral do Commercio do Brasil, New Christians who had been convicted by the Holy Office of lapsing from Catholicism were required to invest in the shares of the enterprise in lieu of having their property confiscated![12]

From the standpoint of colonial development, moreover, the religious policies of the Portuguese governments were in some ways helpful. For the most part, the Lusitanian monarchs were much less rigorous than the Spaniards in screening migrants to overseas territories for religious orthodoxy. In 1535 the country adopted the practice of exiling criminals to these distant locations; after the introduction of the Inquisition, these exiles included religious dissidents such as the Sephardim and those suspected of lapsing from conversion. Consequently, the sporadic outbreaks of persecution in Portugal may well have had the effect of increasing the supply of capital and entrepreneurial talent in the colonial private sector as the Marranos sought shelter in (or were exiled to) places where the Inquisition was comparatively inactive.[13] Studies of early Brazilian development, for example, indicate that the *cristãos novos*, who came from São Thomé and Madeira as well as from Portugal, figured importantly among the early migrants to the colony. At first, as wealthy general traders, they were active in developing initial export items such as brazilwood; later, as skilled sugar technicians and sugar merchants, they fostered the establishment of the important sugar industry.[14] That they would play such a crucial part in providing economic leadership was not, however, attributable solely to their industry and general experience in economic affairs. In a manner which foreshadowed the role of immigrant entrepreneurs throughout Latin America during the republican period, the Sephardic pioneers utilized to advantage their ethnic connections with financiers and traders among the business community of Amsterdam. This both provided capital for Brazilian expansion and served as a vital marketing link for the distribution of Brazilian exports in northwest Europe.[15]

Another long-term advantage for Brazil may have been the typical personality structure of the Luso-Brazilians, which seems to have been perceptibly more plastic and accommodating than the comparatively rigid type associated with the Hispanic temperament.[16] Perhaps because of their greater commercial sophistication, the "management of differences" appears to have moved somewhat farther along in the Portuguese culture area than it did in Spanish America. Much later, during the crucial nineteenth-century period, this was probably a factor in providing Brazil with a relatively stable political environment, while in the interim it was a valuable, if immeasurable, factor in facilitating economic and cultural intercourse with other nations.[17]

THE CHARACTER OF COLONIAL ORGANIZATION

From the very outset, Portuguese colonization of America contrasted sharply with the Spanish American case. Even geography made a difference, for the Portuguese pattern of settlement was a littoral one, dotted along a rather long coastline but concentrated primarily, until the early eighteenth century, around the bulge of northeastern Brazil from São Luiz in Maranhão to Salvador in Bahia. The latter, located in the richly fertile Recôncavo region, was the capital of the sugar coast. The most densely settled parts in this period were around Recife and Salvador. Fortaleza and Natal also had some importance. Until the eighteenth century, Rio de Janeiro was little more than a defense outpost and the highlands of São Paulo were quite sparsely settled. Neither of the latter sites could, at the time, begin to compete for immigrants against the bustling attraction of the sugar coast.

Accordingly, the major centers of colonial Brazil were far more geographically and economically accessible to the mainstream of world trade and commerce than was the bulk of the Spanish empire. The "friction of space" (i.e., transport and communications difficulties) was also less for intracolonial movement as well. Locational proximity and the advantage of cheap maritime transport, moreover, were not only favorable factors in terms of interaction with the main overseas markets but were also advantageous in putting the region close to the labor supply sources in Portuguese West Africa.

This later circumstance was particularly important as the region lacked the large sedentary Indian populations which lived in key areas of the Spanish dominions. As in the case of North America, the indigenous inhabitants were either driven off or rounded up, impressed into slavery, and assimilated as a *mestiço* element.[18] Among the imported African slaves, the process of partial acculturation seems to have proceeded more rapidly than among most of the indigenous people of the Spanish realm. Accordingly, though cultural dualism was not absent from the Brazilian scene, it was less pronounced than in the principal Hispanic colonial areas.

The politico-economic organization of Brazil also differed from that of the Spanish colonies. Centralized state trading had been the device applied to the far eastern spice trade of the Portuguese kingdom, but in comparison with this commerce the early Brazilian trade did not appear to be nearly so promising. Consequently, the American traffic was left preponderantly in private hands outside the main focus of royal control and was conducted by the kinds of commercial companies which were already well evolved in Portuguese foreign trade. Unlike the Spanish imperial system, the Portuguese trading system was not encumbered by the privileged positions and restrictive practices of *consulados*.

Further, the establishment of the early settlements was entrusted chiefly to *donatários*, individuals who had concessions—including economic privileges and considerable powers of a political sort—to settle and develop areas (*capitanias* or captaincies) of Brazil at their own expense.[19] In the manner of the proprietary colonies of Anglo-America, the *donatários* sold land to colonists and promoted various commercial undertakings.[20] Most of the governors of the several captaincies were designated by Lisbon, but some were appointed by the *donatários*. In the beginning, then, colonization was essentially a business venture, combined with aspects of private subgovernment. Altogether fifteen hereditary captaincies were granted, though in time most of these enterprises faltered for want of sufficient resources to develop the grants effectively.

Midway in the sixteenth century a governor-general was appointed to preside over the colonies from Salvador; later, the less important north shore of the Brazilian bulge was detached from the government-general and administered separately. From then until the colonial administration was reorganized by the Marquis de Pombal in the 1750-1777 period, local organization was generally stronger than the loose royal administrative apparatus, which itself was not very centralized.[21] Generally, only the main outlines of policy were set forth in Europe, and the actual implementation and interpretation were left to the governors and municipal councils, the latter being far more consequential in Brazil than in Spanish America. The municipal councils (*câmara municipal*) of Brazil, for example, had broad powers to raise and administer funds for a variety of purposes and in such places as Salvador took an active role in fostering maritime trade.[22]

Actually, the system was even more decentralized than the foregoing would indicate. As such students of Brazilian social history as Gilberto Freyre and Roger Bastide have pointed out, the municipalities were often overshadowed by another institution and were not the nodal points of bureaucratic administration that they were in the Spanish system.[23] Unlike their Spanish

American counterparts they grew up haphazardly, lacked a great deal of artisan activity, and were generally almost devoid of the elaborate physical appurtenances and the numerous personnel associated with the royal administrative bureaucracy supported by Spain. Their councils, instead of being subordinated to the central government, were generally dominated by the *fazendeiros* (owners of the large rural estates or *fazendas*) or the *senhores de engenhos* (sugar mill owners).[24] For much of Brazil, then, the actual administration of day to day affairs was centered in either the large plantations, which were established on the coast for the cultivation of cane, or the *fazendas* devoted to ranching, mainly in the backlands or *sertões*. Of the two, the former was the more decisive in setting the tone of Brazilian life. Thus, the *casa grande* or "big house" of the plantation owner was the center of the social structure, political power, and economic organization and constituted the dominant institution in colonial Brazil for nearly two centuries.[25] On the sugar coast it remained the paramount institution of control for even longer. Patriarchal in character and paternalistic, at best, in its social relationships, the master-slave social system of the *fazendas* set the chief constraints on internal development until the mining boom of the eighteenth century shifted the population southward into a new social setting. From the private sector, rather than from the public sector, came the principal impetus to settlement and social organization.

On the whole, therefore, Brazil was very much a frontier area, left by the metropolitan government to develop on its own devices. The phrase, a "policy of salutary neglect," which was employed by Edmund Burke to describe the treatment of England's North American colonies, can describe much of Brazil's colonial experience. In practice, the colony was largely self-governing, and there was also a certain amount of decentralized regional autonomy. The formal structure of public authority was comparatively unobtrusive in the total scheme of things; until the Pombaline reforms the apparatus of bureaucratic interventionism, which was so conspicuous in the Spanish realm, was of modest proportions.

As in Spanish America, education fell under the purview of the church, particularly the Jesuit order, so that religious personnel played a major role in shaping and developing literature and the arts in Brazil. Politically, churchmen were occasionally active. They took part in evicting the French from southern Brazil, in mobilizing popular sentiment to throw out the Dutch, and in affiliating some of the indigenous tribes of the South with the Portuguese crown, thereby guarding the southern flank of the colony from Spanish expansion. As in Spanish America, convents, churches, and the like were built and lavishly adorned as centers of a rich religious ceremonialism; some were amply supplied with tithe income, endowments, slaves, and even property. But on the whole, the Brazilian church sems to have been much less prominent and influential as a factor in the economic order than the church on the other side of the line of demarcation established by the Treaty of Tordesillas in 1494.

The church in Brazil was not the close adjunct of an assertive imperial power, as it was in the Spanish empire. Its property holdings were less extensive and less valuable. But very likely the minor economic importance of the Brazilian church had a great deal to do with the fact that the commercial export orientation of Brazilian plantations provided the owners with large enough earnings that they had less need than their counterparts in Spanish America to deed properties to ecclesiastical institutions in connection with mortgage borrowing. Furthermore, the greater relative prominence in Brazil of commercialized activity created more accumulations of private wealth and loanable funds as alternatives to church-provided financing. Since the Portuguese crown seems never to have been anxious about granting extensive tracts of land to private settlers, there was also less need to disguise illegal land acquisitions by deeding them to the church and leasing them back for private exploitation. Finally, although other religious orders were active in Brazil, the Jesuits were the most vigorous expression of Brazilian Catholicism up to the time of their expulsion in the mid-eighteenth century; but before that, their opposition to enslavement of the Indians had earned them the implacable hostility of many settlers.[26] This clash of interest between settlers and church in all probability played a part in attenuating the position of religious authority in temporal affairs.[27] In any case, the relative position of the church in Brazilian life was symbolized by a feature remarked by Gilberto Freyre, who noted that the most prevalent expression of the church's presence was the chaplaincy attached to the plantation owner's house.[28]

THE PATTERN OF BRAZILIAN DEVELOPMENT

That Brazil was oriented from the beginning towards export development is partially explicable in terms of the prior evolution of Portuguese national life. Foreign trade was a well established activity in the motherland, and, consequently, the first Portuguese who came to America were primarily looking for new products and supply sources which could feed into the existing international marketing network. Brazilwood and a few other minor products furnished the initial raison d'être for settlement. Around 1520 sugar cultivation was introduced from the Portuguese-held islands in the Atlantic. With the immigration of cane-milling artisans and sugar traders, there began the first of the series of great production and exporting cycles in terms of which virtually the entire course of Brazilian economic history has been writ.

This, too, was an extension of previous Portuguese experience. The technology and organization for sugar production had already been developed to a high state (for the times) on the Azores, on Madeira, and on São Thomé, and the requisite supply of entrepreneurs was available. Access to the chief continental and English markets for the product had been gained through exports from the Portuguese islands, while the export trade links provided also a valuable connection with the major capital markets of Europe.[29] Meanwhile, Portuguese incursions into Africa had opened up an elastic supply of labor which could be applied to the reasonably fertile and accessible lands of the humid Brazilian coast, the so-called *zona de mata*. These lands also had ample rainfall and a supply of fluvial water power for running the mills as well as rivers for internal transport. Locational factors gave the region a further strong natural advantage in sugar exporting, for it was close in terms of shipping costs both to the European markets and African sources of labor. Moreover, adjacent to the *zona de mata* was an uplands zone known as the *agreste* which was unsuited for sugar cultivation but useful for producing food crops—beans, maize, and manioc—to supply the coastal population, as a supplement to the food raised locally on the coastal plantations and the *rocas* (the smaller landholdings of the *zona de mata*). Cotton was also grown, in part for export but mainly for meeting domestic clothing requirements. From land clearing in the *agreste*, as well as on the wooded coast itself, an adequate supply of fuel was assured. Behind the *agreste* was the vast hinterland known as the *sertão* (or *sertões*, in the plural). Useless for cane production and of marginal value for food crop cultivation because of the rainfall pattern [30] and economic distance, the lands of the *sertão* were economically suitable for ranching and, like the *agreste*, developed in a manner complementary to that of the coast. From the extensive ranching *fazendas* of the *sertão* came the livestock needed for plantation transport and for draught purposes in the mills,[31] the meat consumed on the coast, and the hides which were used locally or exported.

Thus, a combination of circumstances made the Brazilian coast a prime sugar producing area, while Spain's preoccupation with developing its mainland American possessions temporarily held off the world market the sugar exporting potential of the most likely competing region, the Caribbean islands. That the Portuguese settlers in Brazil moved so swiftly to realize their strong comparative export advantage was attributable not only to the existence of this advantage but also to the fact that they had few immediate alternative possibilities for converting their rather generously proportioned piece of real estate into a productive asset.

In the state in which they were discovered, the lands claimed by Portugal had only a limited value. The accumulated treasures of Montezuma and Atahualpa lay on the Spanish side of the line of Tordesillas, and the Spaniards acquired the large and settled indigenous population which could be driven into the mines or put to work on the latifundia. Brazil, in contrast, had no evident mineral wealth and the aboriginals were few in number, rather sparsely distributed, and primitive in their level of cultural development. Often nomadic, the Indians were recruited only with difficulty as an agricultural labor force, although the *bandeirantes paulistas*, the frontiersmen of the São Paulo area who had few rewarding alternatives, had hit upon Indian slave-gathering expeditions as the regional export industry in which they had a comperative advantage.[32] Despite the *bandeirantes'* vigor and enterprise in searching for Indian slaves to sell to the northeast, not enough could be rounded up to provide a very substantial labor force.

Unlike the Spanish, then, the Portuguese did not have a supply of servile labor for exploitation as a captive work force. To get the manpower required for agricultural development, they had to make a cash outlay for the purchase of imported Angolan slaves. Consequently, the *senhores de engenho* were compelled, as the *hacendados* often were not, to produce a vendible output which would enable them to recover their initial investment in labor. Moreover, since the purchased slave inputs were mainly imported and since there were hardly any local artisan industries to substitute for the imported processed goods required by the settlers, the marketable surplus had to take the form of export commodities. Accordingly, almost all early Brazilian development depended upon the growth of the external sector—and the complementary domestic production to which it gave rise in the *sertão*, the *agreste*, and the slaving territories of the *paulistas*.

Inasmuch as labor was, in large measure, in the category of international goods, the commercial opportunities of this export-based development pattern were even multiplied. Fortunes could be made not only in sugar production and in the marketing, financing, and shipping of colonial exports and imported specialities; they could also be gained from the mobilization of colonial labor supplies. Thus, the lucrative slave trade was added to the system as a major industry and continued as such down to the early nineteenth century. Although slave-trading firms of other nationalities shared the business, the Portuguese held the paramount interest in it.

Still other mercantile opportunities, of an entrepôt character, were afforded the Brazilians by virtue of the extensive foreign contacts of the Portuguese commercial system and the comparatively unrestrictive trade policies of the Portuguese state. From the first half of the sixteenth century, for example, there appear to have been French and British traders resident in Brazil, and British ships in particular figured prominently in the carrying trade of Portugal. Until formally prohibited by the Spanish crown in 1594, Dutch merchants were also active participants in the Brazilian trade. Even after the prohibition, the commercial connection with the Netherlands continued through Portuguese intermediaries, many of whom were of Marrano or Sephardic origin.[33] Except for certain rather unimportant products which were a royal monopoly, Brazilian colonists generally could, with permission of the *donatários*, send products to foreign ports as well as to Portugal by payment of differential duties—at least during part of the colonial period.[34] Consequently, thanks to the relatively open trading environment of Brazil, the country was also able to function as a way station for the smuggling traffic with the Spanish empire, especially that which moved through Buenos Aires into upper Peru and that which took place in connection with Portuguese participation in the slave trade of the Spanish empire.[35]

Compared with the Spanish dominions, therefore, commercially oriented private sector activities played a much greater role in the colonial growth of Brazil. Marketing, finance, and similar activities were more highly developed. And mercantile capital was, perhaps, the kingpin of the system, although with Portuguese, English, and other interests dominating the marketing structure, it appears that the Brazilians themselves were principally entrenched in the production end of the process. Nevertheless, even the large landowners were mainly committed to a commercial orientation, so that the heights of the social structure were occupied by what amounted to a *Geldaristokratie* which derived its affluence and influence from a market type of economic system.

So long as the overseas markets were expanding, the commercialized agricultural base established by the Portuguese served to sustain a considerable increase in Brazilian gross output and income. While brazilwood, hides, tobacco, cotton, and other minor products entered the export lists, it was sugar that constituted the mainstay. The export trade generated a great deal of the capital required, there was a seemingly inexhaustible supply of labor from Africa, and in Brazil the supply of land was ample. Accordingly, with little or no change in the coefficients of production, the volume of exports rose almost steadily for a century or so by the simple process of pushing the margins of settlement along the coast and bringing in more slaves. The number of sugar plantations and mills grew, and there was even a certain amount of organizational complexity introduced into the system. Some of the land of the plantations, for example, was leased to *lavradores* who, using their own slaves, planted and cut the cane, transported it to the *engenhos* for processing, and shared the output with the millowners who usually collected about 60 per cent as their due. There were also small holders who grew cane on their own land but who utilized the processing facilities of the *engenhos*, generally on a fifty-fifty split with the millowner.

With the growth of the coastal export sector, the complementary economies of the *agreste* and the *sertão* also enjoyed a secular expansion in the first stage of Brazil's historic *marcha para oeste*, or westward movement. Peopled by Portuguese immigrants who failed to obtain land on the coast, by the slaves of these settlers, by fugitive slaves from the coast, and by the *caboclos* or mixed-bloods, these inland areas were cleared by slash-and-burn techniques [36] and given over to mixed farming on a shifting-cultivation basis or ranching. In the *sertão*, both land uses existed side by side. The thorny scrub virgin covering was first removed by *caboclos* for subsistence cultivation, and then, after declining yields set in and crop farming shifted to other parcels, the acreage was turned over as semicleared grasslands for the grazing of livestock. In normal years, the slim margin of subsistence crop farming had only to support the few cultivators, who doubled as ranch hands—and as a private soldiery in the feuds among *fazendeiros*. Primitive as the system was, it worked well enough to support the growth of the export sector towards which it was oriented.

On the basis of this industry framework, Brazil became preeminent as the supplier of sugar to the Western world. By the early part of the seventeenth century, Brazilian sugar and tobacco had supplanted Asiatic spices as the staples of the Anglo-Portuguese trade and Brazilian exports were equally well-known on the European continent.

THE EXPORT DECLINE AND DEPRESSION

By the middle of the seventeenth century the great export boom had come to an end. Sugar shipments to Britain in 1669 were only a tenth of what they had been earlier in the century. In France and the Low Countries, the markets were similarly contracting. Not until the rebellion in Haiti occurred around a century and a half later, when the United States market for sugar was also growing, did the export prospects for the Brazilian sugar industry revive, and even then the effects of these stimuli were transient. For the long interim between these periods, the old center of the colonial Brazilian economy was thrown into depression, and with its decline came a chronic stagnation for the dependent regional economies of the *agreste* and the *sertão*.

The reasons for this reversal of fortunes had comparatively little to do with economics. In spite of the notable absence of continuing technological improvement in the Brazilian sugar industry, the failure to lower the real costs of production did not initially result in a loss of the area's comparative international advantage. Compared with the newly established British-owned sugar plantations, the cost of Brazilian sugar was perhaps as much as 30 per cent cheaper.[37] Nevertheless, economics was not all that was involved in the matter. By the middle of the seventeenth century, the British, the French, and the Dutch had all begun to develop their own colonial supply sources of sugar in the Caribbean and elsewhere. The output from these new producing regions not only received preference in the financing provided from European capital markets but also was given preferential treatment in the major European consumption markets for sugar. Just as Virginia tobacco had, owing to the Navigation Laws, begun to drive Brazilian tobacco from the shelves of English shops, so also the cheaper Brazilian sugar gave way to the output of British plantations which enjoyed the advantage of the same laws. Similar policies displaced Brazilian products in France and the Low Countries.

Because of the nature of their internal cost structure, the sugar plantations lingered on, for the falling cash income was partially offset by declining money costs insofar as slave breeding within the firms offered at least a partial substitute for purchased slave imports. Furthermore, given the heavy fixed costs (mainly the capital invested in slaves) and the relatively low variable costs (so far as downward adjustment was concerned), the region had little choice except to continue in the production of sugar since there were not many alternative production possibilities open for utilizing the same combination of the factors of production. A few changes did occur subsequently as the regional economy attempted to adjust to the changed export situation, but these were rather marginal and never sufficed to reverse the overall trend of economic retrogression.

Some of the *engenhos'* lands, for example, were diverted into subsistence agriculture or into the sharecropping of food production for the growing population of the colony. A tentative beginning was even made towards a broader distribution of land when some of the plantation lands were sold off in smaller units. In a few areas, especially near Salvador, the decline in sugar prices made tobacco relatively more profitable, and so the production of that commodity was increased. Later, around the middle of the eighteenth century, cacao was introduced and grown for export, mainly in the vicinity of Ilhéus.[38] Some cotton had always been grown in the northeast, and in the last third of the eighteenth century a minor export boom appeared in this production when the American Revolution and the War of 1812 temporarily cut off the North American supplies of cotton for the expanding British textile mills. Bahia, Pernambuco, and Maranhão were the chief beneficiaries of these exogenous events. Rice production, carried on for local consumption, was also brought temporarily into export channels by the aforesaid disruptions of the world market which also helped the tobacco trade.

But with all the limited new diversification of output, it was neither strikingly profitable for any protracted period nor carried on with conspicuous efficiency. Primitive techniques and slave labor prevailed, while land quality was also a factor. Repeated plantings of tobacco and cotton, for example, had the same deleterious effects which have been observed in the southern United States. Thus, apart from these sporadically profitable forays into overseas markets, the residue of the sugar boom was a rather large and populous area, extending along the coast and back into the *sertão*, sunk in decadence and poverty.

THE STRUCTURAL CONSTRAINTS ON DEVELOPMENT

The end of the sugar boom threw into bold relief the weaknesses and limitations of the structure which had been so profitable for over a century. The deficiencies of the primitively organized shifting fire agriculture of the *agreste* and the *sertão*, for instance, had already begun to exact the cost which was to mount steadily during the centuries ahead. Deforestation, rapid leaching, and erosion made the system highly unstable and destructive of the soil, and the cleared lands could be worked for only a few harvests before diminished fertility made further cropping unfeasible. Yet, decade after decade, for over three centuries the cycle was repeated to support a gradually rising population; as a result, a large portion of the land was impaired in fertility. Because of the migratory nature of the cropping pattern and because of climate and the low level of the crop technologies employed, the scattered and individually small marketable surpluses were subject to erratic variations in source and volume. This made it difficult to elaborate the supporting marketing and other structures necessary for putting the regional economy on a sounder long-term footing. Storage and transport facilities, fianancial organization, and institutions for the communication of market information and the diffusion of improved techniques of production were stunted in their development. Consequently, the quasi-nomadic *caboclo* farmers of the interior remained rootless, poor, ignorant, and unable to raise their productivity.[39]

Problems no less serious were created on the coast which, for all its commercial orientation, resembled in some ways the contraproductive regime of the Spanish American hacienda system. The source of the difficulty lay primarily in the bifurcated nature of the plantation, the principal economic and social unit. Although the Brazilian plantations were far more capitalistic than the haciendas in their extra-firm relationships and total rationale, their internal relations of production were, because of the reliance on slavery, fundamentally as archaic as anything which prevailed in the Spanish empire. Consequently, while Brazilian latifundism was undoubtedly more effective than the Spanish American variant, at least during the halcyon days of the sugar boom, it proved to have an almost equally negative impact on other elements of the development process, particularly the use of human resources.

The large non-European slave population, for example, was cut off from access to education and the colonial opportunity structure, employed mainly on an unskilled basis, and deprived of the chance to develop initiative for lack of a meaningful incentive system and for want of discretionary authority. Similarly, slave labor, like that of the *peones*, was immobilized geographically, socially, and occupationally and, as in the Spanish American case, neither received money income nor participated in capital accumulation activity or pecuniary management. The labor force was also largely excluded from the monetized domestic consumer market. Thus, in Brazil, as elsewhere in Latin America, the bulk of the human resources were left grossly underdeveloped, and money income, asset holdings, and power tended sharply toward the general pattern of concentrated distribution.

The labor regime in Brazilian agriculture also constricted the total range of domestic development possibilities; in agriculture itself it froze production functions into a mold and impeded technological progress. Moreover, once the initial purchase cost of the slaves had been recovered and their numbers could expand through biological reproduction, the progressive demonetization of labor costs, combined with the relatively insignificant costs of land acquisition, gave the plantation, like the hacienda, a high resiliency in absorbing income variations and hence a high survival capacity as a nonprogressive institution. To the extent that the subsistence requirements of plantation labor could be met by production carried on within the plantation's confines, the corresponding reduction of money outlays to procure the items from outside the firm enhanced this survival capacity even further. Considering (1) the sunk costs in milling equipment and the other accessory capital of sugar production, (2) the lack of owner familiarity with alternative production technologies, and (3) the limitations imposed on investment and production alternatives by the meager domestic market and the risks of branching out into other export products, it can be readily seen how this built-in cost resiliency operated to maintain a monocultural pattern of production on the coastal plantations.[40]

On the coast as in the primitive agriculture and ranching of the interior, conditions were inimical to the emergence of a broader pattern of social and economic development, one which might have been more viable in the long run. Of the windfall profits which were generated by the rise in export prices during the boom, perhaps even less were returned than under the Spanish system into the provision of social overhead facilities by the state or its subsidiary organs. A large portion of the export earnings was appropriated by the Portuguese and other foreign intermediaries who dominated the networks of marketing and finance, while part of the balance was diverted to finance the consumption requirements of the *fazendeiro* households. But even in the reinvested profits, which much have been substantial, there was a long-term difficulty present, for they went primarily to finance the expansion of the existing structure rather than into the promotion of economic change. The main reliance, in other words, was placed on the manipulation of quantitative production variables rather than on qualitative innovation. Consequently, spectacular as it was, the initial boom could not directly lay the basis for sustained and cumulative regional growth.[41]

ECONOMIC RECOVERY AND REGIONAL DIFFERENTIATION

At the end of the seventeenth century Brazil's second major export cycle began. This second era of economic expansion brought into prominence a new part of the Brazilian territory, and, while it began to integrate the various regions of the colony more closely than the previous boom had done, it also helped to accentuate the distinctive regionalism and unevenness of development which have made Brazil what it is today.

Although this spatial discontinuity has meant that the shifting geographical incidence of prosperity left behind a residue of regional stagnation and backwardness, the process has not been without its advantages. While regions once prosperous were subsequently derailed from the track of progress, the shifting frontier did engender a certain fluidity of life which permitted a measure of institutional modification. In a sense, therefore, the new growth cycles could bypass some of the institutional encumbrances laid down in an earlier age. Moreover, since chronological discontinuity accompanied spatial discontinuity in the sequence of export cycles, the historical context shifted along with the geographical context. Consequently, each wave of expansion brought in its wake a different set of economic and social repercussions, and left behind a regional economy of distinctive character.

The new wave of economic growth was launched by the discovery of important gold resources, in what is now the state of Minas Gerais, during the early 1690's. Other strikes followed, both in that state and in Mato Grosso and Goiás. Around 1730, diamonds were also found in the area. Deficient as were the communications facilities of the day, news of the discoveries travelled with extraordinary rapidity and the turn of the century found the previously desolate region swarming with migrants. Between 1690 and 1760, gold production—and, to a lesser extent, the output of diamonds—increased steadily, although exact statistics are not available, partly because of the considerable amount of smuggling which is believed to have occurred in the efforts to evade production taxes. It may well be, however, that Brazil produced almost one-half of the total world output of gold in the eighteenth century. Production began to fall off in the 1760-1780 period, but was still at quite respectable levels even then. Between 1780 and 1800 the output fell below the average of the 1720-1740 period, but even until 1810 it remained higher than the average annual level reached during the first three decades of the boom.[42]

Even though it had long appeared that the Spanish were destined to receive the lion's share of the New World's precious minerals, the Portuguese crown and the private *donatarios* had not altogether written off their Brazilian colony as a possible source of treasure. As early as 1560, government prospectors had discovered a gold mine (which they named Minas Gerais) in the captaincy of São Vincente, but intermittent exploratory ventures sponsored by the *donatários* during the century or so which followed failed to turn up much of promise. Nevertheless, the enterprising but economically disadvantaged frontiersmen from São Paulo were always looking for new economic opportunities as they roamed far and wide in the interior of Brazil, raiding the Jesuit missions in Paraguay for slaves, and setting up ranches along the São Francisco River valley to the north.[43] When slave-hunting activity picked up in the seventeenth century, they crossed and recrossed the area of Minas Gerais where they pursued, in addition to Indians, various reports of the presence of mineral treasures. They eventually discovered the wealth which had proved elusive for so long.

After the boom began, however, it soon reached such proportions that, despite the *paulistas'* struggles to maintain the upper hand, the area became the new hub of colonial economic activity and something of a melting pot for the whole of Brazil as migrants from all over converged upon the region. From the south came the *paulistas*, bringing a more rustic social tradition which differed considerably from that of the sedentary planter in the rich and aristocratically stratified society of Bahia and Pernambuco. Northeasterners, too, decamped from their declining regional economy and poured into the mining area through the São Francisco river route. Included in their numbers were planters who, in hopes of recouping dwindling fortunes, came bringing their slaves with them—thereby occasioning an important intersectoral shift of labor and capital resources in response to the new array of colonial investment opportunities.[44] Still more numerous were the *emboadas*, the new immigrants attracted from Portugal, who soon wrested control of much of the economic and political life of the region from the initial discoverers.[45] Gradually the numbers of people increased until the mountains and hilly uplands of eastern and central Minas Gerais became the most populous administrative unit of Brazil, while in the same wave of migration Mato Grosso and Goiás received their first important permanent settlements.

Spectacular as was the mining boom in itself, it did far more than merely provide the colonial economy with a new lease on life and bring another region to center stage for a while. The array of new economic opportunities it offered during the eighteenth century changed profoundly the course of Brazilian development. While it pulled the economic-demographic center of gravity southward and to the interior and greatly accelerated the rate of European immigration, it also worked important changes in the structure of Brazilian society.[46] Many towns sprang up amid the boom, with all the bustling activity characteristic of mining centers. And with the increase in urbanization, the more diversified and complex occupational structures characteristic of town life increased the size of the Brazilian middle class and expanded considerably the colony's supply of technical and business skills. For the first time, artisan industry acquired some importance in the life of the colony and private bankers emerged to cater to the needs of the mining sector and the growing volume of trade. Since many of the mines were of the placer variety and therefore workable on a small scale with comparatively modest amounts of capital and labor inputs, the range of accessibility to these new opportunities was relatively broad and the returns somewhat more widely distributed than they had been in the old northeast. Even slaves were occasionally permitted to work deposits on their own account, with the opportunity to purchase their freedom as a compelling incentive.

Opportunities for the expression of enterprise were also presented in both regional and extraregional agriculture, because of the rapidly growing urban and mining force demand for food requirements and for a supply of pack animals to carry the volume of overland traffic. Foodstuffs and other agricultural products moved into the region from other parts of Brazil on a growing scale. Foreign commerce opportunities were amplified as well, as the outpouring of gold and diamonds financed a considerably increased volume of colonial imports and renewed the external economic ties which had earlier been on the wane.[47]   European imports (mainly from England) of a wide variety of mining supplies and consumer goods were drawn in to equip and outfit the region's new population, which had proportionately more participants in the market economy than the Northeast.

Minerals other than gold were also discovered, and while they were of no great value then, they were often to prove quite usable in the twentieth century, a deferred but consequential side-benefit of the eighteenth century prospecting fury. Even at that time, though, a few of the other minerals came to be worked on a small scale. For example, iron deposits were exploited and processed with charcoal—apparently with the use of some of the primitive iron-working techniques introduced by slaves from Africa—to make mining tools, iron bands for wagon wheels, and the like.[48]

The mining economy, in short, loosened social stratification, lessened immobility, and gave the new Brazilian heartland a fluidity of structure lacking in the old. Enhanced possibilities for social mobility, together with a diversified and increased range of economic opportunities, created an environment favorable for developing a spirit of enterprise and the structural supports needed to foster its expression. In addition, the more central geographical location of the mining economy better enabled it to function as the nucleus of an embryonic, but nevertheless distinct, colony-wide economic system. From the mining center there spread out certain transregional influences which fostered a derivative response in other areas of Brazil, integrating them together more than they had ever been previously.

Factor mobility out of the old sugar coast was one example of this integrative role,[49] while on the basis of the new *mineiro* markets, even the ranching economy of the northeastern *sertão* was revivified to some extent. With the strong attraction of mining, commerce, and affiliated pursuits, the minerals region could not begin to supply its own agricultural demand, even with the redirection of *sertão* output. Accordingly, the south of Brazil was also opened up by the spread of agricultural and ranching activity. Regions immediately adjacent to Minas Gerais supplied the production of some of these items or, as in the case of São Paulo, benefited from the rising volume of overland traffic converging on Minas Gerais from production sites still more distantly situated. So strong was the pull of the *mineiro* market that it extended even to Rio Grande do Sul where mule and cattle breeding developed on a relatively large scale as the economic basis for the first significant settlement of the area, though subsistence ranching and farming had been practiced there in a minor way for some time before. From there, thousands of mules and cattle were driven northward through São Paulo. A considerable amount of *charque* (dried beef), hides, and other livestock products as well as some wheat and flour [50] also moved out from Rio Grande do Sul in coastal shipping to provision both the inland *mineiro* markets and the growing market of Rio de Janeiro. At the same time that the mining center was fostering an integration of regional economies, it was also, through the channels of interregional exchange (in which its trade balance was negative) dif-fusing the money earnings of mining more widely. Thereby, *mineiro* prosperity supplied the means of payment for financing foreign imports into these other, interacting regions as well. The rapid *mineiro* inflation reported by Antonil, for example, suggests, too, that the buying power transferred to the supply regions was considerable.

Not the least important of the effects of the mining boom was the emergence of the port of Rio de Janeiro. Enjoying a commanding natural advantage based upon its convenient location vis-à-vis the inland *mineiro* population centers and its excellent and easily defended harbor facilities, Rio de Janeiro had been previously a small defense outpost of scant economic consequence. With the minerals boom, however, it moved into the limelight by virtue of its role as the major center for shipping the minerals output abroad and handling the large volume of imported goods financed by the export of bullion and gems. Of the inhabitants of the minerals area, only those of Goiás and Mato Grosso were, thanks to the Amazonian river system, served by another port, that of Belém in Pará. In addition, Rio occupied a strategic role in the most important branch of the limited coastwise shipping of the day: that moving from Rio Grande do Sul through Rio to Minas Gerais. A strong commercial orientation, attuned especially to the field of international trade, thus dominated Rio de Janeiro from the beginning of its major period of growth. From that point on, the shipping facilities, the mercantile houses, the financial enterprises, and the other ancillary business services of the port of Rio were to play a vital role in fostering the further development of southern Brazil. Meanwhile the gold rush brought a tightening up of Portuguese controls, giving greater importance to the apparatus of public administra-tion, and this was also relevant to the growth of the new port. Owing to the clear economic preeminence of the south-central portion of Brazil, Rio was made, in 1763, the administrative center for the whole colony. As the principal seat of government, therefore, the population of Rio was augmented further, and into its market fed a portion of the revenue collected by the fiscal system. Furthermore, the removal of the capital from Salvador helped ultimately to strengthen the hand of southern Bra-zilian interests in the shaping of national policy.

Although the strengthening of public administration during this period caused some dismay, particularly among the *paulistas* who saw it as a means of reducing their share in the wealth of the mining economy,[51] the administrative reorganization was not altogether adverse to economic growth. Since the stricter trade and fiscal controls could not always be enforced effectively, the actual conduct of economic life was less restricted than was formally intended. And under the guidance of Pombal especially, administrative reforms and increased centralized control were sometimes linked with development measures. New mining methods were brought in, new crops were introduced and fostered, and two privileged commercial companies were formed to develop regional resources more effectively. One of these, the Companhia de Pernambuco e Parahyba (1759-1778), came into conflict with powerful commercial interests already established in its trading area and was abolished without having accomplished anything of consequence.[52] The other, however, the Companhia Geral do Grão Pará e Maranhão (1755-1778), had better luck and prepared the way for the only real prosperity the Maranhão area was to know in the colonial period. Heavily capitalized, the company brought in slaves and financed the expansion of rice and cotton production for export to European markets. Came the American Revolution, and Maranhão fortuitously entered upon a striking *fin de siècle* boom.

Pombal's suppression of the Jesuits, however, was devastating to the Brazilian educational system, and equally bad, from a development point of view, were the government's mercantilistic efforts to proscribe many of the colonial artisan industries, except those needed for clothing slaves and the like.[53] It would probably be a mistake, though, to assign too much weight to these latter prohibitive decrees. Very likely the local price inflation born of the gold boom so strongly reinforced the propensity to import that not much domestic industry would have appeared in those days anyway, beyond that which had already come into being during the earlier decades of the boom.

THE AFTERMATH OF THE MINING EXPORT CYCLE

The minerals boom approached the end of its cycle in the closing years of the eighteenth century. With the decline of mining, some of the population drifted westward onto the *planalto central* to increase the ranching activity carried on in Mato Grosso and Goiás. Others began to move to the south. Considerable numbers remained in Minas Gerais, where extensive deforestation had taken place to supply fuel for smelters, forges, and household uses. While the towns declined in size, many remained as small agricultural centers, serving the growing amount of modified subsistence agriculture, commercial farming, and ranching which developed on the semi-cleared lands of the area. Corn, beans, coffee, and rice figured prominently in the food crops that replaced the old mineral base during the late eighteenth and nineteenth centuries.

In the nineteenth century, the area's relatively dense population and its interior location were to permit the growth of a number of small-scale manufacturing enterprises, while its agricultural potential took on new meaning with the revived growth of *mineiro* towns and the continuing expansion of Rio de Janeiro. Following its new line of development, Minas Gerais became in the twentieth century a food-growing, livestock, and dairying region of major importance, second only to São Paulo in the value of its agricultural and ranching products. Unfortunately for the northeast, which had come to depend heavily upon its sales of sugar and cotton in the domestic market, the postmining agricultural expansion of Minas Gerais and neighboring areas to the south included, now that the manpower was available, both of these products. Thus, as time went on, the traditional producers of sugar and cotton had to compete against more advantageously located south-central firms for a share in the most rapidly expanding portion of the domestic market, that of the southern region.

Therefore, the curtain of the eighteenth century fell upon two distinctly separate Brazilian stages. In the north, the coastal-*agreste-sertão* complex lay prostrate, a society nearly immobilized by its internal institutional structure once the old-time dynamism had gone from the external trade links which had carried the region to the crest of its boom some one hundred and fifty years previously. Southward, the first act, based on gold and diamonds, had also come to a close. But there, a rather more versatile and open society remained, poised, as it were, in a sort of developmental entr'acte. Already the stage was being readied for the second presentation—a longer work with coffee as its theme, with a more numerous cast, a more complex plot, and a strikingly different denouement.

Part Three

From Independence to World War I

VI

The Early Nineteenth Century:
Development Reorientation and
Institutional Dislocation

ALTHOUGH most of colonial Latin America, except for Brazil, can be productively studied by looking mainly at the internal structure and functioning of the Iberian imperial system, from the nineteenth century on the conditions of Latin American growth must be viewed in a larger referential context. With marked regional and country variations, the new development pattern was an interaction between two sets of factors, those internal to the culture area and those external to it. To some degree, this interaction had already begun to take shape by the latter half of the eighteenth century. When national independence movements severed the ties with Iberian control centers, these trends acquired even greater importance. Thereafter, most of the significant new developments in Latin America originated in the operations of a world economy organized by an emergent system of international capitalism. Centering on the industrialization of Northwest Europe and the United States, this global system was at its height between 1850 and 1914 when the gold standard came into its own and both international trade and the international transfer of capital and labor were freer than at any time before or since.

The decisive events of the modern period, therefore, have sprung from the relationship of domestic Latin American circumstances to changing influences emanating from the global market. This being the case, the appropriate frame of reference is similar to that developed for the study of recent trends by the United Nations Economic Commission for Latin America (ECLA) in the conceptualization known as the periphery and the center.[1] While one need not accept as valid all aspects of the ECLA theory of the periphery and the center, the basic concept is of analytical utility in that it can be employed to interpret the postcolonial development pattern of the area in terms of an interaction which has forced the "peripheral" Latin American economies to a radical dependence upon the dominant economies of the industrialized "center" countries. As reflex economies,[2] in other words, the Latin American appendages of the global economic system have responded primarily to stimuli coming from the center. The character of their response, like the degree of their responsiveness, was conditioned by two factors: (1) their own institutional heritage and contemporary domestic institutional developments, and (2) the geographical distribution of resources as these were defined by conditions in the center. These components of regional responsiveness account for the pronounced differential development which took place among the individual national economies of the area.

EXOGENOUS INFLUENCES TO AROUND 1850

The stimuli radiating from the industrializing center of international capitalism were powerful because of the very magnitude of the changes occurring in the center. Their complexity and variety precludes a detailed exposition herein, but a summary view should indicate the nature of the new forces impinging upon the recently emancipated countries of Latin America.

Population growth had long been a factor in creating new economic relationships, but in the period in question demographic change was taking place at an accelerated pace. Between 1750 and 1850, for example, the world population may have increased by as much as 60 per cent, while in Europe alone the population seems to have almost doubled in this period of time. After 1850 the rise continued quite rapidly, especially in the North Atlantic countries. Ceteris paribus, this change by itself contributed strongly to a growth of demand for items such as tallow for household lighting, leather for shoes, clothing, furniture, foodstuffs, textile products, and so on. The increase in population, however, was only part of a larger group of changes associated with industrialization, in which two concomitant trends were urbanization and rising per capita income levels.

With an increasing percentage of the center countries' population employed outside of agriculture, demographic growth produced an especially pronounced increase in the demand for rural products. Up until the mid-nineteenth century, much of this increased demand was met by the modernization of agricultural techniques and increases in the European acreage farmed commercially. Even as late as 1850, most countries were still basically self-sufficient in agricultural staples, though England was fast becoming a continuing importer and a sporadic grain trade had developed between western Europe and the central and eastern portions of the continent.

Nevertheless, not all European food needs could be met locally; for example, by the eighteenth century sugar had become the most important single commodity moving in international commerce. As per capita income levels rose along with the growth in population, there appeared also a widening market for new types of goods. Consequently, more of the peripheral export products moved out of the luxury or semiluxury category and entered into popular consumption. Income elasticity of demand, in other words, led to a rising per capita consumption of such tropical goods as sugar, tobacco, tea, cacao, coffee, and, towards the end of the nineteenth century, bananas. There was, in addition, the beginning of a growth in demand for imported salted and dried beef as dietary preferences changed to reflect the new level of comparative affluence. Textiles, too, particularly cotton, shared in the rise in demand which came from the combination of population growth and increases in per capita income. Moreover, with the increased international movement of tropical products, sisal and similar bagging materials experienced a sharp growth in use. For a number of reasons, therefore, it was feasible to increase the cultivated area in the tropical zones of the world and, to a lesser extent, to expand the peripheral livestock industry.

Changes in industrial structure constituted another important contemporary force in shaping the pattern of the world economy. Scored *sempre accelerando*, the mechanization of production began initially in the English cotton and woollen textile industry during the latter half of the 1700's, but spread rapidly both to other production lines and to other areas on the European continent and North America. So quickly did aggregate industrial output rise that even before 1800 there was a growing exportable surplus, which center producers sought to market among the economies of the periphery.

On the one hand, industrialization lowered the price of such basic consumer items as textiles, thereby encouraging a still greater expansion in their demand and, by derivation, that of their raw material inputs. Cotton consumption by the English mills, for example, doubled between 1830 and 1843. On the other hand, the new industrial technology required an accelerated production of producer goods and their associated raw materials, not all of which could be supplied by domestic production in the center. Along with the demand for more coal and iron, most of which was locally available, came an increased need for copper which affected production opportunities in regions as distant as Chile. Furthermore, until substitute types of artificial illumination were developed, the expansion of European mining called for additional use of tallow lighting. And mechanization in industry greatly stepped up the use of hides for leather in machine belting. Because of the acreage requirements of livestock production and the pressure of food demand in the center, which required dedicating the available European land to more intensive uses, both of these industrial demands (together with the aforementioned consumer demand for meat) had to be met increasingly through importation.

Even the modernization of center agriculture was not without resource significance for the periphery. For example, the larger inputs of fertilizer needed by progressive European agriculture initiated in 1841 the export of guano from Peru and ushered in an important period in that country's economic history known as "the guano age." [3] A little later, the same change in demand launched the growth of the nitrate industry which changed profoundly the economic destiny of Chile.

Concurrently, organizational and technological changes were reducing the friction of space and making it possible to bring together economically the complementary resources which were widely separated from a geographical standpoint. Improved channels for the communication of market and production information were provided by the modernization of mail services, the growth of commodity exchanges, the introduction of telegraph systems, and the expansion of news media. Developments in banking and stock exchanges facilitated the growth of corporate structures and other forms of business organization which could coordinate over wide areas the real processes of production by mobilizing and allocating the money units of economic power on a broader scale. To expedite the movement of goods among nations, larger amounts of capital were invested in warehouses, port and harbor facilities, and in more rapid shipping services which had a greater aggregate cargo capacity. At the same time, the new organizational structures and technology were playing a crucial role by facilitating the wider geographical dispersion of people with important economic skills.

As a consequence, world trade grew at a lively tempo during the latter half of the eighteenth century and probably tripled between 1800 and 1850. In the process, Latin America was drawn increasingly into the vortex of the center economies and, thanks to new demand-price and supply-cost relationships, experienced a considerable amplification of its resource base. In a very fundamental sense, however, the resources so created acquired their value primarily from events in the center rather than from anything which was done in Latin America to initiate a process of resource expansion. From the center, largely, came both the demand for the goods and the ability to marshal them effectively to meet that demand. Thus, the resource elements in question were "Latin American resources" mainly in the sense that they happened to be located geographically, but not functionally, within the Latin American borders. For the most part, the Latin American interest in them was solely of a proprietary character.

LATE COLONIAL DEVELOPMENT AND STRESSES IN
SPANISH AMERICA

Latin America's participation in this global growth was conditioned primarily by the ensanguined period of disorder which followed independence. Only a few of the nations—Brazil and Chile being the most outstanding examples—were exempted from the protracted turbulence which engulfed the area. Particularly severe in the 50 years which followed independence, this chronic instability lingered on longer in some countries, even, in some cases, well into the present century.

Signs of the approaching economic reorientation and political break-down were, however, already visible in late colonial times when a series of developments began to undermine the old ideological, administrative, and economic unity of the imperial system. In part the ideological consensus of the ancien régime had been subverted by the spread of ideas from the Enlightenment, by the example of the revolution in North America,[4] and by the weakening of the church which resulted from the Jesuit expulsion and the royal expropriation of the "pious funds" in the *consolidación* of 1805.[5] Though not directly related to the independence issue, sporadic uprisings had for several decades indicated a growing lower class restive-ness. For example, Mexico City was the scene of several *tumultos* or popular demonstrations of lower-class discontent, while the 1765 *tumulto* in Quito was the occasion for considerable lower-class rioting against the local criollo elite. The year 1780 brought the *comunero* revolt in Co-lombia and the Túpac Amaru indigenous rebellion in Peru and Bolivia.[6] Of greater significance still were the armed movements in Mexico during the 1810-1815 period which were led by Fathers Hidalgo and Morelos and by Vicente Guerrero and Guadalupe Victoria. Unlike the actual seces-sionary conflict which occurred shortly thereafter, the short lived Hidalgo and Morelos movements bore the unmistakable earmarks of authentic social revolution.[7] In Venezuela, a revolt occurred between 1810 and 1812 under the leadership of Francisco de Miranda. All of these revolts were unsuccessful, and each was put down according to the Spanish way of doing things, which was not gentle. Yet each was, in its way, a harbinger of things to come.

Curiously though, behind such temporary disruptions of the public order lay a society which was moving forward. The native peoples, now possessed of some natural immunities to European diseases, were growing in numbers, while the composition of immigration shifted from central and southern Spain to the far more economically active northern regions of the peninsula. Enterprising Basques, Catalans, and Galicians came in rising numbers, settling especially in less occupied portions of the overseas dominions: e.g., in Chile and the Argentine, in the Antioquian highlands of Colombia, and in Costa Rica.[8] Though the mining industry of Upper Peru or Charcas (Bolivia) was on the wane, that of Mexico was strongly resurgent. Thanks to important new ore discoveries at such sites as Guanajuato, San Luís Potosí, and Zacatecas, Mexico was producing over half of the world's silver output in 1790. In many areas, too, colonial agriculture was flourishing as never before. Exceptionally capable guidance and direction was also being provided by the governing bureaucracy. For instance, José de Gálvez, visitor-general in Mexico and later minister of the Indies, was a distinguished public servant, even by modern standards,[9] and the adminis-trative vigor and competence of viceroys Bucareli and Count Revillagigedo (the younger) in Mexico left little to be desired. In Nueva Granada, several efficient viceroys contributed to the prosperity of the region—perhaps none more so than José Solís Folch de Cardona who pushed actively a road and bridge building campaign and who set about assembling the statistical data necessary for constructive government.[10]

The Spanish rulers had also finally come around to the long-standing mercantilist practice of authorizing a number of privately financed trading companies to organize and develop commerce in designated areas of the empire.[11] The most famous of these was the Guipuzcoana company, a Basque enterprise whose shares had been placed on the market and sold to the north Spanish bourgeoisie; its major objective was that of monopolizing (with authorization) Venezuela's trade and developing its cacao and livestock production. A second Basque enterprise, the Royal Trading Company of Havana, included the king among its shareholders. The Catalans organized in Barcelona a company to trade with Puerto Rico, Santo Domingo, and Margarita, while a Galician enterprise was launched to exploit the commercial possibilities of Campeche. Excepting the Guipuzcoana Company, however, none was a great success.

Concurrently, European economic expansion, together with the trade liberalization and reform measures instituted by the Bourbon monarchy, was exerting a forceful stimulation on Latin American exports. Moreover, a special stimulus had been given Latin American exports during this period by the Haitian revolution which eliminated that country's previously large sugar exports, and by the revolutionary war of the United States which temporarily enhanced the foreign demand for Latin American tobacco, cotton, indigo, and rice.

Because of the policy expedient of opening ports to neutral shipping during periods of war, new external market links were developed for Spanish America. During the closing years of the colonial era, for example, trading ships of United States registry made their appearance on the scene, opening up an important and growing new market for such specialty exports as hemp and sugar. In turn, North American products began to enter Latin American markets through this aperture, bringing to Buenos Aires, for example, the wheat and flour which Spain was no longer able to supply.

As a result of these developments, the last third of the eighteenth century and the first decade of the nineteenth produced a remarkable upsurge in Spanish American foreign commerce. The criollo elite was surely impressed by the latent economic potential of the resources at their disposition—at their complete disposition should the control exercised by the motherland be removed. Moreover, the potential was widely distributed. Mexico, by 1791, according to von Humboldt, was exporting, in addition to bullion, considerable amounts of cotton—possibly six times that being exported by the United States at the time. Farther south, the Guipuzcoana company, for all its local unpopularity, had revealed to Venezuela the lucrative possibilities of selling cacao and hides in foreign markets. Meanwhile, the slow natural increase of the wild cattle herds roaming over the pampas had eventually supplied Buenos Aires with an exportable surplus of hides; introduction of meat salting techniques in the 1780's added another export opportunity. The Chilean economy was similarly expanding, owing to increased direct trade with ships sailing around the Horn.

At the same time, a series of administrative reforms had fostered the growth of regional self-consciousness, though another aspect of the reform—the replacement of criollos by *peninsulares* in a number of local offices—had, unfortunately for Spain, brought more conspicuous attention to the presence of imperial directive control. In 1739 the Viceroyalty of Nueva Granada, comprising Venezuela, Colombia, Panama, and Ecuador, was separated from Peru. In 1776 the Viceroyalty of Buenos Aires was created to strengthen the Spanish hand vis-à-vis the Luzo-Brazilians in the La Plata area, after which the province of Charcas (Bolivia) was detached from the Lima administrative center and placed under the Buenos Aires jurisdiction. At Havana, Caracas, and Santiago de Chile, new captaincies-general were established which enjoyed a greater measure of independence from the viceroyalties to which they were attached. Here and there, criollos had been appointed to higher-level posts, but real control of the bureaucracy still lay with the Spaniards.

Even within the administrative subdivisions, there is evidence that numerous interregional frictions were developing, precursors of the conflicts which were to trouble the newly established republican governments. Guadalajara, for example, was engaged in feuds with the central Mexican mining districts concerning jurisdiction over agricultural lands lying between the two, while also laying claim to other mining territories in order to supervise the revenues collected therefrom. Northern Mexican provinces quarrelled with the viceregal government in Mexico City over the disproportionate amount of local taxes drained off to the viceregal exchequer; of the 394,301 pesos collected in taxes by the royal treasury at Durango in 1762, the treasury in Mexico City appropriated 362,560 pesos! In both Veracruz and Buenos Aires, the local mercantile groups were themselves divided. *Consulado* members inclined towards more restricted interpretations of trading privileges to safeguard their preferential connections with Spanish suppliers, and nonmembers argued for the advantages of broader relations with non-Spanish overseas firms. Spanish and criollo merchants, in turn, were not without fear of competition from resident foreign merchants.[12] Yet in neither Veracruz nor Buenos Aires were any of the local merchants interested in seeing liberalized trading opportunities extended to other ports in their regions. While both the northern Mexican provinces and Guadalajara were pressing for the opening of the regional ports of Tampico and San Blas, the merchants of Veracruz were joined by the Mexico City *consulado* in opposition to such moves because the competing trade channels could not be dominated by traditional distributors.[13] In the Argentine case, the interests of the Buenos Aires *porteños* were pitted against the up-river ports in like fashion.

Further problems arose from the dislocations which accompanied the changes in administrative organization and trade flows.[14] For instance, wine producers in the inland Argentine province of Cuyo suffered from the competition of European wines entering Buenos Aires, and Panama was sent into economic oblivion when the fleet system was abolished. Even powerful Lima, the emporium of much of South America during the greater part of the colonial period, lost its central position in the commercial scheme of things. The inclusion of Ecuador in the viceroyalty of Nueva Granada reoriented the textile producers of Quito away from the Peruvian markets and sent their output northward along the important new trade route which ran from Guayaquil up through Quito, Popayán, and the Cauca Valley towards the Antioquian gold mining regions. To the southeast, the establishment of the viceroyalty of Buenos Aires meant that the output of the Bolivian mines no longer flowed through Peru but went instead to the new capital on the River Plate. Further, when new sailing routes opened up around the Horn, vessels from Europe could put into the ports of the Chilean coast before reaching Callao, the port of Lima. Thus still another distribution area of the merchants of Peru was carved away—though the change was a distinct boon to the Chileans.

It remained for Napoleon to create the conditions under which the foregoing frictions welled up into outright revolt—though, a bit prematurely, the British had already expressed their interest in the liquidation of the Spanish empire by sending two unsuccessful filibustering expeditions to the La Plata region in 1806 and 1807. As a consequence of the Napoleonic occupation of the Iberian Peninsula and the Spanish resistance, there was considerable confusion in the American colonies over government legitimacy. Just as Spanish capture of the administrative centers of the Indian empires had collapsed the centralized indigenous political structures, so also the highly centralized Spanish system disintegrated when its administrative center was captured. In the course of some rather complicated factional struggles, both in Spain and the New World, a number of the American administrative units in 1810 expelled their top Spanish officials, but nominally declared their continuing allegiance to the crown. However, several of the regions proclaimed themselves fully independent, and, in 1814, the restoration of a Bourbon monarch who appeared intent on reassumption of royal absolutism seemed to confirm the desirability of a complete separation from Spain.

INDEPENDENCE AND CHRONIC POLITICAL DISORDER

The republicans of La Plata, who had already replaced their viceroy in 1810 with one of their own choosing, declared in 1816 in favor of independent national existence. By 1818 the Chileans, who had expelled their Spanish governor in 1810, had attained their independence with Argentine aid. At the other extremity of the empire, Mexican conservatives opted for independence in 1821 and selected an emperorship under Iturbide as the most desirable expedient under the circumstances. Violent battles, bloody reprisals, and a great deal of marching back and forth filled the annals of the 1810-1824 period with martyrs and heroes aplenty before the countries from Bolivia through Venezuela were free of Spanish rule.

From then on, however, it was anybody's game as rival *cabildos* and caudillos vied among themselves for power. For good measure, there followed also a rash of quarrels with the Vatican concerning who should exercise the crown's former patronage rights in replacing the exiled Hispanophile clergy. With the traditional institutional mechanisms of social cohesion impaired or abolished, the civil units which replaced Spanish imperial rule soon began to fall apart.

Paraguay had chosen to part company with the United Provinces of La Plata, as did Uruguay somewhat later. In 1826 Bolivia struck out on its own, independently of both of its former associates, Argentina and Peru. A short while later, however, the Bolivian dictator Santa Cruz marched into Peru and temporarily controlled both countries (1836-1839) until evicted in the course of wars with Argentina and Chile. In 1823 the Mexicans threw out their newly proclaimed emperor and the United Provinces of Central America seceded from Mexico. The name the Central Americans had selected for their new nation, however, proved to be over optimistic. After a decade and a half of disunion, a period filled with revolts and coups, the fiction was formally abandoned and in 1838 Guatemala, El Salvador, Honduras, Nicaragua, and Costa Rica each ran up its own national flag— not, however, without intermittent meddling in each other's affairs thereafter.[15] In 1830, the very nucleus of the Bolivarian vision of regional unity had met a similar fate in what was formerly the Viceroyalty of Nueva Granada. Out of the ashes of the brief experiment of Gran Colombia (1821-1830), the phoenix of nationalism was resurrected as Venezuela, Colombia, and Ecuador.

In an area which was already characterized by a considerable amount of geographical and socio-cultural fragmentation, the termination of Spanish rule added political fragmentation. Thenceforth, the once united region was to experience growth within a framework of compartmentalized national economic units set apart from each other by differing monetary and fiscal systems, trade barriers, and other divergencies in economic policies. Indeed, political fragmentation served to multiply the barriers which severed intrahemispheric ties; with the power of local vested interests stronger in the formation of self-serving policies, former regional rivalries took on a nationalistic guise with independence. Consequently, new obstacles arose to impair the mobility of capital, labor factors, and the intercountry movement

of goods.[16] With the disintegration of the interregional economic relationships laid down by the administered trade network of the Spanish empire,
intra-Spanish American trade swiftly lost its former importance. Whereas
once, for example, the mining prosperity of Peru and Bolivia had fostered
artisan industries in Ecuador and benefited agriculture in Chile and Argentina, there were now new impediments obstructing the regional spread effects
of economic growth.

Further, the divisive forces of regionalism and economic particularism
were present in almost every nation. Highland Ecuador, for instance, joined
Gran Colombia in 1822, the year after the constitution for the confederation had been promulgated, but Guayaquil was not brought in until later
owing to a three-way split among the interests of the port region. One
faction favored incorporation into Gran Colombia, a second supported
joining Peru, and a third group preferred maintaining the local independence from either country which had been declared in 1820. After all of
Ecuador withdrew from Gran Colombia in 1830, Guayaquil was frequently
in conflict over the distribution of trade taxes with the interests of the
national capital at Quito.[17] In Mexico, the colonial economic axis formed
by Mexico City–Puebla–Veracruz endeavored to preserve its hegemony
over the rest of the nation in a controversy which comprehended tariff
policy, port development, and a host of other issues. Merchant importers
lined up against local manufacturers on the question of import duties, but
even the latter were not all of one mind. Though textile manufacturers
located far inland argued for freer importation of cotton, the Veracruz
cotton growers, occasionally joined by the nearby Puebla manufacturers,
pushed for tariff protection of local cotton growers. Yucatán, which wanted
its own ports freely open for trade, nonetheless urged the government to
grant protection for the goods it marketed in the center of the nation.

Argentina, too, was on the verge of disintegration. The *porteño* inhabitants of Buenos Aires city squabbled with the cattle aristocracy of Buenos
Aires province, while Buenos Aires as a whole found the older interior
provinces lined up in opposition to it on many basic points, including
foreign trade policy. Trade liberalization under the Spaniards had already
cost inland domestic producers their Buenos Aires markets, and cheap
foreign goods were spreading further ruin as they moved into the interior.[18]

In country after country, internal clashes of this sort made independence
resemble Pandora's box with its lid askew. With some exceptions, the
nineteenth century was an era filled with both covert and overt strife. In
many instances, conditions verged on outright chaos as coup followed
coup in a dreary succession of juntas, cabals, and cliques. Rule by sheer
force was commonplace in the seemingly interminable and indecisive power
struggles of the day.

Between 1830 and 1903, some forty armed revolts took place in Uruguay.
The country was also involved in the struggles being waged between its

two larger neighbors as well as in the war of 1864-1870 which pitted Paraguay against the combined forces of Argentina, Brazil, and Uruguay and left the "hermit republic" completely crushed from the enormous loss of life and territory.[19] In Bolivia, the situation was even worse, for aside from one war which it won (against Peru) and two which it lost (one against Argentina and Chile, the other against Chile),[20] the 126 years between independence and 1952 brought no fewer than 178 revolts and rebellions—and a grotesque political carrousel of venal chiefs of state. Mexican political development, marred by the war of the Texas revolution (1830's) and a costly war with the United States in the 1840's, was second to none in its presidential turnover rate; the nimble Santa Anna set something of a continental record for the number of times he was in and out of office.

Indeed, the impermanence of high political office was notorious. Colombia, until the presidential office was gained by the Conservatives in 1886, had a stormy political life filled with civil wars and frequent nonconstitutional changes in the presidency. Of Peru's nine chief executives between 1862 and 1885, only two served out their terms of office. Of the 45 persons who, thanks to military coups or dubious elections, sat as head of state in Ecuador during the century or so following independence, only ten served out their full terms; along with its own intermittent civil wars, the country was also involved in wars with both Colombia and Peru. For that matter, the recent president of Venezuela, Rómulo Betancourt, was the first elected president to complete his term of office.

In general, the main relief afforded from the high turnover rate of presidents and dictators were the lengthy intervals of despotic rule provided by such entrenched chieftans as Guzmán Blanco (1870-1888) and Gómez (1908-1935) in Venezuela; Barrios (1871-1885), Estrada Cabrera (1898-1920), and Ubico (1931-1944) in Guatemala; García Moreno (1860-1875) in Ecuador; Francia (1810-1840), C. A. López (1841-1862), and F. S. López (1862-1870) in Paraguay; or Santos Zelaya (1893-1909) in Nicaragua. In Costa Rica, the rule of the caudillo Guardia was the dominant feature of the 1870-1882 period, though otherwise the politics of that nation were comparatively placid by the standards prevailing elsewhere. There was a tendency for these militarily enforced periods of domestic tranquillity to be more common by the latter half of the century, but even then many of these durable leaders owed their longevity more to their skill in quashing uprisings than to their ability in avoiding them.[21]

THE FRAMEWORK OF NATIONAL ECONOMIC POLICIES

Bedazzled by the philosophical currents than sweeping out of Europe and inspired by the example of the Thirteen Colonies in North America, the successors to the Spanish regime proceeded, with few exceptions, to erect a mimetic system of government patterned after the norms of political liberalism. In general, both Indian collectivism and Spanish interventionism were repudiated in favor of policies associated with economic liberalism. Unfortunately, however, the ideologies and structures of both political and economic liberalism were predicated upon a pattern of individual and decentralized decision-making and upon the operation of supporting organizational substructures which had evolved from centuries of historical development in a significantly different stream of cultural tradition. Spanish America was ill prepared by its historical experience to effectively receive these imports; and the conditions which prevailed after independence were hardly favorable for the viable development of these novel ideological and organizational concepts. Thus the effort to install, almost overnight, a regime of economic and political liberalism was predestined to flounder; it did not take into account either the hierarchic historical conditioning of the area's culture or the realities of the inherited power structure. Indeed, the new constitutions and political forms were hardly more than a Potemkin facade of modernity, hastily thrown up around the institutional structures left behind by the departing Spaniards. While the forms themselves could be imported, their substantive content could not.

Political parties appeared, bearing such names as liberals, conservatives, *unitarios,* and federalists. But often these had little substantive meaning and served merely to designate rival political bands which were themselves subdivided into regional and personalistic factions. When such labels did indicate meaningful divergencies in points of view, they tended to revolve chiefly about the issues of secularization versus ecclesiastical privilege, and decentralization versus centralization in the power of national governments. Liberals generally espoused the former position in each controversy; conservatives, the latter. Neither the older theories upheld by the conservatives nor the radically new ones embraced by the liberals, however, were sufficiently persuasive to command general acceptance from the community as a whole, or even to win the continuing allegiance of a decisively large portion of the politically active minority. The whole legitimacy of government had been corroded at its foundations, and disintegration of the traditional fabric of authority and control followed as a matter of course.

Occasionally, political labels correlated loosely with the sort of national economic policies favored. For political liberals, the inherited system of administrative controls and the Hispanic welfare and protective mechanisms had to give way to laissez-faire norms. For conservatives, however, it was impossible to assent to the exotic liberal norms being offered in replacement, and, for the most part, they adhered to the Iberian interventionist tradition. For example, Mexican conservatives, who favored political centralization, were disposed to move slowly in abrogating the regime of economic controls and even went so far as to establish a state-sponsored industrial development bank along the general lines of the mining development bank of the late colonial period. Economic prudence, to them, consisted of introducing new development under the aegis of the state's regulatory policies, a view expressed with particular eloquence by Lucas Alamán.[22] In support of this interventionism, the conservative *consulado* interests, both before and after independence, raised the fear of foreign domination and the specter of the artisan unemployment which had accompanied the freer introduction of imports.[23] According to one *consulado*-sponsored document written to protest the liberalization of trade, the opening of the port of San Blas in western Mexico had put out of work some 12,000 persons in the regional craft guilds. There is evidence, moreover, that European imports were also undermining artisan manufactures in Puebla, Guanajuato, Querétaro, and other former colonial centers of the crafts.

In Colombia and Ecuador as well, the conservative groups usually supported strengthening the central government in relation to state governments and adhered to a protectionist economic position, for in both countries cottage industry dislocation had occurred in the wake of the rising tide of imported European factory goods.[24] Indeed, since similar reports came also from Peru and Argentina, the havoc played on local craft industries, both of the guild and *obraje* varieties, appears to have been a general condition during this age. The decadence of these activities was not ignored by the political leaders of the day. If the liberals could argue on behalf of free trade policies by pointing to the lower prices and superior quality of imported goods, the conservatives could no less cogently point to the obvious damage being worked on various regional economies and to the riots of unemployed artisans that occurred from time to time.

This lineup, however, was not invariable. In the Platine context, by way of contrast, the centralizing advocates (the *unitarios*) of Buenos Aires stood closer to the tenets of Manchesterian philosophy than did the federalists of the interior who saw in tariff policy the main hope for salvaging their domestic industries, which were fast disappearing with the loss of Bolivian markets and the influx of foreign goods. Thus, the *porteño* interests, "liberal" in some respects, wished to conserve the viceregal political preeminence of Buenos Aires; while the faltering artisan industries and mercantile interests of Córdoba, Salta, and Jujuy saw virtue in conserving the internal administrative control of trade but preferred the innovation of political decentralization and greater regional autonomy.

To add to the complexity, policy positions tended to be both fragmentary and shifting. Seldom were the principles proclaimed by new political groupings worked out in a coherent and comprehensive national program, and the party stands themselves changed as one or another of their internal factions gained the upper hand. Early in the national period, for example, Mexican liberals seem to have argued for free trade; later on, however, some of their leading figures championed tariff protection for new industries. In Colombia, the administration of president Mosquera in the 1840's was conservative in complexion, but when the same man returned to power as dictator later on, his policies were inspired by a doctrinaire variety of liberalism.

Factionalism being what it was, public policies often tended to be conceived quite narrowly in terms of group and/or regional interests and were not even so broad as to represent a class interest. Under the circumstances, there were rarely any really "national" policies other than in a purely nominal sense. Literacy and property requirements for voting, for example, effectively disenfranchised most of the large rural population and left only the absentee landlords with political rights, so that most of the policies of the period were formed without a "farm vote" despite the heavily agrarian character of the economic and social structures of the countries.

As the landowners were not of one mind on many matters and had to reckon with military and mercantile interests in the unstable coalitions of interest groups, the result was that policies were generally pursued by fits and starts. The records of the period are replete with policy inconsistencies.

Often, too, policies completely inharmonious with the environment were proclaimed and even passed into law—but just as completely ignored from that point on. Furthermore, for much of the political life of the period, it is futile to search for well-defined points of view in order to ascribe them to political philosophies. Sheer political opportunism almost completely divorced from ideology was often the guiding rule of conduct, and the national stage in many of the republics was intermittently held by a motly assortment of essentially unprincipled caudillos—scarcely a favorable portent for the capacity of Latin America to appropriate beneficially the opportunities presented by the end of Spanish domination.

THE ROLE OF THE PUBLIC SECTOR

By explicitly examining areas of the institutional structure in which maladies were concentrated, one can learn why it was that the social restructuring contemplated, and sometimes attempted, by the idealistic but sanguine *pensadores* met with such general frustration. Indeed, for all the perfervid humanitarianism of many of these leaders, and despite the high hopes they had of emulating the liberalism of other countries, the early republican period simply reinforced many of the features they had most decried in the ethos and social interaction pattern of the colonial age.[25]

The application of law and public policy which had occasionally been arbitrary under monarchical rule now became altogether capricious. If the *obedezco pero no cumplo* formula had formerly generated a certain tradition of illegality, the degree to which the impersonal rule of law was achieved in the independence period is perhaps best indicated by the popular expression *hecha la ley, hecha la trampa* (with each law come the means of evading it). Improprieties of official conduct, which had occasioned much criticism by those who chafed at the inferior position of the criollo population, were to seem picayune by comparison with what followed. If the public business of government had formerly been conducted as a private enterprise of the king, the various cliques which vied with one another for preferment under the new criollo management soon learned that political power could be used for profit and that government itself was the most profitable business of all—especially in a situation of chaos with few of the older checks on the self-aggrandizement of public officials.

The old dispensation had, as nineteenth-century *pensadores* perceived, assigned but meager rewards to economic and technical competence. Yet, under the republican regimes, politics continued to set the dominant cultural tone, entering into everything and extending everywhere. Whereas the struggle for prestige and differential advantage had formerly been confined to plays for royal and bureaucratic favor and to an artful manipulation of the imperial legal system, it was now converted into the often perilous game of national politics, the violently partisan nature of which reflected the higher prizes at stake. Divided into factions and past masters at intrigue, the new criollo ruling groups generally managed to dominate the scramble for political spoils. At the same time, lack of class solidarity prevented them from stabilizing the political order around a new social axis. The booty to be had from control of the government, therefore, was tossed continually back and forth.

The Spanish government had also been indicted by criollo critics for disregarding the welfare of its colonial subjects. Yet the repudiation of Hispanic interventionist controls (because of their supposed incompatibility with the norms of individualistic liberalism) and the new governments' influence in ecclesiastical patronage (which led to the appointment of a hierarchy sympathetic to criollo interests) exposed the indigenous population to an exploitation far greater in scale than had ever existed under the ancien régime. Since the status of Indian rights had been defined by special protective legislation and depended, therefore, on the legal framework and the disposition and efficiency of administrative oversight, the well-being of the aboriginal inhabitants ultimately depended upon who sat in control of the machinery of state. The long-standing conflicts between the crown and the criollos over Indian rights during the colonial age provided a clue to what independence would mean for the Indians.[26] They and their lands, such as remained by the early 1800's, were not the least of the rewards distributed by political contest.[27]

THE DECLINE OF PUBLIC ADMINISTRATION

In accounting for the disparity between what was attempted and what actually came to pass, discontinuities in political development played a major role. The rupture of legitimacy and consensus was one such discontinuity, and another was the deterioration which took place in public administration. A key feature of the social order of the colonial period had been the centralization of formal authority in an administrative bureaucracy manned largely, though not exclusively, by the crown's peninsular subjects. The winning of independence, however, delegitimized this system and put an end to its established personnel policies. Further, it resulted in the eviction or flight of most of the ablest top administrators and experienced bureaucrats, including numbers of the higher clergy who, being crown appointees, not surprisingly harbored royalist sentiments. As the new nations began to function, they did so with a demoralized and depleted bureaucracy, and this greatly jeopardized their capacity to continue the routine business of civil administration, such as the maintenance of law and order, at levels of performance adequate to permit the nations to operate effectively. Indeed, the decline of public administration seriously interrupted the flow of events and relationships which constitute the process of economic development; more often than not, the republican governments checked rather than assisted economic progress. To this untoward state of affairs, four factors seem to have contributed.

First was the departure of so much of the trained talent in public administration. The inexperience of their replacements reflected the political immaturity of the new body politic to which the business of self-rule was altogether novel. Some of the liabilities under which republican regimes operated can be put down simply to the ineptitude of amateurs in the civil service whose role, moreover, was somewhat clouded by the loss of legitimacy in the administrative function. The rather limited previous development of the civic virtues and the lack of a criollo tradition of teamwork only served to make their job more difficult. The frequent changes of regime which followed independence made it exceptionally hard to develop a more professionalized and experienced civil bureaucracy. Since government patronage and patronage expectations were highly useful methods of commanding loyalties and political support, the changes of administration generally involved a substantial turnover of the personnel brought in to share the gains of office with the privileged coterie of insiders.

A second factor was the breakdown of internal control mechanisms and procedures for enforcing bureaucratic discipline. The *visitas*, the *residencias*, and the use of the clergy as a countercheck on the civil servants were discarded at a time when increased supervision might have been required to offset the defects of bureaucratic inexperience. The third factor in the situation was the drastic change in bureaucratic recruitment policies. The shift away from *peninsulares* to *criollos* ushered in widespread conflicts of interests in public administration at just the time that the bureaucratic control mechanisms were discarded. With removal of the peninsular near-monopoly of public office, all the administrative positions which determined such important matters as the enforcement or nonenforcement of regulations, the allocation of government contracts, the manipulation of tariffs and tax policies, the award of privileges, and the like were a matter for political contest. Following dissolution of the empire, not just the favors dispensed by the state but the entire apparatus of the state itself became the main prize. Under Spanish rule, the colonial bureaucracy had functioned, at least sporadically, as a damper on criollo ambitions; but with elimination of this damper, the passion for power and politics, enhanced by the pre-existing leverage of social stratification, assumed unprecedented proportions. To the structure of opportunity and the pattern of social dynamics inherited from the colonial age was added a new form of enterprise, the coup d'etat, and to handle the growing traffic in political power, new social roles developed. Forceful, quasi-charismatic figures known as caudillos took center stage as the typical political leaders of the day. But all around them were the political operators or power brokers who, with infinite reserves of guile, traded in the shifts of factionalism and the personal rivalries of a struggle that was seldom stabilized for long. Under the circumstances, the process which governed advancement to top positions in the management of national economic affairs revalidated for postcolonial times the importance of personalistic relations and skill in the exercise of force. Behavioral attributes such as these, rather than technical competence, constituted the socially defined content of aspiration or "achievement" in the uncertain game of politics and public administration. For politicians with these standards of bureaucratic recruitment, the issue of conflicting interest was an irrelevancy.

A fourth factor in the deterioration of public administration was the internal social and economic conditions which prevailed in the new nations. Given the uncertainties of rewards in the disorganized private economic sector or, in some instances, the near absence of opportunities in a stagnating or slowly expanding economy, the distribution of government jobs with their proximity to the chief flow of appropriable income was for many the major economic opportunity presented in the society of the day. The official remuneration itself was not to be disregarded, but individual enrichment came not from official salaries alone. Deficiencies of administrative control created lucrative possibilities for informal appropriations from the public purse in the handling of public finance, while further remuneration could be garnered in the form of bribes for special favors, preference in the awarding of government contracts, and in the whole scheme of concessionary grants and privileges. For example, notwithstanding the frequent constitutional proscriptions of monopoly, a number of enterprises initiated during the nineteenth century were essentially concessionary in character and dependent in one way or another upon support by public authority. The social expression of entrepreneurship, therefore, had to reckon with *influencia* as an intangible business asset of considerable value and with *mordidas* or graft as a normal item of business expense. Thus it was that the total emoluments of government office were often higher than that to be obtained from nongovernmental employment. Furthermore, in view of the frequent changes of regime and the consequent turnover of governmental personnel, the temporary occupants of public office were under some compulsion to press their advantages while they could.

MILITARISM AS A NEW FACTOR IN THE PUBLIC SECTOR

The turbulence of the age was exacerbated by the presence of a predatory militarism, a factor then quite new in the neo-Iberian institutional setting.[28] This unsettling new element seems to have been definitely involved in the tendency to treat government as a private enterprise. It was permitted maximum latitude for expression by the inability of the politically active to regroup themselves into a viable new consensus.

Civilian supremacy in the state had been unchallenged in Spanish colonialism, even though in the 1760's the crown had, in the interests of building up the security of its American kingdoms, organized a colonial militia in which the criollo elite could obtain certain privileges (*fueros*) as commissioned officers. The winning of independence through armed combat, however, had provided a powerful impetus to creation of a larger military establishment and one which, moreover, was no longer under well-established civil authority. While the dismantling of these forces was inhibited by the domestic disquiet which followed independence, the failure to demobilize contributed in no small measure to the unrest of the times.

> The leaders of the revolutionary armies moved easily and naturally into the political vacuum created by the disappearance of royal authority. Thus at the very beginning of nationhood the armed forces assumed extramilitary (that is, political) functions. And as their military mission, that of defending the new nations against reconquest from Europe, became less meaningful and real, the military rulers, determined to preserve their vested institutional interests, placed more and more emphasis on politics.[29]

Enjoying a degree of independence from government authority and a liberty of action not previously known, the officer-politicians of the Spanish American armies were often able to turn national politics into their plaything. "For more than a generation, nation after nation was subjected to the whims of army-officer politicians who ruled by the sword, perverted justice, and pillaged the treasury."[30] Aside from their personal monetary extractions and the expenditures made to maintain their followers, the military chieftains also saddled many of the nations with a heavy burden of spending to wage the conflicts that grew out of international rivalries among the several states.

Not only was this influential group motivated by objectives which were different from the requisites of economic development, but also its direction of national life moved in a manner antithetical to the development needs of the time. Thus, despite the armed truces which prevailed from time to time under various military regimes, the resultant political stability was seldom linked with national guidance of a sort which furthered the ends of material progress.

FISCAL AND MONETARY INSTABILITY

In the light of what was happening in public administration and politics, it is hardly remarkable that the operations of the public sector generally undermined the process of development during the first half-century of independence. It was impossible to install and enforce effective systems of tax collection, and the cupidity of government officials and the pressure of the military diverted much of the public revenue which was collected into armaments, armies, graft and swindles, and any number of other uses less urgent than the clamant needs of the general population.[31] Even overlooking the elements of fraud and misappropriation, however, the policy and personnel changes which accompanied each alternation of regime occasioned a chronic waste in the planning and implementation of such public investment programs as were undertaken.

With public finance in a precarious condition and with public administration chaotic, the serious neglect of public investment in infrastructure which followed was inevitable. Communications systems deteriorated, road construction was virtually abandoned, and even simple road maintenance left a great deal to be desired, to judge from the harrowing episodes reported by the travelers of the day. Further, the difficulties of enforcing law and order made long-distance overland transport as insecure as it was costly. While in some instances, as in Colombia, obstacles to long-distance commercial exchange provided small-scale local producers with a certain amount of protection against cheap manufactured imports, the more general effect was to contract further the effective size of the republican market areas which had already been circumscribed in their maximum potential by the drawing of national boundaries.

Similarly, the disordered state of the fiscal system insured that, when the diminished fortunes of the church impaired the provision of educational and welfare services, few of the new governments were capable—in the few cases in which they were much concerned with the matter—of replacing them with public facilities. Thus, at a time when the qualitative requirements of the development process for human factor inputs were, thanks to the industrial revolution, commencing a steady rise, the educational systems of most of the Latin American republics were entering a stage of decomposition. Consequently, little or nothing was invested in fostering the intellectual and behavioral changes designated by the term "science," from which might have come the technological advances that gave such inordinate boosts to productivity in the course of western industrialization.

For the ladino population the consequences were bad enough, but in the rural areas there was such a crippling slowdown of the processes of acculturation and assimilation that only negligible progress was recorded in resolving the cultural dualism inherited from the colonial age. Indeed, in most areas all pretense was abandoned of making special efforts to guide indigenous peoples into fuller participation in the life of ladino society. Neither the private property owners nor the state they dominated found persuasive arguments for using a portion of their resources to foster educational advancement.

During the same period, the monetary disorders for which Latin America was to become famous made their first appearance on the scene, in the desperate resort of the new governments to issues of scrip as a substitute for dwindling revenues. Drained of their specie by Spanish bullion withdrawals, by the financing of imported weapons, and by a trade balance which went strongly against Spanish America in the early 1800's (because of dislocations in export production and a rapid rise in the importation of manufactures), the independent governments also found their hard reserves cut off by the general collapse of the mining industry. The sharp reduction in mining production and exports contributed to the local crises of illiquidity and made it almost impossible to service the foreign debts contracted during the liberation struggle.

These external obligations were large, especially when compared with the debilitated economic conditions of the American republics, for a foreign economic penetration almost as great as the foreign ideological penetration of the area had accompanied the separation from Spain.[32] Interested in carving out spheres of influence in the territories liberated from Spain, European governments, England in particular, were not at all reluctant to sanction the loans being promoted by their mercantile and financial communities for the support of revolutionary governments.[33] The merchants and manufacturers of arms and other supplies needed in Spanish America were doubly interested in the public loans, for in the course of securing a new market beachhead overseas they could also, thanks to the loans, receive payment in good European currencies. Investment banking houses, on their part, could collect commissions from the proceeds of bond sales which naturally reflected the intensity of the borrowers' need for external funds.

For the actual suppliers of funds, the investing public which bought the issues out of a mixture of patriotic motives and ebullient, if misplaced, expectations regarding their financial soundness, the matter was another story. The decline of Spanish American mining and the nonproductive character of the loans themselves combined with irregularities in public finance and the fiscal irresponsibility of many postindependence regimes to produce a showdown. Soon the burden of debt amortization and service charges against the export sector, itself in a precarious state, ran up against the propensity to continue imports in unabated volume and the incapacity of the unstable Spanish American governments to honor their debt obligations. There followed a widespread defaulting on almost all the public loans contracted, both domestically and abroad. This, plus the rather negative experience of private foreign investment in the region, eliminated almost completely for several decades the access of Spanish American economies to the important European capital markets. Thus during a period in which the capacity to generate capital internally was diminished because of the untoward effects of political change on the domestic conditions of production, the external borrowing capacity, through which scarce internal resources might have been supplemented by external ones, was also severely impaired. When, later on, Latin America could again approach the international capital market, it was, because of this earlier experience, generally on a rather costly basis. Though often the nominally stated interest rate on the later borrowings was not particularly high, the high brokerage commissions and other payments to insiders and the high discount at which the bonds ordinarily sold reduced considerably the net proceeds of the new loan flotations.

THE PRIVATE SECTOR BEFORE THE 1850'S

Disruption of the colonial institutional equilibrium occurred just at a time when external developments were imposing on the Spanish American economies the necessity of a new orientation and pattern of organization. Yet circumstances in the sphere of political processes interfered markedly with enlarging and securing the foundations of agriculture, industry, and commerce and forestalled the evolution of comprehensive modern money and credit economies in the region. State control of the economy and other aspects of individual and social activity had been commonplace under Spanish rule. But if the traditional scheme of monopoly and restriction was now challenged (by some), the assertive reaction against the familiar conception created so many new difficulties that most of the countries of the region lagged substantially behind in developing the institutional apparatus of modern industrial society. To the limitations imposed by nature on their internal development possibilities were added the limitations imposed by chronic institutional disorganization and the breakdown of the public sector.

The Decline of Domestic Mining. The colonial mining industry, which was expanding within a context of organizational and technological backwardness, suffered a severe setback after independence because of disruptions in the supply of capital, the provision of crucial mining inputs, the labor mobilization system, and the established marketing channels for mineral output.[34] For example, the independence wars cut off the flow of mercury required for processing the ores, while for gunpowder there were, of course, other more immediately pressing uses at hand. The small but promising start which had been made by the crown in developing colonial educational institutions to supply trained mining specialists was abandoned. Not the least of the difficulties stemmed from the weakening of the conventional labor recruitment techniques, especially in those areas where the *mita* system still played a role, and from impairment of the customary mechanisms for channeling capital to the industry, even though these had not been highly developed to begin with.

Private bankers had been hard hit by the general turmoil of the day. The royal exchequer, which had traditionally provided some assistance, was no longer operative, and the public treasuries of the new governments were hardly in a position to take on the additional burden of mining finance. Furthermore, the official colonial mining banks of both Mexico and South America fell on hard times and eventually disappeared altogether. Since most of the mines were located inland, the insecurity of transport and general lawlessness made it particularly difficult to move the mining products out for transshipment overseas. The same conditions also made it extremely difficult to bring in imported mining machinery and equipment with which to improve operations. For a variety of reasons, then, suspension of mining operations often followed the winning of independence; and owing to the ruinous flooding of the mines which this occasioned and to the fact that this, in turn, made it even more expensive to resume operations, temporary suspension was in many instances tantamount to protracted abandonment. In Mexico and Peru, for example, mining declined almost steadily until the middle of the century, while in Bolivia silver mining did not begin to revive until around 1876.[35]

Manufacturing Dislocation. The rapid rise in imports of European manufactures intensified the dislocation of artisan industry, for the simple handicraft firms of the guilds and the *obrajes* had their inception in, and owed their continuous existence to, the insulated, noncompetitive environment erected by Spain's administered imperial economy. Given the rudimentary nature of the marketing system which traditionally handled the output of these firms, the market barriers which had arrested their development, the lack of cooperant capital factors, and the managerial inexperience with technological and organizational progress, most of these firms were ill prepared to withstand the competition of European imports and at the same time cope with the turmoil prevailing in their immediate production environment.[36] Furthermore, while the technological level which characterized domestic manufacturing firms lagged well behind that which had evolved in Europe, the general absence of coal and iron resources in favorable juxtaposition set most of the traditional Latin American manufacturing regions at a grave disadvantage in shifting over to the new industrial technology which was based on these two resources. Consequently, the supply of artisan skills which had developed over the course of the colonial era was of little longer-run significance. Unlike Europe, where artisan development gradually melded with incipient industrialization, the discontinuity of Spanish American manufacturing development, which was occasioned by the fairly quick decline of the handicraft industries, meant that the region was deprived of a potential base in skills and production experience for supporting the rise of domestic industrialization.

From Mexico southward, however, there were sporadic efforts to set up new industrial enterprises along relatively modern lines, in textiles, metal-fabricating plants, and the like. But although some of these ventures managed to survive in a modest way, the general environment in which they operated was such as to make the eventual failure of most of them foredestined. Domestic investment capital was not in plentiful supply and even commercial credit for short-term financing was ordinarily lacking because of the absence of stable banking institutions.[37] Deteriorating conditions in the transport system and the amount of banditry and brigandage which prevailed often made it difficult (or even impossible) to bring raw materials and equipment to the plant sites and to ship the finished products to the various local markets. For that matter, the potential markets were often not very well known owing to the exceedingly imperfect state of the communications networks.[38] And the markets were, in any case, extremely weak in purchasing power and fragmented by geographical, cultural, and economic considerations. Under the circumstances, the inexperienced industrial entrepreneurs of the day were at a considerable disadvantage in competing against foreign manufacturers, and the high incidence of business failures is not surprising.

The Transactional Milieu. A radical instability in the transactional environment militated strongly against enduring success in domestic entrepreneurship.[39] Even the laws incorporated in constitutions were subject to variation, for constitutions embodying quite divergent conceptions of policy and structure often came and went with astonishing frequency. For example, the Peruvian constitution of 1860 was the fifteenth promulgated in that country up to that time. The first three decades in Ecuador's national life gave birth to the first six of the fifteen constitutions which have nominally been in force in that country since 1830, and one dictator (García Moreno in 1860-1875) alone added two more to the list. In Venezuela, Ecuador's erstwhile partner in Gran Colombia, 26 constitutions were enacted between 1830 and 1960. For many years, constitutional replacement almost regularly accompanied the alternation between liberals and conservatives at the helm of the Colombian government. Mexican constitutions were as ephemeral as any of the foregoing, and in Honduras a succession of 10 constitutions attested to the difficulty of stabilizing even a very small portion of the hemisphere.

The frequency of change in what was supposedly the fundamental law of the land, however, falls short of giving a complete picture of the degree of instability obtaining in the transactional environment. Most of the constitutions went generally unobserved anyhow and, consequently, provided few reliable guidelines for the conduct of public and private affairs. The internal political disarray produced national policies which constantly changed and which only rarely were effectively enforced. Further, differential or selective enforcement was a regular feature of the environment, according to the balance in the distribution of *influencia* and favoritism at any particular point in time. When the Hispanic political tradition, with its wide latitude for the exercise of public power, was in the ascendancy, the state tended to intervene at random, albeit generally in an inconsistent and haphazard manner. When liberalism was influential, the state did rather less, except to repeal measures passed under previous conservative auspices. The give and take of contending ideologies, parties, and factions, moreover, created innumerable intermediate policy positions and led to the new nations having neither the advantages of a centrally administered economy nor those of a free enterprise economy.

Thus, the working rules which guided the conduct of business transactions were continually shifting, often in an arbitrary manner, and more variable factors were added to the decision-making process while fewer decision factors remained stable or constant. Together with the imperfect knowledge of the market which prevailed, these conditions increased considerably the possibilities for making erroneous decisions (and misallocating resources)—especially where long-distance and long-term transactions were involved. High risks there were, and in abundance; the uncertainties (i.e., situations which did not admit of a probabilistic basis for making allowances for variables) inhibited effective business decisions even more than the risks. There were, in William Easterbrook's useful conceptualization, both primary and specific uncertainties in such abundance that the wonder is that economic life did not suffer total paralysis.[40] Taxation, tariff, public spending, monetary, and concessionary policies were matters for continuing conjecture, especially considering the expectational ambiguities which lay between written policies and their actual enforcement. The frequent turnovers of government personnel diminished even those risk defenses which could be erected on the basis of personal connections. For mining and manufacturing, in both of which the foregoing considerations were especially aggravated by the relatively large and illiquid fixed capital commitment required, the aftermath of independence was an almost unrelieved episode of disaster.

Postcolonial Agriculture. In comparison with mining and industry, Spanish American agriculture was less adversely affected by the events of the time, although in Venezuela, Mexico, and Uruguay the severity of the war for independence destroyed a good number of livestock operations while civil wars in Peru and elsewhere produced similar, though perhaps not so severe, setbacks for ranching.[41] For the most part, however, the large estates weathered the difficulties of the day because they depended little on capital or short-term financing, already controlled the labor force which they required, and often sold their output in nearby markets. Their internal structural features, in other words, shielded the latifundia from many of the risks and uncertainties which were so prevalent in the transactional milieu for other types of economic activities, for in fewer respects did they have to engage in the extra-firm transactions to which these risks and uncertainties attached. In fact, excepting a few instances such as Mexican sugar and Central American indigo production (which, for different reasons, suffered during the early postcolonial period), the increase in agricultural exports which had begun in the closing decades of Spanish rule continued. This was partly due to the establishment of foreign marketing intermediary firms and to their role in channeling European commercial credit to Latin American producers.[42]

But given the political complexion of the new governments, it is not surprising that little was attempted in public policy to modernize and restructure the agricultural sector except for the occasional adjustments which were made to open it up for export enterprises. In Colombia during the 1840's, for example, two conservative administrations of a fairly moderate hue distributed part of the public domain in small parcels to foster agricultural development, including the cultivation of coffee. In Mexico the ill-fated Banco de Avío endeavored to reestablish a silk industry and to improve sheep ranching. In Peru the government began in 1849 to subsidize the importation of agricultural workers to labor on the export-oriented coastal plantations. On the whole, however, the major changes of the day worked chiefly in the direction of perpetuating and even strengthening the hold of latifundism in agriculture.

The debt peonage system was expanded further, particularly since the landowning class controlled the courts and the instruments of enforcement and coercion, which circumstance also made it easier for the *hacendados* to turn legal disputes over land titles to their own advantage. Because of ambiguities in land titles and the greater vulnerability of small farms to economic disturbances, criollo seizure of power served in more than a few areas to bring about the near-extinction of many of the smaller landholdings, whose continued existence was also jeopardized by the decline of ecclesiastical financing and the consequent need to borrow at usurious rates from private moneylenders. Similarly, the change in the locus of political power facilitated private raids on the public domain on a large-scale basis without even the need of going through the formalities of *composición* procedures. Indeed, grants from public lands were an important means of rewarding political supporters. Mortgages held by the church were often canceled or ignored, and, where conditions permitted, lands held directly by the church were also appropriated as additions to the private latifundia.[43]

The larger landholdings were increased by still another technique which boded especially ill for the conditions of life for the rural populace. After independence several countries substituted the individualistic property norms of liberalism for the Spanish crown's traditional recognition of the validity of collective holdings. Few changes were to affect more radically the distribution of rural sector assets. Since the institution of fee simple individual ownership was neither customary nor well understood among the Indians, the *hacendados* were able to profit from the confusion by buying or simply seizing the individual parcels from their new holders. For example, against Indian resistance sufficiently strong to force temporary suspension of the law in several parts of the republic, the Colombian government passed the law of 6 March 1832 which directed that properties of the *resguardos* (Indian communities) be distributed as individual parcels among the inhabitants. Similar but apparently unrealized decrees had been issued in 1820 and 1821. With an eye to protecting the new freeholders from exploitation, the 1832 law declared such properties inalienable for ten years (later, in the law of 23 June 1843, extended to twenty years). On 3 June 1848 and 22 June 1850, however, additional laws were passed requiring immediate parcellization of communal holdings, thereby canceling the previous regional suspensions. This time, free disposal of land was attached to the newly created individual plots. In 1844 and 1850, laws were also passed to authorize the subdivision and sale of acreage owned by civil corporations.[44]

Peruvian policy moved toward the same end; the famous decree law of 8 April 1824 (ratified by Bolívar on 4 July 1825) authorized subdivision of Indian communal properties. Foreseeing the vulnerability of these new freeholdings, the Peruvian government attempted to proscribe their sale for a rather lengthy period in hopes that the new owners could safeguard their own individual interests by the time of the expiration date. A period of 25 years was stipulated in the decree ratification of 1825, but with the law of 1829 this was modified to read that properties could be sold when their owners were literate.[45] In practice, however, this restriction was seldom adhered to.

Bolivian legislation followed Spanish legal concepts more closely, though in the long run the results were not much different. Asserting the regalist doctrine of property, the government of General Ballivian, in a circular dated 14 December 1842, declared that all lands held by aboriginals belonged to the state, in which status (i.e., as part of the public domain) it appears that considerable tracts were deeded to private owners as payments to members of the army and as a means of retiring public bond issues.[46] Two decades later, however, in the decree of 28 February 1863, the administration of General Achá reverted to the Bolivarian solution incorporated in the Peruvian legislation and declared effective in Bolivia the Liberator's decree of 8 April 1824. Finally, five years afterwards, a latter-day version of the Spanish *composición* process, in combination with special Indian taxation, laid down the basis for a swift transfer of most of the former communal holdings out of the hands of the Indians.

Equivalent measures were eventually instituted in Ecuador and Guatemala, two of the other principal centers of aboriginal inhabitants. In Mexico, the formal abolition of communal property holdings, advocated intermittently in earlier decades, was effected in the liberal reform legislation of the 1850's. For the most part, the results of all of these changes were a widespread loss of the decollectivized Indian properties to the latifundia and the massive proletarianization of the native rural populations. Guatemala was, however, a partial exception, as the growing prominence of coffee cultivation was diverting most of the attention of would-be landowners to piedmont lands which lay somewhat apart from the regions of densest Indian settlement. Accordingly, in the Indian highlands, the passing of Spanish property forms led to the establishment of large numbers of small farms operated on a semi-subsistence basis; these were interspersed with extensive tracts of hacienda properties.[47]

Meanwhile, the advantages of latifundian ownership were also being enhanced on the output side of the process, for with independence came the abolition of the administrative apparatus which colonial public authority had used to regulate price fluctuations in local markets. Since prices were now free to fluctuate in response to changing supply conditions and since local markets were not well connected with each other, the haciendas had greater opportunity than before to exploit their monopsonistic and oligopsonistic positions in product markets—especially in those instances in which the aforementioned land tenure changes had succeeded in reducing the role of competing small-scale suppliers. For a variety of reasons, therefore, the single most contraproductive institutional aspect of colonial times continued to exert a dominant influence in the economic structure of the new nations of Spanish America.[48]

THE MARKETING SYSTEM IN TRANSITION

It is important to review changes in marketing systems which came about with the end of Spanish rule, for it was in this field that, relatively speaking, the greatest immediate headway was made towards developing structures more suitable for fostering economic advance along modern lines. Little change was visible in a great portion of the marketing system which tended to remain labor intensive, with large numbers of petty traders and middlemen handling the distribution of goods among the individually small and geographically dispersed markets in which, for income reasons, the average units of sale also tended to be quite small. Yet, although the nature of this distribution system, which continues to operate to the present day in many regions, has led to recurrent charges that the proliferation of marketing intermediaries burdened the economy with excessively high middlemen charges, such a criticism may not be altogether valid for several reasons.

In view of the nature of the markets, many of which were also in isolated areas of difficult access, a considerable amount of atomistic specialization was required to handle the activities of assembly, bulking, transport, breaking of bulk, and dispersal at different points in the system—especially as the transport and storage facilities then available did not readily lend themselves to larger volume shipments in any case. And owing to deficiencies in the means of communications, additional intermediaries were functionally useful for keeping the small, scattered, and illiterate traders in touch with one another in networks of direct interpersonal connections. In both respects, the low level of fixed capital with which the system operated tended to increase the requirements of working capital, and, therefore, the need to use more intermediaries to speed the flow of working capital (i.e., to accelerate the turnover of inventories). Moreover, given the instability which prevailed in the transactional environment, the dispersion of inventories throughout the many units of a multicellular distributional apparatus was a means of spreading, and lowering, risks while the personalistic element common to interfirm transactions—e.g., through family-linked firms or between firms whose proprietors knew one another— was also a security hedge which operated to stabilize the transactional environment. Altogether, therefore, the large number of commercial intermediaries represented a plausible economic adaptation to the environment in that relatively low-cost labor factors were substituted for relatively high-cost capital investment in transport and communications, storage facilities, education, and the governmental overhead required to stabilize the transactional milieu.[49]

Yet, if many of the features of the marketing system changed little or not at all, there were, nevertheless, other aspects in which constructive change did occur. The abolition of local market regulations may have increased the possibilities for arbitrage and, correspondingly, middleman profits from operating on intermarket price disparities, just as the same change may have enhanced the opportunities for cornering markets to turn freely fluctuating prices to merchant benefit. At the same time, though, the price system could begin to develop and function, however imperfectly, as a guide to business activity. Further, in time a number of the exclusionist features of the colonial mercantile system were gradually abolished or allowed to fall into disuse through the extinction of the guilds and *consulados* [50] and attenuation of the licensing and other regulated privileges of the traditional trading regime. Accordingly, access to participation in marketing was broadened. New firms appeared on the scene to play a role in developing the apparatus of distribution. Some of these were established by immigrant entrepreneurs, especially in the growing external sector. But older firms, too, had somewhat greater freedom in the potential scope of their activities.

Since the spreading of inventories could be used to reduce risks and since inventory investment was an area of capital utilization in which the sacrifice of liquidity could be comparatively brief, the slow growth of mercantile activity gave rise to new, and relatively secure, opportunities for short-term financing in which the windfall gains of inventory appreciation and the speculative gains of market manipulation often provided an additional margin of safety for the lenders. Thus, amid the general turbulence of the age, there was gradually gaining in importance an area of economic activity in which commercial credit could be feasibly employed and, thus, a functional basis for the introduction of more modern types of financial intermediary institutions. When, in due course, these latter were initiated, they often grew directly out of the operations of this emergent marketing system, both in terms of the capital and deposit reserves which were mobilized and the uses of loanable funds to which they catered. Pending the development of banks as such, the wealthier mercantile houses often provided a range of banking services, making loans and holding funds on deposit at interest for others.[51] With the rise of inventory finance came an indirect means of channeling credit into the production process[52]—though, admittedly, to the extent that inventory finance was based upon the marketing of imported goods, the ultimate beneficiaries of the system of commercial credit were often producers located abroad.

EARLY FOREIGN INVESTMENT

A flood of imports was not the only guise assumed by foreign economic penetration. European investors had long been waiting for a chance to tap the alleged El Dorado which lay so tantalizing behind the restrictions of Spanish imperial policy. When Spanish control was lifted, the new republics soon made their first acquaintance with a type who was to figure prominently in their future national development, the foreign business promoter backed up by foreign loans and investment capital. Many were the representatives of this new social role who rushed in to scout out the chances for gain; indeed before the last shot was fired in the battle for independence, these persons had launched new ventures in a number of countries: in trade, transport, mining, and even in manufacturing. For the most part, the investments in manufacturing and transport were injudiciously conceived and suffered from the same adverse conditions which militated strongly against successful operation of domestically initiated enterprises. A discouragingly high number of these initial efforts were simply fiascos. Case histories of the early nineteenth-century textile companies in Mexico, the harried efforts to establish river navigation concerns along the Magdalena in Colombia, and John Miers' dauntless (but finally daunted) attempts to launch a copper manufactory in Chile stand both as monuments to the spirit of hopeful optimism[53] and as classic studies in the extraordinary and frustrating complexities of entrepreneurship in an underdeveloped economy. In mining, the results were equally unrewarding. Often the new ventures were highly speculative, overpromoted, bonanza-type undertakings and, under the difficult circumstances then prevailing, most of the schemes were utter failures. So far as private foreign investment was concerned, therefore, the rosy illusions of European investors were often fairly quickly dispelled. And since foreign finance in the public sector met with a fate no happier, the negative experience in both types of international capital transactions played a part in curtailing the access of Spanish American republics to foreign capital supplies during a period in which their own capacity to generate capital was exceedingly limited.

Thanks to these abortive experiences, the total amount of foreign capital invested in Latin America as of 1850 was comparatively modest. By far the largest portion had been British in origin and placed in the ill-fated public bond issues. By mid-century, these issues had chalked up an unencouraging record of lapses into arrears, defaults, and refunding operations, owing to the recurrent financial crises of most of the new national governments. Many of the early investments in mining, manufacturing, and transport had also been written off as losses—grim testimony to the vexations of doing business in an environment afflicted by what Theodore Roosevelt aptly called "the insurrectionary habit."

Yet, not all the early foreign investments were fiascoes, nor was the trade picture uniformly dark, even though minerals exports had indeed fallen off. Certain types of foreign-initiated firms met with considerable success, notwithstanding all the deficiencies of the business environment, and exports of a number of agricultural commodities rose throughout the disorganized days of the 1810-1850 period. Between 1825 and 1856, for example, the value of exports leaving Buenos Aires had grown from 5.6 million pesos to 16 million pesos.[54] Peruvian exports of wool to England began on a regular basis with a shipment of 5,700 pounds net weight in 1834; by 1846-1856, an annual average of 1.5 million pounds net weight was being exported.[55] In the 1815-1820 period, two or three ships sufficed to handle the annual trade between Chile and Great Britain; by 1847, over 300 ships on this route carried such export products as copper ore, guano, wool, and nitrate of soda.[56] In Colombia the export of hides rose from 125,000 pesos in 1836 to 225,000 pesos by 1856, while between 1835 and 1855 coffee exports had grown from 2,500 bags to 35,000 bags.[57] For Venezuela, the export list in the 1830-1831 fiscal year had included 60,181 bags of coffee, 38,008 bags of cacao, 1,525 head of cattle, and 45,000 hides; in the 1847-1848 fiscal year, the record showed exports of 200,998 bags of coffee, 66,660 bags of cacao, 15,832 head of cattle, and 365,554 hides.[58] In Bolivia, quinine exports had assumed a role of some importance in the 1830-1850 interval, though, as an interesting anticipation of later Brazilian experience with coffee valorization schemes, initial Bolivian efforts to restrict supplies and maintain prices stimulated a competitive production and export of the commodity from Colombia during this period.[59]

Closely associated with these statistics, which can be matched in several others of the countries, were the early foreign investments which were successful. Trading firms they were, mostly, and they provided the crucially important links to overseas markets at a time when the domestic economic environment was falling into disarray. They also were the channels through which foreign capital financed the movement of export goods from Latin America to overseas consuming centers and which, indirectly, contributed to the financing of local production, though the pecuniary requirements of the production process in Latin American agriculture were comparatively limited. By 1822, for example, there were substantial numbers of British traders in the Platine region—39 British-owned mercantile houses in Buenos Aires alone, with other British shopkeepers located in provincial cities. Most of the foreign commerce was in their hands.[60] Locally they also functioned as merchant bankers: when, for example, John Miers travelled overland from Buenos Aires to Santiago in the 1820's, his financial needs for the trip were handled by means of letters of credit, drawn by an English merchant in the port city, on merchants located in the interior provinces.[61]

At approximately the same time, a foreigner residing in Chile observed that in Valparaiso there were several German shops selling glass, toys, and similar goods; a few French shops; a good many establishments run by Yankee traders in such lines as furniture, flour, biscuits, naval stores; a North American consular representative; and a very large number of English commercial houses dealing in hardware, coal, imported textiles, carpets, household furnishings, and even coarse chinaware brought in by English merchants from across the Pacific.[62] Some of these were, as in Argentina, also engaged in finance, and one of the most important Chilean family business dynasties and early banks, the Banco Edwards, grew out of such beginnings. By mid-century in Mexico, French immigrants had established trading firms, set up an agricultural colony in Veracruz, and gone into mining in Sonora and other northwestern parts of the republic.[63] At a fairly early date, some of the French mercantile houses had branched out into domestic textile manufacture, just as many of the early nineteenth-century Brazilian textile factories had been launched by Portuguese and other foreign cloth merchants.[64] North American merchants were also found in pre-1850 Mexico, in which country and Chile they were more numerous than elsewhere in Latin America.[65] Numerous foreign trading firms were established in Peru at Lima, Callao, Arequipa, Tacna, and Trujillo during the decades of the 1830's and 1840's, despite the forced loans often extracted from them by the government and the stagnation of most national exports except wool, guano (after 1840), and, after an interval, silver. Similar reports of the rise of foreign mercantile firms can be found for most of the other countries as well.[66]

It should be recognized that almost none of the estimates of foreign investment in nineteenth-century Latin America appears to deal in a satisfactory way with foreign enterprises of this character. Since, however, foreign capital financed most of the movement of export goods from Latin America to the markets of the industrial center and much of the reverse flow of imports as well, trading and shipping capital were forms of external support no less essential to the expansion of aggregate regional output than the capital invested directly in production installations. Amid the economic disorder of the first half of the century, therefore, the performance of exports and of foreign mercantile capital stood out with singular prominence even though the capital investment represented by the latter cannot be determined with accuracy. Whatever its size, however, the trading investment represented the single most important institutional advance achieved in the first decades of national independence since it extended the compass of the American marketing system and opened up production possibilities on a scale vastly larger than had existed previously.

ENTREPRENEURIAL DEVELOPMENT AND CAPITAL FORMATION

The absence of reliable data makes it virtually impossible to reconstruct the magnitude of various macroeconomic variables during this period. Yet the evidence, sketchy as it is, does permit one to say what was almost certainly happening from the time of the independence wars to the mid-century point. In the public sector, mining, and manufacturing, it seems altogether probable that no net new investment occurred for the Spanish American area as a whole, although in rare instances there may have been regional exceptions to this statement. Indeed, in all likelihood there was actually a substantial amount of disinvestment in these three fields, for it was they which were especially vulnerable to the disorder which was so prevalent during the institutional dislocation produced by the rupture of traditional imperial patterns. Agriculture and trade, however, were more resistant to the deteriorating economic and political environment of the day, and in both, the increase in the volume of transactions—particularly in the operations of the external sector—suggests strongly that capital formation was positive.

In terms of economic organization, little if any progress was made in developing active markets for land and labor factors. Conditions were generally quite unfavorable for the establishment of specialized financial structures, from the operations of which, capital and money markets could develop to mobilize domestic savings for economic growth and diversification. Some shorter-term financing was provided by mercantile intermediary firms, but long-term financing was even scarcer and far more costly than it had been in the colonial period because of the breakdown in the colonial financial system at a time when viable new intermediaries could seldom be established.[67] In short, there were still many barriers to the realization of certain fundamental institutional conditions of capitalistic development: the transferability of property in accordance with production success and the use of money as the controlling instrument of resource use. In addition to the basic obstructions to the free flow of men and resources, the instability in the transactional environment worked almost continuously against the introduction of modern forms of productive techniques. Nowhere, perhaps, was the frustration of modernization plainer than in the social incentive system. Spanish America, with few exceptions, remained a class-divided society with income distributed on the basis of power rather than productivity—one in which the maintenance and increase of wealth had comparatively little to do with savings, investment, and business skill. Neither did the status system accord high recognition to worldly achievement in enterprise, nor did the social allocation of tangible rewards follow, except rarely, in meaningful correlation with success in business activity. Accordingly, the structure of capitalist incentives—the inducements to invent, innovate, and initiate more advanced techniques of production—was weakened at its very core. Meanwhile, the deterioration of an already inadequate educational system depressed further the possibilities of entrepreneurial development by constricting the social diffusion of relevant skills. Social mobility and individual material betterment there were, at least in limited degree, but under the conditions then prevailing a workmanlike attention to productive processes or an adeptness in finance and marketing were about the least promising routes imaginable for those imbued with a motivation to get ahead, except in the field of trade.

In short, the structure of republicanism continued to assign the most meaningful premiums to maneuvers in the exercise of power rather than to achievement-oriented manipulation of technological and economic variables;[68] political astuteness and agility rather than investment sagacity, economic innovation, and market bargaining endured as the primary means of enlarging one's share of the available national income.[69] The weakness of law as an abiding force and the impotence of institutions based on laws and principles made impersonally assessed competence and considerations of efficiency much less germane to the problems at hand than personal associations, such as friendship or family affiliation among peers, and personal favoritism between superiors and subordinates. As the relations between simple economic capacity and economic rewards were as tenuous as ever they had been during the era of imperial interventionism, it is hardly remarkable that the prestige which attached to politics, the bureaucracy, and military service was not shared by business or industrial employment and that the social formation of leadership with a dedication to business enterprise was obstructed.

Underlying this failure at systemic restructuring was the basic fact that the revolution for independence was not in any meaningful sense a social revolution. Consequently, the older institutional inheritance and the pre-existing social structure lingered on with only quite marginal readjustments here and there. The Hispanic system of values and goals and its power-centered social relationships continued to prescribe, in large measure, the patterns of normative conduct in an only slightly altered system of structured roles. So far as the slight changes in structured roles were concerned, the chief novelties were the seizure by criollo interests of sovereign power and the rise of predatory militarism. Given the basic power structure of national life, however, this most often vested the direction of government in those whose rewards came from other than a direct involvement in the processes of production. Accordingly, national goals were identified with the landowner, the politician, and the military, and seldom were national policies well articulated with the requirements for general economic advance—even when, temporarily, the vicissitudes of regionalism, factionalism, and barracks rebellions permitted something approximating a national policy to emerge.

To be sure, a rather superficial mantel of "progressive" policy was sometimes fabricated and draped over the assorted constitutions, governmental decrees, and reform legislation—generally in the name of economic liberalism. But in the absence of supportive institutional substructures, the Spanish Americans were in effect playing, with major organizational handicaps, a new economic game on institutionally unfamiliar territory—just as they were in their efforts to emulate the operations of political liberalism. Hence, removal of the shackles of imperial interventionism did not produce the domestic impetus to economic advance which was hoped for.

Against this background, the incapacity of the new nations to initiate manufacturing development and participate more centrally in the experience of the industrial revolution takes on a particular significance, one which, incidentally, may partially explain the avidity with which national industrialization drives have been pushed in the twentieth century. With supply continuity unassured and market outlets problematical, only the most sanguine (or foolhardy) were inclined to venture their capital in a field where even the physical security of the enterprise was often threatened by political debacles. Some entrepreneurs there were, but their experiences were not such as to inspire a rash of emulators. Yet, if this failure can be readily explained by a hostile environment and the want of the appropriate factor endowments, what was involved was far more consequential than just an inability to develop a particular sector of economic activity. Also forfeited was the broad social significance of manufacturing development and its modernizing transformation of the whole social fabric, its revamping of the system of economic relations, and its shifting of the balance of economic and political power to new groups with different ends in view.

In Latin America, therefore, this inability to industrialize meant a failure to shift resources and the control over resources out of an archaic institutional environment into a more modern, pecuniarily oriented one, one linked intimately with capitalistic incentives to increase productivity, and provided with the congeries of ancillary institutions upon which general economic advance depends. And with the failure to develop domestic power centers alternative to land ownership, Latin America remained a land-based society only partially modified by the appearance of secondary power centers in political structures and military establishments, a society in which the ownership of land conveyed more prerogatives than just the management of the major social asset and the income therefrom. To a very real degree, landownership was tantamount to ownership of government, not only of local government but often of national government as well, with, correspondingly, a dominant role in the determination of tax policies, in the decisions on investments in social capital, in the award of government employment, in the enactment and enforcement of police regulations, and in the conduct of judicial processes.

Landowner influence was not unvaryingly strong in the formation of economic policy at the national level, for there power was intermittently shared with nonlanded politicians and generals. But at the local level and in the market, the owners of the latifundia exerted the uppermost influence in setting the outer constraints on the possibilities of domestic development. Given the ends to which and the manner in which they exercised their decision-making functions, the bulk of the region was deprived of exposure to the larger cultural effects of industrialization: the instrumental reference-set summarized by Veblen as the "cultural incidence of the machine process," the heritage of improvement which has historically issued from the pervasive and contagious effects of technological progress, and the efficiency-oriented increasing specialization of economic roles and functions with which modern civilization, dominated by machine industry, is necessarily concerned. Indeed, the scientific attitude and experimental technique which evolve as practically inseparable accompaniments to mechanized factory production remained as peripheral to the republican scheme of things as they were under the imperial dispensation.

Yet in one sense, the attainment of independence did mark a step forward, for the very disorder which proved so inimical to growth in the short run did loosen the institutional framework sufficiently so that eventually some of the germs of economic change could be implanted. The nature of the domestic order was such as to preclude development of an internal growth dynamic; by latching on to the international market, however, the new countries were able to receive the market-borne changes transmitted from abroad where the institutional foundations for economic growth were more auspicious. Thus, when it came, the impulse to material progress came largely from the outside.

VII

The External Sector and National
Policies From 1850 to 1914

IT was during the sixty or seventy years following 1850 that modern
economic development had its real inception in Latin America. Over
much of the area, the turbulence which followed attainment of nationhood
began to subside somewhat, especially in the closing decades of the period;
and although few countries were yet able to initiate new patterns of growth,
the pull of forces generated in the world market became well-nigh irresistible.
Inasmuch as the first decades of independence had not boded well for self-
generating economic advance, the arguments for placing major reliance
on a foreign impetus—for latching onto the North Atlantic stream of
development—must have seemed especially cogent. In fact, barring a radical
restructuring of domestic institutional arrangements, the recourse to external economic relationships was virtually the sine qua non of any significant economic improvement in Latin America.[1] Though the initial efforts to grasp external stimuli had been to some extent abortive, after
mid-century conditions were generally propitious for a more favorable
outcome. Moreover, the latter half of the century witnessed the spread in
public policy of an exceptionally accommodating attitude towards the
fruits foreign trade and foreign investment might bring. These fruits were
hardly inconsequential. Indeed, so spectacular were the results that until
the era began to draw to a close around the time of the First World War,
it is understandable that the social decision to cast the region's lot with
the dynamism of the world economy appeared, to those who shaped the
decisions, to have been amply vindicated.

EXOGENOUS INFLUENCES ON LATIN AMERICAN DEVELOPMENT

In the countries of the industrial center, the demographic and income
trends noted in the chapter preceding continued unabated. Between 1860
and 1910, for example, per capita incomes probably increased by as much
as 50 per cent in England and France and more than doubled in Germany.
Between 1880 and 1910, the rapidly growing population of the United
States may well have enjoyed a 50 per cent gain in per capita income.
All the while, therefore, effective market demand was being substantially
augmented by both a rising number of consumers and a rise in consumer
purchasing power.

211

By the latter half of the century, European agriculture was increasingly unable to supply the staples of grain, wool, leather, and meat which were consumed by the urban population. There was mounting pressure to utilize lands that were more remotely situated, and the 1850-1914 period saw a great movement into large and relatively unoccupied spaces of the world which were suitable for the production of these goods: Australia, New Zealand, Canada, South Africa, the midwestern and western parts of the United States, Argentina, Uruguay, and southern Brazil. Settlement of these areas meant both bringing into them people, goods, and new techniques of production and moving out of them the staples required at the center. Settled in response to the world market, these areas were fundamentally creatures of the technological changes which lay behind the transformation of the center.

Meanwhile, the continued expansion of scientific farming in Europe was, thanks to the work of Liebig in the chemistry of fertilizers, accentuating the demand for the guano deposits of the Peruvian coast and the nitrates of the Pacific coastal desert. Elsewhere on the American continent, the cultivation of fibers and tropical commodities such as coffee, cacao, and sugar received further impetus from the demand of the center's growing and increasingly affluent population.

During the same period, industrial production in the center was also accelerating; the global aggregate increased more than four and possibly as much as seven times between 1860 and 1914. While both consumer and producer goods industries grew, progress in heavy industry was especially notable and created the basis for an enormous expansion of the output of machinery and other capital goods. Between 1855-1859 and 1910-1913, for example, production of pig iron in the four leading industrial countries rose from 5.1 million tons to 57.1 million tons, production of steel soared from .06 million tons to 53.6 million tons, and coal output increased from 86 million tons to 1,024 million tons.

All of this called for a much greater output of minerals to run the growing industrial plant and, with technological changes, for a more diversified assortment of raw materials as well. Tin-plating requirements soon ran far beyond the production of traditional stannary sources at such places as Cornwall. The rise of the electrical industry augmented the need for copper substantially in excess of the output potential of the European mines. And development of the internal combustion engine and the automotive vehicle industry gave rise to sharp increases in world demand for rubber and petroleum. Lead, zinc, silver, and gold were also required on an ever larger scale.

At the same time, improvements in metallurgy and mining technology, the development of railways for moving bulky goods in volume overland, the introduction of telecommunications systems, and the center's growing exportable surplus of capital (and organizational and technical skills) enlarged the resource base of the periphery. The use of steam engines, for example, spread in mining and sugar milling. Advances in ore-processing methods and earth-moving equipment steadily increased the reserves of minerals which could be economically tapped. And whereas, for instance, in 1840 the world's railway lines totaled only 4,772 miles, with none in South America, by 1870 some 1,770 out of a global total of 130,361 miles of track were located in that continent. By 1900 South American railway mileage reached 26,450 (out of a world total of 490,970 miles). In 1930, when the great railway building age was virtually over, the trackage figures for the world and South America were 795,213 miles and 58,809 miles respectively. From 1866 on, transatlantic cables were laid to connect the major port areas of the two hemispheres. The wireless came into use not long after 1900.

Similarly, improvements in maritime transport, especially with the introduction of steamships, made possible rapid and cheap bulk shipments of goods which formerly had had few or no long distance markets. Between 1850 and 1910, for example, the tonnage of the world's merchant fleets nearly quadrupled, and the annual carrying capacity went up even more owing to the reduction of shipping time. Whereas the travel time of sailing vessels between Buenos Aires and Europe had ranged between three and four months, the introduction of steamships cut this to 50-60 days and further reductions were made before the end of the century. Regular shipments of commodities and processed goods were facilitated by the multiplication of scheduled sailing routes, and marginal adjustments of traffic flows were handled by the flexible schedules of a growing number of tramp steamers. With the development of refrigerated shipping, exports of such new products as chilled meat and bananas were made possible.

On the one hand, therefore, the industrial revolution was opening up new and larger markets for the exporters of the periphery, while, on the other, it was simultaneously providing the technological and organizational capabilities that would enable the periphery to respond with a greater elasticity in supplies. Indeed, where labor itself was scarce, this too could now be provided, thanks to the spread of communications systems and the aforementioned progress in shipping. Consequently, even the sparsely settled regions were drawn into interaction with the center economies. During the heyday of world migration, 1861 to 1920, some 45 million persons moved internationally. The majority of these went to the United States (61 per cent), but approximately 10 per cent migrated to Argentina, and over 7 per cent went to Brazil. Fewer went to the other Latin American countries, but even so their contributions of entrepreneurial and managerial skills were often crucial in shaping the economic capabilities of these relatively less favored nations.

Given the strength of the external market forces which resulted from the foregoing concatenation of trends, it is not surprising that a lopsided development occurred in Latin America in the form of a disparate rate of growth in the export sector as compared with the domestic sector. So far as internally oriented development was concerned, the phenomena of political, geographical, and cultural fragmentation (together with income distribution patterns) functioned to reduce domestic market size at the dawn of a period which attached increasing importance to economies of scale. The drawing of national boundaries led also to a narrowing of the resource base available to each new national economic unit. The enfeebled state of local economic organization and the scarcity of critical capital and skills inputs imposed still further restraints on the range of production options which were feasible for domestically initiated and internally oriented growth throughout Latin America. In contrast, the dynamic expansion of the industrializing center countries gave rise to a strong and resource-selective demand for the few exportable products of each of the Latin American countries. At the same time, the center was able to transfer to the peripheral economies the technical and organizational wherewithal for increasing the output of the products needed to meet that demand.

As time went on, therefore, the differing intensities of demand in these two market alternatives for the goods which Latin American economies could produce and the differing supply elasticities created by foreign and local economic organization led to a situation in which the foreign trade sector functioned ever more prominently in the patterns of gross national product. Further, owing to the resource-selective nature of export demand and the shrunken resource base of each national economic unit in Latin America, the growing relative importance of export-oriented activities served to accentuate the monocultural character of the national development patterns in the countries of the periphery—even though, for the Latin American region as a whole, the total composition of exports was fairly diversified. Virtually all developmental efforts, in other words, were concentrated on exploiting those particular resources in which the peripheral countries enjoyed a comparative international advantage as defined by the needs and production capabilities of the center.

Accordingly, the early decision of the several countries to go their separate ways, to develop along lines which were complementary not to each other but to the metropolitan economies, was critical in reducing the immediate possibilities for product diversification throughout the continent and, hence, in restricting the ability of the individual national economies to adapt to fluctuating conditions in export markets. In the long run, this reintegration of the region into the larger structure of the world market could have been a source of economic strength, and, to some extent, it was. But that it did not contribute more was attributable to the fact that, for a long time, the rewards for connecting with external stimuli were so impressive that most national governments could postpone for decade after decade the difficult task of rectifying their domestic economic systems.

THE EXPANSION OF LATIN AMERICAN FOREIGN TRADE

Responding to the strong pull of overseas demand, Latin American foreign trade underwent a dramatic expansion during the six decades following 1850 and national production patterns changed correspondingly. The temperate zone acreage dedicated to livestock and grain production increased rapidly, as did the tropical and subtropical zone acreage put into plantation crops such as coffee, sugar, cacao, and bananas. Similarly, a host of mining firms began to exploit on an unprecedented scale the heavily mineralized Andean and Mexican mountain ranges and extended their operations even into the northern Chilean desert. Copper, silver, tin, lead, zinc, and nitrates poured forth in almost steadily rising quantities. On the arid coast of Peru, the spread of irrigation led to sharp increases in the volume of sugar and cotton produced for export, while the extraction of guano from the offshore islands dropped millions of libras into the Peruvian treasury from export sales. Before the turn of the century, a wild rubber boom was under way in the vast Amazonian interior. Petroleum also became a major export on the Mexican gulf coast and a minor export from such other countries as Colombia and Peru. Even from Paraguay, once scaled off by the policies of a xenophobic dictator, came exports of livestock products, quebracho extract, timber and bananas. In short, production and export figures registered the quickening pulse of economic life after 1850, and not a country was left untouched.

A few examples may suffice to indicate the general dimensions of the expansion. Between 1853 and 1873, Argentine exports had grown sevenfold, from £ 1.4 million to £ 9.2 million. By 1893 they had doubled again to £ 18.9 million, and in 1903 reached £ 44.2 million. Only seven years later, in 1910, the total value of Argentine foreign sales amounted to £ 74.5 million.[2] Brazil's annual coffee exports rose from an average of 83.4 million kilograms in 1839-1844, to an average of 187.8 million kilograms in 1869-1874, and an average of 740.3 million kilograms in 1901-1905, though the aggregate value of these exports had not increased to the same degree since, during the early 1890's, the rapid expansion of Brazilian output had sharply reversed the upward trend in prices. Even so, the average annual value of all Brazilian exports grew from 150.3 million francs in 1839-1844 to 512.3 million francs in 1869-1874 to 990.1 million francs in 1901-1905.[3]

In Mexico, exports increased from 40.6 million pesos in 1877-1878 to 160.7 million pesos in 1900-1901 to 287.7 million pesos in 1910-1911.[4] Only 23,000 bags of coffee had been exported from Colombia in 1845; with the onset of the coffee boom exports climbed to 107,000 bags by 1880 and in 1915 reached 1,100,000 bags.[5] Venezuela, also caught up in the boom, increased its exports of coffee from 291,000 bags (of 60 kilograms each) in 1850-1851, to 595,000 bags in 1874-1875, to 847,000 bags in 1914-1915; its cacao exports also boomed and rose from 72,000 bags (of 60 kilograms each) in 1874-1875 to 282,000 bags in 1914-1915.[6] Costa Rica's coffee exports moved from 3.3 million kilograms in 1855 to 12.2 million kilograms in 1915, and its banana shipments rose from 111,000 bunches in 1883 to 10,163,000 bunches in 1914.[7] Bolivian exports of tin, amounting to no more than 3,750 metric tons as late as 1897, began an exceptionally rapid rise a year later and reached 16,230 metric tons by the year 1900; in 1913, they reached a prewar high of 44,590 metric tons.[8]

These export increases, which constitute one of the two main features of the period, did not come about solely through the spontaneous response of Latin American economic organization to new market opportunities abroad. On the contrary, supply elasticity was a function of such things as the new railways which were built to link interior regions with deep water ports, the new communications facilities which were installed to connect producing areas with commercial centers at home and abroad, the new technology of production which was applied in mining and agriculture, and the new public utilities and port facilities which assisted the movement of people, goods, and information into organizational structures of a reasonably modern type. Inasmuch as the economic capabilities of most of the countries were at a low ebb by the middle of the century, the sine qua non of export-led growth was massive injection of capital and skills from abroad. This was the second major feature of the 1850-1914 period.

FOREIGN INVESTMENTS IN LATIN AMERICA

An upward trend in Latin American exports was the material outcome of the foreign capital inflows which resumed around the 1850's and which, in spite of a slump during the serious defaulting episodes of the 1860's and 1870's, continued to come to the region in ever increasing amounts from around 1880 to the decade which closed with the First World War. By 1913, foreign investments in Latin America totaled some 8.5 billion dollars. Almost one-third was invested in government obligations. The balance represented direct investments in a variety of enterprises, but especially railways which accounted for approximately 2.9 billion dollars of the total. The largest portion of the remaining investments was in public utilities and mining, and lesser amounts were placed in agriculture, real estate, banking and finance, shipping, commerce, and manufacturing.[9]

These estimates are quite rough and relate chiefly to nominal values. Aside from the incompleteness and quality of the statistical records, there are so many other difficulties involved in making the computations of foreign investment estimates that it is imperative that the figures be taken only in a quite general way. For one thing, stockwatering was certainly present in many of the corporate issues, though to what extent there is no way of ascertaining. In any event, there was a considerable variance between the nominal and real capitalization of many enterprises. Furthermore, the complexities of finance were often so involved that one can never be sure just how much of the stated value of foreign-owned enterprises, especially in the railway and utility fields, represented a transfer of capital from abroad and how much was contributed by various forms of local subvention, some of which, however, also were financed through public borrowing abroad. Still another problem in determining the net transfer of real capital to Latin America stems from the difficulty of segregating the initial and subsequent contributions of external resources from the increases in asset value which were attributable to reinvestment of the earnings generated in the course of production. On the basis of this distinction, for example, some (such as Moura, in Brazil) have contended that foreign investors actually brought in from the outside only a relatively modest proportion of the total value their enterprises eventually came to have, and that the bulk of the capitalization of foreign companies over the long run was, in effect, provided out of the performance of the recipient economies themselves. To the extent that this was true, however, it tends to negate the charge which is also frequently made that foreign investors were "draining" the region of resources through quick repatriation of capital and heavy dividend remittances; it also suggests that perhaps a major contribution of foreign investment activity was not so much its initial addition of external resources to the local factor endowment as its introduction of productive skills and the organizational mechanisms needed for fostering capital accumulation processes within the host regions.

An additional problem in calculating the actual amount of foreign capital available to Latin America during the period in question stems from the difficulty of identifying the nationality of business firms and their sources of capital. A good many enterprises, for example, were operated by resident foreigners who did not raise capital through stock flotations in the European capital markets but who did have recourse to short- and intermediate-term bank credit from abroad. Typical of these were the trading firms which played such an important role in expanding Latin American agricultural exports and which handled a large portion of the imports. But a similar precaution is in order with respect to the small-scale manufacturing enterprises which were started by immigrant entrepreneurs during the period. Moreover, it is probable that all the existing estimates of foreign investment give insufficient recognition to the bank capital and shipping capital which were involved in the marketing of Latin American exports and imports; yet, these were critical to the expansion of regional output.

As for the portfolio investments in public bond issues, two partially offsetting factors must be kept in mind. On the one hand, the nominal values of outstanding government securities represented foreign legal claims more accurately than they represented the actual foreign financial contributions measured by those claims. The discounts at which Latin American governmental obligations were placed in the European capital markets were often heavy and the charges exacted by European investment banking houses were quite high. For example, the Peruvian bond issue of 1870 gave British investors securities nominally worth £ 12 million (bearing a stated interest rate of 6 per cent) at a price of 82.5, while the £ 15 million, 5 per cent issue of 1872 was taken by the British public at 77.5. Some £ 3,400,000 of Costa Rican 6 and 7 per cent bonds were placed in the British capital market during 1871 and 1872 at prices ranging from 72 to 82. On the other hand, if part of the creditors' claims were fictitious in origin, so were the debtors' promises to pay. Debt obligations were often scaled down considerably during the renegotiation of defaulted claims, new bond issues were exchanged for interest obligations long in arrears, and many of the bond emissions subscribed abroad ultimately had to be written off altogether.

Nevertheless, with due allowance for measurement problems of this type, it is clear that between 1850 and 1914 a large number of foreign concerns had responded to the beckoning export opportunities and to the growing foreign investment capability of the center economies by setting up business operations in Latin America. Still larger numbers of foreign investors had made available funds to the various Latin American governments. The prospective returns on investments had become great enough to offer some measure of compensation for the risks of doing business in the area, and the risks had lessened owing to the relatively greater political stability which had been attained in several of the countries by the last quarter of the nineteenth century as compared with earlier decades. Indeed, the three elements —political stabilization, rising trade, and rising investment—were to some extent mutually dependent, inasmuch as the governments of the region soon learned that it was easier to grant lucrative concessions to foreigners in exchange for assistance in securing foreign loans than to get revenue by imposing controversial taxes on their own wealthy classes. For their part, the foreign interests appear generally to have been sympathetic to the more stable, even though authoritarian, regimes in which relatively large military establishments were in substantial measure maintained by loans floated abroad and by taxes levied on foreign trade. The stability these governments could provide for the business environment seemed well worth the comparatively modest investment made in extolling their virtues to the potential purchasers of public bonds in Europe and, later, the United States.

For present purposes, the $8.5 billion estimate mentioned above as the total foreign investment in Latin America as of 1913 should serve well enough to indicate the approximate order of magnitude of the sums involved in this system. The figures to be cited hereinafter, for all their deficiencies, will suggest the relative weight of the constituent parts of the system.

British Capital. Nearly $5 billion of the total foreign stake in Latin America in 1913 had come from Great Britain, which had led off the new era by making heavy subscriptions to government bond issues (two-thirds of the total British investment of £ 180 million in 1880) and investing substantial amounts in the earliest railway lines and public utilities (£ 34 million and £ 11 million respectively, of the 1880 total).[10] During the 1850-1880 period, in fact, British investors had played a direct role in financing 34 railway companies and 24 public utility enterprises, including municipal gas companies, tramways, and waterworks. Steam navigation companies and the earliest telecommunications enterprises were also launched during this era, while lesser amounts of capital went into such activities as mines (£ 3 million), banks (£ 3 million), real estate (£ 494,-000), and meat processing plants.

When the influx of capital accelerated after 1880, British capital was once again clearly in the lead. The stake of the United Kingdom in Latin America nearly doubled in the short span of time between 1900 and 1914 alone. By 1914, Latin America was the site of around 20 per cent of all British overseas investments.

As for the functional fields of investment, approximately 46 per cent of the British capital had by 1913 gone into some 118 railway companies operating in 16 countries; 31 per cent into government bonds; 20 per cent into mining, utility, and other enterprises; and 3 per cent into banking and shipping. Twenty-seven banks or other financial institutions had British owners, as did some 20 oceanic lines engaged in the Latin American trade. River steamers on the La Plata, Magdalena, and Amazon rivers and the steamship line operating on Lake Titicaca were also included among the British holdings. The mining investments comprised 35 nitrate companies in Chile, 23 petroleum companies (half in Mexico, the rest in Peru, Venezuela, Ecuador, and Cuba), and 115 other mining corporations (half of them in Mexico and Colombia, with most of the rest in Chile, Peru, Bolivia, and Venezuela). Nearly every country had some of the 112 public utility companies owned by British interests. Most of the 77 corporate enterprises in real estate, ranching, and plantation agriculture were distributed among Argentina, Brazil, Mexico, Uruguay, Chile, and Ecuador. Of the manufacturing investments, the most important were the meat-processing plants in Argentina, Brazil, and Uruguay. Other British-owned installations were producing tanning materials, beer, textiles, matches, cement, and flour.[11] A geographical distribution of the British holdings is presented in Table VII-1.

French Capital. French capital had been in Latin America from an early date, albeit in much smaller quantity than that supplied from the United Kingdom. During the 1850's, French subscriptions to Peruvian government securities added significantly to the regional investment, owing to the participation of Dreyfus et Cie. in the guano finance system, and during the early 1860's, French investors afflicted with the contagion of Napoleon III's dream of a new empire had made purchases of the bonds issued by the ill-starred regime of Emperor Maximilian in Mexico. After 1870 the flow of French funds to the region stepped up considerably. Between 1900 and

Table VII-1. British Investments in Latin America in 1913

COUNTRY	NOMINAL AMOUNT	PER CENT OF TOTAL
Argentina	$1,860,700,000	37.34
Brazil	1,161,500,000	23.31
Mexico	807,622,000	16.21
Chile	331,691,000	6.65
Uruguay	239,727,000	4.81
Cuba	222,223,000	4.46
Peru	133,292,000	2.67
Guatemala	52,226,000	1.04
Venezuela	41,350,000	.83
Colombia	34,470,000	.69
Costa Rica	33,300,000	.67
Honduras	15,716,000	.32
Paraguay	15,579,000	.31
Ecuador	14,505,000	.29
El Salvador	11,124,000	.22
Nicaragua	6,196,000	.12
Bolivia	2,099,000	.04
	$4,983,320,000	100.00%

SOURCE: Max Winkler, *Investments of United States Capital in Latin America,* p. 280.

NOTE: The estimates presented in J.F. Rippy, *British Investments in Latin America, 1822—1949*, p. 68, are essentially similar. Certain differences appear in H. Feis, *op. cit.,* p. 23.

1914 there was an approximately threefold increase in the nominal value of French holdings in Latin America. In 1914, the French capital in the region constituted some 13 per cent of the total French investments overseas.[12] Investments in government securities constituted around 30 per cent of the French Latin American holdings, while railway investments represented a nearly similar proportion. Banking and finance, mining and commerce, public utilities and manufacturing, and agriculture and real estate were each about 10 per cent of the total of approximately $1.7 billion.[13] Of the $518 million placed in government securities, the overwhelming majority were in Brazil ($176 million), Mexico ($150 million), and Argentina ($128 million). The railway investments of $441 million were about equally concentrated in Brazil ($278 million), Argentina ($120 million), and Mexico ($38 million), as were the other investments in economic enterprises which totaled some $716 million. Of this latter, Brazil again led the list with $246 million, Mexico was a close second with $211 million, and Argentina was third with $152 million.

French investments in banking were particularly consequential in Mexico, Argentina, Uruguay, and Brazil. French-owned minerals properties were located primarily in Mexico (e.g., the important copper mine of Boleo in Baja California), Venezuela, Chile, Bolivia, Colombia, and Brazil. Real estate holdings were concentrated in Argentina, Uruguay, Mexico, and Cuba. Ranching and forest products enterprises were located in Chile, Peru, Paraguay, Venezuela, and Colombia. The French were also active in developing Bolivian rubber. Comparatively little French capital, however, was invested in public utilities, except for minority interests in companies operating in Argentina, Brazil, and Mexico. Numerous mercantile houses were French owned, including some of the most important dry-goods department stores such as the Palacio de Hierro which was established by the French in Mexico City in 1891. Textile, hosiery, paper, and flour mills; cigarette, cosmetics, hat, and perfume factories; distilleries and breweries; glass factories; foundries; and metal working plants were among the manufacturing enterprises set up during this period by French entrepreneurs. Unlike the British, rather little French investment went into meat-processing plants.

United States Capital. Capital from the United States had appeared in a small way before 1850 in Mexico, Cuba, and Chile. It had gone into mining, agriculture, forest products, and mercantile establishments.[14] Various North American shipping lines were servicing Latin America's foreign trade, and Yankees were also to be found operating steamboat lines on the Magdalena and the Orinoco, and in Ecuador.

After the pattern of European investments in Latin America, the last quarter of the nineteenth century saw a marked acceleration of the flow of United States capital to Latin America, especially to Mexico, Cuba, and Central America. By the end of 1897 an estimated $320 million was invested south of the Rio Grande. Among the chief objects of this investment were: Mexican railways ($111 million), Mexican mining ($68 million), Cuban sugar ($32 million), Central American plantation agriculture ($7 million), Central American railways (nearly $6 million), and Colombian and Ecuadorean railways (nearly $6 million). Other mining investments totaling around $9 million had been made in Colombia, Ecuador, Peru, and Honduras. Nearly $7 million had entered the agricultural and forest products fields in Colombia, Venezuela, Panama, Peru, and Brazil, but this was less than the $12 million which had entered the agricultural, ranching, and forestry fields in Mexico. From the 1880's on, North American concerns were especially active in developing telephone companies in Latin America.[15]

Spectacular rises occurred after 1900; by 1914, United States investments in the Latin American region were about five times what they had been in 1897. Excluding investments in cables and shipping, they totaled over $1.6 billion by the end of 1914. Mexico, Cuba, Chile, Central America, and Peru ranked as the major recipients of this capital outflow. Table VII-2 presents one of the more painstaking estimations of the distribution of United States investments at the onset of the First World War, but the usual caveats are in order regarding the exactness of the figures.

Table VII-2. United States Investments in Latin America, 1914: Millions of Dollars

COUNTRY	TOTAL	GOVERNMENT SECURITIES	RAILWAYS	AGRICULTURE	MINING AND SMELTING	PETROLEUM	PUBLIC UTILITIES	TRADE	MANUFACTURING	OTHER
Mexico	848.0	161.4	110.4	37.0	302.0	85.0	33.2	4.0	10.0	105.0
Cuba	279.6[b]	35.0	13.4	129.0	15.2		58.0	9.0[b]	20.0[b]	
Chile	171.4	0.6			169.8	1.0				
Central America	89.7	3.6	37.9	36.5	11.2			0.5		
Peru	90.0	2.0		3.0	69.0	15.0	1.0			
Colombia	21.0			16.0	3.0	2.0				
Venezuela	6.5			1.0		5.0[c]	0.5			
Haiti	10.8	0.4	10.4							
Dominican Rep.	15.6	4.6		11.0						
Bolivia	10.2	8.2			2.0					
Brazil	8.1	6.1			2.0					
Ecuador	8.6		3.6		5.0					
Paraguay	5.0			5.0						
Argentina	26.9	24.7					1.2			1.0
Undifferentiated South America	27.0							20.0	7.0	
Total	1618.4	246.6	175.7	238.5	579.2	108.0	93.9	33.5	37.0	106.0

SOURCE: Cleona Lewis, America's Stake in International Investments, pp. 575–606, 652–655.

aIncludes investments in companies not under U.S. control.
bIncludes trade and manufacturing in other West Indies countries.
cIncludes asphalt.

Substantial discrepancies exist between Lewis' figures and the estimates made by J.F. Rippy, "Investments of Citizens of the United States in Latin America," loc. cit., p. 21. Rippy's country totals, in cases of major variations, are Argentina ($36 million), Brazil ($28 million), Peru ($62.5 million), and Uruguay ($5.5 million), the last mentioned of these not appearing at all in the Lewis estimates. The country estimates made by Max Winkler, op. cit., p. 275, also vary considerably from the Lewis figures in several cases. According to Winkler, the country totals as of the end of 1913 were, in the cases of major discrepancies: Argentina ($40 million), Brazil ($50 million), Chile ($15 million), Colombia ($2 million), Peru ($35 million), Venezuela ($3 million), Central America ($41 million). From the information provided in the three original studies, it is not possible to reconcile the discrepancies, but the differences are not germane to the discussion.

Discrepancies of statistical estimation aside, however, it can be seen that the United States investment pattern differed considerably from the British and French in several respects. Government securities and railways occupied a far less prominent place in the portfolio of United States investors and a larger portion of total holdings was in economic enterprises producing for export to the home country. Indeed, not a few of the United States companies involved in Latin American minerals production were already engaged in similar fields at home, and the overseas investments in rails and public utilities were closely linked, geographically, with the areas of investment in export production. As in the British and French cases, Mexico figures prominently as a site for United States foreign investment activity. Brazil, Uruguay, and Argentina were comparatively ignored by United States investors, who found their other major opportunities in the agricultural resources of the Caribbean and Central America and in the mineral wealth of Chile and Peru. United States investors seem also to have been less prominent than their French and British counterparts in organizing banks in Latin America.

German Capital. By 1914, German investments reached between $677 million and $900 million, or some 16 per cent of the total overseas German investments.[16] Argentina was the primary recipient, accounting, according to Rippy, for around $250 million of the total in 1918. Brazil and Mexico followed with $150 million and $105 million respectively. The next 5 investment areas were Chile ($75 million), Guatemala ($35 million), Peru ($21 million), Venezuela ($20 million), and Bolivia ($5 million). Bonds issued by the governments of Argentina, Brazil, Mexico, Chile, and Venezuela attracted the largest portion of the German capital, but not much appears to have gone into the rail transport field and only a relatively small number of public utilities received investments of German capital.

The few German-owned mining companies were mostly in Chile and Bolivia. They acquired considerable importance in the case of the Hochschild interests, or the Fricke and Francke concerns which were absorbed in the early 1900's into the Aramayo mining combine. Numerous farms and ranches in the Platine republics and Brazil were German-owned. Germans were also active in establishing coffee brokerage houses and *fincas* in Guatemala, Mexico, and Costa Rica and in developing cacao plantations in Ecuador.[17] In Peru, some of the largest sugar properties eventually came under German ownership, such as those of the Gildemeister family which also had interests in Chile and elsewhere.[18] Fairly strong in the export-import business and in shipping (with seven steamship lines operating in the Latin American trade), German firms were especially prominent in the distribution of chemicals, dyes, drugs, machinery, and electrical equipment and supplies.

The first of several German banks in Argentina, the Banco Alemán Transatlántico, was established as a subsidiary of the Deutsche Uberseeische Bank of Berlin in 1893. Other branches of the Deutsche Uberseeische Bank were eventually opened in Peru, Bolivia, Mexico, Chile, Brazil, and Uruguay. By the time of the First World War, other important German-initiated banking firms had been established: the Banco Germánico de la América del Sur, the Banco de Chile y Alemania, the Banco Antioqueño, the Banco Mexicano de Comercio e Industria (which merged with the branch of the German Overseas Bank), and the Brasilianische Bank für Deutschland. Insurance was also a field in which German companies were fairly prominent. They were also active in breweries. Moreover, a considerable number of the early domestic manufacturing enterprises were started by German entrepreneurs.

Rather sooner than their French, British, and United States equivalents, however, a number of the German investment holdings lost their distinctive foreign identity—doubtless because of the rupture of ties with the homeland occasioned by the First World War and subsequent developments in Europe. The Hochschild mining interests, for example, came to be identified with Argentine nationality (with heavy Chilean capital participation) while the Gildemeister holdings were increasingly considered to be Peruvian or Chileno-Peruvian in character. Many of the German-launched trading firms, banks, and other enterprises also eventually took on the attributes of residentiary firms. As events of the 1940's were to show, this was sometimes not sufficient to protect them from confiscation at the instigation of the United States.

Other Foreign Investments. Smaller amounts of European capital came from Belgium (mainly for railways and utilities in Argentina and Brazil), from the Netherlands (chiefly for investments in government securities and petroleum in Mexico), from Portugal (largely for investments in public issues, trade, and textiles in Brazil), and from Switzerland. Spanish capital appeared in Mexican tobacco, textiles (where it was a leading element until French interests took over many of the concerns), and trade; in Guatemalan textiles; and in the Argentine dry goods trade and tobacco production. In a number of countries in South America, Italian enterprises in trade, manufacturing, banking (e.g., the Banco Italiano of Lima), mining, and agriculture were quite important, though most of these seem to have been immigrant-initiated firms which soon took on a domestic character.[19] On the other hand, some enterprises launched initially in Latin America, such as the W. R. Grace Company in Peru and the Patiño and Aramayo mining corporations in Bolivia, expanded their scale of operations during this period to the extent that they evolved into international concerns headquartered abroad and were converted into vehicles for foreign investment in the region.[20]

INSTITUTIONAL IMPACT OF FOREIGN INVESTMENT

The rapid build-up of foreign capital in Latin America between 1850 and 1914 should not lead one to think that the massive transfusion of external resources either contributed to or reflected a fundamental change in the general economic environment of the region. Plenty of difficulties still lay in store for those who attempted to implant modern economic organization. As the previously mentioned wave of defaulting in the 1860's and 1870's suggests, the overall picture was still far from being one of smoothly uninterrupted success.

The first efforts to build Colombian railways, for example, were made around the middle of the century; by 1910, the country had built only about 700 miles of scattered lines of track and quite a few of these had been acquired by the government in the course of bankruptcy proceedings. The costly nature of the roadways, unsound finance, and unstable political conditions each contributed to the riskiness of ventures like the Buenaventura–Cali line and the Medellín–Puerto Berrío line. A concession for the former was first let in 1848, but not until 1914 did the road actually reach Cali; the latter, designed to connect the increasingly prosperous Antioquian capital with a river port on the Magdalena, was begun in the 1870's but not completed until 1929. Notwithstanding the railway fever, the principal transport artery of Colombia in 1913 was still the erratic and discontinuous Magdalena river; shipments from the Atlantic coast to Bogotá had to be unloaded and reloaded no less than seven times en route.[21]

The first railway in Mexico was commenced in 1842, but it was not until 1873 that Mexico City and Veracruz were connected by through rail service. A company chartered to build a line between Mexico City and Toluca was authorized to operate a public lottery as one means of financing construction; during the 11 years between chartering and the time the company passed out of existence, only about 12 kilometers of track were built. Similar negative experiences were encountered elsewhere—by the Keith brothers in Costa Rica, by the unfortunate investors in Mexican rubber, and by the justifiably perturbed holders of Peruvian government bonds, to cite only three of the many instances.[22] Yet the failures, of which there were many, must be set against the fact that for the first time the region began to acquire some experience with the forms and modalities of modern economic life. That the process of social transformation was still incomplete by the time the period drew to a close cannot be gainsaid, but in the long run the institutional changes introduced by foreign penetration were of the profoundest consequence and were, if anything, more important in their impact than the actual foreign material capital itself.

New forms of business enterprise and economic organization were brought in to increase the region's capacity to absorb external capital productively, and from the resultant combination of local resources with those obtained from abroad came the striking output increases alluded to above. Throughout the region, mining corporations and corporate plantation and ranching enterprises were established—often by foreign entrepreneurs, it is true, but not without domestic emulation. Peruvian, Bolivian, and Chilean engineers and prospectors participated importantly in the development of the minerals resources of the Andes. The aforementioned case of the Patiño tin company was only a more striking instance, perhaps, in which Latin American nationals adopted the business techniques and practices, even those of considerable sophistication, which had been evolved in the more advanced portions of the globe.[23]

While railway corporations were, in the majority of instances, set up by foreign promoters, technicians, and capitalists, there were nevertheless several ventures in the transport field in which the enterprise, the capital, and even part of the technical skills were supplied from the local environment—as, for instance, in the case of the Colombian railways in which Colombian engineers played a prominent part. Chilean mining corporations were dominant, or nearly so, in both the copper and nitrate industries up until the War of the Pacific. These firms even moved beyond the national borders to assume the leading role in developing Bolivian and Peruvian nitrate deposits. During the last half of the century, the old sugar industry of northeastern Brazil was, with foreign and national capital, radically reorganized on a large-scale corporate basis.[24] In the south, German immigrants were pioneering in the development of rural cooperative associations and pushing along rapidly the capitalistic organization of local productive activity in agriculture and industry. Indeed, the Brazil of the 1850's and 1860's was gripped by what might properly be described as a fever of institutional reorganization as, in the "spirit of *associação*," joint-stock companies made their appearance on every hand and the still young Rio stock exchange experienced a rather dizzying speculative boom.

Deep in the interior of Uruguay, a British traveler in the 1870's encountered joint-stock ranches organized by Montevideo capitalists, both nationals and resident foreigners. One such corporate agricultural enterprise exemplified particularly well the cosmopolitan flavor of the late nineteenth-century Platine area; owned by Messrs. Ramírez, Jackson, Fernández, and O'Neill, the *estancia* was managed by a congenial individual named Breschi.[25] An increasingly modern and commercialized orientation came to suffuse domestic firms as well as foreign firms in agriculture, even where organizational forms remained comparatively unmodified by the norms of collective, corporate enterprise. Such was true for the tens of thousands of coffee *fincas* and *fazendas* and for many of the *estancias* of the Argentine, and Uruguay.[26] With organizational changes in mining and agriculture there came also technological modernization—as a usual concomitant in the case of foreign enterprises but with some diffusion to nationally controlled concerns. For example, Paul Walle observed in the early 1900's that this demonstration effect was clearly at work along the Peruvian coast where the technical improvements introduced since 1870 on foreign-owned sugar plantations had been copied on the domestically owned properties.[27] Meanwhile, over in the Platine republics the innovations made on foreign *estancias* were generally, if with some lag, adopted by native *estancieros*.[28]

Technical and organizational transformation was, however, hardly confined to the field of primary production or to rails and public utilities. To handle the rising volume of exports and imports, there grew up around the ports, capital cities, and other trade centers an expanding network of firms providing financial, marketing, and other commercial services. Mercantile companies, insurance companies, banks, and even, in a few cases, stock exchanges [29] appeared on the scene to perform the myriad economic functions essential to the modern development process, especially those required to build linkages between Latin American producing centers and overseas markets. In most, foreign entrepreneurs figured conspicuously, but Latin American nationals also contributed to this elaboration of tertiary economic structure—most notably, perhaps, in Colombia, Chile, and Brazil. All over the region, Latin Americans were drawn into the constructional work of the times, and, in many countries, Latin Americans were investing their money and talents in new banks, the export-import trade, insurance companies, mining, petroleum production, public utilities, and even manufacturing activity. Often this was done under the stimulus of examples provided by foreigners; sometimes, however, it was done quite independently of foreign initiative. The Comtian enthusiasm for material progress was at work in the intellectual milieu, and even members of the established elite could in many cases see the advantages of tapping the sources of mineral wealth, of developing export agriculture, and of supporting the railway and road construction programs because of the augmenting effect of improved market access on the value of land. The case of Peru is particularly instructive in that many of the social and economic structures inherited from the age of viceregal splendor have been transmitted in only a moderately adulterated form down to the present day. Yet, as Jonathan Levin has so expertly indicated, native Peruvian entrepreneurial elements were quick to appropriate the opportunities presented by the onset of the guano boom, and, though they soon had to cede way for the participation of foreign interests with superior financial backing, the domestic capitalists created out of the inflow of guano earnings (and government fiscal policy) were eventually strong enough to pressure the government for revisions of policy in a direction more conducive to the material interests of the emergent national bourgeoisie.[30]

For Latin America as a whole, however, it was clearly the foreign migrants and their descendents who played the leading role in the renovation of tertiary sector organization. This was especially evident in the field of banking—particularly if one considers, in addition to the Latin American banks established by foreign corporations, the considerable volume of foreign trade financing carried on by banks located in Europe and the United States and which must be viewed, like the foreign-owned shipping lines serving the region, as an inseparable part of the total production environment of the area. Moreover, even when local financial institutions were established, it was not uncommon that a great deal of their initial support came from foreign-owned firms and/or firms controlled by resident foreigners which needed the ancillary services that banking institutions could provide.

The earliest important bank in Chile, for example, was founded by Augustine Edwards, the son of an English physician practicing in Serena, who at an early age launched his career as a merchant and banker, dealing particularly in mining finance.[31] One of the oldest of the Argentine banks, the Banco Tornquist, grew directly out of the operations of a major foreign trading firm of that name. The combination of mercantile and banking capital represented in the Tornquist enterprises eventually became the basis for one of the larger industrial empires in Argentina.[32] In Mexico, the French business community joined forces to establish the influential and durable Banco Nacional de Mexico in 1880 and also subscribed in 1887 to a substantial share of the stock of the Banco de Londres y Mexico which was reorganized out of the previously founded (1864) London Bank of Mexico and South America.[33] In Costa Rica, the oldest commercial bank was the Anglo Costarricense (chartered in 1863), the name of which speaks for itself. The first Banco Nacional de Costa Rica, established in 1867, was set up on the basis of capital contributed by the government (100,000 pesos), by the British contractor John Thompson (100,000 pesos), and from a loan of 100,000 pesos which Thompson negotiated abroad.[34] Most of the capital of the Banco Italiano, which was established in Lima in 1887, was raised among the Italian colony of Lima-Callao. Resident Italian mercantile concerns also assisted in the establishment of the Banco de Callao which, in 1897, was amalgamated with the Lima branch of the London Bank of Mexico and South America to form the Bank of Peru and London. The close relationship between the Wiese export-import house of Lima and the prominent German-Peruvian bank which later took the name of Banco Wiese provides yet another instance of the rather prevalent association between mercantile capital generated in the foreign trade sector and the earliest modern-type of banking capital in Latin America.

Besides assisting the establishment of banks, foreign marketing enterprise continued to play the decisive role it had assumed during the first half of the century in managing the flow of goods for activities in both the external and domestic sectors. The preeminent position of foreign-initiated firms in organizing the export and import traffic of Central America has been noted above. In Peru, a country which also received comparatively little of the contemporary stream of European immigrants, the commercial life of Lima, particularly the foreign trade sector, centered to a surprising extent around the firms organized by immigrant entrepreneurs from France, Germany, Great Britain, and Italy.[35] Although an early twentieth-century listing of the most important houses engaged in Peru's foreign trade contains some Spanish names, the uncontested majority were foreign names such as Duncan, Fox, and Company, Graham, Rowe, and Company, E. W. Gibson,

Backus and Johnston, Humphreys and Company, J. Ferrand, P. Herrouard, Nosiglia Hermanos, A. and F. Wiese, F. G. Piaggio, G. Berckemeyer, J. Gildemeister—not to mention of course, W. R. Grace and Company. Even the apparent nationality of firm names is misleading and underestimates the role of foreign initiative. Another important Lima merchant of the times for example, was Antônio Sousa Ferreira, a scion of the Portuguese nobility which for a long time had been committed to the realm of international trade and finance. The Casa Ferreyros, which later became the center of one of the major investment groups in twentieth-century Peru, was established in the latter part of the nineteenth century as an export-import house by Spanish immigrants of Galician origin.

Among the larger countries, marketing enterprises established by foreigners were no less important in the general economic structure. In Mexico between 1850 and 1870, for example, the chief commercial rivalry was among resident foreign merchants in that country. French firms gradually displaced the German mercantile concerns which had controlled most of the distribution of imported manufactures. The English, Spanish, and German houses dealing in textiles likewise gave way before the aggressive trade incursions of the French merchants. The wholesale and retail distribution of imported clothing items was virtually monopolized by the French by 1883,[36] although firms established originally by nationals of other countries continued to play an important role in other portions of the trade sector. In Argentina, a preponderant portion of the mercantile sector was also directed by foreigners—especially the British, who helped build the links between the Argentine and its chief overseas market, and the Italians, who, representing about one-half of all the foreigners living in the Argentine in 1895, were ubiquitous as managers of the domestic traffic in goods.[37]

In Brazil, too, British commercial houses were of singular importance for much of the century. There were 75 established in Rio de Janeiro (alongside around 200 Portuguese firms) as early as 1811. By the closing decades of the 1800's, however, Portuguese merchants, backed up by the resources gathered by their agencies and by banks in Portugal, came both to dominate the import trade and to control much of the local distribution system as well.[38] Also significant by the late 1800's were the German-operated foreign trade concerns. Around São Paulo and elsewhere in southern Brazil a sizable portion of local retailing and wholesaling functions was in the hands of Italian immigrants. By 1911, they were facing strong competition in the domestic marketing network from recent arrivals from the Levant.[39]

Nearly everywhere in Latin America, the foregoing examples of foreign-initiated marketing development could be duplicated. While the majority of studies which have been made of the late nineteenth century period of expansion have tended to focus (1) upon the reorganization of primary production by foreign investment activity and the pull of export markets,

(2) upon the field of railways and utility development, or (3) upon the commodity trends and financial relationships recorded in the balance of international payments, one does well to keep in mind that all of these developments required significant innovations in the marketing structure of the Latin American economies. Clearly, the rudimentary mercantile organization left as an aftermath of colonial rule would not suffice to realize the Smithian connection between the extent of the market and economic growth. The economic functions involved in moving increasingly large quantities of imported capital equipment and consumer goods into the region and for disposing of the rising regional product abroad, in other words, presupposed the concurrent introduction and evolution of marketing enterprises which could perform the essential distributional functions implied by the dynamics of economic expansion. Similarly, the spreading commercialization of economic life implied by the transition to a market economy gave new importance to the organizational effectiveness of the institutional machinery of trade and distribution. Moreover, that which, in Europe, the commercial revolution had historically accomplished somewhat prior to the industrial revolution and which had partially laid the groundwork for the full flowering of the latter phenomenon had, in the Latin American case, to be undertaken to a considerable extent concomitantly with the technological revamping of the economy. From this derives the social organizational importance of the pioneering marketing activities performed by the foreign-initiated trade concerns in Latin America throughout the century between the break with Spain and the First World War. Comparatively neglected as objects of scholarly scrutiny, they were nevertheless as indispensable to the formation of modern Latin America as the introduction of rail transport or commercial banking.

The "Domestication" of Foreign Investment. In considering the foreign impetus in banking and marketing development, however, one moves into a field in which the "outside" agents of production begin to take on a character somewhat different from that of the foreign-owned public utility, railway, maritime shipping, mining, sugar, and banana companies. Institutionally speaking, the banks and commercial houses shared some of the aspects of many of the foreign-initiated coffee and ranching enterprises, or of the small-scale manufacturing establishments set up locally by foreign entrepreneurs. In the case of the utility-mining-sugar-and-banana complex, there was a distinct tendency for the control center of the enterprise to remain abroad and the Latin American firm to operate as a subsidiary appendage. Among the banks, the trading companies, the *fazendas-fincas-estancias* of agriculture, and the small factories, there was, in contrast, a certain assimilative tendency. By a process of domestication, these latter enterprises—even when established by foreigners on a rationale which lay, just as much as in the case of mining, in the flow of international trade activity—came to be incorporated into the surrounding economic environment of the host country to a comparatively high degree.

It seems probable, for instance, that most of the banking capital in Latin America, including the financial assets at the disposition of "foreign" banks, grew out of banking operations themselves. Since banking systems tend to grow up in the economies they serve, it is doubtful that any major part of banking resources can be abstracted from the milieu in which they exist. Overall, comparatively little foreign banking capital may actually have immigrated to Latin America, and most of that which did tended to become integrated with Latin American finance and to become far more significant quantitatively after integration than when it first immigrated. Similarly, the Latin American commercial houses established by foreigners may well have received their initial stake from foreign loans and from capital brought over by their founders, and doubtless a substantial share of their business was financed thereafter by means of credits obtained from abroad. But the equity capital of the firms was almost certainly built up chiefly out of mercantile services as intermediaries for internal distribution and as the organizational links between the domestic economy and ultramarine markets and supply sources.

In both banking and mercantile operations, the critical import from abroad was not so much the external capital transfer as the introduction of organizational mechanisms through which capital accumulation was fostered as an integral part of the expansion of the national economies in which these firms were established.[40] Moreover, where conditions permitted, the firms of the tertiary sector tended to remain as permanent institutional features of the domestic structure, directed by the resident foreign owners and, later, by their offspring, either alone or in association with native businessmen and investors.[41] Domiciled in the Latin American republics, these firms often evolved as enterprises in which the "foreign" nature lay largely in the national origin and language of the founder. Otherwise they tended to be indistinguishable, except in caliber of performance and the degree of their continuing contact with foreign markets and institutions, from a "pure" domestic firm.[42] Indeed, many of these foreign-initiated but domestically domiciled firms in trade and finance assumed a prominent entrepreneurial role in feeding back the capital they had gathered from tertiary sector activity into the development of domestic manufacturing firms which often had little connection with the foreign trade sector except for the importation of machinery and equipment and the initial origin of some of their venture capital.

Thus, among these firms, one can detect a rudimentary catalytic process at work which anticipated what was later to become one of the chief values of foreign investment activity. Already there were, in effect, appearing joint participation ventures which combined local capital and talent with foreign capital and/or entrepreneurship. Sometimes the domestic participants were brought in through intermarriage, as in the case of Thomas Armstrong, an Irish merchant-financier in the Argentine.[43] Sometimes they were involved for their influential political connections. And sometimes they were simply attracted to the new projects by the persuasive blandishments of foreign promoters and organizers. In any case, foreign investment activity began its role of inducing an accompanying process of domestic capital formation and gave rise—particularly in commerce, finance, manufacturing, and agriculture—to a process which in some ways resembled the migration of people: the migration of firms (and their entrepreneurs and managers).

PUBLIC POLICIES DURING ECONOMIC EXPANSION

Both ideologically and pragmatically, the public policies adopted in Latin America during the 1850-1914 period of global economic expansion appeared to be vindicated. Social vindication, such as it was, took several forms. Material self-interest was, of course, not the least of these. Even among those who cared little for political and economic doctrines, there came to be an awareness that an expanding and taxable external sector and increased public borrowing abroad were attractive substitutes for heavier local taxation. And with the expansion of government revenues, there were created new sources of income for those in, or with preferential access to, the machinery of state. Military leaders, civilian functionaries, and politicians alike had much to gain from the stepped-up flow of money into public coffers. Large landowners, financiers, and merchants could also profit from the widening array of commercial opportunities and the windfall gains in asset values which came from the economic developments of the time. The exogenous influences described previously were basic to contemporary Latin American economic growth and change; no less important was the circumstance that domestic conditions were receptive to the introduction of policies which took partial advantage of these influences.

Ideological Trends

Although oligarchic rule was a general feature of the region down to 1914, and even thereafter, not everywhere was this oligarchy a totally benighted group. Among the elite, many of whom went to Europe for their education, there were more than a few who were caught up in a general spirit of modernism and material progress. In Latin America, the intellectual ascendancy of these notions was pushed strongly by the thinkers and writers who dominated the universities, who wrote for the press, and who were often very much *engagés* in the political arena. In southern South America especially, the concepts of Saint-Simonianism had been propagated fairly widely by Esteban Echeverría in Argentina and Francisco Bilbao in Chile. Of far greater import in the first half of the century, though, was the diffusion of Bentham's utilitarianism, the philosophical notions of James Mill, and Adam Smith's teachings on political economy. Heavily influenced by these were such key public figures as José M. L. Mora (the chief theoretician of Mexican liberalism), Andrés Bello of Venezuela and Chile (the guiding spirit in the founding of the University of Chile), and José Cecilio del Valle of Central America. But nowhere perhaps were the new currents of thought more articulately propounded than in Argentina, where J. B. Alberdi and Domingo Sarmiento labored incessantly on behalf of libertarian ideals.

Manifesting an admiration of the United States that bordered on adulation, imbued with an apostolic zeal for education, and extending an enthusiastic welcome to European immigration for its broadly civilizing influence, the active members of this eminent band of *pensadores* did much to prepare the way for the gospel of national salvation through foreign investment, trade, and immigration. In keeping with the philosophies they borrowed, most of these exponents of "romantic liberalism" preached a minimal and essentially passive role for the state. Opting for laissez faire in the classic nineteenth-century liberal fashion, they saw progress primarily in the advance of private industry and the spread of progressive attitudes through education.[44] For them, the state was primarily the guardian of the public order. Most of them explicitly rejected the notion of using state intervention to foster and promote economic advance in an active manner.[45] Even among those whose philosophical positions remained more traditional and disposed to interventionism, distinct advantages were sometimes seen in turning to foreign capital with a zest that went beyond simple laissez faire. Conservative that he was, Lucas Alamán espoused many of the ideas of liberal political economy and saw Mexico's main hope in attracting British capital to turn that country's disorganized mining resources to account.[46]

After mid-century, however, certain subtle, and not always explicitly developed, shifts of thinking began to emerge as the positivism of Auguste Comte and Herbert Spencer made considerable headway among intellectual circles of the politically active. Mingled at first with the economic precepts of John Stuart Mill, positivism was later blended with the social evolutionary version of Darwinism. In Argentina, Bartolomé Mitre and Augustín F. Alvárez Suárez were among the outstanding advocates of positivism. In Brazil, liberal republicanism was shaped strongly by the work of such men as Miguel Lemos and Antônio Teixeira Mendes who, aside from founding churches of positivism, succeeded in having the positivist motto, Order and Progress, emblazoned on the national flag. In Chile, José Lastarria and Diego Barros Arana were two of the prominent figures who championed Comtian and Spencerian tenets in the formation of public policy—the latter man, rector of the National Institute, working, as did positivists elsewhere, especially through the vehicle of public education. Mexican positivism got its first real start through the influence of Gabino Barreda who reorganized the educational system under Juárez; but it was Justo Sierra, Porfirian Minister of Education and founder of the resurrected national university, who earned the description given him by José Vasconcelos as the Mexican "high priest of positivism."

Indeed, thanks to the efforts of men such as Sierra, Francisco Bulnes, José Limantour, and others in the coterie of top governmental advisors in Porfirian Mexico (the so-called *científicos*), positivism was elevated to a position resembling an official ideology.[47] All over the continent, "positivism provided the basic structure of Latin American thought during the last half of the nineteenth century, coming to the zenith of its popularity between 1880 and 1900. . . . Nowhere else did positivism achieve a stronger hold upon the directing class of society than in Latin America." [48] Purporting to offer a scientific approach to the problems of organizing national life, positivism came to function as the ideological instrument for forging a consensus among the forces concerned with building a strong (and usually laicized) society and state.[49]

Viewed in some of its aspects, positivism was clearly the offspring of the earlier romantic or utopian liberalism. Like liberalism, it was predisposed to a capitalistic ideology, defending the institution of private property as the basis of society (not merely as the source of *goces personales* as did the theologians) and upholding the private accumulation of wealth as the principal instrument of progress. As an argument for plutocracy, positivism reiterated the liberal view of the absolute rights of private property in opposition to the conditional or contingent character of private property manifested in traditional Hispanic teachings. Drawing upon social Darwinism, it further justified the riches of the upper classes as evidence of mental and moral superiority and argued that economic inequality was necessary to reward intelligent leadership.[50] Positivism also followed liberalism in repudiating welfare regulations and redistributive measures as detrimental to social advance. For the most part, the positivists differed little from their liberal predecessors in denigrating both the Hispanic and indigenous roots of Latin American culture and in upholding foreign economic and cultural models for national progress.[51]

Despite these similarities, the positivistic concept of the state as an active agent of social change and as a principal ordering force in society placed the late nineteenth-century Latin American policy framework somewhat closer to the Iberian and continental tradition of public policy than was the older version of classical liberalism. This was not, however, always clear from the written expressions of positivism. Some—e.g., Gabino Barreda in Mexico and Lastarria and many others in Chile—seemed to favor laissez faire and a narrowly delimited "watchdog" state.[52] But for most positivist leaders, the idea of state economic withdrawal was, partly, one of the impracticable (or perhaps premature) notions of the early romantic liberals and, partly, an ideal the realization of which lay in the future rather than the present. For the time being, active state intervention was justified to promote and encourage what was deemed to be progress.[53]

Accordingly, whatever their abstract preferences, the new national leadership generally favored policies which actually involved the state in doing quite a number of things to install a capitalistic economic system. Indeed, given the inherited weakness of domestic private institutions, it seems likely that complete laissez faire was often not considered to be a meaningful or practical policy alternative. The instrumental role of the state, in other words, appeared as a matter of common sense; however much the international market was counted on to become the prime mover in economic affairs, the state was used extensively to steer the local economy toward that mechanism and to build up the linkages with it.

Thus during the 1850-1914 period when the pull of foreign markets was dramatic and triggered a sizable foreign investment boom, the new wave of foreign investment activity, led initially by railway construction and municipal public utilities, got under way with strong assistance from supporting state intervention. Given the substantial amounts of external resources that were transferred to the public sector by government borrowing between 1850 and 1914, given the generous use of public subventions for various enterprises, and given the franchise nature of many foreign investments (in rails, utilities, shipping lines, and other concessionary ventures), it is clear that much more was involved than mere routine business transactions carried on by free private enterprises in a pure market context.

The point is worth emphasizing, if only to modify the interpretation which has posited a long period of laissez-faire economic liberalism between the interventionistic period of colonialism and what has, on occasion, been described as the neomercantilism of the twentieth century. In view of the frequently encountered nineteenth-century speeches and essays which propounded a minimal theory of the state, it is easy to understand why such a policy deviation should be assumed to have occurred. Yet, when the record of actual policy is examined, it is difficult to detect a rupture of this sort in the continuity of development policy except in a comparatively few instances. Beyond the brief but inconclusive flirtations with laissez faire during the years immediately following political emancipation from Spain and Portugal, and apart from the limited laissez faire policies pursued by Chile and a few other states for somewhat longer intervals, there does not appear to have been any radical departure from a *dirigismo* of one sort or another. Changes in orientation there certainly were between the administered economy of the Spanish system and the interventionism which was introduced under the guise of economic nationalism during the twentieth century. But a certain basic continuity in policy tradition can be detected throughout the history of the area in the role of the state as an active participant in economic processes. It does not follow, however, that the governments of the region were necessarily performing their development functions effectively. In the era of positivism, state intervention was not employed to revamp the domestic institutional framework in any radical fashion. Instead, what was involved was a state-fostered development of the external sector to obtain some sort of maximal economic growth within a context of minimal restructuring of domestic institutions. One way or another, governmental decisions figured significantly in setting the conditions of economic development in the region.[54]

Policies Promoting Property Redistribution

The state intervened in four ways to affect the distribution of rural sector assets. The first of these techniques divested a large portion of the Indian communities of their traditional land holdings and transferred these properties to the large estates. From a regional perspective, this culminated in the Mexican liberal reforms of the 1850's. The shift in control over the means of production also transferred to the latifundia the effective control over a large segment of the region's available rural work force.

The second technique had its origins in the church-state squabbles of the times and in liberal views regarding the desirability of reducing the temporal privileges of ecclesiastical authority. In Mexico, a second long-term result of the liberal reforms of the 1850's was that many of the extensive rural properties of the church passed into private hands, creating new private latifundia as well as adding substantially to the size of preexisting ones. Colombian liberalism dealt in like manner with ecclesiastical estates in the 1860's.[55] When the Guatemalan liberal group returned to power under the dictatorship of Justo Rufino Barrios in 1871, they too confiscated all church properties (including church buildings and cemeteries) and distributed the booty in a manner which hardly corresponded with egalitarian principles. A good many of the church's rural estates in Venezuela were seized by the government of the dictator Guzmán Blanco in the 1870's. Many of the lands of the church in Ecuador were expropriated during the liberal revolution of 1895. Very often in these situations, political cronies and influential landowners were the direct beneficiaries of these asset transfers, but in Ecuador and Peru a more devious method of accomplishing the same end was employed. In both countries, the former church properties were generally transferred to lay or secular "public welfare" societies (*asistencia pública* in Ecuador, *beneficencia pública* in Peru) which were mostly controlled by the landed gentry. As trustees of the societies, they commonly leased the lands to themselves at very low or nominal rates of charge. Regardless of the manner of disposition employed, however, the expropriation of church properties benefited only those associated with the institution of latifundism.

On an even grander scale, the state intervened in the distribution of rural holdings by disposing of large blocs of the public domain during the 1850-1914 period, including tracts of land already occupied by squatters. In some cases, most notably the areas of Spanish America affected by the advent of the coffee boom, fairly large portions of the public domain were ceded to peasant proprietors or medium-scale farmers who had migrated to the appropriate lands to devote them to this increasingly important cash crop. The *tierras templadas* of the slopes of the central and western cordilleras in Colombia were occupied in this manner.[56] A similar pattern of settlement appears to have prevailed in Costa Rica [57] and parts of Venezuela. As time went on, however, the economics of scale available with improvements in coffee processing, the gestation period between initial plantings and subsequent harvests, and the weak position of small producers in times of price fluctuations tended to promote the growth of larger landholding units.[58]

In general, though, small-unit distribution of the public domain was rather exceptional during this era. Even in Costa Rica, the land most noted for the prevalence of family farms, large blocks of the public domain were given away to settle outstanding government debts during the second half of the century. Larger-scale land parcels were distributed in Guatemala too, where coffee cultivation, present on a small-scale basis since the latter part of the eighteenth century, began to acquire importance as an export crop after 1850. Particularly was this the case when Barrios came to office in the 1870's and launched a program to foster agricultural export expansion in an effort to offset the declining indigo and cochineal industries which, after the development of aniline dyes around 1857, were heading rapidly for extinction.[59] Expropriated church lands and lands from the public domain were granted freely or sold at nominal prices, usually in large blocs, to those who would devote them to new agricultural uses such as cattle ranching and cacao, sugar, rubber, and coffee cultivation. Since wagon roads were being pushed into new territories and railway construction had been commenced to link the interior with the Caribbean coast, the lands ceded by the government constituted a substantial developmental subsidy for the export-oriented agricultural activities.

Though generalizations must always be qualified for a period characterized by such mixed trends, it can be said that the Guatemalan disposition of public territory was fairly typical of the land policies of most governments in the region. Indeed, the average size of the land holdings established elsewhere by government grants and sales was undoubtedly far larger than in the Guatemalan case. In several countries of Central America, much more extensive tracts of land were allotted the 20 major companies which pioneered the development of banana culture from the 1870's on. When many of these companies were consolidated into the United Fruit Company in the 1890's, the phenomenon of corporate *latifundismo* reached unprecedented proportions. To promote banana development, public lands were given away, sold for nominal prices, or rented at very low charges to the users.[60]

For a while it appeared that Chile might develop its southern territory on the basis of medium-sized landholding units. This was the pattern of land tenure, for instance, which prevailed in the German colonies established around Valdivia in the middle of the century. But as the warlike Araucanian Indians were driven further to the south, the *fundos* (Chilean haciendas) which already dominated the central valley put in their appearance and came to hold most of the more valuable southern land as well. The same occurred in Argentina, where initially some consideration was given to the possibilities of strengthening yeoman farming with the emphyteusis law. It soon became clear, however, that huge *estancias* would occupy the major portion of the pampa lands which were eventually cleared of Indians by General Roca in 1879. Even beyond the rich pampa region it was the extensive ranch which typified the private holdings which were created from the public domain. In the Mexico of the Porfirian age, the government handed out land on a scale so lavish that possibly only in Argentina were the dimensions of new property units of equivalent magnitude.

Elsewhere in Latin America the story was much the same. While much of the public domain in Bolivia, Peru, and Ecuador lay in the interior, isolated by the Andes and the Amazonian jungles, wherever it did have some actual or potential value, as on the Pacific coast or in the Sierras, it was generally alienated into the hands of the holders of private latifundia. Scarcely anywhere did land policy follow the social and economic criteria incorporated, for instance, into the contemporary Homestead Act of the United States.

Some of these land grants were given as payments to political supporters, while others represented compensation for military services, including service in various Indian wars. Occasionally, "free" land actually occupied by squatters was incorporated into large estates in connection with government measures which permitted denunciation of "unoccupied" lands in order to regularize land titles. In the more arid regions, grants of land with water rights permitted the recipients to add to their acreage by monopoly control of scarce water resources. Sometimes local governments, as in Mexico, sold the lands to which they held title for purposes of raising revenue, and in Mexico, Argentina, Costa Rica, and Bolivia, the national governments used land grants as a means of redeeming public bond issues. Many countries gave land subsidies, often heavy ones, to companies engaged in railway construction; in other instances extensive concessions were given to companies in payment of contracts for surveying the public domain, though the surveys for which payment was given were not always made. Huge land grants, amounting to millions of acres in many cases, were given to "colonization" companies and similar undertakings. These were supposed to develop the territories so awarded, but remarkably little colonization actually occurred in many of these concessions and most, perhaps, were little more than land speculation companies set up with public assets.[61]

In short, the national governments of Latin America, deficient in cash resources, intervened in a massive way with their land resources to affect the conditions of development. Ostensibly, much of this land distribution was oriented toward furthering the development process—by promoting settlement of sparsely inhabited regions, by dedicating more land to commercial production for export, and by financing economic overhead capital. By pacifying the military and otherwise manipulating the spoils system, the land distribution contributed to a measure of political stability. Meanwhile, local population growth, the ever more intensive ultramarine market demand, and the spread of both maritime and overland transport facilities were creating a situation in which public land previously worth little or nothing came to have a value, either actual or speculative, for private owners. The land-grant lures held out by public authority, therefore, were seized with alacrity.

Thus, the commercialization of agricultural life induced by the convergence of international economic forces on Latin America strengthened the system of large landholdings and led to extension of the latifundia on a scale far greater than the colonial period had ever known. Tens of millions of acres passed as a subsidy into the system of large estates, and, by the end of the period, in most countries, nearly all of the most useful lands, or potentially useful lands, had been appropriated by private ownership, either for immediate use, for reserve acreage, for purposes of capturing a labor force, or simply for long-term speculative holding. Though commercial gain was, in a sense, the motivating force, actual commercial use and economic efficiency had comparatively little to do with the process of distribution and subsequent land use in many cases.

Only where significant cost-creating inputs were required to give the land an income value to the new owners did some approximation of commercially effective utilization follow the distribution of public lands to private owners. Such, for example, was the case along the Peruvian coast where irrigation investments were necessary, in Argentina where crop farming had to be introduced to prepare the land for pasturage, in southern Brazil where immigrant workers had to be hired for money wages, and in areas where the production of coffee, cacao, and bananas necessitated land clearing expenses and assumption of gestation-period costs. Even here, however, the size of the farm units and the possibilities for labor exploitation doubtless served to reduce the pressure on the owners to maximize economic efficiency. Elsewhere, the use of land primarily as collateral for borrowing against speculative rises in value, in part produced by the inflationary monetary policies favored by indebted landowners, provided a source of disposable income that had little or no connection with efficiency in land use. Where traditional, nonmonetized techniques of farming were used, scarcely any advance was made beyond the contraproductive regime described in the discussion of colonial latifundism.[62]

Aside from the indirect reallocation of control over rural labor resources which generally resulted from public land policies, some governments of the region intervened more directly to affect the terms of labor supply in the economy. At times, this involved a simple continuation of colonial expedients. In Guatemala, the *mandamiento* regime of conscript Indian labor survived almost intact into the republican era. Under Barrios, an earlier republican law (passed in 1830) was revived to compel all citizens to work three days a year on road construction or else pay a tax as a substitute. For a long period, public magistrates were also authorized to assign a portion of the able-bodied males in each Indian community to work for a specified number of days on haciendas or *fincas*, or in other employment. Later on, this practice was modified to exempt from *mandamiento* service those aboriginals who could supply evidence that they were already working under debt contracts sanctioned in the labor code, but the net intention of government policy was clearly revealed in the instructions issued by Liberal President Barrios in 1876: [63]

> If we abandon the farmers to their own resources and do not give them strong and energetic aid, they will be unable to make any progress, for all their efforts will be doomed to failure due to the deceit of the Indians. You [local magistrates] should therefore see to it: First: that the Indian villages in your jurisdiction be forced to give the number of hands to the farmers that the latter ask for, even to the number of fifty or a hundred to a single farmer if his enterprise warrants this number. Second: when one set of Indians has not been able to finish the work in hand in a period of two weeks, a second . . . should be sent to relieve the first, so that the work may not be delayed. Third: the two weeks work shall be paid for ahead of time through the mayor of the Indian town, thus avoiding the loss of time involved in paying every day. Fourth: above all else see to it that any Indian who seeks to evade his duty is punished to the full extent of the law, that the farmers are fully protected and that each Indian is forced to do a full day's work while in service.

In 1878 the Guatemalan *mandamiento* was finally abolished, though its abolition was not so much a testimony to liberal conscience as to the fact that legally enforceable debt peonage had spread to the extent that the *mandamiento* was no longer necessary. Debt slavery continued until it was outlawed in 1934. After that, a substitute labor mobilization instrument was created in the new vagrancy law which provided that all able-bodied male rural inhabitants between the ages of 18 and 60 and owning less than about 5 or 7 acres of land (depending upon the crop) were required to submit evidence of having worked for a stated period of time (100–150 days) on contract or else be punished as vagrants.

Debt peonage sanctioned by courts of law was the more widespread technique in Latin America for compelling the work force to labor on behalf of the preferred groups of society, especially in agriculture where the *tienda de raya* or company store was utilized to prolong indefinitely the indebtedness of illiterate rural workers to the plantations and haciendas. Moreover, each country had its own version of Barrios' admonition to give "strong and energetic aid" to farmers on labor matters. For example, to supplement the bonds of peonage, Porfirian Mexico relied heavily upon the much feared *rurales*, a national rural police force recruited from former convicts, to instill in the *campesinos* a due regard for the virtues of hard work on the latifundia. A similar debt peonage was by no means unknown in the mining industries of the age. In a practice which recalled the *mita*, as late as 1909 public authorities in certain Sierran districts of Peru could, with a special permit from the central government, intervene directly to "induce the Indians to work at a given mine or plant." [64] Actual slavery, of course, continued to exist until well into the nineteenth century in a number of countries, for example, until 1855 in Peru and until three decades later in Brazil. Convict labor was also employed, albeit on a minor scale, to assist conditions in the labor market, as in the early days of the guano industry.

Compared with the foregoing, other forms of state intervention in the distribution of labor resources were rather more modern in character, although sometimes only marginally so. For instance, to alleviate the labor shortage on the coast of Peru (and, later, as an aid to railway construction), the government subsidized a domestic private company which was given an exclusive concession to import Chinese coolies who could, when landed in Peru, be "sold" to domestic employers on eight-year enforceable work contracts for an average price of 400 pesos each. Between 1849 and 1875, some 90,000 Chinese bonded laborers were imported, at a subsidy of 30 pesos per head—not counting the estimated 10,000 laborers who died en route from Asia.[65] Other countries similarly subsidized the importation of labor, although without the indenture feature of the Peruvian enterprise. Brazil, Uruguay, and Argentina engaged in a variety of means to stimulate the inflow of labor from abroad, advertising (often in misleading terms) the glories of life in the Americas, subsidizing transatlantic passage, and operating employment exchanges and reception centers for the newly arrived. Mostly it was the central government which did this; in Brazil, where state governments were more active, the efforts of the authorities of the state of São Paulo were the most successful along this line.

In southern Brazil, Uruguay, and Argentina, where a reasonably modern system of wage labor came to prevail, alongside a comparatively progressive system of farm tenancy in the latter two countries, government intervention in the labor market was probably all to the good. Elsewhere, however, the policies were such that the commercialization of agriculture contributed little if any to the dissolution of servile relations between landowners and the tillers of the soil, and often, in fact, the servile bonds were intensified.

Public "Fomento" or Development Policies

A host of special promotion measures were brought into play by governments of the 1850-1914 period to modify the variable components of economic decisions taken in the private sector. Agriculture, in particular, was the object of a number of such interventionary measures. Following Spanish precedents, for example, the Guatemalan government established coffee nurseries around the country from which seedlings were distributed free of charge. Coffee producers were granted exemptions from both import and export taxes. To encourage the early banana producers, the Guatemalan treasury paid bounties on new plantings. In 1907 the Chilean government instituted a bounty policy for catches of fish landed by boats of national registry.[66] A wide variety of agricultural products throughout the continent, in fact, were assisted in their beginnings and subsequent development by special bonuses and exemptions from export levies and import duties on the relevant producer goods. Until the 1940's, for example, the United Fruit Company conducted its Latin American operations solely on the basis of special concessionary contracts which exempted it from the payment of income and other local taxes and which either reduced the applicable import and export duties to minor levels or waived them entirely.[67] Occasionally, protectionist measures were employed as well, but generally they were not needed and rarely were they very effective in accomplishing their ends.[68]

Outside of agriculture, the use of cash subsidies was prevalent, especially in the field of infrastructure, as the large public borrowings in foreign capital markets would suggest. The fact that Latin American governments were the main borrowers of external funds is perhaps the most revealing single indicator of the degree of state involvement in economic processes during the late nineteenth century period, for substantial amounts of these funds were employed to modify the economic indicators of the market place and to influence private investment to flow into channels which would guide national economic life towards an export-oriented pattern of development. In other words, during a period in which national private capital was as yet insufficiently developed to assume the leadership in the drive for economic progress, national governments, buttressed by their superior borrowing capacity abroad, stepped in to become the dominant economic force expressing what purported to be the "national interest." Consequently, a very large segment of the foreign capital which came to Latin America between 1850 and 1914 was injected into the local economic processes through the instrumentality of the state, as public investment and as subsidies designed to attract and influence private investment. Given the scale on which the process operated, it would be entirely misleading to construe the era in terms of a simple laissez-faire version of economic liberalism.

Most of the port improvement enterprises, municipal utility companies, and similar ventures, for example, were assisted by public subsidies and, in some cases, also by governmental guarantees of earnings on invested capital. Virtually all of the railway companies which were established in Latin America received heavy subsidies of cash or land or both, and the large majority were given government guarantees for minimum returns on their capital. Investors in Argentine railway concessions were ordinarily guaranteed a 7 per cent return, the guaranteed rate of earnings which seems also to have been typical in the railway concessions of Venezuela.[69] Some states were a bit less generous. Chile guaranteed the concessionaire of the Ferrocarril de Calera a Ovalle only a $5\frac{1}{2}$ per cent interest on invested capital,[70] and the Brazilian railway legislation of 1852 provided for a 5 per cent return, though investors were assured that other railway lines would be excluded from a zone comprising 5 leagues on each side of their right-of-way.[71] Since Brazilian subsidies and guarantees were based on a fixed amount of capital investment per kilometer, it behooved the companies to avoid more costly grades and in consequence lines were apt to meander considerably.[72]

The use of public subvention tended to be employed on a rather indiscriminate basis in the utility and railway field—and not merely because the shortcomings of public administration permitted gross abuses of the privilege. Very often subsidies were used to enhance the profitability of enterprises which were commercially feasible to begin with and which could likely have been built on a nonsubsidized basis. Less frequently, subsidies were used to facilitate the construction of facilities in or to outlying areas to promote the development of these regions and to begin to work towards the attainment of integrated national economies.[73]

In several cases, public expenditures involved the state more directly in the conduct of economic activity, moving beyond the manipulation of market parameters to state ownership of enterprises. As early as 1841, for example, the government of Peru had revised its policy regarding the guano business so as to change, in effect, the institutional character of the industry from that of a licensed private enterprise to a mixed enterprise with a substantial government-held equity interest.[74] Approximately three decades later, the Peruvian government attempted the nationalization of the nitrate deposits as well; this precipitated a disastrous war which resulted in the loss of that valuable asset to Chile. Subsequently, during the ill-fated presidential administration of Balmaceda, Chile launched an aggressive program of economic nationalism which included, among other points, the government's acquisition of key railway lines in the nitrate mining area and, for a while at least, a plan for state operation of a substantial portion of the nitrate industry.[75] In Argentina, direct state participation in the new petroleum industry was inaugurated in 1908.

In the railway field, however, state enterprises were far more common. Peruvian railways were begun as a government enterprise, financed through borrowings against future guano revenues. The bankruptcy which struck the government in 1876 and which was aggravated considerably by the war with Chile eventually forced the state, in 1890, to turn over the operation of the railways to the Peruvian Corporation, an association of foreign holders of the defaulted Peruvian government bonds. In Colombia, Chile, Brazil, and Argentina the state was similarly directly engaged in the railway business, though not as the sole participant in the field. Intermittently the rail lines of Ecuador were also operated by public authority. While most of the lines of Mexico had been initiated as private corporations, the Mexican government revised its railway policy radically in 1906-1907, nationalizing some of the most important lines and incorporating them under public ownership as the National Railways of Mexico; for at least a decade and a half previously, however, the government had been moving increasingly toward exercising a greater degree of centralized social control over the various independent and privately owned lines.[76]

Even outside the agricultural and infrastructure fields, however, the records of the 1850-1914 era are by no means devoid of interventionary measures aimed at promoting development. Some of these measures involved the removal of fiscal barriers to development—as in the case of Chile and Mexico which, to facilitate expansion of the domestic market, terminated, in the 1880's, the old *alcabala* taxes, and the internal or provincial customs duties (*aduanas secas*), while enjoining subnational administrative units against levying tariffs on goods moving in domestic commerce.[77] Other measures had a distinctly nationalistic flavor, as in the case of the Peruvian legislation of 1895 and 1901 in which the government moved to promote the growth of national insurance companies alongside the 15 agencies of foreign companies which then had control of the field.[78] Still others offered encouragement to industrial activity, especially that which was related to export expansion. The government of Brazil, for example, invested in modern sugar mills to revitalize the decrepit economy of the northeast, and, to encourage private capital in the same field, proffered earnings guarantees to sugar milling companies in that region. Similarly, the Argentine Congress in 1887 passed a law guaranteeing a 5 per cent return on capital invested in meat-freezing establishments.

For that matter, hesitant and unsystematic as the steps were, a number of the governments began the first of the protectionist types of measures which, in the twentieth century, were to become the basis for deliberate national industrialization policies.[79] Already by 1900 there was, at least in the larger countries, a small range of nascent residentiary industries— especially in coarser textiles and other lines of simple consumer goods— which could begin to lobby for a more comprehensive interventionary policy as protection against foreign competition.

Argentine tariff schedules, for example, included some protective rates after 1876. A protective policy was inaugurated in Chile in 1897.[80] Aspects of infant industry protection appeared also in the customs schedules of Venezuela and Ecuador. Even in Peru, where the dominant economic interests (cotton, sugar, and minerals exporters) generally favored the cheap importation of manufactured goods,[81] one finds that some protection was involved in the development of the cotton and woollen textile industries during the 1870's and thereafter.[82] By the early 1900's, several flour mills had been established in Peru under the protection of differential duties,[83] and a cement plant was erected at Callao in 1912 with the benefit of an exclusive concessionary award granted by the government.[84] During the latter half of the nineteenth century, Brazilian cotton manufacturing was expanding behind a rising tariff wall; until the 1890's, however, official policy was what Stanley Stein has aptly called creeping protection: i.e., import exemptions, subsidies, grants of lottery proceeds, revenue tariffs so high as to provide protection, and grants of other favors on an ad hoc basis.[85] With inauguration of the Brazilian republic, public policy grew increasingly disposed to push deliberate industrialization through protectionist and other measures.[86] Before 1900, for example, the Brazilian government had made investments in, or given loans to, both textile and sugar mills. By 1916, Brazilian tariff schedules were among the highest in the hemisphere,[87] and it is interesting to note that at least as early as 1908 the now familiar and still lively issue of "internal colonialism" was raised in the Brazilian Congress. Representatives from the less industrialized northern portions of the nation complained that, owing to the policy of protected industrialization, they were in effect having to pay tribute to the more developed states of the south in the consequent higher prices on their purchases of manufactured and other domestic goods.[88]

From the early 1880's on, the former liberal trade policies of Colombia were gradually eroded by experiments with protectionism.[89] By the early 1900's, Colombia's economic policy was consciously influenced by the example of Mexico, the striking industrial progress of which was thought to be attributable in large part to the protectionist measures which had been adopted over the course of many decades.[90] As George Wythe has pointed out, of all the Latin American nations "Mexico has the longest and most consistent record of protectionist measures." [91]

In the Mexican prototype the general policy of the regime of Porfirio Díaz had been to continue the protectionist practices of earlier periods.[92] There is a suggestion, however, in M. P. Arnaud's account of Mexican textile industrialization that some of the high tariffs in question may have been intended originally for revenue purposes and that their protective effect was to some extent unplanned.[93] Intentionally or no, substantial protection was derived from tariffs which, for some categories of textiles, had moved from as low as 5 per cent ad valorem in 1830 to as much as

135-150 per cent ad valorem by the 1880's and 1890's. Mexican tariffs became a major source of complaint on the part of British businessmen and consular officials who saw their overseas markets being captured by national producers. A further deterrent to foreign traders was provided in the intricacy of Mexican customs rules, a de facto protectionist device that probably assisted local producers in other countries as well. "Some British merchants believed that the bewildering array of Mexican laws regarding customs declarations, consular invoices, and ships' manifests were more important barriers to Anglo-Mexican trade than the high charges set forth in the tariff. Many British companies stopped trading with Mexico because they were unable to avoid being fined for violating the regulations." [94]

Mexican textile companies, a good many of which had been established by Spanish immigrants, were the major beneficiaries of this tariff and administrative protection. A further strengthening of the industry came when the influential French mercantile community in Mexico engaged in a series of business maneuvers which, during the 1880's and 1890's, brought an important segment of the textile manufacturing sector under its control. After the take-over, the plants were, with government favors, consolidated and modernized, and their diversified and considerably expanded output replaced formerly imported lines. [95]

French investors also held a large interest in one of the most cherished industrial development projects of the Díaz government: the Compañía Fundidora de Fierro y Acero de Monterrey, S. A., Latin America's oldest integrated steel company. As the region's first state-supported venture into heavy industry, the company received public assistance in a number of ways. The state government of Nuevo León, in which Monterrey is located, facilitated the acquisition of local iron reserves, and the national government adjusted tariffs on foreign iron and steel imports so as to protect the new undertaking. In addition, railway freight rates were lowered to favor the company with cheaper deliveries of coal from the deposits of Coahuila in the northern part of the republic, and special branch lines were constructed by the Mexican National Railways to link the industry with the iron ore deposits at Monclova, Carrizal, and Durango. [96]

Though somewhat less impressive perhaps than the textile and siderurgical cases, a number of other new industries were also launched in Mexico during the Porfiriato with some assistance from the state. Factories producing porcelains, glass, and other ceramic products were established as were an important paper mill and cigarette companies. Not a few of these were also the work of French immigrant entrepreneurs, of whom a good many were merchants—a circumstance which should be kept in mind for the discussion in Chapter VIII. [97]

When Colombia set out to emulate Mexican development tactics, it too moved considerably beyond mere tariff protection. In accordance with the practice of many countries in the area, the Colombian government had long utilized exemptions from import duties and other taxes as a means of strengthening the inducement to invest. Such *fomento* measures, indeed, were fairly common around the continent with respect to investments in infrastructure, agriculture, and minerals. During the 1860's and 1870's, however, the departmental and national governments in Colombia had resorted to a still more varied range of interventionist techniques in what proved to be, ultimately, partially vain attempts to establish basic iron and chemical industries. Subsidies, public loans, governmental purchases of corporate shares, and contracts for governmental purchase of firm output were tried, abandoned, and then revived, along with the guaranteed earnings device customarily employed in the public utility field, to foster the development of textile and other factories in the opening decade of the twentieth century. In general, these special objects of governmental solicitude met with something less than conspicuous success, and one is inclined to attribute the success of the companies which did prosper primarily to factors other than government intervention. Nevertheless, with this assistance and a barrier of protective tariffs, the domestic textile industry expanded gradually, and a few other plants, such as a match factory which enjoyed an exclusive preferential concession on import duties, were able to operate for a number of years.

For present purposes, however, the concrete results of the foregoing industrially oriented interventionist policies were less important than the very existence of those policies. They, and all the other expedients employed in Latin America at the time, measures such as privileged tax treatment and concessions of exclusive regional market rights, attest to an awakening interest in national industrialization and to a growing, if as yet unsystematic, willingness to interfere with the routine functioning of the market in pursuit of ends deemed to be socially desirable. To be sure, most of the intervention, in terms of the actual public resources involved, was still guided by an implicit model of export-oriented growth. Yet a certain basis had been laid, in policy experience and in the formation of new domestic interest groups, for the policy changes which were to come in the post-1914 decades. Following the First World War, interventionism was to increase; it was hardly, in view of the record, introduced de novo. Rather, the policy changes which accompanied the breakdown of the international capitalistic system of 1850-1914 marked a refinement of interventionary measures and a reorientation of their objectives—looking thenceforth primarily inward to the domestic system of economic processes instead of mainly outward to the global market mechanism.

VIII

Enclave Development and Entrepreneurial Growth

AFTER half a century of experience with a pattern of extensive growth based on export possibilities, the economic map of Latin America had by 1914 been transformed, since growth of the export sector played here the propulsive and fructifying role it has played in many other times and places. The supply of capital and labor skills increased, economic organization improved, and at least some external economies accrued to local firms, giving an impulse to the spread of specialization. Out of the stepped-up local flow of money income, there were created potential new sources of investment funds for the private sector, and in the chief urban centers the domestic consumer markets were enlarged by the additional spending power. From taxes on foreign trade and flotations of bond issues abroad, the governments of the hemisphere acquired substantial new fiscal resources for potential investment in the public sector, and this gave encouragement to private investors. The degree to which infrastructure development could potentially have been promoted is indicated by the fact that some three-quarters of the large British capital invested in the region by 1913 had gone into railways, public utilities, and government securities.

There was, in short, a distinct stimulus for the initiation and expansion of various types of residentiary economic activities. Yet the appearance of new elements in domestic economic organization was hardly remarkable, considering the magnitude of the foreign investment and trade flows which induced them. Regional responses to these external catalysts varied, but in all but Argentina and Uruguay, both essentially new countries, there were substantial limitations on the general diffusion of the modernizing influences which emanated from the external sector. Notwithstanding the force of the change agents and the undeniable appearance of a measure of derivative domestic development, in no case did initial expansion of the export sector suffice to bring into being a set of economic relationships which could thereafter sustain national development independently of the external growth dynamic. Indeed, in a majority of cases it was almost as if the external sector were very nearly the sole important manifestation of economic advancement, rather than a catalyst for generalized expansion.

As a guiding development influence, domestic markets remained far overshadowed by the foreign markets that were opened up for Latin American exports. As Latin American economic processes responded to the demand signals of the market place, it was the strong overseas demand rather than the feeble domestic demand which continued to call the tune and to set the pace. Differential response capability was also involved. Throughout the period in question, the external sector's growth fed upon elastic supplies of entrepreneurship and low-cost capital from the more developed economies of the center, while the articulation of Latin American resources with the demand patterns of overseas markets was furthered by the contemporaneous development of larger-scale production and marketing organizations by means of which the whole world was drawn into the trading orbit of international capitalism. For domestically oriented activities, institutional supports were not available on anything like an equivalent scale.

The outcome of this interplay of differential demand and response factors was not merely unbalanced growth, though clearly the incidence of productivity advances and output increases was quite unevenly distributed among the various segments of the economic life of the region. Economic imbalance alone, however, does not suffice to clarify the nature of the development problems encountered, for differential industry and sectoral growth rates are inherent in any dynamic economic situation and are, indeed, functionally related to economic progress. Constructive disequilibria—manifested in the simultaneous existence of leading and lagging sectors and leading and lagging industries—abound in highly developed economics in which expansion at particular points in the system is accompanied by contraction at other points. By virtue of the overall reticulation of the economic systems in which they arise, productivity-furthering impulses generated by such leads and lags are transmitted to appropriate points in the system through an all-encompassing web of market relationships within which productive factors move about in response to the price-registered exigencies of the time. In a proper context, therefore, economic imbalances serve as signals of the directions of the resource shifts which are necessary in any movement to higher levels of aggregate productivity.[1]

By way of contrast, the lopsided development which characterized most of Latin America through the early 1900's had little in common with a pattern of growth in which resources are pulled freely into more productive uses within a comprehensive and integrated market system. Rather, the exogenously induced growth of the external sector occurred to an important degree as a discrete phenomenon, only imperfectly integrated with the totality of national economic existence. For that matter, there were few total national economic systems with which the growth impulses stemming from the external sector could be integrated in order that imbalances might have furthered expansion. Over much of the area, the economic life carried on within national boundaries was, instead, triadic in character: there was only limited interaction among the three coexisting subnational economic systems into which resources were commonly grouped and among which there persisted extremely wide disparities in the levels of technology and organization utilized.

In Mexico and Central America, in the Andean republics and Paraguay, and even among the *caboclo* farmers of Brazil, the economic subsystem which encompassed the bulk of the population and land resources was a modified subsistence agriculture which was often strongly pre-Columbian in character.[2] Largely self-contained on the input side, the semisubsistence sector supplied labor power and a modest amount of agricultural produce and craft items to the other two subsystems in exchange for the use of land and a very small return flow of consumer manufactures. Capital accumulation was minimal, and the semisubsistence subsystem grew very little except in consequence of the absorption of more land and labor factors within a context of static production functions. Monetized transactional relationships, while not entirely absent, were not decisive as a basis for economic organization.

The second subsystem consisted of a colonial institutional residue which set the tone and tempo of life on the haciendas and which also permeated much of the domestic marketing organization and the languishing local crafts in most provinicial towns and cities. Extensive in its geographical spread, the modified colonial subsystem was prevalent throughout Middle America, the Andean republics, Paraguay, and northwestern Argentina and a factor of importance in northeastern and central Brazil and even much of rural Chile. A supplier of minifundia parcels to the semisubsistence sector on which it drew for labor supplies, the modified colonial subsystem related to the third subsystem chiefly as a supplier of agricultural staples for urban consumption and as the source of the money income which the landed elite and petty merchants channeled into a consumption demand for urban services and imported manufactures.

Within this second sector, monetized economic transactions were much more common than in the semisubsistence portion of the tripartate division, but capital formation was at a low level, owing in part to the leakage of the sector's economic surplus into consumption. Financial transactions, beyond those of primitive moneylending, were largely confined to two types: (1) commercial credit "retailed" into the sector by the larger mercantile firms of the modern sector which could draw "wholesale" credit directly from the existing banking enterprises, and (2) the land acquisition and consumption loans which latifundian owners obtained from banking institutions, the real debt burden of which was often eased considerably by monetary depreciation and by the secular rise in land values.[3]

The third subnational system was the modern sector, which centered on the mines, the plantations and commercial ranches, and the railways and utility enterprises, but comprehended also the residentiary financial, marketing, and (to a smaller degree) industrial enterprises that served the foreign trade process and the populations of the central cities where most of these firms were clustered. Examples of such "beachhead economies" could be drawn from every country of the region, although in southern South America, including southern Brazil, the diffusion of economic modernization from the export sector was far greater than elsewhere. These instances aside, however, the modern sector functioned essentially as an appendage of the international market, an enclave which had little to do with the local milieu in which it was geographically situated. Its key input relationships (capital, production and marketing technique, entrepreneurship and organization) came through its linkages with the economies of the center upon whose wide range of well-developed supportive institutions the enclave sector regularly drew. As the principal recipient of foreign capital and organizational inflows, the export sector was inevitably the investment and production leader in each Latin American economy. At the same time, the modern sector's chief output relationships were also with the overseas markets in which the largest portion of its rapidly rising output was disposed of. Through these input and output relationships, productivity advances of no mean degree were registered in the sector as time went on, but the gains of higher productivity often accrued to foreigners, either to the overseas consumers of the products (in the form of lower prices) or to the capital-and-ownership elements of the producer interest as rising net income. And despite the conspicuous connection in the enclave sector between innovative economic reorganization and rapidly rising output, there was a notably slight tendency for the improved techniques of organization and production to be adopted throughout the rest of the economy. Consequently, most of the forces of economic expansion were contained, as it were, within the confines of the modern sector.

THE ENCLAVE NATURE OF EXPORT SECTORS

To understand the circumstances which tended to give Latin American export sectors their enclave character, three aspects of the enclave-domestic-economy relationships must be briefly examined—(1) the technological and organizational characteristics of the export industry itself, (2) the market structures of the host economy receiving the foreign investment in export-oriented production, and (3) public policy in the nations which opted for export-led development. In addition to these, one must keep in mind also the magnitude of the capital requirements for export expansion as these were set by the geographical conditions of the several Latin American nations. Owing to the difficult terrain of Mexico, Colombia, Ecuador, Peru, and Bolivia, for example, enormous amounts of capital, both foreign and domestic, were often required simply to equip the external sector with some of the basic appurtenances of modern economic life—e.g., with rail transport and communications facilities and with power supplies. For the same reason, maintenance costs were high, and little capital was left over, so to speak, for promoting other areas of growth in which the returns were less certain than in export promotion.[4]   Geography likewise operated to restrict the spread effects of overhead capital facilities in many regions.   Whereas, for example, the low-cost railway lines of Argentina, southern Brazil, Uruguay, or central Chile could serve a fairly wide area through inexpensive feeder roads, the territorial accessibility of the expensive lines built in the mountainous regions of the continent was much more narrowly circumscribed.   Undoubtedly, then, natural conditions played a strong role in accounting for the differential diffusion of development from the export and foreign investment base among the several countries of the hemisphere, quite apart from the other circumstances to be discussed.

Technological and Organizational Characteristics of Export Industries.
Although small- and medium-scale mining was prevalent in Latin America through the middle years of the nineteenth century and has, in fact, continued to exist down to the present day in many countries, the technological evolution of the minerals extraction industry was such that by the latter decades of the 1800's the advantage lay increasingly with large-scale, capital-intensive undertakings.   The nineteenth-century copper boom in Chile, for example, was one in which national firms, operating often with hired foreign technicians, were dominant in the export sector, but when the export of copper regained its importance in the early 1900's, a technological shift to mass-mining techniques had given the controlling position to foreign mining corporations with superior capital backing and more sophisticated technological and organizational capabilities.[5]   With headquarters abroad, the foreign concerns not only enjoyed direct access to the cheaper capital markets of the center, whence they also readily obtained the requisite complex machinery and high-level managerial and technical skills, but were also advantageously situated to deal directly with shipping companies and industrial users of their output in overseas markets.

Under the circumstances, the derivative local expansion brought about by minerals export industries tended to be small.[6]   Supplies of the key inputs could generally be obtained more economically through importation and the hiring of foreign specialists than locally, so that only a few residentiary supply industries could develop to service the export sector firms—generally on a repair and maintenance basis, with some custom fabrication of parts and special pieces of equipment.   If the "backward" linkages which could be developed locally were limited, so also were the "forward" linkages, inasmuch as the export products were generally shipped out in an unprocessed or slightly processed state; elaboration of the crude minerals extracted ordinarily required capital facilities and skills which were not easily obtainable locally.

To the extent that these firms were mainly financed from abroad and through internal capital accumulation, they did not contribute a great deal to the development of a diversified and flexible set of local capital and money market structures.   Indeed, insofar as the funds from export sales were largely banked abroad (by foreign export producers and, to some extent, by national export producers as well), only a portion of the sales receipts had to be remitted for deposit in the financial institutions of the host economy to cover wages, taxes, royalties, and the like; consequently, the available bank reserves in Latin American money markets were reduced along with the aforementioned constriction of a local borrowing clientele. Even where residentiary financial institutions did arise to service the local needs of the minerals extraction concerns, these did not, owing to the prominence of external sector finance in their total pattern of activity, acquire much experience in channeling risk capital to a variety of types of new ventures. Moreover, since many of the ancillary services required for the conduct of the mining companies' business (transport, power, and the like) were often provided internally as an integrated part of the export firms' operations, there did not come into being a large number of public-service facilities which could thenceforth serve as a source of external economies to other more diversified and smaller users.

Because the case of entry into these lines of production was not very great, especially for local persons, and because their individually large scale of operations reduced the number of participating firms, the possibilities for generating a domestic supply of experienced entrepreneurs as a by-product of industry operations were small. Although more opportunities may have been provided for moving native workers into semiskilled and skilled categories (e.g., as mechanics, bookkeepers, construction workers) than was the case in agricultural employment,[7] the labor coefficient of the mining industry was but a fraction of that prevailing in agriculture, so that the total number of workers moving upward in this fashion was small.[8]

Of the total income generated in minerals export activities, the production functions of the industry therefore necessitated that a large share be paid to external parties: to the foreign investors and high-level operating personnel, to the foreign suppliers of machinery and equipment, to foreign shipping lines and financial institutions, or to local railways and port utilities which were themselves more often than not foreign owned. With regard to reinvestment, the typical (and rational) investment behavior of the specialized minerals companies ordinarily channeled the internally generated capital back into further expansion of the local mining operation or into the same line of production elsewhere in the world, seldom into nonmining activities in the host economy. A functionally specialized but geographically diversified distribution of the investment funds, in other words, commonly prevailed over a functional diversification in the specific originating locale.

As for the rail and utility enterprises supported by foreign investment, their direct effects on the generation of local entrepreneurship and the diffusion of labor skills were similar to those of the minerals-exporting corporations, and for substantially the same reasons. In like manner, their backward linkage relationships and their relations with domestic financial evolution corresponded to the minerals case, as did also the distribution of their revenues among the differing nationalities of the factors of production involved. In railways as in mining, the output sales strengthened the balance of payments, but gave rise to corresponding charges of substantial size at the same time. The chief difference between the minerals industries and the railway and utility fields lay in the latter's generally greater forward linkage effects; for although a good many of the rail lines were special-purpose railways designed primarily to facilitate the movement of export items, they, and even more the municipal utility concerns, constituted a source of external economies for a small but growing variety of residentiary enterprises. The limitations on their effectiveness in diffusing externalities were not inconsequential but were attributable more to other circumstances, such as geography and public policy, than to the technological and organizational character of the industries as such.

The agricultural-export industries present a more complex case than the foregoing, though, except for ranching operations, the employment multiplier in the expansion of agricultural-exporting firms was considerably greater than in the minerals-extraction or utility fields. Yet, though plantation agriculture had high labor requirements, the character of employment was generally such as to contribute little to improving the quality of domestic labor skills. Consequently, on balance, the growth of export agriculture served no more significantly than did the growth of capital-intensive lines of production to expand the domestic supply of the kinds of work skills which are relevant to initiating and sustaining a modern development process, except for those instances (southern Brazil, Uruguay, and Argentina) in which the industry's labor needs had to be met largely through European immigration. In these latter exceptional cases, the concomitant influx of European workers greatly enriched the host economies by bringing to them all or most of the well-known accessory assets of immigration: namely, the costless (to the recipient economy) quantitative increase and qualitative improvement of its supply of labor factors. Elsewhere, however, the growth of export agriculture simply increased the volume of low-paid unskilled employment.

Inasmuch as the inputs of the agricultural sector were primarily land and labor, together with simple forms of agricultural capital, specialization in such agricultural export products as coffee, cacao, henequen, rubber, and tobacco brought with it rather limited backward linkage effects— though the same circumstance often made entry into the export industry much easier for local entrepreneurs and investors and thereby facilitated the rise of export sectors which were domestically owned and operated. Where this was the case, the local economy also benefited, at least potentially, by retaining a greater share of the export earnings generated in the form of proprietary income and payment for input factors. Moreover, especially in the use of coffee but to some degree in other lines as well, the production functions of export agriculture made possible some derivative residentiary development of supply industries which turned out simple agricultural implements and processing machinery as well as machine parts for the repair of imported equipment. At the same time, however, the potential forward linkages of the agricultural industries tended to be rather slight except for such derivative activities as meat processing and the manufacture of cigars and rum. Thus, much of the output moved abroad with little or no local processing, while the extent of the local demand for processed foodstuffs was curtailed by the prevailing levels of popular income which precluded also much in the way of agricultural diversification.

The technological and organizational character of agricultural export activities was not uniform throughout the sector. The minimum feasible scale of production units and the capital requirements of coffee production, for example, were less than in sugar. Correspondingly, the former industry was more likely than the latter to contain more domestic firms and to generate more domestic entrepreneurial and managerial experience (albeit of a less sophisticated quality) per unit of output.[9] Foreign capital investment and control, in contrast, was more prevalent in the relatively capital-intensive sugar plantations in which the scale of operations was also larger, and accordingly, less of the export proceeds accrued to the host economy. But such distinctions cannot even be drawn invariably on an industry basis. In practice, for example, nationally owned sugar plantations using less modern capital equipment often sufficed for supplying the demands of the home market, while more elaborate installations were required to produce the quality of refined sugar which was exportable.[10] In banana production, the complexities of marketing as well as risk factors and certain economies of scale in production favored the growth of foreign firms as contrasted with domestic entreprises, and gave to these firms (as also in the case of foreign sugar companies) the investment behavior which earlier was described as characteristic of the specialized minerals corporations.

Although some agricultural export industries, particularly sugar and bananas, resembled the minerals industries in their internal provision of overhead facilities, most of them relied upon public service facilities which were potentially available to other users when these should appear on the scene. To this extent, the agriculturally based export sectors were more conducive in still another way to diffused development than were the minerals extraction cases, even though some of the sunk capital in specialized marketing facilities could not readily be put to alternative uses. Yet, if agricultural export firms were also generally more closely tied in with the development of local financial institutions, in which capacity they stimulated tertiary sector growth, they nevertheless had a certain limiting influence on commercial banking loan policies. In most cases, the mono-cultural character of regional export economies largely confined the lending experience of local banks to the forms of bank credit suitable to handling the needs of their major clients in that industry. And as banking customs came to be shaped by the borrowing traditions of the special portions of the money market they served, it would appear that there developed a certain conservative inertia which worked against devising more adaptable or flexible lending practices in order to cater to the needs of new businesses and product lines.

Market Structures in the Host Economies.   It is plain that the sources of the enclave phenomenon lay as much in the economic conditions pre-vailing in the host country as in the characteristics of the export industries themselves. In more highly developed economic structures an expansion at one point in the system is diffused over a network of interrelated and interacting market mechanisms to foster derivative growth and adjustment elsewhere; this action of forces in a constellation of markets thus constitutes a chainbelt for transmitting expansionary influences throughout the system. The situation of most Latin American countries, however, made it exceed-ingly difficult to assimilate the external inducements to growth coming from foreign investment and trade activity in such a manner as to develop effective national institutions fed by national capital. Organizational la-cunae such as the lack of effective national capital and money markets, institutional rigidities such as the land tenure system, and other substantial market imperfections such as deficiencies in domestic economic communi-cations systems intervened to obstruct or dampen the diffusion of exogenous growth stimuli by reducing the market networks over which the influences initiating the external sector could travel and spread.

Owing, for example, to the rudimentary development of savings-mobilizing institutions and the prevailing high liquidity preference which resulted in a high time discount rate, as well as to the differential access of local bor-rowers to the scarce loanable funds, it was difficult to maximize the partici-pation of residentiary firms in either the supply functions of the export sector or the further local elaboration of export sector output. For that matter, direct participation in the production activities of the export sector itself was generally precluded by the same circumstances when the industry which served as the base of that sector was capital intensive in nature. Further, the character of the local market demand for agricultural output, shaped as it was by the skewed distribution of purchasing power, reduced the opportunities for appropriating a portion of the expanded agricultural production as an improved raw materials supply for domestic food proc-essing industries—just as the constricted development of residentiary manufactures in general involved a forfeiting of the potential external economies which might have accrued to such firms from the increased and lower-cost supply of fibers and minerals turned out by the investments in export industries.

Beyond such considerations as these, the domestic paucity and inadequacy of integrative market structures implied that the developmental impetus supplied by foreign capital and the vitality of export markets fed into a generalized pattern of social relationships which drew, for its basic character, upon the relations of production in agriculture and which was, from the standpoint of growth, dysfunctional. Since many of the new enterprises were launched with foreign venture capital and management, the innovationally inclined economic interests were, therefore, often not directly incorporated into, or represented in, the domestic power structure. Thus, a substantial portion of the economic benefits generated locally by the foreign initiated ventures in plantations, mines, railways, and utilities was simply channeled through the same socio-economic structure which had constricted the possibilities for growth before the latter half of the nineteenth century. In a sense, the function of the latifundia-minifundia complex in respect to the diffusion of exogenous growth stimuli was to act as a shock absorber where, from the perspective of the development process, none was wanted.

In the first place, in most rural regions—excepting, mainly, southern Brazil, Uruguay, and Argentina a nonmonetized regime of labor servitude on the estates and the self-perpetuating poverty of subsistence minifundia agriculture kept a large majority of the populace, even those employed in producing a marketed output, ensnared in traditional life styles and archaic forms of social organization, out of direct contact with the commercialized market economy and unexposed to the new influences making for cultural change.[11] Geographical isolation, linguistic separateness, and economic deprivation did not facilitate the general incorporation of nonmonetary sectors into the trading system. Moreover, since the backward conditions of the domestic agricultural sector, the chief (if unremunerative) employment opportunity, governed the wage level of unskilled workers in rural regions and strongly influenced the rate of payment to unskilled nonagricultural workers, both of whom had exceedingly limited options for self-employment, the latifundia-minifundia complex commonly set the terms on which an expanding supply of unskilled labor was put out for hire to the export enterprises. Consequently, export sector wage levels—the major nonfiscal means the local economy had of sharing in the earnings of that sector [12]—customarily reflected the low opportunity costs of the labor employed therein. Hence the rise in export-related employment made only a modest contribution to resolving the problems created by the insufficiency of domestic market size.[13] The more highly paid positions were often held by foreigners who were sometimes even paid in foreign currency and who spent much of that which they did not deposit as savings abroad in the purchase of imports.

In the second place, the contemporary growth of latifundism made it possible for ever larger shares of the agricultural income stream to derive essentially from property ownership per se and the preponderant market bargaining advantages which accrued to large-scale ownership. On the one hand, increasing population pressure against the land was a factor which both depressed the rural wage level to the benefit of employers and continually enlarged the category of income classifiable as land rent. On the other hand, the growing population, the extension of the transport network, and the increased commercial possibilities of agricultural production meant that windfall capital gains of substantial size came to those who could hold on to the land over a period of years, making ever more feasible the traditional practice of multiple hypothecation of properties.[14] Under the circumstances, a rentier type of land ownership was still a passably good substitute for an active and innovative management of land resources, especially since latifundian status brought political and social prestige and the opportunity to acquire additional income as lawyers or corporate directors in the employ of foreign concerns which needed such persons for their knowledge of local rules and for their local political connections. Much of the increase in domestic income, therefore, was appropriated by a comparatively few beneficiaries whose spending and savings preferences were such as to transform rises in income into a higher demand for imported goods or foreign bank accounts. Meanwhile, the growing disparity between living conditions abroad or in the central cities and those of the provincial areas increasingly underscored the appeal of residence away from the estates, so that the age-old tendency for agricultural sector incomes and savings to be siphoned out of the sector as a unilateral transfer payment was stronger than ever before.

On account of these extrasectoral implications of the agricultural relations of production, there was generally only a weak domestic market demand, one which offered little encouragement to residentiary types of economic activities and to the local spread of nonagricultural investment and employment opportunities. At the same time, neither the workers, whose income level was generally so low that savings were not possible to any significant extent, nor the more highly paid foreign officials and technicians, who banked their unspent earnings abroad, seem to have contributed substantially to the local supply of investable savings. Among the wealthy domestic classes, the concentration of savings in the hands of a relatively small group limited the possibilities for developing a really large and active market for securities, while the institution of absentee ownership served to concentrate the domestic savings which were not exported in a small number of urban locales. Similarly, the heavy concentration of property ownership precluded the emergence of a wider range of firms or specialized decision-making units (each providing the locus for exercising initiative and accumulating managerial experience) because few resources and little scope for autonomous action remained for them outside the sway of the controlled domains of the large property units.

Both the parameters of market demand and the restricted access to resources and capital, therefore, inhibited local development of the complex structural differentiation which comes from the establishment of more specialized and more autonomous structural units in the economy, and many of the Latin American economies continued to lack an adequate range of the subsidiary institutions and intermediate social structures which perform the multitude of internal market functions that are central to the viable conduct of a modern economic system. Particularly illustrative of the point was the grossly inadequate development of comprehensive national systems of financial institutions, for there the market-institution lacuna was especially notable.

By the close of the era under discussion, there were still not many banks in most of the countries of the region, and the geographical dispersion of those which did function was so limited that the banking system could neither meet the credit needs of provincial firms nor facilitate interlocal remittances. As late as 1879 in Mexico, for example, there were only four commercial banks operating in the whole republic. Two of them were located in the capital city, one having been established in that year; the other two had just been established in the 1875-78 period in Chihuahua where mining activity was picking up. In other parts of the country, the old-fashioned money lenders and merchant bankers continued to handle financial functions.[15] Furthermore, the access to bank credit—particularly crucial in view of the rudimentary or nonexistent state of capital market organization—was affected by the rather limited dissolution of particularistic restrictions in favor of the money nexus. When, for example, the National Bank of Chile encountered a severe crisis in 1878 and solicited the government for a decree of inconvertibility for the bank notes it had issued, it was discovered that the directors of the bank had lent to themselves, especially during the year of the crisis, an amount equal to half the capital of the bank.[16] Often, in other words, the existing bank lending capacity was available chiefly to insiders, those "*de la casa*," while other would-be borrowers either paid much higher charges for credit or had to do without.

Besides these shortcomings, there was little development throughout Latin America of such specialized financial intermediaries as investment bankers, and, despite the centrality of agriculture in the total economic structure, only a minimal development of agricultural credit facilities generally occurred. Thus, although the new banks of the era met reasonably well the credit needs of the established export trade (the major domestic producing firms, the larger export-import houses and wholesalers, etc.), there were many firms which could not sufficiently qualify as bankable risks to gain access to the established lending institutions. From the standpoint of effectively linking lenders and investors and mobilizing funds for optimal use, the organization of money and capital markets left much to be desired. And in consequence of this limited development of financial intermediaries for channeling savings to investing enterpreneurs, persons who recognized the existing productive opportunities had difficulty in acquiring the money to exploit them while those in control of the potentially available savings were not necessarily those possessed of the requisite entrepreneurial vision.

Public Sector Policies.　Pending the gradual evolution of syndetic market institutions, it is conceivable that state policies might have functioned as a market surrogate in promoting the diffusion of exogenous growth impulses. Yet, in some of the countries the conduct of the public sector was an almost unrelieved tale of misdoings, while in others the organization and operation of public policies was at least as imperfect as the market structure as a means of converting the external sector's expansionary influences into a basis for regenerative or self-augmenting growth.

Part of the difficulty lay in the generally low quality of the political leadership during this period, although happy exceptions to this shortcoming were, to be sure, found here and there. Financed by the swelling revenues from taxes on the external sector, by land sales from the public domain, by overseas loans extracted from gullible foreign savers by investment bankers and promoter-publicists of dubious integrity, and by a growing volume of domestic bank note issues, the public authorities of the region had at their disposition large resources with which to build a system of state-structured choices and actions into the total web of economic relationships. All these resources were, however, channeled into an institutional setting in which the concept of government and law was still not separated from the personalities of men occupying public office; and they were administered by a system of bureaucratic privilege in which the possibilities for political aggrandizement were enhanced by the lack of balance in the distribution of power, the deficiencies of public information systems, the immaturity of the electorate, and the de facto disenfranchisement of the majority of the population.

Indeed, the comparative ease with which funds could be acquired assisted the preservation of authoritarian rule by minority groups, for dictators did not have to go to their people for support if they could rely instead upon the connivance of financial promoters (both national and foreign) in gaining repeated access to the international capital markets.[17] And since most regimes were neither politically nor economically dependent upon majoritarian domestic interests, they were under correspondingly little pressure to justify their fiscal policies in terms of the relation of these to the felt needs of the public. Moreover, the complexion of domestic political processes, where ascriptive norms of leadership recruitment and power-oriented rather than achievement-oriented techniques of political advancement prevailed, was not calculated to generate the sort of competent leadership which could husband the new public sector resources and turn them to the general advantage on the basis of a background in or understanding of the management of economic affairs.

True, there were outstanding exceptions, such as José Yves Limantour, the brilliant minister of finance in Porfirio Díaz' government. But Latin America seems to have had in high public positions more than its share of other types—cosmopolitan aristocrats, parvenu lawyers, shrewd military chieftains, intellectual dilettantes whose preparation for directing a massive development effort was not obvious. One thinks, for example, of the army-backed caudillo president of Bolivia, General Mariano Melgarejo (1864-1871), who, responsible neither to oligarchy nor to a popular constituency, ruled with a brutality as capricious as it was grotesque, and of the Peruvian Minister of Development in 1909 whose qualifications for the job were, according to an effusive press tribute at the time, a "long and distinguished career" as professor of bacteriology, pathology, and anatomy as well as "consulting physician at the Lunatic Asylum." [18]

If the comparative ease with which the public treasury was filled, depleted, and then replenished was a factor which boded ill for popular government, it was also instrumental in fostering an endemic fiscal irresponsibility. Seldom, for example, do the windfall fiscal gains from export booms appear to have been regarded as a special source of development financing.[19] More commonly, the revenues from the external sector were considered simply as a routine part of general revenue and therefore available for covering the ordinary operating expenses of government. These had a way of expanding to absorb all available revenue, so that the chief hope for raising funds for public investment lay in extrabudgetary channels among which foreign borrowing was paramount. The routine governmental expenditures, however, were often made in a context which gave free rein to ineptness and worse. Vast quantities of public funds were dissipated on such unproductive matters as the support of military establishments, the erection of showy public buildings, and the beautification of the capital cities wherein resided the directing elite—not to mention the wastage of public resources which is indicated by the rather overwhelming evidence that improbity and misconduct were pervasive in Latin American public life.[20]

Furthermore, with more money flowing into the public till, Parkinson's law seems to have operated with a vengeance, giving rise to the inflated bureaucracies (the *empleomanía*) of which Francisco García Calderón and others spoke so scathingly. Large outlays, in other words, went to "create new employments in order to assuage the national appetite for sinecures," [21] and the roster of public functionaries swelled pari passu with the rising budgets:

> In the economic life of these Latin American countries the State is a kind of beneficent providence which creates and preserves the fortune of individual persons, increases the common poverty by taxation, display, useless enterprises, the upkeep of military and

> civil officials and the waste of money borrowed abroad. . . . The
> government is the public treasury; by the government all citizens
> live, directly or indirectly, and the foreigner profits by exploiting
> the national wealth. A centralizing power, the State forces a golden
> livery upon this bureaucratic mob of magistrates and deputies,
> political masters and teachers.[22]

Unfortunately, however, the conditions of public administration affected
more than the utilization of current revenues. Proceeds of foreign borrowings were also used to cover expenditures on current account, to pay the
service charges due on previous external loans, or to finance the handsome
commissions charged by European banking houses and reward (formally
or otherwise) the insiders, both Latin American and foreign, who participated in the international capital transfer process. By no means did all of
the balance go into productive expenditures. Deficit financing, as well as
current budgetary management, was a source of misspent public resources
and sporadic difficulties in balance of payments relationships.

Over half the Latin American government loans negotiated in London
during the reckless years of 1869-1873, for example, were in default by
1876. The public outcry which resulted led to an official inquiry by a
special parliamentary committee, and the irregularities which transpired
therein proved to be a harsh indictment of the governments of such countries
as Honduras, Costa Rica, and Paraguay.[23] Nor were questionable practices
a feature limited to dealings with smaller states and the early days of the
massive international capital transfers. The years which led into the Baring
Crisis of 1890 seem to have been notable for the manner in which the railway and banking policies of the Argentine government were manipulated
for the private advantage of officials and friends of the incumbent administration.[24] Indeed, the free-wheeling corruption and favoritism of the period
played no small part in bringing about that crisis in the first place. For that
matter, to the extent that we may place credence in the findings of one
Argentine researcher, whose investigations of the subject appear to be
meticulously exhaustive, there was a certain fundamental mismanagement
in nearly the whole of national railway policy in that country.[25] According
to Scalabrini, the net result of the government's railway construction subsidies and its guaranteed-earnings payments was that a very large portion
of the Argentine railways was handed over, almost as a gift, to foreign
ownership—with ultimately disastrous consequences for the nation's balance
of payments.

Still later—over 55 years after the Select Committee of the House of
Commons had its look into the seamy side of Latin American public life—
the investigations of the U.S. Senate Committee on Finance confirmed the
impression that little had changed in the mode of handling the public's
business in the region. Sometimes it was just a simple matter of influence
peddling and bribery, as when a New York investment banking firm, which

had obtained three Peruvian bond issues in the late 1920's, paid a fee of $415,000 to the son of the Peruvian president-dictator.[26] In certain loan transactions with Cuba, it was the son-in-law of the president who got the fees.[27] At other times, loans were floated but not actually employed for the stipulated purposes. Nearly a third of the Brazilian government loan of $25 million in 1922, for example, was to be utilized for electrification of a railway line owned by the government; eight years later no electrification had been accomplished and the loan was in default.[28]

On still other occasions, outright misrepresentation was involved. The prospectus for the Paraguayan bond issue of 1871 claimed that Paraguay had no funded debt and that "the whole debt of any description amounts to only £213,335." Neither the underwriting company nor any government official saw fit to tell potential investors of the huge indemnities which Paraguay had owed Argentina, Brazil, and Uruguay since the 1870 war settlement.[29] To aid in placing the £1 million Honduran issue of 1867 in the hands of the British public, the government of Honduras pledged as security the receipts from the Amapala customs house—not mentioning the fact that these were already subject to a lien arising out of an earlier loan and that the modest receipts from all Honduran customs houses would not have been sufficient to guarantee a loan of £50,000, much less one 20 times that size.[30] Moreover, both the government and the loan brokers conveniently overlooked the additional fact that all the national customs house receipts were already absorbed simply in meeting the ordinary administrative expenses of the government.[31]

In all fairness it should be mentioned that the foreign partners in these transactions, not just Latin American public officials, also profited from the mishandling of funds. For example, the U.S. Senate committee's exposé revealed how bankers would rig the market for new issues—"dressing up the market," it was called—by entering the market prior to issue in order to bid up the prices on outstanding securities of the country in question. In creating what was, in effect, a fictitious market and in raising bond prices to premium levels, the investment contractors sought to induce the public to view the new bond issues as a good purchase.[32] Substantial profits were to be made in speculative maneuvers of this sort, over and above what the heavy commissions and selling charges generally brought, and apparently the practice was a longstanding one for it was also reported in the earlier British investigation. On occasion, in fact, the funds employed in the speculative manipulation of an issue came from proceeds of the initial sales of the issue itself.[33]

The usual result of all these practices was that only a fraction of the sums the borrowing governments obliged themselves to repay ever reached the treasury. Of the Paraguayan issue of 1871, for example, the investment bankers actually remitted less than half to the government of Paraguay. Consequently, there were built up huge foreign debts for which much less in the way of a real value equivalent had been received by the borrowing economies, and out of which still less had been put to productive use. For decades such debts weighed down burdensomely upon national fiscal systems and balance of payments positions, while all along the wastage of public capital increased the scarcity and, hence, the cost of borrowing for legitimate productive ends in both the private and public sectors. Ultimately the system proved ruinous to the international credit standing of most Latin American countries when economic reverses in the twentieth century led to a reenactment of the widespread defaulting of almost a century earlier. Once again, a considerable external debt and service obligation had been run up without a commensurate increase in the productive capacity of the Latin American economies. Yet one should keep in mind the events which fed into this unfortunate outcome. If the promises-to-pay of Latin American governments turned out to be largely fictitious, so also, from the standpoint of the borrowing economies, was much of the debt obligation which had been incurred.

A full appreciation of the consequences of this improvident fiscal behavior must take into account the opportunity costs of these resources: i.e., the alternative uses to which they might have been put and the gains which might have been realized from these alternative uses had resources been allocated with due regard for the possibilities of forming viable national economies. In particular, the dissipation of fiscal resources on vainglorious presidential palaces, the support of underemployed office holders, the military, and the like was inseparable from the gross neglect of such critically important fields of social investment as transport, communications, and education, for the former claimed resources urgently required for improving the latter.

At first glance, such a criticism might seem excessively negative in view of the substantial public subsidies which were, in fact, bestowed on railway development. But despite the large amount of financing committed to that end, the quality of social control and public economic guidance was such that many of the rail ventures were ill-conceived and poorly executed. Not only did the laxity of public supervision and planning have the short-run effect of creating unnecessarily high capital-output ratios in a field in which the ratio was unavoidably high to begin with; in the longer run, a host of difficulties were bequeathed to the development efforts of later generations by the original socially inefficient use of capital. In retrospect, for example, one can observe that the failure to transcend the perspectives of national (and even regional) particularism maintained the physiographic separateness of the individual nations and market areas. The settled areas of each country remained economically remote from those of neighboring nations for want of transport facilities to agglomerate the scattered domestic markets and supply regions. Yet, if this is too much an ex post facto judgment involving a retroactive projection of development criteria not valid at an earlier period, it can also be observed that only a handful of countries acquired anything approximating a reasonable national coverage in their rail lines while highway extension and improvement were virtually ignored everywhere.

Chile, Argentina, Uruguay, Mexico, and southern Brazil came off relatively well in this respect,[34] but elsewhere the situation more nearly resembled the Colombian case, which the Economic Commission for Latin America has described as follows:

> Mention has . . . been made of the large sums invested by Colombia in the creation and expansion of the transport system. Unfortunately, until not long ago most of this investment was effected without proper co-ordination under over-all programs, and this led to the dissipation of funds and therefore to a relatively low yield from the capital utilized. Moreover, the fact that such investments were largely determined by the requirements of given areas or purely local and circumstantial needs, rather than by an order of priorities established at national level, gave rise to one of the principal defects of Colombia's transport system, namely, its lack of integration.[35]

Scattered, disconnected rail lines were the general rule in Latin America. But even where a broader railway coverage might, from a map, seem to have constituted a national system, integration of the network was generally more apparent than real—as became painfully clear in later years once efforts at domestic economic expansion began to shift traffic flow patterns and needs away from the routings originally required by the external sector. So long, for example, as Argentine traffic flows moved largely from the interior to the port of Buenos Aires and vice versa, the radial lines which fanned out into the interior from the national capital served, if not always efficiently, to move grain and livestock products out for transshipment overseas and imported goods in to the interior consumption centers. Once national development implied a greater volume of cross-system traffic, however, the deficiencies of the system stood out in sharp relief, in part because of the paucity of longitudinal or connecting links between the radii of the network. Cross-country transit was also impeded by the costliness, risks, and delays of unloading and reloading cargoes as they moved from a line of one gauge to another of a different gauge, for on account of failures of social control, the Argentine system developed on the basis of three different gauges.[36] Multigauged rail systems, in fact, seem to have been a quite common feature of the Latin American countries, and everywhere they have tended to detract from the operating efficiency of the capital sunk into this basic infrastructural element.[37]

Besides creating problems for through-shipments of cargoes, the lack of standardization within national railway systems contributed in other ways to unnecessarily high transport costs. Repairs and maintenance charges were exaggerated because of the need to service a variety of equipment, each with different specifications. A Brazilian study of recent years reports, by way of illustration, that switching and interchange have not been feasible as a solution to railway breakdowns, for in addition to different gauge lines, there are nearly forty different kinds of steam locomotives— built to burn a variety of fuels.[38] Furthermore, in Brazil as elsewhere, repair and maintenance requirements have generally been quite high because of past negligence in public regulation and supervision. Poor engineering and faulty construction in the original Brazilian lines have, for example, impaired their effectiveness ever since.[39] Grades that are too steep, poorly constructed track that has never been economically usable, corners that are too sharp, inadequate roadbeds that have unsuitable or no fill—these and other defects have served as a reminder that the basic investments which distribute external economies throughout a productive system can also, when improperly made, distribute diseconomies instead.

In addition to the technical deficiencies of planning, irregularities abounded both in railway finance and construction. Avid in their search for foreign capital, the governments of the region granted literally hundreds of concessions in the last few decades of the 1800's—often upon mere application and with scant regard for the solvency or other characteristics of the applicants.[40] Subsidies were generously proffered; but on account of the predations of promoters and other forms of mismanagement, the concessions frequently lapsed without any material results. Surveying the debacle of railway construction, the Mexican minister of finance issued a report in 1908 which concluded that general disorganization was evident in virtually all aspects of the railway industry.[41] Sometimes tracks had been laid in poorly chosen and difficult locations simply to pass through (or avoid) certain properties; on other occasions the routes were selected solely for the low construction costs they permitted, without regard for the needs of neighboring communities and the centers of production and consumption. The latter resulted, of course, from the promoters' desire to maximize the difference between the subsidy and the actual costs of construction. Elsewhere, lines were extended to unnecessary length in order to run up the kilometer-based subsidy, and for the same reason trackage was also laid in regions of no economic potential.

Because of a multitude of shortcomings in public transport policy during the 1850-1914 era, the external sector, which was relatively less affected thereby, received greater support from the existing infrastructure than did domestically oriented activities, for the internal flow of products in most Latin American economies was especially curtailed by the inadequacies of the system. Agricultural development possibilities suffered from the high freight charges which at once lowered the net earnings of farmers and raised the price of delivered products for consumers, while the range of economically accessible domestic markets was often no greater than it had been in colonial times. Domestic manufacturers were likewise adversely affected, and those in inland locations in particular had also to absorb high transport charges on their imported equipment and machinery as well as on their industrial raw materials. Moreover, domestic producers and consumers alike were continually exposed to exploitive encounters with commercial intermediaries who dominated the scarce transport services and communications channels, for the range of alternative supply sources and market outlets from which the participants in the economy could choose was often narrowly limited by the deficiencies of the transport system.

If public investment policies in transport left much to be desired, the policies regarding research and education—i.e., the investment in human capital formation—were even worse. Remarkably little was spent on improving the system of public education, although the value of elementary schooling was more effectively recognized in the social investment policies of Argentina and Chile than elsewhere. Furthermore, the little which was done to provide schools reflected the almost exclusive concern of governments with central city activities as the machinery of state was virtually entirely in the hands of the privileged segments of the urban populace. Accordingly, rural and provincial regions received practically nothing in the way of educational facilities beyond such few private schools as existed here and there, while even in the major urban centers there was seldom a serious effort made to provide training at the popular level. In conformity with the prevailing scheme of cultural values, education tended everywhere to be concerned almost exclusively with the traditional humanistic curricula, and vocational and technical schools were practically unknown.

The financial support accorded the universities of the region was quite niggardly, but in a few places schools offering specialized higher education were established, e.g., the small national medical, engineering, and normal schools.[42] The Gabinete Topográfico, for example, was founded in São Paulo in 1840 as a sort of precursor engineering school specializing in road construction; its graduates played an important role in the road building of the next half century, including construction of the country's first modern highway, the Estrada União e Industria, on which work began in 1856. On rare occasions, there was even some investment in research—which brought beneficial results, as indicated in another example drawn from Brazilian experience. During the 1890's, the new republican government set up the Serviço Geológico e Mineralógico do Brasil for the purpose of making minerals surveys of the country. Initial exploration was undertaken in the state in Minas Gerais, where an earlier boom had revealed the presence of a number of minerals, and before the Serviço was even 20 years old, its reports on the *mineiro* iron had attracted international attention, precipitating a flurry of foreign investment which pointed the direction for modern development in the state.[43]

Generally speaking, though, the amount of progress attained in cultivating the region's human resources was quite limited, and one should not
overstress the significance of the new developments in education. By 1864,
for example, a number of specialized schools for agricultural, commercial,
and industrial training had been established in Brazil, but the total matric-
ulation of all these schools appears to have been no more than 150 students
in that year. In 1871, when the national population of Brazil reached
approximately 10 million, the total enrollment in secondary schools
amounted to only 9,389 students. As late as 1907, no Brazilian institution
offered advanced education in agriculture, although there were two offering courses in fine arts, ten law schools, seven schools of medicine, two in
pharmacy, and six polytechnic engineering schools.[44] Even Argentina,
which made the broadest educational advances of all the Latin American
republics, had to draw continually upon foreign technical assistance in the
field of livestock production—and has continued to do so down to the
present day. The state of affairs in less affluent and progressive nations is
well indicated by Ecuador, where a foreign visitor in 1867 reported that
the mere 285 students engaged in university work in Quito (the only
"serious" effort at higher education in the country) had to rely on a university library that consisted of 11,000 old and not very useful volumes, since
there was not a single bookshop in the whole capital city.[45]

Even where higher educational facilities were available, the quality and
content of the training were often valueless for purposes of economic
development. Indeed, there is quite a voluminous literature indicating the
nonutilitarian orientation of the available education and its tendency to
foster class prejudice, pseudoaristocratic values, and a disdain for labor.
By all available evidence, including concrete results in economic progress,
the noted Chilean periodical, *El Mercurio,* was indulging in hyperbole
rather than misstatement when it editorialized that a large portion of that
country's university graduates were "true monuments of uselessness, and at
the same time a living indictment of our national educational system."[46]

Owing to the widespread neglect of human resources development, most
of the countries remained comparatively ignorant of their internal resource
potentialities except insofar as foreign prospecting could fill the knowledge
deficit. And in the countries that contained large numbers of indigenous
peoples, little headway was made toward resolving the multiple problems
of cultural dualism by diffusing more widely the values of an economically
progressive culture and by bringing the bearers of traditional culture into
fuller participation in the organized economic, social and political life of
the modern sector. Indeed, among the lower classes generally, the inaccessibility of educational opportunities blocked the routes to economic and social
mobility, and in that sense public educational policies were a factor in
stunting the growth of domestic markets. On the one hand, the uses of
public resources did little to enable the national population to qualify for

the more remunerative and skill-transmitting job opportunities of the export sector; while, on the other hand, the governments contributed little to developing a domestic pool of skilled labor and technical and managerial talent on which residentiary enterprises could draw—a situation which assured the competitive advantage to foreign suppliers of Latin American imports and which inhibited realization of the potential backward and forward linkages of the external sector. Inasmuch as the undiversified character of human resources which resulted from prevailing social investment policies checked the evolution of new comparative advantages in production, public policy was also instrumental in preserving the reflexive dependence on monocultural enclave patterns of economic expansion.

In this connection, the aforenoted rudimentary state of the economic information systems in Latin America takes on special significance. Linguistic barriers, the lack of schools and the pervasiveness of illiteracy, the infrequency and difficulty of human travel and the absence of roads and other transport facilities in many areas, the primitive state of the mail service, and the limited endowment of other forms of long-distance communication, the absence of public statistical gathering and reporting services, the limited circulation and news gathering capacity of available news media—all these conditions raised substantial obstacles to the attainment of accurate market knowledge and to the dissemination of reliable and current financial information. Monopolization of the limited number of information channels and manipulation of information flows were undoubtedly facilitated by these same conditions.

Reliable investment knowledge was difficult to come by for both domestic and foreign investors. The limited spread of communications media from Latin America and the possibilities for "news management" compounded the general foreign ignorance of real conditions in the hemisphere. For these reasons, nearly insurmountable barriers lay in the path of most foreign investors who might have attempted to check on what was being done with their money in distant lands, and consequently, with market knowledge in such an imperfect condition, it is hardly surprising that the social efficiency of the international capital transfer process left much to be desired.

Imprudent investments and financial chicane have been common wherever the system of finance capitalism has held sway. And such unsavory practices as stock watering, the milking of enterprises by insiders, and the flotation of unsound securities through specious information releases and clandestine market manipulation are scarcely unique in underdeveloped areas. If innocent investors sunk tens of thousands of dollars into nonexistent Latin American rubber plantations and if the peddlers of foreign securities lined their pockets handsomely through unethical transactions concealed from the general public, these did not differ in kind from the many corporate abuses practiced in the chief capitalistic nations of the world. Whether at the center or at the periphery, maneuvers aimed at differential pecuniary gain often placed individual interest at cross purposes with the general interest by impairing realization of the material or technological purposes of real investment.

The point, however, is that the laxity of public regulation in Latin America, the virtual absence of social controls on international transactions, and the conditions of the Latin American communications system all combined to facilitate what was almost certainly a much higher proportion of malpractice in the conduct of corporate finance than normally obtained in the advanced countries. Moreover, since capital was far scarcer in Latin America than in the capital-exporting economies, the marginal social value of the losses sustained through injudicious investment and pecuniary sabotage of the capital transfer process was correspondingly greater in Latin America than in the center, even for equivalent absolute amounts of capital loss. In other words, the capital-poor Latin American economies could less afford the costs of private (and public) financial fraud and misjudgment than could the comparatively affluent Europeans and North Americans. Nor could they easily afford the consequences of investor reaction, in the form of diminished capital inflows and higher international capital service charges, which followed upon revelations of these deficiencies in the market mechanism.

In short, because of the instrumental uses of literacy in modern employment and marketing, and because of the other skills requirements of modern enterprise, widespread illiteracy and cultural isolation joined forces to throttle both the appearance of a domestically based expansion and the local spread of benefits from the foreign trade and investment activity of the period. Public policy had encouraged the movement of capital and even, in some few countries, the movement of people, but by and large it had failed to grasp that the movement of information had become the basic organizational principle of the modern age. Since the pronounced underinvestment in social overhead capital occurred at the expense of long-run productivity, the current net gains in growth realized during the 1850-1914 period were, in a sense, consistently overstated—although this was not generally recognized until events of the present century made it impossible to continue with a mode of national economic operation which was essentially parasitical to the external sector.

ENTREPRENEURIAL FORMATION

With the range of domestic growth points truncated by the parameters of market demand and other deficiencies of social organization, it is easy to understand why there should have been such disparities between the development of the external sector and that of the balance of economic activity in Latin America. To some extent, the differential development was accentuated as time went on because of cumulative advantages which made the former a more attractive outlet for investment funds and enterprise than the latter. In addition, there was a certain tendency for the region's pattern of reaction to oscillations in the external sector to be somewhat asymmetric in that foreign trade recessions brought pervasive hardship to the modern subeconomies of the region while foreign trade booms did not usually succeed in triggering a generalized derivative wave of domestic expansion.

Self-Perpetuating Aspects of Enclave-Based Growth. The export sector, for example, enjoyed a more or less continuous improvement in its marketing and economic information system throughout the era, and to it came a growing inflow of specialized productive factors, especially capital and skills, which steadily raised the efficiency of export firms and the adjunctive enterprises which came into being on the basis of external economies provided by facilities associated with foreign trade and investment processes. In contrast, beyond the urban sites which functioned as collection centers for exports and for handling the distribution of imported items, the business environment was quite different. A comparatively primitive domestic marketing apparatus was all that was needed in provincial areas to support the sluggish flow of products moving from agricultural suppliers to the scattered local markets and to handle the meagre counterflow of urban produced goods. Local communications networks for conveying knowledge of production techniques and market signals were similarly rudimentary in character, while the available supply of financial services and human skills was quite limited and not very specialized. For domestic production, the conditions of factor supply were often rather inelastic owing to rigidities in the land, labor, capital, and entrepreneurial markets.[47]

During periods of export expansion, foreign investment flowed in, and from it and the export sales the capacity to import both consumer items and investment goods rose rapidly. Since, moreover, a substantial portion of the populace in most Latin American countries lived outside the money economy, an expansion of employment in the export sector brought about a proportionately greater increase in the level of aggregate money income than it did in total real income and a proportionately greater expansion in bank reserves and other financial assets than it did in total assets. Consequently, demand in the domestic market tended to rise rather sharply while bank lending capacity and private investment followed suit.[48] Government revenues and the state's capacity for borrowing abroad were similarly a positive function of upswings in the foreign trade cycle,[49] so that public sector expenditures rose alongside the increased volume of private sector spending. Thus, the profitability of many investments in the local economy was closely tied to the increased national money income generated by a rise in exports. At the same time, however, during the intervals of export boom the profitability and ease of making investments in the export sector, with its superior economic organization, tended to surpass those of most fields of residentiary activity and the available capital responded accordingly. Since the supply of imported goods was also much more elastic than the supply of domestically produced goods (and since many kinds of imported items were not produced at all in Latin America), a large portion of the increased purchasing power produced by a rise in external sector activity tended to spill over into the demand for imports. The high propensity to import, in other words, functioned to dampen the regional multiplier-accelerator effects of economic expansion and, like the foreign claims to Latin American export earnings, served to divert the impact of these economic amplifiers to the economies of the center nations.

Periods of export recession, on the other hand, occasioned a loss of income to those employed directly or indirectly by the foreign trade sector, and thereby produced a much greater contraction of money income than of total real income—to the detriment of residentiary enterprises catering to the monetized portion of the local economy. Bank reserves and bank lending activity dwindled. Government spending also moved downward with the reduction in trade-based tax revenues and the diminution of external borrowing capability.[50] Owing to the reduction in the capacity to import and the high import coefficient of many types of investment outlays, as well as to the high marginal propensity to import associated with the derivative streams of consumption spending, it was doubly difficult for goverments to take effective countercyclical measures to compensate for a severe downswing in exports. Consequently, during periods of crisis in the external sector both foreign investment and domestic investment were adversely affected. Neither in export booms nor in export recessions, therefore, was there a very strong inducement to invest in diversification of the local economy.

Compounding the difficulty was the fact that recessions in the enclave sector, by affecting precisely that portion of the regional economy in which productivity levels were far and away the highest, fell with special severity upon Latin American economic capabilities. In other words, with contraction in the high productivity sector, the average aggregate level of productivity tended to recede sharply to that relatively low point which typified the extensive colonial remnant and indigenous sectors of the economy. Correspondingly, less of an investable surplus remained to sustain output and employment growth when export demand faltered and foreign capital inflows dwindled. For this problem, there were only quite limited adjustment possibilities available in the movement of resources out of the external sector into portions of the domestic sector which had equivalent levels of productivity.

Most of the more efficient, ancillary institutions for performing distribution, storage, finance, and merchandising functions were geared to the routines of handling a single crop (or mineral product in the case of mining regions), and this influenced strongly the relative profitability of investment alternatives by providing established export production fields with essential external economies quite unavailable to other lines of production. Since departure from time-tested production lines to a more diversified and flexible production mix, however desirable from the standpoint of making better use of resources and effecting a swifter and more accurate adjustment to market changes, also required a whole series of accompanying changes (e.g., changes in firm organization and methods of operation, different production techniques, new managerial and labor skills, more complex types of knowledge, more adaptable and diversified bank credit), institutional inertia and the weight of experience combined with the sunk capital in production and marketing facilities to favor continued dependence on traditional products. Complementary investment supports were, in other words, too rarely available for other lines of production.

Under the circumstances, the vulnerability of the economic structure to vicissitudes in export markets inculcated a pattern of business psychology which ran at cross purposes with the sort of investment behavior required for solid long-term domestic business development. The preference for maintaining high precautionary liquid balances or for sending funds abroad to more stable investment environments was altogether understandable, as was the strong desire for quick, even if not continuable, profits in preference to longer-term, but highly uncertain, gains. Development pricing, for example, was not likely to be practiced when there seemed to be good reason for sellers to extract the maximum advantages of the moment through high markups in boom periods. Perhaps it was the related variability in government revenues as well as the transitory nature of public office which inclined political adventurers to snatch so avidly from the public till. Furthermore, the exceptional insecurity bred by monoculturally accentuated export fluctuations discouraged local investors from taking a long view in measures pertaining to building up enduring domestic enterprises. By increasing the risk of committing capital to more specialized forms (or, alternatively, enhancing the preference for more flexible if relatively unspecialized processes) and by occasioning the periodic underutilization of more specialized production capacity, external sector instability diminished the gains to be realized through business specialization. In addition, the evolution of firms to a larger size—already difficult because of capital costs and the shortage of managerial skills—was arrested because environmental instability tended to produce diseconomies in any scale of operations in which a large number of processes had to be coordinated; the incompleteness of the information available to producers and the difficulty (or impossibility) of routinely extrapolating from previous experience gave rise to the probability of a high degree of error in forecasting the movement of those decision elements on the basis of which the coordination of processes depended.

The existence of entrepreneurs and managers, both domestic and foreign, provides evidence that it was possible to adjust business operations sufficiently to cope with the substantial risks of the age and locale. The point at issue, however, is that which Alfred Marshall raised long ago when he observed that "the struggle for survival tends to make those methods of organization prevail which are best fitted to thrive in their environment; but not necessarily those best fitted to benefit their environment." [51]

Institutional Barriers to Entrepreneurial Development. When the foregoing difficulties are added to other aspects of the economic situation which have been mentioned earlier,[52] it is patent that, quite apart from such things as culturally supplied value and motivational structures, there was a generous supply of more purely economic impediments to local entrepreneurial formation. On top of these, however, various features of the domestic sociopolitical structure also intervened to depress the native capacity for entrepreneurial development.

Most of the participants in the rural economy, for example, were so deprived of significant discretionary authority over resources and so cut off from any meaningful incentive system or opportunities to gain education and useful experience in making business decisions that they figured not at all as potential candidates for economic leadership.[53] A substantial portion of the urban population was no less incapacitated by the prevailing socioeconomic structure to perceive and act upon available market opportunities.

So far as concerns the less disadvantaged portions of the Latin American citizenry, their selection from among the available career options seems often to have been shaped by a fairly rational perception of their comparative employment advantages, and the distribution of these comparative advantages more frequently than not lay in careers of a nonbusiness character. The military, for example, was one avenue for upward mobility in which Latin American nationals were obviously not at a competitive disadvantage vis-à-vis others.[54] In the slow growth of professional employment, there were additional job opportunities for nationals as teachers, physicians, journalists, and writers. Still others found employment as clerks and bookkeepers in the new enterprises in and around the fringe of the external sector. The general situation, however, retarded the creation of more intermediate positions in the socio-economic structure and thus hindered the lateral extension of occupations which typifies modern societies and which creates social differences and distinctions that lie outside the conventional means of assigning social status along a single scale.

More significantly, however, the burst of economic expansion which touched many of the countries between 1850 and 1914 reinforced in several ways the traditional attractions of careers in law and life on the public payroll. For one thing, the enclave nature of the industries which grew from foreign investment activity meant that much of the domestic share in this expansion came from the foreign trade taxes and from the spree of foreign borrowing on which the various national governments embarked. To be in or close to government was, therefore, to gain access to the chief domestic flow of rewards from externally induced growth.

Moreover, the nature of the fields of law and government was such that in them Latin American nationals—trained in their own law and knowing their way around the local power structures—were not at a competitive disadvantage with the foreign technical and business specialists who as immigrants or resident employees of foreign-owned concerns could often, on the basis of superior training and experience in the relevant skills, preempt the new employment opportunities opening up in the process of economic growth. The latter were not, however, likely to have attended the law schools of Latin America nor were they so readily eligible for government employment except in staff positions. Consequently, as retainers providing legal counsel, as bureaucrats able to supply official ratification of what it was the new business interests wanted to do, and as purveyors of useful political connections, well-placed and ambitious nationals could aspire to a share in the export and investment induced affluence which was not otherwise so readily come by.[55]

In addition, sinecures of public office were a socially appropriate means of livelihood for the more impecunious relations of the elite families who, unable to find employment suitable to their status in the constricted domestic economic structure, could readily be absorbed into government by virtue of oligarchic influence in that institution. As T. Lynn Smith has pointed out, the "middle sectors" of contemporary Latin American society, especially those in government jobs and in the socially respectable professions, were formed in part by a downward drift out of the upper social strata—a factor which also infused the "old" middle class's attitudes and value systems with pretentions to aristocratic gentility.[56] Because of cultural conventions, the crude reproduction rate among upper-class families tended generally to be as high as that of lower-class families, but as the former enjoyed a marked superiority in survival rates, upper-class family size was commonly larger than that of the less affluent strata of society. Given the context of slowly expanding economic opportunities, members of the upper class were therefore to some extent forced out of the elite's traditional base in landowning and into other acceptable careers where, through the influence of lineage and their proper education, they could swing a certain competitive advantage over other would-be aspirants for these jobs coming from more humble circumstances. Particularly was this the case insofar as public-service recruitment moved by ascriptive rather than achievement-based norms.

For the elite group, the placing of kinsmen in government office provided a double advantage. It could be used as a means of meeting intra-familial obligations of support, and at the same time it offered a means of establishing useful personal connections in the machinery of state to aid in the manipulation of institutional advantage and to provide a valuable form of insurance against the high levels of instability which pervaded the economic and political environment.[57]

The attraction of legal and governmental careers, however, was far from being confined to the extended families of the elite. For middle-class professionals and even, in some instances, for persons of still humbler origin, the avenues of advancement through public office were also more promising as a source of rewards than business.[58] In bureaucratic positions and as political operators, no less than in the military, members of the subelite classes could on occasion utilize the organizational power of political parties to move up the scale of social preferment, bringing, through nepotism and favoritism, some of their relations and friends along with them. By sharing in the public purse and distribution of the public domain, and through appropriation of church properties and those of political enemies, a certain measure of social capillarity was provided as some of these *nouveaux arrivés* eventually gained entrance into the traditional prestige system and joined the elite segment itself. While one should not exaggerate the numbers of persons and families who were able to cross class lines by such methods, the point is that noneconomic routes for the realization of ambition were often more within the reach of Latin American nationals than were business and industrial leadership roles.[59]

There were in most of the countries some relatively large nonagricultural business holdings which belonged to members of the latifundian class.[60] But most such enterprises were organized along family lines, with ownership and control closely held within groups of relatives and friends who personally held a generous share of the domestic capital which the deficient or nonexistent capital markets were unable to mobilize.[61] In these instances, the political influence wielded by the owning families was sufficient to buy some measure of protection from whimsical fluctuations in public policy, while the ability to cover the firms' assets through political action generally meant that such family concerns could obtain credit much more cheaply than could the multitude whose influence was nil in the continuing struggle for political advantage. The risk premium component of market interest rates, in other words, was varied according to the uneven distribution of political power—in addition to which the landholdings of the privileged classes provided collateral for the chief available type of long-term lending, mortgage credit, which could be used to finance investments both in and outside of the agricultural sector (when the loan proceeds were not used to finance consumption). Besides, it was not at all unusual for persons from socially prominent families to be invited to sit on the directing boards of the new financial institutions which were being established at the time, and this was not a disadvantage when it came to the processing of loan applications. Yet, although the pattern of ownership and control did not necessarily correspond with the social distribution of managerial capacity and entrepreneurial vision, the opportunities were rare for outsiders from the subordinate classes to participate in these domestic business concerns as other than lower level hired employees. Consequently, the characteristic endogamic or in-group pattern of economic opportunity appropriation presented still another hurdle for the more widespread generation of domestic entrepreneurial ability.

Principal Sources of Private Entrepreneurial Development. In view of the manifold structural and other difficulties which attended the successful initiation of national business ventures, it would be easy to come to the erroneous conclusion that foreign investment projects and other export related enterprises constituted the only business innovation to occur in Latin America before the First World War. Although the major business opportunities long lay in the export sector where foreigners often had the edge in industrial experience, market knowledge, and contacts, not to mention access to capital from the lower interest-rate structure of European and North American capital markets (which advantage made it possible for foreigners to invest their funds in long-term amortization projects of high capital density while Latin Americans could not afford to do so), there were other contemporary developments which were gradually laying a basis for eventual economic diversification. To ignore these is to create difficulties for understanding the course of twentieth-century Latin American trends.

For example, it has been widely recognized that the first spurt of rapid industrialization occurred in Latin America during the years of the First World War, at which time the dislocation of European production cut off many of the import sources on which the countries of the western hemisphere had long relied. While, to some extent, United States exporters moved in to displace their former European competitors in Latin American markets, in all of the major countries of the region there was a notable rise both in domestic industrial production and in the numbers of residentiary enterprises engaged in this import-substituting production. Even allowing for the fact that a few, rather exceptional, Latin American nationals had long been engaged in pioneering entrepreneurial endeavors, the elasticity of the domestic supply response to wartime conditions was considerably greater than might have been reasonably expected from the kind of economic environment which has been described thus far in this study. To account satisfactorily for this pheonomenon, it is necessary to examine certain other aspects of the experience of the 1850-1914 era which laid the basis for incipient industrialization and domestic entrepreneurial formation.

In doing so, one finds that while the material output of the external sector was not, for a variety of reasons, a significant basis for derivative domestic economic expansion and structural diversification (at least in the short term), the same cannot be said of the organizational output of that sector. Over the longer term, indeed, the institutional by-products of external sector growth were to provide the critical elements needed for a movement away from the usual nineteenth-century pattern of monocultural export dependency. For purposes of discussion, then, one may divide these interrelated institutional by-products into two categories: the immigrant entrepreneurs and the immigrant firms.

Immigrant entrepreneurs were those individuals who came to Latin America as immigrant laborers, as employees of companies domiciled abroad, as itinerant merchants, and as colonists on land settlement schemes. After their arrival, they began to play a leading role in developing new businesses of a residentiary character for either the foreign or the home market.[62] Immigrant firms were those, particularly in marketing and finance, which were established by foreign initiative with some initial contribution of imported capital but which, in time, gradually came to function as domestic or semi-domestic residentiary enterprises in the countries which were the locus of their operations. In some instances, their original raison d'être was in export management, as in the case of the coffee exporting firms or those handling the grain trade out of the Argentine. In other cases, the firms were set up to handle the internal distribution of imports, either by immigrant entrepreneurs or as branches of foreign firms, as with exporting enterprises. Some were general foreign trade houses involved in both exporting and importing. In addition, it is desirable to include as immigrant firms the financial institutions such as banks and insurance companies which were established, sometimes as branches of foreign financial corporations, primarily to service the foreign trade sector but which mobilized local savings along with foreign capital and came also to have an important function as purveyors of financial services to the domestic economy generally.[63] Before the close of the period in question, the category of immigrant firms also included the earliest branch manufacturing plants set up to serve the local market by manufacturing corporations headquartered abroad, especially in the United States.[64]

While immigrant entrepreneurs and immigrant firms were identical in some cases, the latter category is useful in that it is more inclusive than the former. It comprehends, in addition to the enterprises launched by resident immigrants (with local capital backing in some cases), those which were set up by foreigners who long maintained close business ties with their home country [65] and those which remained, technically, under foreign ownership but which were engaged in operations which integrated them substantially into the domestic market of the host economy.

It would be difficult to understate the contributions made to the Latin American economies by the migrants who came to the region before 1914. Where the pre-immigration population was small in relation to the potential new resources and where a servile domestic work force was lacking or, at least, insufficient for the job at hand, the center supplied the periphery with labor factors in addition to capital and export market demand.

Consequently, Argentina, Uruguay, southern Brazil, and, to a much lesser extent, Chile attracted significant numbers of peripatetic Europeans who brought with them, free of charge to these economies, the labor power, skills, and economic motivation the cost of developing which had been borne abroad. Nor was the contribution of labor factors the only developmental subsidy received by these countries from the immigration process.

Among these newcomers, who numbered in their midst a few Yankees and other non-Europeans, geographical mobility was often linked with a positive attitude toward economic and social mobility, or, to put it plainly, materialistic success.[66] Many of these positively motivated persons, including even those who came originally as laborers, began in time to provide the business leadership which was to figure so importantly in lifting the southern South American area to a level of economic sophistication which was notably higher than that of the other Latin American nations. And while some have suggested that Protestant religious affiliation was, in line with the Tawney-Weberian hypothesis, a contributing factor to the material success of immigrants,[67] the evidence indicates that religious considerations were on balance perhaps less important than the motivation selection process involved in immigration itself. Irish, French, Spanish, Portuguese, Italian, and Levantine immigrants came to figure conspicuously in the roster of Latin American business leadership.[68]

Not all of Latin America was in a position to receive so large a developmental subvention from immigration. Over the largest portion of the region contemporary land tenure patterns and labor systems discouraged the immigration which might have come in response to the attractions of yeoman farming on free lands or even in response to not unreasonably depressed opportunities for tenant farming or employment as wage laborers in agriculture, mining, and construction. But if only three or four countries were able to benefit from relatively large-scale transfers of the crucially important human agents of production, there was scarcely a nation which did not receive some measure of a more specialized, if smaller scale, immigration. All around the hemisphere the increasing activity in the foreign-trade sector attracted foreigners to provide the necessary skills the local society could not supply—and to introduce new attitudes into the domestic cultural environment.[69] Of these, a portion came on temporary job assignments, such as construction and mining engineers, mill technicians on the sugar estates, and specialists in various aspects of public utility operations. Many of these people remained and intermarried with the native population to constitute the nucleus of a new commercially oriented group, both in the towns and, as in the case of the German coffee *finqueros* of Central America, in the countryside. Since in some instances European immigrants could, by entering the local status structure from the outside, marry with the daughters of the upper echelons of Latin American society, their ultimate influence extended even to a marginal transformation of the economic attitudes and behavior of the domestic elite. In this connection one thinks, for example, of the Edwards family in Chile and the financial genius of the Porfirian government in Mexico, José Yves Limantour.

Whether we consider the countries of heaviest immigration or those to which lesser numbers of immigrants and immigrant-firms came, the contribution to economic development made by these new arrivals was quite disproportionate to their numbers. Economically speaking, Argentina was virtually an immigrant nation, for of the 48,779 Argentine firms covered in the 1914 census, 31,483 were owned by foreign-born persons, while another 1,533 firms were owned jointly by foreigners and nationals.[70] It seems likely, moreover, that, since the census of 1895 had indicated that over 80 per cent of the 19,000 business establishments registered in that year were owned by foreign-born persons,[71] a sizable portion of the firms classified as nationally owned in 1914 were controlled by first generation Argentines. Immigration had been heavy, of course, throughout this period, but the immigrant interest in the economic structure far exceeded the proportion of the foreign-born in the total population.[72]

Across the Andes, the Chilean economy had benefited from the work of foreign entrepreneurs since the days when the resident English merchant-financier, Joshua Waddington, had invested heavily in copper mining, railways, and irrigation projects. An English export merchant, Thomas Garland, a partner in the firm of Cousiño and Garland, owned the first Chilean vessels which carried Chilean copper and wheat to England, was the contractor for the San Fernando-Curicó railway, developed the Lota coal fields, and promoted the first tramway, that of Valparaíso, in South America. Previously worthless Chilean copper ores had been given resource value by a new processing method (reverberating furnaces) introduced by the Welshman, Charles Lambert, who engaged in copper mining at Coquimbo. A Yankee shipping entrepreneur, William Wheelwright, established the first important steamship line serving western South America (the Pacific Steam Navigation Company),[73] developed the coal fields of Talcahuano, introduced brickmaking machines to Chile, promoted the Copiapó-Caldera railway line, and moved on to Argentina to cap his career by constructing the Córdoba-Rosario railway and the Ensenada railway and port.[74] In Chilean agriculture, ranching development in the Magallanes territory after 1874 was largely the work of the Englishmen Reynard and Hamilton, the Spaniards Menéndez and Montes, the French Blanchard family, the Portuguese Nogueira, the Swiss Marius, and the Lithuanian Braun.[75] Francisco Encina concluded that around 1890 "almost all industries of any importance in Chile were controlled by foreigners and their immediate descendents."[76] Notwithstanding their lesser numbers, immigrant entrepreneurs were almost as important in Chilean development as they were in the Argentine.[77]

Similar examples of immigrant entrepreneurial endeavor could be cited at length. As promoters of new ventures and as innovators of modern forms of economic enterprise, immigrants did much to reshape the business scene in nearly every republic. Most came to stay in a particular country, or at least ended up staying, whatever their initial intentions, but there was a more migratory breed who were like the aforementioned William Wheelwright. The name of the flamboyant railway promoter, Henry Meiggs, for example, is by now almost legendary and is as interwoven with the economic history of Chile and Peru as that of his nephew, Minor Keith, is interwoven with the development of railways and bananas in Costa Rica.[78] Mexican commercial history would have many gaps indeed if one omitted the role played by such gringos as William Rosecrans, Alexander Shepherd, Arthur Stilwell, and Edward Doheny.[79] More foot-loose in their habits and more transient in their stays in Latin America, they also made significant contributions to the initiation of new undertakings.

It is appropriate to note, at least in a summary way, some of the ingredients in the immigrants' differential advantage vis-à-vis the native population. In the first place, their mentality and motivational patterns were informed by a value system which had been conditioned by centuries of cultural transformation in Europe—a system different from the traditional Hispanic one. In a general way, this in itself probably predisposed the new arrivals to seek out and act upon the available opportunities for material success. In addition their voluntary assumption of the not insubstantial risks of relocating in an alien environment was to some degree an indicator of their repudiation of fatalistic attitudes and acceptance of the status quo. If anything, the selectivity of values implied by migration to Latin America was greater than in the corresponding stream of migration to the United States, for few could have been drawn to the region south of the Rio Grande primarily to realize democratic political ideals or to enjoy religious toleration. The economic motive, in other words, tended to be a paramount consideration. Moreover, as a *nouveau arrivé* group, deracinated socially as well as geographically, the immigrant entrepreneurs were rather clearly characterized by a certain marginality in terms of the existing social structure of their new domiciles. While in some instances this ambiguity of relationship vis-à-vis the Latin American milieu permitted them to enter the local structure through marriage at a fairly high level, it appears that more commonly the advantage in the conventional routes to recognition and approbation lay with the native-born of requisite status. Yet at the same time, the very ambiguity of the newcomers in their identity with the local structure of social relationships probably permitted them a measure of mobility, with marginal acceptance at varying levels, which was not so readily obtainable by those whose social roles and stations were more clearly described in the established institutional framework.

For all its vaunted preoccupation with social lineage (*abolengo*), Latin American culture does have a capacity to overlook obscure backgrounds when really outstanding success is achieved; and with the marginal fluidity which was imparted to class lines by the rise and fall of fortunes in the tumult of republican period politics, the possibilities of the immigrants' gaining eventual social acceptance on the basis of successful performance was enhanced. Old family fortunes were occasionally in need of replenishing, and there was generally a supply of unmarried daughters among these rather large upper-class families. That candidates for marriage with them might be foreign-born was not necessarily a detraction from their qualifications in an age of positivistic accolades for things European and North American. Meanwhile, awaiting eventual acceptance into the domestic social scene, the immigrants could draw some support from others in the growing "enclave" community of the foreign-born while applying their talents and energies to those parts of the social opportunity structure in which their marginal status was not such a disadvantage: the business life of the nation.

In this area, in fact, the immigrant entrepreneurs held the advantage. Their background in a commercialized, industrializing society had equipped them through training, or through the familiarity of long exposure, with the skills relevant for business success. Furthermore, the happenstance of foreign birth provided them with personal knowledge of and, often, connections with the important overseas export markets and foreign supply sources for imported items—no small advantage, indeed, since this particular kind of market and product knowledge coincided with the most rapidly expanding and lucrative portion of the economies in which they sought to earn their livelihood. Foreign consular representatives often constituted a useful liaison with the network of center country suppliers and distributors and served as a source of economic intelligence generally superior to any provided in the host countries. One is struck, in reading the various contemporary consular reports, by the degree to which this valuable overhead facility seems to have served the interests of the resident foreign community as well as firms in the home country.[80] In the reports on visitors and their doings, contained in the periodicals published for the benefit of resident foreigners in Latin America, it is possible to detect a tendency for commercial travelers from the center countries, who were essentially purveyors of economic opportunities, to seek out those of "their own kind" in the course of their journeys through the region.

Thus, the migrants who came to set up shop in the new world were uncommonly well supported by the multitude of information channels at their disposition—and this in an environment in which reliable economic intelligence was scarce. Knowing their way around abroad, in addition, meant that the foreign-initiated firms in the tertiary sector were sometimes able to tap the superior and less costly financial resources of the center countries to a degree not generally possible for native Latin American undertakings.

Many a Portuguese, British, French, or German firm in Latin America, for example, was able to conduct its trade operations with the support of lines of credit with banks in the home country.

These assets—familiarity with business skills, continuing channels of communication abroad, and wider financing alternatives—gave the immigrant entrepreneurs a distinctly advantageous position in the business structure of Latin America and one which tended, when translated into superior earnings capacity and thus a superior basis for firm growth through internal financing, to become cumulative over time. In an environment in which institutionalized capital-gathering facilities were notably deficient, there was hardly a substitute for reinvestable earnings, a source of savings available only to existing firms.

To the foregoing, finally, there must be added a further advantage which, while somewhat more difficult to assess with certainty, nevertheless seems to have played a role in the operating performance of immigrant firms in the American markets. Emilio Willems, for example, notes the presence among the German settlers in southern Brazil of a spirit of solidarity, a sense of group cohesion which enabled them to innovate an organizational form which was at that time virtually unknown in Latin America: the rural cooperative societies through which settlers banded together to establish small factories.[81] A quite similar sort of ethnic cohesion seems to have been involved in the joint action of members of the French mercantile community in Mexico during their successful intrusion into the textile field as M. P. Arnaud has described it, while Stanley Stein's account of the role of the Portuguese community in Brazilian textile manufacturing suggests that there, too, intragroup relations were of a different character from relations of an extragroup nature. Among the existing accounts of Italian immigrant efforts in Latin America one can detect a certain closeness of ethnic association,[82] and within the Levantine groups a similar ethnic loyalty was operative. For that matter, a reading of the books by Mulhall conveys a distinct impression that a special sense of community was characteristic of the resident British in the area.[83]

In specific instances—e.g., the French mercantile-textile consortium, the German cooperatives, the banking institutions backed by members of identifiable foreign communities—some of the economic implications of this factor become clear. The pooling of assets and abilities contributed to an enhanced economic capacity while the special ties with banking institutions were scarcely a disadvantage in the credit-short conditions of the times. But in a larger way the contrast between the internal cohesion of the marginal foreign out-groups and the tenuous interpersonal relations characteristic of the dominant ladino in-group raises at least the possibility that the former may have enjoyed a rather general relative advantage in the collaborative, activity associated with the patterns of modern economic organization.

While the occupational activities of these immigrants were varied and covered virtually the entire range of economic pursuits, three types of immigrant firms in particular require some discussion because of their special long-term contribution to the development process in the region: the mercantile enterprises, the financial enterprises, and the manufacturing enterprises.

As previously indicated, many of the foreign migrants to the Americas helped to fill out the structure of tertiary economic activity by establishing firms engaged in trade, particularly in managing the flow of exports and imports. In Brazil, for example, the British commercial houses, which were of great importance for much of the century in that country's foreign trade, operated alongside numerous Portuguese mercantile firms, and the latter were quite active in the local distribution system as well.[84] Towards the close of the nineteenth century, German-operated foreign-trade concerns acquired some significance; and in southern Brazil, Italian immigrants were widely involved in retailing and wholesaling. Before the First World War, Levantine immigrants also began to play a prominent role in the domestic marketing network.[85] In Argentina a very large segment of the mercantile sector was also managed by foreigners. British firms were particularly strong in exporting and importing, while firms set up by immigrants from other countries, especially Italy, were dominant in domestic wholesaling and retailing.[86] In Mexico after 1850, French-initiated mercantile establishments gradually came to control the distribution of certain lines of imports, and French entrepreneurs were instrumental in setting up many retail concerns of a modern type. Other mercantile firms, however, operated by Germans, Spaniards, Englishmen, and to a lesser extent, resident nationals of other foreign countries, also contributed to the development of Mexico's distribution network for domestic and foreign goods. Among the smaller Latin American countries, the influence of immigrant trading enterprises was, for the most part, no less pervasive and consequential—both for itself and for the demonstration effect of innovations in commercial practice and organization.[87]

Important in their own right, the immigrant mercantile enterprises acquired additional significance as sources of capital and initiative for other activities. British merchants, for example, appear to have added banking functions to their commercial dealings at an early period in the Argentine, while their counterparts in Chile and elsewhere had done the same, as is clear from the previously cited cases of Garland, Waddington, and Edwards. Moreover, when formal banking institutions were established, it was common to find resident foreign merchants among their founders and backers. "English merchants took a prominent part in the first Banco de la Provincia in Buenos Aires in 1822," and "two British merchants . . . were among the founders of the Banco Comercial in Montevideo."[88] In Mexico the Banco Nacional de México, as noted earlier, was initiated with the assistance of the resident French mercantile community, while the Italian business colony in Peru took the lead in setting up both the Banco Italiano and the Banco de Callao. On the basis of their familiarity with the workings of commercial credit and their connections with financial institutions abroad, it was perhaps natural that immigrant marketing enterprises should have been so active in setting up the local financial facilities which they needed to further the conduct of their own operations. In addition, they also had the financial wherewithal to do so, thanks to the trading profits accumulated through the expansion of the external sector.

In the secondary sector, the immigrant firm was also especially likely to be found in the vanguard of manufacturing development. Compared with the growth of enterprises in infrastructure, mining, commercial agriculture, and trade and banking, the field of manufacturing was still in its embryonic stage; but even so, it is impossible to overlook the growing number of small factories which appeared during the 1850-1914 period as a consequence of largely immigrant initiative and of changes in economic relationships and government policies.[89] The impediments to diversified development, in other words, should be thought of as limiting rather than preventive conditions; it was a case of market and other limitations permitting only a limited industrialization rather than (as the matter has sometimes been overstated) a lack of markets precluding the establishment of new industries.

Some of the immigrant entrepreneurs, carriers of the technological skills accumulated abroad, came to the region to establish artisan workshops or small-scale plants which subsequently evolved into larger factory facilities. Julio Vega notes, for example, that in Chile native artisans tended to remain artisans while the not very numerous immigrant artisans, perhaps because of social structural and motivational factors and because of their greater experience with modern technological processes, tended to advance in status and became outstanding as middle class entrepreneurs in industry.[90] In Peru, Bartolomeo Boggio, an immigrant from the Biella mill district of Italy, was credited with being the first person to grasp the possibilities of establishing a woollen factory. His first shop, established in 1888, employed only five workers, but so promising it must have been that within two years the operation was reorganized on a considerably expanded scale with the participation of wealthy and influential Peruvians, after which the progress of the Santa Catarina Industrial Society was "very marked." [91] In several countries, skilled British mechanics and mechanical engineers were often encountered as pioneers in setting up the early foundries and machine shops which, in some instances, endured for many years.[92]

In southern Brazil, many of the artisan shops established by Germans grew into factories for processing local raw materials, utilizing equipment brought from Europe but later often constructing the replacement equipment locally. Technical specialists for these plants were sometimes contracted for in the homeland, while a continuing stream of immigrant skilled workers also helped to keep local technical knowledge up-to-date.[93] Not a few of the German families engaged in Brazilian industry followed the practice of sending their sons back to the fatherland to receive their technical education,[94] and, while the evidence is scanty, it seems probable that other immigrant families may have done the same. The previously cited work by R. Foerster, which is filled with references to the industrial entrepreneuring efforts of Italians in the Argentine and Brazil, seems to indicate that the continuing flow of migrants from Europe was also a factor in enabling these firms to maintain a position of technological leadership.[95]

Not all of the new manufacturing plants, though, were established by persons who came to the Americas for that purpose. A good many were the result of efforts by immigrants who had initially been engaged in another line of activity, including technicians who had first arrived on the scene as employees of the larger foreign investment ventures. Two typical examples of this were the important lumber-milling company founded in Peru by Maurer, the erstwhile Swiss secretary of Henry Meiggs, and the Backus and Johnston brewery established in 1879 as the first in that country by two civil engineers connected with the construction of the Peruvian Central Railway.[96] Stanley Stein reports a somewhat similar pattern in Brazil where foreign textile technicians brought over in the employ of existing firms later contributed their talents to the organization of new concerns. In several of the industrial establishments described in Luis Ospina Vásquez' study of Colombian manufacturing developments, one comes across equivalent cases of skills transfers from foreign companies to new domestic enterprises. This study shows also that even where new factories were launched by native entrepreneurs it was not uncommon for the key technical personnel to be specialists hired from abroad or recruited from among the local foreign communities; often, indeed, this dependence upon foreign technical support continued for many years, the local society being unable to provide adequate replacements.[97] Nevertheless, as examples of joint enterprises which pooled the contributions of local and foreign persons, the companies in question demonstrate rather well one of the most important historical aspects of foreign business activity in Latin America: its catalytic or energizing effect on the mobilization of domestic resources for development.

Besides the foregoing sources of manufacturing initiative, there was one other institutional connection which, then as later, appeared as an exceptionally important aspect of industrial entrepreneuring. Of the several barriers to success in domestic manufacturing ventures, five problems stood out with particular prominence: (1) the difficulty of raising risk capital in a business environment still primitive in its endowment of financial intermediaries and narrow in its pattern of income distribution, (2) the inadequacies of local knowledge with respect to modern product specifications and production processes, (3) the uncertainties of price relationships between domestically manufactured items and imported goods, (4) the paucity of reliable information concerning the size and regional distribution of domestic market demand, and (5) the difficulties of reaching the potential domestic market, wherever it might be located, given the rudimentary development of the national marketing network.

One key group in the local economic structure, however, possessed the means for coping with most of these problems; this was the larger mercantile houses and more especially those engaged in foreign trade. The expansion of exporting and importing activity brought about substantial trade profits, which were accordingly available for further business expansion. Furthermore, this was a group of enterprises which enjoyed access to the lending services of the domestic banks and the branches of foreign banks which had been set up in Latin America. The nature of their trade kept them au courant as far as knowledge of product specifications was concerned, while their overseas marketing connections could be used as a channel for drawing upon the fund of foreign-developed production technology. More than any other economic group, the commercial houses had at their disposition the necessary data concerning price levels and trends of imported goods. In the absence of "public" sources of data on the size and distribution of the domestic market, there was hardly a substitute for the experientially derived information which the established importing firms had available from their internal records. From these, in other words, the major firms dealing in imported manufactures had a reasonably good basis for judging domestic market needs and a means of gauging the possible volume of domestically manufactured substitutes which could be absorbed at varying price levels. The knowledge of the domestic market possessed by the mercantile companies proceeded from the network of distributive outlets they had gradually built up in the marketing of imported items, but which could be utilized to distribute domestically manufactured goods as well.

All things considered, the established houses in distribution were uniquely capacitated to act on such manufacturing opportunities as were potentially attractive, for the risks they assumed in doing so were less than those confronting other would-be industrial entrepreneurs. Moreover, by the closing years of the century many of these concerns had waxed so influential that the possibility of obtaining a sympathetic hearing from government officials concerned with setting tariff and general trade policies was far from being out of the question—particularly as laissez-faire doctrines increasingly lost ground to Hamiltonian and Listian arguments. Not surprisingly, a good many of these concerns acted upon their differential advantage and branched out into the field of secondary production with notable success.

The aforementioned French-sponsored reorganization and modernization of the Mexican textile industry, for example, was enormously facilitated by the mercantile houses' controlling position in the national distribution of cloth and clothing, while French entrepreneurs in the other new Mexican manufacturing lines often enjoyed a similarly advantageous combination of economic roles. Vertical integration, from the ginning of cotton to the whole-sale and retail distribution of mill output, was likewise a prominent feature of the important and long-lived Cantel textile mill in Guatemala. In a strik-ingly close parallel to the Mexican textile case, Portuguese wholesale cloth merchants figured importantly in the late nineteenth-century reorganization of the domestic Brazilian textile industry, replacing single proprietorships and partnerships with more amply capitalized corporate organizations. "With nationally produced cotton at hand, the prices of cheap fabrics con-taining ample cotton fiber were attractively low [compared with the delivered price of heavily taxed imports]. The large commercial houses saw the ad-vantage of producing in Brazil, assuring their chain of distribution a guaran-teed, organized production" [98] and moved, accordingly, into a position of manufacturing leadership.

Bartolomeo Boggio's pioneer woollen mill in Peru must certainly have been helped by the participation of prominent and wealthy Peruvians, but it seems significant that the article describing the Santa Catarina Industrial Society's successful growth also pointed out that the enlarged version of the enterprise included a well-known Italian merchant, Juan Raffo, as man-aging director of the mill and its wholesale and retail stores. [99] In Argentina, where the Tornquist mercantile house had branched out into banking and manufacturing, Torcuato di Tella's industrial empire was born in 1910 with capital put up by the Allegrucci trade brokerage firm, as an employee of which di Tella had "learned the problems of the import-export business, and in doing so, the needs and potentials of the Argentine market." [100] One of the largest South American trading-industrial complexes—known as "El Pulpo" (The Octopus) because of its extensive ramifications—was launched by the Baltic grain traders, Ernest Bunge and George Born, who arrived in Buenos Aires from Antwerp in 1876 and set up a firm, the trading profits of which flowed later into milling and manufacturing. Some 75 years later, the firm was handling around 25 per cent of all Argen-tine wheat exports, manufacturing 85 per cent of the Argentine tin can out-put, operating the largest cotton mill and paint factory in that country, producing a wide variety of food and drug products and other manu-factured items, and conducting a world-wide business in an extraordinary range of items through its branches in 80 countries. Roughly contemporane-ous in its formation was the impressive industrial empire which another shrewd Italian immigrant put together in southern Brazil: that of the rural shopkeeper, hog merchant, and, later, grain and flour trader, Francisco Matarazzo. [101]

Not all of the late nineteenth- and early twentieth-century manufacturing plants were the offspring of firms originally engaged in commerce; the Klabin industrial complex in Brazil, for example, had its genesis in the small plant for converting rags into paper which was established around the turn of the century by four immigrants from Latvia. But so high does the proportion of merchants-turned-manufacturers appear to be among the entrepreneurs of the larger industries that, tentatively at least, one can set it down as a factor of considerable significance in the economic evolution of the region—indicative, perhaps, of the importance of internal economies of scale (achieved through vertical integration) in a general environment not yet sufficiently matured to offer many external economies of scale.

The same circumstances in business sector capital accumulation which tended to favor established firms in the trading field tended also to work to the advantage of the pioneer manufacturing concerns, especially when they were tied in with mercantile concerns and, through them, with banks. Preferential access to loan and venture capital, neither one of which was widely available, supplemented the important role of internal capital formation in the further expansion of the early industrial ventures. Human capital seems also to have been accumulated internally to a large degree; public investment policies being what they were, the limited industrial labor force and local managerial resources were, except for those supplied through immigration, mainly produced by means of skills developed through on-job training in the course of firm operations. Generally speaking, the existing firms gained something of a corner on the scarce factors of production and often enjoyed a monopoly of the locally available market and production knowledge. Furthermore, having built up over time or acquired through mercantile participation in industrial ownership their own distributive networks, early entrants gained a decided edge over those latecomers for whom equivalently serviceable marketing facilities were usually unavailable. Meanwhile, the rather slow expansion of the small domestic markets often meant that there was a lack of potential demand on the basis of which additional firms in any industry could come into being, so that early entrants, through gradual expansion and diversification, could generally cope with the leisured pace of growth in the aggregate national demand for domestic manufactures.[102]

For the long-term development of Latin American economic structure, this period of incipient industrialization should not be underrated. Many of the larger manufacturing concerns operating in the region today had their origins therein, and the industrial experience gained before 1914 was the basis on which an accelerated industrial growth was built thereafter. Moreover, in the narrow economic structure of most countries and in the absence of an abundant supply of systemically provided external economies, there were very definite advantages in taking the lead, advantages which tended to be cumulative in nature and which enabled the firms established early to appropriate many of the economic opportunities which later appeared. Since taking the lead was therefore nearly the same in a goodly number of instances as preempting the lead, the characteristically oligopolistic structure in Latin American industrial sectors thus came into being.

IX

Differential Growth: Regional Variations

IT is desirable to examine the national cases which departed significantly from the implied model of contained development sketched out in the preceding chapter. Differing from each other as well as from the rest of Latin America, Brazil, Chile, and Argentina constitute special situations which tell as much about the general barriers to economic progress as about the exceptional factors which account for their somewhat higher levels of attainment. The fourth case, Mexico, also contains special factors which differentiate it in certain important respects from the other countries of the region, although it remained much closer to the model of contained growth than did the "ABC" countries. The view to be taken of the experiences of these countries is highly selective and is in no way intended to constitute even a summary history of events. Rather, the objective is to discern in each the chief differentiating factors and conditions which enabled it to break away partially from the limitations discussed previously.

Aside from this, there is another reason for considering these four countries individually: that of their economic significance. Each was among the economic leaders of Latin America, having made the greatest material progress between 1850 and 1914. Together, the four countries cover well over half the total land area of Latin America and contain the majority of people in the region. Even today, the four countries generate close to two-thirds of the gross regional product, and stand in the forefront of manufacturing development. In 1914 their share of gross regional product was undoubtedly higher, for other countries have since gained strikingly in relative importance and the relative share of Argentine and Chilean output in gross regional product has slipped considerably over the past decade or so.[1] Accordingly, a special look at the economic history of each of these nations is in order simply to recognize some of the most prominent developments in the Latin American past.

Several circumstances combined to give these countries their special economic prominence. The resource endowment in each was rather more favorable than is common in Latin America. Geography, too, was an advantage, for the most productive regions in each country lie close, in terms of economic distance, to cheap means of placing their exports in foreign markets. The *pampeana* area of Argentina, for example, is easily accessible by economical maritime and fluvial transport, and the Chilean central valley and the coffee lands of southern Brazil are also fairly close to ocean transport services. Merely considering the lay of the land, Brazil, Argentina, and Chile were more favored than Mexico in this respect, but what Mexico lost on account of the ruggedness of its topography was counterbalanced to some extent by its location in the Northern Hemisphere and its proximity to the major consuming centers of the world.

The combination of resources and location endowed the four countries with a substantial supply of investment opportunities which were attractive in terms of the needs of the world market. They received, collectively, the lion's share of the foreign capital which was invested in Latin America during the 1850-1914 era. Probably as much as 80 per cent of the total foreign capital which came to Latin America before 1914 was directed into enterprises located in these four countries. Around a third of the total came to Argentina alone, and Brazil and Mexico each received about a quarter of the total foreign capital stake.[2] Well over two-thirds of the railway trackage constructed by 1914, for example, was built within the borders of the four countries.[3] With capital came other important ingredients of economic performance. The four received the overwhelming majority of the trained and experienced foreign personnel who labored in Latin America during this time. Argentina and Brazil benefited from mass immigration as well. On the output side, nearly 70 per cent of Latin American exports in 1913 originated in the four economies, over 50 per cent from Brazil and Argentina alone.[4] In short, the exceptional performance of Argentina, Brazil, Chile, and Mexico in the 1850-1914 period is obviously linked with the deep involvement of these countries in the international economy, from which they received an intense exposure to the growth-promoting influences of investment and market expansion.

Part of the relative success of these countries, however, lay in their special receptivity to such exogenous stimuli, for the vicissitudes of history had given them—at least to Argentina, Brazil, and Chile—a certain "openness" which enabled them to assimilate the economic trends of the times. They did so, of course, with varying effectiveness. Argentina realized the most nearly complete transformation of any of the four and despite its late start, or more probably because of it, emerged from the period as a comparatively modern nation in many respects.[5] Chile and Brazil were more intermediate cases. In the former the movement ahead appeared gradually to lose momentum and eventually left the country stalled along the route to a modern society; in the latter the forward thrust continued and even gained momentum but tended, more than in Chile, to be somewhat concentrated in its geographical impact.

Of all the four, Mexico contained the most divergent and disparate elements in its socio-economic structure, combining the industrial leadership of Latin America with a residue of traditional culture, both Hispanic and indigenous in character, very nearly as strong as one could find anywhere else on the continent. There, perhaps more than in any other country, the uneasy coexistence of different and essentially incompatible economic arrangements attested to the unresolved contradictions of the age—and to the explosive power inherent in those contradictions.

BRAZIL: CONTINUITY IN CHANGE

Far more smoothly than in any Spanish American country did independence, and eventually republicanism, come to Brazil. In its simplest outlines the easy transition may be sketched out in only a few sentences, but the significance of the change was profound. At a time when the rest of the continent was caught in the throes of governmental upheaval, Brazil sailed placidly, even rather gracefully, out of colonial status and into nationhood, reaping thereby all the developmental advantages of continuity and stability. Without interruption its longstanding participation in the expanding world economy continued into and through the nineteenth century. Indeed, the circumstances surrounding the attainment of independence even enlarged the commitment of Brazil to the international market—and vice versa, for as an attraction for outward moving European capital, Brazil was without peer in the Iberian world until near the end of the century. All during the periods that investors steered clear of the unsettled and delinquent regimes which came out of the old Spanish realm, the Rothschild house and other bankers in London usually managed to float loans for their imperial clients, the Braganzas of Brazil, and private investments followed suit.

Politically, events moved as follows. When Napoleon occupied the mother country in 1807, the Portuguese crown and court set sail for Brazil, crossing the Atlantic with British naval escort. After a short sojourn in Bahia, the whole entourage arrived in early 1808 in Rio, which thereupon became the capital of the Portuguese empire. To mollify local sentiment, as well as to attend to certain diplomatic ends in Europe, the crown raised Brazil to the status of a kingdom in 1815, making it equal in that respect to Portugal. When the king, overdue for a return to his liberated European domain, finally left for Lisbon in 1821, his son remained behind as regent. He declared Brazil an independent nation with himself as its emperor in September of the following year. The step proved to be tremendously popular as the peninsular Portuguese had, after forcing the vacillating monarch to return, given every indication of their intention to restore the former colony to a subordinate status. Thereafter, a form of constitutional monarchy prevailed until 1889 when, with a modicum of friction, the emperor abdicated and the republic was proclaimed.[6] Throughout this long period there had been occasional regional disorders, a couple of wars (one with Argentina and a later one with Paraguay), and the political friction normal to parliamentary regimes was certainly present. Nevertheless, general political stability at the national level was seldom in jeopardy. The empire was free, therefore, to ride the rising wave of coffee prosperity which, commencing slowly in the hinterlands of Rio de Janeiro, swept through the Paraíba Valley and crested spectacularly over the famous *terra roxa* of São Paulo.[7]

The accommodative political system of the Luzo-Brazilian realm was a singular economic advantage, for it provided a reasonably stable environment, one suitable for the effective conduct of business enterprise and conducive to the investment of both native and foreign capital. Continuity in the functioning of the public sector was also far more assured than in the case of the Spanish American countries. In consequence of Brazil's early attainment of more of the political preconditions of development, it seems safe to assume, for both the private and public sectors, that there was a higher level of efficiency in the employment of capital than elsewhere in Latin America. No claim, however, could be made that corruption, inefficiency, and misdirected capital were unknown accompaniments to Brazilian public administration. Far from it. As noted in a previous chapter, the Brazilian railway system suffered most of the defects of those of the other countries, and there were many other common liabilities, including a general neglect of investment in the native human resources. At an early period, too, fiscal policy began to display a marked inflationary bent; the government budget was usually in deficit and the resort to currency debasement and paper money issues was frequent. The case is rather that Brazil was exempted from at least some of the growth-inhibiting conditions that prevailed elsewhere, and this partial exemption was all to the good.[8]

The Evolution of Export Industries. Political stability and continuity may be thought of as permissive conditions for growth, but the fundamental positive force which impelled the economy forward was the export sector. On a small scale, coffee had been grown in several areas of Brazil during the eighteenth century; but the major coffee supply source for the world market at that time, and well into the nineteenth century, was the West Indies. Non-Caribbean producers had received something of a boost, however, when the Haitian insurrection took that important coffee growing area out of the market. Brazil benefited most from this circumstance, for the factors of production were ready and waiting, as it were, for employment in the burgeoning coffee trade. By this time the eighteenth-century mining boom had ended, having pulled both capital and labor out of the northeast into east-central Brazil and made Minas Gerais the most populous region of the country. Many of these factors of production had subsequently shifted into agriculture, particularly into sugar and other food crops for sale to the many towns of the region. With the arrival of profitable opportunities in coffee, there is evidence that a considerable number of people who had accumulated capital in mining migrated—along with workers seeking new jobs—to the Paraíba Valley and nearby areas which were comparatively unsettled and well suited for coffee cultivation. In a good many instances, too, the wealthy *mineiros* took with them not only their liquid capital but their fixed capital (slaves) as well. Hence, the residual wealth of the preceding boom provided the initial stake for the rising coffee industry.

Thanks to the factor mobility which had once before, over a century earlier, enabled the economy to shift to new production possibilities, the reserves of underemployed land, labor, and capital left over from the mining era were moved into coffee and the output thereof increased rapidly. As erosion and diminishing yields set in with the passage of time, cultivation simply moved to the south, onto the better lands of São Paulo state and spread out westward from such centers as Campinas. The effect was, among other things, to continue the geographical shift of the nation's center of economic (and political) power to newer southern regions. The wealth which poured in as Brazil moved to the position of primacy in the world coffee economy came, therefore, into a relatively new and frontier-type region, one with a low density of both population and institutional overlay. It was a region comparatively open to change along a broad cultural front. The very flexibility of social organization in the area was one of the principal reasons why the long-run supply curve was so elastic; by the first years of the present century, Brazil was supplying three-quarters of a vastly expanded global coffee consumption.[9]

Two dimensions of the coffee boom are worth noting, the first being the quantitative increase in output and exports (Table IX-1). Even at the outset, the supply elasticity of the industry was remarkable. From the 1820's through the 1840's there was over a fivefold increase in exports; by the 1880's, another fivefold increase had been realized. During the early period, the increase in output was so rapid that it outran market demand, and between the 1820's and the 1840's there was roughly a 40 per cent decline in price. Nevertheless, because of the cost-structure of the industry—the large sunk investment in coffee trees and slave labor made for

Table IX-1. The Nineteenth-Century Expansion of Brazilian Coffee Exports

DECADE	BAGS OF COFFEE EXPORTED (EA. OF 60 KG.)
1821–30	3,178,000
1831–40	10,430,000
1841–50	18,367,000
1851–60	27,339,000
1861–70	29,103,000
1871–80	32,509,000
1881–90	51,631,000

SOURCE: Caio Prado Júnior, *História econômica do Brasil*, São Paulo: Editôra Brasiliense, 1959, p. 164.

heavy fixed costs and slight variable costs—output continued to expand, and by the 1850's prices were beginning to recover. Thereafter, the price trend was generally favorable to the end of the century. In the first decade of the twentieth century falling prices and overproduction again signaled the emergence of basic weakness in the world coffee market. For the latter half of the century, though, the Brazilian economy received a double-barreled stimulation from its export sector; the growing quantum of exports and the improvement in the terms of trade between the 1840's and the 1890's produced a 396 per cent increase in the amount of real income generated by the coffee export sector.[10]

The momentum built up by the export sector was concentrated in the southern part of the country. Mostly this was in coffee, but eventually the derivative development of other southern regions brought gains in various minor export industries such as the leather and meat-packing industries of Rio Grande do Sul. In the rest of the country, the behavior of the export sector was exceedingly varied.

Sugar, the mainstay of the northeast Brazilian export trade in an earlier day, was virtually at a standstill during much of the nineteenth century. Antillean sugar enjoyed a preference in the British market, and, on the continent, beet sugar production underwent a considerable expansion. Meanwhile, Louisiana production grew as a supply source for the U.S. market. The liberalization of Spanish commercial policy fostered an increase in Caribbean output, which enjoyed substantial freight advantages in reaching the important sugar-consuming centers of the northern hemisphere. Still, some world demand was left over for Brazilian output, which grew slowly during the last half-century on the basis of an expanding domestic market and what amounted to a less than one per cent per annum increase in exports. Sugar export earnings grew more slowly; part of the 33 per cent increase in the quantum of sugar exports over the 50-year period was offset by an 11 per cent drop in prices.[11] Up to the last quarter of the century, when a partial modernization was effected, the industry suffered from several difficulties besides competition in overseas markets. The cessation of the slave trade after the 1840's cut off the traditional labor source. At the same time, the migration of labor (both free and slave) to the dynamic southern regions and the diversion of new slave imports to the same area served further to drive up the price of slaves and, hence, the costs of expanding output. Yet, since it was organized on an extensive basis, the industry depended heavily on increased land and labor inputs for expansion.[12]

As of the early nineteenth century, the technological state of the industry was still primitive as compared with Antillean operations, according to the report of a perceptive foreign visitor to the sugar coast.[13] But a few innovations were introduced thereafter—e.g., the use of bagasse for fuel, animal-pulled plows, steam-driven mills, and a new variety of cane (*caiana*) from the Guianas which had a higher yield and sugar content than the old *crioula* variety.[14] These innovations probably raised productivity sufficiently to offset most of the higher labor (or slave-capital) costs and permitted the gradual expansion of output in spite of these costs and the declining market price.[15] Acreage planted to cane was also expanded, a process greatly facilitated by the introduction of the railway.

During the last quarter of the century, the central and state governments intervened to promote the technological and organizational modernization of the industry. By this time, however, the Amazonian rubber region's competition for labor, the emancipation of the slaves, and the rapid rise of sugar output in competing areas undermined the rather marginal earnings of the industry so that in general it could not be considered a very effective inducement to either regional or national development.[16]

Cotton, which had enjoyed a brief boom in the eighteenth century (especially in Maranhão state), was not in much better shape than the sugar industry with which it sometimes competed for acreage in the northeast. Exports did grow somewhat more than those of sugar—approximately a 43 per cent increase in quantum exported between 1850 and 1900—and there was also a one-third rise in cotton export prices in the last half of the nineteenth century. But, aside from the 1860's when Brazil temporarily supplanted southern United States cotton suppliers in the world market, the chief significance of the industry was that it supplied the raw materials base for the first important wave of Brazilian industrialization. Organized on the basis of slave labor, large plantations, soil mining, and primitive technology, the industry was far from being a stable factor in the expansion of the external sector of the northeast. In any event, its importance as a foreign exchange earner was ordinarily minor (compared with coffee) after the early 1870's.[17]

By the early twentieth century there were three other minor sources of export dynamism. In the state of Bahia, the last decades of the 1800's had seen some shift of factors (mainly ex-slaves as tenant farmers) into tobacco in response to the growing European demand for the product. The combination of rising exports and rising prices brought a measure of prosperity to the locality. Poor production practices, the rents charged the tenants, and eventually, growing competition from African and other producers limited the possibilities of the industry for making a significant and enduring contribution to regional growth. Around Ilhéus (in Bahia) cacao had been cultivated since first transplanted to the region from Maranhão around 1746. The closing years of the nineteenth century saw some expansion underway on a plantation basis; a rising export demand and the decadence of other agricultural lines contributed to the relative attraction of cacao investment. A feverish expansion of acreage after the introduction in 1907 of a high-yielding variety of cacao from Ceylon quickly brought Brazil to a leading position among world cacao exporters[18] and, incidentally, provided the setting and theme for one of Brazil's most socially revealing modern novels.[19] Here, too, however, large-scale landownership and the superabundant supply of labor tended to restrict major participation in the benefits of the boom to a fairly reduced number of persons.[20]

The third minor export boom was the ephemeral, if spectacular, rubber boom of the Amazonian interior. By the end of the nineteenth century, rubber demand and rubber prices were rising rapidly. Under the aegis of both foreign and domestic corporations, many of them quite speculatively organized, there began an intensified penetration and settlement of the Amazonian region which pulled large numbers of *nordestinos* in as laborers to gather the sap of the scattered wild rubber trees.[21] Both the isolation of the region and the cultural level of the labor force facilitated development of an exploitive form of peonage.[22] But social conditions aside, exports of rubber rose from an annual average of 6,000 tons in the 1870's to 21,000 tons in the 1890's. During the first decade of the present century, the annual average was around 35,000 tons, and Brazil was supplying nearly 90 per cent of the world market.[23] Prices continued their rise, too, climbing to £ 639 per ton in 1910, which was over 10 times the level they had been a half century earlier. In 1910, rubber exports were, in value, almost 40 per cent of the Brazilian total.[24]

During the early 1870's, however, the seeds of the *Hevea* had been taken to the Kew botanical gardens in London and, following experimentation, from thence to the East Indies. There, on the basis of scientific selection, experimentation, and a superior labor supply, the first rationally organized production units were established and operating by 1895. Cheap maritime shipping was conveniently at hand, and by 1899 the Asian plantations were making their first shipments to the world market. Against these, the primitive *seringais* or rubber properties of Brazil were no match. By 1921, rubber prices had fallen to less than a sixth of their 1910 level, and Brazil furnished less than a tenth of the world's rubber. With the abrupt end of the boom, all that remained, beyond a small production for the domestic market, were evidences of the wildly conspicuous consumption indulged in during the heyday of the cycle (e.g., the decaying Manaus Opera House) and hundreds of thousands of the migrants who were left stranded in a stagnating and isolated economic region. There followed a widespread retreat into shifting cultivation for subsistence purposes.

Public Policies and Development. For all practical purposes, the long nineteenth-century export boom in Brazil *was* the coffee boom, which was confined largely to the southern part of the country, below the twenty-second parallel of southern latitude. Yet neither the monocultural nature of the Brazilian export sector nor its limited geographical diffusion resulted in a mere enclave-type growth pattern, albeit the other sections of the country, particularly the older colonial regions and the Amazon, were indeed left behind in a state of economic decrepitude.[25] That a more

diffused growth pattern ultimately emerged from the coffee boom is attributable to the special circumstances surrounding the evolution of the coffee
cycle, circumstances which lent a certain quality of receptivity to the environment into which the coffee catalyst was injected. It would be perhaps
overstating the case to say that the movement of the economy south left the
obstacles to growth behind in the north, but something of the sort does
appear to have been involved.

Among the several factors and conditions which favored economic progress, were the domestic political stability and the commercial orientation
of the Lusitanian cultural tradition. Perhaps it was because of these factors
that the government seems to have been disposed to act in a generally
positive way on behalf of the development process, a stance it assumed
from the very year that the Portuguese court arrived in Brazil. This arrival,
according to some students of Brazilian history, was also a stimulus to
development in that it contributed to the further growth and importance
of Rio de Janeiro, which had begun essentially as a commercial center for
the mining boom and continued to expand as an entrepôt for the southern
sugar trade and the coffee trade.

The vastly enlarged administrative functions of Rio de Janeiro added
a considerable government payroll to the urban employment structure, and
the role of the city as the capital of the empire meant that the fiscal
apparatus now began to channel into this urban market area the funds
gathered in by taxation and state loans. On top of this, the crown soon
launched a program of construction and civic improvement to make its
new location more appropriate for royal residence. It should be kept in
mind, too, that into this former provincial center there were moved several
thousand cosmopolitan and sophisticated courtiers, who brought with them
a taste for all the niceties of a European life style and a high propensity
to consume.[26] Their maintenance must have accelerated enormously the
flow of funds in the southern Brazilian economy. It is not surprising, therefore, to find that there appears to have been a very substantial boost to
trade and the regional output of southern Brazil.

In Rio de Janeiro, the immediate consequence was a rapid development
of the institutions of marketing and finance, including those engaged in
the handling of international trade. Both Portuguese and foreign mercantile concerns set up shop in considerable numbers, as did shipping
companies and the other enterprises usually associated with a commercialized urban setting. The royal government, too, had a hand in advancing
the organization of economic life, for among its very earliest measures was
the founding of the first Banco do Brasil in 1808. Among other forms of
support given to the undertaking, the king let it be known that knighthood
would be conferred upon the principal shareholders in the bank.[27] The
first modern style bank in Latin America and as such an indication of
Brazil's relatively more advanced state of economic evolution, the Banco

do Brasil functioned as a bank of issue and as a commercial bank engaged in deposit and discount operations until it closed its doors in 1829.[28] Not until much later were any banks elsewhere in Latin America to attain such a venerable age. Shortly after the bank was set up, the government also authorized the founding of the Rio de Janeiro bourse.

Outside the capital city, the presence of a growing urban center assisted the spread of commercial agriculture in southern Brazil. Sugar cultivation increased in the environs of Rio de Janeiro, and farther afield livestock ranching and other rural products were developed for the ever more numerous consumers of the urban sector. Coastwise shipping also grew. In moving the supplies to market, the ocean routes connecting Rio de Janeiro with the small southern ports enjoyed a decided advantage over the land routes along the escarpment. It was this transport and market system, for example, which provided the economic underpinnings for some 20,000 German colonists who settled in southern Brazil in the first half of the century.

As the founding of the Bolsa of Rio and the Banco do Brasil suggest, the central government's presence in Brazil was not simply limited to providing the amenities of courtly living. The Brazilian monarchs seem to have been more sensitive than most Latin American governments to the possibilities of using the resources of the public sector to promote development.[29] The printing press was finally brought to Brazil. Investment in higher education was initiated, at least to the extent of establishing colleges of medicine and surgery in Rio de Janeiro and Bahia, a naval academy and a military academy wherein engineering training was offered, and, in the 1820's, several schools of law which trained civil servants. A royal library consisting of 60,000 volumes was established for public use. A botanical garden was set up for acclimatizing new plants in Brazil and conducting experiments which would assist agricultural progress. The court also brought European scientists and technicians as consultants and researchers. Naturalists and botanists were among the most notable, but a few specialists were brought over under contract to develop metallurgical enterprises in Minas Gerais and at Ipanema in São Paulo. The important iron works just to the east of Belo Horizonte, for example, go back to the charcoal-fueled blast furnace established in 1818 by a French engineer named Monlevade.[30]

Part of the assistance offered to economic development by the state during this period consisted in repeal of most of the quasi-mercantilist restrictions which had been at least nominally in force during the period of tighter commercial control in the eighteenth century. Beyond this, however, the government experimented briefly with even more direct measures to foster local industrialization. A policy developed during 1808 and 1809, for example, exempted from duties the imports of raw materials and machinery which were destined for use in national factories, while exports of manufactures were—in a hopeful gesture—similarly exempted from duties. Special grants of privileges for a 14-year period were made available to inventors or introducers of new machines, and annual subsidies, raised by a national lottery, were to be provided for such new factories as textile mills and iron works. In addition, government purchases for equipping the military from national producers were contemplated.[31]

For a number of years, though, the pro-industrialization policies were largely nullified by the flood of imported goods which poured into local markets in consequence of new trade policies. Particularly in evidence were British goods, for it appears that, with Europe closed to British exports by Napoleon's "continental system" and with British industrial output growing, England made special efforts to penetrate market areas in Latin America and Asia. Among the areas most susceptibile to British commercial penetration was Brazil, because of the debt owed England by the Portuguese monarch, who arrived in Brazil only through English assistance and whose hope for returning to Lisbon rested largely upon a British defeat of Napoleon. This political leverage the British used to force more favorable terms for the admission of British products into the Brazilian market. Accordingly, in 1810 the crown opened the ports of Brazil to all comers, applying what amounted to a general 24 per cent ad valorem revenue tariff on all imports except those of British and Portuguese origin. British goods received preferential treatment, being permitted to come in with a 15 per cent ad valorem duty which, until 1816, was lower than the 16 per cent duty levied on Portuguese goods.

During the 1820's commercial treaties negotiated with France, Austria, the United States, Belgium, the Netherlands, and the German states reduced the tariffs applied to their goods to 15 per cent as well. The tariff law of 1828 provided for a 15 per cent duty on all imports and marked the peak of the free trade period in Brazil.[32] In the face of such liberal trade policies, few, if any, new factories had much hope of survival. Moreover, the older local handicraft industries such as the textile workshops which had grown up in Minas Gerais under the limited protection afforded by Portuguese colonialism and high transport costs were generally ruined, as they were elsewhere in Latin America during this period, by the rising volume of imports.[33]

At length, however, the trade treaties of the 1820's expired, and trade with countries other than Great Britain grew rapidly, especially trade with the United States. Both developments permitted the Brazilian government to exercise a greater measure of independence in its fiscal policy and foreign commercial relations, especially vis-à-vis England. Over British opposition, the government, in need of more revenues, began to consider raising the level of its import duties. In 1841, the General Assembly authorized a new tariff policy with duties ranging from 2 per cent to 60 per cent, the sense of the debate indicating clearly that not only was this intended to facilitate an increase in public revenues but also that it should afford some measure of protection for local factories. For the time being, however, the extent to which the latter end could be realized was limited by the need of the treasury for tax revenue. By 1844 the general level of ad valorem duties had been approximately doubled to 30 per cent. Interestingly, the reluctance of the minister of finance to raise more duties to protective heights, at a sacrifice of revenue, led to charges in Parliament that he had failed to defend national interests sufficiently against the British.[34]

Even at the 30 per cent level, however, a degree of protection was incorported in the new tariff schedules, so that behind the 1844 tariff wall, the first broad efforts at industrialization appeared as Brazilians and foreigners established cotton textile mills in Bahia, Rio de Janeiro, Minas, and São Paulo. Against charges of favoritism, the state in 1846 and 1847 also revived its earlier policy of granting tariff exemptions for raw materials and machinery imports destined for use by national factories as a means of encouraging domestic industrialization, while the output of these factories was exempted from local excise taxes of various sorts.[35] As of 1852, some 64 factories had qualified for the special status of "national industries" in such fields as textiles, apparel, soap manufacture, beer making, foundries, glassware, vegetable oils, chemicals, and leather working plants.[36]

In 1857, the tariff exemption policy on developmental imports was revoked and, in response to coffee interests which favored cheaper imports particularly of wage goods, the general level of duties was lowered. Nevertheless, raw materials imports were still allowed to come in at a much lower rate (5 per cent) than that applicable to the general run of goods, and the government was forced to move cautiously on tariff reductions for fear of causing capital losses and unemployment in the industries which had already come into being. A moderate level of protection for existing factories was therefore accepted, even during periods of tariff reduction when economic liberals gained the upper hand.

During the 1860's fiscal considerations again led import duties upwards, to a general level of 50 per cent ad valorem. Still further protection was accorded domestic manufacturing in the tariff schedules of 1878, 1879, and 1888, although tariff policy was fluctuating and temporary reductions were occasionally effected in the intervening years. Meanwhile, such adventitious (from the standpoint of local industrialization) developments as the inflationary pressures generated by the Paraguayan war and the repeated devaluations of Brazilian currency (favored for other reasons by coffee producers) seem to have provided significant indirect boosts to the growth of domestic manufacturing output—as did, of course, the long-term increase in domestic market demand which was occasioned by the coffee sector's expansion. Toward the latter part of the century, there were also occasions when the state stepped in to provide direct financial assistance to firms, especially textile firms, which were in difficulty during times of economic readjustment, though this was seen as a temporary rescue operation rather than a matter of continuing policy.

Aside from these measures, however, the principal governmental encouragement of development gradually shifted to a heavy emphasis on railway construction, for which subsidies and earnings guarantees were utilized on a generous scale.[37] In some instances, rail lines were built directly by government. These measures, together with the beckoning possibilities for spreading coffee cultivation, resulted in a substantial extension of the transport system's coverage (see Table IX-2) and increased the effective land resource base of the economy while it augmented the spending streams of the economy.

Toward the end of the century, the state moved still further into the function of spurring economic development in an effort to help the sugar industry out of the difficulties produced by the emancipation of the slaves, the decline in export demand, and technological backwardness.[38] Government-guaranteed earnings, as in railway promotion, were offered to attract capital into the large, comparatively modern *usinas* (heavily capitalized central sugar mills) which began to displace the technologically more primitive and smaller-scale *engenhos*.[39] Tariffs were waived on imports of the equipment needed to get these new, sometimes corporate, enterprises into operation.[40] Legislation stipulated the location of the sugar centrals, and the zoning of supply areas was also a matter of government intervention. In deference to the political influence of the traditional planter class, the *usinas* were originally enjoined from acquiring their own lands for growing cane, although this restriction appears to have been dropped by the 1890's.[41] In at least three instances, a state government went so far as to finance the construction of the *usinas*, which were then leased out to individuals on a concession basis.[42]

Government intervention in sugar, however, was only a foretaste of a more permanent sort of involvement in the agricultural sector, although

Table IX-2. Growth of the Brazilian Railway Lines, 1854—1934

YEAR	KILOMETERS OF TRACK
1854	14.5
1864	474.3
1874	1,283.9
1884	3,302.1
1894	12,260.4
1904	16,305.9
1914	26,062.3
1924	30,305.7
1934	33,106.4

SOURCE: *Anuário Estatístico do Brasil*, Ano V, p. 139.

this later intervention came about not so much because of an insufficiency of development, as in the case of sugar, but because of an excess of development. At the turn of the century, Brazilian coffee production, vastly enlarged in consequence of several decades of rapid expansion in São Paulo state, was outstripping the growth of world demand. Prices weakened and moved downward. This added to the difficulties which already faced the industry since natural variations in the annual coffee crop tended, in the face of an inelastic demand, to produce rather erratic price fluctuations. Therefore, to add stability to the coffee market, the government of São Paulo state, the major producer, in 1902 laid a five-year ban on new plantings of coffee and subsequently extended the ban for another 5-year period. Four years later the state government moved still further with the initiation of the first of the so-called coffee valorization schemes, the Convenio de Taubaté. Using the proceeds of taxes on coffee exports, the state government purchased a part of the coffee harvests, withholding the quantities purchased until market conditions should permit a more favorable disposition of the crop. By 1908 the state government of São Paulo had exhausted its resources and had to begin to borrow abroad to finance the temporary withholding of large stocks from the market. At this point the Federal government entered the picture, as guarantor of the loan. Thereafter, the effects of the ban on plantings began to be felt and price conditions improved. Over the next five years, the market imbalance was rectified, most of the withheld stocks were profitably liquidated, and the foreign valorization loans were retired. The precedent had been established, however, and in less than a decade the regulatory role of the government in the coffee economy was to be revived and amplified.[43]

From 1812 on, the central government was also intermittently active in a development effort of considerable importance to agriculture and the labor market: colonization and immigration. In this the central government was later joined by the southern state governments and private corporations. One of the first two decrees of the new Prince Regent (later Dom João VI) was the concession to foreigners of the same land rights in colonization as were possessed by Portuguese subjects.[44] On the basis of a contract drawn up in 1818 with a Swiss national, one of the first foreign colonization projects patronized by the crown got under way, that of Novo Friburgo. Each of the immigrants received from the Brazilian government the payment of his passage to Rio de Janeiro, transport to the colonization site, temporary lodging, livestock, seed, land, and a maintenance stipend for a two-year period.[45] Twelve years of partial tax exemption was also granted as additional inducement. Some 2,000 Swiss immigrated in connection with this first project. Unlike most of the later projects, these first Swiss colonists seem to have purchased slaves. This was, however, a practice alien to the crown's primary intention in launching the colonization programs, which was that of settling new land and raising the level of agricultural practice by establishing a farming class of medium-scale freeholders.

In 1848 the emperor finally made explicit the prohibition of slavery in colonization areas, and laws and decrees issued over the following decade also clearly differentiated the central government's interest in colonization from the interest of the coffee planter class.[46] While the latter, through private "colonization" ventures and the immigrant-promotion programs of the state governments under *fazendeiro* control, were mainly concerned with recruiting foreign wage laborers (and, in some cases, tenant farmers),[47] the imperial government repeatedly demonstrated its intention to utilize the program to develop yeoman farmers. Such, for example, was the character of the famous series of German colonies which were started in the empty stretches of southern Brazil during the 1820's and early 1830's.[48]

Toward the latter part of the century, the activities of state governments in promoting settlement came to be relatively more important than those of the central government. Most immigrants began to come as wage laborers seeking work in the coffee industry, although both states and private companies continued to promote the establishment of farm colonies and the previously founded settlements gave birth to offshoot colonies. From 1871 on, the immigration agency of São Paulo state played an extremely active role in recruiting European immigrants, subsidizing their passage to Brazil and operating employment exchanges to facilitate the matching of jobs with people. The importance of this work is suggested by the fact that over half of the immigrants who arrived after the late 1870's settled in São Paulo state.

The Diffusion of Coffee Prosperity: Industry Structure. Mention of governmental efforts in promotion of immigration and colonization, in turn, brings one to what was perhaps the crux of the Brazilian economic success: the rapid spread of a commercial export crop, the production of which depended on locally available land, capital, and entrepreneurial factors but which also required considerable quantities of labor inputs, a factor in comparatively short supply. The cultivation of coffee was originally carried on by means of slave labor, but as time went on this became less and less feasible—particularly after the underutilized slave force of the declining mining region had been more or less fully mobilized for coffee production.

In the first place the rapidity with which coffee cultivation spread called for exceptionally large increases in labor inputs, over and beyond that which could be met by means of new slave imports. By 1850 the need for workers was already becoming something of a problem, and several attempts had been made by planters, without notable success, to bring workers over from Europe.[49] During the 1850's the situation became worse because the traffic in slaves had ceased entirely. Meanwhile, according to some writers, the termination of the slave trade released considerable quantities of Portuguese capital which had been tied up in slave finance and which subsequently came, in substantial volume, to Brazil in search of alternative investment (and employment-creating) opportunities.[50] The pick-up in coffee prices during the 1860's, coming after more than a decade without slave imports, precipitated a labor shortage which seems to have been acute and chronic.

The purchase of slaves from other regions in Brazil was no longer satisfactory as a partial answer, for the labor-intensive economies of those regions had only a limited amount of slave labor to spare. Fearing undue loss of the factor on which the whole regional production system rested, the northeastern slave-supplying states attempted by exit taxes and the like to restrict the export of manpower to the south. The southern labor shortage was aggravated still further when the United States Civil War produced a marked revival of cotton cultivation in the older parts of Brazil and led to a renewed interest in keeping the slaves in the region. The flow of slave labor to the south was throttled to a trickle, and labor costs were driven upward.

Owing to the nature of the institution of slavery, the critical scarcity of labor was especially onerous to the would-be *fazendeiros* of the coffee country. An increase in the supply price of labor implied not a rise in variable costs but, rather, a substantial increase in the fixed or capital costs of slave-using coffee enterprises. Given the seasonality of the labor requirements of the industry and the several years lapse between the initial planting of the coffee seedlings and their subsequent maturation to the stage of full production, this conversion of labor costs into fixed, quasi-capital costs both hindered entrance into the industry and elevated the total unit costs of the enterprise to high levels. What the *fazendeiros* clearly needed was a free labor supply which, even if costly on a wage basis, would be nevertheless much more manageable and flexible because of the return of labor charges to the variable cost category. Doubtless it was this fixed-cost squeeze on the *fazendeiros* which helped to spread abolitionist sentiment among the increasingly influential states of southern Brazil.

The alternative—free labor—was not easily come by, for the coffee boom occurred largely in empty territory (or territory quite sparsely settled). To obtain a free labor supply, the wages bargain struck between employers and workers had to rise sufficiently high to compensate laborers for leaving Europe and crossing the ocean to Brazil and to make work on the coffee plantations a reasonable option to settlement on the open frontier. Yet, so long as slave labor was a predominant factor in the industry, it was difficult to attract free labor to the area, though the upward movement of slave costs gradually tended to nudge free laborers' wages higher. Finally, some measure of additional support to the rural wage level was afforded by the possibility of remigration—either back to the homeland or on to labor-short Argentina and Uruguay or, later, into the expanding cities. Having been mobile enough to move transoceanically into the Brazilian labor market, the workers could more readily move out of it again if prevailing conditions deteriorated too greatly. Undoubtedly it was in an effort to "fix" this mobile labor force somewhat that private colonization ventures were established to provide what, in effect, were labor reserve centers on which the *fazendas* of the surrounding areas could draw for peak season needs.

In any event, it appears that by the 1870's the influence of slavery had pretty much vanished from the southern labor market, and with further increases in the extensive margin of cultivation, the demand for labor continued strong and rising. Consequently, with private impresarios and state agencies assisting the process, the immigrants came in mounting numbers to Brazil, nearly all of them to the southern states. The years 1875 through 1879 brought 115,218 of them, and by the 1895-1899 quinquennium the total reached 604,850. After a slight pause, the prewar peak was reached in 1910-1914 with 679,968 immigrants. Altogether between 1875 and 1914, some 3,092,500 persons immigrated to Brazil, and well over a million more came between 1914 and 1940. In descending order of importance, the newcomers hailed mainly from Italy, Portugal, Spain, and Germany—over three-quarters of the total from the first three alone. Many worked in agriculture, some of them eventually moving up from the wage laborer to the tenant status. Others—as they became adjusted and as the coffee frontier moved on, releasing local labor—drifted into the cities to make up an urban, commercial and industrial labor force. Still others, such as the Levantine migrants, appear to have lodged in city life from the outset.

The consequence of the foregoing was that over a period of several decades, (1) the Brazilian population grew vigorously, (2) the proportion of the population in the economically active group was especially large, (3) a high percentage of the labor force, both rural and urban, was involved in the money economy, and (4) as compared with most other Latin American countries, the proportion of money income going to labor factors was high.[51] These conditions created a much broader and more dynamic domestic market than prevailed elsewhere in the Latin American region (except in the Platine republics), and one which was culturally modern; neither subsistence peonage nor pre-Columbian residues operated significantly to diminish the size of the domestic economy of the south. Further, these conditions not only supplied the Brazilian economy with a growing manpower pool, but the process of immigration also served to increase especially the numbers of people who were economically ambitious and therefore positively motivated from a development point of view. The capacity of the regional economy to respond effectively to growth stimuli emanating from the export sector was considerably increased by the diversity of skills and talents the newcomers brought with them.

To some extent, the public subsidization of immigration was, for the short-run, a reasonably effective substitute for investment in education as a means of building up the quality of the human resources in the economy.

What this meant for the possibilities of regional development has been succinctly indicated by the historian Richard Morse whose study of São Paulo stands as one of the most informative regional histories yet written. Noting the rise of a capitalist class in São Paulo between 1872 and 1890, Morse comments: "Foreign immigrants were of course the wellspring that technical and commercial occupations drew upon. . . . The roster of industrial entrepreneurs abounded in such names as Raffinette, Mardelli, Kleeberg, Christofani, Fowles, Weltmann, Sydow, Maggi, Falchi, Stupakoff, Zimmerman, Scorzato, and Witte—while of the proletariat probably 75 to 85 per cent were foreign." [52]

The coffee boom did much to lay the groundwork for a broader regional expansion by creating a domestic market of some importance and by increasing the supply of labor and entrepreneurial factors, but no less a contribution was the strong impulse it gave to the general development of modern forms of economic organization. In agriculture the coffee *fazenda* itself was entirely commercial in its orientation, and, once slavery diminished and free labor gained the ascendancy, it was commercial or market-based in its organization as well. Since the moving frontier of coffee country passed through new territory, land acquisition took place by essentially commercial means. And as the coffee trees grew older and yields diminished, coffee operations shifted to newer lands and the lands once planted to the coffee bean passed on to other uses. Over the cycle, therefore, there was a series of market-directed changes in patterns of land use.

Although for a time it was customary to grow subsistence crops as well as coffee on the *fazendas*, eventually the land of the *fazendas* was too valuable in coffee to permit diversion to other uses. [53] Consequently more and more of the food requisites of the coffee work force were obtained through market purchases, with the result that the expenditure of the money wages earned in the export sector constituted a stimulus to the commercialization of crop production other than coffee throughout southern Brazil. At the same time, the commercialized nature of these sectoral inputs gave added impulse to tertiary sector development for it meant that coffee production itself implied a great deal of necessary financing activity and a considerable elaboration of marketing structure. Coffee production was also one of the few export fields of Latin America in which a derivative industrialization based upon sectoral input requirements occurred. Many of the simpler types of equipment widely employed in coffee processing could be easily manufactured in the small foundries and machine shops which sprang up throughout southern Brazil, and in 1889 the first jute mill was established to make the bags in which coffee was shipped. Since, however, the capital requirements of the industry were comparatively simple, the impetus provided the development of local manufactures was limited.

On the output side of the export sector, an equally pervasive commercialization of life occurred, especially in the cities where the trade in coffee was centered: Rio de Janeiro, São Paulo, Santos. In all of these, useful experience was built up in the conduct of financial and marketing transactions. Moreover, just as the production stage of the industry was readily accessible to native entrepreneurs (alongside immigrants), so also one finds Brazilians actively engaged in the financing and marketing of the product. For example, the *commissários* or factors, who were key figures in the organization of the coffee marketing system, were quite often Brazilians. Considering the intimate links which joined these commission houses with the *fazendeiros*, the native even enjoyed a substantial advantage over the newcomer (who was more likely to be found among the exporting firms). Theoretically, the *commissários* functioned as a selling agent who linked the coffee planter with the exporter and who assembled and bagged the product. In actual practice, however, this was often just the starting point of a relationship—customarily a continuing one—between planter and *commissário* which also involved the latter in advance financing of the crops, in mortgage lending, and in rounding up the various supplies and provisions which were needed on the *fazendas*. Clearly, in these instances the longstanding friendships which were developed among Brazilian nationals, and even passed on over the generations, were practically prerequisite to the trade.[54] It was not unusual for business relations of this sort to be built upon family ties.

Furthermore, as the years passed by, many banking institutions were established by Brazilians on the basis of the capital and financial experience they had accumulated in the coffee business. That the *commissários* should turn bankers is, perhaps, not unexpected, for they were already urban-centered and were in an especially advantageous position astride the interstices of the market so far as concerns capital accumulation possibilities. What is rather more indicative of the advanced nature of Brazilian economic organization is that the *fazendeiro* class was also more than just a strictly rural interest group.[55] From the 1870's, there was a quite discernible tendency for the coffee planters to become progressively more involved in urban economic activities: in banking, in railway companies, in port development, and even in textile plants and other industrial lines. Undoubtedly it was this rather lengthy period of familiarization with the urban sector which assisted the transfer of capital out of coffee and into urban sector business when, in later decades, the fall in coffee prices reordered the array of investment preferences.

Among the several advantages conferred upon Brazil by its export sector, the widespread participation of residentiary enterprises, both national and immigrant in ownership, in coffee production and trade stands out with special importance. In the first place, it seems certain that far more of the earnings of the external sector were retained locally by the labor force and by domestic ownership, financing, and marketing interests than was the case when the export sector was dominated by foreign-owned concerns. Hence domestic capital accumulation, at several points in the system (and not entirely directly in the export sector alone), was facilitated. Secondly, the broad extension, direct and indirect, of the coffee economy served to suffuse and permeate southern Brazilian society with a spirit of commercial activity and pecuniary success.[56] An aristocracy there was, complete with titles of nobility, but it is perhaps not too inexact to think of these barons and others as a group somewhat like the bourgeois aristocrats of nineteenth-century France or Austria.[57] As with the Rothschilds, their patents of nobility were often decidedly capitalistic in origin—a point which bespeaks the commercial ethos of Brazilian life.

Indeed, at a relatively early date, Brazilians had plunged enthusiastically into the intricacies of modern economic organization. The first Banco do Brasil was organized as a joint-stock company. Only a decade later, a joint-stock mining company was formed to develop properties in Minas Gerais. When the mid-century point rolled around, the "spirit of associação" was going strong as corporations were formed on every side. The 1850's and 1860's brought a flurry of feverish speculation to the Rio de Janeiro stock exchange, and between 1850 and 1865, some 180 commercial and industrial corporations were organized.[58] More than 20 insurance companies, at least three savings banks (*caixas economicas*) and well over a dozen commercial banks came into being, along with railway companies, mining companies, urban transport companies, gas companies, steam navigation companies, and assorted manufactures.[59] In addition to the 60 odd so-called national factories, other smaller factories existed as well; the "national factory" category included only the more important undertakings, the ones which were specifically granted exemptions from duties on their raw materials imports.

In a way, Brazilian attainments during this period were epitomized by the most remarkable native-born entrepreneur, Irineo Evangelista de Sousa, a man who rose from middle class origins to become the Baron and later the Viscount of Mauá. Born in 1813, Mauá began his career as a clerk in a mercantile firm operated by Portuguese and, subsequently, British owners. From that time on, however, his fortunes began to advance so that by mid-century he stood out as an entrepreneur par excellence.[60] Indeed, his was a role almost unique in all of Latin America during the nineteenth century, for his activities extended not only throughout Brazil but also to foreign countries and covered many fields. In his native land, he became a leading merchant in the export-import trade; established foundries and metal-working plants which fabricated ships, munitions, agricultural machinery, steam engine parts, sugar mills and saw mills, and iron tubing; organized mining companies and the first railway, gas lighting, and telegraph companies; founded shipping lines for Amazonian, coastwise, and transatlantic traffic; invested in textile mills, colonization enterprises, and rural properties; and achieved a preeminent position in Brazilian finance with at least three banking corporations in his business empire. With agencies and branches in all the important cities of Brazil, Mauá's banks also opened offices in such distant places as New York, London, Manchester, and other European cities.

The arms of the Mauá empire extended even into neighboring South American countries where Brazil's more advanced state of development enabled it, temporarily at least, to assume a certain measure of economic leadership. In Uruguay, where the Baron owned ranching properties, a branch of the Mauá Bank in Montevideo was the first joint-stock commercial bank in the country, supplying with its notes the chief medium of exchange in Uruguay for a while. In Argentina, where banking long had been conducted as an adjunct of mercantile firms and where the only successful early bank was the state institution established by the Province of Buenos Aires in the 1850's, an office of the Mauá Bank was opened in Buenos Aires in 1858. From this, a series of provincial branches were then established around the country. So great was the scope of the Brazilian institution—which engaged in all kinds of financial transactions (investment banking in industry, agriculture, and real estate; discounting and loan operations; deposit banking and note issue)—that Argentine officials soon began to express reservations concerning its weighty influence over the country's economic life. Its success, however, seems to have been a factor in encouraging the establishment of other banks, including the first British ones.[61]

Unfortunately, the far-flung business structure of the Baron eventually came to exceed the bounds of prudence, and, being overextended, it collapsed. But the experience did not deter others, even though it was quite a while before anyone again reached the scale of the operations of Mauá. Factories, banks, and other enterprises continued to appear on the scene, representing a considerable variety of undertakings. By 1889, for example, there were over 100 textile plants; by the early twentieth century, there were also numerous shoe factories; and in 1913 Brazilian entrepreneurs established the first *frigorífico* (refrigerated meat-packing plant) to supply the national market.[62] By the First World War, there was already unmistakable evidence that the seeds of expansion planted by the external sector in the form of capital accumulation and talent had found a reasonably fertile institutional soil in which to take root—at least in the southern clime. But at the same time, it was equally plain that the "two Brazils" described by Jacques Lambert had come into being.[63] Alongside the underdeveloped and backward north, plagued as it was by monoculture and the drought,[64] there had appeared a dynamic *bandeirante*-style economy which kept Brazil in the forefront of Latin American economic progress.

ARGENTINA: THE ADVANTAGES OF LATE DEVELOPMENT

Like Brazil, Argentina enjoyed a distinct advantage in not having begun the development of its modern economic heartland until the nineteenth century.[65] Just as Brazil's colonial economy centered in regions which receded greatly in relative importance after 1800 (the Northeast and Minas Gerais), so also the Argentine transition to nationhood coincided with a definite geographical shift in the economic center of gravity. For most of the colonial era, the economically significant portion of the country extended from around Córdoba northwestward to Jujuy, with a secondary center of some consequence in Cuyo (today known as Mendoza, San Juan, and San Luís provinces). In the former region, the economic base rested upon the production of a variety of goods for which there was a substantial demand in the markets of Bolivia and Peru: sugar, tobacco, fruits, rice, wheat, dried meat, wool and cotton and textiles of both fibers, leather products, carts and wagons. Córdoba was especially notable as a major mule raising center for the transport system of the Peruvian vice-royalty. The *encomienda*, the hacienda, the servile native labor force— these and the other characteristic organizational features of Spanish colonial-ism were established in strength in the region.[66]

Settlements had also been made at such places as Santa Fé, Rosario, and Buenos Aires, but in general the littoral provinces were rather a backwater region of low economic utility and only sparsely settled. Over the pampas and Patagonia roamed fiercely belligerent Indians who were quite unlike the sedentary and more readily exploitable indigenous peoples of Cuyo and the northwest. But even had they not been present, there was little to attract and hold ladino settlers in the region. Along the Paraná River and around some of the marshy sections, it was possible to engage to a limited extent in livestock grazing. Much of the pampean zone, however, had little surface water and few trees and could not be dedicated to systematic ranching until better techniques for well-drilling could be introduced and cheap windmills and fences installed. Agriculture was generally precluded by the prevalence of thick native grasses which were difficult to clear away before the development of the steel plow in the early nineteenth century.

Some subsistence cultivation was practiced to meet the needs of the few thousand inhabitants of the pampean region, and in time the growing herds of wild cattle provided an additional source of food and raw materials. Yet, by and large, the area which was to become the heart of the Argentine nation was left relatively open, with ample room for later growth: room for the people who came as immigrants and "institutional room" for the cultural furnishings the immigrants brought with them. Neither a long-established aristocracy of great wealth nor a large indigenous population reducible to serfdom (and, hence, the source of a persisting sociological dualism) dominated the life of the area, which accordingly entered the

1800's less weighted down with a residue of colonial institutional trappings than many other parts of Spanish America.

To be sure, in the closing decades of the eighteenth century the city of Buenos Aires was lifted from provincial obscurity when, as part of a political reorganization of the empire, it was made the seat of a vice-royalty and, as such, the administrative control center for a large area extending into Upper Peru. But even this move, which initiated the formative years of the area which later established a hegemony over the whole nation, did not mark the inception of the traditional Hispanic ceremonial patterns; at roughly the same time that Buenos Aires became a major governmental center it also took on the commercial functions which ever since have accorded it the preeminent position in Argentine economic life.[67]

Spanish trade policy was liberalized so that the viceregal port was opened to a much greater amount of foreign trade than had legally been conducted in Buenos Aires previously.[68] And with the mineral wealth of Bolivia now channeled down to Buenos Aires rather than northward to Lima, the city became the principal supply and transshipment center for Upper Peru and the interior Argentine provinces. During the same era, the growing population of Europe and the industrial revolution (with its rising requirements for machine belting) made increasingly profitable the slaughtering of wild cattle and the export of hides and tallow. After the 1780's, still another export line was added to the Platine economy as *saladeros* or meat-salting plants were introduced (initially with financial support from the crown) into the region. The first such establishment was founded in Uruguay, but gradually the *saladeros* spread and in 1810 a meat-salting factory was opened in Buenos Aires. To supply the growing demand for salted meat on the slave plantations of Brazil, the Caribbean, and elsewhere, a rising number of ships set sail from the port on the River Plate.[69] Even before independence was achieved, foreign commercial interests, especially British merchants, had established a beachhead in Buenos Aires.[70]

The Rise of Export Latifundism. The formative period of Buenos Aires thus coincided with a marked commercial expansion which made the city the focus of trade in both the La Plata region and the adjacent interior provinces. Strongly pervaded by a commercial and foreign trade orientation and exposed to new European influences, the new viceregal capital gave birth to an urban elite composed mainly of wealthy merchants and liberal minded criollo intellectuals. The nascent rural landowner interest of Buenos Aires province was also essentially akin to that of the urban groups, for, lacking a pool of exploitable native labor, the *estancieros* or ranchers made their living from the export trade. The provincial caudillo, Juan Manuel de Rosas, who lorded over Buenos Aires as dictator for two decades, not only stood for the *estanciero* interest of the countryside but also was an owner of one of the early *saladeros* in Buenos Aires and an exporter of meat (on his own vessels) to Rio de Janeiro and Havana.

With independence there began a long struggle between mercantile *porteño* interests and the varied interests of the interior of the country, an economic conflict which lay behind the squabbles of such rival provincial caudillos as Rosas of Buenos Aires, Quiroga of La Rioja, Urquiza of Entre Ríos, and López of Santa Fé. Gradually, the economy of the old interior provinces suffered dislocation and decline, while the *porteño* economy moved ahead into ever closer interaction with the overseas markets for Buenos Aires exports.[71] The first British Chamber of Commerce, for example, was established as a combined commercial and social center for the growing British resident community in 1811; by the early 1830's, the British community in Buenos Aires numbered at least 4,000 persons and possibly as many as 5,000 or so, among whom the merchants were the wealthiest and most influential.[72]

The policies of Rosas were far from conducive to economic development, but the export economy flourished nevertheless: first, on the basis of hides and salted meat and later—as the quality of sheep was gradually improved through the introduction of Merino, Southdown and Rambouillet strains— wool. Still later, British *estancieros* brought over the Lincoln sheep, when refrigerated shipments of mutton acquired importance. Whereas wool exports amounted to only 384,000 kilograms in 1829, the year Rosas took control of Buenos Aires, by 1850 they had risen to 7.7 million kilograms. By the 1880's, wool exports averaged over 109 million kilograms, at which time they represented 50 to 60 per cent of the total value of Argentine exports.

Under the Rivadavia government of the 1820's an interest had been displayed in the possibilities of colonization and immigration, but neither then nor in the subsequent Rosas decades was much actually done officially to promote settlement by Europeans. Nevertheless, the expanding opportunities of the situation themselves advertised the advantages of coming to the Argentine. In addition to the English merchants and artisans who sailed to the River Plate there came several thousand Basque, Scottish, and Irish herders of sheep who brought the skills and experience which were lacking locally. By the end of the Rosas regime in 1852, there were an estimated 4,000 Irish shepherds in Buenos Aires province alone, a number which increased almost tenfold by the 1870's.[73]

An export-oriented economy and substantial immigration were not, however, the only harbingers of things to come. By 1850 a third basic characteristic of the modern Argentine economy had also put in its appearance: the large *estancia* or ranch. Although the Rivadavia administration had first hoped, in its policy of emphyteusis, to raise funds and foster commercial development by the long-term leasing of public lands, the policy was soon abandoned in favor of outright sales and grants of large tracts of land. As early as the 1820's, some 20 million acres were alienated from the public domain, while Rosas, as the Indians were pushed farther to the south, indulged in a massive give-away program. Large grants were given to the military for service in the Indian wars, other large parcels were turned over to holders of public bonds, and still other estates were created out of grants and sales to favored political supporters. Speculators in both Argentina and Europe formed land corporations to acquire additional hundreds of thousands of hectares. By mid-century, therefore, a concentrated distribution of land ownership had been thoroughly entrenched as a basic institutional fact of life in the Argentine; and powerful landed oligarchs emerged as a dominant force in the political and economic life of the nation.[74] After Rosas, the process continued unabated.[75]

Argentine latifundism did not, however, result in the kind of extreme anti-developmental bias which inhered in large-scale landownership elsewhere, although, beyond peradventure a more moderate distribution of property would have been far more desirable in the long-run. For one thing a goodly number of the *estancias* were foreign-owned or organized by immigrants as commercial ventures from the very outset, and on these came many of the improvements which, when emulated after a lapse of time by native *estancieros*, contributed so much to agricultural efficiency in the Argentine, starting with the importation of steel plows, well-drilling machines, and cheap standard windmills.

In 1844, for example, the first wire fence was installed on the *estancia* of Richard Newton who, in 1866, helped organize the Sociedad Rural as an association of progressive ranchers for the purpose of encouraging technical improvements. In consequence of the introduction of fencing, selective breeding of livestock became more feasible, and with protected fields, the simultaneous conduct of ranching and grain cultivation was facilitated. In 1848 another British *estanciero* by the name of White imported the first Durham bull, thereby beginning the process of upgrading the Argentine herds which subsequently continued with the importation of Herefords. The invaluable contribution of foreign ranchers and ranch managers to development of the sheep raising industry has already been mentioned, while later on, in 1876-1884, a further technological advance of momentous consequences for the Argentine rural economy came from abroad as a result of French development of refrigeration techniques. In 1876 the first refrigerated ship crossed the Atlantic, and in the year following, the Sociedad Rural dispatched the first export cargo of refrigerated Argentine beef to Europe. Subsequently, French and English companies commenced regular refrigerated-ship service between the River Plate and Europe, and in 1882-1884 both English and French entrepreneurs established the *frigoríficos* in the Argentine.

During the eighties, advances were made in the quality of pasturage as the planting of alfalfa gained popularity. Since it was discovered that the

conversion of natural grasslands to planted pastures was made more efficient
by an intermediate, preparatory stage of crop cultivation, the shift also
gave rise to a greater demand for temporary tenant cultivators who farmed
the land a few years before moving on and leaving it planted in an improved
cover. Immigrant *estancieros* and their associates in the Sociedad Rural
appear to have worked closely in support of all of these developments.

While native ranchers seem generally to have lagged some distance behind
the foreigners in making these technical improvements, eventually they
followed suit and, indeed, often brought over European specialists to manage the properties for them. There was every reason for them to do so,
for as there was no indigenous labor force which could be impressed into
servitude, the lands acquired by the beneficiaries of government largesse
could only provide an income when put into commercial development.
Even mere land speculation depended upon such factors as the deliberate
promotion of immigration and population growth and the extension of
transport facilities. Consequently, large-scale landownership almost necessarily carried with it a certain interest in general developmental measures
and in the commercial operation of rural properties.[76]

Owing to the foregoing circumstances, then, there emerged in Argentina
a society dominated by *porteño* and exporting interests, one ruled, rather
undemocratically, by a comparatively enlightened oligarchy made up of
estancieros, merchants, and bankers who were able to draw upon the talents
of such well-educated and progressive national leaders as Mitre and Sarmiento. From the 1860's on, a relatively high level of political stability
prevailed—as is suggested by the fact that the constitution of 1853 endured
until the 1940's—while, playing to the strength of a dynamic export sector,
the incumbent governments pursued policies which on the whole were more
favorable than not to the development process.

Public Policies and National Development.   Foreign capital was offered
considerable inducement to come to the area, and in response to the generally favorable situation, huge amounts flowed in and came to control
much of Argentine economic life—urban transit systems and other city
utilities, railway lines, modern port facilities, and the like. From the 1880's,
in response to the superior Argentine export possibilities and in consequence
of the relatively smaller domestic capital accumulation capacity, the amount
of foreign capital invested in Argentina surpassed even that which had been
sent to Brazil. The major portion of this foreign stake in the Argentine had
come from Great Britain, which country was also far and away the chief
consumer of Argentine exports and the principal supplier of Argentine
imports.[77] For the time being, the influx of foreign capital exerted a powerful influence in favor of development, even though its preeminence was
later on (in the 1930's) to become the source of acute conflict when British
political and economic pressure was brought to bear in support of these
foreign investment interests.

Closely related to the strong encouragement given foreign investment was the government's railway policy, for all sectors of the oligarchy were strongly in favor of railway construction because of its effects on land values and the volume of trade. Attracted by generous subsidies and earnings guarantees, capital flowed into railway investment and, in the process of opening up the rich pampa area to full utilization, stimulated the development of out-lying regions at the same time that it connected the various parts of the national market to the *porteño* metropolis (see Table IX-3).[78] By the early twentieth century, Argentina possessed more kilometers of rail lines than any other Latin American country, and on a kilometers-of-railways-per-capita basis it also far outdistanced other Latin American countries. As of 1909 Argentina had, for every 10,000 inhabitants, 23.59 miles of track. The equivalent figures for other countries were: Uruguay 10.96, Mexico 7.12, Brazil 6.49, Chile 3.98, and Venezuela 3.0 miles.[79] Most of the trackage was owned by private, albeit state-subsidized, companies, but some 6,000 kilometers of the approximately 35,000 kilometers of total trackage in 1915 were held by state-owned and state-operated companies. In general, the state lines were constructed to open up to development the more remotely situated portions of the country.

It should be kept in mind, however, that Argentina enjoyed very special natural advantages in building its transport system. It both lacked the internal geographical barriers which fragmented so many of the other Latin American nations and possessed a richly productive and relatively flat economic heartland which was readily accessible at low cost by the rail lines which fanned out of Buenos Aires and by the fluvial transport route of the Paraná. Thus, internal traffic was facilitated, while nearly all of a region which contained the most fertile soils of Latin America and which was almost ideally suited to the production of grains and livestock was comparatively close to cheap water transport. Yet not only the export-oriented *pampeana* region benefited from the locational advantages. Extension of rail lines produced a certain measure of redevelopment in older areas as

Table IX-3. Growth of Argentine Railway Lines, 1857—1935

YEAR	KILOMETERS OF TRACK
1857	10
1875	1,956
1885	4,502
1895	14,516
1905	19,794
1915	34,607
1925	37,225
1935	41,376

SOURCE: Adolfo López Mayer, *Transporte en la Argentina*, Buenos Aires: 1946.

well.[80] The old and rather stagnant sugar industry of Tucumán, for example, was rapidly reorganized and expanded on a modern basis after the arrival of the railway from Rosario in 1876. Up to that time, the burden of transport charges had confined the marketing of Tucumán sugar to the provinces immediately surrounding, but following the modernization of the industry which occurred as a result of railway development, the region was able to place its production in the growing market of Buenos Aires. Between 1870 and 1910 the area planted to cane increased from about 2,400 hectares to 72,000 hectares. In the long-settled Cuyo region, the acreage planted in grapes underwent a dramatic expansion as immigrant Spaniards and Italians arrived to develop a wine industry to serve the expanding national market, but realization of these possibilities awaited completion of the rail line in 1885. In 1887 some 27,000 hectoliters of Mendoza wine were shipped out by rail to the littoral markets; in 1890-1891, regional wine exports reached 268,000 hectoliters. Along with railway development, a rapid expansion of the telegraph system was promoted by the government, so that in 1874 there were already some 3,100 miles of telegraph lines in the country. By 1908 the extension of the telegraphic system was ten times this length.

In the instances just cited, the resource development which occurred in response to public investment in transport and communications was privately organized. It should be noted, though, that the state was also directly engaged in resource development in the minerals field, notwithstanding provisions in the Mining Code which seemed to proscribe such action.[81] Beginning in 1902, for example, the Dirección de Minas, Geología, e Hidrología of the Ministry of Agriculture initiated a vast plan of exploratory drilling to determine the subsurface features of the country. Toward the end of 1907, petroleum was located in one of these perforations in the Comodoro Rivadavia area, and follow-up drilling completed in the subsequent three years verified the presence of valuable subsoil resources. Thereupon a larger program of development drilling was launched, and an assortment of petroleum producing and refining facilities was installed to exploit the reserves of the 5,000 hectare petroleum zone which was set aside in 1910 for government development. Shortly afterwards the state also reserved to itself a 7,500 hectare zone in a second oil field, the Plaza Huincul. The petroleum produced therefrom was used on the state railways in Patagonia, by the military, and by the Italo-Argentine Electricity Company and other electrical generating companies in the Buenos Aires region. Thus was launched, in the era of high capitalism, the government's oil company, the Yacimientos Petrolíferos Fiscales or Y.P.F., alongside which private companies were eventually allowed to operate.

Of considerable importance over the long run was the public investment which went into education—a social outlay which was a fairly painless one to the determining classes because of the substantial increase in government revenues that attended the swift expansion of the foreign-trade sector.

During the first half of the century, the state of education in the country was nothing less than deplorable. Both Brazil and Chile had made educational advances which surpassed anything achieved elsewhere in Latin America by the 1850's, but Argentina was closer to the general level of ignorance. As late as 1869, the year of the first national census, only 22 per cent of the population was literate. The year before, however, had brought to the presidency a distinguished Argentine, Domingo Sarmiento, who in his earlier years of exile had become acquainted with the educational programs of Chile (where he was appointed director of the government normal school) and the United States.[82] Impressed by his observations abroad, he launched with the assistance of yankee teachers trained in the philosophy of Horace Mann, what was eventually to become the Argentine public school system.[83] Despite the rapid growth in population over the following years, the literacy rate was increased to approximately 50 per cent by 1895 and to nearly 66 per cent by the time of the First World War —a record not matched elsewhere in Latin America, even though, of course, the quality of the education offered often left something to be desired from a developmental point of view.[84]

Finally, from the 1850's on, the government revived the Rivadavian policy of encouraging immigration and colonization, an effort in which it was joined by private colonization companies, by railways, and by individual large landholders.[85] A good many of the colonization companies were essentially fraudulent and were in reality land speculation companies, which amassed large land grants but actually settled few people. Furthermore, the extent of Argentine latifundism deterred many immigrants from coming, for it reduced substantially the possibilities for that immigration which came in search of land ownership.[86] Nevertheless, the employment opportunities opening up in railway construction, in port and urban modernization, in the expanding sheep and cattle industries, and in derivative urban trades began to pull increasing numbers of people to Argentina—from many countries, but especially from northern Italy and Spain. To help matters along, the government, composed of landed interests who needed more laborers and who perceived the highly desirable relationship that existed between population growth and land values, advertised abroad and subsidized immigrant passage to the Argentine. At the time of the first national census in 1869, approximately 12 per cent of the 1.8 million population consisted of immigrants. By 1874, another 280,000 immigrants had arrived, over 70,000 of them in 1874 alone.

Accelerated Development and Modernization. The 1870's brought changes which vastly accelerated the pace of immigration. The use of planted pastures (planted by tenant cultivators after a few years of crop farming) spread rapidly, upping the labor requirements of the economy substantially. Meanwhile the pacification of the frontier regions and the extension of the rail network (which itself called for more labor inputs) enabled certain types of ranching to be shifted to lands farther removed. In response to the growing world demand for grains, an increasing amount of pampean acreage was transferred to grain cultivation and this again raised the labor component in the economy by a considerable degree. Up into the early 1870's, Argentina was a net importer of grain; but from around 1876 on, it maintained an export position, sending a rising volume of maize and wheat abroad to the expanding European markets.[87] Between 1872 and 1895, the amount of pampean acreage under cultivation increased 15 times, while between 1895 and 1905, the acreage planted to wheat, maize, lucerne, and linseed alone more than doubled. Argentine wheat exports, which were 34 million bushels in 1891-1892, reached 109 million bushels in 1905-1906. By 1911, Argentina was the world's largest exporter of maize and chilled and frozen meat, was second only to Russia in wheat exports, and was second only to Australia in wool exports.

Given the foregoing changes in economic activity, it is not to be wondered that immigrants came in large numbers to work as laborers, tenants, and sharecroppers in Argentine agriculture and in the tertiary sector activities which accompanied agricultural expansion. By 1895 the national population had grown to around 4 million persons of whom approximately 25 per cent were foreign-born. In 1914, nearly 30 per cent of the total population of 7.9 million were foreign-born while many of the native-born were first- or second-generation descendants of immigrants.[88] Not only did the economy benefit from the enormous developmental subsidy represented by immigration, but there was also an especially neat adjustment of the labor supply to labor requirements, one which made for an exceptionally economical utilization of labor factors. Cheap ocean passage on rapid steamers and the reversal of seasons on either side of the equator made possible the periodic migration of harvest hands between Europe and the Argentine (the so-called *golondrinas*).

With the immigrants came all the ancillary benefits which have been noted before: the new technical and organizational skills and aptitudes, the spirit of enterprise and achievement-oriented motivation, the useful commercial connections abroad, and so on. As early as 1869, for example, although immigrants composed only 12 per cent of the population, they held around 80 per cent of the bank deposits.[89] In the early 1900's, the immigrants outnumbered natives as proprietors in commerce and industry in the ratio of three to one. Moreover, the nature of the agricultural sector was such that it tended, as time went on, to release people for nonrural employments, while eventually the slackening rate of railway construction worked to the same effect. Many immigrants, too, came only to acquire a stake from temporary work in agriculture, whereupon they moved into the cities, while others came to work in the towns and cities to begin with, as artisans, shopkeepers, workers. Consequently, with immigration there came a rapid expansion of the city population—e.g., Buenos Aires grew from

178,000 in 1869, to over 400,000 in 1895, to 1.5 million in 1914 (of whom half were foreign-born)—from the ranks of which there emerged a middle class of some size and a skilled urban labor force. After 1890, for example, the middle class Radical Party appeared as an increasingly strong contender for power, vying with oligarchy on various issues such as monetary policy,[90] while around the turn of the century the formation of the Socialist Party attested to the influence of European ideologies among the nation's more sophisticated labor force.

Together with processable raw materials (sugar, leather, meat, milk, flour, quebracho wood, etc.), the congregation of these human elements in Buenos Aires, where capital equipment could be brought in cheaply, represented the country's chief resource for industrialization—a process which was further assisted by the advanced state of economic organization that had accompanied the rise of the foreign trade sector and mass immigration. During the 1860's and thereafter, for example, the various resident communities of foreign businessmen involved in the Argentine foreign trade had been active in establishing banks which catered to their credit needs and handled the finances of companies of the respective nationalities.[91] British merchants and British-owned railways and shipping lines had helped establish such banks as the London and River Plate Bank (1862), the British Bank of South America (1863), and the Anglo-South-American Bank (1888). The Italians founded the Banco de Italia y Río de la Plata (1872), the Nuevo Banco Italiano (1887), and the Banco Popular Italiano (1899). French interests established the Banco Francés del Río de la Plata (1886) and joined Spanish capital in setting up and expanding the Banco Español del Río de la Plata (1886). Altogether, 25 of the 143 banks operating in the republic in 1913 were foreign institutions, as were 33 of the 85 insurance companies.[92]

Foreign-initiated concerns were also prominent in developing such specialized fields as mortgage finance: e.g., the Banque Hypothécaire Franco-Argentine, the Société de Credit Foncier de Santa Fé, the Dutch Mortgage Trust of the Río de la Plata, and the Société Hypothécaire Belge-Argentine. As early as 1811 the British Chamber of Commerce was performing some of the functions of a bourse. In December 1834, the Sociedad Bolsa de Comercio was formally founded, thenceforth exercising a growing influence over the commercial and economic life of the nation.[93]

Banking development, however, was neither entirely a foreign-initiated field nor a field given over entirely to private enterprise, even in economically liberal Argentina. Some of the earliest, if somewhat ephemeral, nineteenth-century efforts to establish banking institutions had been governmental or quasi-governmental in character: e.g., the Banco de las Provincias Unidas del Río de la Plata (1826). After the fall of Rosas, the Banco de la Provincia de Buenos Aires was set up (or revived) in 1854 by the government of the most important province of the country. From 1872 until its collapse in the crisis of 1890, there was operating the Banco Nacional which was established by the federal government as a mixed public-private enterprise. This was replaced, in 1891, by the Banco de la Nación which came to play a major role in the nation's banking structure, receiving deposits, engaging in loan and discount operations, and, in particular, channeling credit to agriculture. By 1916 the Banco de la Nación had 158 branches and was far and away the largest financial institution in the nation in terms of deposits, capital, and other measurements. From 1886 on, still another state bank was operating in the Argentine credit scene, the Banco Hipotecario Nacional, which soon became a chief participant in the field of long-term mortgage finance.

Aided by these organizational supports and strengthened further by (1) a rapidly growing and skilled population of relatively high income which was almost entirely involved in the money economy, (2) an expanding geographical frontier which added steadily to the land resources available, (3) a pronounced trend toward urbanization, (4) unparalleled locational, topographic, climatological, and soils advantages, (5) a vigorously expanding foreign demand for national exports, and (6) the favorable attention of foreign investors, the Argentine economy surged forward on the basis of astonishingly high rates of capital formation [94] to become, without question, the most modern and prosperous national economy in Latin America—as Brazil might have become had it been relieved of the economic dead weight of the Northeast. Within its expansive climate a growing variety of nonagricultural enterprises took root and flourished.[95] The census of 1913, for example, reported 48,800 industrial establishments, a 50 per cent increase over the number of such firms operating in 1908 and more than double the number reported in the 1895 census. At the same time, the industrial labor force numbered some 410,200 workers, a 240,000 increase over 1895, while the installed horsepower in 1913 was three times the capacity registered in 1908.[96] Although food industries still bulked large in terms of total capitalization and employment, other newer lines were developing as well: metal working and machinery companies, furniture, textiles, clothing, paper, and so on. By 1914 local industries supplied roughly 40 per cent of the value of the processed and manufactured goods consumed in Argentina, and the nation seemed almost certainly to have crossed the threshold between economic backwardness and modern, development-sustaining economic organization.[97]

CHILE: ARRESTED MODERNIZATION

Together with southern Brazil and the Argentine, the long, narrow Republic of Chile was among the most promising nineteenth-century sites in Latin America for a successful transition to modern economic society. There, too, the historic interplay of geography and cultural trends created certain special advantages, albeit of a different nature from those enjoyed by Chile's large transandean neighbor and with a rather different influence on the course of national development. In some respects Chile would appear to have been even more favored than Argentina, but it had some relative disadvantages as well.

To review the latter first, it should be noted that, as compared with the heartland of modern Argentina or Southern Brazil, Chile began the nineteenth century in a rather more occupied state. Santiago had been founded in 1541, Concepción in 1550. And while the occupancy of Chile was not thereafter uninterrupted, because of the belligerent propensities of the Araucanian Indians, the ensuing two and a half centuries saw the gradual appropriation of most of the land in the central region, along with a more or less steady increase in the population. Consequently, there was relatively less "room" in the country for immigration as the nineteenth century unfolded its expanding array of economic opportunities, and less amplitude for the cultural changes which elsewhere were aided and abetted by large-scale immigration. The immigrants who did come to Chile made an invaluable contribution to its development, but they were only a small fraction of the number who came to Argentina, Brazil, and Uruguay.

Furthermore, by independence the hacienda regime in agriculture (the *fundos*, as the larger Chilean haciendas are commonly called) was already a dominant feature of Chilean economic life and took up much of the land in the rich central valleys of the heart of the nation, although smaller farms known as *chacras* were also operating here and there. Peonage of the sort found in Mexico or Peru had not developed to such a large extent on the Chilean *fundos*, since there were fewer indigenous peoples to impress into servitude. Nevertheless, there had emerged a widespread system of resident agricultural labor known as *inquilinaje* which was somewhat intermediate between the regime of colonial peonage and the comparatively more progressive and modern tenancy systems of the Argentine. Thus, although the *inquilino* generally received some cash wages as well as the use of a plot of land and was perhaps several cuts above the peon of prerevolutionary Mexico, he had far less mobility and earned much less than Argentine tenant farmers or the workers on the Paulista coffee *fazendas*. While the latter were related to landowners through a cash nexus, the *inquilino* was in effect tied to his estate by long-standing bonds of tradition, family life, personal dependence, and work obligations to the landowner and could rarely skip off to other estates or acquire property to improve his lot.[98] *Inquilinaje* was, in other words, a rather static, modified colonial kind of relationship. It has persisted until the present day as a regressive feature in Chilean agricultural organization.

Yet, if Chile entered its national period with certain of the liabilities of colonial agricultural organization, there were, nevertheless, offsetting advantages which enabled it to overcome these impediments to a considerable extent. Geographically the country was well favored, for the land of the central valleys was fairly fertile, and the climate benign. Within the main region of settlement no difficult topographical barriers intruded to create marked regional differences or to disrupt the geographical unity of the ecumene. Because of the lay of the land, the chief population and resource centers lay close to the coast and therefore enjoyed ready access via low-cost water transport to each other and to foreign markets and supply centers.

The native inhabitants of this landscape had been neither especially numerous nor culturally very advanced. Some, the Araucanians, were warlike. Hence, the original inhabitants of the area were either driven off or fairly rapidly assimilated—the latter process being hastened by the Spaniards' devotion to the Biblical injunction to be fruitful and to multiply. In consequence, the lower classes—the *inquilinos* and the *rotos* (laborers in general)—were largely mestizo in ethnic composition, so that they did not remain so isolated from the cultural fabric of the nation as did the rural populace of Indo-America. Furthermore, eighteenth-century immigration had counted for relatively more in building the total Chilean colonial population than was the case in the parts of the empire which lay farther behind the frontier, and the emigration from Spain shifted in that century to the harder-working and enterprising Basques, Catalans, and Galicians.[99]

The Continuity of Economic Expansion. The arrival of these more economically gifted immigrants coincided with a period of expansion in the colonial economy. During the eighteenth century, the extension of land settlement produced an increasingly large exportable surplus of agricultural products, an output which was marketed primarily in Peru and Bolivia. With the late-colonial trade liberalization measures, trading vessels could legally begin to sail around the Cape to Peru, stopping in Chile en route. The provisioning of these vessels, together with the expanding shipping facilities they provided for Chile's own foreign trade, proved to be an additional impetus for the rise of commercial interests in the area. The stimulating effect of these developments was twofold; along with expansion in the volume of exports came a distinct improvement in the terms of trade. Late colonial times brought also a pick-up in Chilean mining activity (silver, gold, copper, and some coal), and fostered development of still another nonagricultural interest group of some size. In general, Chilean mining operations tended to be smaller in scale than was the case in the rich lodes of the viceroyalties of Mexico and Peru.[100] Consequently, somewhat as in the Antioquian case, the beneficiaries of Chilean mining development were rather more numerous, if individually less princely in the magnitude of their wealth.

By the time national independence was won, a full-fledged production and foreign trade boom was well underway. As early as 1821, Chilean products were being exchanged directly with places as far away as England and Calcutta.[101] Thereafter, trade rose for several decades; between 1845 and 1860 alone, the foreign commerce of Chile tripled.[102] New silver deposits were opened up, permitting a considerable increase in output up into the middle of the century. For example, the fabulous Chañarcillo mine, which was to produce somewhat over half of the total nineteenth-century Chilean silver output, began operation in 1832.[103] Other valuable strikes were made from time to time, although the rich Caracoles vein which was discovered in 1870 was the most important later element in prolonging Chilean silver production. Meanwhile, copper acquired such importance that by the 1840's and 1850's, Chile was the leading copper producer in the world. Coal mining in the 1820's through the 1840's supplied, among other users, the new Pacific Steamship Company which Wheelwright had established with the backing of English capital.

Small-scale exploitation of nitrate deposits began around 1812, but after the 1830's their export-directed development began in earnest.[104] With continuing increases in output, the export value of nitrates even exceeded that of copper by the 1870's. Later in the century, after the War of the Pacific had delivered Peruvian and Bolivian nitrate resources to Chile, the nitrate export tax revenues were so great that most internal taxes were abolished, though government spending increased so rapidly that it was still necessary to obtain frequent loans abroad.

Agricultural exports, the most important colonial Chilean exports, continued to play a role in the republican era, as Chilean products moved even beyond the older markets in such countries as Peru and Argentina. At mid-century, for instance, agriculture had received two additional boosts. Discovery of gold in California in 1848 made Chile an important provisioning center for ships rounding the Cape, especially until the Central American crossings were developed for those heading west in the gold rush. Chilean foodstuffs were even exported in considerable volume to supply the Californian markets before farming was well developed in that territory. Around 1852-1854, Chile was also a supplier of foodstuffs to Australia, which was just beginning to develop. From 1865 to the end of the century Chilean wheat was exported to the English market.[105]

The beneficial effects of this long foreign trade boom were greatly enhanced by the fact that Chile was one of the few Latin American countries to attain a fairly stable political structure soon after independence. After a decade or so of anarchy, the conservative oligarchy consolidated its position in the highly centralist government which came into being in the 1830's under the political guidance of the wealthy merchant Diego Portales. Alone among the Latin American constitutions of this era, the Chilean Constitution of 1833 lasted for over 90 years. Not only was the financial position of the government improved by the relative stability which accompanied the foreign trade boom,[106] but the condition was also conducive to the development of business enterprises which could take advantage of the new economic opportunities of the day.

A good many of these new firms were initiated by the immigrant entrepreneurs who were attracted to Chile by its prosperity and stability, or by their immediate offspring. Manufacturing development was almost entirely the work of such men, but in other sectors they were also important. Thus, for example, John MacKay was, along with other foreigners, among the pioneer innovator-organizers of Chilean coal mining in the 1840's, while Matías Cousiño, an entrepreneur of French derivation, not only made a large fortune in coal mining but also became a leading figure in nitrate development. In copper mining, too, foreign entrepreneurs and technicians contributed much to the progress of the industry. British-founded mercantile establishments in Valparaíso, Santiago, and elsewhere assisted greatly in getting Chile's growing foreign commerce underway in a satisfactory manner. Modern livestock ranching was brought to Chile by men with such names as Ricardo Price, Oscar Schoueman, Tomás Eastman, Nathan Miers, Manuel Bunster, and Tomás Bland.[107] Around mid-century, between three and four thousand Germans settled as farm colonists in southern Chile in the vicinity of Valdivia, developing prosperous middle-sized farms and contributing so much to the progress of the region that some Chileans were later moved to recommend an immigration policy which would be specifically aimed at bringing in other German settlers.[108] In general, however, the number of immigrants who came to Chile was not large. Most of the settlement of the southern frontier region took place on the basis of large estates and a movement of people out of central Chile.

The Rise of National Entrepreneurs. The achievement of domestic stability came at a time when trade possibilities were rapidly expanding and before international concerns domiciled in the advanced countries could reach out to dominate completely the economic activity of the periphery. For the larger part of the nineteenth century, Chilean development was to an impressive extent an accomplishment of domestic enterprises founded by criollo or immigrant entrepreneurs; and native capital, originating mostly in mining and trade (or, indeed, the two combined), played a leading role in acting upon the widening range of economic opportunities. From an early date, for example, a group of merchant-financiers known as *habilitadores* were the main suppliers of capital in the form of money and goods to the owner-operators of copper mines. They contracted to take the output of the mines in repayment; a portion of this was then remitted abroad (e.g., to England or Calcutta) in payment for imported items.[109] Immigrant interests were of course represented in this branch of trade, but, generally speaking, Chilean businessmen—some, for example the Ossa family, of late colonial economic prominence—predominated. Located chiefly in such ports as Coquimbo, Copiapó, and Huasco, the *habilitadores* often functioned as agents or branches of the large trading establishments of Santiago and Valparaíso and emerged as a major source of capital accumulation in the early national period. As nitrates gained in importance, many of these same Chilean firms (e.g., Gallo, Puelma, Custodio, Ossa)—joined by firms founded by immigrants or the offspring of immigrants (e.g., Augustín Edwards, Antonio Gibbs)—grew larger still in the financing of that industry. Often, the foreign mining firms which were established in copper and nitrates during this era received their financing from the established Chilean mining capitalists.[110] The Chilean coal industry was similarly developed largely on the basis of national capital, even though there, as in copper, foreign technicians brought in the important technical improvements.

Given this development, it was only natural that economic modernization should be carried further by these domestic capitalistic ventures. The earliest banks, for instance, were established primarily by Chilean capital—particularly that which grew out of the combination of trade and mining-finance noted above. In 1854, the Banco de Bezanilla, MacClure y Cía. began operations, followed in two years by the banking firm of Ossa y Cía.[111] Not long afterwards, the Banco Edwards was established, with branches in London, Paris, Vienna, and Boston. Also in the 1855-1860 period, the government established the Caja de Crédito Hipotecario (National Mortgage Bank) to make long-term loans to agriculture.[112] Significantly, all this occurred several decades before the opening of the Bank of Tarapacá and London in 1888 brought British branch banking to Chile. Still other aspects of capitalistic organization were also not long in appearing. The Bolsa de Comercio of Santiago, the more important of the two bourses in the country, was established in 1893. The Bolsa de Corredores of Valparaíso, which was incorporated in 1898 (and officially recognized in 1905), grew out of an earlier organization, the Bolsa de Comercio of Valparaíso, which had been founded before 1840.[113]

So dynamic, in fact, was Chilean business enterprise that it eventually led to a conflict with the country's northern neighbors in an interesting case of intra-Latin American "imperialism." Backed by some foreign (mostly English) financing, Chilean capitalists had formed companies to develop nitrate deposits in territory belonging to Bolivia and Peru. They rapidly assumed a commanding position. Thereupon Bolivia, in contravention of an earlier treaty with Chile, began to levy heavy taxes on the Chilean companies, while Peru even went so far as to expropriate the Chilean companies, issuing certificates to the expropriated owners but not paying the promised compensation. War ensued, with the consequence that Chile acquired the extremely valuable nitrate territories from its neighbors in a classic "imperialistic" maneuver.[114]

As in the case of Brazil, therefore, a Chilean national bourgeoisie had come into being by mid-century—an aristocracy of wealth based upon commerce, mining, and banking which shared with the older landowning elite the positions of social and political prominence. When, in the early 1880's, a survey was made of the 59 largest personal fortunes in Chile, only 24 were found to be of colonial origin; the others had been built up in the nineteenth century.[115] The two moneyed groups could not, however, be clearly separated, as by the later decades of the century there had been a considerable degree of intermingling. On the one hand, the older landed gentry appears to have invested in urban enterprises and to have looked with favor upon marriages with financially successful immigrants and their descendants; on the other hand, as time went on an increasing number of the urban rich (and, later, even the less rich) purchased rural properties.[116] What emerged, then, seems to have been a sort of hybrid *haute bourgeoisie*, comprising wealthy urban capitalists and the old rural upper classes in an ever closer economic and familial union that dominated both the apparatus of finance and the machinery of state for a considerable period of time. More modern in the nature of its origins and in the character of its economic base than the upper class counterparts in many other Latin American countries, the Chilean plutocracy was at the same time limited in the degree to which it could promote social structural changes, for its dual origin gave it interlocking interests which by the end of the century made it something less than receptive to programs for either rural or urban reform.

Undoubtedly, too, the heavy involvement of this class in the export sector throughout much of the period in question was an important factor in exempting it from the necessity of doing more to facilitate the internal development of the country, although as time went on, the Chilean elite became increasingly marginal (and somewhat parasitic) in its relation to the activity of the external sector. Events following the War of the Pacific put much of the nitrate industry into foreign hands, while the twentieth-century revival of the copper industry—based on heavily capital-intensive mass-mining techniques—demanded a complex technology and management and a capital investment which were far beyond the capacity of the Chilean business community to supply. Accordingly, when Chilean copper production began to pick up after 1900, it did so as a largely foreign controlled industry.[117] In any case, the kind of historically premature stabilization of social structure to which this class fusion gave rise became eventually a strait jacket which tended, in the present century, to restrict the range of policy options available to the government in its efforts to diversify the domestic production structure; in particular, the road was blocked to a continued modernization of the agricultural system.[118] Perhaps it is significant that, notwithstanding Chile's agricultural potential, a Dirección de Servicios Agrícolas was not set up until 1915 nor was a Ministry of Agriculture established until 1924.

The Prelude to Policy Changes of the Twentieth Century.   Before these limitations were reached, however, the economy and social structure manifested what was for Latin America a remarkable degree of modification, a modification which was signaled politically by the formation of the Radical Party in 1862. Perhaps few of the entrepreneurs (many of them immigrants) connected with the small industries which were springing up had yet entered the ranks of the elite, but from the time of its founding in 1883 the Chilean Society for Industrial Development (Sociedad de Fomento Fabril) campaigned for, and often managed to obtain, various forms of state assistance in the national industrialization movement: subsidies, tariffs, and preferential treatment in governmental purchasing contracts.[119] From 1897 on, tariff policy moved clearly into protectionism; but long before, the state had begun, somewhat unsystematically, to intervene to promote the growth of domestic manufacturing. In the 1840's, for example, the first sugar refinery had been established with state protection, including reductions of and exemptions from duties. During the same period, the state also guaranteed, for eight years, a 5 per cent return on capital invested in various kinds of textile mills, in copper metallurgy plants, and in glass and bottle factories.[120] More general assistance to economic growth came through a variety of pro-developmental policies which the mercantile-influenced state pursued over the years in the promotion of commerce: e.g., port improvements at Valparaíso and elsewhere, the promotion (despite some conservative opposition) of education some 30 years before the larger Argentine effort got under way,[121] the reduction and eventual abolition of *alcabalas* (internal trade taxes) to promote the domestic movement of goods, and (over some landowner opposition) the encouragement of road building and railway construction.

Flour mills, breweries, leather factories, and furniture factories appeared on the scene, though perhaps less as a result of direct protection than of general economic progress. By the 1880's, the growth of copper mining and the nitrate industry, together with the expanding public works program, had brought into being a surprisingly large number of foundries and metal-working establishments which turned out such products as nitrate equipment, some types of copper and silver mining machinery, agricultural and milling machinery, parts for railways, and military equipment.[122]

During the administration of President Balmaceda (1886-1891), the most interesting developments in economic policy appeared. In a manner which was anticipatory of the twentieth-century policy scene, there was launched a state-directed and state-encouraged program of economic modernization.[123] Strongly nationalistic in flavor, the Balmaceda government incurred the enmity of foreign interests by proposing to "Chileanize" the nitrate territory railway, which was then owned by British interests and which had been used as a means of strengthening the British hand in the field of nitrate production, and by proposing to use the still extensive public reserves of nitrate lands to regulate both the production and sale of the commodity. At first the administration intended to operate nitrate fields as government enterprises and set about arranging a loan from the Rothschilds for the purpose of buying up nitrate properties. A bit later, though, the government's position switched in favor of private Chilean capital; and by denying foreign companies access to the remaining public reserves, it was hoped to augment the role of domestic companies in nitrate production and exportation.

Ownership of the nitrate fields, it should be mentioned, had become a significant public issue during that time; one of the consequences of the War of the Pacific had been a substantial transfer of nitrate deposits from Chilean to alien ownership despite a Chilean victory in the war. When the Chilean properties in Peru had been expropriated just prior to the war, the compensation certificates issued to the former owners of expropriated properties took on a decidedly speculative character owing to the uncertainty of their eventual redemption. British and other European speculators apparently bought up large quantities of these certificates at bargain prices, and when the properties were restored to certificate holders after the war by the Chilean government, much of the industry passed thereby into foreign hands, among whom Colonel John T. North, the Nitrate King, figured prominently.[124] Just how much of the industry was actually alienated is not altogether clear. Some authors cite evidence that over half the deposits remained under Chilean ownership by the early twentieth century, while others claim that the Chilean interest was reduced to but a small fraction of the total.[125] Whatever the exact amount of foreign interest, however, it was sufficient to raise a twentieth-century sounding charge of foreign domination, particularly when during the 1880's the interest of the nitrate cartel in restricting output conflicted with the government's desire to keep up production in order to collect more export taxes.[126]

Foreign capital interests (and some domestic employers) were further antagonized by the comparatively tolerant attitude adopted by the Balmaceda government toward labor strikes in the nitrate fields during the late 1880's, although the government's eventual repression of the striking miners cost it proletarian support without really winning it the backing of the moneyed interests of the nation. Indeed, to judge from the relative apathy of the proletariat during the anti-Balmaceda revolution of 1891, it would seem that a chief flaw in the Balmaceda program lay in its failure to achieve a broader base of popular support which might have sustained it against oligarchic and foreign attack. Apart from a stated intention to use the profits of a government-owned national bank to finance worker housing, there was not much in the administration's activity to enlist mass enthusiasm except for the general pro-developmental posture of the regime. At the same time, however, important interests, domestic as well as foreign, were alienated by the government's conception of its proper role vis-à-vis the development process.

Oligarchic interests affiliated with the private banks were threatened in several ways by the government's proposal to establish a government central bank on the basis of nitrate revenues. For one thing, the profligate and inflationary note-issuing policy of these banks had favored the heavily mortgaged landowners and the exporting interests whose income was received in foreign currency and whose costs lagged behind the general increase in the price level. Yet the government seemed bent on ending this convenient arrangement by conferring on the central bank a monopoly of note issue. Thereafter the forced savings generated by the government bank's expansion of the money supply would serve to transfer more resources to the public sector for the aggressive public works campaign.[127] Furthermore, the avowed intention of the government bank to stimulate development through low-interest loans and easy lending policies was a threat to established private banking interests, while it diminished the differential advantage of those who long had enjoyed a privileged access to bank credit.

The Balmaceda government also proposed to plow nitrate revenues into the public investment program, utilizing higher internal taxes to cover the routine costs of administration; but at the same time, an impasse developed between the oligarchic congress and the executive branch of government over the national budget with the result that a substantial fiscal deficit appeared and inflation became a symbol of the affront given to entrenched interests. The public works program—road building, railway construction, expansion of the school system—added more problems to the scene by drawing labor from agriculture and exerting an upward pressure on rural wages, thereby putting a squeeze on the landed interests. Moreover, the government's plan for using the public works program as a springboard for industrialization (e.g., by placing large orders with national metal-working plants for metal bridges and flat cars), however well-intentioned, merely exposed the administration to charges of favoritism and graft.

The government-generated inflation, the transfer of resources to the public sector, government intervention in banking, state ownership of railways and regulation of the nitrate industry, and presidential defiance of Congress eventually disturbed so many established powers that revolt broke out. The mainstay of public finance, the nitrate revenues, was cut off from the central government by a naval blockade which was thrown up between central and northern Chile, the nitrate companies disregarded a government order to shut down and diverted their tax payments to the anti-administration forces, and the Balmaceda government was brought down. Thereafter, the legislature deprived the presidency of much of its power and a period of more conventional oligarchic rule ensued until 1920.

As it happened, however, the period of parliamentary rule was transitional, for the forces which lay behind the Balmaceda phenomenon gradually gathered strength and came to the forefront once the interwar economic crises hit. As early as the 1880's, several of Chile's most distinguished economists, including former proponents of laissez faire, had begun to call for government regulation of nitrates: e.g., Miguel Cruchaga Montt and Francisco Valdés Vergara. Expansion of mining brought increasing numbers of *rotos* into the industrial proletariat, and general domestic development brought an unprecedented shift of people from the rural areas to the towns and cities,[128] while the growth of cities in turn amplified the urban occupations which constituted the base of the middle classes. With the growing relative importance of more organizable urban labor, trade unions appeared,[129] and the Socialist Party was founded in 1912.

During this period, the established order of society came under increasingly bitter attack—for example, in the widely read *Sinceridad: Chile íntimo en 1910* by Alejandro Venegas.[130] An ever more outmoded agrarian structure began to weigh heavily on the possibilities of development as agricultural exports lost their dynamism and agricultural imports began to rise.[131] In addition, perhaps because of its relatively more advanced state of socio-economic evolution, there appeared at an early date that chronic inflationary process which has often in Latin America accompanied the intergroup struggle for political and economic power and which, in recent decades, has seemed to be epidemic in the hemisphere. This too, a symbol of the arrested transformation of Chilean society and of the resultant institutional instability, ultimately took its toll on the process of economic growth. Thus, the pattern of development which began so promisingly in the nineteenth century grew less and less viable in the twentieth— aided and abetted, of course, by unfavorable exogenous changes in the Chilean export situation.[132]

MEXICO: ANTECEDENTS OF REVOLUTION

Like the other three countries surveyed in this chapter, Mexico was a major beneficiary of the quickening economic tempo of the late nineteenth century, although its participation in the global wave of expansion was, as in the Argentine instance, belated. It was, in fact, largely compressed into the last quarter of the century, a circumstance which served to differentiate Mexican experience from the rather more lengthy involvement of Brazil and Chile in the growth of international capitalism and the correspondingly greater degree of societal elasticity achieved in the latter two countries. At the same time, however, the Mexican case differed radically from the Argentine experience. In the latter country, externally impelled growth opened up a comparatively new and unsettled region to modern modes of economic organization. In Mexico an overlay of modernity, impressive enough in its own right, was superimposed upon a complex established institutional structure that contained a substantial residuum of archaic economic elements, was afflicted severely by cultural dualism, and which was already quite unstable because of the deep-seated social and political cleavages that had troubled the life of the nation throughout most of the century.

Brazil, somewhat more than Chile and Argentina, shared these internal disparities, but there the division between the old and the new was to a considerable extent a segregation of geographical regions: the anachronistic

Northeast and the booming South which met each other only marginally in such intermediate areas as Minas Gerais and Bahia. In Mexico, though, the dynamic, and unsettling, elements of the new order were interjected into the very midst of antecedent arrangements, so that the internal disparities, brought side by side, were far more sharply defined. Perhaps, indeed, nowhere else among the Latin American nations was this contrast brought into such clear focus.

Expansion of the External Sector. Part of the story lay in Mexico's resource and locational advantages. The rich endowment of minerals and the variety of agricultural products which had made the country the most valuable overseas dominion of Spain served to awaken anew the interest of foreigners in the investment opportunities of the land—particularly with such technological advances as the development and extension of rail transport, the introduction of new cyanide processes in mining technology, and the rise of the petroleum industry. Moreover, the country, located as it is in the Northern Hemisphere relatively close to the many shipping lines plying the Atlantic and the Caribbean, was well situated to participate in the accelerating commercial life of the age. The well-developed Caribbean and Gulf of Mexico shipping services were, for example, especially instrumental in facilitating exports of such important items as henequen (the mainstay of the Yucatecan regional economy), the coffee and sugar crops of the hinterland of the port of Veracruz, the rubber production of southern Mexico, and, in the early twentieth century, the rich outpouring of petroleum from the fabulous Golden Lane, an area lying along the Gulf Coast between Tampico and Veracruz.

Not the least advantage in this respect was the fact that Mexico was next door to the United States, which was, of course, one of the principal world centers of industrial and general economic expansion. To this important market Mexico was linked throughout the period by the shipping facilities of the Gulf of Mexico; but after the United States railway system reached the Mexican frontier at several points in Texas, Arizona, and California during the 1880's, economic interaction between the two countries was greatly intensified. From that time on, the extension of the Mexican rail lines northward (with generous public subsidies) to border connecting points took on special significance in adding to the resource base of the country.

By way of illustration, one might observe that traditionally the Gulf coast had been the major supply center for the Mexican cotton textile industry. When rail lines were pushed to the northern border, however, such areas as Sonora, Nuevo León, the Valle de Mexicali, and Coahuila quickly moved into cotton production, for the improved transport conditions made the northern part of the republic far more accessible than ever before. Domestic and foreign capital flowed in, combining with foreign managerial ability to establish a capitalistic organization in regional agriculture. Farm machinery was imported from the United States, and between 1884 and 1910 the famous Laguna district of western Coahuila, served by the Mexican Central Railway, emerged as the dominant cotton producing region of the country—mainly for the expanding domestic consumption of cotton but also, in the early years of the present century, with an occasional small amount for export (although Mexico was a net importer of cotton throughout the era).[133] In like fashion, the introduction of United States capital into extensive cattle ranching operations in the northern states of Mexico converted still other areas of previously low utility into areas of resource value.

In some ways, however, the new agricultural development of northern Mexico should probably be taken as the realization of external transport economies originated by the even more consequential minerals development of the area. In the closing decades of the nineteenth century, the center of the Mexican mining industry gravitated northward where, thanks to the new railway lines, it was closely integrated with similar operations carried on concurrently in the western portion of the United States.[134] Mexican lead, for example, was shipped in considerable volume across the border for smelting in Texas and Colorado (notably at Leadville) until an increase in United States duties in the Windom Act impelled a number of North American minerals companies to set up ore processing facilities in Mexico itself.

Among the minerals opened up to exploitation in the northern and western states were lead, copper, tin, iron, silver, antimony, and zinc. Owing to these developments, the nation's external trade moved substantially toward a more diversified pattern that included not only a variety of industrial minerals but a number of different agricultural products as well. In addition to the crops and minerals mentioned previously, the following were also significant export items at some time during the Porfirian period: graphite, cattle and hides, chick peas, vanilla, guayule, ixtle, and chicle. If, on the one hand, the nation benefited as did no other Latin American country, except possibly Peru, from the varied character of its export industries, the same degree of diversification implied, on the other hand, a fairly comprehensive geographical incidence of the export-induced push toward modernization. Few major areas of the Mexican countryside were left altogether untouched by this pervasive, yet limited, involvement with the new industrial age.

Public Developmental Policies and Organizational Modernization.   Locational advantages and the complementarity of Mexico's resource base to the needs of foreign markets were, however, only a part of the picture. No less important were events of an institutional order. After the ill-fated French intervention of the 1860's, the country moved gradually into the most stable political period it had ever experienced as an independent nation. While liberal-sponsored reforms cut deeply into the accumulation of ecclesiastical assets that had been slowly rebuilt after the plundering associated with the separation from Spain, this despoilation seems to have given a new impetus to the circulation of wealth in the private sector of the economy, at least among a slowly increasing, if still rather small, number of the new elite. Indeed, in the *nouveaux riches* of the Reform—bent on enhancing their recently acquired fortunes in a manner they viewed as identical with national progress—there is a curious prefiguring of the role of the so-called Revolutionary millionaires of a later age. Estimates of the total value of the properties shifted to private ownership vary considerably, but it was far from inconsequential, despite the previous erosion of church assets. George McCutcheon McBride, for example, estimates that over 40,000 properties were expropriated from the church after the Reform.[135] Both McBride and Andrés Molina Enríquez, however, note that the wealthy and the politically influential reaped most of the benefits of this state-directed multimillion dollar transfer operation. Subsequently, under the authoritarian and in many ways unattractive regime of Porfirio Díaz, whose long tenure commenced in 1876 and lasted until 1910,[136] a heavy-handed sort of rule made the country a more hospitable place for the conduct of business enterprise and provided the opportunity for an inner coterie of positivistic advisers known as *científicos* to install their version of modernizing national policies.

The implications of the Porfiriato were not lost on foreigners, who soon came to view the "new" Mexico as "an ambitious marcher in the procession of nations." And lest they should miss out on the march, foreign investors rushed in to lead the parade. United States investments alone rose from only a few million dollars to around a billion dollars during the Porfiriato. Typical of the foreign interpretation of the changed situation in Mexico was a series of articles which were offered the readers of *Harper's Magazine* in 1897 under the title, "The Awakening of a Nation," and which proclaimed:

> She is no longer old Mexico; while in the United States we have been achieving a material development, she has wrought the political and social miracle of the century. Within less time than has elapsed since our Civil War invented millionaires, Mexico has stepped across as wide a gulf. From a state of anarchy tempered by brigandage, she has graduated to the most compact and unified nation in the New World. She has acquired not only a government which governs, but one which knows how to govern, and, contemporaneously, a people which has learned how to be ruled. Only those who seriously knew the country in the old days can at all conceive the change from the Mexico of a generation back to the Mexico of now. There was no touring then, and nowhere was travel more unsafe. By every country road, even into the very heart of cities, the *bandido* robbed and murdered. There were even lady Turpins, and some of them were geniuses. There

were no railroads, no telegraphs, practically no commerce; at the bottom of all, no security. Today Mexico is—and I say it deliberately—the safest country in America. . . . As for stability, the record speaks for itself. Mexico had sixty-two viceroys in 286 years—not very tumultuous; but it also has had fifty-two presidents, emperors, and other heads in fifty-nine years of this century. *Now, one president for twenty years. Some will say that this is not republican. Possibly not, but it is business.*[137]

The attractiveness of Porfirian Mexico was not, however, simply the result of a perennial president and the eradication of banditry by the dreaded *rurales.*[138] In 1884 and 1889 new codes of commercial law were promulgated, imposing a more modern system of transactional rules uniformly upon the whole nation. The 1889 Mexican Code was issued to take into account the improvements made in 1885 in the Spanish Code, the latter constituting the prototype for the Mexican codes of 1854, 1884, and 1889. Trademark laws were also brought up to date, while the metric system, first adopted by the Mexican government in 1857, was finally put into force on a fairly comprehensive scale in the 1890's, to the great benefit of commercial transactions between Mexico and European countries. Internally, the government took steps to remove the local customs duties which had long impeded the movement of goods from one state to another in Mexico, despite Article 124 of the 1857 Constitution which had previously provided a basis in fundamental law for their abolition. Legislation in 1886 attempted to make that article of the constitution less of a dead letter, but it was not apparently until 1896 that the central government was able finally to suppress these internal barriers to trade.

In 1887 a substantial stimulus was given to one basic production sector, that of minerals exploitation, when a new mining code was promulgated. Under this and subsequent mining laws enacted in 1892 and 1894, tax burdens were lowered on the mining industry and the procedures for registering claims and conducting mining operations with foreign capital were greatly simplified. In fact, during the Porfiriato the whole fiscal system was renovated, and a quite unaccustomed orderliness was introduced into the budgetary operations of the national government. The bad reputation acquired by Mexican public securities during the century made this an achievement of no little difficulty since part of the task involved refinancing and consolidating the nation's external public debt. Throughout the early Porfirian period, moreover, the fluctuating and generally declining price of silver, the standard of monetary value, presented the government with additional difficulties. Nevertheless, these problems were overcome so that the system of public finance, if still regressive and unsatisfactory in a number of other respects, was vastly improved in comparison with its state in the pre-Díaz era.[139]

Important as were these legal and fiscal modifications in providing a climate more auspicious for economic growth, they were by no means the sole measures employed by government to foster expansion. The minerals boom of the late 1800's and early 1900's, for example, was essentially the creature of an amplified rail system, in which undertaking public policy was a vital element. Government subsidies of both money and land were granted with liberality, and if there was an enormous amount of chicane and waste in the program, it was nevertheless an accomplishment of considerable importance that the less than 580 kilometers of track in use in 1875 had been extended to over 14,500 kilometers by the end of the century. Ten years later, Mexico had nearly 25,000 kilometers of track.

Much of this railway construction was designed, as elsewhere in the economically peripheral regions of the world, primarily to move export items to foreign markets. Yet because of the scattered locations of the export industries and the central position of the capital city and major Mexican markets, the rail connections built to link these with the Gulf Coast ports and with the transshipment points along the United States frontier gave Mexico the skeleton of a reasonably well-distributed rail network. Around the turn of the century, the qualitative deficiencies attributable to the lax social control which had been exercised over rail construction were so glaring, however, as to elicit public remedial action. Under Limantour, the minister of finance, the government began the nationalization of the railways. Communications development was also fostered by the Díaz regime. By 1900 there were over 45,000 kilometers of telegraph lines throughout the republic, while the postal system, still organized by the old colonial ordinances until 1883, had been administratively reformed in 1883 and 1895.[140]

Domestic industrialization was encouraged by tariffs that were increasingly protective after the 1867-1876 period, though the trend toward local manufacturing was also assisted by monetary depreciation and by the transport charges added to imported goods as they moved to the interior markets of the country. Both federal and state governments, however, went even further than simple tariff policy, for there appears to have been a decided growth of Mexican protectionist sentiment throughout the Porfiriato as increasing doubt was expressed regarding the universal applicability of liberal economic principles.[141] Tax exemptions and reductions, waivers of duties on capital imports, rebates on export duties, and special concessionary grants for new firms were among the measures employed to promote the initiation and growth of new industries,[142] which were also, of course, favored by the aforementioned suppression of internal customs duties and by the notable urbanization of the times.[143] In some instances—e.g., the new iron-and-steel industry at Monterrey—the government role in assisting the establishment of the plant was considerable, as was mentioned in an earlier chapter.

From the standpoint of private enterprise, virtually all the foregoing policies were conducive to developmental investments, and the response of business was impressive. In the field of mining, for example, the number of concessions increased rapidly after 1887, and production, thanks to the introduction of mechanized mining, grew correspondingly. Lead output rose from around 22,000 tons in 1890 to 81,000 tons in 1900. Copper production, only 4,300 tons in 1890, amounted to 16,000 tons by 1899. Gold production, which was about 1,000 kilograms in 1889, reached a level of almost 14,000 kilograms by 1901.[144] Petroleum production, just entering the early stage of successful commercial development at the turn of the century, had expanded so considerably that by 1911 Mexico ranked third among the world's petroleum producing nations.[145]

Commercial agricultural output increased in a similarly striking manner in a number of lines. For example, refined sugar output, which was probably around 25,000 tons in 1877, reached 137,000 tons in 1911. Much of the growth in mining and agriculture depended, of course, on the possibilities of export sales, and in this connection it is significant that between 1877-78 and 1910 there was approximately a sevenfold real increase in foreign trade.[146] In constant pesos (of 1900-01 value), exports of merchandise and precious metals rose from 40.6 million pesos in 1877-78, to 74 million pesos in 1888-89, to 287.7 million pesos in 1910-11.

The changing composition of imports reflected additional evidence of structural developments in the Mexican economy. Total merchandise imports amounted to 76.9 million pesos in 1888-89 and reached 213.5 million pesos in 1910-11. In the former period, imports of consumer goods accounted for 53 per cent of the total, while producer goods represented the other 47 per cent (25 per cent being nondurable producer goods, and 22 per cent durable producer goods). By 1910-11, the proportions of imports represented by consumer items and producer goods had been exactly reversed, reflecting the rising volume of investment activity in Mexico. Moreover, the Mexican economy was making headway toward meeting its own raw materials requirements in the new investment fields, for most of the increase of imports represented by producer goods was in imports of capital goods such as machinery and equipment. In 1910-11, durable producer goods imports accounted for 30 per cent of total merchandise imports; nondurable producer goods, 27 per cent.[147]

While extractive industries represented the backbone of the Porfirian modernization effort, the pace of manufacturing development was sufficiently rapid to place Mexico at the forefront of Latin American manufacturing nations by the close of the era in question. Import merchants, faced with a potential loss of their markets as tariff policy grew more restrictive, reacted by taking the lead in setting up local production facilities.[148] Others, especially immigrants, followed suit. Paper mills, cotton, silk, woolen, and linen textile factories; vegetable oil plants and soap factories; glass and glassware industries; leatherworking plants, tanneries, and garment companies; furniture-making establishments; a jute mill; tobacco, food, and beverage factories; brick and tile plants; an iron and steel mill; a cement factory, foundries and machine works; explosives manufactures; and agricultural implements manufacturers—such were the varied new industries which came into some prominence during the Porfiriato. Much of this was concentrated in the federal district, at Monterrey, or in or near Puebla, but manufacturing enterprises of various sorts were also to be found in such places as Chihuahua, Torreón, Celaya, León, San Luís Potosí, and Querétaro.

There was also some headway made with respect to laying down the organizational infrastructure of a modern economy, over and beyond the legal and fiscal modifications noted earlier. On 21 May 1887, the government authorized establishment of the Bourse of Commerce and granted a 50-year concession to a private company to operate the bourse, which functioned as a securities exchange as well as an organized market for registering the prices at which wholesale merchandise transactions were effected. The Bank of London, Mexico, and South America (established in Mexico in 1864 as the first modern commercial bank in the country) was eventually joined by other institutions. The years 1875-1880 brought three more banks of issue into operation. Two of these—the Banco Santa Eulalia (later the Banco Minero de Chihuahua), which was established by a North American entrepreneur named MacManus, and the Banco Hidalgo—were set up in the northern mining districts of the country. The third was the Monte de Piedad, the sole surviving financial institution from the colonial period, which in 1879 received permission from the government to operate as a bank of deposit, discount, and note issue. In 1881 and 1882, three other banks were added to the list; the Banco Nacional Mexicano (the chief shareholders in which were associated with the Franco-Egyptian Bank), the Banco Mercantil, Agrícola e Hipotecario (primarily involving Spanish capital), and the Banco Hipotecario Mexicano.[149]

Several of these institutions began to engage in branch banking through offices which they opened in several parts of the republic, and in subsequent years still other banks of deposit, discount, and issue were opened in the principal towns and cities of the country. By 1901, some two dozen banks, not counting branches, were in business. Comprehensive regulation of financial institutions had been attempted in the conservative general banking law of 1897, but of the usual weaknesses of new banking systems Mexico appears to have had its share.[150] Perhaps the state of the new financial intermediaries was not quite as anarchic as some Mexican writers have suggested (it seems to have been not so bad as the era of "wildcat banking" in the United States), but the situation was still sufficient to give cause for a growing concern for the soundness of the banking system in the late Porfirian period.[151] Inadequate provisions for reserves, overcommitment of funds to less liquid long-term mortgage paper, depreciation in the quality of mercantile bills handled, repeated extension of loan maturities, excessive issue of bank notes, costly competition for deposit business (through high interest payments)—these and other deficiencies led to the thorough revamping of banking legislation in the reform law of 1908.

The Sharpening of Internal Contradictions. By 1908, defects of the banking system represented a comparatively superficial problem in the larger Mexican economic scene. In the closing years of the decade, a number of trends converged to expose the serious deficiencies in Porfirian prosperity, particularly its overreliance on the external sector and its failure to attend to an adequate internal participation in the benefits of export-led expansion. Prices on several of the principal export products declined; the amount of new foreign capital coming in for investment diminished. Credit extension was gradually curtailed, loans were called, the difficulty of debt collection increased, and security sales dwindled. In the process of retrenchment, the artificiality of many financial transactions of the preceding era of expansion was glaringly revealed, and a number of financial institutions went under. Current government revenues shrank, forcing the government to borrow more abroad, while a failure in the maize crop compelled the government to resort to imports of grain in an effort to allay the mounting popular discontent.

A significant element in this widespread disgruntlement was the small but articulate middle class which had been created and sustained by the processes of economic development and urbanization, although, when compared with southern Brazil, Argentina, or Chile, the Mexican middle class was neither so proportionately large nor so widely involved in the economic life of the nation. Lacking the skills and advantages for upward mobility which immigration and/or political stability had accorded the middle classes of those other countries, its position in the socio-economic structure was more precarious and marginal to the total scheme of things. Nourished intellectually by the slim but appetizing diet of education provided by the Díaz government,[152] this urban-based class appears, from all accounts, to have become increasingly disaffected in the closing years of the Porfirian era.

On the one hand, the educational opportunities available to this class increased its awareness of prevailing conditions and problems at the same time that they (and all the official propaganda about national progress) stimulated the economic and social aspirations of at least the more ambitious members of the class. Moreover, just to the north there existed a country which presented an alternative socio-economico-political model, a system with far greater ambit for the development and realization of middle class ambitions. On the other hand, the desires of the middle class for political participation were continually frustrated by the manipulated authoritarian structure of the Porfiriato, for the formation of public policy was monopolized by a small group which was insensitive if not outright hostile to the interests of the rest of the body politic.

On the economic side, some of the *petit bourgeois* members of the class may have been harmed by the breakdown of local commercial and producer monopolies which followed upon the expansion of the railway system and the freeing of domestic trade from the trammels of state customs levies. A larger number of the class may well have suffered during the recession which hit the country near the close of the Porfirian period. In any event throughout the long period of economic expansion it was clear to this class that the national pattern of sharing in the benefits of this expansion was heavily skewed in favor of the privileged few: the rich, the politically influential, and the foreigner. Far more so was this the case in Mexico than in Brazil, Argentina, or even Chile. Furthermore, it appears that the structure of the system left much to be desired, from a middle-class point of view, in opportunities for advancement. Participation in political decision-making was debarred by a select in-group's preemptive control of the process. And opportunities for significant class participation and advancement in economic decision-making processes were widely blocked by the competitive superiority of foreign businessmen and technicians as well as by the control of the opportunity structure retained by local influentials and their kin. Indeed, while official adulation of things and people foreign verged on the incredible, this high-level xenophilia was increasingly met, at the middle rungs of society, by an understandable resentment which merged into xenophobia.[153]

In this connection, it is important to keep in mind that, for geographical and economic reasons, it was the United States which exerted the dominant foreign influence on the country, an influence which was in nature political and cultural as well as economic. In the latter area alone, however, the influence was overwhelming, for as the chief provider of foreign investment funds, United States capital emerged as by far the principal foreign owner in a land in which foreign ownership per se was subject to growing criticism. Around three-quarters of the mining industry and over half the oil industry were in *yanqui* hands—as were many of the railways and the large plantations and ranches. In Baja California where four foreign companies held a total area of over 40,000 square miles, one United States company alone, the Mexican International Colonization Company, owned more than 20,000 square miles of the land.[154] Between a half and two-thirds of Mexican imports came from the United States while around three-quarters of its exports moved to the markets of the large northern neighbor. Yet, for historical reasons (the Texas secession and the American-Mexican War) the United States was bound to be the prime target for any anti-foreign feelings which might be born of Mexican nationalism. Under the circumstances, Mexican nationals could probably be pardoned for fearing that the Colossus of the North, having already seized half the national territory by war, was now bent on gobbling up the remainder.[155] Whereas Argentina may have used equally lavish inducements to entice foreign capital, there it served mainly to "fill up" an empty country; in Mexico the anxiety, particularly acute in the middle class, was that the effect would be rather more one of displacement.

Displacement was more than an anxiety, however, among many of the lower class, particularly in the rural areas. It was an accomplished fact. Under Diaz, in what was probably the worst policy blunder of the regime, the Juárez Reform Laws were so interpreted as to open the door to a wholesale destruction of the small, indigenous properties. As many as 2.3 million acres of communal lands were redistributed into individual parcels that could be more readily absorbed by the adjacent large estates, while in other instances village lands were simply appropriated by the so-called colonization companies as part of their grants (a practice which was nominally in contravention of the law) or taken over under legal proceedings which permitted individuals to "denounce" and claim public lands.[156] Perhaps only 10 per cent or less of the native villages retained any lands at all by the close of the Porfiriato, the others having been absorbed by the haciendas. In a comparatively short period, vast numbers of people were added to the rural proletariat and deprived of the tiny margin of security, probably more psychological than real, their small parcels and community claims had formerly afforded. Rural violence was often generated—in Jalisco, in San Luís Potosí, in Querétaro, and Guanajuato, and in the even more violent open rebellions in Sonora and Yucatán—but the rape of the Indians' lands continued with scarcely a pause.

On a larger scale, in terms of the actual acreage involved, was the alienation of the public domain. Early in the Díaz period the government had entertained the idea of using public lands to attract a stream of immigrants to the country, although there were a few at the time who correctly foresaw that the latifundian system would render such an effort futile.[157] To support the notion, the government instituted a policy of making large concessions of territory to surveying and colonization companies, out of which concessions land grants in fee simple ownership could be claimed subject to various conditions stipulated by law. For example, the maximum grant which could be made to any one person was stated. In addition, certain portions could be transferred to the companies as payment for the services they presumably rendered in staking out the unoccupied lands for settlement. Hardly any settlement was in fact realized, however, and the colonization programs as such had practically no success at all. The comparatively few immigrants who came to Mexico settled in towns and cities where they quickly became prominent in the commercial, financial, and industrial activity of the day. The colonization and land development companies, though, profited handsomely, becoming, in actual practice, land speculation enterprises.

Lax enforcement and lenient interpretations of the applicable land laws were common. In the 1890's, the legislative provisions concerning disposition of the public domain were liberalized even further, to remove the nominal requirements that the land be actually settled or turned to use and to remove the restrictions on the size of claims. Thanks to the liberalization, recourse to fraud was less necessary than previously, but otherwise the pattern of land distribution continued to follow accustomed lines. In mostly large blocks, some 38.8 million hectares of land passed from public ownership to private control during the Porfiriato and went to individuals, land companies, and railway companies.[158] The size of the transfers varied from region to region as well as from case to case, but in the arid northern states, the land holdings built up in this fashion were, in a number of instances, over 1 million hectares in extent.

To be sure, the lot of the peon was not everywhere equally bad. Owing to the commercialization of agriculture in some regions, and to mining, railway construction, or expanding urban economies in others, there were new opportunities for a limited number of rural workers to shift to more productive and remunerative employment.[159] As a consequence, not a few *hacendado* employers complained that the new geographical and intersectoral mobility of labor was producing a shortage of hands. Nevertheless, the general conditions of life for rural people were so glaringly unsatisfactory that in the early years of the twentieth century even such respectable circles as those represented at a series of Catholic congresses began to propose a variety of reforms to deal with the situation; these included minimum wage levels, limitation of working hours, establishment of worker commissaries for the sale of goods at cost, provision of decent worker housing, creation of mutual savings societies for *campesinos*, and introduction of profit-sharing systems on the estates.[160] By contrast with the lot of the upwardly mobile rural workers in southern Brazil and the Argentine, the Mexican peon was far poorer; and even in comparison with the typical *inquilino* of Chile, the Mexican was often more disadvantaged by virtue of his greater cultural and linguistic isolation from national life and the less productive land with which he had to work.

For the nonagricultural worker, money wages—and very probably real wages—were higher than those of his rural counterpart. Nevertheless, save in exceptional cases, the pay was low, the hours long, and working conditions grim.[161] But whereas efforts to improve the lot of the agricultural worker availed little, in large measure because of the general lack of organizational strength among the *campesinos*, the urban labor force associated with the industrial development of the times soon came to exhibit the character it has displayed in other national settings.[162] As early as 1853 the first mutual benefit type of workers association was formed, and in the decades following, a number of other groups of this nature came into being. In 1870-1872 a labor central, the Gran Círculo de Obreros de

México, composed of such mutualist associations, was formed.[163] From at least 1882 on, somewhat similar Catholic workers' associations were established with the support of various members of the religious hierarchy, though, after publication of the *Rerum Novarum* encyclical, the Catholic social movement began to assume a more militant stance which earned for it the denunciation as "socialistic" or "communistic" by the capitalist press of the Porfiriato.

Still other varieties of reformism, socialism, syndicalism, and anarchism—some emanating from the Knights of Labor and the I.W.W.—were introduced into the intellectual climate of the times, and by the late 1880's and 1890's the more modern sort of trade union organizations were appearing in textiles, railways, and mining. Before the nineteenth century had ended, there had been at least six years—1881, 1884, 1889, 1890, 1891, 1895—in which a notably large number of strikes occurred, while the opening years of the present century witnessed an almost steady rise in the level of industrial conflict that culminated in the bloody textile and mining strikes of 1906-1907.[164] Of these latter occasions of violence, it was the Río Blanco textile strike which was the more sanguinary in terms of the actual number of workers killed and wounded. But in a sense the issues—not only of the strike itself but of the age as well—were crystallized and publicized as never before in the upheaval at the foreign-owned Cananea copper mines in 1906.[165] It was there that the conflicts bred by class disparities in the sharing of national wealth and power were joined with the conflicts that pitted nation against foreigner. Perhaps, indeed, in a curious way the Cananea episode can be taken as the symbolic opening of a period of upheaval and change the resolution of which was symbolized, a third of a century later, by a very similar sort of labor dispute. In the Cananea case, the basic issues were raised and left open to fester in the subsequent years of turbulence. With the settlement of the petroleum strike some 30 years afterwards, the work of national consolidation was begun in earnest.[166]

Part Four

From 1914 to the Present

X

The Origin of Economic Policy Changes in the Twentieth Century

CONSIDERING that a type of market-guided development was being attempted in what was in many important respects still a premarket institutional setting, one must judge the results in late nineteenth-century Latin America to have been remarkable. Although a severe problem of social anachronism remained to hamper the spread of growth and although the pastiche of policies employed during the century following independence contained an abundance of contradictory and ill-conceived elements, modern economic development was nevertheless introduced into the region. Despite the lack of genuine constitutionalism in actual practice, the state had nevertheless to respond to the major pressures brought to bear on it, paying at least some heed to modern-minded intellectuals, a number of whom had their origins in the governing classes. Largely this was so because their views of appropriate policy happened to coincide with the political need of the state to obtain more resources without extracting them by taxation from the domestic holders of wealth. Among other things, then, the requirements of this situation compelled the state to present a correct image to foreign investors and businessmen in order that the desired resources might be more painlessly gathered from a growing volume of transactions in the external sector.

Through the rapid rise in relative importance of the external sector, there occurred, despite the enclave character of that sector, a certain amplification of the received institutional framework as new economic organizations were added, facilitating the utilization of new technology. Foreign enterprises, immigrants, and immigrant firms arrived on the scene and made up in part for the lack of a native tradition of entrepreneurial endeavor. Uniquely identified with the economic expansion of the times, these newcomers, both permanent and transient, were generally at the forefront of private sector advance. With their greater experience in modern technology and forms of business organization, their valuable connections in the world market, and their frequent ability to rely on the backing of superior capital resources, they established in Latin America the organizational seedbed within which modern technology could begin to take root in the area. Through them and the whole institutional apparatus of foreign investment and trade, a pipeline was also laid down through which Latin America could begin to tap the superior technological research and development of

347

countries which were far more advanced in economic evolution. In consequence, substantial increases were realized in the land resources and the capital stock of the region. Although growth impulses deriving from the external sector encountered numerous hindrances, some very real headway was nevertheless made in enlarging the supply of economically relevant skills. During the closing years of the era, 1900-1913, the build-up on both counts was particularly significant.

Closely related to these economic changes were a number of promising social changes, for in the partial decomposition of traditional cultural forms a certain loosening of the system of social stratification took place. In the cities, the nearly polar, or two-class, system of old gave way to a class structure which was characterized by increasing complexity. From its incubation in the bureaucracy and the professions—and, to some extent, in enterprises associated with foreign trade and increasing urbanization—a native middle class began to develop, fortified in varying degree by the upwardly mobile immigrants. Mining, construction, utility enterprises, and the scattered new factories brought also into being a working class which was quite different in a number of important respects from the voiceless and amorphous throng that had labored on the land for centuries. Since, as H. F. Dobyns has observed, enlightenment and skills are strategic components of power, such changes were bound to be portentous.[1] The traditional social system of the haciendas had permitted the overlord to monopolize enlightenment in order to maintain the traditional exploitation of Indian serfs who were excluded from the enlightenment process. However, the gradual diffusion of knowledge and skills marked by the social structural changes of the 1850-1914 period was accompanied by a corresponding gradual diffusion of power. Even before the year 1900, parts of Latin America had come to know, or at least to taste, the possibilities of middle class radicalism, and an embryonic unionism imbued with both an ideology of social consciousness and a bent for political action.

Yet, by its very nature, the nineteenth-century movement towards capitalism was limited, albeit ultimately quite consequential. While growth-conducive features were added to the Latin American institutional environment, the inherited growth inhibiting features nevertheless remained. Owing to the lack of integrative structures, the two continued to function in inharmonious juxtaposition, producing an economic and social dissonance that grew especially loud from around 1910 on and which attested unmistakably to the presence of unresolved contradictions in the social fabric of Latin America. In the countryside, the pauperized masses had, thanks to the land-tenure policies of the age, been largely converted into a rural proletariat, a tractable labor force deployed essentially as so many beasts of burden. Victimized economically by the prevailing institutional arrangements, they lived under conditions of social disrespect with few avenues of mobility open to them. Except for the Platine region, the large majority of the populace, urban as well as rural, lived under social structures which denied them effective participation in national processes of modernization. Lacking opportunities for education and access to managerial roles, deprived of the purchasing power with which to exercise consumer sovereignty, and possessing no discretionary control over wealth, they had little share in the decision-making processes, either economic or political.

On the one hand, the industrial growth of the center countries had demonstrated to Latin America the potential for economic advance contained in the productive new technology. On the other, the political and economic system of the nineteenth-century world had proved incapable of fostering a sustained and socially satisfactory utilization of the new technology in that area.

INTERNAL TRENDS LEADING TOWARDS POLICY CHANGES

Intellectual and Policy Shifts. Although for some the reality of export sectoral development was taken as equivalent to national progress, the turn of events produced by World War I and its aftermath exposed such an equation as an example of misapplied synecdochical expression. Thereafter the dominant policy trends in Latin America reflected unmistakably the need for seeking a more viable development route. Long before this, however, there were clear signs that the briefly held belief in the efficacy of economic liberalism was on the wane, even though the espousal of classical economic policy was seldom, in practice, an unqualified one in Latin America.

The whole existing order had come under increasing attack from some of the hemisphere's leading intellectual figures. Ranging in temper from Hispanophilic romanticists writing threnodies for a bygone age to apostles of dialectical materialism, these critics raised a multitude of questions about the policies and relationships which had once seemed so promising. From Lima, Manuel González Prada (1848-1918) delivered his thundering indictment of the social infirmities of *fin de siècle* Peru and inspired a whole new generation of articulate reformers, among them José Carlos Mariátegui, the founder of the Peruvian Communist Party, and Victor Raúl Haya de la Torre, the founder of the Aprista movement. In Mexico, Andrés Molina Enríquez's dissection of "the great national problems" (the title of his influential book, *Los grandes problemas nacionales*) marked a head-on confrontation with the amour propre of the Porfiriato. The avid anti-imperialism of that other great and internationally read Mexican, José Vasconcelos (1882-1959), exemplified the growing uneasiness of Latin Americans about the influence of foreign powers. In Chile the writings and speeches of Valentín Letelier (1852-1919) raised questions with quasi-Marxian overtones, while Francisco Encina's classic exercise in critical scrutiny, *Nuestra inferioridad económica*, was given first as a series of university lectures in

1911 and appeared in published form for wider circulation in the year following.[2] Across the Andes, it was José Ingenieros (1877-1925) who expressed the reservations of many concerning the course the Argentine nation was following. At length, the voices of dissatisfaction mounted to a whole chorus of strong and diversified dissent.

If the climate of opinion was changing, so also were actual economic thinking and policy—and very much in the same direction. By 1914, for example, the Chilean government was owner of 64 per cent of the railway kilometrage of that country. Early in the century, one of the most prominent Chilean railway experts was, while acknowledging the usual European arguments for laissez faire, pointing out the special justification for state intervention in young countries such as Chile, holding it to be not only useful but also necessary.[3] During the 1880's and 1890's, the beneficent role of foreign capital in Chile had been fundamentally questioned in the course of a rather acrimonious public debate over the desirability, from a national point of view, of permitting foreign (largely British) interests to dominate the nitrate industry through a variety of cartel-like arrangements.[4] Moreover, as the British nitrate interests were to discover, the reservations regarding their role were by no means confined to the avowed nationalists of the Balmaceda regime; it soon became apparent, with the post-Balmaceda restitution of congressional rule, that such suspicions transcended party lines. Significantly, the controversy grew particularly acute whenever adverse conditions befell the nitrate export market. Meanwhile, in 1883 the government itself had lent its support to the creation of the Sociedad de Fomento Fabril,[5] an association for promoting industrial development. By the turn of the century, policy makers were increasingly attentive to protectionist arguments for encouragement of the domestic manufacturing sector.

In Argentina, too, late nineteenth-century export recessions had become occasions for antiforeign invective and for consideration of policies with a nationalistic flavor—a development which presaged much of the twentieth-century policy style.[6] Moreover, direct state participation in the new petroleum industry had been decided upon before the First World War. As early as 1876 the proponents of Argentine industrial development had succeeded in adding a protectionist element to the tariff measures of that year, developing the now common argument that free trade in manufactures is an appropriate policy only for advanced countries.[7] Eleven years later, the Unión Industrial Argentina was formed out of a merger of two pre-existing associations of manufacturers and obtained government recognition as the authentic voice of local industrial interests, in which capacity the Unión was consulted by government on tariff policy.[8]

Under Limantour's direction, the Mexican government of Porfirio Díaz had begun around 1906 the nationalization of its rail lines in an attempt to repair the deficiencies of the private concession system, but this was only one of a number of policies through which the national government was stepping in to influence the pattern of the country's development. There, as in most of the major nations by 1900, tariff policy had veered in the direction of protectionism, though the Mexican drift into industrial promotion through tariffs came even earlier than it did generally in Latin America. As noted previously, the Mexican success in promoting new manufactures was already, by the first decade of the present century, a matter for favorable discussion in such other countries as Colombia.[9]

In Brazil as early as 1882, distinguished spokesmen such as the Baron de Paranaguá were questioning the wisdom of pinning national fortunes to a monocultural export pattern. In the same year the conservative *Jornal do Comércio* of Rio de Janeiro even argued that the nation should seek diversification of the economy away from its agricultural base. The notion was, needless to say, received with favor by the Brazilian Associação Industrial, which was then devoting its energies to fighting proposed reductions in tariffs.[10] For that matter, almost three decades earlier the voices of economic nationalism had already been raised in the Brazilian parliament, and in the 1860's a prominent public figure, the Viscount of Itaboraí, had inveighed against an absolutist attachment to principles of economic liberalism on the grounds that this would impede the industrialization which was considered indispensable to the prosperity of the country.[11] Industrialization, the viscount argued, was much more advantageous than agriculture as a mainstay of national life in that it was far less vulnerable to the fluctuations induced by climate and the like and not nearly so limited by natural conditions.[12] Between 1859 and 1881 the dominance of those advocating classical economic liberalism in Brazilian universities had yielded to those more inclined toward interventionist schools of thought.[13]

During the last three decades of the nineteenth century, a number of Bolivian ministers of finance began to suggest that a protective interventionism would, in fostering national manufacturing development, help relieve the country of its balance of payments problems. Though very little was done to implement the notion, the discussion developed still another theme which since has figured prominently in the twentieth-century rationale of deliberate industrialization.[14] Even in conservative Peru, where the newly established Sociedad Nacional de Industrias found little receptivity for views in favor of national manufacturing development, there were policies which anticipated the characteristic aims of the twentieth century in respect of nationalism. Beginning in the 1850's, the government used its interest in the guano industry to place a greater share of the guano export contracting business in the hands of national entrepreneurs, a policy which was augmented in the subsequent decade but later abandoned as a result of fiscal considerations. In 1909, however, a government company took over the distribution of guano to the domestic market after the competition from Chilean nitrates had virtually eliminated the former export markets for guano. Earlier, following the War of the Pacific, the government had also moved, as noted previously, to "Peruvianize" the insurance business.

Around the continent, therefore, there were signs of a growing disenchantment with what was later, somewhat mistakenly, believed to have been a market-guided pattern of development. Critics of the left were charging that basic social needs had been neglected, but, as in the Mexican Catholic social action conferences of the early years of this century, spokesmen from other parts of the political spectrum were articulating somewhat similar views. In Brazil, possibly with a view to providing a greater inducement for immigrant laborers to come to work as agricultural hands but with very distinct reformist and modernizing objectives at the same time, a Catholic group led by Deputy Ignacio Tosta succeeded in early 1903 in inducing the government to issue a decree authorizing the formation of rural labor unions even before urban unions were encouraged.[15] Although the measure was not, for various reasons, effective in establishing stable organizations of agricultural workers, it nevertheless signaled the point of departure for what was later to become a substantial body of legislation defining new socio-economic relationships within the Brazilian body politic. Thus, even under essentially conservative regimes, steps had been taken which were to involve the state increasingly in the economic life of the hemisphere, so that long before the turn of the century there were seldom, in practice, any clearly defined or specified boundary conditions between the polity and the economy.

The Growth of Nationalistic Sentiment. That a certain xenophobic tendency should have been mixed with the foregoing intellectual and political trends was understandable on several counts. For one thing, foreign interests were conspicuously identified with the emergence of the external sector. When, as during periods of xport recession, that sector was unable to perform according to expectations, responsibility for the difficulties which insued was easily, if not altogether logically, transferred to the most prominent institutions operating in that sector. Undoubtedly, a factor which facilitated this assignment of culpability was the knowledge that not a few foreign promoters had been implicated in the numerous fiscal and policy irregularities of the day. Meanwhile, in reaction to the dominating influence of imported cultural norms and ideoligies, a mild but vigorous sort of *Kulturkampf* which reasserted the superiority of Hispanic values was getting underway under the inspiration of *pensadores* such as the Uruguayan José Enrique Rodó and intellectual societies such as the Mexican *Ateneo de la Juventud.* Incorporating a certain bias against the allegedly inferior and materialistic values of the outsider, this new intellectual climate thus lent philosophical support to the tendency to deprecate foreign contributions and to magnify the deficiencies of foreign undertakings.

As a further reinforcement, the historic experience of people in Latin America had predisposed them to think essentially in terms of an exploitive theory of wealth, a frame of reference in which a stable or at best slowly expanding output had been customarily divided along the lopsided lines of existing power relationships. Under such conditions, one group's gains represented a corresponding loss for others linked with that group through the network of economic and political transactions. As the alternative concept, that of mutual gain from a rapidly expanding aggregate output based upon technological advance and rising productivity, was as yet comparatively unfamiliar, the way was open for a projection of the domestic understanding of wealth to international transactions. It must surely have seemed to many, therefore, that the unmistakable affluence of the principal foreign powers was obtained in large measure at the expense of the less fortunate regions, including Latin America, with which they were related through trade and investment processes. Moreover, the fact that foreign ownership was a prominent feature of the economic landscape—in land, minerals, public utilities, and the public debt—did little to allay the misgivings that somehow there had occurred an alienation of the national patrimony. On the contrary, the scale of this ownership probably served, at least in the popular mind, to create an identity between large foreign owners and domestic latifundistas.[16]

In addition, it was plain that not many people had benefited, at least in any directly obvious way, from the spate of foreign investment activity, for the highly technical character of many foreign operations and the rather limited growth of new residentiary activity pulled what was, after all, only a relatively small portion of the native population into jobs where they could acquire new skills and more favorable earning opportunities. On the face of it then, it appeared that the more highly paid managerial rungs of business organization were simply taken as the prerogative of foreigners while most of the natives employed in such enterprises were confined to low-skill jobs in which the remuneration was comparatively meager. Although in retrospect one can see that this was mainly a consequence of the economic drag posed by the domestic institutional framework, a framework which held to a minimum the "trickle-down" process of benefit distribution, the source of the difficulty was not at all generally understood at the time. In any case, given such conditions, foreign economic interests were both institutionally conspicuous and the objects of a suspicion which was generally latent and sometimes overt. And since trade and investment relations with the United States were gradually increasing in relative prominence during this period, it is not surprising that much of this suspicion should eventually have come to focus upon inter-American relationships.

In order to understand fully the rise of nationalistic feelings throughout Latin America, it must also be recognized that the record of dealings with the economically strong nations had been anything but unblemished throughout the nineteenth century. Foreign political and military interventions related to commercial objectives had become part of the historical record in a number of nations, even before the United States embarked upon its Caribbean military ventures during the second decade of the present century and still longer before the Roca-Runciman agreement of the 1930's (and its revision) made humiliatingly clear to the Argentines the ability of the United Kingdom to use market leverage to exact further concessions from a dependent supply source. For example, British military intrusion into the La Plata region in the early nineteenth century had been followed by the British occupation of Falkland in 1833, an Anglo-French intervention in support of Uruguayan independence, a French naval blockade of the Argentine coast in 1838-1840, and a further blockade of Buenos Aires in 1845. In 1863, British vessels had also imposed a brief blockade on Rio de Janeiro and seized several Brazilian ships.

At the northern extremity of Latin America, a French blockade of Veracruz in 1838 came close on the heels of the *yanqui*-engineered secession of Texas and was followed in less than a decade by an invasion from the United States which cost the Mexicans a sizable portion of their national territory. During the early 1860's, an intervention in Mexico by France, Great Britain, and Spain turned into a full-fledged military occupation of the country by French forces which were apparently intent upon establishing a puppet regime to further Napoleon III's imperial ambitions.

Along the Caribbean coast of Central America, where the British had been present in Belize and the so-called Mosquito Coast of Honduras and Nicaragua for decades, it was not until 1860 that foreign forces withdrew from the latter two countries. Even then they remained in control of the Belize territory claimed by Guatemala. In the interim, Salvadorean ports had been subjected to a short British blockade around mid-century, while the 1850's witnessed an attempted take-over of Nicaragua by the yankee soldier of fortune, William Walker—apparently with the backing of New York financial circles which were interested in frustrating the operation of a Vanderbilt company established in that country during the Californian gold rush.

As early as the Grant administration there had been public discussion in the United States of the possibilities of annexing Santo Domingo and Cuba; but with the conclusion of the Spanish-American War in 1900, the United States settled instead for the annexation of Puerto Rico and the imposition of the Platt Amendment on the newborn Cuban nation. Two years later, British, German, and Italian naval units blockaded Venezuela. In 1903 Colombia was faced with a rebellion which, with poorly disguised support from the United States, separated the Isthmus of Panama from its sovereign jurisdiction.[17]

With incidents of this sort on the record, therefore, there developed in Latin America a self-conscious colonial mentality that found difficulty in distinguishing between economic dependence and political subjugation. Indeed, in the arenas in which public policy discussion often took place, there appears to have evolved rather a predisposition to look at foreign properties in utilities and extractive enterprises in somewhat jaundiced terms so that, irrespective of the economics of the case, the negative political experiences of the past ineluctably came to be incorporated into contemporary economic reality.

The Growth of New Domestic Interest Groups. Still other internal developments were converging to force Latin America to embark upon a distinctly new course in economic policy, as the socio-economic changes referred to at the beginning of this chapter had created new domestic interest groups who, being located primarily in the urban sector (and especially in the capital cities), were in a favored position to press public policy towards some accommodation of their diverse objectives. That most political systems were structured to give a preponderant weight to the urban electorate undoubtedly hastened the process, as the rural majority was, most often, only passively related to the political processes through which national policies were developed.

Literacy requirements for voting, for example, disenfranchised most of the rural populace, but literate urban dwellers could, with far greater ease, band together in temporarily effective, if often transitory, pressure groups which had to be recognized as forces to contend with in central city politics. Moreover, the educated urban middle classes were not without articulate spokesmen for their interests. From this social level came many of the teachers, journalists, writers, and other shapers of public opinion in the region. Thus, even at a stage when the economic structure of national life vested little financial power in these subdominant groups and when, accordingly, they could make only limited progress by using economic (or nongovernmental) means to improve their lot, there were available at least some possibilities for seeking satisfaction of group aims through political and governmental processes. The power of the state, therefore, was sought first as a substitute for the economic power which the new groups did not yet have and, secondly, as an instrument by means of which the economic rewards that were otherwise unobtainable could be procured.

For some of the aspirants, the immediate objectives were fairly straightforward, and the answers, at least during times of economic expansion, comparatively simple. Local business people, in general, favored public spending programs which would increase the earnings and employment opportunities in urban commercial pursuits, while others in the middle class—professionals, public functionaries, and those in military life—could always be counted on to support policies which would lead to an expanded volume of employment in the government sector itself. With these groups, there was ordinarily little problem, until the increase in their numbers began to press upon the limits of fiscal resources or when, as in the late 1880's and early 1890's, a world depression and money panic reduced these resources through a serious recession in export price levels and a contraction in the flow of foreign investment funds.

Indeed, the general success of these elements of the middle class in obtaining their aims was for some already a cause for alarm in the early twentieth century. Two observers of the Argentine scene in that day, for example, noted with concern the fact that expenditures on public administration and military support were rising as rapidly as the fiscal resources, leaving little for productive public investment.[18] The same could have been said of the other countries. By the early 1900's, however, the middle class had everywhere grown more numerous while trade disturbances were becoming more frequent and unstabilizing in their effects on Latin American government finance. From that point on, therefore, new answers had to be found for meeting the ambitions of even the most entrenched and generally conservative portions of the middle class; these ambitions would be realized by expanding public employment more rapidly, by fostering the growth of domestic concerns, and by remolding the external sector into a stronger source of local employment opportunities.

There were two subdominant groups in particular, whose rise in relative importance revealed the political dynamics of economic change in Latin America: the domestic industrialists and urban labor. Even prior to the turn of the century, the former were not altogether without influence. Long before the accelerated industrialization produced by the First World War increased their numbers and voice (and, concurrently, the political weight of the urban work force), industrial associations had already appeared to lobby for measures to protect and encourage national manufacturing development.

It is clear from the record, of course, that it was not conscious protectionism which originally called these domestic industries into being, although higher tariffs for revenue helped to do so and currency depreciation did, on occasion, provide an indirect form of protection in that import prices were raised by the amount of the depreciation while local producers' costs were affected only to the extent that they used imported raw materials and required new imported equipment, from which differential they gained a margin of advantage. In like manner, the depreciation of Latin American currencies was also to function as a stimulus to foreign investment in local manufacturing since it reduced the dollar or sterling cost of setting up facilities for local production. For this as well as for ordinary cost considerations,[19] by the opening years of the present century foreign concerns were establishing branch plants in Latin America, including assembly industries which subsequently served as a springboard for further manufacturing development.

All along, however, the evolution of economic conditions was gradually providing a more ample base for domestic industrial growth, quite apart from public policy inducements to manufacturing—a point which must also be recognized in considering the latter day industrialization of the continent. Through immigration and the demonstration effect, the supply of industrially oriented entrepreneurs had increased. In Argentina, Uruguay, southern Brazil, and Chile the supply of workers possessing industrially relevant skills had also been improved. Moreover, the accelerating tempo of trade and the modernization of commercial organization was giving rise to accumulations of mercantile capital which, when suitable opportunities were presented, were available for transformation into manufacturing capital. At the same time, the natural resource base of the national economies of the region was being expanded under the primary impetus of increases in export demand and foreign investment activity. In addition, foreign investments in utilities and railways, together with the financial and distributional institutions which were developed in the growth of the external sector, provided other external economies which could be utilized to advantage by domestic manufacturing establishments.

In the larger countries, especially, the normal process of manufacturing growth based on improved factor supplies and externalities was also helped along by the gradual increase of purchasing power in domestic markets. Indeed, since urban growth was also a feature of this period—one which implied changes in consumption habits and the shift of consumption (and, correspondingly, the organization of production) from a household basis to the commercial sector—and since domestic income increases tended to be concentrated in urban areas,[4] moving the general level of living there considerably above the line of mere subsistence, it seems reasonable to suppose that, in accordance with the Engel-Schwabe Law, discretionary disposable income and, hence, the local demand for manufactures were increasing much more rapidly than aggregate income. Thus, national markets for fabricated goods, while still small, were probably growing at a relatively high rate. Transport costs (especially overland transport charges in the case of the inland market areas of Mexico and Colombia) in conjunction with tariff charges helped to widen the range of domestic goods supplied in these markets, over and beyond the portion of fabricated products which are inherently domestic rather than international goods, while here and there local supplies of raw materials created particularly favorable cost situations for the initiation of domestic processing industries.

Thus it was that between 1850 and 1914 the inventory of newly-established manufacturing facilities included such enterprises as ice plants, coal gas plants, building materials plants (sawmills, brick and tile plants, and even small cement mills in at least seven countries), ceramics and glassware companies (producing houseware, bottles, plate glass, etc.), simple pharmaceuticals and drugs, soap factories, tanneries, shoe factories and other leatherworking concerns, match factories, tobacco mills and cigarette factories, and furniture and carriage-making factories. By the time of the First World War, food processing plants included sugar and flour mills, beef extract plants, meat-packing companies, breweries, distilleries, manufacturers of carbonated beverages, salt works, mechanized plants for processing coffee and dairy products, and factories turning out candies, pasta, and vegetable oils.

Cotton gins appeared fairly early in such countries as Mexico, Brazil, and Peru, and by the end of the century local mills producing the cheaper cotton textiles on a more-or-less modern basis had begun in these countries plus Ecuador, Guatemala, Chile, Argentina, Uruguay, Colombia, and Venezuela. In Mexico, Argentina, Chile, Ecuador, and Peru small woollen mills were established in the latter half of the century, to be followed by knitting and hosiery mills. The last quarter of the century brought the initiation of clothing factories in all of the larger countries and some of the smaller ones (e.g., Uruguay) as well. Some paper-making plants using rags, local pulp, and imported raw materials were founded in the major countries. In the field of heavier industry, relatively modern ore smelters began operations in such countries as Mexico and Chile, while petroleum refineries were established in Mexico, Peru, Argentina, and Colombia before 1910. The large integrated iron and steel works established in northern Mexico in 1902 produced pig iron, steel, and mill products; but already by 1870 at least two iron works with blast furnaces had been installed in Colombia, and in Brazil a small steel and rolling mill had been set up in the state of Minas Gerais by a Belgian immigrant around mid-century. During the early years of the twentieth century, still other small-scale siderurgical mills were able to begin operations on the basis of a growing availability of scrap metal.

Even where local raw materials were not at hand, differences in the transport costs of imported raw materials and of finished products sometimes presented favorable opportunities for the establishment of local manufacturing enterprises. Such was often the case, for example, in the many small foundries and metalworking plants which found it economical to import sheet and bar metal which they cast and milled locally to the required shapes, producing hardware, light farm implements and machinery, rails for railways, bridge girders, and, indeed, a rather astonishing variety of products. Sometimes they turned out custom-made equipment which was not readily available from abroad but which was needed on a limited scale to meet the specialized requirements of local production activity: e.g., the mining equipment used in several countries, equipment for sugar mills, the simple machinery used in Colombian and Brazilian coffee processing.[21]

In other instances, the advantage in the local production of metal products was reinforced by an additional factor. Railways, streetcar companies, electric utilities, mining companies, sugar mills, and textile factories had to install, or utilize locally installed but separate, facilities for repair and maintenance. But once the foundries for the production of castings and the welding and milling facilities were in place (the capital costs having been assumed for the above purpose), the significant costs for manufacturing new equipment such as rolling stock and machinery components were often only the incremental costs. In such cases, the local producers could turn out a limited volume of finished items on a basis thoroughly competitive with the imported products.[22] Originally, for example, the Eagle Foundry and Car Works of Arequipa, Peru, was established in the 1880's with this function in mind, but by 1911 the enterprise could advertise that it was producing on order such varied products as turbines, pumps, boilers, Pelton wheels, ploughs, mills for grinding ores and sugar cane, steel bridges, bells, iron fences, fountains, bedsteads, wagons, and carriages.[23] In centers of still greater economic importance, there were numerous manufacturing companies which had their inception in this kind of cost relationship. By 1904, for example, the metallurgical section of the Unión Industrial Argentina included 43 foundries and metal-working firms in its membership, a figure which probably included only the more important establishments in Buenos Aires at the time.[24]

Not a few of the small light industries launched in Latin America between 1850 and 1914 were to mature into nationally important sources of consumer goods during the twentieth century. Similarly, the small foundries and machine shops which had often been set up initially for repair and maintenance operations eventually turned out to be the nucleus of a more general, if rudimentary, engineering industry as they began to build rolling stock for railways and tramways, assembly parts, and machines of various kinds.[25] In the light of these trends, therefore, the chief impact of the First World War and subsequent events was essentially that of accelerating a cumulative process rather than initiating a new economic process. It is extremely doubtful that the war-induced spurt of domestic manufacturing development could have materialized to the extent that it did, had not this preparatory period of industrial development preceded it.

Yet, even if this incipient process of industrialization owed much to the automatic operation of market forces within the changing socio-economic structure of the period, it nevertheless laid the groundwork in two important ways for policy changes which would lead increasingly to public intervention in the market mechanism. In the first place, it created a new industrially oriented group of urban entrepreneurs who had a common interest in pushing for protectionist measures to enlarge their share of the domestic market. That they had, prior to World War I, already succeeded through their associations in getting a measure of protectionism built into public policy was, as will be seen in a moment, a significant factor in the developing political dynamics of the day. In the second place, the early stages of industrialization had helped to increase the numbers of urban wage laborers, adding further to the ranks of those who worked with the railways and utility companies, in the port works and construction, and so on.

Although not yet generally strong enough to achieve significant economic gains through collective bargaining procedures because of conditions normally prevailing in Latin American labor markets, this urban labor force, with its newly formed trade unions, was not entirely defenseless in its quest for a more humanly acceptable way of life. By promises of political support and through strikes and other civil disturbances which disrupted the tranquility of life in the principal urban centers, it was possible to exert an essentially political pressure aimed at extracting concessions for labor from government in the form of interventionary decrees which gradually involved the governments of the hemisphere ever more deeply in the matter of influencing the terms and conditions of employment.[26]

For better or for worse, the fortunes of the labor movement came to be closely tied in most countries with the evolution of new political alignments and the growth in power of central government authority. Thus it was, for example, that, during Batlle's ascension to power in Uruguay in the first decade of the present century and during the Alessandri administration in Chile in the early twenties, organized labor was pushing for a strong central power which could intervene in support of worker demands—a relationship between labor and the state which has been reproduced so many times in the other countries that it may be taken as one of the more valid generalizations which can be made about contemporary Latin America. Whatever the deficiencies of the system of labor relations which was in the making at the time, it is difficult to envisage that, under the circumstances then prevailing, there was any practicable alternative. In consequence of this emergent system of political bargaining, state intervention in the labor market soon became a part of the Latin American scene and the way was opened to a comparatively early introduction of labor and social legislation which in the more advanced countries came much later in the process of industrialization.

To be sure, the gains from such intervention were hardly general. Foreign enterprises were most susceptible to governmentally induced settlements on behalf of domestic labor though considering the generally superior productivity of such concerns it is probable that they were the ones who could most afford to raise the returns to labor.[27] Rural workers, on the other hand, were virtually untouched by such measures, except insofar as they might be employed on foreign-owned plantation enterprises where some improvement was occasionally obtained. Workers in domestic industrial concerns and in some service enterprises were able to gain at least a share in the new benefits (except where evasion was practiced), for governments in which landowner influence was still an important factor could contemplate, without insurmountable disturbance to self-interest, the possibilities of making Bismarck-style concessions to urban workers so long as the rural labor force was left comparatively unaffected and the costs of such concessions were borne by less influential domestic interest groups.

It was in this connection, however, that the spread of industrial protectionism became politically, as well as economically, significant. Thanks
to the consequent reduction in the degree of competition in national markets,
the way was open for governments to make concessions to urban labor
without undue opposition from the new national industrial interests; with
greater freedom in pricing policies, these in turn could in some measure
shift the burden of higher labor costs on to the consuming public at large.
Thus, even before the major policy trends of twentieth-century Latin
America took clearer shape, internal adjustments in the alignment of
economic interests and the balance of political power were leading in these
directions.

From the point of view of domestic circumstances, the persisting inability of many Latin American countries to structure a stable and enduring
political consensus was a factor of considerable relevance in the foregoing
connection. Regimes which could not command the allegiance of a decisive
portion of the body politic for any substantial length of time were almost
forced to cast about for means of obtaining at least temporary support
from the most promising available quarters. In a sense, therefore, a
situation was created in which the struggle for power among contending
parties and factions could be said to have forced the pace of marginal
accommodation to the more vocal new interests in the formation of
public policy, even though the same situation did not provide the conditions in which a decisive new consensus could be reached and appropriate
new policy lines clearly worked out and implemented on a continuing
basis.[28]

For that matter, one finds in this set of enabling conditions the political
rationale for a great many of the twentieth-century economic policies we
shall subsequently examine in more detail. Although these policies are
not without a certain economic logic, in spite of the strong aspect of
improvisation their development has often presented, they have also been
imbued with political values which, in a number of instances, may have
been of more immediate importance than the economic implications of
such measures. Whatever else has been achieved, the policy innovations
of the past five or six decades have equipped the governments of the
region with a more diversified set of expedients with which to effect an
apparent accommodation of new interests in the socio-economic system.
Even if over the longer run the benefits gained through accommodation
have sometimes turned out to be in part illusory (as, for example, in
general price rises which negated the real value of increases in money
wages, or in cases in which the elasticity of demand prevented higher profits
from being realized through manufacturers' price increases), the political
advantage to the government of these accommodative policies has been
three-fold.

In the first place, immediate gains to particular groups have tended
to be eroded only gradually so that a political value has been realizable

in the interim between initial concession and subsequent erosion. Where the time horizon is foreshortened because of increasing uncertainty in the longer term future, a high but quick return may (in politics as in economics) be valued over a lower periodic return spread out over a longer interval of time. In the second place, the invocation of a variety of accommodative policies has generally made it difficult to ascertain fully the incidence of the costs of such policies; thus the real net balance of any particular group is left somewhat in doubt, its concessionary advantages being clearer than its share in the costs of concessions to other groups. The distribution of the costs of interest-group accommodation has tended, in other words, to be both concealed and, in some degree, socialized or dispersed rather widely throughout society. Finally, given wide disparities of participation by various social segments in national political processes, the policies which governments have employed to effect accommodations among stronger interest groups have on occasion been of such a nature as to shift the burden of policy costs to less organized and less articulate sectors of society.

EXTERNAL CONDITIONS CONDUCIVE TO POLICY CHANGES

While domestic socio-economic changes were gradually pushing public policy in new directions, exogenous events from around 1914 on supervened upon and coincided with these changes in such a way as to reinforce the new policy trends. The long, halcyonic era which closed with the First World War was not unmarked by problems in the export sector, but the experiences of many countries after 1914 were anything but conducive to maintaining a widespread trust in the reliability of the external growth dynamic. Indeed, for manifold reasons the external sector now began to take on such a minatory aspect that it raised grave doubts as to the wisdom of continuing any policy structure which placed a major reliance upon foreign investment and export growth as the twin propellants of Latin American economic expansion.

The Growth of Export Competition.   Just prior to the First World War, for example, the enthusiasm generated by the success of Brazil's first coffee valorization experiment had been somewhat offset by the swift collapse of that country's promising rubber boom when European science and business enterprise succeeded in installing a more productive competitive supply source, organized on a modern plantation basis, in the colonial territories of Southeast Asia. Thus the fate which earlier befell Latin American exporters of dyestuffs (because of the activities of the British East India Company in the late eighteenth and early nineteenth centuries), quinine (with development of alternative supplies in the Dutch East Indies), and vanilla (with French-sponsored introduction of improved techniques of cultivation in Madagascar) was replicated on a larger and, from a Latin American point of view, more devastating scale.[29]

Meanwhile, even the prospects for Brazilian coffee exports were far from assured, and a second valorization program had to be launched in the late 1910's. While the fortuitous occurrence of a severe frost made the program once again successful because of the consequent reduction of Brazilian output, the contemporaneous expansion of output in other producing countries, especially in Latin America, soon led to renewed conditions of oversupply in export markets. By the mid-twenties, a third Brazilian coffee valorization scheme had to be introduced to support badly sagging coffee prices. These had dropped from 19 cents per pound (the New York wholesale price quotation for Santos No. 4) in 1920 to 10.4 cents per pound the year following.[30] For about six years the program was able to maintain higher price levels, but world production continued to rise and with the onset of the world depression prices declined more sharply than ever, forcing the physical destruction of coffee stocks on a huge scale.

The Latin American sugar industry had long contended with the rapid expansion of sugar beet production in Europe and North America (and with domestic cane producers as well in the United States). So considerable had been the expansion of beet cultivation, that during the last decade of the nineteenth century and the first decade of the twentieth century European beet sugar output exceeded the total world output of cane sugar. Subsequently, cane production staged a rapid comeback, but Latin American cane sugar exporters now had to face a world market in which rapid increases in exportable output were resulting from a particularly heavy investment of capital in such colonial and semicolonial areas as the Philippines, Hawaii, Formosa, Java, Mauritius, and the Caribbean Islands. By the time of World War I, huge surpluses had produced such price declines that the industry seemed headed for complete disaster. While the war provided temporary relief by curtailing European beet sugar production, the postwar revival of beet cultivation, coming on the heels of a vigorous expansion in cane, again created a severe condition of oversupply and depressed prices.[31]

The experience of rubber and sugar with increasing competition in export markets was to be repeated many times over in the present century though not necessarily always with quite such harsh consequences. Bolivian tin was faced with the sizable growth of exportable production in Southeast Asia and wild gyrations in export prices. Chilean copper, despite its twentieth-century resurrection with the introduction of mass-mining techniques by foreign enterprises, was selling to markets in which heavily capitalized concerns in North America, the Belgian Congo, and elsewhere figured as formidable rivals. For example, drawing upon cheap African labor and strengthened by political and economic control of the area, British investment developed Rhodesia as a major copper exporter during the first half of the twentieth century. Similarly, the cultivation of cacao and coffee were being fostered in Africa as a means of increasing colonial exports, while export-oriented petroleum development shifted first from Mexico to Venezuela and thence to the Islamic area and elsewhere.[32]

To an important degree, comparative advantages provided by nature played a role in these displacements.[33] But in more than a few instances the alternative supply sources which were being developed were in areas directly controlled by colonial powers, and this control was often exercised to facilitate provision of supporting infrastructure and orderly administration as well as to insure an especially favorable political climate for the foreign capital placed in export industries.

In addition, owing to the resource-creating aspect of modern industrial technology, Latin American exporters of certain items came to be confronted with a new form of area competition that was based upon inter-product or intersectoral competition. Thus not only was the Latin American position in export markets undermined by growing competition from colonial supply sources, but also the advanced countries themselves gave birth to new industries which, in a number of instances, competed with Latin American products. The nineteenth century had already witnessed the displacement of cane sugar by beet sugar, but more typical of this new source of export instability was the development of coal-tar dyes by means of which the European chemical industry put to route the various exporters of natural dyestuffs in the underdeveloped portions of the world, including some of the Central American economies which were already faced with rising Asiatic competition. Later on, chemical discoveries in the period between 1865 and 1900 eventuated in the production of synthetic fibers which made increasing inroads into the markets for such natural fibers as cotton and, more recently, wool.

Less gradual, however, was the effect of the synthetic production of nitrogen which grew out of the successful experiments of the German chemist, Fritz Haber, in 1913. As late as 1910, Chilean nitrates supplied some 420,000 tons of a total world production of 656,500 tons. Ten years later, Chilean output had risen to 430,200 tons, but world production had grown to approximately 993,800 tons. Thereafter, notwithstanding considerable improvement in the efficiency of the Chilean nitrate industry, which was brought about with the introduction of the Guggenheim process, the competitive superiority of synthetic nitrogen became steadily more pronounced. By 1930, Chilean nitrate production had entered a period of decline, falling to just under 420,000 tons in that year, while global production of nitrogen reached a new high of 2.2 million tons.[34] While aggregate Chilean exports were bouyed by the concurrent growth of Chilean copper production, copper itself encountered growing competition both from other supply sources and from the newly important aluminum industry. The aluminum industry also offered new competition to tin in such uses as foil, tubing, and vessels of various sorts.

A further threat to the expansion of Latin American exports was the increasing efficiency with which the industrial plants of the developed nations used their raw materials inputs. Development of electroplating processes in the manufacture of tin plate, for example, had by 1946 reduced the tin content in a ton of tin plate to an average of 11.9 pounds as compared with 27.1 pounds of tin per ton of tin plate in the older immersion or hot-dipping method. Similarly, development of improved copper alloys permitted a more sparing use of that metal in several fields. In addition, progress in the technology of scrap metal recovery—in such fields as lead, copper, iron, and tin—considerably enhanced the relative importance of secondary sources of supply, which are mainly located in the advanced countries. For instance, secondary copper production as a percentage of total copper consumed rose from less than 25 per cent in 1919-1920 to well over 50 per cent in the mid-1930's, although the late 'thirties saw some reversal of this trend.

Because of the more economical use of raw materials in industrial technology, the growth of manufactured output has not, it is claimed, led to commensurate increases in the demand for raw materials exports. On this score, however, the evidence is not altogether clear, for while the raw materials inputs per unit of output have undoubtedly been reduced in a number of instances, it may well be that consequent cost reductions in final products have contributed to a larger total output of the various manufactures using raw materials imported from Latin America so that the aggregate demand for such exports has not necessarily been adversely affected. Be that as it may, the threat of technological displacement has appeared sufficiently real that it has often been called into use in support of national policies designed to diversify patterns of production and trade.

Natural Variability in Exports. If growing export competition (whether apparent or real) from a number of sources often became an ingredient in national economic policy deliberations in Latin America, a chronic export instability arising from natural conditions was in other cases also a factor to contend with. And although instability of this character is not, strictly speaking, a problem distinctly associated with the twentieth century, it nevertheless became far more troublesome in recent decades as domestic expansion based upon past export growth gradually geared the economies of Latin America to a higher level of requirements with regard to export sector performance. For coffee exporting nations, the susceptibility of coffee crops to the vagaries of weather—a problem which has been greatly accentuated in Brazil by the southward migration of coffee cultivation onto lands in Paraná state which are more vulnerable to frost damage—has compounded the difficulties that stem from the normal variations in yearly yields which are inherent in the production cycle of the crop (see Table X-1). Furthermore, because the large Brazilian production

Table X-1. Brazilian and World Coffee Production 1920–1935: Millions of 60-Kilogram Bags

YEAR	BRAZILIAN PRODUCTION	TOTAL WORLD PRODUCTION
1920	7.5	14.0
1921	14.5	22.0
1922	12.9	20.7
1923	10.2	18.3
1924	14.9	24.2
1925	14.6	24.3
1926	15.5	26.6
1927	15.8	26.4
1928	27.1	39.4
1929	13.6	26.1
1930	28.2	40.8
1931	16.6	29.4
1932	28.2	41.3
1933	19.8	34.0
1934	29.6	42.9
1935	18.2	31.5

SOURCE: V.D. Wickizer, *The World Coffee Economy with Special Reference to Control Schemes*, Palo Alto: Stanford University Food Research Institute, 1943, pp. 248–249.

exerted such a preponderant influence in world coffee markets, the fortunes of other exporting countries, already variable because of their own production fluctuations, were further subjected to a second order of fluctuations which were attributable to changes in the exportable output of the major producer of the commodity.

For that matter, the very nature of coffee as a perennial tree crop tended to create a situation in which world coffee supply adjusted only sluggishly to changed conditions of demand. The initial gestation period of several years duration before peak yields are attained from new plantings necessitated a fairly long-term and difficult anticipation of future demand conditions. Since, in addition, this initial interval entailed a considerable outlay of funds followed by a period of unremunerative waiting, the risks of inaccurate demand prediction were high. Consequently the upward movement of prices ordinarily had to be substantial in order to provide the "stimulating profit rate" which was necessary to induce capital investment to flow into new plantings in an amount sufficient to raise supplies to meet demand. Once the gestation period was past, however, the protracted bearing period, extending over an interval of several decades of gradually declining yields, created a situation in which the large sunk investment in coffee plantings had to be exploited even if prices subsequently fell to a point where only variable costs were covered. Indeed, over the short run prices could drop even below that level without producing a significant reduction in production capacity, as planters would scarcely have destroyed expensive tree capacity which could only be replaced over a lengthy interval so long as there lingered a hope of improved market conditions. Consequently, supply curtailment tended to be as lagging in response to downward demand and price changes as supply increments had been to upswings in the market; in both directions price movements were accentuated by conditions of supply inelasticity.

To a somewhat lesser degree, production rigidities of an essentially similar sort also plagued exporters of cacao, cane sugar, and bananas. The susceptibility of cacao and bananas to disease presented further complications. With the rapid spread of the "witches broom" blight in 1916 and 1922, for example, the Ecuadorean cacao export industry was brought to almost total ruination. In Central America, the infection of fields with the Panama disease during the 1920's forced the abandonment of many banana plantations along the Caribbean coast of Nicaragua and Costa Rica, and in the Bocas del Toro region of Panama. Shortly thereafter a second blight, sigatoka, appeared in Trinidad in 1938 and spread to the continent, accelerating the movement of the industry to the drier leeward sections of the Central American Pacific coast where the disease was more controllable than in the humid environment of the Caribbean side. Particularly was this the case in Panama, Costa Rica, and Guatemala. In the process, though, many of the smaller producers were forced out of business by the high cost of disease fighting equipment and procedures, as the laying of ground pipes for spraying was approximately as expensive as the initial cost of putting ground into banana production.[35] Further, the shift to the Pacific coast raised initial investment costs and reduced the ease of entry into the industry inasmuch as banana production there required the installation of costly irrigation equipment because of the comparative dryness of the climate.[36]

To illustrate some of the effects of such natural catastrophes, it could be remarked that Nicaraguan banana exports fell to insignificant levels in a comparatively short period of time, Honduran exports dropped from 27.7 million stems in 1930 to 11.2 million stems in 1938, Colombian exports declined from 7.6 million stems in 1939 to slightly over 5 million stems in 1940, and Mexican exports dropped from nearly 17 million stems in 1937 to only 6.6 million stems in 1940.

Other Sources of External Sector Instability. To the forgoing sources of twentieth-century external sector instability must be added the severe dislocations of export and import trade flows which were occasioned by two world wars and the intervening depression. Repeatedly, the traditional supply sources of imports were partially cut off while access to normal export markets was similarly disrupted. Except for the 1930's, however, some adjustment was possible insofar as the United States displaced Europe as a supplier of Latin American imports and as a customer for Latin American exports (see Table X-2).[37] Moreover, in the period bracketed by the two global conflicts, the commercial policy of the developed nations tended to move in an increasingly restrictive direction. Tariffs, quota systems, and import licensing requirements, for example, tended to close continental European markets to the exports of Latin American cereals and meat products, as such countries as France, Germany, and Italy moved toward self-sufficiency in these agricultural lines. Tariff barriers rose to historic highs in the United States during the late 1920's. Even Great Britain, long the champion of liberal trade policy, adopted the imperial perference scheme and through the Ottawa Conference imposed a quota system on the imports of meat from South America.[38] Concurrently, nearly all the major sugar consuming countries began to establish preferential controls

Table X-2. Latin American Exports and Imports, 1901–1948;
Indices of Latin American Export and Import Volumes: 1938 = 100

	1901–1905	1913	1925	1928	1937	1938	1948
IMPORTS							
Total imports	58	111	111	123	103	100	183
Imports from Europe	89	163	108	128	108	100	91
Imports from U.S.	30	65	120	129	112	100	329
EXPORTS							
Total Exports	48	75	86	105	121	100	124
Exports to Europe	62	92	83	113	125	100	81
Exports to U.S.	47	70	121	118	121	100	179

Values of Latin American Exports and Imports
(Millions of Current Dollars, f.o.b.)

	1901–1905	1913	1925	1928	1937	1938	1948
IMPORTS							
Total imports	515	1,226	2,066	2,083	1,396	1,309	5,101
Imports from Europe	347	793	908	973	702	635	1,323
Imports from U.S.	126	317	844	831	577	494	3,205
EXPORTS							
Total exports	823	1,590	2,741	3,005	2,360	1,771	6,535
Exports to Europe	523	963	1,361	1,600	1,207	922	2,329
Exports to U.S.	234	441	1,005	947	672	453	2,356

SOURCE: Economic Commission for Latin America, *A Study of Trade Between Latin America and Europe,* Geneva: United Nations, Department of Economic Affairs, 1953, p. 3.

on production and trade which worked to the disadvantage of noncolonial sugar exporters.[39]

Given the role played by exports in such economic variables as fiscal receipts, national income, exchange rates and monetary conditions, and rates of saving and capital formation, it was widely believed that the fluctuations of the post-1914 period were inimical to the orderly conduct of economic life in Latin America—even though there is no real empirical confirmation for an association (causal or otherwise) between export instability and low rates of growth. Annually as well as cyclically, the period registered marked variations in export prices, export quantities, and export proceeds which were not offset to any important degree by corresponding fluctuations in import prices, and the export sector was viewed as a source both of recessions and chronic inflationary pressures. Table X-3, for example, provides one of the several measures through which the erratic behavior of this sector can be traced.

Closely associated with the events of the post-1914 period was a substantial interruption of the flow of foreign capital, particularly from Europe, into Latin America. Since the export sector had been the locus of a considerable amount of foreign investment activity, the deterioration of export prospects served to diminish the attractions which the region could offer the foreign investor. In addition, the outflow of European capital was limited by large-scale war mobilization programs as well as by postwar economic rehabilitation efforts and the general contraction of capital availability which was produced by conditions of recession and depression.

Table X-3. Year-to-Year Fluctuations of Latin American Export Proceeds in Real Terms

ITEM	PERIOD	AVERAGE PERCENTAGE FLUCTUATION PER YEAR
Argentine wheat	1914–1950	32.2
Argentine wool	1923–1948	15.3
Brazilian coffee	1902–1950	21.0
Brazilian cotton	1904–1950	41.4
Brazilian cacao	1910–1950	25.8
Peruvian cotton	1905–1950	25.9
Peruvian copper	1902–1950	20.2
Chilean copper	1902–1950	20.5
Chilean nitrate	1914–1950	21.4
Bolivian tin	1902–1950	16.8
Uruguyan wool	1923–1948	17.7
Mexican copper	1902–1950	21.8
Mexican petroleum	1913–1950	16.5

SOURCE: United Nations, Department of Economic Affairs, *Instability in Export Markets of Under-Developed Countries,* New York: United Nations, 1952, pp. 48–49.

Table X-4. Argentine Capital Formation as a Percentage of Gross Product: Annual Averages

PERIOD	TOTAL INVESTMENT	OF NATIONAL ORIGIN	OF FOREIGN ORIGIN
1900–1904	25.9%	14.1%	11.8%
1905–1909	48.2	30.2	18.0
1910–1914	42.2	21.4	20.8
1915–1919	13.0	9.6	3.4
1920–1924	26.4	22.8	3.6
1925–1929	33.3	28.5	4.8
1930–1934	22.2	19.0	3.2
1935–1939	23.7	21.2	2.5
1940–1944	18.2	16.7	1.5
1945–1949	24.4	24.3	0.1

SOURCE: United Nations Economic Commission for Latin America, Análisis y proyecciones del desarrollo económico: V. El desarrollo económico de la Argentina, Mexico: United Nations, Department of Economic and Social Affairs, 1959, Vol. I, p. 71.

While Argentina was perhaps uncommon in the degree to which its economy was linked with European foreign investment, its experience is nevertheless instructive indicating the kinds of adjustments which were necessitated in Latin America in consequence of the drying up of European capital sources in the post-1914 era (see Table X-4).

To the end of the 1920's, the sharp diminution of new European investment in Latin America was, in some countries at least, offset by the concurrent growth of United States investment in the region. With the onset of the depression of the 1930's, this too declined precipitously until the early forties brought a strong resumption of the upward trend in the amount of United States capital flowing south. Thus, the external resources available to most of the countries of the region were subjected to two partially interrelated sources of instability—variations in both export earnings and capital movements—both of which had constituted in the preceeding era the main engines of economic expansion.[40]

AN OVERVIEW OF PUBLIC POLICY REACTIONS:
THE SEARCH FOR ECONOMIC VERSATILITY

The national problems associated with these externally induced difficulties were intensified by (1) the relative lack of domestically oriented investment and employment opportunities which could take up the slack in the economy caused by fluctuations in the external sector and (2) the comparatively rudimentary development of the institutional mechanisms needed for facilitating resource shifts among alternative uses. Moreover, the fixed nature of the commitment of specialized agricultural, mining, and transport capital—e.g., special purpose railways in particular areas; installations such as mining shafts and equipment, sugar mills, coffee drying mills; large scale plantings of agricultural perennials of long maturation—made much of the existing capital stock relatively immobile. This also reduced the mobility of the cooperant factors which were involved in export production. Similarly, the mobility of land resources (and, correspondingly, the cooperant factors applied thereto) was often relatively slight, given the limited alternatives uses of soils under prevailing climatic conditions and transport costs. The limited range of technical skills which had been developed locally presented still another problem in the adaptation of resource use to changing market conditions. All three conditions lessened the resiliency of the Latin American economies in their reactions to fluctuations in export market conditions, while the magnitude of the consequent adjustment problems both reconfirmed the deeply engrained cultural skepticism of market-guided activity and underscored the apparent logic of interventionism. Accordingly, the deliberate development of more diversified domestic sector uses for a larger portion of national resources became a prime concern of Latin American policy.

Not all countries were equally involved in this policy drift, for it was generally more pronounced in the larger countries than in the smaller ones whose slight domestic markets afforded much less opportunity for an internally oriented development strategy. These latter, of necessity, remained far more externally oriented and even, in some cases, made some headway in effecting a diversification of their export sector—although in the recently inaugurated Central American Common Market there is evidence that several of the smaller countries have sought means of giving a more domestically oriented cast to their development policies. Before this, the most notable exception among the smaller countries was Uruguay, which at a comparatively early date adopted policies that turned the focus of concern inward. There, however, for want of sufficient domestic market size, such efforts were not altogether successful, and severe problems—in the form of chronic inflationary pressures, weak domestic industries, and a rather poor showing in export sector performance—have resulted from the policy change. Among the larger countries, Peru came somewhat belatedly to the new policy style, for the unusual diversity of its exports reduced the pressure to turn towards an internally oriented pattern of growth. Yet even allowing for qualifications, it is reasonably accurate to conclude that the dominant new concern in the Latin American policy field has been a preoccupation with measures for forcing the pace of domestic development.

In part, this concern implied policies which would modify the pattern of control over resource use, both by encouraging national ownership over foreign ownership and by substituting administrative signals for free market signals in the allocation of resources. National ownership was seen as a value not only in terms of its bearing on the distribution of rewards from resource use and hence a means of retaining more income within the domestic sector of the economy; it also appeared desirable as a device for placing control over resource use more directly under the purview of public authority wherein, presumably, national policy objectives could be more effectively realized than amid the conventional indicators of the market place. Pursuit of these objectives, therefore, involved the extension of public policy to an increasing number of the pivotal decision-making points in Latin American society, a trend which, in several respects, resembled a recommitment to the elementary values and norms of Hispanic culture and a return to the neo-Iberian commonsense tradition of interventionism with its predilection for a centrally administered social organization.

Essentially what was involved in this policy shift was a summation and synthesis of Latin American historical experience, based on the assumption that the postulates and values of liberal society and industrialism lacked, in the Latin American setting, the structural supports to maintain them. Accordingly, the traditional Hispanic static conception of society in which the state functioned as the principal ordering agent was combined with the more dynamic conception of society of the nineteenth century to produce a social philosophy in which the state now appeared as the chief agent of change. The conservative preference for centralized and paternalistic government was linked with the liberal desire to promote social progress, while liberals and conservatives alike were often able to agree on the desire to foster industrialization and structural diversification of their economies. This new policy direction—with its focus on the construction of distinctly national economic, political, and social systems—represents perhaps the only era in Latin American development to which the term mercantilism can be very appropriately applied, for it would appear that by the early 1900's the events of the nineteenth century had finally built up in that area the social preconditions of a mercantilist policy stance in which the consolidation and internal integration of the nation state became a central objective of public authority.

The logic of new policies also implied measures which aimed primarily at fostering national capital accumulation as a partial replacement for foreign investment.[41] These policies were conditioned not so much by immediate comparative advantages as by the relative ease with which the formation of domestic capital resources could be induced in various sectors of the economy. In other words, in the effort to increase the aggregate supply of domestic capital the approach has been more towards a search for the easiest places to encourage investment rather than identification of the optimal places in terms of productivity criteria—a consideration which may account for the comparative neglect of agriculture since encouragement of increased capital formation in that field runs into complicated institutional hindrances.

While promotion of national capital formation has been generally valued as a means of transferring resource control in line with the objectives mentioned above, the domestication of capital resources has sometimes been further justified on the grounds that the relevant investment alternatives tend to be different for domestic investors as contrasted with foreign capitalists. According to this argument, the former consider mainly the investment options presented within the national economy when looking for further uses of earnings, whereas the latter, operating in a geographically more extensive context, may reinvest earnings gained from local operations in enterprises located abroad if these correspond to company strategy and if they appear, at the time, more promising.[42] Thus, it has been contended that domestic capital tends, with somewhat greater certainty than in the case of foreign capital, to enhance the national capital stock over the longer run, although evidence contrary to this assumption would seem to be offered by the notorious domestic capital flights of recent times. In any case, it has patently been the expectation that higher rates of domestic investment would reduce the susceptibility of the Latin American economies to exogenously produced disturbances, notwithstanding the limitations imposed on the fulfillment of this expectation by the high import coefficient of many types of domestic investment outlays.

Finally, no doubt because of the general flimsiness of domestic political structures, the heavy setbacks produced by wars, depressions, and changes in the commercial policies of the economically advanced nations have forced public authority to cast about for means of stabilizing the economic environment, even at some cost to the long term growth of material output, if, indeed, the latter end can be meaningfully separated from questions of political stability. Given the difficulties of political consensus building, it is doubtful that the choice between immediate security and future progress and expansion was often a real option for most of the governments of the region. Thus, insofar as the new policies which looked to insulating domestic politico-economic structures from externally induced shocks may have entailed certain sacrifices of comparative advantages, they may be interpreted both as efforts designed to force the pace of evolution of new comparative advantages and as acceptable, or politically tolerable, means of socializing the costs of economic stabilization—a sort of national insurance premium, as it were.

The other policy goals of the post-1914 period—the quest for a limited degree of autarky, accelerated national industrialization, the imposition of social controls on foreign capital interests, and so-called national integration measures—have been, for the most part, subsidiary to the broad objectives mentioned above. Taken in conjunction, they seem to have had as their overriding intent the internalization or domestication of the growth dynamic which formerly was largely foreign in origin. This is not, however, to say that at all times individual components of this policy mixture have been argued solely by reference to this dominant objective, for they have often been propounded on grounds more narrowly drawn.

Industrialization, for example, has frequently been proposed for a variety of other reasons. Among other things, it has been justified as a means of reducing the import leakage in the national income and employment multiplier effects, as a necessary employment outlet for productively absorbing the redundant rural population during agricultural modernization, and as an essential measure for coping with general population growth. Still other arguments have tended to place great emphasis on the supposed cultural influence of industrialization: its role in engendering a spirit of technical modernization and its contribution to the diffusion of productive new skills, habits, and attitudes. More recently, industrial promotion has been supported on the grounds that the technological and investment multiplier effects—the so-called backward and forward linkages—are normally greater in the manufacturing sector than in the agricultural sector, so that investment and growth in selected industries automatically tend to induce further investment and growth in related lines of production.

During the post-World War II period, a wide acceptance has also been accorded the argument that local industrialization is required in order to maintain equilibrium in the balance of payments. Since it is contended that world demand for the primary products exported by Latin America is less elastic with respect to income than the demand of Latin America for manufactured goods, economic growth in the absence of import-substituting industrialization would, it is believed, simply produce a chronic tendency toward disequilibrium in the balance of payments. Thus, local industrialization is seen as an indispensable means of filling the gap between the desired rate of increase in national product and income on the one hand and the less rapid rate of increase in the capacity to import on the other.[43] In this argument, however, one returns to the fundamental policy objective: the desire to free domestic growth possibilities from constraints imposed by the external sector.[44]

In all of this, the policy outcome has involved an interplay of both external and internal trends which, during the period in question, have tended to converge or to be mutually reinforcing in determining the shape of the policy response. Domestic groups of a pro-industrialization bent were, for example, strengthened in numbers by the noticeable bursts of industrial growth which came as a result of the curtailment of competing imports during wartime and postwar recovery periods when acute shipping shortages made it difficult to obtain imports and erstwhile foreign suppliers turned their productive capacity to other ends. The same occurred during depressions when foreign suppliers were often financially prostrate and when diminished export sales reduced the capacity to import. Once established, the new domestic manufacturing interests could then demand and generally obtain the enactment of heavily protective duties on their products as a safeguard against foreign competition when world conditions became more normal.

For example, domestic industry, which supplied only 40 per cent of Argentina's final demand for industrial goods in the 1905-1910 period, was able by the 1925-1929 quinquennium to supply 49 per cent of that demand, thanks largely to the strong development impulse received during war years.[45] In Brazil, the number of manufacturing firms grew from 3,250 to 13,336 between 1907 and 1920, while the capitalization of these firms rose from 666 million cruzeiros to 1,816 million cruzeiros (in constant cruzeiro terms) during the same interval.[46] Between 1915 and 1923, the number of plants in the Chilean industrial sector, excluding smaller artisan type establishments, grew from 2,406 to 3,196.[47] The effects of the depression and the Second World War were essentially similar. Currency depreciation and the foreign exchange and trade controls imposed to cope with balance of payments difficulties afforded still further protection to domestic industrial interests.

At one and the same time, then, the disordered conditions of the world economy lent cogency to arguments raised in behalf of economic nationalism while they diminished the effectiveness of arguments advanced by groups which were oriented to the external sector and which saw the expansion of foreign trade and investment as the most reliable growth agency if not the *primum mobile* of development. The same set of conditions also worked generally toward strengthening the local economic position of the nationalists while undercutting the economic power base of groups which previously were nourished by the growth of the external sector. Moreover, as in the case of the southern Brazilian coffee growers who began in the 1930's to shift capital out of coffee and into other lines of investment (primarily in the domestic sector), the situation also encouraged at least a partial transformation in the character of these later groups. Thus, damaged by the First World War and broken by the depression of 1929-1933, the classical worldwide system of trade and multilateral payments balancing was brought to the verge of complete destruction by the economic nationalism of the 1930's and the Second World War.

XI

The Orthodox Approach to Development

Retrospectively, it is possible to distinguish three main policy patterns or styles in Latin American economic life during the twentieth century, although no individual country has adhered consistently to any one of these styles throughout the whole period. Moreover, there are certain shared or common elements in these different policy approaches. Nevertheless, most of the policy experience of the past four of five decades may, for analytical convenience, be sorted into these three patterns: (1) the orthodox approach (Chapter XI), (2) the neo-orthodox approach (Chapter XII), and (3) the approach of developmental socialization (Chapter XIII).

As ideal-type constructs, the three policy configurations are useful for identifying different sets of assumptions regarding the possibilities of the economic situation and the different approaches to problem-resolution which have sprung from the respective sets of assumptions. In the actual policy tendencies which have emerged from these different points of departure, one finds distinct evidence of a varying assessment of the relative importance of different variables or considerations in the development process. Over the years, there has also been discernible within each of these approaches a distinct evolutionary process, a certain refinement of policy technique and elaboration of program rationale which have helped to clarify the differences among these policy styles. Particularly has this been the case since the Second World War. More recently still, especially insofar as the Alliance for Progress may be taken as the chief development policy statement of the 1960's, a process of synthesis has been in evidence. In the program implied by the Punta del Este Charter, and before that the Act of Bogotá, one finds elements drawn from each of the three main policy streams along which economic life moved in the preceding decades.

Of the three approaches to development, the one which has represented the least deviation from the theoretical policy mold of the pre-1914 era and which, accordingly, might be termed the most conventional or relatively orthodox of the three is that which has been pursued, albeit somewhat incompletely, by many of the smaller countries of the region for whom an inwardly oriented development pattern was less practicable. Some of the larger countries, however, have followed this route at times, as in the case of Argentina, Brazil, Colombia, Peru, and Venezuela during the twenties. The policies followed by the conservative governments of the Argentine during the thirties and those adopted in Peru by the Odría and Prado administrations after 1949 would also exemplify fairly well the sort of development style referred to in this regard.[1] A partial, and rather inconclusive, return to economic orthodoxy was even attempted in Argentina during the post-Perón struggle to rehabilitate the national economy, when efforts were made to restore the strength of the agricultural export sector and to encourage the inflow of foreign investment capital.[2]

This too was, up to recent times, the position generally upheld by the United States in discussions of inter-American policy, particularly in the emphasis on the role of technical assistance and private foreign investment, and in the various trade-fostering concessions effected under the Reciprocal Trade Agreements Act.[3] In the work of numerous advisory missions from the International Bank for Reconstruction and Development and the International Monetary Fund, the orthodox view of development received, during the post-1945 period, what was probably its most sophisticated and comprehensive expression.

As a matter of actual practice, of course, no country in the hemisphere ever fully realized the policies implied by this approach—just as there was substantial departure in practice from the theoretical norms which formally held sway in the prior era. Yet, as an ideal towards which actual policy tendencies have on occasion aimed, it seems appropriate to posit this as one of the major policy predispositions of the present century.

POSTULATES AND ASSUMPTIONS OF THE ORTHODOX APPROACH

While it is difficult to characterize in summary fashion the complex considerations involved, the basic orientation of the orthodox approach can be indicated by reference to what appear to have been its main points of emphasis. Three of these in particular serve to establish its connection with the previous historical pattern of development: (1) a continuing effort to foster the growth of primary industries and export earnings, (2) a concern with the development of infrastructure, and (3) the attention accorded measures designed to create an investment climate capable of attracting foreign capital with all its ancillary benefits.[4]

Grounded on the not unreasonable assumption that domestically available Latin American resources are insufficient for attaining an acceptable rate of growth, the policy aim has been that of augmenting domestic factor supplies with resources generated by the operations of the external sector. As a corollary, increased efficiency of domestic resource use has been sought through taking advantage of existing and potential comparative advantages in trade. The programs recommended by this approach have usually concentrated on increasing the output of products which depend mainly upon employment of the region's relatively abundant labor and land factors, except where, as in the case of power generation, inflexible production coefficients dictate a capital-intensive technology. From the higher real incomes gained thereby would presumably come the wherewithal for pushing domestic development forward more rapidly. Furthermore, it has been argued, creation of a favorable investment climate for foreign capital would also redound to the benefit of domestic business interests, encouraging higher rates of national capital formation alongside the growth of the external sector.

Typical of the measures adopted in this general strategy of development were the liberal concessions which were granted, up to the mid-1940's, to foreign companies operating in the Venezuelan petroleum industry and the encouragement later extended by the Pérez Jiménez government of that country to foreign capital for development of the valuable iron ore deposits of the Orinoco region. Similarly, the orthodox budgetary policies pursued by the Galo Plaza administration of Ecuador (1948-1952) and the inducements offered by his government to investors in the export sector—which paid off handsomely in the form of rapid increases in the production of coffee, cacao, and bananas—were also squarely in line with orthodox development advice. No less so were the maintenance of free convertibility for capital transactions and the new mining and electricity codes promulgated in Peru during the early 1950's, for all three measures were aimed at fostering foreign investment and expanding the volume of Peruvian exports.

Meanwhile, the inter-American policy of the United States was offering strong support for externally oriented development policies in Latin America. Subsequent to the reciprocal trade treaties, the United States Congress in 1939 initiated a program of technical assistance to Latin America, giving special emphasis during the early 1940's to expanding agricultural and mining output. In addition, the wartime period provided a further stimulation of Latin American exports through the large purchase contracts which were negotiated by various United States government agencies for strategic materials produced by the other countries of the hemisphere. Later, in the expectation that special protection against various risks would promote more foreign investment in Latin America, the policy of the United States came to incorporate still another innovation as special investment guaranty treaties were negotiated with Bolivia, Colombia, Costa Rica, Cuba, Ecuador, Guatemala, Haiti, Honduras, Nicaragua, Paraguay, and Peru.

The assumptions underlying such policies seem to have been, apart from those postulated at the theoretical level in conventional economic doctrine, somewhat as follows. In the first place, the major disturbances in the world economy during the first half of the twentieth century have been viewed as essentially transitory in nature and hence not an appropriate basis for longer run policy formulation, at least insofar as they might be thought to justify a shift to a more autarkic approach to development. In the secular expansion of the world economy, it was supposed that underdeveloped countries could anticipate a continuing growth in the demand for their exports, while real earnings from foreign trade could also be enhanced by the increases in productivity which would come from utilizing modern production and marketing techniques. The latter achievement would permit the export sector to function as a source of strength even in the face of declining prices so long as real production costs could be lowered more rapidly than prices declined. But lurking behind the orthodox developmental approach there seems to be some expectation that over the long run such trends as the spread of industrialization and the growth of world population might conceivably shift the terms of trade in favor of the producers and exporters of primary commodities. Whatever the direction of future export price movements, however, there would appear to be ample justification for a concerted effort to insure that productivity advances place Latin American exporters among the more efficient producers for the world market rather than among the marginal group for whom shifts in prices tend to wipe out profits.[5]

For the smaller countries, of course, the weakness of their internal markets and the narrowness of their natural resource base afforded scant hope for attaining a more autarkic pattern of economic organization in any case, although Uruguay, the wealthiest of the smaller countries and the one richest in its human resources, did indeed make some efforts along that line. While the very real problems of instability in the export markets for primary products could not be brushed aside, the chief remedy has been seen in a systematic cultivation of the possibilities of export diversification: e.g., cotton and cattle in Central America, iron ore and fish products in Peru. To this end, a recurrent theme stressed in the country studies made by World Bank missions has been the identification of unrealized potential comparative advantages in international trade. At the same time, it is indicative of the general attachment to market-guided development which is inherent in this approach that international commodity stabilization schemes, an alternative means of dealing with external sector instability, were ordinarily viewed with disfavor (by those outside of Latin America) because of the latent risks in such proposals for a chronic misallocation of resources.[6]

The second major assumption is that, barring exceptional circumstances, the supply of foreign capital would be reasonably responsive to investment opportunities in the capital-short underdeveloped areas. These opportunities would be created by the postulated growth of export demand and the domestic expansion derivative thereof. With sound public policies, these investment opportunities would also, it was expected, elicit a greater supply of domestic private capital. There has also been, in this policy style, a disposition to consider the supply of private economic initiative and the character of private economic organization as potentially adequate to the tasks of development—with the corresponding corollary that the role of government, while by no means construed in minimalist terms, would properly be confined to the execution of more fundamental tasks so that the public sector would function in a service role to the private sector. Essentially, then, the strategy has sought to work as far as possible within the framework of market economies, turning the market system to maximum advantage for development.

It cannot be said, however, that the orthodox approach to development, with its emphasis on the external agents of growth, has altogether overlooked the need for institutional reordering in the economic systems of Latin America. Indeed, all along this has been one of its major concerns. As early as the 1920's and 1930's, for example, important changes in the banking structures of a number of countries were instituted as the result of the work of such foreign monetary experts as Kemmerer, Triffin, Max, and Niemeyer.

While Uruguay had had a central bank since 1896 and in Bolivia the Banco de la Nación Boliviana had performed a special role since its establishment in 1914 (as had similar institutions in Nicaragua since 1912 and in Paraguay since 1916), the formative period of Latin American central banking may be said to date from 1923 when the Banco de la República de Colombia was set up under the guidance of E. W. Kemmerer. Subsequently the Kemmerer efforts resulted in creation of the Banco Central de Chile (1925), the Banco Central de Ecuador (1927), the Banco Central de Bolivia (1929, a reorganization of the earlier institution mentioned above), and the Banco Central de Reserva del Perú (1931, a reorganization of the Banco del Perú which had been established in 1922). During the same decade, two other countries acting without foreign advice had established central banks, the Banco de México (1925) and the Banco Central de Guatemala (1925), the latter utilizing to some extent English central banking experience.

The following years saw a continuation of efforts along these lines, with the Chilean economist, Hermann Max, assisting in the establishment of the Banco Nacional de Costa Rica (1936), the Banco Central de Venezuela (1939), and the Banco Nacional de Nicaragua (1941). Meanwhile, the British specialists F. F. J. Powell and Sir Otto Niemeyer participated in setting up the Banco Central de Reserva de El Salvador (1934) and the Banco Central de la República Argentina (1935). During the same era, the central banking institutions in Mexico (1931) and Ecuador (1937) were reorganized to function more exclusively as central banks rather than as banks which also dealt with the public, and a considerable body of legislation was enacted with a view to improving the operations of national monetary systems.

Finally, thanks at least in part to the collaboration of specialists from the Federal Reserve System, further changes—either through reorganization or through the initiation of new institutions—were effected in the central banking regimes of Paraguay (1944), Bolivia and Guatemala (1945).[7] Over the years, too, a few countries were able to effect modest improvements in their fiscal systems, as, for instance, in the case of the Kemmerer-inspired budgetary reforms in Colombia in 1923 and 1931.

Throughout the late 1940's and the 1950's, the United States and such agencies as the IBRD and the IMF were almost continuously urging the desirability of other domestic reforms in a variety of fields. These promptings were, moreover, reinforced with a host of technical assistance missions (e.g., the Joint Brazil-United States Economic Development Commission of the early 1950's) and the so-called *servicio* arrangements for assistance in agriculture, health, and the like. The studies and recommendations of these groups, incidentally, charted new ground by increasing the availability of economic data on the structure and performance of the economies which were the objects of their analyses. Similarly valuable advisory service in the field of institutional reform was rendered by the Food and Agriculture Organization and other specialized agencies of the United Nations.

It is perfectly true, of course, that there was often a substantial disparity between the policies and programs recommended on the one hand and the actual portions of these which were subsequently implemented on the other, a fact which has led some to consider the information-gathering function the chief accomplishment of these missions and agencies.[8] Nevertheless, even the unimplemented aspects of this perspective on development merit consideration in order to clarify the differences between it and the principal alternative policy approach which was adopted up to around 1961. A rather vocal body of opinion in the contemporary policy debate has often held the orthodox approach to be both inadequate to the present needs of Latin America and disregarding of the dominant aspirations of the peoples of the area, particularly to the extent that nationally oriented development and industrialization have come to be viewed as the touchstones of economic success. On balance, however, such an assessment would appear to be a not altogether accurate interpretation of the developmental implications of orthodox policy.

ELEMENTS IN ORTHODOX DEVELOPMENT PROGRAMS

View of Industrialization. It is true that adherents of the conventional development approach have generally tended to underscore the importance of strengthening the export sector and have interspersed their statements with strictures against a certain overreadiness to launch new industries on the basis of highly protective commercial policies and other forms of subsidies.[9] It seems fair to state, however, that this has not been attributable to any animus against the industrialization of backward areas or to a desire to safeguard the export markets of the manufacturing nations. Rather, it is because they have favored a more indirect route to industrial development, one in which the rise of new manufacturing establishments occurs as a normal consequence of the free play of market forces once there has been created an environment conducive to industrial growth. From this has sprung the apparent bias in favor of private enterprise as contrasted with direct state investment and intervention in industrial development.

Present market-size constrictions on industrial development would, for example, be gradually relaxed as basic government development programs were implemented, bringing with them a multiplier effect on the volume of expenditures. Cost-price reductions could be effected with the attainment of increased efficiency and would augment the quantity of products which could be absorbed by a given volume of purchasing power. Extension of national transport systems and agricultural modernization would be pre-eminently important in enlarging the size of the available domestic markets for national industries. In a phrase, then, the difference between the orthodox approach to manufacturing development and that of the chief alternative policy styles may be thought of as the difference between induced or derivative industrialization on the one hand and deliberate industrialization on the other.

Some industrial promotion policies have been admitted in this school of thought: e.g., the establishment of agencies to publicize industrial investment opportunities, a cautious use of tax exemption programs, and carefully selected and temporally limited grants of tariff protection.[10] The Puerto Rican model has often been cited as a sound guide for manufacturing promotion elsewhere in the hemisphere. But such other devices as direct public investment in industry, broad tariff and exchange-policy protection, and the subsidized provision of cheap power have ordinarily been held to be antieconomic in the long run. For the most part, the proponents of this point of view have emphasized the importance of measures which might be thought of as constituting the preconditions of industrial development and have, with respect to industrial policy as such, mainly been concerned with pointing out the possibilities for establishing new industries (or modernizing and expanding existing ones) both on the basis of processing presently available or prospective domestic supplies of raw materials and as producers of agricultural requisites with domestic farmers as their primary customers.

For example, the World Bank's recommendations for Venezuela placed in the category of "preferred industries" such fields as food processing, beverages, dairy products, meat products, hides and leather, animal feeds, vaccines and serums, agricultural implements, fertilizers, insecticides, fibers and fiber products.[11] For Nicaragua, the promising areas of industrialization were identified as feed mixing plants, slaughter houses and meat refrigerating plants, vegetable oil plants, cotton gins, sawmills and hardboard mills for forestry development, cement, wire products manufacturing, textiles, leather, and food processing.[12] For Colombia, the most appropriate fields of manufacturing expansion were seen as including textiles, shoes and leather goods, sugar, simple chemicals (based especially on sugar chemistry), fats, mineral water, glass, cement, petroleum derivatives, and scrap and pig iron.[13] The bulk of these manufacturing opportunities have been justified mainly in terms of the internal needs of the Latin American economies, but, since they are predicated on local raw materials sources and tend to be projected on labor-intensive rather than capital-intensive coefficients of production, some hope has also been held out that this correspondence with factor endowment might well provide the basis for new comparative advantages in the export of manufactured items.

In short, by means of comprehensive recommendations for certain lines of industrial development as well as through the work of special technical assistance missions aimed at lifting productivity levels in various lines of Latin American manufactures, the exponents of the orthodox development route have recognized the case for a measure of industrialization even while they have focused major attention elsewhere. Generally speaking, though, they have urged that other matters should take precedence at this point in the area's economic evolution. These matters include reforms of such key elements of development as monetary and fiscal systems,[14] substantial investments and organizational improvements in such "enabling" sectors as transport, power, health and education,[15] and above all, perhaps, rehabilitation and modernization of the agricultural sector. Indeed, the dominant note struck in virtually all of the literature issuing forth from these sources has been not so much the magnitude of investment requirements but rather the repeated emphasis on the role of economic organization as a crucial factor in economic development.

Reform in Public Administration. No theme has been reiterated more frequently than that of the need for more effective public administration, unless it be the repeated references to the inadequacies of the fiscal system and the agrarian system. Even the frequently mentioned shortcomings in the supply of credit and banking services have their origin, at least in part (because of the extensive development of governmental banking), in the antiquated modes of handling the public business.

Time and again, the deficiencies of the information-gathering functions of government have been underscored, along with the problems these have created for the formulation of adequate plans and policies. No less insistent have been citations of gross malfunctioning in the provision of basic government services.[16] The absence of sound studies as a basis for public investment programming and the lack of continuity in the planning and execution of public works programs have both been singled out as additional defects which call for remedy. It has also been observed that totally inadequate provisions for maintenance have often reduced the value and life of public investment projects even when they have been brought to completion. Empty hospitals and workers' housing units, skeletons of buildings left unfinished for years, schools built so as to be visible from the main highways rather than where needed—such constitute the evidence of administrative malfunctioning. Nowhere have the conditions common to many countries been more forthrightly condemned than in the World Bank's *Report on Cuba:*

> In Cuba, public works rarely follow a long-term plan. They usually just occur in cycles . . . due, in part, to the belief of political leaders that the Cuban people will judge their merit by the volume of public works . . . which are visible, even if unfinished, at election time.
>
> Since tangible evidence of activity is what matters for this purpose, from the political point of view it is not necessary for projects actually to be finished, as long as they can be seen. It does not matter for instance, whether new schools or hospitals are adequately staffed and furnished, whether roads run all the way to their projected destination, or whether bridges actually serve their purpose of carrying traffic. The important thing is to have something to show the people—something under construction which gives employment.
>
> Since the next administration may not care to endorse the policy of its predecessor by completing its projects, Cuba today is littered with unfinished public works projects.
>
> In the past decade, the public works "cycle" has operated on the following lines:
>
> A new administration comes to power and finds that the public funds have been exhausted by the previous one. For a while, therefore, it does not—indeed cannot—carry out many public works and there are only a few signs of activity. Around the middle of its term, however, the government has to start to think about its political future. So funds are accumulated . . . and the work gets slowly started. When the administration comes to the end of its term, the work, whether finished or not, stops. This wasteful pattern is not, of course, invariable and some projects are brought to completion over several administrations; but it is sufficiently common to be typical of much public works activity.[17]

Thus, although the condition of public administration was not intended to be the specific concern of economic advisory missions, the subject became inevitably a matter of analysis and recommendation because of the limitations imposed by administrative capacity on policy choices and the increased likelihood of erroneous decisions occasioned by the prevailing lack of information on resources and other economic factors. At long last, it became impossible to sidestep the fact that the historic treatment of government as a private preserve of the oligarchy had impeded its being reorganized in a way more compatible with the requirements of a responsible public undertaking.

From the explicit concern with development came, in the first place, the recognition that when the conventional functions of the state are not properly discharged, the added burden of development functions cannot but result in further strain on the conduct of government operations. In fact, when the new calls upon the state involve a complexity of talent and technique that public administration is ill-prepared to supply, the expansion of governmental functions is almost certain to be accompanied by a deteriorating performance of most of those functions, including the limited basic ones. But beyond this, it has been stressed that the possibility of utilizing even limited government action as a tool of development is considerably blunted —perhaps so much so as to be ineffective—when public administration is faulty. Poorly administered tax systems make it difficult to employ fiscal measures to direct investment into preferred fields, while duplication and lack of coordination among agricultural agencies render almost hopeless the task of agrarian modernization.

In sum, even though the conventional approach to development has ordinarily placed a major reliance on private enterprise, reserving for it nearly the whole arena of directly productive activity, and notwithstanding the explicit preference in this approach for consigning an essentially supportive role to public investment, the incompatibility between outmoded structures of governmental organization and the rising technical demands on the modern state has necessitated assigning the subject of government structure and staffing a top priority in development analysis and programs.

At the action level, such a priority found concrete expression in the field of technical assistance, where, during the 1950's, a number of programs were undertaken in several of the countries to improve the quality of public administration.[10] With U. S. assistance, specialized schools of public administration were established in Brazil, Colombia, and Costa Rica, the latter serving also the other countries of the Central American region, while experts from various U.S. universities (and elsewhere) were also called in as advisers for administrative improvements in Peru, Bolivia, Panama, Chile, Ecuador, Venezuela, Uruguay, and Paraguay. While the accomplishments of these efforts are not to be minimized, neither should they be exaggerated. At most, only a bare beginning was made in providing better training and more effective governmental organization.

Fiscal Reform. Inseparable from the foregoing theme has been the attention accorded the parallel need for fundamental fiscal reform, an area in which only a very moderate headway had been made earlier in the century. Indeed, from the assessments of prevailing fiscal systems contained in the country studies and other analyses, there can be little doubt that poor fiscal organization has been one of the chief local impediments to the expansionary effects associated with new investment and the growth of trade.

Because of defects in this field, Latin American governments have been unable to mobilize tax revenues from the external sector and channel them into productive capital formation, a prerequisite for enabling the rest of the economy to reach higher levels of productivity and for resolving the problems of economic dualism. Thus, even though the orthodox policy position has favored investing public funds in such a way as to provide a basis for collateral private agricultural and industrial investments rather than state management of the whole economy toward development, the requirements for basic social and economic overhead capital are so considerable and urgent that public capital formation must necessarily play a significant role for the present in national investment processes.

This being the case, improvement in the organization and operation of the fiscal system has been held to be of high priority not only in order to mobilize the resources needed for investments in infrastructure but also to prevent faulty fiscal systems from becoming the chief source of a malignant inflation which would, in turn, aggravate the scarcity and misdirection of savings. Nearly all the writings of this development approach assign important values to price and monetary stability; for ever since the post-1914 abandonment of the gold standard nationalized money and placed in the hands of the state another instrument for control over the economy, the consequences of fiscal disorder have been magnified by monetary disturbances.

Fiscal reform has also been called for to remove distortions of the capital allocation pattern which are attributable to discriminatory features in the tax structure, as for example, in the case of Peru where income from rental properties has been much more lightly taxed than income from industrial activity.[19] Other changes have been urged in order to strengthen the financial position of subnational levels of government which, nourished for the most part by exceedingly slim fiscal resources because of the predominant centralizing tendencies in national tax systems, have been generally unable to perform their necessary functions in anything like an adequate manner. While some of the national constitutions in Latin America assign local governments a variety of public works and service functions, it is not unusual to find that in practice few municipalities actually carry out these functions. Thus, despite constitutional provisions for local government projects, these are either carried out by the appropriate central ministries or not at all; few channels have been provided for the expression of local initiative in such matters.[20]

Still other proposed reforms have sought to increase the progressive character of the fiscal system, not only through modifying existing tax rates and shifting the reliance from indirect taxes to direct taxes but also through changes in tax administration and more rigorous enforcement of tax laws. Among the benefits sought through more progressive taxation (in combination with the proposed public spending programs) have been: (1) a broader domestic distribution of purchasing power which would alleviate present market demand constrictions on investment and growth, (2) a curtailment of conspicuous consumption which would free domestic resources for other uses, and (3) the stronger balance of payments position which would result from reducing demand for foreign luxury goods. Further, by shifting purchasing power to lower income groups whose simpler consumption demands might more readily be met from local production, and thus creating new possibilities for realizing economies of scale in the production of standardized goods for a wide market, the import leakage which has historically dampened the stimulating effects of public spending and foreign trade multipliers upon national income and employment levels would also be diminished. Since there is some evidence that even in Brazil, the largest Latin American market, the prospects for continued industrial expansion have become less bright because of a pattern of industrialization which has, of late, catered increasingly to the limited demand for a broad range of durable consumer goods among high-income groups, the redistributive aspects of a movement to more progressive taxes take on additional value.[21] For a number of countries, the probable, and in some cases substantial, economies which might be realized from changed procedures of tax collection have also come up for consideration.[22]

Throughout the discussion of tax reform, it has been pointed out that the ramifications of fiscal change are quite widespread and by no means confined to the mobilization of adequate resources for public use or even to the general repercussions on other sectors. One advisory mission report, for example, has observed that in Argentina the reliance on import duties has, because of the high import coefficients of national industry, tended to inflate domestic manufacturing costs to the detriment of developing both the local and the export markets. Yet, given the reliance of the fiscal system on indirect levies, the state would find it hard to forego duties on imported capital goods and intermediate products; other dutiable goods (consumer items) had been displaced by the very process of import-substitution industrialization which increased the importation of the former categories of products. Therefore, without a substantial recasting of the fiscal structure, efforts to reduce the cost structure of domestic manufacturing by lowering the import charges on investment goods would simply create, or accentuate, other problems. The shifting composition of imports would tend, for instance, to reduce the share of government revenues in national income and so contribute to deficits in the fiscal system.[23]

In this respect, the Argentine predicament is hardly unique; examples of similar difficulties requiring remedial tax changes abound in the literature on Latin American development problems. By the early 1960's, however, comparatively little progress had been actually realized in the field of fiscal reform in most of the countries, although a great deal of knowledge had been gained which would be useful for implementing desirable changes in later years.

Human Resources Development. Besides organizational changes in government operations, orthodox development advisors have stressed the desirability of concentrating public sector investment in limited but critical fields of action rather than in a broad range of state enterprises. Programs in the long-neglected areas of health and education have been held especially vital in improving the quality of human resources: to increase the mobility of labor, to lift productivity of the abundant human factors, and to provide new skills required to sustain the development process. To this end, primary and technical-vocational education have tended to receive the major stress, in part to assist the preparation of a suitable industrial labor force but, perhaps more especially, to ease the path towards agricultural modernization by facilitating the spread of market information and innovations in production techniques.

For some countries, education has further been viewed as one of the chief means of bridging the cultural chasm which has persisted through the centuries in the form of coexisting but disparate cultural traditions. Where a substantial sector of the populace has not yet even learned the national language, the basic implement of cultural communication, much less assimilated the relatively newer traits of organization, conceptual universes, and value systems of commercial-industrial civilization, the argument for a heavy educational investment has been cogent indeed as a means of bringing more people into participation in the money or market economy—if not necessarily so cogent as to prompt an adequate response in action. But even where cultural bifurcation is less pronounced, the general case remains strong for the kinds of educational programs contemplated by the orthodox development advisory groups.[24]

Yet notwithstanding the persuasiveness of the case, by the end of the 1950's the accomplishments in human resource development were rather limited. Most countries had expanded somewhat the number of schools in operation and had benefited from the foreign private and public financial support which had been provided for training their nationals abroad in specialized disciplines. Here and there, constructive innovations were also introduced into national education systems, such as the rural radio schools sponsored by UNESCO and the Catholic church in Colombia or the vocational training programs sponsored jointly by industry and government in Venezuela, Brazil, and Colombia. Higher education, too, was strengthened in a number of countries, particularly the more advanced ones. Meanwhile, public health and sanitation services were gradually improved in practically every economy, as, indeed, demographic trends would suggest. With all due allowance for these and other gains, however, it was clear that the major task of human resource development had not yet, anywhere, received the degree of attention recommended for it by advocates of the orthodox development strategies.

Transport and Communications Development.   In terms of actual financing dimensions, the field of transport and communications has almost invariably been singled out as the area requiring the greatest immediate investment outlay in the public sector, despite the fact that it was exactly this field which was the prime recipient of foreign investment (in railways) in the preceding century.[25] In part the continuation of this priority attests to the severity of the basic transport problem which faces most of the countries of the hemisphere and which leaves potential resources (and markets) either untouched or underutilized for want of adequate ways to reach them. But in part—particularly insofar as a not insignificant portion of this investment effort was thought necessary for the rehabilitation of national railway systems —it also stands as testimony to failures in the social management of past investment, as well as to the process of disinvestment which seems to have occurred in the railways of several countries. Additionally, a part of the accumulated transport capital from preceding decades had simply become outmoded. Having been constructed originally to move raw materials to seaports, many of the Latin American railways were adequate neither for the correlation of manufacturing and agricultural industries producing goods for the domestic market nor for handling the distribution of those goods.

In consequence, land which could be cultivated remained idle while other more accessible agricultural areas suffered resource degradation from being overworked. Transport losses on perishable commodities have customarily been heavy, while the incentive to produce marketable agricultural surpluses has been impaired for lack of expeditious means of moving them to urban consumers. Furthermore, information on market conditions and new production techniques has spread only slowly as a result of poor transport conditions. For industry, the problems have been no less onerous. Suspension of production and partially idle productive capacity have often been occasioned by breakdowns in the supply flow of fuels, raw materials, and machine parts, while the effort to compensate for such transport uncertainties has necessitated an expensive level of inventory maintenance. In most countries, the existing transport system, aggravated by high rates of damage and pilferage, has tended to raise the costs of production and put the price of output beyond the reach of potential customers, a goodly portion of whom are beyond the effective compass of existing transport services anyway. Development of an internal transport network has therefore appeared as a necessary form of capitalization for industrial and agricultural activities catering to the local market as well as a support for programs which aim at strengthening, through lowered costs and diversification, the external economic position of the Latin American countries.

For several reasons, then, the amount of "unfinished business" in this fundamental sector has struck many students of the development process as one of the most serious of the present obstacles to the efficient functioning of the Latin American economies, a handicap which has lowered the productivity of capital and the other factors employed in industry, agriculture, and commerce and which has imposed a heavy burden of costs upon producers and consumers alike.[26] Because of lowered net returns, producers have been less able to accumulate the capital needed for expansion, while the high prices of final output have served to shrink further the already limited volume of effective market demand. Consequently the range of development options has been severely restricted by bottlenecks in the transport sector and the shortage of goods has been intensified. In addition, the grave technical and managerial deficiencies of government-operated rail lines (and of public utilities in general) have often resulted in persistent financial losses—deficits which have been financed, with inflationary consequences, out of the fiscal system.[27]

Relying heavily upon the logic of external economies, development orthodoxy has consistently urged a concentration of public investment efforts in the transport and communications sector and has employed the powerful sanctions of external financial assistance to attempt to lend further weight to the argumentation presented in its reports and analyses. Nearly a third of the lending of the Export-Import Bank to Latin America in the 1934-1958 period (exclusive of balance of payments loans) was directed into the transport and communications field, a portion which represented the largest single share of that institution's financial commitments to economic development activity in the hemisphere.[28] Similarly, the World Bank, from the beginning of its operations through 1959, devoted an almost equal percentage of its Latin American loan commitments to the same ends, although in that case loan obligations for the development of electric power resources (over half the total Latin American loan commitments) somewhat exceeded the resources allocated to transport and communications projects.[29]

In a few instances, most notably Colombia and Mexico, there has been some emphasis on the geographical extension of the rail network.[30] For most cases, however, the thrust of rail transport modernization has involved the rehabilitation of existing facilities: replacement of roadbeds, rails, and rolling stock, abandonment of no longer economical lines, and modernization of service installations. By and large, the main emphasis in the extension of land transport routes in these programs has turned to highway construction.

For one thing, the lower initial cost of highways as compared with rail lines makes them decidedly attractive in a context of capital scarcity. They can more readily be constructed by labor-intensive means with domestically available resources, thereby helping to boost domestic employment levels. The relevance of this advantage is emphasized since one of the overriding objectives in these programs has been that of substantially increasing regional access to national transport systems by extending routes as widely as possible. For another, the capital investment in highways can more feasibly be adjusted to the anticipated economic usefulness of particular roads than is the case with railway lines, where a very high minimum investment is normally required. As one of the basic purposes often sought in the transport program has been the opening up of new areas for commercial agricultural development, the possibility of adjusting the type of penetration road built to the near- and intermediate-term needs of the areas being settled constitutes another major argument in favor of the highway approach. In the third place, highway routes appear to be far more flexible in that they can be used by all types of vehicles and can therefore easily serve a variety of transport needs, from local farm-to-market hauls to long cross-country traffic.

This latter point is particularly important, for few of the development programs to which these transport recommendations have been attached envisage the near-term generation of the sort of heavy minerals and industrial traffic which would ordinarily require rail facilities over and beyond that which could be accommodated by modest adjustments in the present railway pattern. Instead, most of the projected new traffic patterns relate in an integral manner to the larger design of the development programs advocated by orthodox advisory groups, a design which places agricultural improvement at the forefront of concern. Correspondingly, this overall development program orientation has implied a need for the kinds of transport services which would be most appropriate for (1) the cheap and rapid movement of diversified farm products to and among various urban markets, reducing both the wastes of spoilage and the spread between farm and city prices and for (2) facilitating the distribution of urban sector output (fertilizers, tools, consumer goods, etc.) among scattered rural markets. Under the circumstances, then, the recommended concentration on road building programs would seem to be entirely logical.[31]

Finally, the modernization, and in some cases the new construction, of port facilities has come in for a share of attention in transport improvement programs, primarily to lower the delivered costs of imported goods (especially producers' and intermediary goods) and to enhance export efficiency.[32] For two countries, Brazil and Chile, port improvement has also a role to play in internal transport as the geography of these nations suggests a significant role for coastwise shipping in the domestic movement of goods among producers and consumers.

Of all the elements of the orthodox development approach, perhaps none had been more widely accepted than the emphasis on transport development. The Pan American Highway, for example, was gradually extended along the length of the continent, with a few breaks in Central America, while additional roads, of a generally lesser quality, were constructed to the more outlying regions. In Peru, Bolivia, and Brazil the first of the penetration roads into the Amazonian interior were built. Not uncommonly, the chief impetus behind highway construction was the inadequate service provided by railway lines, for often the new roads began to carry bulky products which, under normal conditions, would have gone by rail. By the middle of the century, substantial progress had been registered in highway development in Brazil, Chile, Colombia, Mexico, Peru, Uruguay, and Venezuela. Argentina had also acquired a fairly widespread network of roads which were, however, for the most part in poor repair and often inadequately surfaced. Mexico and Colombia, as noted earlier, also made gains in extending their railway lines, and throughout the continent air transport service enjoyed a particularly rapid growth, being employed for freight cargoes as well as passenger traffic.

It would be erroneous to assume that the record was devoid of shortcomings. Almost everywhere, for instance, road maintenance was seldom provided at an adequate level, and in Argentina the highway building program reached its peak in the 1930's, after which public investment in road development declined considerably. Notwithstanding its substantial highway expenditures, Brazil was still far short of possessing anything like an adequate network of good all-weather roads. Quite generally, moreover, the effort devoted to constructing feeder highways and farm-to-market roads was manifestly insufficient for national needs, while political and organizational rigidities often severely hampered the implementation of programs to improve the operating efficiency of telecommunications and port facilities, just as they frustrated the renovation of Argentine and Brazilian railways. Even so, at least a fair start had been made towards developing one area of public policy which, politically if not economically, was relatively noncontroversial when compared with other elements of the approach.

Power Development.   On the logic of external economies, investment in electric power has figured prominently in the development programs which have been prepared by proponents of the more conventional approach to economic progress. While the details of the proposed power programs have naturally differed from country to country, in general there has been a preference for limited projects designed to meet the existing critical power shortage. Less favored have been the more ambitious, but less economical, programs that have often been proposed in Latin America for anticipating possible longer-run changes in demand and for using the lure of large blocks of cheap (subsidized) power as a stimulus to industrialization.[33] The highly capital intensive nature of the power industry is, with due recognition of the high cost of capital, the basic element in this conservative approach to the subject, a feature which also helps to explain the related tendency to favor foreign investment in this field of endeavor whenever feasible.

Perhaps the most distinctive feature of the orthodox approach to power development, however, has been its endorsement of the cost-of-service principle in the pricing of energy output, a position which runs counter to a rather widespread predilection for holding power rates at uneconomically low levels in the belief that such practices are necessary for fostering general economic development. As one report summarized the position, "It seems clear that Latin America's need is for *more* electricity, not for *cheap* electricity." [34] Accordingly, the "full cost" concept of pricing has been repeatedly supported, not only on the grounds that such a policy would help preserve the integrity of market directives in the use of resources (including power resources) but also on the grounds that this is the most desirable means of insuring an adequate financial basis for the necessary expansion of the industry:

Public regulating authorities are apt to be attracted by policies of so-called 'cheap' power, to such an extent in some cases that rates do not even fully meet direct operating costs. Experience in many countries has shown that such power is not cheap in the end; and that, if development of an economy is not to be retarded by deterioration of plant and severe shortages, rates should cover all costs and also provide some contribution to the financing of future expansion. It has been said that the really expensive kilowatt is the kilowatt that an economy needs but does not have. In all its lending for power, therefore, the Bank lays great emphasis on the need for adequate rates.[35]

Additional justification for the orthodox energy policy has been drawn from the relation between energy pricing and monetary stability. A fairly prevalent position in Latin American governmental and academic circles, for example, has held that electric power installations should be run at little or no profit in order to subsidize industrial development, although such a position rests upon an uncritical assumption, which seems difficult to support, that cost-of-service pricing would deter the growth of economic industrial users of electricity. In any event, since in practice there has been a tendency among some governmentally owned electric power enterprises to disregard the cost of capital, the sale of subsidized energy has necessitated a resort to inflationary methods of finance on the part of the governments sponsoring such ventures.

The degree to which the orthodox development position on energy investment has been incorporated into actual development practice in the Americas has been mixed. On the one hand, the comparatively noncontroversial engineering character of power projects has meant that, as in the case of transport development, it has been easy for the governments of the region to endorse the general idea of energy investment. With foreign technical assistance, a goodly number of project proposals were prepared and then implemented, with substantial financial backing from both the Export-Import Bank and the World Bank. On the other hand, however, the general predilection for low rates, which has sprung from political considerations as well as from the desire to subsidize manufacturing development, has meant that both private and governmental energy enterprises have found it difficult, or in some cases, impossible to finance additional facilities out of earnings. Moreover, private companies have often been unable to attract new capital for expansion purposes, and foreign power companies in particular have been strongly discouraged from bringing in capital from abroad. Although exceptional cases exist—for example, in Peruvian policy—the more usual result has been that underinvestment in public-service power facilities has created chronic energy shortages and obliged industrial users of electricity to install their own generating facilities to provide power on a supplementary or stand-by basis.

Agricultural Development.   The final point which emerges unequivocally in the orthodox development perspective is the prime importance accorded agricultural development. Indeed, on this score the statements of policy emphasis have been most explicit, leaving no doubt whatever that the agricultural sector is viewed as the mainstay of most of the Latin American economies and that the primacy of agriculture is, for the projectable future, a necessary and continuing characteristic.[36] Through this priority, in fact, the essential historical orthodoxy of the theory of secular economic change implicit in this development approach comes most clearly to the forefront, for it conceives the development process basically in terms of Western economic experience in which a sweeping agricultural revolution was antecedent to the industrial revolution. In all reports, therefore, if not in actual practice, considerable attention has been devoted to the various means of encouraging a widespread shift from subsistence to commercial agricultural production and to the correlative changes implied thereby in grading and marketing, storage, transport, and processing facilities.

Broadly speaking, there are five ends sought in the recommended agricultural programs. First, to feed a growing and increasingly urbanized population and to raise nutritional levels (and the productive quality of human resources), the goal has been a substantial increase in the aggregate volume of food production. Such an objective, needless to say, takes on further importance in the light of the high income elasticity of demand for food which apparently prevails throughout most of Latin America. Realization of this goal would, it has been argued, also help relieve one of the major sources of inflation in the hemisphere and, through its effect on the cost of wage goods, contribute to bringing the structure of industrial costs down to a more satisfactory level. Second, these programs have sought diversification through the introduction of new crops and animal products, both to broaden the export base and to meet new demands (of consumers and industrial users) which inevitably appear in the domestic market in the course of development, thereby curtailing expenditures of foreign exchange for agricultural imports.[37] Inasmuch as agricultural diversification would go hand in hand with changed patterns of land use, it would also promote, through permitting a better adaptation of crops to environmental conditions, a higher level of productivity throughout the agricultural sector.

A rising level of agricultural productivity has constituted the third main objective of these programs: partly to raise the real income of the rural populace since virtually all of the reports hold that an improvement in the standard of living has to start with agricultural productivity, partly to lower the supply prices of food and agricultural raw materials to the urban sector, and partly to improve the competitive position of export crops. A fourth objective which is mentioned explicitly in a number of reports and which is implicit in all the others is the expansion of employment opportunities in agriculture. Sectoral differences in production functions being what they are, the employment multiplier of additional capital inputs in agriculture would appear to be superior to that realizable in the industrial sector. For this reason, a generally cautious view has been taken regarding the socially desirable forms of rural mechanization since it is feared that premature movements in this direction would, given the limited availability of capital elsewhere in the Latin American economies, simply accentuate through labor displacement the already troublesome problems of unemployment and underemployment. Finally, the income and employment effects of the foregoing objectives, were they to be attained in any substantial measure, would encourage a derivative expansion of industry: those which utilize agricultural output as raw material inputs and those (the producers of agricultural requisites and consumer goods) which have, or could have, farmers as their primary customers.

Up to a point, the measures which have been recommended as leading to the attainment of these objectives are fairly standard. A part of the answer has, for example, been sought in extension of the acreage under cultivation through land reclamation projects, irrigation projects (especially smaller scale ones), and colonization and resettlement schemes, mostly of the semidirected rather than totally planned or purely spontaneous sort. In most cases, though, more of the increase in output and productivity has been expected to come from improved practices developed and demonstrated by research and experimentation agencies, disseminated through technical and extension services, and supported by improvements in farm credit facilities.[38] Better seeds, fertilizers, and pesticides; improved breeds of livestock and progressive livestock management; improved pastures and crop rotation practices; afforestation programs and techniques of erosion control; improved storage facilities; and dissemination of the simpler agricultural tools and implements (of the types which could be domestically manufactured, especially) exemplify the modernized practices in crop production and animal husbandry which have been seen as crucial to agricultural development. In addition, virtually all such programs have called for further support through renovated agricultural research and extension services, an appropriate adaptation of farm credit measures, and a careful use of price and stabilization policies.[39]

While many of these functions tend to be of a public character and, for that reason, a part of the governmental action program recommended for agrarian modernization, it should be kept in mind that a supplementary thrust towards rural progress is inherent in the kinds of agriculturally related manufacturing enterprises which have usually been proposed in the field of industrial development. In this view, the deficiencies of agricultural extension work in Latin America have not stemmed solely from failures in public administration and education; they have also been attributable to the general backwardness of business enterprise. Consequently, the marketing of agricultural requisites and incentive goods in a more progressive or enterprising manner would gradually build up a comprehensive privately organized "agricultural extension" system (whose "extension agents" would be salesmen of new seed varieties, fertilizers, and the like) alongside public efforts in this field—as has, of course, happened in the more advanced Western economies.

Both the public and private aspects of the orthodox approach indicate that the kind of agricultural programs proposed have been informed by the probably valid assumption that the chief sources of long-run gains in rural productivity may depend less on the internal organizational forms of agricultural firms (i.e., on internal economies) than on those aspects of the general production environment which provide significant external economies to agricultural firms whatever their forms of internal organization: e.g., suitable transport and marketing arrangements, research stations and extension centers, educational and credit facilities, and so forth. In agriculture, as in transport, power and human resources development, the orthodox approach has thus tended to center on programs which structure additional external economies into the national production scene.

In contrast to its position on the industrial sector, therefore, the orthodox program for agriculture has generally envisaged a considerable amount of governmental guidance, particularly intervention of a promotional character. So great are the demands of this task upon the machinery of the state, especially when taken in conjunction with the other area of basic reform already mentioned, that it would appear both realistic and consistent for proponents of orthodox development strategy to take the more restrictive position they have held regarding the propriety of governmental intervention in other areas of economic life, particularly in the industrial sector. The efficacy of broad interventionism, in other words, has been circumscribed more by a realistic regard for practical limits on the capabilities of the state for constructive economic action than by any basic philosophical commitment to the tenets of economic liberalism as such. This being the case, it does not seem altogether just to criticize the orthodox programs, as some in Latin America have done, of following a route linked with political conservatism—much less with a desire to shore up capitalism, as the Marxian critique has held.

For that matter, it is also in the field of agricultural policy, at least as this has been enunciated by foreign economic advisors, that one can find evidence that supporters of the more orthodox path to development have not been necessarily wedded to the socio-political status quo—even if there were room for doubt on this score after studying the implications of their recommendations for education and fiscal reform. Although official missions from international agencies have been somewhat constrained in their treatment of Latin American agricultural problems by the fact that they have been working with governments and have therefore had to confine their recommendations mostly to those actions which could practically be implemented by existing governments, they have nevertheless on several occasions called explicit attention to the desirability of effecting fundamental institutional or social structural changes in the agricultural sector as a part of a program of agrarian modernization. Perhaps no other of the country studies has been so outspokenly critical of the traditional institutional milieu as the World Bank's devastating *Report on Cuba*, but even so there has been an explicit recognition of the need for corrective measures to cope with the inefficient use of land which has stemmed from prevailing land tenure systems. Moreover, throughout much of the analysis there runs the assumption that such conditions as absentee ownership and insecure tenancy generally operate to thwart efforts to improve rural productivity.[40]

Admittedly, discussion of the details of dealing with this critical, and politically sensitive, issue has generally been somewhat circumspect and so limited as to appear a bit vague, particularly in contrast to the lengthy expositions devoted to more routine development subjects. But doubtless it has been here that the aforementioned constraints of official accreditation have been most operative. Making due allowance for this consideration then, one can find in the World Bank reports of the 1950's a number of policy recommendations which, if implemented, would tend to democratize the pattern of control over agricultural resources and broaden the participation of the rural populace in the fruits of agrarian progress.[41]

For example, the programs for substantially increased rural education and extension efforts and for a modification of farm credit systems were aimed at improving the lot of the small- and medium-sized farmers, while the land settlement proposals were generally framed in such a way as to increase the relative importance of these groups in the total size distribution of agricultural holdings. To reinforce the economic position of these groups further, most of the development recommendations went on to propose a vigorous governmental program to assist in the formation of credit cooperatives, machinery and farm implement pools, and cooperative marketing organizations. Through such associations, the member farmers could gain more of the economic advantages of scale while at the same time the cooperative organizations would serve as the institutional links through which governmental programs of agricultural modernization could be conveyed to the ordinary *campesino*, who historically has generally been beyond the effective reach of programs of this sort.[42] Eventually, or at least so might one surmise from the context, the new cooperatives would provide the means for a decentralization of government activity and control in the agricultural sector.

Concerning the latifundia problem proper, a number of approaches were advanced, ranging from the suggestion that Swiss legislation against absentee ownership might be considered for possible emulation to changes in tenancy legislation which would promote greater security of tenure through long-term leasing contracts.[43] It was also felt that public control over irrigation projects might usefully be employed as a means of gaining social leverage over the larger landowners: for example, by limiting the supply of water to a stipulated maximum number of hectares per owner.[44] In the main, however, the favored approach to land reform appears to have been the fiscal approach,[45] in which tax powers would be used to coerce idle land into use and, in other cases, to force the conversion of ranches into economic-sized farms devoted to crop cultivation. Apart from shifting the intensities of land use, the taxation device was also seen as helpful in depressing inflated land values (thus making access to land ownership easier for some farm families) and, in opening the land to more intensive cultivation, as a means of absorbing more rural manpower into productive employment. Through the imposition of heavier fiscal charges on lands not occupied by the owner, it was hoped further to discourage the institution of absentee ownership and to promote a wider spread of incentives throughout the agricultural sector.

The potential efficacy of this route to agrarian reform would, of course, depend greatly on modernization of systems of tax administration (which would be enormously complicated by the addition of a land tax of the sort proposed) and on attainment of a considerable degree of monetary stability to avoid an inflationary erosion of the real tax base. Given the problems inherent in assessing on a national basis the values of rural properties with only rudimentary land classification and cadastral surveys available and without sufficient numbers of trained personnel to administer such a program, the fiscal approach to agrarian reform turned out in practice to be a quite unworkable instrument of reform. Yet, even so, it must be recognized as one of the earliest proposals made in the post-1945 period for coping with a basic problem which, in the more dominant currents of development policy, went largely unattended amid the preoccupation with national industrialization measures.

SHORTCOMINGS OF THE ORTHODOX APPROACH

With its general emphasis on agricultural modernization, transport improvement, human resources development, and fiscal reform, the orthodox approach to development may be credited with anticipating many of the central points of concern which today, reformulated in the context of a more sweeping (and, perhaps, more arresting) vision of socio-economic change, shape the course of hemispheric development policies. At the same time, the very fact that so many of these measures were still awaiting effective implementation in the 1960's is evidence of the rather limited success with which the advocates of conventional development met during the earlier period, though, to be fair, it must be admitted that the very magnitude of the problems which confronted them virtually insured that only a modest amount of headway could have been made in any case.

On balance, the record of achievement was a spotty one. Peru, in virtue of its free exchange policy and its new mining and electricity codes favoring private investment, was able to make good on its resource potential in both fields, recording impressive gains in each during the 1950's; more striking still was its flourishing fishing industry which quickly rose to international prominence under the aegis of private initiative. Under the direction of Premier and Minister of the Treasury, Pedro Beltrán, a man strongly given to support of the principles of economic liberalism, at least a beginning was made in the difficult and unpopular task of enforcing the taxation laws more rigorously, and a relative degree of monetary stability was also achieved. Colombia, as mentioned previously, made significant progress in integrating its national railway system with construction of the rail route to the Caribbean coast and, by various means, registered notable gains in the output of a number of agricultural lines. Thanks to the efforts of local religious authorities and to the collaboration they received from UNESCO, Colombia was also able, in the development of the Sutatenza system of rural radio-schools, to claim credit for one of the few significant educational experiments in Latin America during this time.[46] Guatemala, in the post-Arbenz period, instituted a few (quite limited) tax reforms, endeavored to stimulate private enterprise, stepped up its highway construction program, launched a modest program of colonization and resettlement, and even achieved a measure of progress in export diversification. These achievements, notwithstanding, however, it was (and is) still a very considerable distance removed from the "free world showcase" of development which a famous foreign president predicted it would become following the overthrow of the communist-infiltrated Arbenz regime.

Guatemala's enterprising neighbor to the south, El Salvador, similarly launched an active program of road building and employed with considerable success a variety of measures to expand the output of crops other than coffee, which was traditionally the mainstay of the economy. In Nicaragua the growth of cotton cultivation made such rapid gains that it came, in the postwar period, to overshadow the importance of coffee, while a new livestock industry was developed to the extent that ranching products began to figure importantly in the nation's export lists during the 1950's. By the end of the 1940's, Venezuela's long-standing open door policy towards foreign investment had paid off quite well in the form of three decades of rapid expansion in petroleum production and exports; however, some critical reaction had occurred (in the form of the short-lived Acción Democrática government of the late forties), in part because of the manifest failure of the oil investments to promote greater collateral economic growth in that country.[47]

In Argentina, the partial introduction of orthodox development policies in the post-Perón period led to some recovery of production capacity in the export agricultural sector. The encouragement given foreign investment brought rapid gains in the national production of petroleum, with corresponding savings in the foreign exchange previously spent to finance petroleum imports.

Monetary and banking reforms and the institution of less complex exchange rate systems were also brought about in several of the economies, but more than offsetting such scattered examples of economic advancement were the policy areas of continued gross neglect. For all their contribution to development thinking in the Americas, one must conclude that the exponents of economic orthodoxy had failed to give sufficient attention to considerations lying in the realm of the institutional parameters of economic growth and change, considerations which might be said to constitute a necessary part of the preinvestment stage of social reorganization.

To cite only a few instances of these gaps or, perhaps more accurately, these leaps in development planning, it could be observed that although several of the World Bank reports allude to the role of "noneconomic" barriers to efficiency which originate in the social structure and the culture of the countries studied, the attention devoted to means of alleviating these shortcomings (e.g., "the cultural isolation and defensive attitude of the Indians" of Guatemala) would seem to be altogether inadequate. In like manner, despite the admitted centrality of agrarian modernization and the importance of rural forms of social organization such as the village, comparatively little was said regarding ways in which community development might be employed to transform such units and integrate them into a modern type of economy, in the process adding to monetary investment a probably not inconsequential amount of investment in kind through capturing the productive potential of underemployed rural labor. That a revitalized rural community structure—through such vehicles as strengthened civic structures and *campesino* organizations—might further have a vital political role to play in generating the pressures needed to redress ancient social and economic imbalances seems scarcely to have been considered.

Similarly, for all the emphasis given to fiscal reform and public investment, one must search quite far in order to find adequate discussion of the influence of political power in controlling and apportioning the funds spent from the national treasury. Yet in the absence of such considerations, discussions of far-reaching changes in this area tended to take on a certain air of unrealism. To a degree, the same might even be said of the whole question of agrarian reorganization. Illuminating though the orthodox analyses have been, they scarcely ever went far enough to indicate clearly how the Latin American countries might go about instituting something more substantial than the placebo reform programs which were characteristically enacted prior to the 1960's. In a different but related area, namely that of human resources development, one would be hard put to find a convincing example of a new national educational program which bore any resemblance at all to the kind of effort proposed as essential by advocates of the orthodox development route. Here, too, the disparity between recommendation and accomplishment has been so great as to suggest that important analytical links were somehow omitted between observed need and designed response.

Perhaps the whole issue which is involved here was crystallized in the frame of reference employed by one of the more elegantly conceived and well-reasoned development programs of the postwar period, a report which was prepared by a group of foreign economic experts for the Prado administration of Peru. Echoing a notion which was mentioned in the World Bank's Nicaraguan study, the report quite correctly noted in its opening paragraphs that

> . . . the national effort for economic development must be as quick and as sweeping as a mobilization for war. Like a war effort, it must have the support of all sections of the nation. Unless the spirit of the national effort is grasped by labor and business, by farmers, miners and city workers, by all classes and political groups, the chances for success will be small.[48]

Yet notwithstanding the laudable sentiments expressed in this exhortation and despite the fact that the ambitious program subsequently presented was clearly predicated upon establishment of an environment conducive to the concerted social action called for, not a word of advice was further offered on the subject other than a casual reference to the desirability of "placing less immediate emphasis on expenditures for socially motivated projects." [49] Since the situation then existing in Peru was anything but the sort of milieu suggested as appropriate for a national development effort, the impression is inescapable that not all matters worthy of attention were in fact receiving it. A not dissimilar developmental myopia appears to have afflicted most of the otherwise praiseworthy efforts at Argentine economic recovery during the aftermath of Perón, with the result that a solid beginning was yet to be made in that direction a decade following Perón's flight from the country. It seems reasonable to suppose, therefore, that the limitations of the conventional or orthodox development route were manifested not so much in its sins of commission—for on the side of actual policy prescription the recommendations carried a great deal of validity so far as they went—as in its sins of omission. For these, the acts of reparation were to come in the 1960's.

XII

The Latin American Neo-Orthodoxy in Development

$\mathbf{F}_{\text{AR}}$ more pervasive than the orthodox development approach, and, indeed, often interlaced with it in actual practice, has been the policy style outlined in a general way at the end of Chapter X. Quasi-autarkic objectives, deliberate industrialization, a suspension of free-market directives in the allocation of resources, a variegated assortment of welfare policies—all these, tinged with differing hues of nationalism, have formed an approach to development in which a fundamental aspect of public policy has been the broad and in many ways culturally recidivist commitment to the principle of state intervention. No less fundamental has been the reorientation of development efforts: from the externally oriented growth policies of the nineteenth century and the orthodox strategy of recent times to an internally oriented pattern of development. Just as aggressive public sector action was, in earlier decades, utilized to connect local economic processes more closely with the workings of the world market, with the twentieth-century reorientation of policy, the operations of the public sector became the chief buffer of the domestic economy against the pressure of external events.

At first devised on an ad hoc, piecemeal basis in response to the troublesome exigencies of economic life in the present century, eventually the new policies assumed a more ample character and rationale, as well as a certain permanency. As they came to be increasingly integrated into the fabric of national economic life in the hemisphere, the new policy configurations became, ultimately, a type of neo-orthodoxy within the Latin American setting, with an acceptance as widespread and conventional as any policies which had been previously espoused.[1] Indeed, so pervasive has been this interventionist revival that its features have both transcended national boundaries and cut across a variety of political regimes.[2]

As the doctrines embodied in the work of the World Bank and similar agencies imparted a more systematic quality to measures previously related only within the general structure of traditional economic theory, so also a similar process of evolution has been perceivable within this alternative policy stream. The development style enunciated by the United Nations Economic Commission for Latin America (ECLA), in inspiration as well as by conscious intent the lineal descendant of the earlier interventionistic pragmatism, has in effect provided a comprehensive justification and systematization of this policy orientation during the post-World War II era.

Especially has this been true with regard to the role and direction of central economic planning, a theme which, in one form or another, has been recurrent in this approach for a number of years, however much, for better or for worse, actual practice has regularly fallen short of the projected ideal. More recently, the logic of the national integration efforts of the past has, with ECLA pointing the way, led directly into present-day attempts to bring about some form of regional economic integration.

ASSUMPTIONS OF NEO-ORTHODOXY

Thanks to the outpouring of economic discussion and analysis in contemporary Latin America, both in and out of ECLA, the assumptions on which internally oriented development policies have been grounded have been considerably clarified. Consequently, it is possible to trace the main lines of variance between them and the alternative set of assumptions which underlie the more orthodox development approach.

In part, the approach in question assumes that some of the forces postulated by traditional economic doctrine do not, for various reasons, operate in actuality; this failure gives rise to problems which can be handled only by a recourse to national action on the part of the countries experiencing these problems.

For example, the mutual economic benefits derived from free commercial exchange in the world market have been questioned repeatedly. In fact, it would appear that sometimes a considerable portion of the traditional principle of comparative advantage has been rejected on the grounds that the international division of labor does not, as conventionally supposed, automatically function to the benefit of underdeveloped countries. While in vulgar discourse such an indictment has often been couched in the simplistic language of "selling cheap [raw materials] and buying dear [manufactures]," more sophisticated arguments have also been adduced over the years in support of this contention. Beginning with the crude notion that exporters of primary products are in a position to claim only an inferior portion of final product value, because of the (presumably superior) processing-value-added claims of the industrial countries, the line of argumentation became more elaborate and rather more plausible during the era between wars, when its advocates remarked the relative instability of raw-commodity prices as compared with the prices of the manufactured goods moving in world trade. Because of differences (i.e., the degree of competition prevailing) in market structure and organization as well as differences between the more controllable production situation of the factory as contrasted with that of the farm (i.e., the supposed congenital weakness of agriculture which derives from its dependence on nature), it was claimed that commodity-exporting nations would necessarily encounter greater difficulty than industrial nations in adjusting to cyclical disturbances. Indeed, given initial slim economic margins and inherent vulnerability to natural catastrophes, the additional market fluctuations generated within the business enterprise system were adjudged nearly insupportable by the peripheral economies.

At least an element of this reasoning entered into the intellectually more complicated case devised during the late forties by ECLA in support of the need for interventionistic policies of industrialization.[3] In its reading of historical data, ECLA purported to find evidence of a secular trend of deterioration in the Latin American (or the periphery's) terms of trade. Particularly manifest between the 1870's and World War II, the trend resumed, according to ECLA, in the 1950's. From that point onward, ECLA contended, the trend would be, *ceteris paribus*, a condition hindering the development of the periphery by (a) making the periphery's capital imports more expensive and (b) at the same time making it increasingly difficult to augment the periphery's earnings of foreign exchange. Part of the difficulty, it was claimed, stemmed from the disparity between the center and the periphery in their income elasticities of demand for imports. On the one hand—because of the operation of Engel's law, increasing technological efficiency in the use of raw materials, and the development of synthetics— the center's demand for imports from the periphery would tend to grow more slowly than the center's aggregate growth rate. On the other hand— because of generally high income elasticities of demand for manufactures and the capital-import requirements of development programs—the periphery's demand for imports from the center would normally tend to grow more rapidly than the periphery's rate of increase in national income. Therefore, demand factors alone, given the relatively inelastic demand for raw materials and the more elastic global demand for manufactured items, would tend to depress the prices of periphery exports while sustaining the prices of center exports.

To the tendencies postulated in reciprocal demand analysis, the ECLA case went on to add certain assumptions regarding the behavior of supply, which on the whole reinforce the divergent export price movements occasioned by the former. Technological progress (and increasing productivity) was taken as a feature common to the export sectors of both the center and the periphery, though rather less in evidence within the domestic sectors of the peripheral economies. While classical economic theory assumed that the benefits of technological advance would tend to be widely distributed through some combination of lower prices on output and higher producer incomes, the ECLA analysis of center-periphery relationships disputed this contention. Instead, it asserted, what ordinarily occurs is a quite asymmetrical distribution of the gains from trade in favor of the center countries, a conclusion reached on essentially the same analytical grounds as those propounded in the familiar Singerian argument. In other words, the basic assumption made in reasoning to the conclusion that the center is in a position to appropriate most of the increases in world income which result from increased productivity is that the product and factor markets of the center are not nearly so competitive as those of the periphery. Owing to the presence of strong labor unions and oligopoloid industrial structures, the main result of productivity increases in the center's export sector is an increase in factor rewards (i.e., higher wages and profits), not a fall in the prices of the center's exports; hence, on this side of the trading relationship it is primarily the producers who benefit from productivity gains. In contrast, throughout the periphery the labor market is such that increased productivity cannot easily be appropriated by labor factors in the form of higher wages (a point which the ECLA argument borrows from W. A. Lewis); meanwhile the relatively competitive structure of the periphery's export product markets prevents capital-ownership interests from appropriating the productivity gains in the form of higher profits. Consequently, technological progress in the periphery's export sector tends to be translated into lower export prices—to the benefit of center-country consumers.

The combination of these conditions, then, produces a situation in which the slowly rising center demand for peripheral exports encounters a rapidly expanding supply of the latter, because of technological progress. The outcome of this interaction: a long-term downward pressure on the price level of peripheral exports. Concurrently, center export prices tend to hold steady or even to increase, owing to (a) the strong demand of the periphery for imports and (b) the ability of productive factors of the center to enforce their claims for income by holding export prices at levels consonant with those claims. In either case (i.e., steady or rising center export prices), the outcome would be an increase in the price of periphery imports (center exports) relative to the price of periphery exports (center imports).

On the basis of this presumed secular deterioration in the Latin American terms of trade, ECLA-minded advisers tended to discount the value of a development program geared primarily to an expansion of exports. To the extent to which their underlying theoretical assumptions are valid, a significant increase in exports would mainly tend to lower unit export prices rather than to increase aggregate earnings of foreign exchange. And were market forces permitted to follow their course unimpeded, the underdeveloped nations of the periphery would steadily lose in their share of total global product to their trading partners of the center.

An adverse movement in the terms of trade or a lopsided sharing of the benefits of technological advance do not, of course, indicate that there are no gains whatever from the trade process for the nations which benefit relatively less; their position would remain superior to what it would be in the absence of trade—a matter which the ECLA school of thought has never denied in its discussion of the limitations of export expansion as a source of financing for Latin American development. It has, however, used the foregoing analysis to argue that given the parameters of (a) existing and foreseeable demographic growth rates and (b) a rate of increase in per capita income which is high enough to be politically tolerable and socially acceptable, Latin America could not reasonably expect, in a purely free market context, to satisfy its need for goods through the normal processes of trade expansion. The rate of increase in the Latin American demand for imports being in excess of the growth rate of the demand for Latin American exports, the result would be, or so it has been contended, a goods deficit which, in the absence of interventionary measures, would frustrate attainment of the target Latin American aggregate growth rate.[4] To forestall this eventuality, a deliberate modification of the international division of labor was held to be in order so that the growing gap in Latin American trade balances, the disparity between the countries' capacity to import and their development objectives, could be met from new internal production.

Since the supposed gap consists largely of manufactured goods, the needed new internal production would consequently involve a process of domestic industrialization. And while, in the interests of maintaining high domestic investment levels, the new industrialization would be pushed initially in the consumer-goods field (thereby displacing imports of manufactured consumer goods in order to release foreign exchange to finance the producer-goods imports needed for investment expenditures), this would represent only one dimension of "import substitution industrialization," the term which has been used to describe the ECLA policy position. In the aggregate, the level of imports would not necessarily be diminished by such policies; rather it is the composition of imports which would be changed. In a more fundamental sense, therefore, the import-substituting aspect of the industrialization process recommended by ECLA consists of developing new domestic industries to substitute for the aforementioned goods deficit, that is, the needed "imports" which could not be obtained because of limitations on the capacity to import.

Needless to say, as the deliberate industrialization measures justified on such a basis would involve, and have in actual practice involved, the creation of new domestic industries whose cost levels are higher than those of their counterparts in the center countries, this departure from the pattern of development dictated by the traditional formulation of comparative advantage theory has implied an acceptance of some measure of protectionism as a more or less permanent feature of public policy in the peripheral economies.

Within Latin America, the foregoing line of reasoning has been accepted as a convincing description of the preconditions of development. Accordingly, country after country has incorporated some version of import-substitution industrialization doctrine into the core of its national development program. To be sure, a country's judgment of the situation may be inaccurate, but it is with the reality of the judgment and not its inaccuracy that we must deal. As a corollary of this approach, international commodity-control agreements have been favored by ECLA economists and the Latin American bloc in general. By shifting real income distribution in favor of the underdeveloped countries and thus redressing the assymetrical sharing in the gains from trade which would prevail in an unfettered market situation, such schemes have been endorsed for their utility in assisting the region to make an easier transition to more diversified production patterns. With a floor placed under the level of export earnings, Latin America could proceed, it has been argued, to develop more systematically its internal supply sources of manufactures in order to fill the goods deficit created by the gap between developmental requirements and the limited capacity to import.

Still other points of conventional economic theory have been disputed. Although little has been said in Latin American neo-orthodoxy about the possibilities of improving the climate for private foreign investment in order to encourage the inflow of external resources for development, it seems to have been believed that international capital movements do not necessarily take place in accordance with differences in earning ratios. Consequently, despite the generally high profit returns which accrue to capital in Latin America, there is little assurance that foreign investment will respond in adequate volume. The remedy envisaged: governmental negotiation of public loans and grants on terms other than those which would prevail were the judgments of the market to determine them [5] Similarly the routine operations of the market economy have long been thought inadequate to the job of marshaling resources, both external and domestic, for development—an oblique recognition of the problems created by the institutional framework of the Latin American countries. Since it has been assumed that the automatically available supplies of investment capital and entrepreneurial ability are insufficient to maintain an acceptable growth rate, the conclusion has been drawn that public intervention in allocating resources, directing investment, and controlling foreign trade is indispensable. Thus, controls are justified to guide foreign-exchange earnings (and foreign capital) into "productive" investment, especially, in the light of the terms of trade argument, into the development of the key secondary industries rather than primary industries.

In the process of lifting the growth rate in this fashion, inflationary price movements might well emerge as the means of effecting forced savings, but the predisposition has generally been to attribute such upward price level changes primarily to the influence of structural features, or supply inelasticities, in the Latin American economies and hence to depreciate the effectiveness and the feasibility of conventional counter-inflationary measures.[6] While it is recognized that such traditional counterinflationary techniques as fiscal surpluses and monetary restraint could, if pressed vigorously enough, halt the rise in price levels, proponents of the Latin American neo-orthodoxy have usually argued that the results would, apart from generating possibly unmanageable political tensions, gravely impair the drive for development by damping the rate of aggregate investment.[7]

The view of inflation, in turn, brings up the second major category of differences between Latin American neo-orthodoxy and the body of conventional development doctrine. Even where the relationships and forces postulated in traditional economic analysis are accepted as valid descriptions of reality, there has been so much dissatisfaction with the social consequences of the operations of such forces that a regime of governmental allocations and controls has been favored as a means of achieving a more socially desirable result. For this reason, it has also been argued that international equilibrium cannot be attained and maintained in a tolerable way by such automatic correctives of the market as deflation and devaluation. Thus, a resort to trade and exchange control, including the selective devaluation implied in multiple exchange rates, has been justified as a more acceptable manner of correcting maladjustments in the international economic position of the Latin American countries.

Similarly, even where it is admitted that international capital movements do occur in response to profit considerations, the general expectation of neo-orthodoxy appears to be that the allocational pattern as well as the amount of such investment would not be satisfactory. Consequently, tariffs, quotas, advance deposits on imports, special import duty concessions, import and exchange licensing, differential exchange rate policies, and a variety of other restrictions have been widely employed to channel international transactions in what are believed to be more socially desirable directions.[8]

In the adoption of exchange and trade control systems, however, it is clear that the Latin American governments were actually moving much further than a mere regulation of international economic relationships. Given the significance of the external sector in domestic economic life, the nationalization and state operation of the foreign trade sector (which is what such control systems, in effect, have meant) has placed public authority in control of the important intervening variables which link the world economy with domestic economic processes. By expropriating foreign trade flows, in other words, the state was placed in a position to determine for the domestic private sector such key relationships as the relative prices (in domestic currency) of foreign and domestic goods, the cost of capital investments and the level of operating expenses (when these involved imported capital goods and imported intermediate products and raw materials), and the profitability of the export sector. Indeed, the whole array of domestic investment preferences and production opportunities was thereby subjected to state determination, since the controls exercised by government over the import components of domestic economic activity could be used to modify the relative cost-price and earnings structures obtaining in all sectors of the national economy.

In addition to the arsenal of regulatory devices applied to the external sector (with their direct and indirect impact on internal economic relationships), most of the governments of the hemisphere have moved even further. By supplementing the ordinary techniques of fiscal and monetary policies with state entrepreneuring and direct governmental investment, governmental lending, price controls and subsidies, special tax incentives, and credit controls, neo-orthodox policy has attempted to fashion a course of development different from and hopefully superior to that which would result from the normal functioning of the market economy. Indeed, it is just for this reason that the assertion of national control over economic life has played such a central role in the policy trends of recent decades. The nationalization of railways and other public utilities, the creation of government banks, the organization of public enterprises in the petroleum and electric power fields, the initiation of state-owned steel mills, and in fact, the general disposition to use public investment to foster the development of pivotal or basic industries—all these widespread efforts to domesticate the key sectors of the economy and to use the instrument of government to fill the gaps in national production and resource patterns have had at their core one essential rationale. The same may be said of the measures which have been employed to modify the labor market by requiring the employment of nationals in foreign-owned firms, or those affecting the capital market by favoring domestic ownership of stock in foreign-initiated corporations—both of which types of measures have aimed at a partial domestication of foreign enterprises. Every one of these cases has reflected a dissatisfaction with the decisions that automatically result from the free play of market forces, and every one of them documents an instance in which the social decision was taken to abridge or suspend the market mechanism by organizing resources through the major public institution that stands most independently above the market: the state.

In handling the problem of economic leadership, then, the neo-orthodox approach has commonly tended to assume that the private-sector capacity for leadership is limited, being circumscribed for lack of wider cultural underpinnings at a number of crucial points in the economic environment. Accordingly, it has placed major, if possibly sanguine, reliance on public-sector leadership in the drive to reestablish the countries of the region on a sounder economic footing. In contemporary Argentina, for instance, 84.5 per cent of the capital and reserves included in the ten largest enterprises of the country belongs to firms in the public sector; for the twenty largest enterprises, the corresponding figure is 67.9 per cent. For Chile, excluding the nitrate and copper companies, government ownership holds 75.9 per cent of the capital and reserves of the ten largest enterprises and 68.3 per cent of those of the top twenty concerns. In Brazil, the equivalent ratios are 78.1 per cent (for the top ten enterprises) and 68.2 per cent (for the top twenty); while in Venezuela, excluding the petroleum companies, the extent of state ownership is 87.7 per cent and 77.8 per cent, respectively. Even in Colombia, where the interventionist pattern of neo-orthodoxy has not been quite so fully developed, public-sector equity investments account for 69.4 per cent of the capital reserves of the ten largest concerns (again excluding petroleum) and for 58.9 per cent of those of the twenty largest enterprises.[9] While in some few cases publicly owned enterprises are under private management, most are managed directly by the state or by autonomous state corporations. Furthermore, in all of these cases and in others as well, the governmental guidance represented by the enterprises of the public sector has commonly been extended by a vast network of regulatory intervention to encompass very nearly all aspects of national economic life.

Much less commonly, it must be said, has there been an equally critical scrutiny of the leadership capacity of the public sector,[10] of the problems of misspent government savings, and of the difficulties produced by public enterprises operating with neither market nor fiscal discipline. Rarer still has it been fully recognized that the significance of an amply defined latitude for government intervention must be seen in the light of a rather restricted access to governmental decision-making processes. Instead, there has been discernible a pronounced tendency on the part of many spokesmen of the new policy style to fall captive to the arresting vision of the salvific state and to leave such questions to the side, either largely unexplored or else discussed in writings of sibylline obscurity.[11] Yet while the leadership capacity of the public sector is certainly open to question, one may in justice ask if that of the private sector has been any better.

Finally, the spread of a latitudinarian attitude regarding state intervention has not sprung directly from ECLA doctrines. Quite often, in fact, the use of the ECLA thesis has served only to rationalize interventionist measures that would have been taken anyway, or to make them more respectable. While ECLA has frequently been viewed as the great villain who has destroyed "free enterprise" in Latin America, there is little in the historical record to support the view. More creature than creator, the regional commission has, in the main, merely reflected and articulated a doctrinal position which long antedated its appearance on the contemporary policy scene.

THE GEOGRAPHICAL INCIDENCE OF THE NEW POLICY STYLE

To describe more specifically the policy trends and institutional innovations which together have made up the neo-orthodox development style as well as to provide some indication of its prevalence in Latin America, a summary account of its appearance in various countries is appropriate. Of these national instances of its occurrence, three in particular have been selected for a more detailed discussion in the belief that each of the cases chosen is especially illustrative of certain features of the new policy course. In part, this is so because in all three countries it may be said that the neo-orthodox policy synthesis has received a particularly ample expression, perhaps to a degree equaled only in Brazil among the rest of the Latin American nations.[12] Hence, the very fullness of this evolution of economic policy and practice provides, as it were, a helpful map of the phenomena which elsewhere have been less completely developed. Throughout each country case, note references will indicate the appearance of similar policy changes elsewhere on the continent. Yet, among the three cases there have also been notable differences—in emphasis, in surrounding circumstances, and in outcome—and these too are, for present purposes, instructive.

In the case of Uruguay, the first of the three, the political impetus behind neo-orthodoxy stands out clearly. Without excessive simplification, the case may be constructed as a conflict which pitted the city (especially the dominant metropolis) against the countryside, although the eventual resolution of the dialectic contained concessions to rural interests in the name of national development. Of the several interwoven themes of the new policy style, the welfare and national control aspects seem to have predominated in the Uruguayan setting. A developmental drive and industrialization, though present, have tended to occupy a secondary position. Finally, the Uruguayan experience demonstrates unusually well a major limitation of the neo-orthodox development route: namely, the restricted development possibilities which result from efforts to launch a self-contained growth process upon a not very diversified natural resource base and a small national market.

The second case, that of the Argentine, shares a number of common elements with the Uruguayan experience. But south of the River Plate the transition to a new mode of public policy was delayed, while the stakes involved in the contest between old and new were substantially higher. Correspondingly, the lines of stress and tension in interclass and international relationships were greatly intensified—to the point, in fact, that the country resorted to an authoritarian political regime in order to maintain temporarily a semblance of national cohesion. Furthermore, when the shift finally came, the process of domestic industrialization, with its concomitant effects on socio-economic structure, was already far more advanced than it had been in Uruguay when that country broke with the past.

For this reason, and because of the larger Argentine resource base and internal market, national industrial development entered much more centrally into the policy deliberations and concerns of the government in Buenos Aires than it did in the official circles of Montevideo. Indeed, all the circumstances together interacted to produce a distinct exaggeration of both the industrial orientaion of public policy and nationalistic motivation, as well as of the problems encountered in reconciling divergent class interests sufficiently to produce a social consensus capable of sustaining public policy on a reasonably stable basis. Nearly all of the other countries of Latin

America have shared these characteristics in varying degree, but by virtue of their exaggerated manifestation in Argentina, it is relatively easier there to identify the developmental policy deficiencies which have sprung from such sources.

The case of Chile, the third one to be singled out for extended consideration, involves a country which stands somewhere between the first two examples in several respects. As the second Latin American country to opt for the new policy synthesis, its encounter with the problems of transition has been more gradual and its domestic and international relationships less stressful than in Argentina, although not so gradual or so smooth as in Uruguay—at least up to the present time. At the same time, owing to its minerals and power resources, the size of its internal market, and the fact that the nation embarked upon the new policy course after the First World War had provided an initial stimulation for domestic manufacturing growth, the Chilean commitment to an industrial orientation in development policy has been significantly stronger than the Uruguayan, though less frenetic than the Argentine.

Behind all of these aspects lies Chile's long involvement in the nineteenth-century pattern of world economic expansion. For a combination of reasons, then, the Chilean version of the new policy style has been more comprehensive in the scope of its objectives than the Uruguayan version and more matured or more fully evolved than the Argentine. Indeed, considering both of these dimensions, it may be taken as the most complete statement of the neo-orthodox development framework in Latin America. As such, the pervasiveness of its interventionist features affords an example of almost every policy element which has subsequently been employed elsewhere on the continent.

The most significant limitation on the illustrative usefulness of these cases stems from the fact that none of the three countries, thanks to the composition of their population, has had to cope with a serious internal problem of cultural dualism. Though rural Chile more closely approximates such a dualism than do the other two nations, even there the situation stands at a considerable distance from, say, that of its Andean neighbors to the north, or of Mexico or Guatemala. Yet it may reasonably be contended that this limitation does not in any important way detract from suitability for purposes of examining the chief aspects of the neo-orthodox policy framework. The reason is simply that nowhere in the Latin American experience with this framework is there any convincing indication that it contains the significant elements of an answer for this problem.

URUGUAY

Curiously enough, it was in Uruguay where state control first sprang once again into the ascendant. A country which in no small part owed its national existence to the desire of commercially important foreign powers to maintain an independent buffer between Brazil and Argentina in the rich Platine precincts, its pastoral economy had, despite the checkered internal political life of the nation, participated extensively during the latter part of the nineteenth century in the rapid commercialization and expansion which transformed the resources of the south Atlantic coast of Latin America. As in other areas, the growth of the export-oriented sheep and cattle industries had occurred within a context of a latifundian land-tenure system. Because of the suitability of much of the limited land area for livestock pursuits, the enclosure-type movement associated with the rise of commercial ranching on an extensive basis precipitated a migration of rural workers into the towns and cities of the land, especially to Montevideo, the capital. There the rural migrants were mingled with the large new wave of immigrants from Europe who had come to the country, attracted to the employment opportunities created by foreign investments in utilities and meat packing and by the generally fast tempo of trading activity.

With passage of the tariff law of 1875—an act which reversed the liberal, revenue-oriented customs law of 1861 and which provided protective duties for goods which could be produced in Uruguay while exempting from duties imports brought in for domestic processing [13]—the structure of the urban economy had taken on a new character. New factories appeared in food processing, shoe and woollen-goods manufacturing, furniture making, leather working, and the like. Again, the focus of these developments was chiefly upon the politically strategic area of Montevideo, where civic life was increasingly influenced by the intellectual and ideological perceptions held by the new immigrants and their offspring. By 1900 almost a third of the total Uruguayan population resided in the capital city. Thus, while the older economic interests associated with exporting and importing by no means ceded their position of dominance without contest and, in fact, resisted on several occasions the policy drift implied in the 1875 tariff legislation, the balance of political power was changing in favor of the urban sector with its new preoccupations and concerns and its self-assertive bourgeoisie and newly organized workers. By 1903, when José Batlle y Ordóñez was elected to his first term, the transfer of authority to the new socio-economic sectors was almost complete. Although a civil war soon ensued, it ended in defeat for the conservative opposition. By the second Batlle administration, 1911-1915, the way was open for the reform program to begin in earnest. [14]

To reduce economic inequality by measures favoring consumers and workers, to diminish foreign economic control, and (in lesser measure) to promote internal development—such were the principal goals of the new regime. Inasmuch as the implementation of these objectives was representative of the pioneering effort in Latin America to devise a new policy style, it is worth noting the particular forms the program of change assumed.

In line with the government's commitment to new ideals of social justice, and to build a popular base of political support, early in the second Batlle administration, measures were introduced to facilitate labor's right to organize, as were minimum wage laws, an eight-hour day, a system of old-age pensions, regulations of working conditions, severance pay provisions, and a workmen's compensation program. Although administrative capacity was not sufficient at the time to insure a comprehensive enforcement of all these measures, nevertheless new ground had been broken in a field which later was to include such innovations as unemployment compensation, paid vacations, and family allowances. In 1943 the industrial Wage Councils, composed of government, management, and labor representatives, were established on an ad hoc basis to settle wage demands and handle other problems in labor-management relations.[15] Significantly, the inauguration of the new policy style elsewhere in Latin America has almost always commenced with just such an activation of the labor movement and the introduction of similar types of social legislation. And even where it has proved impossible to realize immediately these changes on a comprehensive basis in actual practice, as in the Uruguayan experience, the start toward their enforcement has usually begun with the larger urban-industrial firms, particularly those under foreign ownership—a practice which has linked the welfare aspect of intervention with the correlative goal of controlling foreign interests.

With the twin objectives of combatting foreign domination in the economy and of benefiting consumers through lower charges for services, the Batlle government also, in 1911, created the State Insurance Bank (Banco de Seguros), an entity which was empowered to write fire, life, and marine insurance at low rates, and later, to handle the several social insurance programs and the workmen's compensation scheme. As of 1926 the Insurance Bank was granted a national monopoly of several categories of risks; and while old-line private companies (of which several were foreign) continued to do business in a number of areas, the state enterprise gradually came to occupy an overwhelmingly dominant position in the insurance field.

A further effort to aid consumers, and to promote certain developmental objectives at the same time, came in 1912, when the government set up the State Mortgage Bank (Banco Hipotecario). Initially designed to finance home purchases, the bank later undertook to make mortgage financing available to small businesses and to promote the growth of small farm ownership, both on an individual basis and in colonization programs.[16] In this the Mortgage Bank was adding still further to the supply of lower-cost state credit available to businesses, for the first-established of the three state banks, the Bank of the Republic (Banco de la República), had all along been conducting, as it conducts to this day, a commercial banking business. A major source of loans for rural producers and the depository of the bulk of individual savings accounts, the Bank of the Republic had been chartered in 1896 as a mixed enterprise and converted to a state corporation in 1903. From that year on, it functioned as the sole bank of issue and as the fiscal agent and depository of the government in addition to its commercial banking activities. In 1931 and subsequently the Bank of the Republic also administered the foreign exchange regulatory system. On the whole the state banks appear to have done a reasonably good job of providing banking and insurance services to the entire country, although the considerable, and possibly undue, expansion of private commercial banking facilities in recent times has made this less important and there is now a great need for the Bank of the Republic to exercise stronger central banking controls over the entire credit system to cope more effectively with inflationary conditions.

To furnish low-cost utility services and ostensibly to promote the electrification of the Uruguayan hinterland, the state enterprise in electric light and power (Administración de Usinas y Teléfonos del Estado, or UTE), which had been established in 1889 and granted monopoly rights for the Montevideo market in 1906, was given in 1912 the exclusive right to sell electric energy in the whole nation.[17] Thereafter, the profits earned by UTE from sales in Montevideo (at prices which have not been particularly low) were used to extend service to the rural areas, although rural light and power services generally continued to be more expensive and of poorer quality than in the city. Eventually becoming the largest of the state companies, the UTE took, in recent decades, a leading role in developing the country's hydroelectric power resources. By operating, as a whole, on a profit-making and technically efficient basis, it remained, along with the banks, among the financially stronger of the approximately two dozen autonomous economic agencies of the state, most of which have constituted a drain on the fiscal system.

The creation of UTE also signaled a changed attitude toward foreign-owned public utilities and industries in general. In 1915 the telephone system was taken over as a public corporation (the postal and telegraph services having been state owned and operated since 1877), and the first governmentally constructed railway was built to compete with an existing British railway company. Not until 1948, however, the year after nationalization of the British-owned tramway company of Montevideo, was the rail system completely nationalized and placed under the jurisdiction of the National Railways (Ferrocarriles Nacionales) agency. Long before, however, a favorite project of the Batlle political group had finally been implemented as a check against the foreign meat-processing companies operating in Uruguay: the organization in 1928 of the State Meat Packing Plant (Frigorífico Nacional). Thereupon, the State Meat Packing Plant was given a preferred position in supplying the home market in hopes of raising prices to producers while lowering the prices paid by the consumers. But poorly administered, the plant required substantial subsidies from the government and never really succeeded in accomplishing either of its main objectives.

Shortly after the venture into meat packing, in 1931 the National Administration of Fuels, Alcohol, and Cement (ANCAP) was organized to monopolize the importation of those goods, although in practice the agency has dealt principally in the importation, refining, and distribution of petroleum products, with some local drilling for oil as well.[18] Apart from this, ANCAP operated mainly as an importer of cement and coal for governmental use. Financially solvent, the enterprise has generally conducted its business in an efficient manner.

Throughout the years, there were also scattered efforts to use the power of the state of promote domestic development, even though this objective was generally less prominent than other policy goals. The previously mentioned lending policies of the state banks worked somewhat to this end, as did, of course, the rural electrification and hydroelectric power development programs of the UTE. Moreover, quite early (1916) the government sought to attract more shipping business by organizing the port works of Montevideo as a public corporation which could keep port charges low—although in subsequent years the record of the port authority was, to say the least, undistinguished. To supplement these measures, however, the state moved even further, both through regulatory intervention and through direct participation. With respect to the former mode of promotion, the tariff law of 1912 reasserted strongly the protectionist trend which had been in evidence during the last quarter of the nineteenth century, and added to the tariff shield a variety of tax exemptions and exemptions from duties on imported producer goods (raw materials, intermediate products, and capital goods) for the purpose of giving still further encouragement to domestic manufacturers.[19]

Since 1912, in fact, protectionism has been a continuing feature of Uruguayan public policy, for thereafter tariffs were seldom adjusted in any other way than upward.[20] During the thirties, yet another instrument of development guidance was fashioned when the exchange control and import licensing regulations which were set up (initially on a temporary basis) to deal with balance-of-payments problems began to assume a more permanent character.[21] By their manipulation, public authority acquired new means of subsidizing the growth of favored lines of production—as when relatively unfavorable exchange rates were applied to export sales of raw wool in hopes of encouraging the domestic processing thereof and the exportation of manufactured woollens.[22] Yet, though multiple exchange rates were generally manipulated to favor import-substitution industrialization, they also, for years, were used to discriminate strongly against types of agricultural exports in which Uruguay had a comparative advantage, a practice which ultimately did much to undermine the strength of the economy.

To provide more direct assistance to domestic development, the government formed in 1911 the State Fishing Institute (Servicio Oceanográfico y de Pesca, or SOYP) and in 1912 the Institute of Industrial Chemistry (Instituto de Química Industrial). Originally conceived as research and training agencies, both institutes eventually branched out into production and distribution activities. Beginning in the 1920's, the chemical institute initiated the first production of what was, over the years, to become a varied line of fertilizers, sheep dip, insecticides, and basic industrial chemicals such as sulfuric acid and caustic soda. On the whole, the state chemical industry appears to have been a reasonably profitable undertaking. Less successful was the record of SOYP. As the largest fishing enterprise in the nation, SOYP has been, since 1937, operating fishing fleets and fish processing and marketing facilities—but almost continually at a loss. On the other hand, another almost contemporaneous excursion of the state into the production of goods met with somewhat better fortune, for the government-organized monopoly, the National Milk Producers Cooperative, which replaced the private dairy firms expropriated by the state in 1935, apparently made some headway in increasing the supply of milk and milk products while achieving productivity gains in the processing of these goods.[23]

On balance, the different elements of the post-Batlle programs have varied considerably in their impact. Some of the new autonomous entities and decentralized agencies have operated effectively, the most notable case being, perhaps, the UTE which has succeeded in almost doubling the installed electric generating capacity of Uruguay in the years since World War II. Others, such as the National Railways, accomplished little or nothing of merit and even, through operating losses, became a source of inflationary pressure in the economy. Taken as a whole, therefore, it cannot be said that the new Uruguayan policies were an unqualified economic success.

To the country's credit, however, the result has been a socio-economic system in which welfare and security elements have helped to reduce social tensions and to support and enlarge the middle class, a development helped along also by the increased (but probably excessive) number of public functionaries and by the comprehensiveness of the Uruguayan educational system. The degree of institutional stability achieved was exceptional, at least until the 1960's, and the country enjoys what is probably the most equitable internal distribution of income in Latin America. Considering the conditions which prevail throughout most of the continent, it must be recognized that these accomplishments are far from negligible.

On the other hand, the end result to date may also be appropriately described as stagnation at what, by Latin American standards, is a relatively high level of per capita income; for from the standpoint of economic development, the policy course begun in the early years of this century has reached a dead end in recent times. Since 1957, in fact, the per capita gross domestic product has been falling by almost 2 per cent a year, the chief sustaining feature in this decline being the unusually low rate of population growth.

Manufacturing, which in 1945-1954 expanded with some rapidity, at a cumulative annual rate of 8.5 per cent on the average, later ceased to play a significant role in leading the economy forward. Between 1954 and 1962, for example, the rate of growth in manufacturing output was less than $\frac{1}{2}$ per cent per annum. And in spite of the barriers placed in the way of importations from abroad, the unmistakable evidence of saturated conditions in the exiguous internal market made it impossible to attract more than a quite modest amount of foreign investment in manufacturing. Neither does there appear to be much immediate likelihood of relaxing this restraint on national industrial growth by expanding manufactured exports, for the means by which the industrial sector was built up in the first place have resulted in a pattern of manufacturing enterprise characterized by small, high-cost producers. Indeed, owing to the introduction of security-inspired make-work policies aimed at relieving unemployment, the productivity per worker employed in industry has even tended to fall in recent years. As a consequence, in contrast to the relationship which generally obtains in most Latin American countires, the Uruguayan industrial work force, which includes 23 per cent of the economically active population, generates only 19 per cent of the gross domestic product.

Even the widespread welfare system—which was, perhaps, the major achievement of the reform-minded government—became a source of considerable difficulty, as a recent ILO study made plain, owing to the complexity of the schemes, the division of programs among several administrative institutions with overlapping activities, and general mismanagement. Avoidance of contributions, favoritism in the distribution of benefits, frequent duplication of payments, the payment of unemployment compensation to many people who are in fact working, and the rather low age requirements for eligibility for several types of payments have impaired the effectiveness of the welfare schemes, while depletion of funds by the central government and high administrative costs have brought several parts of the system to the verge of bankruptcy.

Meanwhile, the hope of Batlle and his followers that somehow their largely urban-centered reform program would eventually, if indirectly, promote agricultural change and progress never materialized. And in the absence of constructive public policies for the rural sector, the potentially high productivity of that segment of the economy remained untapped; agricultural technology failed to progress and for many years actual disinvestment in agriculture may well have occurred. For the past thirty years agricultural production has been practically stationary; its 1.6 per cent annual growth rate ranks as one of the lowest rates of increase in agricultural output in the hemisphere. Inasmuch as a partially subsidized domestic consumption was rising at the same time, especially in Montevideo, the exportable agricultural surplus, long the mainstay of the Uruguayan external sector, gradually dwindled away, so that by the early 1950's less than 30 per cent of the total production in the agricultural sector was available for export. Revealingly, although between 1950 and 1960 both the volume and the aggregate value of Uruguayan exports declined, the drop in volume substantially exceeded the fall in value.

From 1954 on, every year brought a deficit on current account and a threatening increase in short-term foreign liabilities. Within a decade, therefore, the precarious condition of the nation's balance of payments left no further room for doubt that the time had come for a thorough reassessment of the policy course which in prior decades had seemed so innovational. Welfare interventionism, valuable as it was in its own right, would finally have to be joined with a stronger admixture of developmental objectives.

ARGENTINA [24]

For many years the Uruguayan policy model, the main features of which were already evident by the time of the First World War, stood unique in Latin America although for a brief period it seemed that there might be some prospects for a similar line of development in neighboring Argentina when the Radical government of Yrigoyen came to power in 1916. Based largely upon the urban middle class and expressing a sympathetic concern for the problems of the working class, the new administration seemed to evince a political complexion not unlike that which brought Batlle to the presidency in Montevideo. Its inauguration, consequently, took place amid enthusiasm and high hopes. Yet those who expected better things to come were very soon undeceived.

A few laws were enacted to facilitate the organization of labor, and retirement funds were established through new social legislation. But much of the industrial goodwill (to use Commons' helpful concept) which might have been gained thereby was dissipated in the harsh and sanguinary measures the government employed to suppress the strikes which broke out in early 1919. In another field of economic endeavor, the State Tanker Fleet was organized in 1921 to handle oil shipments for the State Petroleum Enterprise (the Yacimientos Petrolíferos Fiscales), which in turn was formed to operate the oil fields formerly developed by the Bureau of Mines. Beyond this, however, the achievements of the government were minimal or worse. Throughout the Radical era, which ended with rioting and a coup d'etat in 1930, machine politics were combined with the autocratic personalism of the president and a scramble for the spoils of office to produce a period noted for its corruption, administrative chaos, and general governmental irresponsibility. The administrative incapability of the new group in power, a condition which, at least in part, was a function of the inexperience of the new people brought into the government, made it impossible to move forward toward the desired reforms.

In retrospect, it seems highly probable that the inability of the Radical administrations to make good on promises of reform was an important factor in explaining the intensity of the public policy changes which finally came to Argentina in the forties with the advent of *Peronismo*. Meanwhile, there was to be further frustration of popular expectations when, from 1930 to 1943, the discredited middle-class Radical leadership gave way, and conservative oligarchic rule was restored. Thereupon, labor-movement activity was curtailed, discussion of reform was muted, and election procedures were rigged (as they had also been by the Radicals) so as to render ineffective the voices of political opposition.

Nevertheless, it is not without significance that even under the guidance of the conservative governments of the thirties there was a gradual movement away from the observance of market economics, thanks at least in part to the exigencies of coping with the depression. Exchange controls were adopted in 1931, and although they were later relaxed as the economic recovery of the mid-thirties took place, quantitative trade controls were applied with increasing frequency. Behind the shelter of the new trade controls, domestic industrialization gain considerable momentum; and in such lines as woollen textiles, vegetable oils, chemicals and pharmaceuticals, electric light globes, and rubber and aluminum products there was registered a quite marked expansion. Of the 57,957 industrial firms reporting in the 1941 industrial census, some 40 per cent had been established between 1931 and 1941. In the fields of agriculture and trade, new organs of public intervention were formed with the creation of national regulatory commissions for sugar (1929), quebracho extract (1933), meat (1934), dairying (1934), edible oils (1934), yerba maté (1935), and cotton (1935). Even the vital grain business came in for control when the National Grain Board (Junta Reguladora de Granos) was set up in 1933. At first established on a temporary basis, the regulatory functions of the agency were renewed and augmented in 1940.[25]

Under conservative rule, a start was also made in purchasing the rundown British-owned railways, and additional leverage was gained over the railway companies when the government instituted a large-scale national program of highway construction. The highway program, incidentally, provided such a strong stimulus to the growth of the domestic cement industry that by 1939 Argentina's eleven cement plants were producing about two million metric tons of cement annually, almost half of the total Latin American production. In the field of finance, finally, the Central Bank was created as a semi-autonomous institution in 1934 to increase the efficacy of monetary policy.

At the same time, however, there was enough of the traditional external orientation in the conservative program to insure that when the eventual reaction came it would take on an aggressively nationalistic character. For example, during the Justo administration of 1932-1938, generous—and widely unpopular—concessions were made (not without the odor of corruption) to foreign capital interests, among them the French-controlled port company of Rosario, the Belgian-owned light and power company in Buenos Aires, and in an especially provocative case, the British-owned tramway company in Buenos Aires. The last-mentioned of these was, moreover, outstandingly ill conceived, since it was exacted as part of the price for British consent to renewal of the Roca-Runciman pact of 1933, an agreement which had already generated much adverse public response at the time it was negotiated. Seldom in Latin American history, in fact, were the implications of economic imperialism so nakedly revealed.[26] As a consequence, the later nationalization of foreign utility and railway companies as well as the strident controversy of the late 1950's and early 1960's concerning foreign petroleum concessions were, politically speaking, foreordained in spite of the negative repercussions these measures were to have in the domestic economic situation.

Together then, these conditions—the long containment of social structural changes and the Esau-like transactions with foreign economic powers—contributed to the formation of the new policy style which rapidly took shape after 1943 and which was subsequently to be christened with the name of *justicialismo*. Between 1943 and 1955, the development approach which was pioneered in Uruguay reached its zenith in the Argentine, although within the compass of the Second Five Year Plan (prepared for 1953-1957) and associated legislation there was already a distinct veering back toward the path of economic orthodoxy.

Recognizing the political potential latent in the confused and splintered Argentine labor movement, the Peronist leadership began its work with a display of solicitude for the working class. Older social legislation, such as the forty-hour work week which had been passed in 1933, was rigorously enforced for the first time, and new welfare legislation was added in such areas as minimum wages, workmen's compensation, paid holidays, medical benefits, and dismissal indemnities. A number of the benefits of this legislation were even extended to full-time and part-time agricultural workers, an occurrence sufficiently rare in Latin America to deserve being recorded. For tenant farmers and sharecroppers, protective measures were also enacted. During 1944-1945, a National Social Security Institute was formed to administer the advanced social insurance programs which were being introduced, including pension systems with cost-of-living escalation provisions. A decade later in 1954, by which time the regime was in other respects adopting a less benevolent attitude toward labor, the pension schemes were vastly expanded to cover rural and independent workers as well as employers. Eventually, the accumulation of social charges amounted to at least 60 per cent of the direct wage bill in many lines of employment;

but if this created certain problems in some parts of the economy, it was also, owing to the substantial margin of in-payments over out-payments in the system, an important source of savings for financing other aspects of the government program.

With strong governmental encouragement, unionization was pushed into sectors of industry which were previously unorganized, and even the organization of rural workers was aided. Concurrently, however, on the basis of various devices such as the power of the government to grant or withhold legal recognition of unions, and its power to "intervene" workers groups (by substituting government administrators for union officials),[27] independent and anti-Peronist worker organizations were gradually undermined or eliminated, and most of the recognized unions were gathered together in the Confederación General del Trabajo (CGT), the comprehensive central labor confederation.[28] While on the one hand this regrouping of the labor movement rendered it more amenable to governmental control, there were, at least up to the early 1950's, many advantages to labor in the arrangement. Throughout this time, the Secretariat (later Ministry) of Labor and Social Welfare intervened extensively in collective bargaining to effect settlements favorable to the workers. Meanwhile, the spread of industrial development, itself a prime public-policy objective, contributed still further to an improvement in the real income accruing to labor.

With the labor movement enlisted in support of the administration, the government soon turned its attention to organizing other groups as a means of extending the influence of the state. Organized interest groups had of course existed in Argentina for a long time, and the three most powerful— the Sociedad Rural, the Unión Industrial, and the Cámara Argentina de Comercio—together constituted a broader associational front known as the Asociación de Instituciones y Entidades Libres (ACIEL). These had not always, however, been notably well disposed toward the philosophy and policies of the government, and their considerable strength was at least potentially a challenge to the directive authority of the state in domestic economic matters. Against them, the Peronist-dominated labor movement afforded some leverage, while the old, established state banks inherited by the Perón regime could also be employed to advantage in steering the economy: the National Mortgage Bank (Banco Nacional Hipotecario) and the vast Bank of the Argentine Nation (Banco de la Nación Argentina), which functioned in part as state banks for the agricultural sector.[29] Moreover, from its inception the government had at its disposition the whole array of foreign exchange and trade controls—e.g., multiple exchange rates, import and exchange licensing requirements, a multiple-column tariff system—which had been evolved by previous administrations. All of these could be drawn upon to build an organizational constituency for the regime.

For agriculture, the chosen instrument was the cooperative, the formation of which was promoted by preferential treatment in both the allocation of scarce items such as tractors and other farm machinery and in the lending policies of the state banks.[30] From 1948 to 1953, for instance, the loans made to the growing number of agricultural cooperatives increased approximately twenty times. As it happened, given the intrasectoral distribution of cooperative associations, this meant that official resources were being channeled primarily into that segment of the rural sector which produced for the home market rather than into the segment which traditionally furnished the major export staples. Additional encouragement for the cooperative movement came in 1951 when the government declared its intention of eventually dismantling its large state trading enterprise, IAPI, and of turning IAPI's marketing functions over to the cooperatives of the agricultural sector, although as things turned out, this never came to pass.

During the same general period, with the ostensible purpose of setting up bargaining groups for negotiations with trade unions, the government began also to build rapport with elements among employer interests by promoting the organization of what in some respects was or came to be a parallel group of associations rivaling the ACIEL cluster. Within the new Confederación General Económica (CGE), as the overall entity was designated, there were formed as counterparts to the old-line associations the Confederación de la Producción (in agriculture), the Confederación de la Industria, and the Confederación del Comercio.[31]

Apart from the foregoing moves, the Perón regime embarked quite early upon a campaign to establish the preeminence of the state in Argentine economic life by attempting what elsewhere might have been called a "socialization of the commanding heights of the economy." To compensate for the inadequacies of the rail and highway systems and to gain a degree of leverage over the private shipping companies operating on the important Paraná River route, the government created in 1944 the State Fleet, thereby adding to the State Tanker Fleet which had been formed in the 1920's and to the State Merchant Marine (Flota Mercante del Estado) which had been acquired in 1941 when the government expropriated over two dozen foreign ships which were then in Argentine ports. A few years later, in 1949, the Perón administration extended its role in water transport further by placing under government ownership the large overseas and river fleet belonging to the Dodero Lines, an Argentine company which had bought the shipping enterprise from British investors in 1931. Two other, smaller private shipping lines were also nationalized in 1949.[32] Though given preferential treatment under the foreign trade regulatory system, the Merchant Marine nevertheless operated at a loss and required substantial subsidies from the state.

The year 1944 also brought the beginnings of a larger state role in the financial sector when the State Industrial Bank (Banco Industrial de Argentina) was established, which was to become virtually the sole source of medium- and long-term financing for small- and medium-sized manufacturing firms. Two years later the Central Bank—which had been created in 1934 as a semi-autonomous institution, directed by a board made up for the most part of representatives from the large foreign banks in Buenos Aires—was nationalized and placed in control over the three other state banks and all commercial banks.

Concurrently, the Argentine Institute of Reinsurance was established, first as a mixed company excluding foreign firms from participation (Instituto Mixto Argentino de Reaseguros) and later as a wholly owned state enterprise (Instituto Nacional de Reaseguros). Its function was to nationalize most of the country's reinsurance business and, by so doing, to prevent the export of reinsurance profits. Domestic insurance companies, which were given preferential tax treatment over foreign firms, were obliged to do all their reinsuring with the Institute, while all companies doing business with the government were, in turn, required to engage domestic firms to write their insurance. Foreign insurance companies were required to transact at least 30 per cent of their reinsurance business with the Institute, which was also empowered to write direct insurance in fields where a private market did not exist.

Even bolder than the 1944 interventions in transport and finance was a measure which enabled the state to take a decisive role in shaping relationships in the all-important external sector: the expropriation as public utilities of the large grain elevator companies of Buenos Aires and La Plata which had traditionally held a key position in the marketing of Argentine exports. As in transport and finance, this too was but the point of departure for a further extension of state control, for in 1946 the Argentine Institute for Promotion of Trade (Instituto Argentino de Promoción del Intercambio, or IAPI) was established. At first, its chief authorization was to monopolize the handling of wheat exports, in which connection the National Grain and Elevator Institute which grew out of the 1944 expropriation was converted into an IAPI subsidiary. Very soon thereafter, however, it assumed control of the foreign sales of other staple exports, including meat (through another IAPI subsidiary, the National Meat Institute). In addition, IAPI began to operate as a major importer of a variety of goods needed in the new development program: ships, tractors, vehicles, machinery and equipment, iron, copper, newsprint, sugar, rubber, and the like. As late as 1953, some 63 per cent of the country's exports and 20 per cent of its imports were handled on IAPI account.

As might be expected, the prominence of IAPI made it a target for criticism, and it was saddled with much of the blame for the ills which beset the economy throughout the life of the agency. For the first half-decade of its existence, IAPI's trading profits were substantial and constituted an important source of financing for much of the government's program, including retirement of the foreign debt. Its profits, in turn, derived from the wide spread the state trading company was able to maintain, as the sole exporter of the main agricultural lines, between the foreign sales prices (which were rising in the 1940's) of its goods and the low prices it paid the domestic producers of these items. Until commodity prices turned downward in the early fifties, IAPI was in a position to capture as its profit a considerable portion of the net income of the rural export sector. So great, in fact, was its monopsonistic levy that the disincentive effects seem to have contributed to the deterioration which was then in evidence in export agriculture and ranching, though, for the sake of explantory completeness, it must be recognized that other factors were also undermining the export sector: adverse weather conditions, the increasing shortage and costliness of rural labor, and the difficulty (and costliness) of obtaining adequate supplies of agricultural producer goods because of the preference accorded manufacturing sector imports throughout the late 1940's.

It was also true that a rising domestic consumption of the staples of the export trade was cutting into the exportable surplus, while there may have been, in addition, some shifts by rural firms away from the production of exportable commodities, whose prices were held at low levels by IAPI, and into the production of other commodities for which the domestic market provided a strong and growing demand. In any event, in the early fifties IAPI attempted to repair the damage to local production which had been caused by its previous low buying prices and began to raise the prices it paid farmers and ranchers for exportable commodities. But since this change in the agency's domestic purchasing policies coincided with the decline in export prices, the result was a deficit in IAPI operations which had to be covered by large governmental subsidies. From then on, the IAPI controversy merged with the debate over inflation.

All the while that it was extending state control over domestic interests, the government was engaged in radical economic surgery to reduce the influence of foreign capital in the economy. Foreign-held bonds were redeemed, and drawing upon the country's substantial accrual of foreign earnings, the government launched a nationalization spree which was perhaps unequaled in Latin America until the Castro regime was installed in Cuba, although, in all fairness, it should be noted that contemporary British restrictions on foreign-owned sterling balances limited, for the time being, the alternative uses of a substantial portion of the Argentine foreign exchange reserves. Once again it was 1944 which contained the portents of things to come. The nationalization in that year of the British-owned gas company of Buenos Aires was swiftly followed by the purchase of several provincial utility companies which were subsidiaries of the American and Foreign Power Company. In 1946 the same treatment was applied to the telephone systems of the country. Two years later, the mostly British-owned railways—which for many years had been in a dilapidated state—likewise passed into government ownership, to be used thereafter, through the substantial expansion of employment on the railways, as a means of providing public relief to the supporters of the regime. By the end of the 1940's, in short, the foreign debt had been retired, and the major traditional foreign equity interests in the economy (exclusive of the meat-packing concerns) had been liquidated.

However understandable these measures were at the time in terms of the government's basic commitment to economic nationalism and in the light of twentieth-century Argentine political history, this lavish use of foreign exchange reserves to effect a large-scale repatriation of foreign capital was, along with the discriminatory treatment of agriculture, a most serious economic error of the regime. For that matter, even the fancied emancipation of the economy from foreign control which was sought through these means turned out to be ephemeral. With the exhaustion of the nation's foreign reserves, the illusory character of "economic indepedence" quickly became manifest as the level of foreign indebtedness began to rise again, reaching eight hundred million dollars by the end of the Perón era.

Whatever the wisdom, or lack of it, in the policies outlined in the foregoing paragraphs, at least one objective had been achieved: that of subjugating economic interests (though not economic forces) to the power of the state. Within this new national economic structure, however, direct investment by the government was, aside from the governmentally controlled utility and transport companies and the petroleum industry, less than one might have expected, considering the dominant philosophy of *étatisme*. Some of the direct public investment, in fact, came about more through force of circumstances than through deliberate design.

The National Administration of State Industries (Dirección Nacional de Industrias del Estado), for example, was set up in 1947 to operate companies which had been expropriated from their former owners in the Axis Powers during World War II. Other equity investments, amounting eventually to around a billion pesos in corporate securities (many of them of dubious value), were acquired in the course of politically influenced manipulations by the Joint Security Investment Institute, an agency which was established in 1947 for the purpose of moderating the movement of prices in the stock market.[33] Other than these and the various minerals deposits exploited by the National Department of Mines, the state industries consisted mainly of factories run by the armed forces. For example, the State Aeronautical and Mechanical Industries, which operated under the jurisdiction of the Air Force, produced an assortment of motorcycles, cars and trucks, and parts for airplanes, but not on a commercially significant basis. Some sixteen factories and two small blast furnaces (at Zapla), which produced around 40,000 tons of pig iron annually, were operated by the Military Manufactures Administration of the Army.

The most ambitious direct venture of the state into the industrial field, and the one which was most characteristic of the developmental intervention theme in Latin American neo-orthodoxy, did not occur until 1949 when the Sociedad Mixta Siderúrgica Argentina, S.A. (SOMISA) was formed. A mixed enterprise, 80 per cent owned by the government, SOMISA was founded to build and operate a large, completely integrated steel mill at San Nicolás on the Paraná River. With this step, the Argentine government finally began to do what several other countries had by then already been doing; namely, to employ direct public investment as a means of establishing basic industries on which other technologically derivative industries could then be built up. Just as government initiation of basic chemicals industries had elsewhere in Latin America been used as a springboard for the development of, say, fertilizer and plastics plants, in SOMISA the Argentine government was, along with other governments in the hemisphere, pushing the expansion of basic steel works in order that a more widespread development of domestic metalworking industries could take place without running into balance-of-payments difficulties.[34] Unfortunately, severe balance-of-payments difficulties were already near at hand by the time SOMISA was organized. Because of the economic retrenchment occasioned thereby, it was only after the end of the Perón regime that the new mill reached completion and commenced production.

To coordinate the policies of the government, attempts were made beginning in the mid-forties to set up mechanisms for centralized guidance of the economy. At first, the National Postwar Council, and later IAPI, served as the key policy-formation agencies, but in 1947 the directive function was transferred to the newly created National Economic Council. The Council presided over the First Five Year Plan which was promulgated in late 1946 to cover the years 1947-1951. Although the plan was comprehensive in its coverage of various sectors except agriculture, defects in plan preparation and implementation, not to mention financing, resulted in a general failure to achieve many of its objectives. Even so, the program ended by costing some three times the original estimate, in part because of the inflationary pressures generated by the central bank borrowing which was resorted to in an effort to finance the plan. Worse still, the attempt to accomplish more than the administrative and financial capacity of the public sector would permit produced a host of new problems for the economy. What was involved was a fundamental incompatibity between the economic and political goals of the regime, both of which, however, were rooted almost equally deep in the experiences of the 1916-1943 era.

The practical achievements of the 1940's lay mainly in an expansion of hydroelectric generating capacity and in a not altogether viable growth of industry, especially in the light industry sector, continuing the strong surge of manufacturing development which began during the thirties and picked up momentum during World War II. From an annual average of 2,160 million kilowatt hours in the 1935-1939 period, the output of electric energy rose to an annual average of 5,180 million kilowatt hours in the 1950-1954 quinquennium.[35] During this time, according to data contained in the 1939, 1946, and 1954 industrial censuses, the number of registered industrial plants rose from 54,000 in 1939 to 86,000 in 1946 and 152,000 by 1954. The corresponding figures for workers in industrial employment were 620,000 (1939), 917,000 (1946), and 1,056,000 (1954).[36] Light industry figured prominently in this growth as indicated by an ECLA study which shows that from 1935-1939 to 1950-1954 the proportion of imports represented by consumer goods fell from around 34 per cent to just under 13 per cent.[37]

At the same time, as the above-cited figures suggest, between 1946 and 1954 industrial development tended to center, except for a few large projects, on the proliferation of relatively small enterprises; for despite the greatly increased number of registered firms, the accompanying increase in industrial employment was modest. Moreover, a closer look at the time sequence of actual production changes indicates that, for all the vaunted policy emphasis on industrialization, the main period of growth in manufacturing output was actually over by 1947 or 1948. Except for an almost insignificant increase in 1951, which was followed by a decline, the level of output in the manufacturing sector was practically constant from 1947 through 1954. Not until 1955 was there again a meaningful increase.[38] Over the same period, national agricultural output grew much more slowly than industrial output and reached its peak in 1947-1948, with most of the production gains occurring in items consumed in the domestic market. From that point on, however, agricultural output declined until 1953-1955, during which period it recovered to a level only slightly higher than that of 1947-1948. Further, after years of neglect or worse, the agricultural export sector was ill-prepared to cope with the downward slide in export prices which soon began to materialize and which was a chief feature of the decade of the 1950's.

Owing to the ambitious industrialization program which had been set in motion, the import requirements for intermediate goods and capital equipment were considerable. Beyond that, more foreign exchange was needed if the older Argentine manufacturing industries were to modernize. Still additional amounts of imports would have been called for had there been any serious effort made to raise production and productivity in the agricultural export sector in order to put that portion of the economy in a position to earn the wherewithal for the development program.

Finally, much of the Argentine infrastructure, including almost the entire railway system (which had suffered at least two decades of disinvestment), was in urgent need of expensive and extensive rehabilitation, in connection with which heavy foreign currency expenditures would have been incurred. In short, it was precisely during a period in which the implications of national growth pointed to the necessity of increasing the external resources available to the economy that the political objectives of the government compelled it to engage instead in capital exportation. By the same token, the nationalization of railways and other public utilities forced the Argentine government to assume, in a context of general capital scarcity, the primary responsibility for maintaining and increasing investment in the most capital-intensive sectors of the economy. Given the high cost of capital factors, few other steps could have been taken which would have placed such a heavy burden upon a fiscal system that was none too strong to begin with, once the accumulated wartime balances had been drawn down.

By the early fifties, the penalty for these mistakes—compounded by an adverse movement in the terms of trade—was forcing a different policy course upon the government. The attempt to sacrifice the traditional sources of economic strength to the attainment of novel policy objectives had, in other words, entailed a cost which ultimately was too great for the economy to bear. For want of the foreign exchange which had been used to nationalize foreign investments and for want of the export earnings which a more constructive agricultural policy might have provided, agriculture itself remained seriously undercapitalized, the level of technological obsolescence had risen in much of Argentine manufacturing, and the railways were in worse shape than ever. The latter condition was made especially critical by the fact that the highway contruction program, and even highway maintenance, had not received significant support for years. Indeed, it appeared that the Argentine situation, with its newly developed manufacturing margins encompassing a deteriorating economic core, was essentially a case of a "hollow frontier" pattern of industrialization, to borrow the useful term by which Preston James has characterized the Brazilian pattern of land settlement. Even in the fields of electric power and petroleum, both of which experienced some expansion, output could not keep pace with the demands of the urban-industrial sector, so that power shortages were hampering the efficient operation of industry while rising petroleum imports were placing a heavy strain on the nation's increasingly weak balance-of-payments position. Consequently the failure of the First Five Year Plan, compounded by the problems it and related government policies had created, led to the institution of new policies which were much nearer in conception and orientation to the kind of development approach recommended in conventional economic doctrine.

The Second Five Year Plan, promulgated to cover the years 1953-1957 but canceled with the fall of Perón, made clear this change in course.

In it there was a pronounced de-emphasis of industrialization (excepting, chiefly, the field of agricultural machinery production) as the prime development objective, and a corresponding new emphasis was placed on transport improvement, petroleum expansion, and the revitalization of the export agricultural sector as a means of obtaining the foreign exchange needed for financing developmental imports. In pursuit of these goals, IAPI raised the prices it paid to farmers and ranchers for exportable items; and while credit stringency was applied to industry and commerce, a policy of credit ease was applied to agricultural borrowers. At the same time, the importation of agricultural requisites was facilitated by changes in the administration of the exchange and trade control system. Public works of a social welfare character were assigned a much reduced role, and around 1953 the government began to adopt a less generous attitude toward labor and to speak of the need for greater labor discipline and increased productivity. Wages as well as prices were frozen in the anti-inflation controls introduced during that year. Further, amid more frequent expressions of concern for the well-being of private capital, the government announced its intention to divest itself eventually of many of the state enterprises which had been accumulated through the years. Finally, as if to remove all shadow of doubt about the extent of the public policy revision, a welcome was extended once again to foreign capital, for in August of 1953 a new law was passed to give strong encouragement to foreign investment in industry—especially in motor vehicles, tractors, and of all things, the long sacrosanct petroleum field.[39]

To be sure, the encouragement of foreign investment in secondary industry was not necessarily, of itself, a departure from the policy framework of Latin American neo-orthodoxy; it has in fact been quite common for Latin American nations to encourage foreign investment in this field, even while restricting its access to other sectors of the economy. Moreover, many of the attributes of the neo-orthodox approach were to remain, perhaps indefinitely: the protection of national industry, the social and welfare legislation, the state banks and steel mill, the state-owned public utilities, and some degree of central economic guidance. Yet, the overall set of changes outlined above nevertheless suggested that, for the time being at least, the Argentine version of the new policy style had passed its zenith. Even so, the long period of domestic turbulence which followed, not to mention the subsequent repudiation of the changed treatment of the petroleum industry, demonstrated that a viable alternative would hardly be found by simply embracing a traditional design for development.

CHILE [40]

The same loose political grouping which had brought Batlle to the presidency of Uruguay in 1903 and Yrigoyen to the presidency of Argentina in

1916 was also emerging in Chile by the early part of the present century. There, as in the other two countries, social structure had become somewhat more fluid, urbanized, and Europeanized than in the rest of Latin America. A radicalism similar in inspiration to the parties of Yrigoyen and Batlle had appeared as the preferred philosophy of the Chilean middle class, while Marxist and syndicalist influences were spreading among an urban proletariat which, like its counterparts in Uruguay and Argentina, was less submissive than the labor force of most of the Latin American countries. When the decline of the nitrate industry commenced, bringing with it administrative and financial difficulties for the government, a basic prop of the old regime was undermined. And with the election of Radical-supported Arturo Alessandri in 1920, the era of uncontested upper-class rule was brought to an end. For a few years conservative opposition in the national congress blocked enactment of the legislative program of the new administration, but following a brief intervention by the armed forces, Alessandri returned to office in the mid-twenties with military backing and put through a new constitution (1925) which, by strengthening the power of the executive branch of government, greatly diminished the force of the congressional opponents of reform. Thus began a period in which the economic policy of the nation was to be considerably reshaped

Under the leadership of Carlos Ibáñez, Alessandri's successor in 1927, the new direction of public policy received still shaper definition with the inauguration of a vigorous public works program and the creation of new organs for governmental intervention in the economy. The depression of 1931 brought the downfall of the Ibáñez government and an interlude of turmoil unusual for Chile, during which a short-lived "socialist" government took office. Political order was soon restored, however, as Alessandri returned to the presidency (1932-1938), this time with conservative backing. While the public works program was curtailed rather sharply in the name of fiscal and monetary orthodoxy, this proved to be only temporary, and on the whole the net effect of the "conservative" Alessandri government was to continue the institutional and policy innovation which was ushered in during the 1920's. In the meantime, both the Radical and Democratic Parties moved leftward on the political spectrum, the newly formed (1931) Socialist Party began to grow, the Communists continued to gain strength (particularly in the labor movement), and the Christian Socialists, the predecessors of the Christian Democrats, made their entrance upon the political scene. So strong was the leftward movement, in fact, that in the 1938 elections a Popular Front government came to power. After this broke apart in 1941 because of a falling out among the erstwhile partners in coalition, a variety of center-left coalitions, generally dominated by the Radicals, held control of the government until 1952. From then until the elections of 1964, the political complexion of the executive branch of government drifted back to the right, at first under the second Carlos Ibáñez administration (1952-1958) and later under Jorge Alessandri (1958-1964), a member of the same family as former president of that name.

Between the two Alessandris, however, an irreversible shift had occurred; and at least up until the mid-fifties, behind all the vicissitudes of the political scene, public policy moved falteringly but clearly toward a new synthesis involving substantial economic activity and direction by the state. Thus, although Chile was the third of the major South American nations to move away from the established political moorings, following Uruguay and Argentina in that respect, it was actually the second country to launch the socio-economic policies which had been initially charted in Uruguay. In Chile, unlike Argentina, circumstances were such that there was not the protracted delay between the shift in political alignments and the subsequent realization of that shift in public policy.

As in Uruguay, the Chilean experiment opened on a welfare theme when, in 1924, laws were passed providing for governmental encouragement of consumer cooperatives and, more importantly, a variety of new measures were enacted in the field of labor legislation. Therein, the state began unmistakably to assume the role of the principal integrating mechanism in the Chilean socio-economic system, a function somewhat broader than that of serving as a means for facilitating mutual accommodation among subsidiary groups. Subsequently consolidated in the Labor Code of 1931 and extended by such provisions as minimum wage laws and family allowances, the 1924 sally into public control of employer-worker relationships covered legislation regarding the workers' rights to organize, collective bargaining procedures, strikes, holiday and dismissal pay, and the eight-hour day.[41] Also included was a measure which was later to be widely emulated in Latin America: the requirement that a minimum percentage (75 per cent, later raised to 85 per cent) of the work force of firms operating in Chile should consist of Chilean nationals.[42] The same year saw the beginnings of the social insurance system when laws were passed establishing insurance programs for sickness, disability, and accidents and old-age pensions. What with the thousands of additions and extensions which were made during the following decades, the system, if such it can be called, came by the late 1950's to comprise 52 institutions, including 41 social security funds for different groups in the population and 11 health and welfare organizations.[43] In addition to operating hospitals and food and clothing stores, the system gradually began to acquire investments in certain industrial stocks and came to control both the largest producer of vaccines in the nation (the Instituto Bacteriológico de Chile) and the country's largest medicinal manufacturer (the Laboratorio Chile, S.A.). For the most part, however, after passage of enabling legislation in the mid-thirties as part of an effort to stimulate construction and public works, the considerable reserves of the social security system went into the financing of low-cost public housing and mortgage loans.

Before the decade of the twenties ended, the government had also entered the field of banking and finance. Or perhaps more accurately, it had expanded considerably the small beachhead it already had in that sector since the creation of the Mortgage Credit Institute (Caja de Crédito Hipotecario) in 1855 and the National Savings Bank (Caja Nacional de Ahorros) in 1910.[44] In 1921 the Government Pawn Shop (Caja de Crédito Popular) was opened to make small loans throughout the country and (until 1949 when these were transferred to the National Savings Bank) to accept savings deposits.[45] Four years later the Central Bank (Banco Central de Chile) was established to handle the government's finances, to administer monetary controls, and to engage in a general banking business. Shortly afterwards, in 1927 and 1928, a number of special-purpose banks were inaugurated as state enterprises. Financed by contributions of capital from the government budget and loans from the Central Bank, the new banks were authorized to extend short- and intermediate-term credits to nationally controlled firms in several fields.[46] The more important of these state lending institutions were the Agricultural Credit Institute (Caja de Crédito Agrario), the Mining Credit Institute (Caja de Crédito Minero), and the Industrial Credit Institute (Caja de Crédito Industrial), the last-mentioned of which was intended to play a role in the rather vague six-year program announced by the Ibáñez administration for stimulating domestic industrial development. In addition to these there were also created two small regional development institutes (the Institutos de Fomento Minero e Industrial of Tarapacá and Antofagasta), an Institute for Nitrate Development (Caja de Fomento Salitrero), and a Coal Financing Institute (Caja de Crédito Carbonífero) through which state subsidies were channeled into the coal industry.[47] During the same period, in what was to amount to no more than a gesture in the direction of resolving Chile's critical agricultural problem, the Agricultural Colonization Institute (Caja de Colonización Agrícola) was established. Although not, strictly speaking, a state bank, the Colonization Institute was envisaged as a financing agency for promoting the establishment of colonies of small farmers on lands which it acquired by purchase or expropriation.[48]

Approximately twenty-five years later, in 1953, the National Savings Bank, the Mortgage Credit Institute, the Agricultural Credit Institute, and the Industrial Credit Institute were merged to form the Chilean State Bank (Banco del Estado de Chile).[49] The two regional development institutes were concurrently absorbed by the Chilean Development Corporation which had been set up in 1939 (see below). At the same time, the Mining Credit Institute, which in 1938 had absorbed the Coal Financing Institute, was reorganized as the Mining Credit and Development Bank (Caja de Crédito y Fomento Minero, or CACREMI). Subsequently, in 1960, CACREMI was reorganized again in a consolidation with one of the Mining Credit Institute's chief projects, the ENAF (Empresa Nacional de Fundiciones) copper smelter which began operations in 1952, to form the National Mining Enterprise (Empresa Nacional de Minería).

Gradually, therefore, the array of interventionary financial institutions was restructured into a more systematic pattern of organization. Although for a good many years following their initial creation the volume of financing actually directed through these state entities was comparatively modest, their establishment was nevertheless quite important in at least three ways.

In the first place, they represented the first really significant Latin American effort in the present century to forge a new policy instrument, the special-purpose state bank. By providing services not readily forthcoming (if at all) from established economic institutions and by applying the positive sanctions of credit allocation to both private and public enterprise, the banks were to assist the government in attaining a variety of developmental objectives.[50] During the decades following, this sort of direct intervention in the money market was to become a technique that would be repeated in almost every country on the continent, as indeed the previously mentioned Banco Industrial of Argentina would suggest.[51]

Secondly, the evolution of these special-purpose state banks was to demonstrate the diversified range of functions, not excluding the entrepreneurial one, which would often be added to the operations of such institutions in the course of carrying out their more routine investment and commercial banking activities. Banks they might be, but of a most unconventional sort. More accurately, they should probably be viewed as parafinancial institutions. The Mining Credit Institute and CACREMI, for instance, became major buyers of several types of ores (both on their own account and on commission), built roads, acquired a railway, and operated minerals-processing plants (for the beneficiation, concentration, and smelting of ores) in addition to making loans for developing mines and processing ores.[52] The charter of the Chilean State Bank was even more ample in this respect, for in addition to providing a full range of commercial, mortgage, savings, and investment services for firms in agriculture and industry, it was authorized (a) to establish and operate deposit warehouses, fertilizer plants, and agricultural processing installations, (b) to intervene in the management of industrial enterprises, (c) to engage in foreign and domestic trade, and (d) to carry on other operations of an agricultural, industrial, and commercial character. For this reason, it may also be said that the special-purpose state banks were anticipatory of the more comprehensive development authorities which have been created in a number of Latin American countries, including Chile itself.

A third feature of the sectorally oriented state banks should probably be made explicit as well: namely, that their continuity in business would not necessarily depend upon their adherence to conventional economic criteria of success. Susceptible on the one hand to the political influence of their clients and endowed on the other hand with access to central bank rediscounting privileges and/or supplemental appropriations from the budget of the central government, they have been able to continue to operate—as, for example, in the case of CACREMI—even in the face of recurring deficits. Thus, the multiple purposes served by these institutions have, for better or for worse, commonly included political as well as more narrowly economic objectives.

At the time that the first development banks were being set up, the theme of national control of economic processes was also emerging as a dominant concern. To express it, a further group of policy innovations was introduced which was to enlarge considerably both the role of the state as a direct participant in the economy and the regulatory intervention of the government.[53] By decree in 1927, for example, the insurance field was reserved to Chilean companies, except for those foreign concerns already in business at the time—a measure which resembled in some ways the Uruguayan legislation of the year preceding. The following year brought the formation of the Chilean Reinsurance Institute (Caja Reaseguradora de Chile), an official agency vested with a monopoly of all foreign reinsurance assignments and with permission to form domestic reinsurance pools as well. Much later, public intervention in insurance moved still further when, in 1953, the State Insurance Institute (Instituto de Seguros del Estado) was organized to monopolize the fire and casualty insurance written for the central government and its official and semiofficial agencies.

In the natural resource field, a series of laws were promulgated between 1926 and 1928 which reversed the position taken in the Mining Code of 1888 by reserving to the state the ownership of all petroleum deposits. Since 1931, refining as well as exploration and development have also been exclusively (with very minor special exceptions) a governmental function. Until 1943, regular governmental departments conducted these matters,[54] but in that year the Chilean Development Corporation was given responsibility for developing the oil fields in the southernmost part of the country. After these had become quite consequential, the National Petroleum Enterprise (Empresa Nacional de Petróleo) was established in 1950, with a nationwide monopoly of exploration, development, and refining, a charge which, incidentally, it has fulfilled in an exemplary manner.

While over the years the state petroleum industry was to become an undertaking of major importance, its institution in the late 1920's was at the time overshadowed by still another experiment in intervention, which had national control as one of its objectives. In what was ultimately to prove to be a vain effort to salvage the faltering nitrate export industry, the Chilean congress in 1930 authorized the establishment of the controversial Chilean Nitrate Company (Compañía de Salitre de Chile, or COSACH). A mixed enterprise, with a 50 per cent government participation,[55] COSACH was empowered to monopolize the production and sale of nitrates. The drastic consequences of the world trade depression soon forced the dissolution of COSACH, but even though production was returned to private hands, the exportation and sale of nitrate (and iodine) were retained as a monopoly by the successor to COSACH, the Chilean Nitrate and Iodine Sales Company (Compañía de Ventas de Salitre y de Yodo de Chile, or COVENSA), which was organized in 1934. As a mixed enterprise, with a 25 per cent governmental participation in earnings (increased, in 1956, to 40 per cent), COVENSA was, practically speaking, an extension of the public sector through the government's control of the company's board of directors.[56] In time, COVENSA rescued the industry from insolvency, despite the growing competition from synthetically produced nitrates, and gradually reestablished the nitrate trade on a sounder, albeit much reduced, scale.

In view of the strong initial impetus given state interventionism and in the light of contemporary political trends, it is not surprising that for over two decades following the early Alessandri and Ibáñez governments the evolution of an administered economy should have proceeded rapidly. Indeed, as the foregoing paragraphs have demonstrated, the policy innovations of 1925-1930 were but a prelude to a course of development which did not begin to abate until around 1956. Even then, the institutional work of the previous decades was by no means undone, and with the election of the Frei government in 1965, it seemed certain that the interventionist pattern of guided development would be resumed and perhaps intensified. This being the case, it is in order to summarize others of the post-1930 changes which amplified the role of the state in economic life.[57]

Exchange controls were first decreed in 1931 and supplemented by the institution of import quotas and licensing in the following year. During the subsequent eight years or so, the exchange controls evolved into a comprehensive system characterized by a complex structure of multiple rates, and import restrictions grew ever tighter.[58] In the early forties, such controls were at their peak as various government agencies received authorization to determine what could be imported and exported, to fix quotas (and require licenses) for both categories of transactions, to pay import subsidies and export bounties, and to engage directly in foreign trade transactions. Originally instituted in the 1930's as a measure to conserve foreign exchange, the Chilean exchange- and trade-control system was therefore, like its equivalents in other countries, perpetuated into the 1940's as a means of implementing other national economic policies. All this, of course, was in addition to the continual adjustments of tariff levels, for since the turn of the century tariff protection for domestic industries had been a settled policy. Sharp upward revisions in the tariff wall began in 1928, and further increases were effected throughout the thirties and thereafter. Behind the shield provided by these changes and currency depreciation, domestic industrial production (exclusive of mining and construction) rose by 88 per cent between 1925-1927 and 1941, while between 1941 and 1949, despite serious difficulties encountered in obtaining capital imports, a further increase of almost 36 per cent was realized.[59]

In 1932 new executive decrees authorized the imposition of sweeping controls over the production, pricing, and distribution of all goods considered to be prime necessities, including the power to requisition such goods and to expropriate the producers thereof for failure to obey regulations or for permitting production capacity to go unutilized.[60] The patent objective of the decrees, of course, was to enhance the market-regulating activity of the state which had been initiated in a small way in 1930 with the inauguration of the Agricultural Export Board (Junta de Exportación Agrícola), an agency which had been authorized to intervene in agricultural marketing processes through price supports, export subsidies, export licensing, export embargoes, and trading in agricultural commodities on its own account. While in actual practice the more radical controls were employed sparingly except during World War II (and the expropriation provisions were not invoked at all), the basic authority has remained as a potential instrument of policy ever since.

Indeed, at least with respect to the application of public controls to the domestic marketing of staple foodstuffs, a more or less permanent or institutionalized form for expressing the general intent of these decree laws was provided in the establishment of the Instituto Nacional de Comercio as a state trading agency. By means of foreign and domestic trading, including the exercise of monopoly powers for some imports such as wheat and frozen meat, the INC endeavored throughout its existence to regulate the available supplies and the prices of basic food items in the domestic Chilean market. Essentially the same functions were assumed by its successor agency in 1960, the Empresa de Comercio Agrícola.

In the field of industrial regulations it is interesting to note that as early as 1932 a decree similar to the later Mexican "industry saturation law" was promulgated which permitted the government to prohibit or otherwise control new investment in fields thought to be afflicted with "overproduction." While the law has actually been applied in only a few instances, and only in 1940 and 1941, it was never revoked and remains as one of the several available sanctions the state could employ in directing capital formation into chosen channels. In view of the supervisory powers conferred upon the Chilean Development Corporation, however, the "overproduction" law would appear to have become redundant.

In 1933 the second of what was to become a varied assortment of tax remission and incentive measures was enacted to stimulate the construction industry [61] (the first of these modern developmental fiscal concessions was passed in 1929 for the encouragement of iron mining). Special provisions of a similar nature were later extended to promote investment in such fields as the metallurgical and fishing industries as well as to encourage the decentralization of industry.

At the same time, however, and doubtless under pressure of the need to find new revenue sources to replace the nitrate taxes, tax increases were assuming a new and important function in the panoply of public policies. Such was the case with respect to the vital copper industry, for here the intention was to enlarge the participation of the domestic economy in the export sector by tapping its earnings through taxation. During the mid-1920's, the export earnings retained through the new taxes imposed by the social legislation of 1924 marked the first step in that direction, a step that was quickly supplemented by the establishment of an income tax in 1925 which taxed gross profits at an effective rate of 12 per cent. From the standpoint of the local economy's participation in export earnings, these measures, together with the unionization which was encouraged in the copper industry, provided a partial offset to the decline in aggregate export sales which occurred during the depression. With the introduction of exchange controls in 1931 and multiple rates shortly thereafter, still another means of harvesting a growing share of copper export sales was instituted,[62] while in 1934 the income tax rate was raised to 18 per cent. A further elevation of the income tax rate to 33 per cent was applied to the copper companies in 1938.

Thus, by virtue of the higher rates of direct taxation, the effects of the charges set forth in the social legislation, the newly instituted indirect taxes implied by the exchange control system, and the upward movement of basic wage rates, the benefits flowing to the domestic economy during the upswing in the copper market of the 1930's increased much more rapidly than did the total amount of copper export sales. During subsequent years, the taxation scheme applied to the copper industry was revised repeatedly so that by 1955 the share of the gross profits claimed by direct taxes reached the level of 68 per cent, at which point the continuing debate over possible contraproductive effects of the tax regime took on new vitality.[63]

Since it is far from being uniformly certain that increased export taxes in Latin America necessarily result in any lasting contributions to domestic economic growth, the quality of public organization being what it is, it is worthy of note that in 1939 the Chilean government took specific steps to insure that there would be at least a measure of correspondence between the taxes collected from the export sector and domestic capital formation. More-over, it did so in a move which, while not without antecedents in the Chilean experience of the late 1920's, nevertheless constituted an important new precedent in Latin American development policy. In 1939, on the basis of financing drawn in part from an earmarked portion of the 1938 income tax increase on copper mining, the first of the Latin American general develop-ment authorities was born in the guise of the archtypal Chilean Develop-ment Corporation (Corporación de Fomento de la Producción, or CORFO). The scope of its authorization as the key state mechanism for the planning and promotion of economic development was sweeping. But while CORFO has been essentially a government-controlled enterprise, it has also, by including representatives from the major private economic associations on its board of governors, attempted to evolve a type of collaborative guidance for the economic system.[64]

Not only was CORFO empowered to collaborate with other governmental and semigovernmental institutions and with private institutions in devising programs for increasing production in existing or new lines; it was also charged with drafting a comprehensive plan for national development which would embody a due regard for intersectoral and interregional balance while strengthening the country's international balance-of-payments position. In line with the foregoing, it was assigned the task of preparing appropriate policy recommendations for the implementation of such plans, whether of program or project dimensions, and with insuring that the whole endeavor would be formulated in a manner consistent with the goal of increasing the participation of Chilean interests in the industrial, commercial, and agricultural life of the nation.

As a matter of actual practice, CORFO's efforts in the development planning field were chiefly limited to project planning, with some attention to sectoral development programs and, as in the case of the Plan Chillán which began in 1954, to participation in regional development schemes.[65] No real general or national development plan was ever drawn up until the 1960's, the closest previous approximation having been the eight-year plan for agricultural and transport development which was prepared for the years 1954-1961. However, as this earlier plan was predicated on substantial foreign aid, which was not, as it turned out, forthcoming, the attainments were actually quite limited in the broader areas of planning.

Besides the planning function, CORFO was also granted far-reaching powers to assist in the actual execution of plans and projects. As a supervisory agency for all sectors of industry, its authorization was required both for starting new production facilities and for expanding existing plants. To facilitate industrial development, CORFO also provided technical assistance by acting as engineering consultant, marketing agent, and purchasing agent, as well as engaging in the importation of the machinery and equipment needed for approved projects and assisting in obtaining foreign financing therefor.[66] In its capacity as a government bank, CORFO made loans to private firms, mixed enterprises, and state agencies and corporations and also made equity investments in partnership with private (and primarily Chilean) capital, both as a majority and as a minority stockholder. In investment areas where private interests had not gone either at all or (from the government's point of view) on a sufficient scale, CORFO moved even further by exercising its power to organize and initiate companies, subsequently operating them as either state undertakings or selling them in whole or in part to private investors.[67]

In the course of its operations, CORFO loans were granted to hundreds of enterprises in a wide variety of fields, and up to the end of 1958, investments had been made in the stock of some 66 companies, in 41 of which CORFO had held a majority interest.[68] The industries represented by these investments have been exceedingly (and in the eyes of some thoughtful critics, excessively) diversified: mining and metallurgical companies; metal processing and machinery plants; agricultural and stock-raising firms; colonization companies; electric power and electrical products companies; lumber and forestry concerns; cement, chemical, and fertilizer enterprises; rubber manufacturing; fishing and fish-processing companies; beet sugar refineries; hotels; wine companies; refrigerated meat processing installations; vaccines; a motion-picture studio; poultry supplies; and so forth.

Beginning in the mid-1940's, however, with the organization of the National Electricity Enterprise (Empresa Nacional de Electricidad), an entity which operated by 1958 over 62 per cent of the public-service electric generating capacity, the investments and loans of CORFO tended to be directed in more concentrated fashion. Following the hydroelectric program, which received the largest single allocation of CORFO support,[69] the National Petroleum Enterprise ranked a close second. Among the other larger investment projects were a copper rolling mill and wire plant (Manufactureras de Cobre, established 1944), the beet-sugar refineries operated by the National Sugar Industry (Industria Azucarera Nacional, established in 1952), a national hotel corporation (Hotelera Nacional, organized in 1951), an agricultural machinery and equipment company (Servicio de Equipos Agrícolas Mecanizados, formed in 1946),[70] the largest rubber manufacturing plant (Industria Nacional de Neumáticos, organized in 1941 in cooperation with the General Tire and Rubber Company and since sold to private interests), and the national steel mill (Compañía de Acero del Pacífico, developed from 1944 on, with production beginning in 1950).

To summarize the Chilean case is not an easy matter, and to evaluate its accomplishments is even less so. On the one hand, it resembles the Uruguayan situation in that the neo-orthodox approach had become a firmly implanted part of the Chilean politico-economic reality by the mid-twentieth century; but as a point of difference, the Chilean experience was even more productive than the Uruguayan counterpart in the extent of the institutional innovation it incorporated. Going beyond the welfare interventionism which sat entrenched in Montevideo, the Chileans went on to pioneer a goodly number of the new instrumentalities of public economic direction which, taken together, might be most aptly characterized as developmental interventionism. They did so, moreover, in a fashion which was on the whole far less impulsive and probably more enduring than that which gave such an air of perpetual crisis to the *justicialista* variation of the new policy style in Argentina. Indeed, it is not going too far to state that it is in the developments which occurred in Chile between 1920 and 1960 that the fullest dimensions of Latin American neo-orthodoxy stand revealed.[71]

At the same time, the limitations of this developmental approach also stand out with particular clarity in the Chilean experience, for there they were not obfuscated so much by either the very small market and resource-base restrictions which operated with such severity in the Uruguayan case or the excesses of nationalism which caused the Argentine experiment to come to such an unsatisfactory end. The shortcomings of the Chilean route to development are, in other words, those which in greater or lesser measure have afflicted all the countries which have followed the neo-orthodox pattern of internally oriented development.

There there were, in fact, shortcomings in Chile's developmental interventionism cannot be gainsaid, even though allowances must be made for the adverse effects on national growth possibilities which stemmed from the secular deterioration in the Chilean terms of trade throughout most of the period in question. Perhaps no other Latin American country had been so hard hit as Chile by the depression of world trade which took place in the 1930's, and despite the boom in copper export prices which occurred in 1954-1956, for example, the Chilean terms of trade had still not regained the level of 1925-1929. Brief recessions in copper export markets had also marred the decade following the end of World War II, while the 1954-1956 boom was, in turn, followed by a sharp break in copper prices which brought the value of copper exports down from a peak of 56 cents per pound in 1956 to 20 cents per pound in 1958 before recovery set in. Needless to say, from this, as well as from the undesirable consequences of various domestic policies, the country suffered an almost chronic disequilibrium in its balance of payments with the rest of the world.

All this, it must be recognized, created an environment anything but favorable for the development programs which were being attempted at the time. Nevertheless, the general weakness of the external economic position of the country cannot be made wholly accountable for the fact that during most of the postwar period the Chilean aggregate growth rate was among the lowest in Latin America. While the Latin American gross product increased at an average annual rate of 6.3 per cent between 1945 and 1955, that of Chile increased by only about 2.7 per cent per year during the same period. Moreover, notwithstanding the explicit commitment of the Chilean government to accelerated development and in spite of the progress which was made in shifting the composition of imports in favor of producer goods (from 48 per cent of imports in 1925-1929 to 61 per cent in 1951-1953), the Chilean rate of capital formation during the postwar period was also one of the lowest in the hemisphere. And of the capital invested, a rather high percentage, even by Latin American standards, appears to have gone into residential construction.[72] Meanwhile in the output of manufacturing industry, which had experienced intense growth during the thirties and forties, there were by the 1950's clear signs of a weakening in the momentum toward further expansion. Scattered gains of even impressive proportions were registered in certain lines of manufacturing production after 1950, but on the whole the general rate of increase in manufacturing output may not have exceeded a 4 per cent annual average between 1950 and, say, 1962.

For this state of affairs, internal policies must bear some share of the blame. Though it is true that the capacity to import was eroded by terms of trade movements, and this may have created a certain bottleneck for investment expenditures because of the import coefficient of domestic capital formation, it is also true that amid the preoccupation with internal structural elaboration very little was done to diversify the export trade of the country as a means of overcoming the difficulties associated with the overwhelming reliance on a single export product. For that matter, even the strength, such as it was, of the traditional export items was undermined by policies which ultimately functioned as deterrents to an improvement in the export situation, in spite of their logic as means of increasing the returned value benefits which the local economy derived from the export sector.

Consequently, the capacity to import was not only impaired by the adverse terms of trade movements but suffered further from the virtual stagnation in export volume which was a feature of most of the postwar era. The faltering nitrate industry, for example, was (until the reforms of 1954) long deprived by the exchange and taxation systems of the financial resources needed for modernization of its production facilities. Far more important, the combination of domestic inflation, high taxation levels, and discriminatory exchange-rate policies served artificially to convert Chile from a relatively low-cost copper producer to one whose production cost level was quite high in comparison with the cost levels prevailing at alternative production locations elsewhere in the world. Therefore, until reforms were introduced in 1955 in the public policy regarding copper, the attractiveness of Chile as a site for investment in copper mining was considerably diminished. Reflecting this condition, Chilean copper production declined from a World War II peak of around 500,000 metric tons to less than 400,000 metric tons in the early 1950's. Even the strong 1954-1956 rise in world copper prices only returned the level of Chilean output to about 480,000 metric tons. Not until 1959 did the country's copper production begin to surpass the levels reached in the first half of the 1940's. In the meantime, world copper production increased rapidly in the postwar period, so that the Chilean share of the market declined from 20 per cent in 1944 to only 13 per cent in 1954.

Although some of the resources extracted from the export sector through penalty rates in the exchange control system were used to subsidize the importation of capital goods, preferential rates were also employed to subsidize the importation of items for consumer use, or of intermediate goods and raw materials required by the consumer goods industries which had been brought into existence during the deliberate industrialization drive. The latter category of imports, in fact, made for a growing rigidity in the import structure, a rigidity which began by the 1950's to plague not only

Chile but also the other countries that had set up import-substituting light industries. Both domestic industrial production and employment levels, in other words, came to depend upon the ability of the external sector to supply the new factories with a steady flow of fuel, raw materials, and intermediate goods for processing. Whereas formerly a contraction in the capacity to import had brought discomfort mainly to the upper- and middle-class consumers of imported finished goods, the consequence of foreign-exchange shortages now became even more far-reaching. In addition to the limitations imposed on the industrialization process by domestic market size, therefore, it was becoming clear that there were also limitations which might emerge from the evolving structure of imports.

Besides the imports which had to be continued simply to keep established consumer-goods industries going, there was another development in the import structure which was even more ominous. This was the rising portion of the limited amount of available foreign exchange which was being expended to bring in, on a subsidized basis, imports of foodstuffs. Although as recently as the interwar period Chile had been a net agricultural exporter, it became during the forties a net agricultural importer. Worse yet, the national agricultural production deficit was even increasing in the postwar years. From 8 per cent of total imports in 1947-1950, agricultural imports rose to over 25 per cent of total imports by the mid-1950's.

Behind such trends lay a serious case of rural sector stagnation, for between 1942-1944 and 1950-1954 the increase in agricultural output was only 8 per cent for the entire period. On a per capita basis, therefore, agricultural production was actually declining—by 15 per cent from pre-World War II to 1950-1954. A modest improvement did occur for a while in the later 1950's, but between 1950 and 1962 the overall gain was very low. Moreover, of the slight increases in output which were realized during the forties and early fifties, a substantial portion may have been attributable simply to the addition (through growth of the rural population) of more labor factors, as the period appears to have been characterized by disinvestment in the agricultural sector, with the disinvestment even more pronounced when figured on a per-worker-employed-in-agriculture basis than when measured on a gross basis.

Part of the explanation for the poor showing of Chilean agriculture is doubtless to be found in the inherited structural features of agricultural organization, i.e., in the old persisting problems of the latifundia-minifundia complex. Almost nothing had been done throughout the period of developmental interventionism to change the basic framework of rural land tenure arrangements, for the achievements of the Agricultural Colonization Institute were so paltry that they need not be assigned any significance. There seems, too, to have been little accomplished in the work of the supportive agricultural agencies (agricultural training schools, extension services, and the like) or the special agricultural credit institutions, whose loan policies generally fell on the short side of providing the rural sector with genuine development credit in a manner which would maximize agricultural output. For that matter, the credit allocations of the official institutions may merely have served as a cheaper substitute for loan capital which otherwise could have been obtained from private lending institutions, and there is no assurance that the borrowers—often the owners of the larger rural properties—who benefited from the preferentially low interest rates did in fact always invest their loans in the agricultural sector. That they may not have been inclined to do so, however, was itself at least partly a function of other public policies which, by fostering the subsidized importation of agricultural imports and imposing unrealistically low price ceilings on domestic agricultural output, worked for a long time in the direction of providing strong disincentives for local rural producers.

The disincentive effects of agricultural price controls were in turn aggravated by the chronic and intractable inflation which afflicted the country for most of the period in question. Attributable in some degree to the high propensity to consume of the Chilean bourgeoisie, the chief beneficiaries of the welfare and public employment programs,[73] the inflationary trend was fueled also by the automatic wage increases that were needed to placate a restive and militant labor force and by the ambitious development programs which were launched on the basis of a very much outmoded fiscal structure. Thus, since the whole development undertaking—with its array of price supports, subsidies, new lines of industrial development, and welfare and housing programs—almost continuously exceeded the capacity of the system of public finance to mobilize resources except through inflationary forced savings, the result was an almost unbroken series of budgetary deficits which had to be financed out of currency expansion. Considering the distorting effects of virulent inflation on investment preferences and on the cost-minimizing functions of production management, and considering, too, the tendency of market signals for resource allocation to become lost amid the welter of interventionist measures, the real wonder, perhaps, is that any vestige of efficient resource utilization managed to survive at all.

Significantly, it would appear that the brunt of the problems of adjustment consequent to the foregoing situation fell upon the private sector, which, for all the props and protections afforded by the system, was still, relative to the public sector, more vulnerable to the impact of adverse economic forces. In contrast, the public sector—based, as it was, ultimately upon the powerful sanctions available to the state—could more readily continue to operate, at least until the burden of adjustments forced upon the rest of the economy exceeded tolerable proportions. Just prior to the modifications introduced in the mid-1950's, therefore, it is revealing that the public sector accounted for 72 per cent of the overall low rate of gross domestic investment, a proportion between public and private shares which was almost the exact reverse of that prevailing in Latin America as a whole. Moreover, notwithstanding the rather minor, albeit generally salutary, changes of policy effected there-after, the prospects for a strong economic recovery remained dim. That a viable way out of such problems was exceptionally difficult to discover was possibly best indicated by the mounting political crisis which afflicted the nation and which, prior to the elections of 1964, seemed even to pose the threat of driving the country altogether out of a democratic, evolutionary course of development.

OTHER COUNTRIES

Among the remaining Latin American nations, the policy orientation which evolved so distinctly in Uruguay, Argentina, and Chile was not always so clearly focused for two reasons.

In the first place, some of its elements were often introduced without a further commitment to the other parts of the program. Particularly was this the case in the field of social and labor legislation, where even tradi-tionalist regimes otherwise hostile to the growth of a strong labor movement were sometimes moved to promulgate measures that on paper looked like concessions to the spirit of the times. Guatemala, for example, enacted its first modernistic labor code as early as 1926, while in 1920 and 1936 Venezuela also instituted new codes of labor legislation. Ecuador did so in 1938, Cuba followed suit in 1940, and similar codes were promulgated in Bolivia in 1943 (a measure under consideration since 1939) and Costa Rica in 1943. By 1940, moreover, all the countries had on the books at least some legislation regarding hours of work, workmen's compensation, union-ization, and other related matters. Social welfare and insurance programs of varying degrees of elaborateness were passed in Ecuador in 1935 and 1942-1944, in Peru in 1936 (expanded in 1941 and subsequently), in Venezuela in 1940-1941, in Costa Rica during 1941-1942, and even in Paraguay in 1943, to cite only a few examples. Behind the legislative façade, it is true, the actual implementation of such measures was often quite a different matter, and some of the labor codes and other labor measures appear to have been designed mainly to place the trade union movement under strict governmental tutelage. Nevertheless, even gestures in the direction of never before recognized elements in society were indica-tors of the general drift of events. Similarly indicative has been the rather prevalent propensity to establish special-purpose state banks and develop-ment agencies, even in countries where the basic orientation of policy has remained tied to an externally oriented pattern of growth.

The second difficulty encountered in tracing the spread of the new policy style is the occasional brevity of the regimes which purported to embrace it. A case could be made, for instance, that some fairly close approximation of welfare and developmental interventionism was the professed inspiration of the governments which came to power in Peru in 1945 (i.e., the Bustamante-Aprista alliance), in El Salvador in 1948, and in Panama in 1952. But in two of these cases the administration's tenure of office was cut short (by a military coup d'etat in Peru, by assassination in Panama), while, in the third, internal maneuvering among the directing group led eventually to a measure of withdrawal from the original program commitments. A brief flirtation with a neo-orthodox policy trend may also have been a feature of Bolivian experience in the 1936-1939 period, though here the evidence is quite inconclusive. Less ambiguity attaches to the case of Guatemala, which threw out the durable dictator, Jorge Ubico, in 1944. Notwithstanding the intellectual fuzziness of "spiritual socialism," by which term Ubico's successor, Juan José Arévalo, chose to identify his program, the labor and land reform clauses of the new constitution of 1945 and the rapid creation of the institutional apparatus of the interventionist state made plain the fact that a basic reorientation of national policy had occurred. The reorientation was aggressively antiforeign as well, as was placed beyond all doubt when the Agrarian Law of 1952 was enacted—primarily, it would seem, with the intention of expropriating the land reserves of the largest foreign investment interest in the nation, the United Fruit Company. By this time, however, the more authentically Guatemalan policy elements had come to take a back seat to the tactics and stratagems of the cold war. Under Arévalo's successor, local communists became increasingly influential in remolding public policy to fit ends not necessarily related to national development objectives at all. And since their ouster in 1954, Guatemalan public policy has not, for the most part, been very clearly headed in any discernible direction except as it has linked the country more closely to its neighbors in the Central American economic integration program.

These two different kinds of problems aside, however, it is still quite valid to think of welfare and developmental interventionism as a general policy tendency toward which a significant number of Latin American nations have been gravitating in recent decades. The reforming zeal manifested in the Alfonso López administration of Colombia during 1934-1938, for example, succeeded in 1936 in putting a number of controversial amendments into the constitution which enlarged the state's power of expropriation, basically modified the nature of private property rights (by reasserting the old Hispanic social function of property concept), and pledged the state to give special protection to labor. While the official zest for reform abated somewhat under subsequent administrations, the elaboration of interventionist mechanisms and the gradual shift of national concern to industrialization and internal development continued through both Liberal and Conservative as well as military and civilian governments down to the present day. Indeed, the essential continuity of this policy evolution is perhaps all the more significant in that it has proceeded in a relatively uninterrupted manner despite the serious and tragic political disturbances which have frequently beset the country in the past twenty or so years.

In Costa Rica, a greatly expanded role for the state in the development of the national economy and the promotion, through the nationalization of certain foreign properties, of national economic independence became the major and minor themes of public policy when the revolution of 1948 placed the National Union Party in control of the government. For a full decade thereafter, the government moved accordingly, and even when the leadership of the National Union Party was interrupted for a term by the election of a conservative president in 1958, the consequent change at the policy level was more of emphasis rather than outright repudiation of what had been achieved up to that time.

Not altogether different has been the experience of Venezuela since the first Acción Democrática government acceded to power in 1945. Thereupon, the new political leadership gave labor a wholly unaccustomed freedom of action, passed extensive educational and social legislation, drastically increased (through royalty and tax obligations) the country's claim to the earnings of the petroleum export sector, and enacted a new constitution that was anticipatory, as most such documents have been, of a host of corrective and normative measures to follow. At the same time, the preexisting government banks for industry and agriculture were revitalized and a new national development authority was established, thereby providing the country with the basic instruments for a state-sponsored industrialization drive into which a portion of the now larger petroleum earnings were reinvested. Exchange controls, high customs duties on imports, and direct or quantitative import restrictions were also enlisted in support of the drive. Although harsh political repression and close government control of the trade union movement were unattractive features of the military dictatorship which was installed when the Acción Democrática government was thrown out of office in 1948, the national industrialization effort continued undiminished, while several state development agencies even enlarged the scope of their operations.

Positive action by the state to further economic development processes, including again, especially domestic industrialization, also became the keynote of the Estado Novo program espoused by the long regime of Getúlio Vargas who ruled Brazil from 1930 to 1945 and again from 1950 to 1954 on the basis of an army-labor-bureaucracy coalition.[74] The one administration which lay within the Vargas period, that of Dutra in 1946-1950, departed not at all from the institutions and policies of the Vargas regime and even carried the national control objectives a bit further by purchasing all but one of the major foreign-owned railways of the country. In like manner, the post-Vargas governments of Kubitschek, Quadros, and Goulart were, from the standpoint of economic policy, post-Vargas only in point of time, for the basic framework of economic development was only a modification of that which had been created during the thirties and forties.

The details of this policy framework may be skipped, just as one may pass over the particulars of other countries' experiences with neo-orthodox national development programs. For present purposes, it is sufficient to note that most of the rather ample assortment of Brazilian interventionist measures, which approximated the Chilean case in the extent of their elaboration and utilization, has consisted of techniques and institutions which are not significantly different either in form or objective from those which have already been described. Exchange and trade controls, protective tariffs, public promotion of and investment in siderurgical enterprises and other basic industries, governmental banks for development, national development "plans" and sectoral development programs—all these features and others equally familiar have been incorporated into Brazilian economic structure since 1930. If more distinctive elements are to be found therein, they would be, perhaps, the somewhat greater concern devoted to agricultural colonization and new land settlement [75] and the comparatively prominent economic role played by state governments alongside the national government, especially in the development of electric power resources.

Though afflicted, like the countries of the case studies, by chronic inflation and balance of payments problems and though, also as in the other three cases, little or no progress was made in diversifying the export sector, Brazil was nevertheless able to attain a substantially better national growth rate than Uruguay, Argentina, or Chile during most of the postwar era. Indeed, in this regard Brazil ranked higher than the average of all Latin American countries, though it was outpaced by Venezuela and Mexico among the larger countries and by a number of the smaller countries such as Ecuador, Guatemala, El Salvador, and Nicaragua. By the 1950's, moreover, Brazil had become the foremost industrial producer in Latin America, in spite of the fact that at least half of its labor force was still employed in agriculture. It does not follow from this, however, that the Brazilian version of developmental interventionism has been more effectively structured and employed than that of Uruguay, Argentina, or Chile, though it might be said that in Brazil such policies were possibly more appropriate to the setting.

That the Brazilian experiment with guided development turned out so well was partially attributable to the improvement in the country's terms of trade, an improvement produced by the sharp postwar rise of coffee prices which lasted into 1954. Since export volume was increasing as well during this time, the overall trade position functioned as a powerful stimulant for economic expansion up to the middle fifties, giving the country a momentum which carried it forward for some time even after coffee prices broke from their peak highs. External economic assistance from the United States and international institutions was also a positive factor in the situation, for a third of the nonmilitary loans and grants which the United States government channeled to Latin America between 1946 and 1958 went to Brazil. In access to World Bank financing, Brazil was the leading Latin American borrower, having received over a quarter of the IBRD loans to Latin America up to 1960, even though for several years World Bank lending operations in Brazil were suspended because of an impasse which developed between the Bank and the Brazilian government. During the first five years of its operations, the International Finance Corporation, an affiliate of the World Bank, also made approximately a quarter of its total Latin American commitments to enterprises operating in Brazil.

The large size of the Brazilian domestic market and the relatively diversified resource base of the country were further conditions which favored internally oriented industrial development in the eyes of foreign as well as national investors. From the former, especially those from the United States, the response was impressive. Whereas as late as 1943 Brazil had ranked sixth among Latin American nations as a recipient of United States private foreign investment, by 1950 it was second to Venezuela in this respect, the amount of private investment from the United States having approximately doubled in the preceding seven years. By 1958 the amount of United States private capital invested in Brazil had more than doubled again. Furthermore, unlike the case of Venezuela, where the bulk of foreign investment went into the petroleum industry, the flow of foreign capital and technological competence to Brazil went primarily into the burgeoning manufacturing sector, where domestic investment was also substantial but where the import-substitution process of industrialization was quickly approaching its final and most difficult phase. Since public investment, which was running at high levels, was also going substantially into basic industrial and energy fields (until the pell-mell construction of Brasília diverted public funds to a less productive use), the direction of capital formation in Brazil was generally conducive to generating rapid increases in aggregate output. During the 1952-1961 decade, the real increase in gross domestic product averaged 6 per cent annually, though in 1963, after a very slight decline in 1962, it fell to only 1.6 per cent. Consequently, with all the foregoing circumstances working in favor of the country's economic growth, it was not until the decade of the sixties that public attention was forced to reconsider the long-term viability of the pattern of development which had been adopted.

CENTRAL AMERICAN ECONOMIC INTEGRATION

In the project for Central American economic integration, five economies, whose very small individual sizes had severely limited the possibilities of separate domestic industrialization programs,[76] joined together in the hope that collectively they might more successfully pursue the kind of inwardly focused growth programs which the larger Latin American countries had adopted earlier.

Following the lead of El Salvador, which had begun to negotiate bilateral free-trade treaties with its neighbors, the five countries (with support from ECLA) in 1951 established the Organization of Central American States to foster political and cultural cooperation within the region. In the following year the Central American Economic Cooperation Committee was set up to work toward a broad integration of the region's economies. During 1954 the Advanced School of Public Administration was organized as a regional institution, and in 1956 the Central American Institute for Industrial Research and Technology was set up to prepare and encourage technical studies and to assist governments in promoting industrialization. Later on, a program was launched to coordinate higher education among the participating countries.

By the middle of 1958, two conventions were ready for signing: the Multilateral Treaty on Free Trade and Central American Integration, which set forth a ten-year schedule for building a regional customs union and abolishing internal restrictions on the movement of goods, and the Agreement on the Regime for Central American Integration Industries, which laid down the basis for developing new industries whose economic scale would require immediate free access to all the markets of the member countries. Before the end of 1961 a Central American Economic Council had been set up to give more direction to this tropical *Zollverein*, and the Central American Economic Integration Bank was created as a regional development authority. In the same year the deadline for completely free intraregional trade and for uniform external tariffs was advanced somewhat, while the Treaty of Economic Association, signed by a majority of the countries in 1960, had been amplified by a General Treaty of Central American Economic Integration, an agreement signed by all the countries except Costa Rica, which went into effect in June of 1961. Not long afterwards, the Costa Rican government decided to cast in its lot with the other countries of the region and moved toward full participation in the regional integration scheme.[77]

With these steps the number of Latin American countries remaining committed to the traditional externally oriented pattern of development was reduced still further, for, owing to a variety of circumstances, the Central American common market project got under way in remarkably short order and moved swiftly toward realization in the 1960's. From 1950 to 1963, for example, the volume of intra-Central American trade rose from $8 million to $66 million, and in 1964 it reached $105 million. In the period 1961-1964, intraregional trade grew at a rate of 42 per cent a year, as against an average annual rate of 11 per cent for Central American trade with the rest of the world. Whereas intraregional trade accounted for 4 per cent of total imports in 1958, by 1964 the ratio had increased to 14 per cent. Significantly, in 1964 trade in manufactured goods made up 39 per cent of total intra-Central American trade, while the structure of foreign investment in the common market had shifted notably into such industrial fields as manufacturing and petroleum refining.[78]

Undoubtedly, the small size of the individual participating nations was a factor in hastening this evolution, for it made the necessity of regional economic integration both compelling and obvious if industrialization was to be attempted in any significant degree. The same condition, having precluded much previous industrial development in each of the countries, had also prevented the emergence of a substantial number of protected local firms which might have functioned as vested interests in opposition to regional integration. Furthermore, although the level of development varied among the several countries entering into the scheme, the variation between one country and another was much less extreme than that encountered among the nations which have joined together in the Latin American Free Trade Association. Unlike the LAFTA, which stretches from Mexico to southern South America, the Central American nations also enjoyed a locational advantage in that the participating members of the common market were adjacent to each other, a factor which made for far greater ease in establishing closer communication and transport linkages among them. The fact that they adopted the common market rather than a free trade area approach to integration was probably an additional feature which resolved some of the difficulties that have stalled the realization of the larger Latin American economic integration program. In any case, by the mid-1960's, the countries of Central America, excepting Panama, were moving well along their new development route and emulating the import-substitution industrialization which earlier had spread among the larger economies of the hemisphere. Almost certainly, though, the process would not go very much further before attention would have to be focused more concertedly on the complicated problems of agricultural development.

THE CONTRIBUTIONS AND LIMITATIONS OF NEO-ORTHODOXY

In appraising the problems associated with Latin American welfare and development interventionism, several things, which are in the nature of extenuating circumstances, must be kept in mind lest the criticisms made of it appear to present a wholly negative picture. In actual fact, a great deal has been changed for the better, and the overall balance of the record would seem to be one of net accomplishment.

In the first place, the industrialization process which has been attempted is without doubt one which is comparatively complex when set against the industrialization efforts of an earlier time. The internal organizational and technical structure of individual industries (including even the textile industry, which historically was at the forefront of the mechanization movement) is vastly more complicated nowadays than formerly, and the whole thrust of modern technological development has been to create an intricate network of interindustry relationships in consequence of which productivity levels at any particular point in the system tend to be strongly influenced, either negatively or positively, by the quality of performance attained in other areas of the system. Here Veblen's well-known comments concerning the interconnectedness of the modern industrial apparatus are very much to the point. Owing to the growing articulation of component segments within the total economic complex, an increasing share of the operating efficiency of individual industries is actually imputable to the degree of systemic efficiency realized in the structure at large. Therefore, until the entire network is sufficiently elaborated and matured, as it were, many if not most of the individual parts of the structure will tend to function under a handicap for want of the Marshallian external economies which are transmitted through the interstitial transactional flows of the system.

For this problem the possibilities of cross-cultural borrowing offer only a limited solution, since the sophisticated technological and organizational skills needed to support a modern industrial system may require a considerable length of time to be assimilated by a less advanced society. Consequently, the special difficulties which Latin American countries have encountered in forcing the pace of industrialization are fundamentally attributable to an environment in which the underpinnings of industrial growth are still deficient. If particular infant industries have found it difficult to grow up, this is a function of a probably unavoidable lag in the development of collateral portions of economic structure.

Complicating the matter further is the fact that technological progress, the crux of the growth process, has been primarily the achievement of other more advanced areas of the world. Thus, modern technology has developed in a geographical setting and under conditions of factor distribution and factor costs quite different from those prevailing in the borrowing economies. Ideally, the process of technological borrowing should be accompanied by an adaptation of the borrowed technology of production to a new geographical and economic setting. Unfortunately, in the new setting skilled adapters are likely to be few. Temperate-zone agriculture and timber exploitation, for example, have been brought to their present high degree of development in large part through support from the chemical and mechanical industries of the temperate-zone center countries; still largely lacking in the underdeveloped nations are comparable industrial-sector facilities for devising the new techniques, instruments, and equipment appropriate to the quite different problems of tropical agriculture and forestry.[79] Similarly, if it is commonplace that less developed countries borrow for their new industries the capital-intensive production technology originally developed for the resource patterns of the center economies, this is ordinarily because of the difficulty of working out new techniques which, exploiting the possibilities of labor-capital substitution and a certain degree of technological dualism, would be better suited to their own circumstances. Thus, the capital accumulation requirements and the import coefficients of economic expansion have been increased while the employment multiplier of new investment outlays has been reduced.

The design of more suitable production processes, in other words, would ordinarily require skills of engineering and economic analysis which are anything but plentiful in the areas needing to make the adaptations. For an indeterminate period, therefore, the initial stages of agricultural development and industrialization are bound to be afflicted with problems of the sort for which only time can provide some hope of amelioration. To be sure, more sensible policies would have helped matters along, whereas actual policies have often aggravated the difficulties. For example, the choice of capital-intensive production functions which are inappropriate to national factor endowments in Latin America has certainly been fostered strongly, if unintentionally, by state policy in most of the countries of the region. On the one hand, since much of the social welfare system has been financed by payroll taxes rather than out of general taxes on net income, the direct costs to firms of employing labor factors have been raised by substantial percentages. On the other hand, the cost to firms of investing in capital equipment has been reduced by such development incentives as preferential interest rates and favorable exchange rates as well as by tax incentives which are based mainly upon new outlays for fixed capital (i.e., plant, machinery, equipment) rather than new investments in working capital (including the labor payroll). Moreover, the frequent combination of fixed or stable exchange rates with domestic inflation has, by overvaluing domestic currencies in terms of foreign currencies, operated to lower the price of imported capital relative to the price of domestic labor and thereby encouraged the substitution of the former for the latter. Artificially, therefore, relative factor prices have been modified so as to encourage the kinds of investment expenditures which do little to relieve unemployment and which result in higher real costs to the economy. In addition, the ability of foreign-owned enterprises to draw their capital requirements directly from lower-cost capital supply sources abroad has also tended to favor the installation of capital-intensive production technologies in many of the newer industrial fields.

The third extenuating circumstance is that the process of Latin American industrialization has been attempted in a cultural environment which, despite its long history, has had only about a hundred years, at most, of experience with modern economic life—a short time, indeed, in which to develop the whole set of institutions, habits, and skills which are required for supporting the industrialization process in this era. With only a limited capacity for endogenous innovation in economic affairs, the institutional heritage made it also difficult to ingest and digest influences coming from the outside during the nineteenth and early twentieth centuries.

With this in mind, it is evident that the essence of the economic modernization effort of the past few decades would almost necessarily consist, as it has, of a great deal of institution-building of an innovative sort. It could hardly be otherwise, since economic functions do not simply occur by themselves but are performed by social organizations (or more accurately, the interaction of social organizations operating within a system). While it has nowhere been denied that additions to capital stock—e.g., through loans, investments, and grants—play an important role in the task of fostering sustained economic growth in Latin America, it has also been acknowledged, both in practice and in discussions, that a matter of possibly even greater urgency has been the need for institutional renovation in order to make more effective use of the resources already at hand, as well as to increase the domestic capacity to absorb productively the capital which might come in from abroad.

It would be fanciful, however, to imagine that the creation of permanent institutions capable of making continuing contributions to economic development might have been a comparatively easy process, especially when much of it was undertaken in Latin America prior to the postwar blossoming of knowledge in the field of development theory and analysis. Necessarily, in the absence of any comprehensive body of economic doctrine on the means of developing backward economies, much of the policy experimentation and institutional pragmatism had to proceed into a social territory which was only partially mapped by theoretical guidelines. The process was made even more difficult because of the need for moving somewhat away from the pattern of a market-directed economy. All along there has been at least an implicit awareness that as the market expresses the institutional order (whatever it may be) and as this latter was in Latin America in many ways inimical to economic growth, economic development has correspondingly implied a certain logical necessity for abridging or suspending the operations of the market mechanism in the process of reconstructing social organization in a more growth-conducive fashion. At the same time, a reform approach of this nature has involved acceptance of the risk of a possible loss of some of the economically serviceable functions of market signals.[80]

The Accomplishments of Neo-Orthodoxy

For all its indisputable deficiencies, the state in its direction of the public sector and its regulation of the private sector has had to play a vital economic role in largely uncharted fields of action by virtue of its capacity as the major restructuring agent of society. And with due allowance for its own condition of organization, the limited professional and technical skills at its command, the general lack of accurate data, the instability of the political order,[81] and the pressures, both internal and external, which have been brought to bear on it, it has on the whole performed in a more socially responsible manner than at any previous time in Latin American experience, if only because the state has come to respond to a wider sector of society than ever before.[82] Such costs as have been incurred in the process may be taken as a more or less unavoidable social outlay—a deferred charge for past failures in the area of social change, which finally has had to be met. From a different perspective, the costs may be viewed as the costs of having selected what is, hopefully, a speedier way of reaching a different pattern of economic and industrial organization and changing the structure of comparative advantage.

For example, the reduction of market risks through protectionist trade and exchange policies may in a number of instances have helped to induce local initiative to respond to the new profit opportunities created thereby and in the process encouraged a shift of funds from consumption flows and/or capital exports into domestic capital formation. Even when occurring in theoretically "uneconomic" industries, such investments may nevertheless have been more socially beneficial than the alternative uses to which such funds would otherwise have gone, however far from the optimum allocational pattern the end result might remain. For that matter, in evaluating the waste of domestic resources which has resulted from misallocating them to "uneconomic" industries, it should also be kept in mind that the net loss implied thereby from a theoretical standpoint may, considering the practical realities of the situation, sometimes appear rather more a case of less-than-maximum net gain. In other words, a good many of the so-called uneconomic manufacturing plants may have enabled resources to be used with higher productivity than they had in preexisting uses: e.g., in subsistence or latifundian agriculture, in conspicuous consumption, and in residential construction. Pending a more nearly complete transformation of institutional structure (especially that obtaining in the agricultural sector), the social opportunity cost of the labor employed in the industrialization program may, within the existing context, be set at zero or very near it, so that the discrepancy between firms' pecuniary costs and social opportunity costs might render the new industries less uneconomic than they would appear to be on an enterprise accounting basis.[83]

Furthermore, in some cases the threat of market deprivation implied by deliberate industrialization policies may actually have stimulated foreign investment in what might be called a process of anticipatory preemptive industrialization. That is, in the knowledge that national purchasing power is so limited that the first firms established in particular fields may be able to saturate the market, leaving little unfulfilled demand for later would-be entrants into those lines of production, foreign firms have hurried in to set up local manufacturing facilities before trade barriers were imposed and before balance-of-payments strains made it more difficult to obtain the requisite investment imports. In so doing, they preempted scarce production factors and in some cases, distributional outlets, as well as local demand. Yet, these types of foreign investments, no less than those associated with a more open-market economy, have brought the various ancillary benefits that make foreign investment far more valuable to the host economy than the addition to capital stock alone would indicate.

This last point can be extended more generally as another consideration which bears on any assessment of the costs of deliberate industrialization in Latin America, for to some extent the costs may be legitimately inter-preted as an investment in systemic change, the returns on which are realized through time in diffused form as the broad cultural influence of industrial activity. The growth of a spirit of business enterprise has undoubtedly been one such benefit, while the more rapid development of human skills—i.e., the accumulation of entrepreneurial and managerial experience, the development of a skilled labor force through on-job learning experience—has constituted another. Far more than Latin American agriculture, the new industrialization has increased the interest in technical training be-cause of its insistent demand for new skills, while the urbanization that has accompanied industrialization has facilitated provision of such educa-tional services as have been available on a modest scale. Inasmuch as developments of this nature work ultimately in the direction of increasing the familiarity with technical and scientific processes and enlarging the domestic supply of engineering and research skills, a plausible case could be made that the Latin American countries have also put themselves in a more favorable position than prevailed previously to generate the kinds of external economies an industrial civilization can offer in support of agri-cultural modernization.

Both the new business leadership and the industrial workers and em-ployees have been able to make good their claims to a portion of the national product, the former through protected profits and the latter through a combination of unionization, governmental intervention in wage setting, and social welfare programs. At least a beginning has been made, there-fore, toward effecting a wider distribution of income and wealth. More-over, just as the industrialization policies have tended to overcome trans-port difficulties by concentrating and enlarging national markets (i.e., through the movement of consumers and purchasing power to the major cities), thereby widening the range of investment opportunities, so also the joint processes of industrialization and urbanization have, by facili-tating communication and intensifying interaction, created a wider aware-ness of the possibilities of change. From this and the modifications induced in the structure of political power, it may reasonably be argued that, witt-ingly or unwittingly, the deliberate industrialization policies of the past several decades have helped considerably to accelerate the pace of cultural change and to that extent have built an environment more conducive to long-term economic expansion. More than a few advocates of neo-orthodoxy have implied, not unmindful of the social consequences of industrial development, that one of the advantages of developmental interventionism has been its utility in forcing the evolution of a new domestic power structure, bypassing rather than directly attacking (at least for the time being) the entrenched agrarian-based system.[84] Eventually, it was correctly foreseen, urban socio-economic changes would, by stimulating popular expectations, developing nontraditional leadership, and arousing the rural populace, generate forces which would render less and less tenable the vestigial institutional apparatus of old.

All these together—the new classes, attitudes, and abilities—must properly be included among the cultural and social effects which represent at least a partial repayment of the initial costs of industrial development, over and beyond the actual goods produced. Yet whereas the new and relatively costly "uneconomic" industries need not last forever, since their capital investment is amortizable in a comparatively short period and since resources can be reallocated to other uses with the passage of time, the cultural return on the investment constitutes a yield of a more enduring nature.

The Shortcomings of Neo-Orthodoxy

In considering the limitations of the neo-orthodox development approach, it should be kept in mind that the preoccupation with national industrialization has been a function of two major political constraints. In the first place, the political and social difficulties, quite apart from the technical difficulties, in directly tackling and reforming the structure of the agricultural sector have made the industrial route less controversial and therefore more politically attractive to date. In a number of cases the channeling of substantial aid to agriculture rather than to the industrial sector would, under the existing unreformed agrarian regimes, have been tantamount to aiding the political opposition. Hence, the neo-orthodox policy route arose from the dilemma that, politically, governments could neither give strong encouragement to agricultural development nor institute a basic reformation of that sector's organizational arrangements. Instead, the hope has been essentially that of Batlle's Colorado Party: that industrial growth would eventually elicit agricultural modernization without a controversial intervention. In the second place, owing to internal migration and the high natural rate of demographic increase in the cities (because of the concentration of health and sanitation improvements in the major urban areas), public authorities have for many years been operating under severe pressure from the urban populace to concoct policies to absorb unemployed production factors in the urban sector. The relatively uncontroversial basic welfare (and population-increasing) measures which had been introduced fairly early to meet popular expectations for state action were not matched by the more difficult fundamental reforms of the production structure which would have been required to lift national product commensurately. Accordingly, the state was forced to seek less controversial means of providing new employment and income opportunities at the points of most intense demand. Both political constraints, therefore, tended to give national industrialization the look of a panacea.

As a panacea, however, the policy expedient of internally oriented industrialization was to have only a temporally limited value. By the latter half of the fifties, the development cushion afforded by the foreign exchange reserves accumulated in the early forties had been used up, the temporary stimulus of the Korean crisis was past, and the postwar boom in coffee prices had changed abruptly into a sharp recession. The sluggish performance of the United States economy made that export market a dubious source of support for the Latin American external sector, while the introduction in the United States of certain trade restrictions protective of domestic interests seemed hardly a good augury for the future.

Even more ambiguous, perhaps, were the long-run implications of European economic recovery and integration. During the immediate postwar period, the United States had argued that the economic rehabilitation of western Europe was a first-order priority claim against the available foreign aid resources. Not only was this justified on the grounds that it was essential to meet a grave political threat from communism but it was also claimed that a restored economic vitality in Europe would, by strengthening Latin America's second-most important export market, ultimately redound to the benefit of the Western Hemisphere's development potential. In the same interval, the modest scale of the foreign aid program for Latin America had been further justified by reference to (a) the large external reserves built up by Latin America during the early forties and (b) the rapid growth of private foreign investment in the region. Both factors, together with the lending power of the Export-Import Bank and the World Bank, seemed sufficient to meet the major needs of Latin America for external resources up through the early fifties.[85]

Thereafter, however, European economic growth, and to some extent the prospects of European economic integration, began to pull a larger share of United States private capital exports across the North Atlantic. Meanwhile the emerging relationship between the European Economic Community and formerly dependent African regions raised the specter of discriminatory treatment against Latin American exports in the very market which had formerly been counted on to enhance the external economic position of Latin America. Also problematical were the prospects for Latin American trade with the countries of the European Free Trade Association, because of commonwealth ties and special trade connections with countries and territories of the African continent. When resolution of the Suez crisis and the opening of new petroleum fields in North Africa led to a drastic fall in the level of new United States private foreign investment in Venezuelan petroleum, still another source of external stimulation was removed. Not long afterwards events in Cuba served to dampen the interest of foreign investors in Latin America even more generally.

By the late fifties, in short, a combination of events and circumstances had undermined both the trade and investment components of the Latin American external sector, while the charges against foreign earnings arising out of previous capital transactions were steadily mounting. Against such a deteriorating background, the weaknesses and imbalances of neo-orthodox interventionism became so manifest as to compel a renewed search for more viable policy alternatives. In essence, what had been accomplished up to the mid-twentieth century was a second, rather limited, organizational renovation, one mainly designed to meet the most immediate exigencies of the industrialization process just as the earlier period between 1850 and 1914 had witnessed the elaboration of certain new mechanisms for promoting the expansion of the external sector.

Institutional innovations at the margin of the structural core had added some significant new possibilities to the growth patern, and the value of the accommodative adjustments devised to meet the demands of new functional interest groups should by no means be discounted. Both, beyond peradventure, accentuated social and political trends which were corrosive of the older institutional arrangements and which, by sharpening the internal contradictions of the received order, would ultimately precipitate the more fundamental changes that are the central concern of the policy scene today. Yet, disregarding the longer-run implications of the new development policies, the more immediate outcome of Latin American neo-orthodoxy was simply the grafting on of a species of state-sponsored industrial capitalism to the trunk of agrarian anachronism which had previously been modified only enough to permit the export sector to sprout.

While the earlier modification led almost ineluctably to the second, to an impressive degree the deepest roots of the old order were still barely touched. Whereas the earlier export growth experience had eventuated in the appearance of an externally linked enclave phenomenon, the new industrialization was also less than comprehensive in the sweep of its impact on national socio-economic structures. In a sense, it had brought into being a domestic sort of urban enclave which was still only partially integrated with the total pattern of national life. For this reason the phrase, "the twentieth-century policy revolution," which has sometimes been used to describe the compass of welfare and developmental interventionism seems ill-chosen, if not altogether inaccurate. Evolution there surely was, but the fundamental reordering suggested by the term revolution was largely absent.

That this is not too sweeping an assessment of the policy style launched by Batlle and, later, the Chileans can be indicated by a look at the salient shortcomings of the period. First and foremost among these has been the general, if understandable, failure to institute a radical reorganization of the rural sector in order to strengthen the base of the Latin American economies. Because of this failure to open up agrarian institutional structure, most of the modernizing efforts of the past several decades have been concentrated in the more flexible urban sector. For the most part, the agrarian programs of the period have been essentially of either a make-shift or placebo nature, and hardly ever was any serious and sustained effort made either to diversify agricultural exports or, for that matter, even to exploit, in a rational manner, the import-substitution possibilities of the agricultural sector. Locked in traditional practices of earlier times and deprived of the external economies which would have come from a greater social investment in institutions and services for modernizing agriculture, rural life in Latin America remained, to a considerable extent, under the direction of an ascriptively selected management whose function was more that of the passive rentier than that of the active entrepreneur.

The widespread emphasis on measures to enhance the attractiveness of industrial investments may actually have jeopardized the possibilities of an improvement of the agricultural scene by drawing enterprise and capital out of the rural sector and by increasing the price of the financial and material inputs of that sector.[86] For example, prices of material agricultural inputs have tended to rise where revenue duties have been collected on imported equipment and supplies, where farms have been forced to buy such items from more costly domestic supply sources, and where the artificially stimulated demand of the manufacturing sector for foreign exchange has bid up the exchange rate applicable to agricultural-sector imports. Similarly, the artificially stimulated demand of the industrial sector for domestic loan capital has tended to increase the interest rate for competing agricultural borrowers. In addition, discriminatory exchange and trade controls on agricultural exports, subsidized agricultural imports, and price controls on domestic rural production have also, on occasion, hampered national agricultural performance. Further, the overall system of industrial protectionism exacted an enormous subsidy from consumers in general for the benefit of national manufacturers and the privileged segments of the domestic industrial labor force.

For a variety of reasons, therefore, agricultural productivity lagged badly—so badly that a number of countries actually experienced a declining per capita agricultural output over the past two decades. Higher food and materials prices and rising expenditures of foreign exchange on agricultural imports have followed from the consequent supply inelasticities of the situation, and often there has been considerable difficulty in expanding and diversifying exports. For some countries, the discriminatory treatment of agriculture has also resulted in an inability to realize greater net returns from foreign sales of presently exported agricultural products. No less serious has been the persisting problem of the great mass of the rural population, whose opportunities for advancement, amid a confining latifundism and a retrograde minifundism, have remained either negligible or nonexistent. From the standpoint of employment conditions, the obstacles placed in the way of agricultural progress have inhibited expansion of precisely the sector most generally characterized by labor-intensive production functions and have thereby contributed to unemployment, underemployment, and low rural earnings. At the same time, alienated from effective participation, whether as producers or consumers, in the national economy, the low-productivity-and-income farm population has in most instances constituted a prime market limitation on further expansion of the urban-industrial sector.

It is not going too far to assert that the heart of the whole problem of income-distribution disparities lies in the unreformed nature of the agricultural sector, for even a considerable portion of the urban manifestation of that problem is attributable to the unsatisfactory state of affairs prevailing in the countryside and to the depressing influence of agrarian structure on the growth potentialities of provincial population centers.[87] Driven by mounting population pressure in an atrophied agricultural setting, increasing numbers of people have been induced by the cultural disparities existing between the provincial regions and the favored industrialized urban areas to move to what they believe to be a more advantageous opportunity structure.[88] Yet, inasmuch as the traditional cultural setting of the hinterland gave the migrants little or no preparation in the skills and attitudes needed for industrial life, the result has often been simply to shift the locus of unemployment and underemployment, and to bring into the metropolises a potentially disruptive mass which had not yet been effectively inducted into the shared beliefs and values and the common body of ideas of the dominant social sectors.[89]

Moreover, owing to the constrictions of the market served by urban industry, and to the kind of domestic demand pattern presented by a concentrated distribution of income, the relatively labor-intensive types of industries which came into being early in the process of import-substitution (e.g., nondurable consumer goods) began to lose their dynamism in the late forties and fifties. Latter-day industrial expansion shifted increasingly to the production of more elaborate consumer durables for the high-income consumers, and to the manufacture of producer goods. Since in all countries the absolute size of the domestic market was small to begin with, it is obvious that problems of economic scale in production would inevitably loom larger as industrial diversification gave birth to a wide range of goods and services, each of which represented only a minute fraction of the total market. Especially was this the case insofar as the more recently instituted lines of production tended to be in industries characterized by high minimal sizes of optimal-scaled plants. In these latter lines, the density of capital has been generally higher and the use of labor correspondingly lower, while the types of labor skills involved have also become more sophisticated than in the light industries established in previous decades.

Consequently, the recent growth of industrial diversification has displayed a marked tendency to require ever larger capital inputs to turn out goods purchasable by a diminishing portion of the population, all the while absorbing manpower at a declining rate. Owing to both the employment requisites of these more recently initiated industrial undertaking (i.e., their absorption of a comparatively small number of highly paid skilled workers) and the concurrent growth of monopoloid features in industrial structure (since the small size of the domestic market permits only a very few of the larger-scale ventures to be established in each line), the new income generated by these new lines of activity has tended to become progressively more concentrated among a smaller portion of the population, thereby restricting the scope of the employment and income multiplier effects on the rest of the economy. Because of the heavier capital outlays, with their high import coefficient, and the advanced technological and organizational skills required to set up the newer lines of industrial production, not to mention the difficulty of operating at an economic scale in the face of the small domestic demand, increasing difficulty has been encountered in maintaining at acceptable levels the national rates of investment and growth, let alone the rates of increase in new nonagricultural employment.[90]

Far more quickly than was the case in the first, light-industry stage of import-substitution industrialization, the second, more complex, stage of import-substitution industrialization ran up against the problem of market saturation. In addition to redundant agrarian employment, the problem of structural unemployment of unskilled labor in the urban sector assumed increasingly serious proportions in recent years as a result of the continuing strength of the rural-urban migration, overall population growth, and the changing character of domestic industry.

In the wake of the threatened, and in several major cases already evident, deceleration of domestic economic expansion, sharp questions were raised regarding much of the accomplishments of recent times—particularly where the continuation of inflation generated acute social tensions by accentuating the hardships suffered by those left out of the narrowing channel of growth. For one thing, it became difficult to justify the allocation of resources to new industries turning out consumer durable goods of a luxury or semiluxury nature for a small segment of the population while there was still such an obvious unmet social need for goods of a more utilitarian character. In particular, the unsatisfied potential demand of lower-income rural and urban people for the products of light industries suggested that a renewed expansion of this portion of the industrial structure would, because of its labor intensive character, require less new capital investment and less imported complex (and costly) machinery while it would also contribute more employment opportunities to the economy. In this, the requisites of continued industrial expansion lent cogency to the arguments derived from criteria of social justice. Similarly, the tendency of the heavier new industries to boost price levels upward, because of the high cost of capital for capital-intensive production functions and because of the cost problems encountered in the choice between suboptimal scale plants or underutilization of capacity in optimal-sized facilities, afforded further grounds for objection to the outcome of recent economic policy—not only from consumers but also from other producers who were forced by trade policies to buy investment goods from high-cost local manufacturers.

Since it was the shape of domestic market demand which determined the present course of industrial evolution, the criticism of industrial growth patterns ultimately came to focus on the income distribution parameters of economic growth. And this brought to the forefront of concern both the old agrarian latifundism and the newer urban "latifundism" which had emerged in the concentration of power in industry and finance. Tainted with the suspicion of collusive agreements and based, in part, upon quasi-monopolistic positions carved out of the economy through political pressure upon government to pursue highly protectionist policies, the new urban-sector version of latifundism has not been so obviously efficient in its use of resources as to fend off public criticism of its performance. It has, in fact, in at least the more sophisticated countries become as socially unacceptable as the agrarian prototype.

A further serious defect of much of contemporary Latin American development policy was the casual attention given to measures for stimulating exports and earning much needed foreign exchange. In a number of cases overvalued exchange rates even reduced the attractiveness of Latin American export goods to foreign buyers, while the indirect taxation of local export firms through multiple exchange rate systems undoubtedly discouraged further investment in these lines in several countries.[91] Yet, as import-substitution continued to be pushed, the initial requirements for imported capital equipment and often for imported fuels, raw materials, and intermediate goods as well, increased the need for foreign exchange, particularly as the drive for industrialization moved into the heavy industry sector. Meanwhile, the long gestation periods of certain of the new investments meant that these projects were often slow to yield their anticipated foreign-exchange savings.[92] Furthermore, the new income generated in urban areas by the inwardly directed investment process commonly raised the domestic demand for imported goods, as well as for locally produced items, beyond the level which resulted directly from the import coefficients of the new investment outlays themselves—an effect which on more than one occasion was intensified by a combination of domestic inflation and the control of exchange rates at unrealistic levels. Concurrently, as was noted in the case of Chile, the gradual displacement of less essential imports by more essential imports had given a much greater rigidity to the import structure, leaving less room for adjustment to unfavorable export variations. The latter were aggravated by the general lack of success in obtaining greater export diversification and/or the failure to achieve substantial advances in the productivity of export industries.

Accordingly, a good many of the nations were saddled with a growing burden of external repayment obligations, which, by the late fifties and the sixties, led repeatedly to refinancing operations designed to stretch out debt amortization periods and, predictably, to more clamorous demands for softer lending with longer terms, substantial grace periods, and minimal interest charges. During this period, balance-of-payments bottlenecks often made it difficult to assure a continuing supply of imported producer goods sufficient to expand aggregate output to meet the rising flow of money-spending in domestic markets, and domestic price levels responded to reflect this constriction. Here, too, the predicament of the export sector may be traced at least in part to somewhat the same set of circumstances which produced the deteriorating situation in agriculture. In both instances, in the absence of the sectoral reforms which the governments were not yet capable of effecting, a favoring of production would have involved a politically unpalatable support of traditional economic interests, both domestic and foreign.[93]

Not dissimilar policy constraints operated to obstruct the flow of foreign investment into the vital public utility field, with equally detrimental consequences for the possibilities of national investment. In some instances the result has been a persistent bottleneck in the provision of infrastructure services, which has raised the capital-output ratio of existing investments through interruptions of production flows. In other instances it has raised the initial capital investment requirements of new industrial ventures by necessitating a concomitant provision of private electric generating capacity on either a permanent or standby basis. In both cases, however, costs of production were elevated and price levels responded accordingly. Where the state stepped in directly to cope with the problems created by its regulatory system, the consequence was generally to add to an already overworked fiscal system the substantial burden of responsibility for capital provision in the most capital intensive sectors of the economy. Perhaps because of the urgency of this sort of demand on the limited resources of the state and because of the prevailing predisposition to focus on urban sector development as such, the general tendency has been to allocate wholly inadequate sums to transport construction and maintenance. Thus, agricultural development has been handicapped while industries have suffered from the uncertainties and high costs of intranational movements of materials and supplies as well as from the difficulty of economically reaching customers in extra-metropolitan markets. In short, the insufficiency of the resources devoted to infrastructure formation brought debilitating consequences for virtually all aspects of the productive superstructure.

An additional pervasive shortcoming of the interventionist policy configuration has been the failure to modernize national fiscal systems and systems of public administrations.[94] The result has been to leave the region with obsolete tax and spending systems which are not only inflexible, for being so closely tied to indirect taxes and the external sector, but often contraproductive as well. Thus, although government was widely employed as an instrument of development, it was often a rather blunt and clumsy instrument. Along with a general inability to curtail unproductive expenditures, it was usually difficult to mobilize all resources possible in order to induce them to flow into productive investment channels. In particular, since the prevailing revenue systems were unable to generate more resources for the public sector at a time when the public sector was expanding its activity, the consequence was often—aggravated by inadequate monetary controls—recurrent budgetary deficits financed out of central-bank borrowing, rapid monetary expansion, and an endemic inflationary condition, which among other things, has encouraged a diversion of savings into such relatively unproductive fields as inventory and real estate speculation in quest of effortless windfall gains

Further, owing to overexpansion of the governmental apparatus, with its attendant problems of inflated bureaucracies and defective internal coordination, the waste and administrative absorption of resources within the machinery of government has usually been substantial, featherbedding and inefficiency being only the beginnings of a lengthy list of abuses of public responsibility. On the output side of the public sector, the lack of long-range strategy, the propensity to guide public investment by sporadic and piecemeal plans lacking in consistency and continuity, and the frequent inability to follow through on public programs even when they were well conceived have both lowered the productivity of the public sector itself and contributed to the widespread inability to coordinate public and private sector investment for maximum effectiveness. Consequently, the reduced portion of public-sector expenditures actually eventuating in increases in national productive capacity added still further impetus to the inflationary pressure deriving from fiscal deficits.

At subnational levels of the fiscal structure, revenue starvation has been especially common. As a result, the inability to undertake local and provincial programs for constructing economic and social overhead capital served, in the course of time, to maintain and even to increase regional disparities in the investment environment, all the while contributing further to the supply inelasticities which have depressed the level of systemic economic performance. Paralleling subnational level fiscal limitations, it has also been generally the case that centralized control over local government—extending, for example, in the Colombian and Peruvian cases to centrally appointed, rather than locally elected, district prefects and municipal mayors—has operated to suppress local governmental initiative and to avert community control over local resource use. Save for unusual instances, scarce administrative talent with genuine civic dedication has not at all been attracted into these lower levels of government, where social control lies perhaps closest to the deployment of rural resources.

It must also be noted that, with the chief exception of Uruguay, a major deficiency of Latin American fiscal systems has been their lack of success in modifying significantly the highly unequal distribution of income and wealth, a distribution which has frequently failed to support in practice the historical justification for inequality on the basis of its presumed contribution to higher savings and investment coefficients.[95] Quite apart from the socially and politically unsettling effects of high affluence in the midst of poverty, the failure to redistribute income on a broader basis has undoubtedly played an important role in the reduction of national market size for many light industries and in encouraging the previously noted proliferation of new industrial ventures into increasingly uneconomic directions: into the production of consumer superfluities of a luxury nature, into more capital-intensive lines with complicated technologies, and into areas in which the optimal-scale plant tends to be high (with the result that either suboptimal plants are established or large plants are set up but operated at partial capacity).

Among the other policy shortcomings of the period under review, two may be noted as being especially significant for the present analysis: financial organization and education. So far as concerns the former, it may be observed that for all the developmental innovation which has occurred in the field of state banking, the network of financial institutions has manifested a chronic inadequacy in mobilizing private savings and allocating them among alternative uses in a manner compatible with the expressed national development objectives. Consequently, overinvestment in certain fields has coincided with underinvestment in others. Beyond this, however, the functioning of the capital and money markets has also been a factor in fostering the growth of urban "latifundism." For its part, commercial banking seldom extended the compass of its operations in a really imaginative way to elicit and gather up popular savings.[96] But if inflation—itself partly the result of the laxity of monetary controls—has had a role in discouraging thrift, there is also reason for believing that the popular mistrust of banks has been at least in part attributable to the failure of the old-line banks to serve the public. There is some evidence, for example, that recently established competing credit institutions, which have attempted to meet popular needs, have not only been able to encourage the habit of saving but also have induced depositors to bring in previously hoarded sums which formerly were not available as loanable funds. In general, it appears that the established commercial banks have existed to serve a very small privileged clientele, especially those *de la casa* (i.e., those having close connections with banking ownership), and that conventional banking practices have normally functioned to deprive substantial sectors (e.g., domestic agriculture), regions (e.g., the provincial areas), and numbers of firms (e.g., small and medium-sized businesses) of access to bank credit except, occasionally, on the most costly lending terms.[97] With access to bank credit on achievement criteria so poorly democratized, the long-standing and profitable practice of relending—by those enjoying the favor of lending institutions to those to whom the banks' doors were closed—has persisted to the present day. Where branch banking has been the custom, it has been further charged that the main effect of such arrangements has been to drain the provincial regions of loanable funds in favor of the ascriptively preferred borrowers of the central cities.

Still less progress has been made in developing meaningful capital markets in most of the countries, a defect which has constituted a special hardship for new enterprises in need of venture capital. To some extent this has been the case because prevailing patterns of income distribution forestalled the emergence of a sizable class of small investors. To some extent it has reflected the savings-depressing consequences of inflation. And to some extent it has resulted from monopoloid industrial structures and lenient tax enforcement which, by enhancing business profits and the possibilities of internal business savings and financing, have reduced the necessity for established firms to submit their requests for capital to the test of the impersonal market judgments.[98] Among the latter firms, their privileged access to bank credit seems not rarely to have enabled them to raise a portion of their capital needs by means of renewed term-loans from ordinary banking institutions—a practice encouraged on the one hand by interlocking corporate directorates and on the other by the commanding degree of economic (and political) power which qualifies them beyond question as prime credit risks. At the same time, the resort to debt financing in preference to equity financing has enabled established investing groups to avoid diluting their control of the major production enterprises.

Given the predominance of closely held private corporations, comparatively few top-quality shares have customarily been available for active trading on the existing security exchanges. The general absence or weakness of laws for safeguarding minority stockholding interests, for requiring public disclosure and authoritative scrutiny of relevant business information, and for enforcing verified and standardized accounting practices have served both to increase the risks of security purchases for small investors and to conceal the knowledge required for investors to allocate their funds on a rational basis. The very thinness of the market which has resulted from these circumstances has, by reducing the liquidity of stockholders, constituted still a further barrier to a broadened participation in the ownership structure of the national economies of the region.

Finally, for all the lip service paid the ideal of national development, there has been a singular reluctance to invest substantial amounts in popular education, a deficiency which, revealingly, has been most conspicuous in the field of rural education, where the bulk of the population generally resides and where a spread of knowledge and the increase in human capabilities would clearly prove disruptive of settled power relationships in the countryside.[99] Even where school facilities have been provided, the content of education has often been such as to render the investment largely disserviceable from the standpoint of propagating the supply of economically relevant skills. On both counts—i.e., the quantitative insufficiency and the qualitative inadequacy of schooling—the result has been to impede technological improvement, to retard the development of a skilled labor force and middle-management personnel, and to depress the supply of entrepreneurs alerted by education to the available economic opportunities and capacitated by appropriate knowledge to act upon them.[100] And just as the scarcity of skilled labor has exerted a strong upward movement in certain wage areas (pushing costs and prices upward), so the whole set of shortcomings in national educational programs may be charged with being one of the principal bottlenecks (or structural blockages) to an increased output of goods and services and, to that extent, a prime source of inflationary potential. On the whole, the customary attitude toward investment in knowledge—in general education and scientific development—bears the earmarks of a society in which an unequal distribution of income is accompanied by an unequal distribution of political power. As has often been noted, the development of a broad educational system under such circumstances brings few obvious gains to those who would have to provide the bulk of the tax revenues for the educational investment.[101]

It is germane also to recognize that the social contribution of such education as has been available has frequently been diminished by a pervasive tendency toward ascriptive recruitment, especially at the higher levels of economic organization. Thus, there has not always been a meaningful relationship between educational preparation and the assignment of economic roles. From the standpoint of the quality of economic leadership, the effects of this disparity have been serious. For example, the reports of various technical assistance missions sent to Latin America by the Council for International Progress in Management amply document the high degree of inefficiency prevailing in much of Latin American business organization because of defective management: indifference to rationalized production techniques, lack of interest in marketing analysis and proper marketing management, and a failure to employ cost accounting as a tool of managerial decision making.[102] Fairly common, too, have been the experiences with lax delivery schedules, unreliable adherence to product specifications, and highly variable quality-control procedures. Since firm inefficiency is translated into systemic inefficiency through the network of inter-firm transactions, the end result of this poor management behavior has been to create relatively unfavorable capital-output ratios in broad sectors of most of the Latin American economies and to diminish the possibilities for using national manufactures as a means of diversifying the export sector.

To counteract this problem, the routine sanctions of the market have been only weakly utilizable for several reasons. For one thing, the incapacity of the limited local markets to support a large number of firms in particular fields of production has stifled the pressure of domestic competition, as has the imperfect organization of domestic financial markets. Government trade and exchange policies have ordinarily insulated national producers from foreign competition, while fiscal policies have provided, through inflation, still additional coverage for production inefficiency.[103] Beyond these permissive conditions, however, the very extensiveness of interventionism has created a situation conducive to "politicized" managerial behavior rather than efficiency-oriented management.

For many of the major firms, profitability has depended less upon a combination of market judgment and cost-reducing measures in production than upon an astute cultivation of the favors of the administrative apparatus of the state. On the one hand, the inadequacies of bureaucratic control procedures have kept the door open to a particularistic use of government; on the other, the spread of economic controls has provided an increasing number of administrative decisions which can be manipulated for differential pecuniary advantage: tax policies, government contracts, import quotas and tariffs, government loans, exchange licenses and exchange rates, variably enforceable labor and social legislation, and so on. Under the circumstances, ascriptive patterns of staffing, for all their detrimental consequences on instrumental efficiency, have continued to be validated by the nature of the prevailing socio-economic system within which business enterprise has operated.

In surveying the limitations of the neo-orthodox policy configuration, it is patent that the major shortcomings of the period have not been merely happenstance. On the contrary, all of them—whether in the field of agrarian structure, or in income and property distribution, fiscal structure, financial organization, or educational development—have possessed a significant common denominator. In every case, the relatively unreformed institution has been one which lies especially close to or has intimate links with the distribution of power in Latin American society. Behind the considerable amount of policy experimentation and organizational innovation which characterized the past several decades, the fundamentals of the power structure survived in what was, all things considered, an only partially modified form.

Even the one area of actual reform which might appear to have modified the power system most significantly, namely, the achievements in labor and social legislation, in most cases did not radically change the system; there was an observable predisposition to withhold or soften the application of social legislation in areas which impinged directly upon deeply entrenched domestic economic interests.[104] Government intervention in industrial relations may, in fact, have impaired somewhat the longer term prospects for building greater organizational strength in the trade union movement, for labor union leaders were probably encouraged to see their main avenue of advancement in the governmental relationship rather than in the union movement as such. At the same time, the politicizing of labor-management relations may also have had the effect of undermining the commitment of rank-and-file members to their unions by shifting worker loyalties to extra-union political operators who could assist in affecting the desired settlements.[105] Government, as the dispenser of favors, instead of union strength in collective bargaining, became the kingpin of the system, and with this came the possibilities of subordinating union objectives to those of government and political parties. Consequently, with few exceptions, such as the Unión de Trabajadores Colombianos, it has proved exceedingly difficult to establish truly independent worker organizations capable of consistently representing worker interests in the forum of public debate. More often than not, trade unions have existed on the suffrance of those in control of the machinery of the state.

Indeed, within the crisis precipitated by the coincidence of adverse external developments and the gradual loss of dynamism in internally oriented growth processes, it is precisely the new awareness of the staying power of inherited institutional arrangements that has charged the contemporary search for a better development policy with such a high degree of social and political malaise. Thus, for example, despite Chile's forty years of experience with neo-orthodox development programs, the 1964 elections in that country still revolved about the issue of a fundamental restructuring of the social and economic order. Even the comparatively resilient Brazilian political system in the same year came close, perhaps closer than ever before, to a major breakdown. In Colombia, the paralysis of national policy making and a resumption of violence gave grim testimony in the mid-1960's to the extent of past failures in systemic modernization. Meanwhile, eleven years after the ignominious flight of Perón from Argentina, the citizens of Latin America's wealthiest nation had yet to find a clear way out of their chronic internal difficulties.[106] Across the River Plate the state of affairs in Uruguay, the initiator of neo-orthodoxy, was better only in that the acrimonious debate over economic failures was being conducted within a slightly more tranquil political environment.

From the foregoing, it is clear that one of the salient problems in contemporary Latin American development, that of inflation, is far from being solely attributable to monetary mismanagement and is, instead, symptomatic of the essential incompatibility between the projected new social goals and the limited institutional adjustments which have thus far been effected for attaining them. While monetary permissiveness has played a role in allowing the price level to respond to a wide variety of inflation-propagating factors, the propagating factors themselves have originated at a number of points in the system and are only partly a consequence of the behavioral reactions and structural rigidities which fiscal deficits and easy money policies have engendered.

As Roberto Campos and others have suggested, the international demonstration effect has operated somewhat asymmetrically in Latin America. While it has influenced in a decidedly expansionary manner both popular consumption habits and social expectations regarding overall systemic performance, it has had much less influence on the organization of production.[107] Consequently, the impetus for development has reflected more a pull from the demand side of the market than a push from the entrepreneurial or supply side. On the latter side, backward production and organizational technologies and a whole congeries of institutional obstacles, such as imperfections in factor markets and impediments to factor mobility, have inhibited the responsiveness of intersectoral and interindustry shifts of resources to a growing and increasingly diversified set of demands on the system. Meanwhile the domestic unrest generated by the excess of competing claims over present resource availabilities has aggravated the situation further by discouraging the inflow of foreign capital which might have relieved inflationary pressures, by encouraging the flight of domestic capital, and by forcing governments increasingly to operate on the basis of short-term political expediency rather than judiciously conceived long-term growth policies.

In the face of such besetting difficulties, whose manifold sources have been traced out previously, it is not to be wondered that symptomatic-level therapy has generally proved so unavailing. The problem of inflations, therefore, must be seen as one which is solvable primarily in the context of reforms more pervasive and radical than conventional contrainflationary fiscal and monetary policies imply. Both the monetarist and structuralist schools of thought regarding inflation recognize as much, the differences between them, on the policy prescription side, being the degree to which they see wisdom in working within the ordinary market and price system of resource allocation in the reconciliation of growth and stability objectives.

ECONOMIC INTEGRATION

Similar internal quandaries have been accountable for the almost geologic pace with which the larger Latin American countries, and some of their smaller neighbors, have moved toward realizing the plans of the Latin American Free Trade Association. Notions of unions, both economic and political, have long been discussed in Latin America, but during the 1950's the Economic Commission for Latin America began to lay the groundwork for a more serious consideration of regional economic integration by preparing a series of studies which indicated the prospective advantages of such a move.[108]

The times were especially propitious for a favorable hearing of integration proposals, for during the same decade the economies of Latin America had already begun to confront the problem of market saturation and the diminished dynamic this implied for import-substitution industrialization. At first this was evident in the light-industry sector, in which, after a considerable period of growth, overbuilt production capacity began to appear in such lines as textiles and artificial fibers, chinaware, glass and porcelain, plastic articles, and shoes. Even more swiftly, market saturation appeared in the newer heavy industry and consumer durable goods fields which had provided the main source of industrial expansion during the later 1950's: e.g., in chemicals, cement, machine tools, electric appliances, and automobiles. In both the light- and heavy-industry sectors, excess capacity had resulted from building ahead of demand, while in the latter case suboptimal-sized plants had also been established. In consequence, capital-output ratios were unfavorably affected, and productivity levels suffered. Accordingly, during the period in which ECLA was raising the new possibility of uniting national markets into a larger regional market, the countries of the region were faced with the unpleasant prospect of a faltering rate of expansion in industrial investment, output, and employment; and given the priority accorded the industrial sector, a slowing down of investment in that sector implied, other things being equal, a serious depression of the national coefficients of capital formation.

It was clear that significant areas of heavy industry could not be initiated at all on any potentially economic basis because of the insufficient size of existing domestic market demands for producer goods, while the predicted gap between development needs and the capacity to import seemed to rule out the possibility of obtaining these goods from abroad in adequate quantities. The expectations of ECLA and many others regarding the possible future expansion of primary commodity exports were, it must be recalled, decidedly pessimistic. And in spite of, say, the rather efficient modernized textile industry of Colombia or the comparatively satisfactory production ability of Brazil in a number of industrial lines, it was not generally believed that there were promising prospects for a substantial expansion of exports of Latin American manufactures to the highly competitive world market.

On these assumptions, export earnings were not expected to grow sufficiently to maintain existing ratios between national income and imports, so that increased import substitution was prerequisite to continued growth. Yet, as the ECLA studies remarked, the projections of regional growth requirements for the 1955-1975 period indicated that there would clearly be an area-wide demand for a variety of new goods which, even allowing for probable imports, would be sufficient to justify Latin American production of these items, provided that the new industries established to produce them could sell to an integrated regional market. For such fields as specialized steels, chemicals, machinery, railway and construction equipment, and automobiles and heavy vehicles, future industrial expansion could be based on a combination of growing domestic markets and supplementary export markets within Latin America itself.

By the end of the fifties, technicians in many of the major countries had seized with alacrity on the concept of regional economic integration as a *deus ex machina* which, by transcending the narrow markets of individual economies would enable the growth of the industrial sector to continue, especially in the intermediate goods, heavy industry, and consumer durables fields where considerations of scale are more important than in the light-industry sector. The essential logic of Latin American economic integration, therefore, was initially pinned to expectations that such a step would open up new horizons in industrial investment, options which had been foreclosed in the previous era of separate national development.

Regional tariff preferences and the like, in other words, would be utilized to reduce the risks and uncertainties that had previously inhibited the development of industrial lines which needed to sell to export markets from the outset in order to spread production costs over both export and home-market sales. Unit costs and prices, in turn, could theoretically be reduced for both portions of the market. And with more investment goods being produced within the integrated area, investment levels would be freed from the constraint long presented by the high import coefficient of most capital outlays. The advantages of this would theoretically accrue to both the private and the public sectors, especially insofar as it would permit fiscal policy to be employed more effectively to compensate for fluctuations in the external sector, although insofar as the LAFTA agreement would increase the elasticity of imports from other member countries it might be more effective as a restraint on inflation in particular instances than as a support for national antirecession measures.[109] The latter could conceivably be rendered more difficult because of the relation between imports and the domestic spending and employment multipliers.

Within the new context, the already encountered limits on import-substitution industrialization could be relaxed, the general development dynamism restored, and the depressing effects of excess and suboptimal capacity on levels of industrial productivity reduced. Alongside the deepening of the industrial structure, which would come from initiating new manufactures that are predicated on the existence of a large market and a corresponding high volume of output, it was felt that, following the insight of Adam Smith concerning the relationship between the extent of the market and the degree of specialization, new opportunities would also be gained for increasing the specialization of national industrial investment efforts, with consequent advantages in efficiency. As was pointed out in various of the integration studies, intra-industry specialization had already begun to emerge within the larger economies of the region in such fields as metal manufacturing and the engineering industries. For example, in the production of electric motors, sewing machines, electric and gas ranges, metal furniture, and the like, there was an observable tendency to subcontract to specialized firms the foundry part of the production process and even such functions as stamping, forging, and thermal treatments. In Brazil, with the accelerated development of automobile production, the few relatively large plants which initially produced a wide variety of components were giving way to a larger number of specialized smaller plants, each producing one or two parts. With integration, it was argued, additional opportunities for intra-industry specialization would appear in fields such as pulp and paper, cotton textiles, steel and nonferrous metals, railway equipment, motor vehicles, chemicals, and so on, on the basis of which further congeries of specialized satellite supply industries could be evolved. Somewhat paradoxically, the shift to larger scale output at the industry level would permit a functional proliferation of smaller scale enterprises clustered about the new lines of manufacturing promotion.

To the extent that the foregoing objectives could be attained, the case for the formation of LAFTA was strong indeed. From them would come the internal and external economies of scale which would enable the participating countries to realize increasing returns from their factors of production. The rise of the marginal efficiency of capital in the industrial sector would, in turn, doubtless elicit a higher rate of capital formation, both domestically and as a consequence of the new attractions held out to foreign investment, for the previous experience with import-substitution industrialization on a national scale had already served to increase considerably the elasticity of the supply of capital to residentiary manufacturing enterprises. Over the longer run, the resultant increases in employment and real incomes would both provide the basis for a larger amount of domestic capital accumulation and feedback into the system to expand the size of the several domestic markets—thus, presumably, circumventing the institutional obstacles which were difficult to tackle directly as a means of enlarging domestic market size.

Politically, if a certain Machiavellian motive may be imputed to the plans, not the least of the ways in which LAFTA would function as a powerful inducement to growth lay in its strengthening of the position of the socio-economic groups which, in previous years, had been most closely linked with the drive toward systemic modernization. Moreover, as an additional political corollary of the projected evolution of LAFTA, it was also suggested in the course of discussions that the regional economic integration scheme might constitute an instrument for improving the terms of trade between member countries and the rest of the world. On the one hand, the organizational framework of LAFTA was proposed as a mechanism for facilitating the development of a common policy and joint controls on exports, although the degree to which exports could be stabilized thereby would obviously depend upon enlisting the cooperation of nonmember exporters of competing commodities. On the other hand, the LAFTA structure was envisaged as a potential means of increasing the bargaining power of member countries in negotiating concessions from other nations and groups, such as the European Economic Community, though since LAFTA was not designed originally as a customs union, it was difficult to see how it might deliver effectively on promises of reciprocal tariff reductions. Yet, insofar as it served to amplify the resource and industrial base of Latin America, there was at least the possibility that an increased elasticity of demand for outside products might give some negotiating advantage in setting the terms of trade.

The orientation of the LAFTA agreement which was signed in February of 1960 was aimed primarily at realizing the so-called dynamic benefits of economic integration: i.e., the freeing of an anticipated future intercountry trade potential on the basis of which the large number of similar imports the member countries obtained from the rest of the world could be translated into complementary lines of domestic development through import substitution. Pending the evolution of the free trade association into a common market, a development urged with increasing frequency by the mid-sixties, there were only limited opportunities for achieving the static advantages of economic integration: i.e., the shift of demand to lower-cost producers within the integrated area, concentrating production at the most efficient points and giving a better use of resources already being utilized. Although it was true that one article of the Montevideo treaty urged members to grant tariff reductions on goods not presently traded among the signatory powers, most of the trade liberalization measures appeared to apply mainly to the existing items of intra-Latin American trade, while in practice the reciprocal concessions on "not presently traded items" were, in line with the dominant objective of the agreement, largely confined to those items which were also not produced significantly by the membership.

Accordingly, the vagueness of the treaty language, in conjunction with the realities of internal politics in each of the LAFTA states, left in limbo the status of a third significant category of goods—namely, the output of existing manufacturing industries which had previously developed in each of the major countries behind protectionist and import-substitution policies. Competitive rather than complementary on an area-wide basis, the intercountry similarity of this sheltered light-industry production (plus some consumer durables and a few intermediate-goods industries) precluded their figuring significantly among the goods traded among the Latin American countries and therefore in the trade categories most liable to liberalization measures. And although some economists such as Jacob Viner have argued that competitive economies benefit more from economic integration than do complementary economies (because of the static advantages to be gained from more intensive competition), there were reasons for believing that this would not easily result from the structure of the LAFTA agreement.

Past industrialization efforts conducted in a national context had indeed reduced the complementarity of the Latin American economies in the manufacturing field, but, significantly, the ambiguous escape clauses provided in the treaty authorized the member countries to suspend or revoke tariff concessions when balance-of-payments reasons should indicate a need to reduce imports, or when imports should have or be "liable to have, serious repercussions on specific activities of vital importance to the national economy."[110] Moreover, the complex item-by-item annual negotiating procedure set up for implementing trade liberalization gave wide latitude for vested interests in each country to exert pressure to stall on particular concessions, to a degree not possible in the across-the-board, layer-by-layer reduction approach adopted in the European Economic Community. For that matter, the potential benefits from heightened competition in manufactures were also reduced for two other reasons which were independent of the LAFTA organizational structure: the de facto protection offered by high intercountry transport costs (or nonexistent overland transport facilities) and the grossly underdeveloped state of regionally comprehensive market information systems and distributional channels for the conduct of intraregional trade.

If it be assumed that the existing geographical distribution of manufacturing facilities among the LAFTA members does not necessarily correspond to the intraregional distribution of comparative advantages in various industrial lines, the mode of operation chosen for the development of the scheme not only sacrifices certain of the potential static advantages of integration but also involves a risk of accentuating the misallocation of resources. Under the circumstances, the chronological incidence of particular trade concessions applicable to the area as a whole remained quite uncertain,[111] especially since there have been widespread doubts that the economic integration scheme would reach its successful conclusion anyway in the allotted twelve-year period. In the interim, capital and other resources could continue to flow into particular national fields of production which were uneconomic when compared with potentially competing facilities located elsewhere in the region, while expansion of the most efficient producers would be inhibited because of the uncertainty of the period in which they could reach out to sell to other markets in the LAFTA area.

In fact, to the extent that certain LAFTA-based investments should induce a rise in national incomes and, hence, the purchasing power in any national market, there was little to prevent this development from eliciting further investment in expanding the production of (at least temporarily) protected lines of manufactures catering to the domestic market, irrespective of whether or not such facilities enjoyed a comparative advantage from the standpoint of LAFTA as a whole.

Adding to the problem of anticipating the temporal and spatial incidence of concessions, was the use of weighted averages in computing the value of concessions. Thus, considerable variability from year to year was introduced into the distribution of concessions by product lines. For some items, initial reductions in tariff duties and other restrictions were not followed up, in subsequent negotiating periods, by further progressive reductions on the same items. For other goods, no concessions at all were arranged by certain of the member states during the initial years of the scheme. Overshadowing the whole procedure was the difficulty of anticipating when individual countries would become disposed to accord preferential treatment to high-cost manufactured imports from other LAFTA members instead of buying cheaper imports, of possibly better quality, from nonmembers—or, indeed, instead of reserving the home market for their own high-cost producers who, in any case, were in a position to influence national policy more strongly than could their would-be competitors from other LAFTA countries.

The static advantages of economic integration could conceivably be realized in fields other than manufactures, in the production of items which already constitute the bulk of intra-LAFTA trade. Yet the advantages to be derived from freeing this trade should not be overstated. Nearly half of the trade, for example, is in foodstuffs, where the diversity of soils and climates suggests a sound basis for agricultural complementarity and hence a point of departure for increased agricultural development built on trade among LAFTA markets. It may be doubted, however, whether export market constrictions are the chief obstacles to agricultural progress in the case of most of the countries; and in any event, for the near and intermediate term future the likely LAFTA demand will most probably represent only a very small portion of the total export demand for the commodities each of the countries supplies to external markets. The intra-LAFTA trade in agricultural produce, even more than the trade in industrial items, will also depend for its development upon the creation of cheaper transport facilities for handling bulk shipments within the region.

These considerations, together with the fact that in Latin America the minimum efficient scale of operations ordinarily tends to be much smaller for agricultural firms than for industrial firms, lead one to believe that the developmental impetus to be derived from a growth in LAFTA markets will not be among the important inducements to improved agricultural efficiency. By and large, substantial scope exists for improving agriculture quite independently of the wider LAFTA markets potentially available.

In the past, intercountry shipments of industrial raw materials and liquid fuels have accounted for the bulk of the remaining intra-LAFTA trade. While such shipments undoubtedly will expand as economic integration moves ahead, their expansion, like that of agricultural goods, will depend heavily upon substantial progress in the field of regional transport. Similarly, for many years the LAFTA demand is likely to be much less consequential than the export demand of nonmember countries as a condition affecting the development potential of suppliers of industrial raw materials in the several exporting countries. As for petroleum, the chief regional supplier of this product to other Latin American countries, Venezuela, was not until quite recently involved in the evolution of the LAFTA scheme. And while Brazil should continue to provide a major regional market for Venezuelan petroleum for a good many years, several of the other principal LAFTA members either have already achieved a near self-sufficiency in petroleum or, as in the case of Argentina, are likely to do so as present exploratory and developmental drilling activity proceeds.

For a number of reasons, therefore, the LAFTA structure fell short of creating a satisfactory framework in which the participating members could begin *ab initio* to direct their resources into the lines which would represent an optimal distribution of productive factors after the transition to free trade had been completed. Compounding the problem, both the physical and the organizational means for promoting the intraregional mobility of goods and productive factors were and still are in a very rudimentary state of development, except among a few adjacent countries in southern South America. Transport facilities and transport policies are only now beginning to be coordinated with a view to furthering intraregional traffic, while still embryonic, at best, are the comprehensive economic information systems and marketing structures which are prerequisite to an effective linkage of supply and demand in the evolving integrated system of product markets. Factor markets, being only primitive, for the most part, within the several member countries, have years or even decades to go before they can function as positive adjuncts to development on the larger scene.

Meanwhile, great variations exist in national policies regarding monetary matters, fiscal structure, wage and labor benefit systems, and tariffs and other controls on trade relations with nonmember countries. Foreign-exchange systems with multiple rates are still to be found, and varying degrees of overvaluation remain in national currencies. These and the variety of special investment inducements offered in the form of tax concessions, exemptions from duties, low-cost loans from state banks, and the like, all tend to influence the distribution of investments and the location of industry in a manner which may or may not accord with the distribution of comparative advantages within the integrated trading bloc as these would be determined by other criteria.[112] To date, moreover, only in rare instances have national planning and development programs been designed with a view to attaining a complementary intraregional balance among the several national development efforts, even as regards the new industries which supposedly are to lead the way to regional integration.

It would be idle at this point in time to conjecture at any length upon the ultimate larger economic consequences of the LAFTA program, to consider, for example, whether in the long run the balance of concessions would lead more in the direction of trade diversion or more toward trade creation. Despite the original intentions expressed in the Treaty of Montevideo, which called for a twelve-year program for realizing the aims of the treaty, it is now clear that regional economic integration will require a much longer period to become effective and that the experience of the first half of this initial experiment will likely result in a considerable revamping of the original structure, possibly in the direction of a customs union or common market.[113] Although intra-LAFTA trade grew by roughly 75 per cent between 1960 and 1964, with each successive bargaining conference the negotiations became more difficult, and the number of concessions placed on the National Schedules diminished, owing to domestic protectionist pressures and other problems. During the first session, some 3,246 concessions were made by the participating countries,[114] and in the second session the number of concessions made totaled 4,347. In the third and fourth sessions, however, the concessions agreed to amounted to only 655 and 307, respectively. Moreover, during the third and fourth bargaining conferences, half or more of the total concessions granted were made by only two of the member countries, Argentina and Mexico, and meanwhile a number of countries had made either few or no concessions at some of the sessions or actually withdrawn concessions granted previously. Practically no start at all was made towards reducing the widespread administrative protection which hampers foreign trade in Latin America.

The growing difficulty in dismantling tariff barriers and the failure to achieve substantial progress toward the creation of a vigorous trade in new products suggest that the main value of LAFTA thus far has been that of indicating the desirability of some alternative approach to economic integration.[115] Still other problems tend to reinforce this supposition. For one thing, to the extent that a new trade in manufactures may develop, it seems reasonable to expect that the major beneficiaries will be concerns with foreign ownership, particularly those which in the past have been exporting to the several national markets; for in the course of such business, these firms have developed the necessary market information and the marketing channels on a comprehensive regional basis which would give them a decided edge over purely national manufacturers in taking advantage of the wider market potentialities. More widespread marketing implies also a larger scale of production, and with greater management experience in large-scale operations as well as access to larger blocs of capital, foreign firms are better prepared than their native counterparts to establish the kinds of production facilities that economic integration is intended to call into being. Moreover, the capital and management of such firms, coming in large measure from the outside, undoubtedly have greater mobility in seeking the most promising locations for investment within the LAFTA region than do domestic Latin American capital and management. Should foreign firms reap the lion's share of integration benefits, new difficulties of an internal political nature would surely emerge to vex the subsequent evolution of the integration scheme.

In the second place, even the special concessions granted in the LAFTA treaty structure to the poorer countries may not suffice to retain the adherence of these nations to the scheme should the latent agglomerative tendencies of integration be realized.[116] The importance of water transport to intra-LAFTA traffic flows, for example, seems certain to increase the concentration of economic activity in the littoral regions of the continent without doing a great deal to open up the interior. Beyond, this, the marked disparity among participating regions and countries in their share in the available supply of externalities would seem to favor the concentration of new industrial investments in those locations already the most advanced, creating inequalities even greater than those which exist at present. While economically advantageous, in terms of its bearing on increases in total regional output, such a development would engender additional political tensions in an area whose supply of conflict situations is already by no means exiguous.

Finally, it must be recognized that the contribution of LAFTA to regional growth is to some extent proportional to the degree to which intra-American trade restrictions have been, in relation to other growth-inhibiting factors, important barriers to economic development in Latin America. As S. S. Dell has observed, a plausible case can be made that the internal structural features of the Latin American economies are far more consequential than tariffs and foreign-trade quotas as obstacles to economic progress.[117] Indeed, it may well be that, as much as deficient public understanding of the complicated subject of integration, the fact that LAFTA can be construed as a substitute for a frontal attack on the difficult domestic structural hindrances to growth accounts for the notable lack of general public enthusiasm for the project.[118] Given the dubious reliability of a trickle-down process of benefit diffusion in Latin America, it is difficult for many to see LAFTA as a very satisfactory alternative for well-conceived national reform and development programs. The fear has even been expressed that, in the absence of suitable mechanisms for coping with cartel agreements (such as might arise out of the industrial complementarity agreements) and the like, LAFTA might entrench more solidly the monopoloid features of the existing socio-economic structure. Moreover, whereas the Rome Treaty which set up the European Economic Community "concerns itself vaguely with social issues, the Montevideo Treaty goes much further: it ignores them completely." [119]

Objections or reservations of this sort seem hardly captious, for more than once, historically, innovations in doctrine and policy—such as import-substitution industrialization—have been used to dodge more fundamental issues of development. Already, for example, the allocation of considerable resources to the production of manufactured consumer superfluities rather than to expansion of the output of more utilitarian goods for meeting basic consumer needs has given rise to questions regarding the type of industrialization which has been fostered—and would be stimulated, *ceteris paribus*, by economic integration. The production of high-priced passenger cars, fashion shoes, luxury stoves and refrigerators, and so on versus the production of utility vehicles such as trucks and buses, small tractors, simple stoves, agricultural implements and work shoes is for many a more cogent statement of immediate allocational alternatives than merely a greater or lesser production of the former category of items. Similarly, the benefits to be derived from an increased intra-LAFTA trade in agricultural goods appear, to a considerable number of observers, to be small when compared with those derivable from changes in the domestic organization of agricultural production and marketing.

For some countries, it may be asked if the advantages of searching for supplementary markets in other Latin American economies are really so strong that the scarce human and organizational inputs devoted to the effort could not be more effectively employed in widening the domestic market through income redistribution, educational, and other reform programs which would incorporate into the home economy the rather large portion of the population excluded from effective participation therein. From the fuller employment of existing industrial capacity which would result, capital-output ratios and production costs would be lowered and the goods turned out by national industries would stand a better chance of becoming competitive in export markets, whether in LAFTA or elsewhere. For that matter, it would appear that in many instances the managerial and marketing practices of residentiary firms fall considerably short of meeting the standards of adequacy even for their immediate home markets, a circumstance which leads to skepticism regarding the potential efficacy of their performance in the more difficult and competitive field of export marketing. While this managerial backwardness reduces the gains to be anticipated from regional economic integration, it renders almost altogether vain the hopes more recently expressed by Latin American representatives at the United Nations Conference on Trade and Development that a removal of trade barriers on the part of the center countries would facilitate the expansion of manufacturing exports from Latin America.

In short, although the general value of regional economic integration commands acceptance as useful supplementary development policy, a very justifiable concern began to emerge in the sixties lest it, like the national industrialization policies which preceded it and gave it birth, divert attention from developmental problems of a more basic nature.

XIII

Development and Socialization

IN at least three cases, and to some extent in a fourth, contemporary economic development has been predicated on changes considerably more comprehensive than those involved in Latin American neo-orthodoxy. Bolivia, after its revolution of 1952, began to struggle towards a basis of national development which was profoundly different from that which had prevailed up to that time. Before the decade of the fifties had closed, Cuba had similarly abandoned the economic and social arrangements which had served as the matrix of development since independence from Spain. Almost half a century earlier, however, the Mexican nation had embarked on a radical new experiment which, as in the Bolivian and Cuban cases, began with a revolution that overturned the political and social structure of the antecedent era. In all three countries the revolutionary alteration of the economic system was unmistakable.

The fourth and more equivocal case is Venezuela, a country wedded to the externally oriented pattern of growth until the forties. During that decade the hallmarks of neo-orthodoxy were stamped on the system in the form of a policy of "sowing the petroleum" to foster internal development. With the return of the Acción Democrática government in the late fifties the acceleration of agrarian reform, educational improvement, and trade union development, not to mention the democratization of political processes, interacted with rapid urbanization and industrialization to produce realignments in social, political, and economic relationships which were de facto almost as sweeping as those which had evolved over the course of decades in Mexico.

Yet in Venezuela the process of systemic transformation, while accelerated, was nevertheless imbued with greater continuity than in any of the other three countries. Not only was there less of a political upheaval along the route (although irregular changes of government were involved), but also throughout the period the external sector continued to function as a valuable source of strength for the rest of the economy. More than that, it provided, with the tax changes of the forties, massive resources for the state to use in its various programs of socio-economic reconstruction. In revolutions as in other matters there is an undeniable advantage in being rich.

Of the three clear-cut examples of revolutionary development, the Mexican version is perhaps the most instructive. From the standpoint of assessing the effects of social reorganization on economic growth processes, the Cuban episode is still too recent, and too much colored by extraneous factors introduced by global politics, to permit very satisfactory study. Leaving aside the essentially polemical literature which has poured forth in volume from both advocates and opponents of the current regime, the more objective information which remains conveys little more than the not especially novel conclusions that administrative amateurism is exceedingly costly in a centrally planned economic system and that a state of belligerency and trade dislocation also have their costs. If certain undeniable advances have also been in evidence, it is apposite to remark that the imperfections of the prerevolutionary system were such that, in many areas of policy, almost any change was bound to constitute an improvement.[1]

The Bolivian case is similarly limited in its value for present purposes, although for somewhat different reasons.[2] Still young, as social experiments go, the Bolivian revolution is nevertheless old enough to have demonstrated already its capacity to produce constructive changes in a number of fields which bear on the long-term development possibilities of that country. For the first time in Bolivian history, notable headway has been made in integrating the large indigenous element into the social fabric of the nation, educational processes have been extended (often at local initiative) to include classes of the population formerly denied access to opportunities for self-improvement, and the agricultural sector has begun to show an unaccustomed measure of vitality. In rural and provincial population centers, especially, occupational structures have evolved in a more diversified and complex direction which seems to testify to an increase in the purchasing power generated and retained in local markets.

At the same time, however, the economic accomplishments of the Bolivian revolution are still overshadowed by the enormous liabilities with which geography and history have conspired to saddle the nation. On the former count alone, the lay of the land, its resource endowment, and locational factors would have presented substantial handicaps to the growth of national wealth irrespective of the type of economic policy selected. As for the latter, few nations had ever received so little benefit over the years from the growth of the export sector, even in Latin America, and the tin industry inherited by the revolutionary governments was, in spite of its critical role in the nation's balance of payments, one which was in a sadly deteriorating condition by 1952.[3] The postrevolutionary behavior of the labor force in mining—with its near-pathological concern for job security and its demands for wage settlements and fringe benefits which were excessive for prevailing levels of productivity—was an entirely understandable, if economically unfortunate, reaction to an environment in which current employment options were still quite limited and in which disproportionate gains had historically been reaped almost exclusively by the owners of minerals resources.[4] Never had these latter displayed the exemplary standards of socially responsible conduct to which foreign critics, apparently, expected the organized workers to adhere in the fifties and sixties.

Aside from the assertive, and often negative, reaction of trade unionists to programs for rehabilitating the vital mining industry, the administration of the nationalized mines and of much of the public sector generally has reflected the low level of managerial competence and inexperience which are the inevitable products of decades of disregard for progressive social investment policies. That a certain element of *revanche* should have colored the behavior of peasants, urban workers, and others in the system for several years following the revolution may have had adverse repercussions on the operating efficiency of the economy, but it was no less attributable than the foregoing to the circumstances of historical conditioning.

Thus, for much of the time since 1952 the Bolivian economy has been paying off bills in the "deferred social charges payable" account and in liquidating this liability, which could no longer be postponed, it has only recently begun to attain a position in which the post-1952 transformation could be reasonably expected to yield positive returns in the form of a higher national product. Redemption of the legacy left by over a century of republican mismanagement, not to mention the heritage of colonialism, has so far dominated the workings of economic processes in Bolivia, and it is thus premature to look to the Bolivian case for instruction on matured relationships between comprehensive social change and economic development.

At the same time the Bolivian and Cuban cases do serve to indicate a point which must be kept in mind also in examining the Mexican version of revolutionary change. In all three instances, a higher output of goods has been only one of the objectives of the contemporary development programs. The effectiveness of these programs, therefore, cannot be assessed altogether accurately by reference to an hypothesized optimum allocation of resources which takes its meaning from only one (i.e., material output) of the several ends being sought. On the contrary, the progress made towards realizing other ends in these "multiproduct" endeavors, though difficult to measure in a quantifiable way, must nevertheless be taken into reckoning.

This much said, one may go on to summarize most of the other objectives —which are, after all, as valid as the objective of increased income within the traditional framework of economic analysis—under the term developmental socialization. What has been sought in Mexico, Bolivia, Venezuela, and Cuba is the progressive socialization of economic life, and beyond that, the socialization of other areas of national relationships as well. The economic dimension is conjoint with important political and social dimensions. Moreover, as is indicated by the current Christian Democratic program in Chile, the historic principles of the Aprista ideology in Peru, or even the rather fuzzy outlines of Perón's *justicialismo* and Arévalo's "spiritual socialism," [5] the objectives of socialization are by no means confined to the particular countries which have moved most concertedly towards their attainment. At the same time, the diversity of means selected for socializing national economic life in the several Latin American countries should serve as a *caveat* against the simplistic equation of socialization with state ownership and operation of enterprises, i.e., with socialism in its conventional nineteenth-century meaning. Instead, the meaning of the term "developmental socialization" is much more complex, and its implications more profound. By a variety of measures socialization has been utilized to promote (a) a wider access to the opportunity structure, (b) a broader participation in economic decision-making processes (through spreading the control over productive assets), and (c) an expanded sharing in the fruits of the economy (through a wider distribution of income and social benefits). To provide a milieu more propitious for the linking of economic growth with these ends, the directed emergence of supportive social organization has been a central feature of public policy, which has also been employed deliberately to protect and enhance what has been conceived as the collective interest. Thus, in recognition of the contemporary importance of various collectivities and of conditions which have historically militated against individual mobility, the restructuring of social relationships involved in the socialization process has generally aimed at providing organized groups with greater advantages (and opportunities for group mobility) under the social system whose design became an explicit concern of public policy.

POSTULATES AND ASSUMPTIONS OF DEVELOPMENTAL SOCIALIZATION

The distinctive policy content of developmental socialization has been, at least until the early sixties, less readily identifiable than that of either the orthodox or Latin American neo-orthodox approaches to development. For this there are several reasons.

For one thing, in the formulation of orthodox and neo-orthodox perspectives, professional economists have played a larger role, elaborating their underlying economic rationales and enunciating the policy implications of these rationales. In contrast, the insights and goals of developmental socialization, which has shared certain features with the other two approaches, have emerged over the years out of the practical programs of political parties and the doctrines propounded by political and other intellectual leaders, few of whom have been professionally trained and practicing economists. Of late, a growing number of economists from several of the Latin American countries have begun to reappraise the historical experience of the region with a view to extracting more systematically from it policy implications which are linked with the perspective of developmental socialization— e.g., Edmundo Flores of Mexico, Celso Furtado of Brazil, and Aníbal Pinto and Jacques Chonchol of Chile. But by and large, the major outlines of developmental socialization have been evolved through a whole series of pragmatic adjustments to changing political and other circumstances.

In this evolutionary process, the most notable common feature has been a predisposition to utilize as a basic point of departure the assumption that the social, economic, and political systems which dominated most of Latin American history have become so discredited that nowadays they are productive more of conflict and a variety of other disutilities than of anything else. The remedial action sought, however, has not always been precisely defined. Often both diagnosis and therapy have been couched in an ideological mode of expression which borrows in varying degree from Marxism, or as in the space-time continuum of early-vintage Aprismo, from even more exotic and nebulous thought systems. Since such conceptualizations of the problem and its cures have frequently been employed mainly for their expressive or affective values, in a manner which verges on ritualistic formalism, there is a certain difficulty in deriving from them the policy specifications to which they lead in the field of economics. Here, in fact, the construction of a policy pattern by inference from actual experience would seem to constitute a more satisfactory means of ascertaining the content of developmental socialization.

The experiential approach itself is not without other difficulties. For one thing, as in any complex social phenomenon, the organizational behavior in question has been characterized by goal succession and multiplication in the course of time—e.g., the interweaving of industrialization and agrarian modernization objectives between 1930 and 1950 in Mexico. As new interest groups have come into being, deflecting organizational resources to ends other than those originally proclaimed as paramount, goal displacement has made its appearance as a further source of distortion—though, in practice, the allocation of resources to non-goal activities may simply have represented an unavoidable aspect of attending to those intrasystemic relationships which were necessary to maintain the new organizational system. If, for example, the Mexican Revolution has moved far afield from some of its early egalitarian objectives, this need not lead one to the conclusion that the Revolutionary development route has been abandoned or that it was a failure. As is now commonly appreciated in social analysis, goal succession and the diversion of resources to non-goal uses *may* be interpreted as a means of attaining the greater long-term organizational flexibility needed for adjusting to external and internal changes.

Finally, the very nature of the process of developmental socialization complicates the task of deriving its significance for and tracing its impact on economic policy, given the present state of knowledge in the development field, for the boundaries of the process far transcend that area of social existence which is conventionally placed within the "economic" sphere. In all of its variant manifestations, developmental socialization has involved an assumption or perception (not necessarily clearly formed at all times however) that the modernization of national life should be the chief focus of public policy, a focus which entails more than incremental changes and even more than macroeconomic structural shifts of greater magnitude, although these are subsidiary to the total process. Rather, the proper context of the process of developmental socialization is that of macrosocietal change. Alternatively stated, the full modernization of the social system is the over-riding concern, within which economic development constitutes a subobjective, one of the several lines of action which are bound up in the process of improving the institutional capability of the societies in question to meet growing and increasingly diversified demands.

With this broader end in view, the devising of new structures has been held essential to sanctioning values different from those prevailing previously, particularly for the purpose of developing the general institutional values, behavioral commitments, and attitudes which are characteristic of a society adapted to the industrial order. The educational system, for example, ceases to be a means for ratifying received insights and becomes instead a mechanism for feeding new skills and perceptions into the system; but to reinforce new values adequately, it is obvious that much else has to change as well. Other institutional innovations have been advocated and adopted to integrate the various participants in the system into national life through new relationships—relationships aimed at creating new sharing patterns in the distribution of power and a greater measure of social solidarity. Such, for instance, is the import of the several schemes through which industrial relations systems have been revamped to give a greater weight to worker interests as well as of the spread of popular education programs which constitute the chief link of the general populace to the modern communications network and the acquisition of skills (thereby reducing the monopolization of information and skills as an element of differential social advantage). In like manner, the long-term democratization of the credit system through such innovational instruments as governmental savings and lending institutions, credit cooperatives, workers banks, and mobile banking has sought to modify attitudes and habits no less than the distribution of power over resource use. Associational development through the public encouragement of trade unions and farmer organizations has played its role as well. But perhaps no measure has been quite so central to the process as the introduction of agrarian reform to restructure directly the relations of production in agriculture, and indirectly the larger national pattern of social dynamics.

Inevitably, all such efforts, which are subsumed under the primary objective of building a viable and modernizing society, require some resource inputs and must necessarily, therefore, be included among the contending claims which have to be met in the resource allocation process. For example, the redirection of resources to nurture the growth of social groups whose political influence is presumably cast on the side of policies which promote national modernization involves a corresponding measure of resource deprivation for the institutions and social groups whose actions are believed to be antithetical to this effort. Similarly, additional claims against current resource availabilities have been generated through the implementation of a variety of programs which have had as their aim an enlargement of the boundaries of the economic opportunity structure so that the network of material incentives relates more meaningfully to a larger portion of the citizenry. Still further claims on the use of resources have arisen out of the fundamental necessity for maintaining the new and evolving system as a going concern. Thus, social or systemic viability has emerged as a major allocational criterion with ramifications extending considerably beyond the mere level of the output of goods and services which are measured in national product and income accounting. Material output represents but one of several resource-using elements which the new allocation patterns of developmental socialization have attempted to increase, even though it is the one which is most susceptible to quantification and measurement in the conventional framework of economic development analysis.

If for this reason it is difficult to apply routine economic analysis in an altogether satisfactory way to the multi-output endeavor which is here called developmental socialization, there is another problem which stems from a further common assumption embodied in this conceptualization of the development process. Not only is the total output of the resource inputs hard to evaluate; a precise and measurable specification of the input-output relationships postulated by the exponents of developmental socialization is also very nearly impossible. Yet one of the fundamental assumptions of that approach is that in the long run the aggregate volume of resources (or inputs) available for allocation is a function of the less readily measurable outputs in previous production periods. In other words, most of the public policy activity of the approach is predicated on the assumption that economic growth depends, ultimately, upon a substantial and comprehensive renovation of social organization, including a restructuring of some existing institutions, the abandonment of others (such as the hacienda), and the formation of new intermediate-level structures to reorganize relationships among economic and social processes in a growth-supportive manner.

The use of current resources to build new communications networks to disseminate market information and production knowledge on a broader scale is one rather obvious example of these postulated input-output relationships. The wider dispersion of incentives throughout the various strata of Latin American society is another. The intent, clearly, has been that of restructuring the system of socio-economic roles in such a manner as to shift the relation of participants in the system from a passive to a more active engagement. Thus, the formerly submissive peon becomes a farmer; the subsistence-sector consumer becomes a member of an emerging mass market wherein he contributes to creating a more salubrious climate for industry and agriculture and to raising the productivity of the existing stock of capital. Correspondingly, because of the wider array of investment opportunities and the concomitant greater inducement to save, the native businessman becomes less a passive manager of stable relationships and more an enterprising figure, taking a growing role in the shift from customary means of production to an era of changing technology. In the context of a more active labor market characterized by an expanding array of job opportunities, the worker becomes less a mere jobholder, clinging tenaciously to whatever employment circumstances may provide, and more a production agent with opportunities for expressing his initiative through improved skills and upward mobility.

The creation of institutions for handling intergroup conflict through negotiation and the evolution of consensus-building structures represents still a third type of postulated input-output relationship, one which aims at avoiding the production losses occasioned by such things as industrial strife, capital flights, and conflict-generated inflationary movements. In like manner, agrarian reform, itself a multipurpose measure, has been deemed prerequisite for putting an end to the centuries-old underutilization of land and labor resources, just as this and other policy measures have been aimed at curtailing the losses of future output which would ensue from a continuation of expenditures primarily intended to attest to high status. For that matter, the use of resources in various ways to legitimize and stabilize the political authority of central governments is also intended to be related to the long term growth of material output in several respects: by providing greater continuity and a longer-term time horizon for planning and public policy implementation (thereby reducing the wastes of ineffectual and shifting policies), by increasing the feasible range of choices in the formation of public policy, by permitting the accumulation of greater experience on the part of public-sector personnel, and in general, by enabling the public sector to assume a greater measure of authority in the allocation of resources and power, thereby extending the role of the state from that of maintaining order to that of actively managing the processes of change.

The very listing of some of the new input-output relationships postulated by the developmental socialization approach to economic growth reveals the elusive nature, from the standpoint of empirical verification, of many of the policy assumptions most central to this conceptualization of the growth process. Intuitively, the majority of these assumptions seem sound enough, but inasmuch as they lack the (perhaps misleading) analytical clarity of the orthodox and Latin American neo-orthodox positions on growth policy, they have not yet eventuated in explicit and reasonably systematic policy statements such as are available for these other development strategies. This being the case, it is perhaps advisable simply to move on to a consideration of the experience of the country which has had the longest record of identification with developmental socialization: Mexico.

THE MEXICAN REVOLUTIONARY PATTERN OF DEVELOPMENT

In asserting that the Mexican path to development contains important distinctive features and that it has, on the whole, been consistently more successful over a longer period of time than the developmental approaches practiced elsewhere in Latin America in recent decades, one must also make explicit certain matters which are not, properly speaking, a part of those assertions. The modern Mexican experience with economic growth has attracted more attention from abroad than efforts in any other Latin American country. Further, as a testimony to the success of the Mexican experiment in cultivating domestic intellectual resources, it has engendered copious discussion, analysis, and debate among the Mexicans themselves. Although fairly impartial and thoughtful studies are now abundant for one or another aspect of the Mexican development process, it is still a subject which tends to evoke emotional or ideological reaction, and private preconceptions have a way of intruding into much of the discussion even, or perhaps especially, when they are not always forthrightly confessed. To reduce confusion it is therefore well to clarify a few points at the outset.

Common Features with Neo-Orthodoxy. To say that the Mexican encounter with economic modernization is distinctive is not the same as saying that it is unique. Indeed, institutional formulae associated with Mexican social processes are common to the whole tradition of Latin American neo-orthodoxy. As in many of the other countries of the hemisphere, the twentieth century has brought in Mexico a repudiation of liberal economic norms; the Revolution, as Daniel Cosío Villegas has succinctly expressed it, "assigned to the state, as of old, the role of principal promoter of the nation's material and moral well being." [6] Accordingly, most of the interventionist techniques previously noted have also been employed in Mexico. [7]

Beginning in the late thirties, the railway lines were completely nationalized. With the creation of the Federal Electricity Commission at about the time that the petroleum industry was expropriated in 1938, the operations of the public sector began to expand steadily in the basic energy field, a development which culminated in 1960 in the government's purchase of the major remaining privately owned (and foreign-owned) public-service power companies. As early as 1925 the government had made its first move to subject the money market to closer public control with the establishment of the Banco de México as a central bank which had, until the banking reforms of 1932, commercial banking functions as well. In 1926 the first of the state-operated sectoral banks came into being when the National Agricultural and Livestock Bank (Banco Nacional de Crédito Agrícola y Ganadero) was set up, while the subsequent three decades brought the initiation and development of a broad array of government banking institutions which operated directly in and extended the coverage of the national money market. [8] Alongside the evolving system of public credit institutions, the government took steps in the early thirties which involved the state increasingly in the organization and management of a national capital market. And over the years, a number of regional development authorities were set up as well.

Concurrently with the other interventionary measures of the thirties, public authority was extended to encompass the foreign-trade sector, mainly by means of tariffs and import quotas and licenses rather than through exchange controls and multiple exchange rates, which in Mexico were employed for a much briefer period than elsewhere in Latin America. Not to be overlooked in this connection is the attention accorded by the government to the export side of the external sector through such public entities as the National Foreign Commerce Bank (Banco Nacional de Comercio Exterior, established in 1937) and a variety of governmental commissions which were charged with fostering the development of particular crops. In the internal marketing system, government action has been expressed in many ways—the regulation of basic commodity prices, the establishment of a system of supervised slaughterhouses, the creation in 1936 of a National Warehouse Company (Almacenes Nacionales de Depósito), to mention only a few. With the establishment in 1937 of the Mexican Export-Import Company or CEIMSA (Compañía Exportadora e Importadora Mexicana), the state moved further and more directly still into the field of marketing by buying (locally and abroad) and distributing at bargain prices the foodstuffs consumed by low-income segments of the population. After CEIMSA was reorganized and absorbed into the National Popular Subsistence Company or CONASUPO (Compañía Nacional de Subsistencias Populares) in 1961, state merchandising operations were extended also to the handling of soft goods of a mass-consumption character. Yet most of these public forays into the business field had their equivalents in a number of other Latin American countries, as did the Federal Labor Law of 1931, which required the hiring of nationals by foreign companies.

Again, just as in other larger Latin American countries, deliberate industrialization has been a prominent theme in Mexican development. Even in the early turbulent years of the Revolution, national leaders were not unaware of the ultimate desirability of building upon the industrial base which had been constructed during the Porfirian era, although other matters required more direct attention at the time. During the 1920's, domestic manufacturing revived and began to grow again, thanks to the effects of public works programs and other trends,[9] while these and the repercussions of the world economic dislocations of the thirties provided the environment for a continuing elaboration of domestic manufacturing structure. During this period, too, the newly established Nacional Financiera, a state financing institution charged, among other things, with strengthening the securities market, began its first experiments with industrial financing—a function which, in conjunction with actual industrial entrepreneuring, became the dominant activity of the institution during the forties and fifties.[10] By the forties, the cumulative expansion of domestic industry, furthered by wartime conditions and increased governmental support, made it seem to many that the Mexican Revolution had become synonymous with the accelerated promotion of industrialization. With the backing of both domestic and foreign capital, new manufacturing enterprises appeared in ever-increasing variety, and public policy pronouncements not infrequently reflected the import-substitution doctrines being propagated by ECLA.

In brief, a great deal of contemporary economic history in Mexico displayed the policy hallmarks familiar over much of the hemisphere.

Special Favoring Circumstances. Though it cannot be maintained that Mexican experience has been altogether different from that of other Latin American countries, neither can it be asserted that Mexican economic achievements have been entirely attributable to wise direction by Revolutionary public authority. The country had an advantage in being able to build upon the accumulated economic experience of the Porfirian period, from which it inherited a number of key railway lines and other types of infrastructure, a variety of manufacturing and extractive enterprises, and the nucleus of an industrial labor force. The diversity of its domestic resource base and its large population—second only to Brazil in Latin America—were also favorable in their bearing on the possibilities for installing internally oriented development policies.

Moreover, there was "available" a fairly long period of time in which the country could experimentally begin to evolve its present system. While internal frictions were often acute and even sanguinary during the earlier decades of the Revolution, the impact of externally induced tensions stemming from the cold war struggle or even, simply, the international demonstration effect was probably less, over much of the period, than it is today among many of the less developed countries. Though hostile foreign pressures were by no means totally absent, especially those which were exerted intermittently from the United States, techniques of external interference had yet to reach the levels of sophistication and intensity which are now fairly commonplace. At the same time, this circumstance was not an unmixed blessing, for, throughout much of the period since 1910 Mexican policy makers were necessarily operating without benefit of such developmental guidelines as modern economic theory has adduced in recent years. And for three decades or so, foreign aid figured hardly at all among the resources available to those in charge of developing the Mexican national economy.

The proximity of the country to the United States, for all its disadvantages in certain respects, was also beneficial in more ways than one. Cross-cultural influences which generally supported the modernization of attitudes and skills, along with less desirable traits, flowed southward from the northern border of the republic, and the ease with which the Mexican economy could be linked with the wartime production effort of the United States undoubtedly accentuated the stimulation given to the Mexican economy by the Second World War. Geographical proximity facilitated the supply of developmental imports, while creating a readily accessible foreign market for various Mexican export items.[11] Of more than modest importance were the opportunities this latter aspect provided for expanding the nation's dollar earnings from tourism, and until termination of the practice in the mid-sixties, from the exportation of seasonal labor.

While one would not wish to detract from the accomplishments of the Mexicans themselves, such factors as the foregoing must be recognized for making important contributions to the success of the country over the long run.

Deficiencies in Mexican Development. Although impressive material and social progress has been realized in Mexico, giving that country one of the higher and more stable growth rates in Latin America during recent times, there is a considerable distance still remaining between the present state of the Mexican economy and any plausible version of an abundant society. For reasons best known to themselves, some foreign observers have seemed to feel that the failure of Mexico to reach the millennium constitutes a self-evident indictment of fundamental weaknesses in the Mexican system, if not a failure of the Mexican Revolution itself; and repeatedly the conclusion has been drawn that just around the corner a drastic showdown lies in wait. Within Mexico, too, there have been Jeremiahs enough and of sufficient variety to satisfy almost any conceivable ideological shade of pessimistic inclination.

One need not, however, resort to cataclysmic prophecies of deep dilemmas and irresolvable contradictions in order to recognize that errors of policy have been committed, that many problems await a resolution, and that in any complex society where open dissent is permitted there are normally conflicting interests and views regarding alternative courses of policy action. That Mexico has not been exempted from political stresses and has encountered certain difficulties in assuring the long-term maintenance of a high growth rate would seem to indicate that it has not yet hit upon a policy line more infallible than those followed by many more economically advanced nations—a somewhat pedestrian conclusion which is perhaps rather less surprising than the views of those who appear to find this circumstance exceptional and worthy of extended comment.

In any event, leaving aside the various criticisms which have been made of the political arrangements of the country, it may be useful to summarize a few of the more significant problems with which development policy will have to cope in the future. Of these, one of the most serious—the rising rate of population growth, which has already diluted the aggregate GNP growth rate when figured on a per capita basis—has as yet received the least explicit response in the discussion of public policy. The problems it creates are so familiar in the literature of development that further comment is not needed beyond remarking that the demographic growth rate itself is a testimony to the advances in health and nutrition which have been made heretofore. Closely related to the demographic predicament is another problem, which has been accorded more attention, that of investing sufficient resources to improve the quality of the ever more numerous human factors of production and reorganizing the educational system to supply the sophisticated and specialized technical skills which are now required by the economy in virtue of its past successes in development.

Particularly troublesome for those who would solve the foregoing problems is the growth in numbers of the low-income segments of society, where a good many people have been bypassed in the national drive towards modernization, both in the urban and rural sectors, even as the middle and upper income groups have increased in numbers and in economic strength. To make headway, however, in linking lower-income segments more productively into the system would obviously require a transfer of resources away from the more privileged members of the social and economic structure and thus a reduction of the marked interclass disparities in income and wealth which rapid economic growth has fostered. Though, economically speaking, the positive gains to be realized from such a reallocation of resources would tend to offset a possible contraproductive reaction on the part of those relieved of some of their income, the political resistance to redistributive measures resembles the difficulties which have almost always attended the initial implementation of such programs elsewhere in the western world. At the same time it must be recognized that the very existence of potential clashes over policy appropriateness between the directors of the public sector and the leadership of the business community testifies to the success of past interventionary policies in stimulating a vigorous growth of domestic private entrepreneurship out of the shambles of the Porfirian collapse.

For a large portion of the poorer group in the Mexican nation, future social investment programs, to be effective, must necessarily be tied in with more complex institutional changes, such as major improvements in the provision of agricultural extension and rural credit. Nowhere is this required more than in the case of the small farmers and *ejidatarios* (members of collectively owned but not necessarily collectively operated farms) of the central and southern regions of the republic where population growth has led to the progressive subdivision of rural properties and where primitive agricultural practice has caused erosion and impaired soil fertility. Thus a broader policy question overlaps the income distribution controversy, the problem of human resources development, and the issue of persisting rural poverty—namely, the conspicuous disparities in regional participation in national modernization and development processes. Although regional backwardness is not necessarily objectionable from the standpoint of national economic growth, and while in Mexico the controversy over interregional differences has not become so sharp as in Brazil and has in fact been muted by the outward consensus maintained by the ruling political party (the PRI or Institutional Revolutionary Party), there have nevertheless been occasional political reverberations sufficient to produce a governmental response to the problem in the form of assorted regional development programs.

More generally, however, the regional-disparity issue has been properly viewed as a derivative of a complex of particular economic relationships, and it has been on these that remedial measures have tended to concentrate, though perhaps in an insufficiently concerted or coordinated manner.

At the same time, the questions of persisting rural and regional backwardness must be seen in the context of the entire national record of development. If, for example, the relative income position of certain population groups and areas has evidently deteriorated, this has often been less a matter of absolute deterioration than of the marked advances registered in other portions of the economic structure: e.g., the concentration of a great deal of the industrial expansion in such locations as the Federal District and Monterrey and the notable progress which has been made in, say, the agriculture of northwestern Mexico. Not surprisingly, available investment resources have more often been channeled according to potential productivity criteria, as in the case of agriculture, than according to abstract notions of maintaining regional parities. In the process, some groups and regions have been left behind. Even on these, however, the Revolutionary regime has often conferred some benefits in the form of the subsidized distribution of mass-consumption items, the provision of rudimentary social services, and grants of subsistence farm parcels (on *ejidos* and land-settlement schemes) which have afforded at least a measure of protection against arbitrary treatment by rural employers. In the long history of unremunerative lending which has characterized the operations of the Banco Nacional de Crédito Ejidal (National Ejido Credit Bank) since its establishment in 1935, one finds additional evidence of the compensation prizes awarded by the government to those who were otherwise bypassed in the drive for national development.

Not to be discounted either is the undoubted psychic value of the status of *ejidatario* (a member of an *ejido*) as contrasted with that of the landless peon. In the long run one of the most important aspects of the Revolutionary program may well turn out to have been its ability to generate, during earlier and more critical decades, a fairly ample output of psychic rewards and elements of status, e.g., the welfare-service symbols of governmental concern and recognition, official support of trade union expansion, ejidal property ownership, and membership and offices in the political party structure and new interest-group organizations. By this expansion of the status system, nonmaterial components of welfare could be distributed much more widely than could material and financial resources, which had to be allocated more sparingly in the interests of economic growth. Although the trade-off ratios between these two categories of rewards have begun to change in recent times, it would be incomplete to ignore the value of these substitution possibilities during earlier periods—or, for that matter, the reservoir of goodwill which has remained up to the present day in the form of a wider latitude for selection among alternatives in development policies.

Notwithstanding scattered manifestations of lower-class discontent, and the hopes of some for capitalizing these to political advantage, it must be conceded that the lively public discussion which has attended such controversial and sensitive issues as the problem of income and wealth distribution has highlighted the contrast between the fundamental stability of the Mexican system and the more vulnerable structures of other Latin American countries. Furthermore, the fact that the present relevance of earlier institutional solutions adopted by the Revolution, even the *ejido* itself, has come to be openly questioned in the forum of public opinion is at least as much an indication of growing national maturity as it is of the shortcomings of the system.

Finally, by virtue of its past attractiveness for foreign public and private capital, Mexico has begun to reach a point at which the foreign debt service obligations have risen to a high level in relation to export earnings and current import requirements, which are mostly goods used in sustaining national investment levels. Furthermore, as in the other more developed Latin American countries, the newer industries require a comparatively large market for successful operation. Without denying the difficulty of transcending these obstacles, one must nevertheless assess the bearing of these considerations on future growth possibilities in the light of the record of past performance. For a number of reasons, the prospects are not necessarily dim.

In the first place, the domestic market, which has already demonstrated a remarkable capacity for expansion over several decades, should continue to grow over the years ahead, with far less rigid limitations than are customarily encountered in most of the other Latin American countries. Cultural dualism, for example, has been on the wane for years, while growing urbanization (a geographically widespread phenomenon notwithstanding the particularly accentuated rise in the population of the metropolitan area centering on Mexico City) and the comparatively well-integrated national transport and communications networks lend further support to the market amplification process. Moreover, in appropriate social investment policies, such as further strengthening of the agricultural extension services and popular education programs, and in an assortment of income-redistribution measures, such as the recently inaugurated national profit-sharing scheme, the government has available the experience and the means for stimulating national investment through policies which would accelerate the expansion of the mass market. Given the deepening of the industrial structure which has already been effected in past decades, it seems reasonable to anticipate that a considerable growth of the light-manufacturing sector could occur with a declining import coefficient in investment, while at the same time the growing breadth of the derivative demand for producer goods should facilitate the continued expansion of intermediate and capital goods industries. The increased elasticity of internally available supplies (of a steadily growing variety of goods), of course, has given the government a certain leeway in using public sector expenditures to stimulate domestic prosperity which is often absent in other Latin American countries where balance of payments constraints reduce the room for maneuvering in fiscal policy.

Although it may be true that the capital-output ratios tend to be higher in the newer lines of Mexican industrial development than in some of those which enjoyed a major period of expansion in years past, it would appear to be questionable to assume that future growth would necessarily involve any substantial increase in this relationship at the aggregate or national level. For one thing, the investments made between, say, 1940 and the present, have already included substantial outlays in a number of critical capital-intensive areas such as electric power and hydraulic projects, transport development, and the petroleum, chemical, and siderurgical lines. Consequently, the future investment needs in these and similar fields are often more a keeping up with the growing domestic demand than a catching up with demand after a protracted period of underinvestment, as is the case in many of Mexico's sister republics. Indeed, it is logical to expect that increasing returns will be realized in the years ahead from many of the past investments in infrastructure and basic industries.

Mexico has also long demonstrated an ability to direct capital into fields which make a relatively high contribution to growth, as a consequence of which the nation has been able to maintain a more favorable relationship than other Latin American countries between national capital formation levels and the expansion of GNP. For the future, there are a number of reasons to expect if anything, a further improvement in this relationship—i.e., in systemic operating efficiency—which should help to compensate for any rising tendency in the capital coefficients of particular fields of production, though, obviously, the situation is made more difficult by the directly unproductive expenditures required to meet the pressures of population growth. Broadly speaking, the basis for optimism lies in the not unreasonable expectation that the Mexican economy is moving into a period in which it should also realize increasing returns from past investments in human resource development and organizational modernization.

In respect of the former, notable progress has been made during the past two decades in the field of formal education and training. Technical and scientific fields of instruction have been improved, not only in the pure sciences but also in the applied and social sciences. Not least in importance among these advances have been the renewed concern for training agricultural specialists (at Chapingo and elsewhere), the steadily improving instructional facilities for engineers and business specialists (at the Monterrey Technological Institute, the Polytechnic Institute in Mexico City, the National University, Ibero-American University, and so on), and the recent efforts to improve the quality of economics training (at such places as the Colegio de México and the University of Nuevo León). But perhaps of at least equal importance has been the in-service training and experience distributed throughout the economy in the work of public agencies, especially those most directly involved in development efforts, and the operations of private sector industrial, commercial, and financial enterprises. Even the now terminated *bracero* program seems to have made a distinct contribution to upgrading the production competence of Mexican agriculture. Out of all of these sources of human resource development a labor force has taken form, possessing a growing variety of skills, with a substantial qualitative improvement in most of them, and a steadily expanding supply of managerial and entrepreneurial capabilities. In the nature of the case, these social processes tend to be cumulative, which augurs well for further growth.

On the organizational level of the economy, the sizable amount of industrial and business experience which has been accumulated over the past several decades also argues strongly for a growing efficiency in the performance of production, marketing, and financial functions. A modern style of manufacturing organization, for example, is already quite common among Mexican firms, not only those in the Federal District and Monterrey industrial complexes but also those located in such newer industrial sites as Chihuahua, Guadalajara, Salamanca, Toluca, and Torreón.

In marketing and merchandising, organizational changes since World War II have produced a virtual revolution in the field of distribution. Public markets have been modernized on a widespread basis, and product standardization and quality control at the manufacturing level were joined with new mass distribution techniques in self-service supermarkets, chain department stores, and lately, discount houses. Fixed pricing with lower unit markups, consumer credit, market research, and dynamic marketing promotion have been but a few of the other innovations enhancing the efficacy of the articulating or integrating functions of the marketing apparatus vis-à-vis the primary and secondary sectors of the economy. Meanwhile, the rapid growth of the banking system—reflected in the increased assets of the central bank and privately owned deposit banks and even more vigorously in the increased scale of operations of other state-operated credit institutions and the private *financieras* (investment and financing companies)—indicates the steadily more important role played by the processes of financial intermediation in the economic life of the country.[12]

> With the institutional development which occurred, and also with the greater sophistication of financial instruments and market practices, transactions of all sorts were facilitated. Not only were investable resources augmented as a result of the development of the financial system, but also because those resources were given greater mobility they were able to contribute more to the efficiency and growth of the overall economy. Furthermore, the easier movement of goods from producers to consumers also contributed to economic growth.[13]

Systemic operating efficiency should continue to benefit in the future also from the progress which has been made in building up the technical research competence and the general economic leadership capabilities of the public sector.[14] For years a reasonably effective and somewhat co-ordinated guidance was provided the national economy by four key development instruments of the state: the central bank, the Nacional Financiera, the Ministry of Finance, and the Ministry of the Presidency. Meanwhile, in the creation of scores of ministries, departments, decentralized agencies, and other entities having state participation, the government evolved a comprehensive, yet flexible set of intermediary institutions which were integrated with the various sectors and geographical regions of the national economy and which constituted the means of implementing the decisions taken in the central institutions of economic guidance. In the work of the Investment Commission of 1954-1958, a rather closer coordination was introduced into the operations of the multitudinous action agencies, while further steps towards a more integrated national planning and policy implementation were taken with the creation of a central planning office in the Ministry of the Presidency in 1958 and the establishment in 1962 of the Interministerial Planning Commission. Even though the most probable eventual outcome of these efforts is a planning system akin to that practiced in France or the Netherlands, it is reasonable to expect that they will issue in a more systematic and efficacious definition of public sector developmental priorities as well as an improved coordination of public investment programs with private sector efforts.

Finally, if there are good reasons for believing that the internal economic arrangements of Mexico will continue to evolve in the direction of higher productivity, it must also be recognized that improvements in the social organization of resources have, in facilitating the mobility of resources among alternative uses, already produced an economic structure which is more resilient than those which obtain in most of Latin America. In particular, the economy, in both public policies and private sector responses, has demonstrated a considerable ability to adapt its external sector to changing conditions in foreign markets; for unlike the usual Latin American case in internally oriented development policies, the Mexican development pattern has not neglected to improve the performance capacity of its export industries. The postwar cotton boom provides one illustration of a government-supported export industry, as does the strong encouragement given the export-oriented shrimping industry. Similarly, the successful efforts undertaken to increase the exports of lettuce, tomatoes, strawberries, and other agricultural products to the growing markets of the United States and the rapidity with which Mexican sugar output was raised to take advantage of new export opportunities occasioned by the Cuban Revolution provide further testimony to the long-term ability of the economy to strengthen its external position. Not surprisingly, Mexican exports, including exports of manufactures, have figured quite prominently in the trade flows released by LAFTA, and in this one also finds evidence of a trend evident elsewhere in the changed complexion of the Mexican external sector—namely, the conscious efforts which have been made to diversify export markets as well as export products.

Thus, while the future relaxation of balance of payments constraints on Mexican growth is by no means assured, there are nevertheless grounds for assuming that the prospects need not be pessimistic. At the very least, the organizational modernization which has occurred in Mexico has, in both its fostering of internal economic integration and its stimulation of export versatility, given the country a far more favorable position in this regard than is common among the other Latin countries of the hemisphere, including, as in the case of Argentina or Brazil, some which have potentialities superior in many respects to those of Mexico. In Mexico the pattern of development which has been attained thus far also rests upon a degree of political stability and continuity which is altogether singular among the larger Latin American countries. An advantage of no mean consequence in its effects on national and foreign investment levels, the stability of the Revolutionary regimes carries the additional benefit of permitting the government greater latitude in pursuing public policies conducive to future national growth without the convulsive political reactions which have accompanied the search for an enduring basis of development elsewhere in Latin America.

The Socialization of Development Processes. In looking for what has been distinctive and typical in twentieth-century Mexican experience, one is impressed with the extent to which the Revolution functioned as a jolt to set the nation in motion along a path fundamentally different from the course of development before it occurred. While the initial impact of the upheaval was to shatter a narrow and constrictive institutional framework and thereby open the system to comprehensive changes among nearly all aspects of the culture complex, in time the complicated social phenomena associated with the Revolution provided the dynamism for both an extensive renovation of the agricultural sector and a modern industrial transformation. That it did so seems largely attributable to the success of the Revolution in socializing national economic processes no less than its attainments in socializing the political processes of the nation. Indeed, the two are inseparably related, for out of the "mobilization system" created by the dominant political party during some three decades of efforts to organize the entire population under a strong central authority came what is perhaps the most striking and creative characteristic of the Mexican system: [15] the growth of its institutionalized capacity to build other institutions as needed to support modernization.[16]

At the risk of artificiality, the institution-building aspects of the Mexican Revolution may be summarized under three categories.

(1) Basic to the whole process was a series of institutional reforms which radically shifted the controlling structure of authority away from earlier elites and placed the augmented powers of the state in the hands of new leadership groups among whom narrow self-regard and ideological differences were often enough present but who had an interest in change and in an expansion of the domestic opportunity structure. While the eradication of former vested interests freed the government to experiment, with a greater flexibility than was customary in contemporary Latin America, in the formulation and application of economic policies, the necessity to evolve a new political consensus compelled, as it were, the national leadership to search for policies which could be plausibly related to the welfare of larger portions of the electorate. Of the several institutional changes which worked to these ends, the one which was the crux of the entire Revolutionary program was the land reform and redistribution campaign, a measure which in time virtually eliminated the domestic latifundian class as a significant political influence [17] and which also undermined the influence of foreign capital, a portion of which had gone into landholdings. New labor legislation which gave the government a major role in labor-management relations and the government's de facto sponsorship of various trade union organizations afforded additional leverage over both domestic and foreign capitalists, while nationalization of the petroleum and railway industries in the thirties and the amplification of public electric-power programs after that time diminished the political power of foreign capital interests which in prerevolutionary days had been a prominent element in national policy formation. Export and import controls, and intervention in credit policy to channel more funds to national enterprises simply reinforced the subordination of external economic influence to national development objectives.

(2) At the same time, the liquidation of latifundian and foreign-investor power and the nature of the Revolution's political base both permitted and, in a sense, forced public authorities to undertake programs of general benefit, especially for the rural constituency where the restructuring of the land tenure system had provided an environment in which incentives could be more widely operative than previously. Accordingly, during the second decade of the Revolution the government began, with the limited means at its command, a program of public investment which was, over the years, to channel gradually increasing resources into basic development fields. In 1925, for instance, the National Irrigation Commission and the National Road Commission began their work of expanding the agricultural land base of the economy and of consolidating the scattered producing regions and consuming centers into a national market—a measure which also supplied an impetus to domestic manufacturing development and increased the mobility of productive factors as well as of farm products and industrial output. In 1926 the first of the long series of public agencies designed to step up the supply of credit and auxiliary assistance to the

agricultural sector was set up in the form of the National Agricultural and Livestock Bank.

(3) Even earlier, the Ministry of Education had been organized (in 1921), and under the creative leadership of José Vasconcelos and others the modern educational program was commenced.[18] Rural as well as urban schools were constructed with a rapidity which was unusual, considering the available resources, and in subsequent years the content of the educational program was turned toward life-oriented teaching or practical activities and the fostering of attitudinal change. By 1936 three central agricultural schools and nine regional agricultural schools were operating, a national economics school and a national polytechnic institute had been established, adult education programs were receiving rising support, and such innovations as motor truck libraries had been employed to extend the compass of the human development effort. Meanwhile, beginning with the early "cultural missions" which were sent into rural areas, efforts were made to incorporate the indigenous population more fully into the life of the nation.

All three areas of institutional action fed into the objectives of national integration and development by increasing the extent of participation in decision-making processes, by making public policy more responsive, even if imperfectly, to broader segments of the national body politic, and by distributing the benefits of economic advancement more widely (though not, of course, equally). All three categories of institution building activity, therefore, played a role in socializing the economic life of the nation. Though interventionism was a paramount feature of the socializing policies, in the long run the private sector was also substantially revitalized; for by distributing incentives and diffusing the access to the opportunity structure more broadly, the socialization programs lessened the importance of resource deprivation as a barrier to the social diffusion of entrepreneurial roles.

In later years, public investment in the foregoing programs continued to expand, and by the late forties additional public sector resources were directed into such basic fields as power development (electrification programs and the petroleum industry) and the rehabilitation of the railway system. More or less contemporaneously, the first of the multipurpose regional development commissions was created to attend to the material advancement of outlying areas, and subsequently land settlement or colonization programs were expanded to take up unutilized or underutilized farming areas as well as to relieve (even if only modestly) the growing population pressure in the more densely settled parts of the nation. Altogether, then, the ability of the government to command general acceptance of its policies—to benefit, as it were, from a popular presumption that the state was operating for the common welfare—enabled the resources of the public sector to be ploughed into basic development fields on a scale and with a continuity which were rare in Latin America.[19] Significantly, in Mexico, almost alone among the republics of the region, rapid industrialization was accompanied by a notable increase in agricultural modernization and output.

The decades of Revolutionary guidance also saw a progressive elaboration of the institutional infrastructure necessary for operating a modern economic system; both directly and indirectly public policies were employed to promote the development of a wide variety of enterprises and specialized institutions in the financial, industrial, agricultural, and marketing fields, ranging from sugar-producing cooperatives and mobile banking offices through trucking firms (encouraged by low-price petroleum products and highway construction programs) to steel mills, fertilizer factories, and petro-chemicals plants. The enhancement of the inducements to invest no less than the provision of mechanisms for encouraging and gathering savings, encouraged national capital formation to play a larger role in the national development program, so that whatever adverse effects some of the regime's policies may at times have had on foreign investment, especially during the mid-thirties, national capital formation was not necessarily lowered by the (temporary) deterrence of foreign capital inflows.[20] The same set of policies which reduced the attraction of foreign investment in certain fields, in other words, were generally conducive to a rise in domestic capital accumulating (and managerial and entrepreneurial) ability, a circumstance which probably laid a sounder basis for self-generating growth over the long run.[21] Moreover, insofar as national policies tended to increase the range of accessible production alternatives and to heighten factor mobility, they also enhanced the opportunities to shift resources from less productive to more productive, if not necessarily optimal, uses, and in so doing, helped to build up a body of domestic economic experience which in time would assist in deploying an enlarged stock of resources in closer approximation to optimal combination patterns.[22] Over the long run, then, mistakes in capital allocation tended to be at least partially self-correcting.

Aside from the relationship of these institution-building efforts to the performance of a multitude of economic functions, the expansion and growing complexity of the occupational structure loosened class lines and fostered social and economic mobility, while lending support to the exercise of ambition and the general aspirations for material advancement. Together with the mass-education programs, which were aimed at inculcating a desire to break with tradition and expanding the horizons of popular awareness, the important social by-products of such efforts in institutional reconstruction have been a diffusion of the materialistic incentive system, a greater experience in collaborative interaction or organizational processes, and a more widespread involvement of human talent in the processes of production and exchange.[23] Labor commitment, entrepreneurial formation, and a rise in private investment were not the least of the advantages which fed back into the system to support the rate of economic growth. On a broader scale, the dissolution of the prerevolutionary traditional social structure and value system and the growth fostered by national policies stimulated the rise of a "fairly abstemious and frugal" middle class based primarily "on talent, personal services, education" rather than on petty property holdings, devoted to modernization and education, and recognizing "economic achievement as a worthwhile end."[24] A performance-oriented group, it dominated the political processes through control of the communications and educational systems and the party and governmental bureaucracies; with the wide interventionary powers of the state at its disposition, it was in a position to exercise a command over resources which, more often than not, corresponded to the requisites of development.[25]

As an extension of the socialization process to the national decision-making level, an ample use of Revolutionary ideology as a basis for consensus was combined with the dominant political party, structured to include the major popular interest organizations, to build a communications (and control) system second to none in the hemisphere in the comprehensiveness of its coverage and its ability to mobilize the general population behind the development program. Further, in the government-sponsored formation of semi-official associations representing employer and business interests which did not fall within the formal structure of the major political party, institutions were built by means of which other important economic groups were given a consultative access to the national decision making apparatus. Thus, over the course of decades a nationwide structure was evolved to reconcile divergent interests in a process closely akin to that which Charles Lindblom has called partisan mutual adjustment.[26] Within this context, a high degree of overall stability and peacefulness was attained because of the possibilities of using the pragmatic devices of negotiation, bargaining, and compromise to effect social agreement and coordination, while by virtue of the reliance on these processes a degree of reciprocity which is decidedly unusual for Latin America was also structured into the system.[27]

From several standpoints, therefore, the socializing aspects of the Revolutionary pattern of development, which explicitly abjured the growth strategy which prevailed prior to 1910, may be taken as the distinctive feature of the Mexican experience. Formed, not without hardship, mistakes, and struggle, over several decades of experimentation, the institutional restructuring involved in the process amounted to a fundamental reordering of the system and of the set of socio-economic dynamics it contained. Paradoxically, the result was a development policy which realized more profoundly the national integration objectives of the neo-orthodox internally oriented growth strategy while at the same time it incorporated many of the developmental priorities upheld by the orthodox approach to growth. On the whole, the long-term growth prospects of the country appear more assured and less susceptible to the impact of political disturbance than in most of the other members of the Latin American bloc, and this position seems attributable to the peculiar combination of policy objectives—and to the framework of socialization from which the synthesis of economic growth and systemic change evolved.[28]

THE ALLIANCE FOR PROGRESS

In Latin America as a whole, the four decades following the First World War did much to extend the organizational infrastructure and to build up modern business units and the supply of skills. Yet, by the close of the fifties, the realization was inescapable that the neo-orthodox policies of industrial interventionism, even with regional economic integration, would not suffice to establish economies with a solid potential for autonomous growth. By that time, too, the rather spotty history of United States aid and other external aid to the region left little doubt that a search for more efficacious ways of fostering development was in order. Well-intentioned though the individual foreign assistance programs doubtless were, the novelty of a large-scale semipermanent commitment to assisting overseas development virtually insured that the effort would for a number of years suffer the defects of inexperience.

In the first place, the realization in the United States that a long-term commitment to foreign aid was necessary was slow in coming, and accordingly, the whole program had about it an air of contingency and improvisation. Appropriations varied from year to year, with little assurance of continuity over the longer run, and foreign assistance efforts were scattered over a multiplicity of agencies, both national and international, among which there was little, if any, coordination. Indeed, several times during the late forties and fifties, a substantial portion of the United States foreign economic assistance program underwent reorganization; and with each transmutation, the shifting emphasis in program objectives, the turnover in personnel, and so forth added a further complication to the business, as did the changes of regimes which occurred in the countries of Latin America. On both sides of the aid process, the policies for recruiting, training, and retaining capable personnel were frequently inadequate, a circumstance which together with the aforesaid reorganizations made it difficult to realize the advantages of cumulative experience.

Both the multilateral and bilateral assistance efforts were geared to a project-by-project approach, with insufficient regard by either donors or recipients for how specific undertakings and project loans might fit into the context of a comprehensive plan of attack on the problems of economic backwardness. Notwithstanding the planning assistance provided in the Economic Development Institute of the World Bank or that forthcoming from the planning agency of Puerto Rico, and ECLA, scant headway was made in implementing procedures for defining national development priorities in terms of which the piecemeal project assistance might have been related to a concerted program of action. While the need for particular forms of assistance was usually clear enough, the relative need was often conjectural. Consequently, given the ambiguity of policy objectives and the diffusion of efforts which characterized the period, resources were often dissipated and the effectiveness of all the projects was reduced, even though approximately $4 billion or so of external assistance had been made available to Latin America in the 1950-1958 period from the I.B.R.D., the Export-Import Bank, and various U.S. agencies alone.[29]

For a number of years, the deficiencies of the aid program were masked by circumstances which created an aura of growth in the hemisphere. In the immediate postwar period, for example, the accumulated reserves from wartime export sales cushioned the expansion of the region, as did the terms of trade which were moving in a generally favorable direction for Latin America from the late thirties to the mid-fifties—though the comparatively slight gains in the volume of Latin American exports already betrayed an underlying weakness in the situation. Moreover, up through 1957 there had been a dramatic rise in the amount of private foreign capital going to Latin America, which received more U.S. private investment than any other underdeveloped area. During the latter half of the decade, however, the terms of trade worsened, foreign investment fell off sharply, inflation continued to plague a number of major countries (and some minor ones, too), foreign exchange reserves dwindled away, and balance-of-payments crises became chronic. As political instability mounted, alongside the deteriorating economic scene, the U.S. policy towards Latin America was reexamined once again.

Evolution of a New Inter-American Policy. While an earlier policy review delivered in 1953 by Milton Eisenhower had remained largely unimplemented, the Nixon report of 1958, which, among other things, suggested a new look at the case for commodity stabilization and greater foreign assistance, came at a time when conditions were ripe for a more sympathetic hearing. The same year, the U.S. Secretary of State reversed the earlier opposition of the government on a special hemispheric bank—a proposal first discussed just prior to the Second World War—and proposed the creation of the Inter-American Development Bank, an institution which was established the year following on the basis of a sizable U.S. capital contribution. More or less concurrently, the United States announced its approval of the new LAFTA program. On all three occasions, therefore, the United States adjusted its policies in the direction favored by the Latin American bloc for a number of years previously.

An even bolder policy change was adumbrated in 1958 when the president of Brazil issued a call for a program known as Operation Pan America. On the assumption that the persistence of low income levels would precipitate social unrest and disrupt the development of democratic institutions, President Kubitschek explicitly recognized the political dimension of economic development and solicited a deliberate multilateral effort to promote growth on a hemisphere-wide basis. In the discussions which followed, the goals of accelerated industrialization were linked not only with regional integration and commodity stabilization but also with a reduction of trade barriers in the center countries, land reform, and improved social services. Furthermore, an annual growth target (a 5½ per cent per year increase in gross product) and a date (1980) were mentioned for bringing per capita income up to a level of $500, on assumptions which seemed to borrow from Rostow's then current concept of the take-off and Leibenstein's concept of a critical minimum effort. Whereas formerly the attraction of foreign investment had been relied upon to facilitate Latin American growth, it was now proposed to set the growth objectives and on that basis marshal external resources in the amount needed to sustain the target rate of expansion.

Eventually the so-called Committee of Twenty-One which had been convened in October of 1958 by the O.A.S. to respond to the Kubitschek proposal completed its deliberations, and a somewhat clearer definition of the program framed by Operation Pan America emerged from the Bogotá Conference of 1960 in the Act of Bogotá (September 1960). Again, the position taken was essentially that of adding social reform to economic growth in order to attain political ends (i.e., a more assured evolution towards democracy). Besides the customary appeal for commodity stabilization, the Act called for an increase in long-term loans to stabilize foreign exchange availabilities, endorsed the traditional U.S. position on the urgent need for fiscal and monetary reforms to promote savings and domestic resource mobilization, and set forth the general nature of program requirements in such fields as agrarian modernization, the development of housing and community services, health and sanitation improvements, and education or human resources development. Concurrently with the Bogotá meeting, the Congress of the United States authorized a $500 million appropriation to be administered by the Inter-American Development Bank (as the Social Progress Trust Fund), the International Cooperation Administration, and the O.A.S. as a source of soft loans and grants for financing welfare projects, planning development, and technical assistance. Partly an acquiescence to Latin American appeals for more flexible lending policies, the measure also indicated the willingness of the United States to make outright (and disguised) unilateral transfers of additional resources to its southern neighbors in order to consolidate the organizational infrastructure of development.

A synthesis of prior policy positions taken by the United States and the Latin American republics, the policy changes which occurred between the summer of 1958 and the fall of 1960 incorporated a number of features which soon afterwards would reappear in the structure of the Alliance for Progress.

Most important, agrarian reform was finally brought into the limelight as a formal commitment of the signatory parties to the Act. Thereby, it was publicly recognized that agricultural backwardness and the social system associated with it have constituted since colonial times a major brake on the progress of the region. Save in exceptional instances, the lengthy period of urban development had not provided sufficient stimulus to promote a widespread modernization of agriculture by means of the interplay of market forces, i.e., through increasing the commercial demand for farm products and creating labor shortages in the rural sector. Indeed, in view of the lack of a continuum between urban life and the rural hinterland, a lacuna manifested in the concentration of modernity in the principal cities and the stagnation of provincial towns and secondary cities, the relative weakness of the urban network as a whole evinced the presence of serious structural impediments to the automatic diffusion of growth-eliciting influences to the countryside. Accordingly, the Act admitted that remedial action would necessitate a reformation of the institutional framework if an effort to install an improved agrarian regime was to be made.

Beyond this, clauses in the agreement of Bogotá touching social welfare and human resource development bespoke a new awareness that even in the cities prevailing conditions have not permitted a great deal of individual mobility. In consequence, the nonrural populace included millions of marginal urban dwellers, often physically segregated in their residential zones from the locus of city life, who lived in many ways detached from urban culture.[30] At once a threat to political stability and an underutilized resource for economic growth, the urban fringe also required the implementation of special policies if it was to be better incorporated into national growth processes.

In the third place, the importance of development planning, on both the national and hemispheric level, was explicitly acknowledged as a means of establishing priorities to guide resource allocation and, through its reduction of uncertainty and risk levels, as a device for strengthening private investment performance.[31] While lip service had often been paid by Latin American governments to the planning principle, little had ever been accomplished in fact; for the United States, the insistence on planning in Latin America was even more novel. In any event, this, in conjunction with the other reform and welfare objectives, made plain the multilateral rejection of market indicators as a sufficient guide for development and expressed the recognition that special measures were essential, given existing institutional structures, to resolve the disproportionalities of the historic patterns of growth in Latin America and to insure a socially desirable diffusion of the benefits of growth. In both the Operation Pan America proposal and the Act of Bogotá, as well as in the subsequent Alliance for Progress, the recommended incorporation of reform and welfare objectives into the development planning program attested to an awareness that simple economic growth, in the form of higher national incomes and products, was inadequate, even if it could be attained, for assuring the stable future development of the region. The recent experience of the higher-income countries of the area—Argentina, Uruguay, and Chile—argued strongly against making a simplistic connection between comparative affluence and a viable social system.

If any dominating insight can be said to have emerged from the policy discussions of the period, it might be summarized as a more realistic perception of the actual relations which exist between market economics and secular economic growth. Over the long term, in other words, neither the market context nor an institutionally deflected partial interventionism could necessarily be relied upon as the *primum mobile* of material advance, for both, in the last analysis, merely give expression to underlying institutional arrangements as these interact with the state of the industrial arts. Depending upon the circumstances, the resultant interaction pattern may or may not be conducive to viable growth. In the particular case of Latin America, with the chief exception of Mexico, it was abundantly clear by the 1960's that, on the whole, the domestic institutional order which was registered in national market relationships and in neo-orthodox policies was not growth conducive. With much of the population culturally and some linguistically isolated in subsistence agriculture (and the disguised unemployment of the urban service sector), and with money income and wealth so concentrated and the access to economic opportunities so limited, disenfranchisement was as much a factor in the operation of consumer sovereignty in the market as it was in the exercise of citizen sovereignty in the political process. Consequently, the customary resource allocational patterns were anything but consonant with social needs. In addition, the coverage of the market was foreshortened further by the imperfections of market knowledge, while the rigidities and inelasticities inherent in national economic structures raised still other obstacles to a productive expression of market dynamics. From many standpoints, therefore, a restructuring of the received social order and a deliberate abridgment of the market mechanism appeared prerequisite to attaining a more autonomous basis for economic expansion.

Essentially, the concepts of development needs which informed the discussions of the 1958-1960 period constituted the core of the Alliance for Progress program. Launched by President Kennedy in two speeches during March 1961, more detailed guidelines for action were set forth in the Punta del Este Declaration which was issued by an inter-American conference in August of the same year. From the neo-orthodox policy tradition, the Declaration incorporated such elements as the desirability of accelerated industrialization (including the development of capital-goods industries), regional economic integration, and commodity stabilization.[32] From the orthodox policy tradition upheld by the United States and various international agencies came the emphasis on fiscal and monetary reform, more efficient public administration, rural development,[33] rehabilitation of the educational systems at all levels, expanded technical assistance programs, and an explicit reminder of the special need to stimulate Latin American export industries. Drawing implicitly upon the example of Mexico and the 1958-1960 policy reappraisals, the Declaration went on to stress the critical role of development planning, reforms in land tenure systems [34] and other socio-economic relationships (e.g., the strengthening of the labor movement and improved industrial relations systems), the desirability of reducing military appropriations,[35] and the urgent need for such popular welfare measures as better low-cost housing, public health services, and municipal water supply and sanitation systems.[36] Of the chief development problems of the hemisphere, only the population question was entirely avoided.

Specific targets were set in a number of action areas,[37] the whole program was enunciated as a decade-long effort, and as a principal innovation of the Alliance, the United States committed itself on a long-term basis to guarantee that a certain amount of external resources would be forthcoming for development programs framed along the lines of the Alliance objectives. Of these, approximately $1 billion annually were to be supplied by U.S. government lending agencies: including grants and loans with maturities extending up to fifty years duration, with low or near-zero rates of interest (especially for social projects), and with deferred amortization periods. A third of a billion dollars was to be obtained from the various international lending agencies, and another third of a billion was expected to come from private investment as the Alliance program increased the attraction and capital absorptive capacity of Latin America. The balance ($0.3 billion) of the $2 billion which were estimated as representing the annual external resource requirement (exclusive of export earnings) of the program was, hopefully, to be supplied from public and private sources in Europe and Japan—though how the cooperation of these, and private capital in general, was to be obtained was a matter for conjecture.[38]

Ostensibly, the external finance so provided was to be mainly in the nature of program financing, or project financing which was integrated into a larger program, while the mobilization of external resources on a massive scale for development plans meeting the conditions of the Punta del Este Declaration was viewed as a means of supplying sufficient leverage (coercion or inducement, depending on one's point of view) to effect the internal structural changes deemed necessary for the success of the venture. Technical assistance in planning and program development was to be channeled through the U.S. Agency for International Development, the OAS, ECLA, and the Inter-American Development Bank, and, later, the Inter-American Committee on Agricultural Development (or CIDA); and an annual review of the progress of the Alliance was made the duty of the Inter-American Economic and Social Council. The Inter-American Development Bank, which also administered the Social Progress Trust Fund, was envisaged as a major financial channel for the program, both as a direct lender and as an intermediary for drawing investment funds from investment consortia in Europe, the United States, and elsewhere.[39]

As might be expected, however, the aforementioned possibility of external leverage was not lost upon the negotiating nations, and the whole question of program supervision and the coordination of efforts proved to be the most controversial issue of the Punta del Este conference. It was here, of course, that the implications of contingent but systematic external financing for the actual implementation of national reform measures were crystallized, and the resolution of the *contretemps* which developed over the issue seriously weakened the effectiveness of the Alliance framework—perhaps fatally. In the original version of the proposal for coordination and direction, the United States and the head of ECLA, joined by some of the smaller countries (who feared preferential treatment for the larger countries under alternative arrangements), endorsed the idea of creating a seven-member council of experts to review and evaluate all development programs for internal consistency and for their compatibility with Alliance objectives.[40] By this means it was also hoped to coordinate individual national plans in a manner appropriate to regional economic integration. The *siete sabios*, as the council was derisively labeled, would, on the basis of approved plans, coordinate aid requests and make recommendations on the allocation of loans and grants, in effect operating as an intermediary between the Latin American countries and the sources of external finance.

Opposition to the review board soon developed on the part of the larger countries,[41] and in its stead was substituted a nine-member committee which was empowered to function only in an advisory capacity. Neither were individual nations required to submit their plans to the Committee of Nine, nor were they debarred from directly soliciting external financing without approval by the committee of their programs. Left, thus, in a state of functional limbo, the Committee of Nine was eventually joined, or even overshadowed, by another "key" board (with an equally ambiguous role): the Inter-American Committee for the Alliance for Progress (CIAP). By the middle of 1966, the practical significance of the Committee of Nine had been so eroded to a ceremonial function that its members resigned *en masse*. The move—which came after a period of wandering policies in Washington as the original design of the Kennedy years lost its focus under a new administration—occurred amid such contradictory trends in Latin America that it symbolized particularly well the uncertain future of the whole Alliance for Progress program.

The Context of the Alliance. Although the Alliance for Progress may eventually be abandoned, if indeed it has not already been discarded in practice, a variety of circumstantial reasons make it premature, at this point in time, to judge the impact of the program as such. In the first place, the new approach to development embodied in the Alliance was introduced somewhat belatedly, in terms of the various conditions which might have facilitated a program of basic, and costly, changes; and, inevitably, the program inherited an especially difficult political and economic situation.

As mentioned previously, the terms of trade for most of Latin America had been deteriorating for several years running by the time the Alliance got underway. Meanwhile the balance of payments problems had been compounded further by the financial mismanagement of Latin American governments (and overseas lenders), which had permitted, or even encouraged, the excessive contracting of suppliers' credits and other short-term debt obligations at high rates of interest. In consequence, between a quarter and a half of the Alliance financing disbursed to Latin America during the first four years of the program was diverted from developmental uses into balance-of-payments operations designed to rescue foreign, and largely European, creditors from the predicament into which they had got because of their own misjudgment and the unsound practices prevailing in Latin America during the late fifties and early sixties. While a moratorium on the short-term debt and a scaling down of the principal obligations had much to recommend them from the standpoint of economic realism, there being no compelling reasons to bale foreign creditors out of their past mistakes, the looseness of the Alliance control mechanisms was such that little could be done to forestall or prevent what amounted to a substantial dissipation of development funds. In addition, it might be added, the expected new contributions of funds from Europe and Japan for Latin American growth never materialized, at least at the levels anticipated at the outset of the program.

Concurrently, before and after the Punta del Este Declaration, the attraction of western Europe as a site for investment was on the rise, a factor which served both to retain European capital at home and to deflect outgoing private U.S. capital from the underdeveloped areas at large and from Latin America in particular. That the latter was afflicted with severe balance of payments problems and a political risk symbolized by the contemporary manifestations of Castroism (and other forms of social protest expression) served to accentuate further the negative appeal of the region for foreign private venture capital. Accordingly, net new private foreign investment in Latin America had, by 1959, declined sharply from its peak in the 1950's. Thereafter, it rose only enough to cover, during the first four years of Alliance, about a quarter of the projected needs for new foreign private direct investment in the region (i.e., $300 million for the four years as contrasted with the hoped-for inflow of $300 million per year).

The circumstances which repelled the influx of private foreign capital were, of course, not hidden from domestic Latin American capitalists; the admittedly scattered evidence suggests that these, for their part, were also investing heavily abroad, both before the inauguration of the Alliance and thereafter. Yet, virtually no efforts were made to stem the flight of domestic capital, or to retrieve that which had already gone abroad. In fact, capital exportation (or repatriation) was even deliberately promoted, as when Brazil bought out the interests of a number of foreign-owned utility companies and Argentina decided to purchase the assets of the foreign petroleum companies operating in that country. In these instances, as in the case of domestic capital flights, the slack administration of Alliance financial assistance in effect provided the exchange cover for an actual removal of capital from the region.

Because of the foregoing short-term and long-term capital movements and the service obligations on outstanding debt and investments, the net resource transfer to Latin America during the initial years of the Alliance fell far below that which had been anticipated, even though the authorizations of aid from the United States ran very close to the promised levels. For example, according to the data compiled by the International Monetary Fund's *Balance of Payments Yearbooks*, the gross capital inflow to Latin America declined from $2 billion in 1957 to $1 billion in 1959. By 1962 it had risen again to $3 billion, but subsequently it fell off to around $1.6 billion in 1964. When repayments of principal and the repatriation of foreign private direct investment are taken into account, the trend of net capital inflow ran as follows: $1.3 billion (1957), $689 million (1959), $1.7 billion (1961), and around $900 million in 1964. Even worse was the record when the interest and dividend charges on foreign capital are taken into consideration; for, with these included in the computation, the net resource transfer to Latin America moved from $837 million (1957) to $109 million (1959) to $926 million (1961) to only $6 million in 1964. Thus, in order to supplement Latin American resources with the annual $2 billion of external resources which were viewed as the conservative minimum requirement during the Punta del Este discussions, it gradually became clear that, in practice, there was needed a far higher amount of gross capital inflows than the program had originally contemplated— though where the additional injection would come from was by no means certain as late as 1966.

Meanwhile, even though there was some improvement in the terms of trade for Latin America during the initial years of the Alliance and although regional export volumes had risen somewhat, the rate of growth in the per capita value of regional exports was comparatively modest and nowhere near a level which would permit the export sector to supply the dynamic which international capital transfers could not provide. Furthermore, the significance of the 5.2 per cent annual rate of increase in exports which was reached as an average during 1960-1965 was conditioned by the fact that, during the same interval, external dividend and interest payments were increasing by 8.1 per cent while amortization payments were also rising. Consequently, for the five-year period of 1960-1964, payments for profits, interest, and amortization together represented 27.4 per cent of current export earnings. A good many of the countries, particularly the smaller ones, enjoyed a much stronger external position,[42] but for several of the larger economies the situation grew especially critical. By the mid-sixties, for instance, the external public debt service obligations of Chile amounted to 22 per cent of export earnings, the equivalent ratio for Argentina was 37 per cent, and that of Brazil was probably at least as high, if not greater.

To be sure, the problems of export expansion inherited by the Alliance were not the sort which could be alleviated in a few years' time, but certain developments in evidence by the mid-sixties created potentially troublesome problems for the future. Increases in coffee prices, for example, appeared to be accompanied by a declining per capita consumption of the product, at least in the U.S. market. Similarly, the striking increases in copper prices which occurred in 1966 produced a reaction on the part of copper users which seemed to portend a permanent shift to substitute products in a number of lines. In the meantime, little had been done to insure that the growing closeness of relations between Europe and Africa would not bode ill for Latin American exports, while in the United States the restrictions on imports of Latin American sugar, petroleum, lead and zinc continued in force and the subsidized exports of U.S. cotton provided a running throat to Latin American exporters of that commodity.

Future problems aside, however, the fact of the matter was that the combination of circumstances described above resulted in a diminished per capita level of imports from 1959 through 1963 when compared with the quinquennium just preceding. In other words, whereas the level of per capita imports in 1954-1958 averaged $50.40, the average level for 1959-1963 was only $45.60, which was almost exactly the average level of per capita imports maintained in the 1948-1952 quinquennium. Considering that an increased per capita volume of importation of capital equipment and other essentials was indispensable for accelerated growth, the relative stagnation in import capacity functioned both as a brake on expansion and as a symptom of more deepseated difficulties.[43]

If external economic relationships were scarcely a major source of strength for the Alliance development efforts, internal conditions in Latin America were at least equally unpropitious. During the first five years of the Alliance effort, difficulties of a political nature impeded, for varying lengths of time, the effective conduct of government in Argentina, Bolivia, Brazil, Chile, Colombia, the Dominican Republic, Ecuador, Guatemala, and Peru. Moreover, the quality of public leadership was sometimes such that a popular attitude of cynicism or indifference towards the Alliance appeared entirely justified, for the new program name, after all, as the latest in a long series of alleged reform-and-progress programs, the previous ones of which had, more than anything else, been productive of disenchantment and frustration. Under the circumstances, it was perhaps remarkable that between 1960 and 1965 investment levels in the region only declined from 17.3 per cent to 16.3 per cent of the total regional product—a change which nevertheless permitted an absolute rise in fixed investment over the period in question.[44] Although the rate of increase in capital formation was near that of the population growth rate, and to that extent was not contributory to an improvement in the economic scene, much of the failure of investment to expand more rapidly was attributable to the fall-off in externally available savings after 1961. Correspondingly domestic savings came to play a larger role in financing regional investment. Somewhat encouragingly, public investment (in such fields as infrastructure and social services, particularly housing) made an increasing contribution to capital formation, growing at an average annual rate double that of private investment between 1960 and 1965. Yet, whatever the positive changes realized, the net result of the period was that an improvement in the rate of regional capital formation was not attained and little headway was made in reducing the amount of unemployment (and underemployment) to more tolerable levels.[45]

In retrospect, therefore, it would appear that the Alliance for Progress had been somewhat unrealistically oversold from the beginning. Not only did it underestimate the difficulties which were to be encountered and the amount of external assistance required for moving the Latin American economies ahead, but also it conveyed the impression that certain goals could be attained much sooner than could reasonably be expected. Without denying, for example, the data-collecting and educational value of the planning process which was stimulated by the Alliance, and without denigrating the usefulness of the process in forcing national policy makers at least to consider various alternative forms of resource allocation, it should have been evident from the outset that few, if any, meaningful comprehensive ten-year plans could have been prepared to guide the evolution of the Alliance program. For many countries, the formulation of an adequate long-term plan of the sort contemplated could not realistically have been expected before the later years of the Alliance, if then. For others with a greater planning competence, there was still an unresolved problem of how to assure that the plans would actually be implemented. Consequently, in some cases, such as that of Bolivia, the development plans submitted resembled exercises in fantasy, while in others—e.g., Colombia—the ten-year plans received practically no implementation.[46]

Complicating further the whole conduct of the Alliance, including the implementation of reforms and development plans, was the previously mentioned failure to establish effective control mechanisms in the administration of the Alliance. Just as few countries made any serious efforts to establish an adequate internal public information structure in order to involve and mobilize the various segments of their societies more fully in the development programs,[47] so also the multinational agencies associated with the Alliance were generally unable, or unwilling, to coordinate the program more systematically and to gear the provision of external assistance to the criteria originally set up. Consequently, the reported distribution of aid during the first years of the Alliance followed no discernable pattern of priorities and criteria, at least from an economic point of view. Most notably, perhaps, Mexico, which had long since implemented most of the reforms called for in the Punta del Este Declaration and which clearly possessed the capacity to utilize external assistance with great effectiveness, received a per capita portion of the Alliance aid which was less than half that received by Colombia, which did little in the way of reform, and less than a third of that allocated to Brazil, where hardly anything constructive was accomplished until quite recently. Similar anomalies abounded throughout the aid apportionment record.

Finally, instead of accelerating the pace of internal institutional reform, the actual operations of the Alliance program could be construed in a number of instances as having provided sufficient aid to enable the participating governments to procrastinate on the implementation of really serious reform measures. For example, except for a few instances, agrarian reform programs have resembled merely token measures, military spending has continued at its accustomed level, and the degree of rigor embodied in ostensible fiscal reforms is indicated by the slight number of prosecutions undertaken for tax evasion as well as by continuing ostentation in the consumption habits of the privileged in nearly every country. Indeed, if the Alliance was in some ways conceived as an attack on privilege, which, presumably, is one of the implications of the social revolution it was supposed to abet, then one must conclude that the defenses of privilege have in most cases proved to be distressingly durable.

The Significance of the Alliance for Progress. In time, the apparent growing tendency of many of the Latin American participants to view the Alliance program as simply the latest of the conventional foreign assistance programs of the United States suggested that a number of the central premises of the original conception had, for one reason or another, fallen by the wayside. Among the more prominent casualties was the conception which dominated the initial presentation of the Alliance when it was first sketched out in the Washington speeches of March 1961, the conception which drew most heavily (albeit perhaps not consciously) upon the experience of the Mexican case: namely, the functional relationship between economic development and the socialization of national economic structures.

By some, both in Latin America and the United States, the deemphasis of socialization was held to be a change for the better, though for reasons which were not the same in all cases. Among the Latin American partisans of the resumption of a business-as-usual and aid-as-usual approach were, naturally, the elements which felt most immediately threatened by the reformist objectives of the Alliance design: landed interests and even nonagricultural business interests which thought that development planning and more rigorous taxation were tantamount to socialism. From such quarters, particularly the latter, there was often a failure to appreciate the long-run advantages which would accrue to the private sector from a present emphasis on public investment in infrastructure, an assessment which seemed to reflect a preoccupation with short-run costs (and intersectoral reallocations of resources) and a heavy discount of future benefits. On the other hand, it must be recognized that the past performance of governmental operations in Latin America had not always been conducive to a belief that a transfer of resources to the public sector would promote systemic efficiency. Moreover, the matter of fiscal reform, with its corollary of higher effective rates of taxation, did indeed lead into the question of possible disincentives for business investors so that it could be claimed, at least hypothetically, that a rise in public sector capital formation might entail the risk of a decline in private sector capital accumulation.

For these contentions, there were few absolutely certain answers, in part because of the lack of sufficient empirical evidence on actual relations between tax structures and investor reaction in the Latin American setting. Yet, it could be observed that, historically, the prospect of higher taxation has almost always been countered by allegations that serious disincentives for investment would result, without convincing evidence, however, that such an outcome would invariably be the case. Further, the present state of fiscal technique provides an option for designing tax systems which draw their increased revenues at the expense of consumption flows and less socially productive investments, without any necessary detriment to the incentives for more useful categories of investment outlays. For that matter, the very utility of special development-oriented tax-reduction incentives depends, to a large extent, upon the general level of effective taxation; in an environment in which regularly assessed taxes are minimal and also widely evaded, the offering of tax incentives to encourage particular lines of investment is very nearly meaningless.

As for the ostensible fear that agrarian reform might result in a lowering of production, which was the customary argument advanced against that aspect of the Alliance program, the desirability of the change must be considered in the light of several factors. In the first place, the chief reason that the whole question of agrarian reform had received such prominence lay in the fact that much of Latin American agriculture was, for reasons discussed elsewhere in this study, manifestly inefficient in its use of both land resources and the human agents of production. In consequence of this inefficiency, the rural markets for urban output were quite limited because of the meager purchasing power of the rural populace, the balance-of-payments position of a number of countries was weakened by the necessity of food imports, and there was a constant threat, in the form of food shortages and higher food prices, to the real income position of politically strategic sectors of the urban population. Beyond these, the possibilities for a more vigorous development of secondary population centers were also impaired. Not only did the foregoing constrictions on the further progress of the urban sectors of the economy make it difficult to maintain expansion at a rate sufficient to generate an adequate number of employment opportunities. In addition, the same set of circumstances meant that the contribution of the agricultural sector to national capital formation was limited (owing to low productivity levels and the spending habits of large landholders), while the whole situation in agriculture, including the power of politically influential landed wealth to resist fiscal obligations, circumscribed severely the national tax base and, hence, reduced the public sector's ability to supply essential public services and economic infrastructure. In this connection, of course, the danger of placing an excessive burden of taxation on urban firms was functionally related to the low level of fiscal productivity in the rural sector.

For a great deal of Latin American agriculture, therefore, the risk of reducing aggregate output through agrarian reform seems rather low, precisely because the system, as it stands, is already operating, in general, at such an ineffective level.[48] And although the costs of an agrarian reform have been repeatedly mentioned as a further obstacle to implementing this aspect of the Alliance program, four considerations would seem to suggest that the "costliness argument" should not really carry much weight in actual policy formation. In the first place, the fact that agrarian reform and modernization, if they are to result in higher levels of productivity, necessarily imply a need to finance a number of complementary programs (e.g., agricultural research and extension, the development of more effective marketing structures, rural education, better agricultural credit programs, etc.) is valid, but largely beside the point. Such outlays are required in any case to improve the performance of agriculture and to foster general economic development, and there is no reason to assume that they must be joined with the existing land tenure regime to achieve their effects. On the contrary, they are exactly the kinds of programs which generate the external economies that have made farm firms elsewhere so productive and, as such, are the measures which hold considerable promise for converting peasants into farmers, by providing the requisite institutional supports for agricultural entrepreneurship within the context of a more widely distributed incentive system.

That, generally speaking, the average post-reform size of rural property holding would be smaller than that prevailing at present is not necessarily a relevant consideration, except insofar as a number of the recent studies of Latin American agriculture seem to indicate that smaller units tend to make a more effective use of their available factors of production than do latifundian units. In many instances, the advantages of scale in agriculture can be realized through cooperative organizations, while, of course, many of the existing haciendas are, in actuality, simply large-scale ownership units rather than large-scale production units. Moreover, the usual arguments which link the need for large-scale landholdings with the advantages of mechanization are predicated on an entirely misleading analogy with the factor proportions and production coefficients which typify the agriculture of the United States (and, of late, western Europe). As the experience of Vicos, Peru, not to mention that of Japan, has demonstrated, however, there are many types of agricultural improvements which are more appropriate to labor-intensive crop farming patterns than the land-extensive, labor-displacing mechanization employed in highly developed economies: e.g., improved seed selection; the application of fertilizers herbicides, and pesticides; terracing, irrigation, and better water control in general; the expansion of horticultural activities; the provision, through labor-intensive construction techniques, of improved farm-to-market roads to increase the market value of agricultural output; better crop storage facilities; improved rural education; and so on. Many of these innovations simultaneously provide additional employment and raise productivity, and few, if any, depend upon the presence of large-sized firms for their effectiveness.[49]

In the second place, the supposed necessity for indemnifying, at great expense to the fiscal system, the former owners of properties taken for purposes of redistribution is quite debatable. Considering the usual burden of unpaid taxes, defrauded wage liabilities, and misleading declarations of taxable value which have been associated with hacienda ownership in the past, and considering also the social function theory of property which has been incorporated for decades in the constitutional law of most countries, neither legal formalities nor general institutional propriety suggest a valid basis for extensive compensation, which would, in any event, serve no useful social or economic purpose. To the extent, therefore, that compensation for past mismanagement is presented as a costly impediment to agrarian reform, the argument should be recognized for what it is and not accorded a validity which it does not, in fact, possess.

A third potential cost element of an agrarian reform is somewhat more complex. Were those properties presently operated in an efficient manner to be subjected to redistribution, there would likely be a cost to the economy in the form of a reduction of output. Indeed, the very threat of expropriation, particularly if present over a protracted period, would in all probability result in the same outcome because of the detrimental impact of uncertainty on levels of agricultural investment. Not only would net new investment suffer, but also there is a probability that actual disinvestment would occur as landowners withdraw capital from agriculture in anticipation of possibly impending expropriation. Under such deteriorating circumstances, current levels of production would be adversely affected, while the post-reform situation would be made even worse. Since the existing relations of production in Latin American agriculture are, in general, so socially and politically unacceptable, it may reasonably be argued that the realistic question to raise at this point in time involves a comparison of the costs of a systematic agrarian reform with those of a deferred change in agrarian relationships *plus* the intervening costs of uncertainty.

In this context, therefore, there is much to be said for a strategy of development which moves as swiftly as possible to a resolution of uncertainty factors. Thus, to the extent that it is possible, in short order, to identify the more inefficient large agricultural properties and to utilize them, without delay, for redistributional purposes, the chances would seem to be enhanced for reducing the political pressures for further changes in land tenure arrangements. Accordingly, paradoxical as it might seem at first, a fair case can be made for the proposition that an aggressive implementation of agrarian reform and land redistribution measures offers, over the long run, the best hope for salvaging intact those efficient property units whose reorganization would, in truth, constitute a real loss to the development effort. Both the Mexican and Bolivian experience with agrarian disruption are instructive of the kinds of costs which are incurred from a failure to implement reforms when public sentiment has reached the point of considering that such changes are long overdue.

This leads to the fourth item which must be considered in conjunction with the costs of agrarian reform: namely, the costs to the economy at large of not having an agrarian reform. Leaving aside the immense opportunity costs which the present agrarian regime has entailed in the form of underdeveloped human and land resources, it may be observed that the political instability generated by rural unrest has long created costs which extend to many other segments of the national economic processes. Irregular changes of government with consequent losses of efficiency in the performance of public sector functions are only the beginning of a list of such charges which, to be accurate, would also have to take into account the depression of national capital formation rates by flights of domestic capital, the deterrent effects of instability on foreign capital inflows, the high risk premiums incorporated into the interest rate structure (particularly contraproductive in the case of long-term credit supplies), the strong liquidity preference with its resultant bias in the patterning of investor behavior, and so on, not to mention the military expenditures required to suppress various manifestations of rural discontent. For academic and theoretical purposes it is useful to define rather narrowly the range of variables and the parameters which bear upon the analysis of particular economic problems, but in practice it is difficult to ignore the more diffused, and theoretically less manageable, social and political phenomena which condition and modify the behavior of economic relationships. Thus, in the actual search for viable development routes, it would seem to make a great deal of difference whether a country is still debating how to handle the land-tenure problems inherited from the past or whether it is able, as Mexico has recently done, to contemplate the rather different problems involved in setting up a Museum of the Hacienda. Between the two situations lies the significance of the original conception of the Alliance for Progress.

Finally, as the foregoing comments have perhaps suggested, much of the present controversy regarding the proper future evolution (or abandonment) of the Alliance for Progress derives from a continuing predisposition to view social reform as essentially an appendage, or even a postscript, to the economic development process—a luxury which prudent judgment would defer to a later point in time when, presumably, present abstention from consumption (of social reform benefits) would have created a larger wherewithal to distribute. Similar in character to the productionist-consumptionist controversy in the field of labor policy, and having a certain affinity with the "primitive capital accumulation" concept of Marxian theory, this view of the relation of socialization to growth processes has enjoyed an intellectual support rather more respectable than that which has often been adduced to counter the arguments for fiscal and agrarian reform.

A representative example of this line of reasoning may be taken from an appraisal of the Alliance for Progress which, after noting that the Alliance was "biased" in favor of "social change" rather than "economic development" (which was "given lesser attention"), goes on to assert categorically that "reform-redistribution-welfare activity [i.e., social change, in the author's definition] is *not* economic development." [50] The policy conclusions drawn from these premises led, of course, in the expected and familiar direction: namely, a reversal of the relative emphasis on the supposedly separate goals and a caution that "the United States should not be overeager to 'force' reforms on the aid-receiving countries." Significantly, while positing a certain antithetical relationship between "economic" goals and "reform-redistribution-welfare" goals, the latter figuring essentially as consumption rather than investment variables in the development process, the aforesaid analysis included among the social-welfare objectives such categories as housing, education, and health and sanitation. [51]

Of itself, the study just alluded to need not concern us further, though it is only fair to acknowledge that elsewhere it raises provocative and meaningful issues. What is more significant is the point of view it articulates regarding the most central features of the Alliance, for by all indications the detachment of "social change" from "economic development" which makes the former a possible by-product of the latter became the overriding perspective in the post-Kennedy years of the program. Yet, as S. Herbert Frankel observed years ago, the conventional formula, "the social consequences of technical change," may, historically, have less to recommend it than the alternative statement of the relationship: "technical change as a social consequence." [52] Referring to Ashton's famous work on the industrial revolution (to the effect that the phenomenon was "not merely 'industrial' but also social and intellectual"), Frankel argued convincingly against dissociating different aspects of a process which, in fact, constitute a single whole. Very much the same may be said of the relationship between socialization and economic development in Latin America today, for in reality they appear as two sides of the same coin.

Just as the economic life history of Latin America leads one to the conclusion that the dysfunctional imbalances of the economies of the region are rooted in the preceding unbalanced development of social structures and the whole institutional apparatus of economic growth, so also the prospects for future material development seem inseparably bound up with measures aimed at building a more constructive social order. In this sense, therefore, social reform, or what is more accurately described as socialization, is neither a consequence nor a prerequisite of economic growth but is, rather, an integral part of the process itself. Consequently, to divorce the objective of economic growth from social reconstruction involves more than a somewhat dated and mechanistic view of social processes in general; it implies, as well, an artificiality which may, at times, be valid or even essential for purposes of restricted analysis but which is seriously misleading when proposed as a policy guide for actual historical circumstances. Nowhere is this clearer than in the resultant tendency to construe social reforms as, like consumption, resource-using while disregarding the investmentlike or resource-creating aspects of the process. Only a few examples should suffice to clarify the point.

So much has been written of late concerning the importance of human-resource development that it would appear altogether needless to belabor a conceptual framework which would consign educational expenditures to a noneconomic, "welfare" category. The same may be said of health and sanitation expenditures, particularly for an environment in which endemic diseases and parasitical infestations impair work efficiency and even, quite probably, learning ability. Yet, it should be noted that while these types of public investment programs are tied in with productivity objectives through their effects on the qualitative improvement of the human agents of production, they also (especially in the case of education, industrial apprenticeship programs, and the like) express the objectives of socialization by spreading more broadly the ownership of the skills needed in a modern economy and, hence, the earning power derived from those skills. Moreover, the latter aspect is a well-nigh inseparable concomitant of the former.

To treat the provision of popular housing (as distinct from luxury construction) as a quasi-consumption expenditure is no less questionable, for it overlooks the utility of an accelerated (labor-intensive) construction program as a transitional educational device for imparting a modicum of mechanical skills and industrial discipline to a labor force which is often still in the process of leaving the quite different social context of traditional agriculture. As a means of stimulating the growth and capabilities of basic construction industries which are required also for the satisfactory development of other sectors of the economy, a popular housing investment program can be justified additionally for its employment-multiplier effects, especially among the unskilled and semiskilled who are difficult to absorb in manufacturing. Moreover, being an industry which draws primarily upon internally available resources, it constitutes one area of employment expansion which makes fewer direct claims on the limited capacity to import.

Insofar as wage payments bulk large in construction outlays, the indirect pressures on the balance of payments may be minimal as well, for the pattern of consumer preferences which characterizes the typical construction laborer in Latin America is such that his demand is more likely than not to be directed against the kinds of products the local manufacturing sector is already capable of supplying. Thereby, of course, a second order of employment and investment expansion is introduced into the system at a point where supply elasticities tend to be greater than elsewhere. For that matter, to judge from the experience of recently established popular-level savings-and-loan associations in Latin America, the potential availability of financially accessible and economical housing itself appears to function in an incentive role, fostering the habit of thrift among those for whom the previous paucity of attainable incentive objects made the act of saving less meaningful. Once again, therefore, objectives of development and reform appear conjoined.

In like manner, it may be noted, the democratization of the credit system implied by another of the Alliance-sponsored reform-and-welfare programs, i.e., the promotion of credit unions, has already demonstrated (in some cases, in the face of opposition and harassment from the established banking institutions) an impressive capacity to familiarize broader segments of the population with the workings of a modern credit system. Simultaneously with increasing the access to loan capital and reducing the imperfections in the money market, upon which the traditional practice of usurious moneylending was based, the development of credit cooperatives and savings-and-loan associations has also provided some confirmation of the hypothesis that the savings function may be institution-elastic as well as income-elastic. Although the evidence is, as yet, insufficiently studied to permit more than a tentative statement on the matter, both the monetization of previously dispersed hoards and an increase in the savings effected from current income appear to have been involved in the rise of the financial holdings of these institutional innovations.[53]

Indeed, it would appear that most, if not all, of the reform measures contemplated by the Alliance for Progress, both in the design of the Punta del Este Declaration and the early action programs launched pursuant thereto, were imbued with this dual aspect of development and socialization. The rural cooperative societies which were intended to strengthen the income position (and, hence, the welfare) of small farmers were no less aimed at increasing production and productivity by bringing economies of scale to their members. The community development programs and other measures which looked to the democratization and strengthening of local governmental institutions were, at the same time, devices for encouraging local economic initiative and tapping underemployed human resources to build up overhead capital in the form of water systems, school facilities, farm-to-market roads. The reforms sought in the machinery of public administration not only were directed to increasing the integrity of the administrative personnel; they also had as two of their objectives a more efficient provision of basic public services and the allocation of these on a more universalistic and less particularistic basis. Further, with a more competent handling of the public business, it might be expected that the corruption and disincentive effects associated with ill-conceived and inefficiently administered internal controls (price controls, physical controls, and the like) would also be reduced, to the benefit of firm productivity and, ultimately, gross national product.

From what has been said already concerning the double effects of fiscal and agrarian reform, it is evident, therefore, that the bulk of the measures of a reformist or socializing character in the Alliance conception of development implied also a restructuring of the relationships among socio-economic groups which was generally positive in its bearing on the possibilities of economic progress. Consequently, to speak of a reduction in class and other institutional barriers to vertical mobility and to enumerate the measures which increase the access to the array of opportunities is, in large measure, merely to describe from another point of view the process by means of which a larger portion of the population moves from a position of marginal participation to active engagement in the economic life of the nation.

The Alliance and the Alternatives.   There are, finally, two further points, which may be drawn from the experience of Mexico during the past century, that seem more than tangentially relevant to an adequate historical evaluation of the development approach contained in the Alliance. The first of these relates to the sources of economic initiative, while the second pertains to the balancing of long-term growth targets with shorter-term exigencies. Alternatively stated, the issues involved are those of developmental dynamism and viability.

With respect to the first, it seems clear from the record that over the greater portion of Latin American history the principal impetus to economic and social change has come from outside of the area—at first in the guise of colonial administration, later, in the form of foreign investment, export demand, and immigration. With the inception of neo-orthodox policy, the attempt was made to internalize the dynamic of economic development, but only a partial success was achieved in the effort. In time the inability of the countries to carry through a more far-reaching overhaul of their domestic economic and social arrangements gave birth to the development quandaries of the present era, when, once again, an appeal was made for external assistance in continuing the process of systemic transformation and modernization in an orderly manner in lieu of the violent mode of change which seemed the only alternative in many instances. Of itself, the resort to Operation Pan America and the Alliance for Progress confessed the evident lack of a sufficient internal impetus to compel the adoption of adequate public policies and to foster the evolution of more productive institutional relationships, for the claim that resource scarcity lay behind the appeal must be discounted on several grounds. In both the private and public sectors, existing resources were often being employed with an inefficiency which belied their scarcity, while in addition there was good reason to believe that substantial holdings of wealth belonging to Latin American nationals had been transferred abroad.

In view of these conditions, therefore, the chief value of a renewed program of external assistance would seem to lie less in the temporary supplement of resources it might provide than in the leverage such inducements would afford for initiating and pushing domestic reorganization in a direction which would thereafter be supportive of a more autonomous pattern of development. Without a reordering of the internal institutional framework, in other words, there would be little assurance that either the resources already at hand or those made available from abroad would be utilized effectively, in which case a program of external assistance would prove, at best, to be a mere stop-gap measure. Ultimately, then, the logic of external assistance presupposes that its deployment rearranges the power structure of the recipient social system by nourishing the initial development of domestic groups whose interests correspond to the requisites of national development: e.g., a public which can demand of its government the necessary educational and transport improvements, an electorate strong enough to press for fiscal reforms, consumer-voters with a stake in policies which force national industries to become more efficient, a farm bloc with a concern for and an ability to obtain agricultural extension services, and industrial entrepreneurs who can assert the need for improved organization in capital and money markets. At the same time, the process of nourishing such development-related groups implies a corresponding reorganization of the prevailing incentive and opportunity structure which previously arrested their evolution and a formation of new institutions from which they can mobilize the resources to reinforce their initiative.

In the complex phenomena of the Mexican Revolution, more clearly than elsewhere in Latin American history, one glimpses the comprehensiveness of the changes in social relationships which appear prerequisite to cultivating a domestic leadership which is capable of developing, with minimal external public assistance, effective growth-oriented institutions and policies in both the private and public sectors. There, for example, the broader and more enduring economic significance of the agrarian reform is missed if one looks at it within the limited framework of analysis which treats the change as a mere input-output problem fully describable in terms of calculated investment priorities and the like. Rather, in relation to the larger power structure of society, there can be little doubt that the reform, for all its shortcomings, played a prime role in opening the whole structure of the system to the possibility of constructive change along a broad front: with effects on law, politics, social investment alternatives, the social distribution of opportunities, and new types of economic leadership roles and sanctions. Similarly, in their existential context, other reforms of the Revolutionary regimes—in finance, labor relations, and education—appear also indissociable from the productive accomplishments of the country in economic matters. Though the example of the Mexican experience does not lead to the conclusion that equally sweeping changes need be sought by external aid programs in all the other Latin American countries, the connection between social reform and self-sustaining internal economic drive in the Mexican case seems, nevertheless, sufficiently close to warrant the presumption that a development program devoid of a reasonably heavy reform content runs a serious risk of becoming merely another palliative applied on a hemispheric scale.

The second point on which Mexican experience is somewhat illuminating relates to the problem of reconciling the maximization of long-term growth through heavy current investment with the pressure for an immediate increase in the sharing of current gains in output—a problem which is not altogether eliminated by the fact that a number of the forms which an increased sharing may take are also conducive to long-term increases in productivity. Even allowing for the latter, however, it must be recognized that, whatever other considerations may bear upon the planned social distribution of income in the course of development, the historically oppressive conditions of labor in Latin America are ineluctably exercising a strong reactive influence upon contemporary policy formation. As a result, the distribution of resources must be worked out within the constraints set by an entirely understandable desire to repudiate the lopsided relationships of the past. In part, therefore, the development problem reduces to one of social bargaining.

Viewed in this light, a central task of development planning and policy becomes that of devising measures which modify interorganizational relations and the exchange relationships of socio-economic groups in such a

way as to enable the various participants in the economic system to rede-
fine the terms of their interdependence. In this, the contribution of planning
to the facilitation of collective agreement would seem to consist of its
utility in clarifying transactional alternatives and their opportunity costs—
in providing, as it were, more information on the next best alternatives so
that, in ignorance of those, none of the "bargaining" groups find nonagreement the only alternative to its preferred choice. The role of development
policy, in turn, appears, among other things, to involve the implementation
of measures which bring closer together the equilibrium positions of the
"bargaining" parties by influencing the least favorable terms each will
accept in its interactions with the other socio-economic groups. For example, measures which restrict the possibility or likelihood of domestic capital
flights reduce the withholding power of propertied interests. In like manner,
measures which operate to provide non-income components of welfare (e.g.,
better working conditions, greater economic security, improved status recognition, the reduction of ascriptive privilege) may, by creating a feeling
of general economic improvement, serve to restrain the claims against
potential savings by wage-earning interests. On both counts, the post-1910
Mexican experience is instructive.

Yet, if the record of Revolutionary Mexico illustrates the constructive
possibilities for linking social bargaining with growth objectives, that of
Porfirian Mexico, and its immediate aftermath, is no less germane for an
appraisal of development models which focus one-sidedly on the acceleration of investment and output variables while taking distributional elements
as parameters. Inasmuch as the dislocation of the 1910-1925 period was
a functional outgrowth of the system which prevailed from 1875 to 1910,
the only meaningful context in which the efficacy of the growth-*sans*-reform
policies of the Porfiriato can be evaluated is in terms of the net material
gains of the fifty-year period as a whole—in which case, the implied development model of the Porfirian epoch must be judged an utter failure. Moreover, in the last analysis, the debacle of Porfirian policy derived from a failure of the development strategy to permit the occurrence of sufficient social
bargaining to recast, in an evolutionary manner, the exchange relations
among the different segments of society. With nonagreement and withdrawal of commitment to maintaining the system the only acceptable alternative for many of the participants in the process, the "growth" policies of
the era may be said to have led directly to the substantial asset losses
which ensued with the overthrow of the Diáz regime.

If, therefore, the historical experiences of Mexico—and for that matter,
those of Bolivia and Cuba as well—contain any insights at all which are
relevant to the design of contemporary development policy in the Americas,
they would seem to demonstrate emphatically the advisability and realism
of structuring mutual gains and benefits more broadly into the process of
economic growth, if for no other reason than the quite practical one of en-

abling the Latin American economies to continue to operate as going concerns. Ill-equipped, by virtue of their historical conditioning and the institutional deficiencies derived therefrom, to attain such a system in the normal course of events, the republics of the region would appear at present to face the necessity of deliberately socializing their economies as part and parcel of their planning for long-term development. Although the design of the Alliance for Progress contained its quota of errors, on this, its most central and controverted point, it seems not to have been amiss.

Notes

NOTES FOR CHAPTER I

1. United Nations, Economic Commission for Latin America, *Posibilidades de desarrollo industrial integrado en Centro-América*, United Nations: 1963.

2. A phrase first used by von Humboldt in an eighteenth-century study. Both before and after von Humboldt's time, there has been a general predisposition to view Latin America as a region exceptionally rich in resources, the evidence notwithstanding. In the late sixteenth century, for example, Sir Richard Hawkins commented, in regard to Chile, that "it hath no Silke, nor iron, except in mynes, and those as yet not discovered." Richard Hawkins, *Observations of Sir Richard Hawkins in His Voyage into the South Sea in the Year 1593,* London: The Hakluyt Society, 1847, p. 158. Several centuries later a network television report on Brazil informed its U.S. viewers that the Amazon basin had a food-producing potential sufficient to feed not only all of Brazil but a goodly portion of the Western Hemisphere as well!

3. Brazil's "March to the West," which inspired the inflation-breeding construction of Brasília, may well constitute a similar case in point. Although the program was directed towards opening up new territory for settlement and agricultural development, many experts believe that a greater potential expansion of agricultural output would be realized from developing the intensive margin (i.e., the modernization and redevelopment of already settled lands) rather than the extensive margin of the rural sector. While many Brazilians dream of emulating the westward movement of the United States, it is lamentable that the South American giant has nothing at all comparable to its North American "prototype": namely, a productive western extremity and a highly developed eastern extremity bracketing a mineralized and agriculturally rich interior.

4. Brazil has some 27 per cent of the Latin American hydroelectric power potential, while together Peru, Chile, and Mexico have another 35 per cent. Colombia and Argentina each have about 7 per cent of the total; Venezuela, 5 per cent. United Nations, Economic Commission for Latin America, *Energy Development in Latin America,* Geneva: U.N. Department of Economic and Social Affairs, 1957, Chap. 4.

5. Half the known Latin American coal reserves appear to be in Colombia, and

531

about a fifth are in Chile. Approximately 13 per cent are located in Mexico and Brazil. Smaller amounts are found in Peru, Argentina, and Venezuela. *Ibid.*

6. According to Stephen Haden-Guest, ed., *A World Geography of Forest Resources,* New York: The Ronald Press Co., 1956, pp. 205–207, North America has some 770 million acres of accessible forests (of which 545 million acres are in use) and 300 million acres of inaccessible forests. In contrast Latin America has 850 million acres of accessible forests (of which 220 million acres are in use) and 1,400 million acres of inaccessible forests. It should be mentioned that European technicians have been engaged in research which indicates some new possibilities for substituting certain tropical hardwoods for temperate-zone varieties in a number of uses. Organization for European Economic Cooperation, *Tropical Timber: Production and Consumption Prospects,* Paris: 1955, p. 27.

7. In modern times a number of Japanese colonies in South America have experienced some success in the conduct of tropical agriculture, but other undertakings, such as the Le Tourneau-sponsored venture in eastern Peru, have been much less fortunate.

8. Charles Wagley and Marvin Harris, "A Typology of Latin American Subcultures," *American Anthropologist,* Vol. 57 (June 1955), pp. 428–451.

NOTES FOR CHAPTER II

1. Alvaro Gómez Hurtado, *La revolución en América,* Barcelona: Editorial AHR, 1958, p. 13.

2. In recognition of this essential cultural unity of Latin America, John Gillin has concluded that "there is a common pattern of customs, institutions, and ethos that characterizes modern Latin American society as a whole." John Gillin, "Ethos Components in Modern Latin American Culture," *American Anthropologist,* Vol. 57, No. 3, Part I (June 1955), p. 488. Similarly, George Foster has detected this same cultural unity, Hispanic in origin and distinct from other world areas, as underlying all Latin America, giving it a common cultural stamp which was "manifest in . . . character, personality, personal habits, and beliefs . . . [and] perhaps even more sharply in a philosophy about God, sovereign, State, and man which was remarkable as much for its effectiveness as a guide to action as for its internal consistency and completeness." George Foster, *Culture and Conquest: America's Spanish Heritage,* New York: Wenner-Gren Foundation for Anthropological Research, 1960, p. 2. Elaborating, Foster has enumerated the modalities of this cultural unity as consisting of language, a relatively inflexible class structure, elaborate courtesy and highly stylized external human relationships, pride, *dignidad* (a concept akin to the oriental "face"), an authoritarian tradition in religion and government, respect for personal force rather than impersonal law, a customary avoidance of law and regulation which fosters an anarchic type of individualism, a view of work as a necessary evil rather than a positive value, a belief in luck, and the prevalence of *personalismo* (i.e., an "effective personal working relationship with the right people") rather than the impersonal principle in government and business. *Ibid.,* pp. 3–4.

3. S. B. Clough and C. W. Cole, *Economic History of Europe,* Boston: D. C. Heath and Company, 1952, pp. 206–215. Melvin W. Knight, in his *Introduction to Modern Economic History* (Berkeley: 1940, pp. 71–72) also notes that in contrast with other European powers of the colonization era, Spain "went in heavily for direct public management," and that owing to this and to "minute state supervision, private business organization remained crude," there being little room for the development of the great private chartered trading companies which elsewhere operated on the basis of broad powers delegated to them by the state.

4. The Belgian sociologist, Roger E. Vekemans, S. J., for example, has observed that Spanish Catholicism has traditionally differed considerably from the manifestations of Catholicism in Germany, Holland, or the Anglo-Saxon countries. According to Vekemans, who formerly directed the sociology department of the Catholic Pontifical University of Chile, Hispanic Catholicism has generally been overspiritualized and sentimental, prone to mysticism, and not an "incarnational Catholicism" which is much concerned with "humanizing conditions of life in this world." From the resultant sharp clash between religious affectivity and intellectual rationality, Vekemans sees a danger that Hispanic Catholicism may be unable "to assume the new set of values of a rising technical civilization." R. E. Vekemans, "Is the Church Losing Latin America?", *Ave Maria,* Vol. 91, No. 2 (9 January 1960), pp. 5–10.

5. T. B. Veblen, *Absentee Ownership and Business Enterprise in Recent Times,* New York: B. W. Huebsch, Inc., 1923, p. 121.

6. While the Spanish colonial regime has often been indicted for its explosive treatment of the native population, through debt peonage and absentee ownership, its monopolistic character, and the shortcomings of venal officials, it is well to bear in mind that these were hardly unique to the Spanish system. For comparable defects in another colonial undertaking, see Clive Day, *The Policy and Administration of the Dutch in Java,* New York: The Macmillan Company, 1904, pp. 51–61, 63, 100–105, 117–119, 157–160, 348–352, and 368. See also, George Masselman, *The Cradle of Colonialism,* New Haven: Yale University Press, 1963.

7. A prime case in point is the early study of colonial development written by A. G. Keller (*Colonization,* New York: Ginn and Company, 1918). Similar in vein is the description of Spanish immigrants to the New World as "adventurers, seekers of fortune, often from aristocratic Spanish society, the type which naturally would not take to arduous tasks," in Clarence F. Jones' *South America,* New York: Henry Holt and Company, 1930, p. 9 (see also pp. 8, 10, 86). Still more reflective of an unsophisticated acceptance of the *leyenda negra* tradition is E. W. Shanahan's *South America: An Economic and Regional Geography,* London: Methuen and Company, Ltd., 1940, pp. 41–49, 64–67, and 291 ff.

8. With the economic motive paramount, enslavement of the Indians was at first permitted on some grounds, although there was continuing dispute among jurists and clerics as to the morality and justice of the practice. Thanks, however, to the work of Zumárraga, Vasco de Quiroga, the Franciscans of Guatemala, and Bartolomé de las Casas, the practice was condemned and, in the New Laws promulgated in 1542, prohibited altogether. As for the general quality of Spanish policy, it is worth noting the conclusion of the historian L. B. Simpson that "the fact is that the viceroys of New Spain, with singularly few exceptions, even in the slovenly period of the seventeenth-century Hapsburgs, were admirable public servants, trained for their profession, and possessing a high degree of personal responsibility .... Men of distinguished ability succeeding one another in a long and rarely broken line." Lesley Byrd Simpson, *Many Mexicos,* Berkeley: University of California Press, 1963, p. 46.

9. Aside from the well-known studies on this point by Heckscher and Schmoller, see J. W. Horrocks, *A Short History of Mercantilism,* London: Methuen and Company, Ltd., 1924, and Maurice Dobb, *Studies in the Development of Capitalism,* New York: International Publishers, 1947, especially Chaps. 2 and 5.

10. In his classic essay, "Spanish Mercantilism Before 1700" (in *Facts and Factors in Economic History,* Cambridge: Harvard University Press, 1932, pp. 214–239), E. J. Hamilton has shown that Spanish mercantilism was actually not much more than a rather crude bullionism, while Ramón Carande, in his *Carlos V y sus banqueros, la vida económica de España en una fase de su hegemonía,* 1516–1556 (Madrid: Revista de Occidente, 1943), has shown that during the important reign of Charles V, mercantilism was largely foreign to Spanish thought and policy. Navigation acts and shipping subsidies were employed; a host of restrictions and prohibitions (with drastic pun-

ishments for violators) were placed on the export of treasure and even domestic shipments of specie; commercial policy was designed to eliminate a passive trade balance and to assure that payments for imports would be made in the export of Spanish goods; and restrictions were placed on both imports of finished goods and exports of many raw materials (to encourage local finishing industries to develop); but many policies incompatible with mercantilism were present as well. Tariffs were used for revenue purposes more than for protection; to deal with inflation and goods shortages, imports were sometimes encouraged while exports were prohibited; trade restrictions were often temporary and seldom were general and absolute, numerous exceptions being permitted (on payment of fees) for trade counter to legal restrictions. On occasion foreign traders even enjoyed certain exemptions not enjoyed by the Spanish. Spanish policy towards trade was shifting with no observable guiding principle of consistency, and, as Colmeiro has demonstrated, mercantilist doctrines grew slowly and without order and never succeeded in forming in Spain a new system. Consequently, for approximately two centuries or more, Spain's commercial policy was a web of contradictions, with many policy shifts in response to the expediencies of the moment and pressures of various groups and with still further deviations arising out of contraband and bribery. For an extended discussion of these inconsistencies, see M. Colmeiro, *Historia de la economía política en España*, Madrid: Librería de D. Angel Calleja, 1863, Vol. II, pp. 315—355.

11. For the insights of this group, which included, among other things, a fairly modern understanding of the spending and tax multiplier effects, see Bernardo de Ulloa, *Restablecimiento de las fábricas, y comercio español*, Madrid: Antonio Marín, 1740; Bernardo Ward, *Proyecto económico, en que se proponen varias providencias dirigidas á promover los intereses de España, con los medios y fondos necesarios para su plantificación*, Madrid: Por la Viuda de Ibarra, Hijos, y Compañía, 1787 (4th printing; written in 1762); and Joseph del Campillo y Cosio, *Nuevo sistema de gobierno económico para la América*, Madrid: Imprenta de Benito Cano, 1789. All were critical of the previous commercial policies of the government.

12. José Ortega y Gasset, *España invertebrada*, Madrid: Revista de Occidente, 1946, pp. 97—116. Ortega y Gasset acknowledges that feudal elements were found in Spain but argues that they were so weak that the Roman tradition of the state and of central rule by law (with its emphasis on the collectivity) won out over the personal ties and individualism of feudal pluralism.

13. The noted Spanish historian, Rafael Altamira y Crevea, for example, observes that feudalism was mainly found in Catalonia and Aragón and was largely absent from León and Castile where the crown retained more power. Another historian, Antonio Ballesteros y Beretta, agrees that, although elements of feudalism were to be found in the kingdoms of Castile and León, the social structure and political organization of these influential parts of Spain, which played a major role in Spanish institutional development, were a far cry from central European feudalism. R. Altamira y Crevea, *Historia de España y de la civilización española*, Barcelona: Librería de Juan Gili, 1900—1902, 2 vols., Vol. I, pp. 299—301, and A. Ballesteros y Beretta, *Historia de España y su influencia en la historia universal*, Barcelona: Casa Editorial P. Salvat, 1922, Vol. III, pp. 328 ff. Similar reservations about the relatively weak or special development of feudalism in Spain and the correspondingly greater role of monarchical power are expressed in Sergio Bagú, *Economía de la sociedad colonial; ensayo de historia comparada de América Latina*, Buenos Aires: Librería "El Ateneo" Editorial, 1949, pp. 31—55; José Arias y Miranda, *Examen crítico-histórico del influjo que tuvo en el comercio, industria y población de España su dominación en América*, Madrid: La Real Academia de la Historia, 1854, p. 23; and J. P. Oliveira Martins, *La civilización ibérica*, Mexico: Cuadernos de Cultura, 1944, Vol. II, pp. 21—23.

14. C. H. Haring, *The Spanish Empire in America*, New York: Oxford University Press, 1947, p. 28.

15. J. M. Ots Capdequí, *El estado español en las Indias*, Mexico: Fondo de

Cultura Económica, 1941, pp. 15—16, 21.

16. Sergio Bagú, *op. cit.*, pp. 97—143, attacks strongly the notion that the economy of the New World dominions of Spain was feudal and stresses its commercial ethos and the extent of specialized production for the market.

17. German Arciniegas, *América, tierra firme,* Santiago: Ediciones Ercilla, 1937, p. 173. Arciniegas views the conquistadores as capitalistic entrepreneurs, albeit individualistic ones who did not use the chartered-company technique of English capitalism (p. 178), and makes much of the point that they financed, or obtained financing for, ventures under crown contract in exchange for a payment of a portion of the gains to the crown. In return, the conquistador-entrepreneurs sought positions as governors (*gobernadores*) of the areas they claimed. As Arciniegas admits, however, these supposed capitalists had not only to contend with Indians, pirates, and, sometimes, their own unruly soldiers, but they were also soon set upon by the *jueces de residencia* (royal magistrates) with their staffs of lawyers who, unless bought off, often deposed the "capitalistic" *gobernadores* and took over the government (p. 177). Gervasio de Artíñano y de Galdácano, in his *Historia del comercio con las Indias durante el dominio de los Austrias* (Barcelona: Talleres de Olivia de Vilanova, 1917), also argues that Spain brought the commercial spirit rather than feudalism to the Americas, since the discovery of the New World resulted, in the first place, in the course of a search for trading routes and greater profits from foreign commerce; thus, in this sense the commercial motive was antecedent to the settlement of the Indies. De Artíñano contends (pp. 60 ff.) that just as the merchant guild, or *consulado,* of Cádiz monopolized the trade with the west African coast, the merchant guild (*consulado do comercio ul universidad de comerciantes*) of Seville was formed around 1543 as a cartel-type agency handling trade with the Indies, performing insurance functions in that trade, and acting in an advisory capacity to the government's Council of the Indies (Consejo de las Indias). As a cartel, the merchant guild held a limited juridical authority and performed certain administrative functions respecting private trade.

18. The Welsers, who had banked the Spanish crown on a number of occasions, obtained permission to form in 1528 a trading company to monopolize the trade of Venezuela, but the concession, the only one of its kind for the first two centuries of the colonial period, was abandoned in 1546 without having produced notable economic results despite the severity of the exploitive measures employed by the concessionaires. An account of this venture and its aftermath (the resumption of full royal control of the life of Venezuela) is found in Eduardo Arcila Farías, *Economía colonial de Venezuela,* Mexico: Fondo de Cultura Económica, 1946.

19. A radically different assessment of the character of colonial organization is to be found, for example, in Richard Konetzke, "Estado y Sociedad en las Indias," *Estudios Americanos,* Seville: Escuela de Estudios Hispano Americanos, Vol. 3, No. 8 (January 1951), pp. 33—58.

20. The original, full statement of the thesis is found in F. J. Turner, *The Frontier in American History,* New York: Henry Holt and Company, 1920, and runs to the effect that the conditions of life on the frontier were conducive to the rise of individualism, social mobility, and democracy by weakening the checks of settled forms of social organization and partially disintegrating ancestral institutions. Somewhat simplistic in the Turnerian version, the thesis was later subjected to substantial criticism and modification which did much to refine the theory rather than to refute it on an across-the-board basis. In particular, the exponents of the so-called "germ theory," by emphasizing the institutional antecedents of American life, helped to remove the crude environmentalism of the Turnerian statement and recast the theory in a more acceptable culturological frame of reference. For an excellent summary of this work, see George R. Taylor, ed., *The Turner Thesis Concerning the Role of the Frontier in American History,* Boston: D. C. Heath and Company, 1956. One of the most ambitious efforts to synthesize Turner's insights with those contributed by latter-day scholars of the frontier is Walter

Prescott Webb's *The Great Frontier,* Boston: Houghton Mifflin Company, 1952, in which Webb interprets the North American experience as but the terminal stage of a four-centuries' long frontier movement which profoundly affected the institutions, habits, and attitudes of the culture region of the North Atlantic community. See also: D. R. Fox, ed., *Sources of Culture in the Middle West,* New York: D. Appleton-Century Company, 1934, and Louis B. Wright, *Culture on the Moving Frontier,* Bloomington: Indiana University Press, 1955, both of which draw heavily upon the germ theory of frontier interpretation.

    21. The contrasts between the Spanish American and the North American frontier settings have been mentioned, in passing, by Walter P. Webb, *op. cit.,* pp. 86–88, and Isaiah Bowman, *The Pioneer Fringe,* New York: American Geographical Society, 1931, pp. 296–345. Also helpful in the comparative study of frontiers is Silvio Zavala's essay on "The Frontiers of Hispanic America," in W. D. Wyman and C. B. Kroeber, editors, *The Frontier in Perspective,* Madison: The University of Wisconsin Press, 1957, pp. 35–58, although Zavala does not dig deeply into the institutional aspects of frontier existence in Latin America. For revealing examination of this latter, critically important point, see Herbert E. Bolton, "The Spanish Occupation of Texas, 1519–1690," *The Southwestern Historical Quarterly,* Vol. 16, No. 1 (July 1912), pp. 1–26; H. E. Bolton, *Outpost of Empire,* New York: Alfred A. Knopf, 1931; H. E. Bolton and T. M. Marshall, *The Colonization of North America,* New York: The Macmillan Company, 1963, esp. pp. 54, 233–235; Victor A. Belaúnde, "The Frontier in Hispanic America," *The Rice Institute Pamphlet,* Houston: The Rice Institute, Vol. 10, No. 4 (October 1923), pp. 202–213; Jorge Basadre, *Historia de la República del Perú,* Lima: Editorial Cultura Antártica, 1949, Vol. I, pp. 25–27. E. Arcila Farías, *op. cit.,* confirms in several places the relevance of the observations of the foregoing writers for Venezuelan conditions, while the same is done for the Chilean frontier by H. Douglas-Irvine in "The Landholding System of Colonial Chile," *Hispanic American Historical Review,* Vol. 8, No. 4 (November 1928), pp. 449–495. The point made by nearly all of these writers is that, as Belaúnde put it, the frontier societies of Spanish America were "born old" in the sense that fairly rapidly the main institutional props of Iberian life were implanted on the very margins of the Empire, leaving little room for the social organizational fluidity which Turner found as the dominant characteristic of the North American frontier. In this, the Spanish experience closely approximated the frontier described by Paul L. MacKendrick in his essay, "Roman Colonization and the Frontier Hypothesis," in Wyman and Kroeber, *op. cit.,* pp. 3–19. For an excellent portrayal of the vast juridical hierarchy which was intricately interwoven with the administrative system in one of the frontier regions of the empire, Chile, see Enrique Zorrilla Concha, *Esquema de la justicia en Chile colonial,* Santiago: Universidad de Chile, Seminario de Derecho Público de la Escuela de Ciencias Jurídicas y Sociales de Santiago, 1942. The maturity and urbanity of this comprehensive apparatus contrasts sharply with the simplicity or even rusticity of the institutional life on the Turnerian frontier.

    22. Some have argued, on the whole convincingly, that this was so as early as the tenth century of the Christian era; see, for example, Lynn Whyte, Jr., *Medieval Technology and Social Change,* New York: Oxford University Press, 1962.

    23. Frederick W. Maitland, *Selected Historical Essays,* Cambridge: The University Press, 1957, pp. 97–115. John R. Commons, *Legal Foundations of Capitalism,* New York: The Macmillan Company, 1924.

    24. F. W. Maitland, *op. cit.,* pp. 127–147. William S. Holdsworth, *A History of English Law,* London: Methuen and Company, Ltd., 1924, Vol. IV, pp. 54–299.

    25. Henri Pirenne, *Economic and Social History of Medieval Europe,* New York: Harcourt, Brace and Company, no date given, p. 2.

    26. That the particulars of the Pirenne thesis have been questioned quite extensively is not especially relevant to the present study, for virtually all scholars are in agreement that important changes did take place during the Middle Ages in the economic

and political organization of northwestern Europe. See, for example, Alfred F. Havig-
hurst, ed., *The Pirenne Thesis: Analysis, Criticism, Revision,* Boston: D. C. Heath
and Company, 1958.

27. The contrast has been explicitly noted, among other places, in Karl A. Witt-
fogel's *Oriental Despotism: A Comparative Study of Total Power,* New Haven: Yale
University Press, 1957. The contrast between the two culture areas is also developed
at length in John L. La Monte, *The World of the Middle Ages,* New York: Appleton-
Century-Crofts, Inc., 1949, a book notable for its extensive treatment of the Eastern
Empire as well as of western Europe.

28. Archibald R. Lewis, "Did the Dark Ages Exist?", *The Texas Quarterly,*
Vol. 2, No. 3 (Autumn 1959), pp. 40–56.

29. Such, for example, is the clear conclusion in F. L. Ganshof, *Feudalism,* New
York: Longmans, Green and Company, 1952. Ganshof, incidentally, specifically notes
that, except for the region of Barcelona, Spanish feudalism differed in many respects
from the classical feudalism of the Carolingian area. *Ibid.,* p. 60. See also J. L. La
Monte, *op. cit.,* Chaps. 11, 12, 21, and 28.

30. R. H. Tawney, *Religion and the Rise of Capitalism,* New York: Harcourt,
Brace and Company, 1926, Chap. 1.

31. To be sure, the process was not one of steady advance; witness the savage
massacre of the Irish by English armies in 1604–1654 which began a repression of long
duration and of a severity not substantially lighter than anything handed out by Spain.

32. For a useful interpretation of the significance of the religious factor in this
process, see William Warren Sweet, *Religion in Colonial America,* New York: Charles
Scribner's Sons, 1942. Sweet describes the cultural pluralism and religious diversity
of early North America and the implications of these for political organization. The
prevalence of dissenter and nonconformist views among the varieties of "left-wing
protestantism" which were espoused by the immigrants who came in increasing proportion after 1660 is also assessed in Sweet's *The American Churches, an Interpretation,*
New York: Abingdon-Cokesbury Press, 1948, pp. 14–33. According to Sweet, the
Scotch-Irish, Germans, and Huguenots who predominated after 1660 deemphasized the
institutional character of religion, substituted individualistic for collective Christianity, and supported free speech, self-government, and individual rights. In the process,
religious emphasis shifted from formal creeds and doctrines to personal conduct and
practical results.

33. Seldom has the process been so lucidly depicted as in Daniel J. Boorstin,
The Americans; the Colonial Experience, New York: Random House, 1958, and in the
sequel volume by Boorstin, *The Americans; the National Experience,* New York: Random House, 1965.

34. F. W. Blackmar, *Spanish Institutions of the Southwest,* Baltimore: The Johns
Hopkins Press, 1891. While unabashedly ethnocentric in its value judgments, this
early work had the merit of clearly recognizing the strong and distinctive Roman cast
of the Spanish institutional order. Especially useful are Chap. 2, which deals with
the Roman origins of Spanish colonial organization, and Chaps. 8 and 9, which shed
considerable light on the highly organized institutional life of the frontier regions of
settlement.

35. C. H. Haring, *op. cit.,* p. 28.

36. Continuity, rather than disjunctive development, was the essence of the
Spanish experience in economic organization and institutional life generally, as has
been emphasized by Charles Verlinden in his "Les origines coloniales de la Civilisa-
tion Atlantique: Antécédents et types de structure," *Cahiers d'histoire mondiale,*
Paris: Commission Internationale pour une Histoire du Développement Scientifique et
Culturel de l'Humanité, Vol. 1, No. 2 (October 1953), pp. 378–398. While Verlinden
traces the continuity between the Spanish colonial effort and the Italian trading and
colonization ventures from the eleventh to the sixteenth centuries in the Levant and

elsewhere in the Mediterranean (which trade involved an active commerce between the Italians and the Iberians), Clough and Cole, *op. cit.*, p. 58, have pointed out that many of the techniques of foreign commercial policy practiced by the Italian city states of the Middle Ages were borrowed, in turn, from the Byzantines.

37. In Protestant countries, persecution of religious dissidents was also, of course, a customary practice and, as in Spain, was also perhaps more of a political measure than a religious one. Nevertheless, the longer-term consequence of the religious break in northern Europe was to diminish the effective sanctions of ecclesiatical authority much more than in Spain.

38. As A. P. Usher had indicated, few of these other European institutions could match the durability of the Barcelona Deposit Bank (1401–1713), but while Barcelona had been very active in medieval commerce and the Mediterranean trade of later times, it was not until comparatively late in the colonial period that the mercantile and financial interests of that exceptional city were permitted to participate directly in the trade with the Americas. For an account of this early banking house, see A. P. Usher, *The Early History of Deposit Banking in Mediterranean Europe*, Cambridge: Harvard University Press, 1943.

39. Verlinden, *op. cit.*, remarks the role of the Italian business contingent (navigators, financiers, merchants) in Seville during the Atlantic expansion of Spain. Considering that Spanish policies had done great harm to the once flourishing Sephardic community of the Iberian peninsula, the importance of the availability of Italian business talent should not be underrated.

40. Although the merchant guild of Seville was centrally involved in the transatlantic trade, only a very limited sort of capitalistic organization developed in that city. In the beginning, private trade between Spain and America was hindered by close royal control of any exchanges with the natives and by the tendency of Spanish industrial firms (until their decline) to carry on the bulk of their business with the colonies on their own account. Later on, other factors appear to have arrested capitalistic development. André E. Sayous, "Partnerships in the Trade Between Spain and America and also in the Spanish Colonies in the Sixteenth Century," *Journal of Economic and Business History*, Cambridge, Massachusetts: Vol. 1, No. 2 (February 1929), pp. 282–301.

41. J. P. Oliveira Martins, *op. cit.*, Vol. I, pp. 67–89; A. Ballesteros y Beretta, *op. cit.*, Vol. I, pp. 347–363.

42. A. A. Vasiliev, *History of the Byzantine Empire*, Madison: University of Wisconsin Press, 1952, pp. 48, 53–54. René Guerdan, *Byzantium, Its Triumphs and Tragedy*, New York: G. P. Putnam's Sons, 1957, pp. 17 ff. Charles Diehl, *Byzantium: Greatness and Decline*, New Brunswick: Rutgers University Press, 1957, pp. 71–78.

43. A. A. Vasiliev, *op. cit.*, pp. 58, 60–65; Charles Diehl, *op. cit.*, pp. 27–29, 32–37.

44. A. A. Vasiliev, *op. cit.*, pp. 116–128.

45. This tradition of regalism has, with the support of historical circumstances, persisted strongly throughout Iberian and neo-Iberian development. So deeply ingrained has it been, in fact, that even in the context of nineteenth-century political liberalism and twentieth-century republican government, the chief executive has frequently held, de facto if not de jure, powers considerably in excess of those assigned his office in the Anglo-American version of republican government. State and local governments have, for the most part, been quite feeble, and this concentration of political authority has had important consequences for the shape of national economic policy and the pattern of resource mobilization.

46. Charles Diehl, *op. cit.*, pp. 66–68; A. A. Vasiliev, *op. cit.*, pp. 116–128, 143–149, 159. Alipio Valencia Vega, *Fundamentos de derecho político*, La Paz: Librería Editorial "Juventud," 1954, pp. 66, 91, 407.

47. For a useful description of the Roman colonial structure in Spain, see R. Altamira y Crevea, *op. cit.*, Vol. I, pp. 101–119. A more general exposition of the Ro-

man system is found in W. T. Arnold, *The Roman System of Provincial Administration,* Oxford: B. H. Blackwell, 1914.

48. A monumental guide to the early development of this legislation is Clyde Pharr, *The Theodosian Code and Novels and the Sirmondian Constitutions,* Princeton: Princeton University Press, 1952. This contains both a translation of the imperial enactments and a useful commentary. See also the brief survey of relevant developments in A. A. Vasiliev, *op. cit.,* pp. 101–102, 143–147, 158–159.

49. Paul Collinet, *Etudes historiques sur le droit de Justinien,* Paris: L. Larose et L. Tenin, 1912, Vol. I, pp. 23–25.

50. At the same time, Justinian law modified the oldest Roman law considerably in regard to the institution of property, especially by removing the absolute, individualistic character of those rights. By asserting the extension of the power of the divinely ordained emperor to the domain of privately ordained things, the Justinian code laid a foundation for broad interventionism and the right of eminent domain. The modification of private property implied was carried further by the teachings of the church fathers on the nature of property (i.e., the stewardship concept). An exposition of this development is found, among other places, in Gonzalo Canal Ramírez, *Función social de la propiedad: prospecto histórico, filosófico, y jurídico,* Bogotá: Antares Imprenta-Editorial, 1953, pp. 30–57.

51. Constantine had made himself virtually the head of the church; the organizational and administrative functions of the church fell to the state, and the successors of Constantine carried on in the same way. The patriarch was limited in his role to spiritual matters, while the emperor claimed for his sphere all administrative offices, whether of church or of state. The inception of this tradition is significant, for though we are not here concerned with either political or religious history, the public sector of the colonial Spanish American economy and, indeed, the entire pattern of colonial social integration rested upon this traditional unity. For a discussion of the Byzantine "sacred monarchy," which was essentially a return, under Roman auspices, to the underlying social tradition of the ancient East, see Charles Diehl, *Les grands problèmes de l'histoire byzantine,* Paris: Librairie Armand Colin, 1943, pp. 9, 49–50, 57–59, 65–66; and Ernest Barker, *Social and Political Thought in Byzantium,* Oxford: The Clarendon Press, 1957, pp. 7–12, 27–29, 105–109.

52. Christopher H. Dawson, in his *Medieval Essays* (New York: Sheed and Ward, 1954, pp. 12–94), observes that Christianity was a chief conveyor of the Roman-Byzantine cultural order to the western part of Europe.

53. Charles Diehl, *Byzantiun; Greatness and Decline,* pp. 89–90; René Guerdan, *op. cit.,* pp. 88–98; Charles Diehl, *Les grands problèmes . . . ,* pp. 107–110. The excessive state regimentation of industry and commerce which had become the norm in both the Hellenistic and western portions of the ancient world by the fourth century of the Christian era is documented repeatedly in Clyde Pharr, *op. cit.;* see also W. A. Brown, "State Control of Industry in the IV Century," *Political Science Quarterly,* Vol. 22, pp. 494 ff.

54. Karl Polanyi, C. M. Arensberg, and H. W. Pearson, eds., *Trade and Markets in the Early Empires,* Glencoe, Illinois: The Free Press, 1957.

55. Max Weber, *General Economic History,* Glencoe, Illinois: The Free Press, 1950, p. 331.

56. One of the themes which runs most strongly through contemporary Latin American life is the tradition of comprehensive government responsibility. The tradition is a long-standing one in Iberian culture. There is no quarrel here with the nature of the social arrangements implied by this tradition, but two observations do seem to be germane. For one thing, the assumption of a wide functional role by public authority means that the efficiency with which the assumed functions are performed will depend heavily upon the operational efficacy of the structure of public administration. For another, the tradition at least raises the possibility that national wealth will be distributed more

by government decrees than by economic forces and that the allocation of resources will be similarly determined.

57. While the absolutism of the crown eventually (before the New World venture was established) terminated the experiment with constitutionalism made during the Middle Ages in Spain, it is interesting to note that not until Bourbon centralism was installed were most of the *fueros* surpressed, and even then they endured in Galicia, the Basque country, and Catalonia. Thus in many ways the centralism of monarchic authority was more completely realized in the ultramarine kingdoms than in Spain itself, particularly in northern Spain.

58. A. Ballesteros y Beretta, *op. cit.,* pp. 515–530; M. Colmeiro, *op. cit.,* pp. 113 ff., 135–140.

59. Martin A. S. Hume, *The Spanish People,* New York: D. Appleton and Company 1911, p. 54; J. P. Oliveira Martins, *op. cit.,* p. 128. In his study of colonial municipal government in Spanish America (*El cabildo en Chile colonial,* Santiago de Chile: Ediciones de la Universidad de Chile, 1940, pp. 19 ff.). Julio Alemparte Robles traces the democratic features of municipal organization to the Germanic influence brought to Spain by the Visigoths, a view which is supported by the Spanish authority, Eduardo de Hinojosa, in his *Estudios sobre la historia del derecho español,* Madrid: Imp. del Asilo de Huérfanos del Sagrado Corazón de Jesús, 1903, Chap. 1.

60. José Ortega y Gasset, *op. cit.,* p. 100; R. Altamira y Crevea, *op. cit.,* Vol. I, pp. 166, 189–190, 197–199; J. P. Oliveira Martins, *op. cit.,* pp. 122 ff. The Lex Romana Visigothorum, which was in force from c. 500 to 654, preserved important elements of imperial Roman law, while the Liber Judiciorum of 654, which prepared the way for the famous Fuero Juzgo of 694, continued this influence. J. T. Vance, *The Background of Hispanic-American Law,* New York: Central Book Company, 1943, pp. 33–44.

61. Manuel Colmeiro, *Elementos del derecho político y administrativo de España,* Madrid: Librerías de Don Angel Calleja, 1858, pp. 8–11, 15–20, 22–27. The Fuero Juzgo or Lex Romana Visigothorum and the Breviarium Alaricianum of this period drew heavily upon the Theodosian Code; M. A. S. Hume, *op. cit.,* pp. 69–70; A. A. Vasiliev, *op. cit.,* pp. 101–102. See also the discussion of the historical background of Spanish law in Gustavus Schmidt, *The Civil Law of Spain and Mexico,* New Orleans: privately printed, 1851, pp. 9–90. According to J. T. Vance, *op. cit.,* pp. 53–57, the Gothic element was dominant in this landmark of legal development, but the point is disputed by other authorities. According to the writer of the article "Derecho Romano" in the *Enciclopedia Universal Ilustrada* (Tomo XVIII, pp. 300–301), Roman law triumphed over Gothic law in the Fuero Juzgo.

62. M. A. S. Hume, *op. cit.,* p. 63, 72; Luis G. de Valdeavellano, *Historia de España, de los orígenes a la baja Edad Media,* Madrid: Manuales de la Revista de Occidente, 1952, pp. 296–301, 304, 309–318, 561–569.

63. R. Altamira y Crevea, *op. cit.,* Vol. I, pp. 177–178, 181, 192–194.

64. M. Colmeiro, *Historia de la economía . . . ,* pp. 197–198, 375–377; R. Altamira y Crevea, *op. cit.,* Vol. I, pp. 262–266; Christopher Dawson, *op. cit.,* pp. 117–127; Julius Klein, "Medieval Spanish Guilds," in *Facts and Factors . . . ,* pp. 164, 167 ff.

65. Antonio Ballesteros y Beretta, *op. cit.,* Vol. III, pp. 341 ff., 354 ff.; José Arias y Miranda, *op. cit.,* p. 28.

66. As J. T. Vance has pointed out (*op. cit.,* pp. 46 ff.), the intimate relationship built up between the church and the state identified Christian unity with national unity and gave clerical lawyers a major hand in shaping the legal tradition which governed that national unity. See also the excellent study of Richard Konetzke, *El imperio español,* Madrid: Ediciones Nueva Época, S. A., 1946, pp. 81–90, for a discussion of the development of a unitary state which fused faith with politics.

67. Rafael Altamira y Crevea, *A History of Spain,* Princeton: D. Van Nostrand Company, Inc., pp. 225–228, 263–264, 310–313. Richard Konetzke, *El imperio español,* pp. 11–12.

68. J. T. Vance, *op. cit.,* pp. 73–78.

69. Rafael Altamira y Crevea, *Historia de España . . .* , Vol. I, pp. 301–303, notes the rise of free towns and leagues of cities (*behetrías* and *hermandades*) in this period.

70. Gustavus Schmidt, *op. cit.,* p. 13; Antonio Ballesteros y Baretta, *op. cit.,* Vol. III, pp. 315–316; Rafael Altamira y Crevea, *A History of Spain,* p. 316; J. T. Vance *op. cit.,* pp. 86 ff., 93–103; "Derecho Romano," *loc. cit.,* p. 299. The Siete Partidas contained a strong assertion of the powers of the monarch, admitted the *fueros* as compromises of necessity, and borrowed from Roman and canon law their traditional doctrines of the state. See also Carlos Román Celis, *El estado administrativo como forma política del mundo moderno,* Mexico: Universidad Nacional Autónoma de México, Facultad de Derecho, 1956, pp. 25–53, 61, and José Cepeda Andán, *En torno al concepto del estado en los reyes católicos,* Madrid: Consejo Superior de Investigaciones Científicas, Escuela de Historia Moderna, 1956, pp. 50–54, 71 120.

71. By 1476 the trends evident in the Siete Partidas were accentuated when a juridical system dependent upon the crown was established, which in principle (if not in practice, owing to exemptions later granted) obliged all classes to contribute to the state and to submit to the same monarchically centered jurisdiction of law. Richard Konetzke, *El imperio español,* pp. 75–78. In the Leyes de Toro, promulgated in 1505, the elements of Roman law were strengthened further. J. T. Vance, *op. cit.,* pp. 117–120.

72. Rafael Altamira y Crevea, *A History of Spain,* p. 310; Antonio Ballesteros y Beretta, *op. cit.,* p. 350.

73. Antonio Ballesteros y Beretta, *op. cit.,* p. 307; Julius Klein, "Medieval Spanish Guilds" in *Facts and Factors in Economic History,* pp. 169–187; M. Colmeiro, *Historia de la economía política en España,* Vol. I, pp. 300–306, 215–325, 359–367, and Vol. II, pp. 237–240, 273–286.

74. The municipal and parliamentary democracy of Spain was gradually lost as the crown found ways of raising funds without the consent of the taxed. From 1273 on, the *Mesta* (or sheep-raisers guild) paid revenue to the crown for rights to establish a sheepwalk extending from above Burgos into southern Spain. From around the middle of the fifteenth century, additional income was raised for the royal treasury through payments of the Cabaña de Carreteros, a national carters guild, which moved over national roads. The discovery of America, which enabled the crown to extract heavy trade duties through the Casa de Contratación and which provided rising royalties from mining, virtually completed the process of establishing the fiscal independence of the monarchy from the municipalities and the parliament (the Cortes). With these funds, a series of industrious sovereigns, impatient with democratic processes, were able to finance internal political fights in the various Spanish cities and so contribute to their devitalization as centers of power.

75. The point is explicitly made, for example, in F. García Calderón's *Latin America: Its Rise and Progress,* London: T. Fisher Unwin, Ltd., 1918, pp. 285–286.

76. The theory of the state developed by these men was in marked contrast to that propounded by Locke and Rousseau. It had quite different implications for the possibilities of intervention and, hence, the nature of private property rights. The germ of the idea was contained in Vitoria's "De Potestati Civili," which is to be found in Francisco de Vitoria, *Relaciones teológicas del maestro Fray Francisco de Vitoria,* Madrid: Imprenta la Rafa, 1934, Vol. II, pp. 169–210. For an exposition of the structure of Vitoria's theory, see Herbert Wright, "Vitoria and the State," in *Francisco de Vitoria,* addresses in commemoration of the fourth centenary of his lectures "De Indis" and "De Iuri Belli," Washington, D.C.: Catholic University of America, 1932, pp. 25–36; and Luis Recasens Siches, *Las teorías políticas de Francisco de Vitoria,* Madrid: Sucesores de Rivadeneydra, S.A., 1931, pp. 10–11, 29–38, 57–59. The theories of Suárez ran along the same lines and, like those of Vitoria, constituted a definite rejection of any notion of individualistic natural harmony such as that contained in Smithian economics. See Herbert Wright, "Suárez and the State" in *Francisco Suárez,*

addresses in commemoration of his contribution to international law and politics, Washington, D.C.: 1933, pp. 29–43; and Luis Recasens Siches, *La filosofía del derecho de Francisco Suárez,* Mexico: Editorial Jus, 1947, pp. 83–107, 154–160, 169–187. For the core of Suárez' theory, see Francisco Suárez *Tratado de las leyes y de Dios legislador,* Madrid: Hijos de Reus, 1918–1921, Book II, Chaps. 13–15, and Book III, Chaps. 1–4.

77. Despite rebellions against inquisitional activity, such as occurred in Aragon in 1484, in Catalonia in 1487, and in Mallorca in 1490, the Inquisition continued its persecutions, involving even one of the primates of Spain and members of the religious orders as well as converted Jews.

78. José María Gironella, *The Cypresses Believe in God,* New York: Alfred Knopf, 1955, Vol. II, p. 643.

79. Towards the end of the fourteenth century, anti-Jewish pogroms occurred, in spite of papal condemnations, in Seville, Castile, Aragon, and Catalonia. Because of these, many persons, in order to save their lives and possessions, became *conversos* (converts to Catholicism), and many of the *conversos* prospered in both business life and the professions. Some, such as Alonso de Espina who was a Franciscan friar and rector of the University of Salamanca, even rose to high positions in the nobility and the ecclesiastical hierarchy. Indeed, especially after the holocaust of 1391, Spanish Jewry, as such, was quite weakened and disorganized, and economic leadership passed to the *conversos,* who were particularly important in public finance, private finance, manufacturing, and international trade. Abraham A. Neuman, *The Jews in Spain,* Philadelphia: The Jewish Publication Society of America, 1942, Vol. I, pp. 163–169, 191, and Vol. II, pp. 183, 221 ff.; Cecil Roth, *A History of the Marranos,* Philadelphia: The Jewish Publication Society of America, 1932, pp. 21 ff. Virtually all the writers on the subject, it may be noted, identify the *conversos* as of key importance in the capitalistic developments of the day. Note, for example, the treatment of the subject in Julio Caro Baroja, *Los judíos en la España moderna y contemporánea,* Madrid: Ediciones Arión, 1961, Vol. II, Chaps. 1–5.

80. Commercial intercourse among the regions of Spain had been hampered by differing laws and customs while the kingdoms were administered separately, but as the *aljamas* (the Jewish communities in the towns and cities) were quasi-autonomous and lived according to laws which were similar from region to region, the Jewish communities enjoyed a special institutional advantage in long-distance trade.

81. The Moriscos were expelled in 1609, and may have numbered 200,000 to 300,000 persons. Cecil Roth, *op. cit.,* pp. 29–53, 74 ff., related the degree to which the *conversos* were harrassed by the Inquisition.

82. For this reason Spanish religious policy merits mention, for religious persecution was hardly unique to Spain. Protestant-sponsored terrorism and persecution were practiced, for example, in Basel (1528), in Holland (1619), and in England under Elizabeth I, but for circumstantial reasons these instances had not the economic significance of the events in Spain.

83. While the nobility of southern Spain was permitted to invest in trade and shipping, the crown, as a general policy, which reflected its mistrust of the group, discouraged and even prohibited the nobility from undertaking expeditions to the Americas on their own account and risk. Richard Konetzke, "Entrepreneurial Activities of Spanish and Portuguese Noblemen in Medieval Times, " *Explorations in Entrepreneurial History,* Vol. 6 (1953–1954), pp. 116, 118.

84. Robert S. Smith, *The Spanish Guild Merchant, A History of the Consulado, 1250–1700,* Durham, North Carolina: Duke University Press, 1940, documents the origins of the *consulado* in medieval Spain along the Mediterranean coast, whence the institution spread to other Spanish cities and to the New World. As Smith makes clear, the *consulado* was, like the municipality, one of the chief, feudal-derived and non-Roman institutions of Spanish life which arose out of the crown's grants of exceptions and privileges to particular groups. As such, it was one of the few instances in which a social group obtained a certain measure of independence of action from direct state

control and was, therefore, a form of limited self-government.

85. The characteristic melding of political and economic activity is evidenced by the many Sevillian merchants involved in trade with the New World who endeavored to purchase patents of nobility and seats on the municipal council in order to avoid payment of duties and influence royal officials to forego inspection of their shipments. Ruth Pike, "The Sevillian Nobility and Trade with the New World in the Sixteenth Century," *Business History Review,* Vol. 39, No. 4 (Winter 1965), pp. 441, 444.

86. By the sixteenth century, the Mesta (the Castilian sheep-raisers guild) was probably, along with the *consulados,* the chief exception to the generally weak array of private institutions, and in the absence of countervailing interests, its influence upon government policy was quite powerful—though detrimental from the standpoint of economic development. That its influence was so strong derived from the fact that it was useful to the crown: as a source of loans and as a source of tax revenue (on the merino wool which was exported). In the colonial period the merchant guild of Seville attained some importance, but its influence was not so much an independent development as one which was created by the crown itself when, to control the American trade, it confined that trade to the Guadalquivir port. For a discussion of the Mesta, see Julius Klein, *The Mesta: A Study in Spanish Economic History, 1273–1836,* Cambridge: Harvard University Press, 1920.

87. A useful account of economic controls, with a particularly good discussion of the extraordinarily complex tax system of Spain, is found in G Desdevises du Dezert, *L'Espagne de l'ancien régime, les institutitions,* Paris: Société Française d'Imprimerie et de Librairie, 1899, pp. 197–203, 365–418. Desdevises du Dezert indicates how the cumbersome nature of the tax system restricted commerce while at the same time it necessitated the employment of an army of functionaries for its administration, thereby occasioning high costs of collection.

88. Lesley Byrd Simpson, in his article "Unplanned Effects of Mexico's Planned Economy," *The Virginia Quarterly Review,* Vol. 29, No. 4 (Autumn 1953), pp. 514 ff. succinctly states the case by observing that "Planning in Mexico is as old as the Conquest. The first planning agency was the Council of the Indies, established in 1524 by the Emperor Charles V. It was given the assignment of organizing and governing the whole New World. The civil, religious, and economic structures were all set up according to blueprints drawn in Spain. The result was a managed, authoritarian society run by a vast bureaucracy." Desdevises du Dezert, *op. cit.,* pp. 95–102, 126–133, and 138–163, indicates the strong parallels between the domestic institutions of Spain and those of colonial organization: e.g., the Council of Castile and the Council of the Indies, the viceregal office, and the *corregidores* (intermediate agents of royal power).

NOTES FOR CHAPTER III

1. There were certain modifications in the system. While some, for example, have traced the governmental forms utilized in the New World to Old World origins, recent investigations have turned up an assortment of innovative features in the colonial organization. Sigfrido A. Radaelli, for instance, in his "La Institución Virreinal en las Indias, Antecedentes Históricos," *Revista de Indias,* Madrid: Instituto Gonzalo Fernández de Oviedo, Consejo Superior de Investigaciones Científicas, Vol. 14, Nos. 55–56 (January–June 1954), pp. 37–56, finds no precedent in the European vicroyalties for the American viceroyalties of 1535 and after.

2. See, e.g., Germán Arciniegas, *América, Tierra Firme,* Santiago de Chile: Ediciones Ercilla, 1937, pp. 173–181; Silvio Zavala, *Los intereses particulares en la conquista de la Nueva España,* Madrid: Facultad de Derecho, Universidad Central, 1933; and Volodia Teitelboim, *El Amanacer del capitalismo y la conquista de América,* Santiago de Chile: 1943. Lesley Byrd Simpson also verges on this interpretation in some of his writings: e.g., "New Lamps for Old in Latin America," in University of California at Los Angeles, Committee on International Relations, *The Civilization of*

the Americas, Berkeley: University of California Press, 1938, esp. pp. 4—8.

3. References to such innovations are numerous in most of the contemporary and later studies of the colonial period. A particularly useful overview of the many Spanish contributions in agriculture is to be found in Ricardo Cappa, *Estudios críticos acerca de la dominación española en América,* Madrid: Librería Católica de Gregorio del Amo, 1890, Vols. V and VI, "Industria Agrícola-pecuaria Llevada a America por los Españoles."

4. Aside from the various tribes of central Mexico and the Indians of the Inca empire, the Chibchas of Colombia had also attained a fairly high level of civilization. The Maya of Central America, however, were already on the decline by the time the Spanish arrived, and most of the other Indians of the Americas were more primitive.

5. Even the well-organized Inca empire was, at the time of the Conquest, "embroiled in dynastic schism and civil war." Charles Gibson, *The Inca Concept of Sovereignty and the Spanish Administration in Peru,* Austin: The University of Texas Press, 1948.

6. See E.W. and A.E. Stearn, *The Effect of Smallpox on the Destiny of the Amerindian,* Boston: Bruce Humphries, Inc., 1945; George Kubler, "Population Movements in Mexico, 1520—1600," *Hispanic American Historical Review,* Vol. 22, No. 4 (November 1942), pp. 606—643; S.F. Cook and L.B. Simpson, *The Population of Central Mexico in the Sixteenth Century,* Berkeley: University of California Press, 1948. The Stearns note that measles, typhoid, and syphilis were also brought in along with smallpox, with ravaging effects on the native population of the Americas. Moreover, in the wake of the smallpox and other epidemics, a shortage of harvest hands often produced famine conditions which contributed further to depopulation.

7. Under Spanish rule, the "public" food storage facilities used by the Incaic system were not maintained, and with the introduction of sugar cultivation on the coast, large amounts of irrigation water and land were diverted from the production of crops for the native populace. Since mining was substantially increased by the Spaniards, larger numbers of Indians were put to work in that industry, usually under harsh conditions, and correspondingly less manpower was available for the conduct of agriculture at a time when the consumption claims of the ladino population against that sector's output were mounting.

8. As George Foster has expressed it in *Culture and Conquest: America's Spanish Heritage,* New York: Wenner-Gren Foundation for Anthropological Research, 1960, p. 10, the aim of Spanish colonial policy was purposeful, guided change involving "the extension of an ideal Spanish culture and culture values to all parts of America where it was physically possible, a policy not duplicated elsewhere in modern times." The culture so transmitted, which Foster sees as essentially conservative in nature (p. 20), was patterned mainly on Castilian models (p. 14). For a contemporary foreign observer's view of Spanish imperial aims, a view contrasting them favorably with French policies, see François R.J. de Pons, *Voyage à la partie orientale de la Terre-Firme, dans L'Amérique Méridionale, fait pendant les années 1801, 1802, 1803 et 1804,* Paris: de l'Imprimerie de Fain et Compagnie, 1806, Vol. II, pp. 4—15.

9. Royal jurisdiction even moved into the spiritual sphere under this scheme of social organization, so that the king exercised a quasi-pontifical authority over and beyond his jurisdiction regarding temporal matters and personnel appointments. Rafael Gómez Hoyos, *La iglesia de América en las Leyes de Indias,* Madrid: Instituto Gonzalo Fernández de Oviedo, 1961, presents a thorough examination of this relationship.

10. Paradoxically, a "dynamic traditionalism" might be the most accurate description of the Spanish system. However static in conception the venture was, it was not a milieu from which social change was absent, largely as a result of exogenous factors and forces: e.g., population decline and subsequent recovery, foreign wars and intermittent interruptions of the empire's trade organization, mining booms and declines, the subversion of the system introduced by the Enlightenment, the growth of foreign trade in the eighteenth century, etc. Moreover, it must be kept in mind that there were sundry

impediments to full exercise of the royal authority which was asserted in law.

11. R.D. Hussey, "Antecedents of the Spanish Monopolistic Overseas Trading Companies, (1624–1728)" *Hispanic American Historical Review,* Vol. 9, No. 1 (February 1929), pp. 1–30.

12. Roland D. Hussey, *The Caracas Company, 1728–1784,* Cambridge: Harvard University Press, 1934. In 1734 the Company of Galicia was given certain limited trading rights with Campeche and Veracruz in Mexico, while in 1755 the Barcelona Company was chartered to try to revive Spanish trade with the Caribbean islands. Eduardo Arcila Farías, *Economía colonial de Venezuela,* Mexico: Fondo de Cultura Económica, 1946, pp. 32, 312–313 ff., discusses the conflict which developed between the private trading interests in Venezuela and governmental authorities.

13. The "Ordenanzas sobre descubrimiento, población y pacificación de las Indias" promulgated by Philip II in 1573 forbade, with severe penalties for violations, anyone to make discoveries without royal license, and the foundation of towns within areas already discovered was to be undertaken only on license from the viceroys, the *audiencias,* and other royal agencies. The rigidity with which these rules were adhered to is exemplified by the early history of San Jose, California. Originally located in accordance with the instructions given by a Spanish governor, the site involved the settlers in conflicts with a neighboring mission and was also subject to inundation. The colonists petitioned the governor to move the town to nearby higher ground, but their petition had to be forwarded for a ruling to the *comandante-general* in Sonora who, in turn, referred the matter to a royal attorney. The decree authorizing the move was eventually issued, almost two years after the petition was submitted. Frederick Hall, *The History of San Jose and Surroundings,* San Francisco: A.L. Bancroft and Company, 1871, pp. 46–48. See also E. Arcila Farías, *op. cit.,* pp. 30–32.

14. José Arias y Miranda, *Examen crítico-histórico del influjo que tuvo en el comercio, industria y población de España su dominación en América,* Madrid; La Real Academia de la Historia, 1854, p. 58; Richard Konetzke, "Estado y Sociedad en las Indias," *Estudios Americanos,* Seville: Escuela de Estudios Hispano Americanos Vol. 3, No. 8 (January 1951), pp. 33–58. The most complete statement of the accepted official doctrine of the day was, perhaps, the treatise written in 1629–1639 by the noted regalist theoretician, Juan de Solórzano y Pereyra, *Política Indiana,* Madrid: Imprenta Real de la Gazeta, 1776, 2 vols.. Solórzano's work, which also worked out in a definitive way the pro-monarchical concept of ecclesiastical patronage, was banned in Rome for its espousal of a type of caesaropapism which interposed the authority of the crown, as "Vicar of the Indies," between the Papacy and the Catholics of the Spanish Empire, For a modern interpretation of the organizational rationale and structure of the Spanish system, see Richard Konetzke, *El imperio español,* Madrid: Ediciones Nueva Epoca, S.A., 1946. Also informative is Silvio Zavala, *Filosofía de la conquista,* Mexico: Fondo de Cultura Económica, 1947.

15. Of enormous value to an understanding of the legal disposition of mineral rights, together with an appreciation of the extent of governmental regulation of the mining industry in colonial times is Francisco Xavier de Gamboa, *Commentaries on the Mining Ordinances of Spain,* London: Longman, Rees, Orme, Brown, and Green, 1830, 2 vols.. Private rights in mining were of a usufructuary nature and conditional upon: registration of minerals discoveries before a justice, payment of royalties to the crown, and continuous working of the mines on an officially set minimum scale. Gamboa, *op. cit.,* Vol. I, pp. 152–154, 310–312; Vol. II, pp. 57–70, 74–102. Gamboa, a distinguished Spanish jurist, wrote his comprehensive study in 1761.

16. Eduardo Arcila Farías, *op. cit.,* p. 60; Oscar E. Reyes, *Breve historia general de Ecuador,* Quito: Editorial "Fray Jodoco Ricke," 1955, Vol. I, p. 203. A clear statement of this point of view was expressed in 1795 by the regalist Spanish economist Jovellanos, who saw, in fact, the desamortization of civil property as an issue even more important than the freeing of religious property. See Gaspar Melchor de Jovellanos, *Informe sobre la ley agraria,* Madrid: Instituto de Estudios Políticos, 1955, esp. pp. 147–148 ff.

17. *Real ordenanza para el establecimiento é instrucción de intendentes de exército y provincia en el Reino de la Nueva España,* Madrid: De orden de su Magestad, 1786. Article 61 of the ordenance set forth clearly this social utility concept of property. Article 62 instructed the intendants to promote the cultivation of various crops by distributing vacant lands of the public domain or private lands which were uncultivated (except for communal properties). The distributed lands were to be granted only in a usufructuary degree; the instructions provided further that if the land grants were not put into use, they would be regained by the crown and reassigned to cultivators who would use them as intended.

18. For recognition of the Hispanic roots of this and related social doctrines now current in Latin America, see Moises Poblete Troncosco, "The Social Content of Latin American Constitutions," *Social Forces,* Vol. 21 (1942—43), and José Domingo González, "El Problema de la Tierra en el Perú," *Revista Universitaria,* Lima: Anõ XXIV, Vol. III (September-December 1930), pp. 639—734.

19. As Pedro M. Oliveira pointed out in his *La política económica de la metrópoli,* Lima: Imprenta La Industria, 1905, pp. 67—68, the justification presented for the *mita* regime of conscript labor was that the members of a society must work to contribute to the collectivity—i.e., the state— and that since the mines were necessary for the public good, forced labor in them was legitimate on grounds of public utility. For an example of the manner in which native labor was organized and regulated for "public utility" work, see José Toribio Medina, ed., *Colección de documentos inéditos para la historia de Chile,* Santiago: Imprenta Elzeviriana, 1901, Vol. 28, pp. 294, 322, and Vol. 29, pp. 144, 416. Since agriculture, the usual employment of native labor, was also in the public interest, the sources cited indicate that forced labor in the mines was sometimes limited to the off seasons in agriculture—an interesting early attempt to tap underemployed rural labor for development purposes.

20. Useful to an understanding of this point, which has also been widely revived in modern times, are José Cepeda Adán, *En torno al concepto del estado en los reyes católicos,* Madrid: Consejo Superior de Investigaciones,Escuela de Historia Moderna, 1956; and Francisco Porrúa Pérez, *Teoría del estado,* Mexico: Editorial Porrúa, S.A., 1954, pp. 38, 145—152, 165—173, 187—188, 229—242, 370—376.

21. John H. Parry, *The Spanish Theory of Empire in the Sixteenth Century,* Cambridge: The University Press, 1940.

22. Reflecting the centralistic rather than the feudal legacy of Spain, the bulk of the laws of the New World was administrative law emanating from the decrees of the crown, the Council of the Indies, the viceroys, the *audiencias,* and lower-level agencies of government. From this experience came the strong Latin American tradition of administrative law and interventionism.

23. Foreigners could occasionally, with the express consent of the crown, receive licenses to trade and reside in the New World, while foreign skilled artisans and clerics could emigrate relatively freely—as could those foreigners with Spanish wives who had resided in Spain for at least a decade. See, for example, the legislation on this matter noted in Luis Rubio y Moreno, *Inventario general de registros cedularios del Archivo General de Indias de Sevilla,* vol. V of the series *Colección de documentos inéditos para la historia de Hispano-America,* Madrid: Compañía Ibero-Americana de Publicaciones, S.A., 1928, pp. 154—156. During eighteenth-century Bourbon rule, the restrictions on French travel and settlement in the empire were particularly relaxed, while the licensing of other foreigners seems also to have been administered with more leniency.

24. Octavio Paz, *El laberinto de la soledad,* Mexico: Fondo de Cultura Económica, 1959, p. 91. "Colonial society is an order made to last, . . . a society ruled according to principles of law, economics, and religion which are fully consistent with each other and which established a vital and harmonious relation between the parts and the whole."

25. Denis W. Brogan, *The American Character,* New York: Time, Inc. Book Division, 1962, pp. 4—6, 33—34, 82—83. In this, of course, Brogan has simply reaf-

firmed that which earlier had been observed by Crèvecoeur and de Toqueville.

26. Note, for example, the system described in E.B. Greene, *The Provincial Governor in the English Colonies of North America,* New York: Longmans, Greèn and Co., 1898, for its contrasts with the complexity of the Spanish overseas administrative structure.

27. For a good description of this process in the frontier region of Chile, see H. Douglas-Irvine, "The Landholding System of Colonial Chile," *Hispanic American Historical Review,* Vol. 8, No. 4 (November 1928), pp. 449–495. The article is particularly revealing of the web of regulations which governed economic life and relationships on the frontier, even to the extent that the government restricted the mobility of the settlers by forbidding them to leave the area of their settlement except for short periods. Also especially relevant are E. Arcila Farías, *op. cit.,* pp. 30–32, which deals with the Venezuelan case, and Oscar E. Reyes, *op. cit.,* Vol. I, pp. 177 ff., for Ecuador.

28. Especially instructive is the manual on Spanish law prepared by a royal official for the use of governors, *corregidores,* judges, and other colonial administrators: Alonso de Villadiego Vascuñana y Montoya, *Instrucción política, y práctica judicial conforme al estilo de los consejos, audiencias y tribunales de corte, y ortos ordinarios del reyno* . . . , Madrid: Con privilegio, por Juan de la Cuesta, 1617. Containing models of various legal documents and instructions on procedural law (as well as a concise exposition of relevant Spanish legal sources), the manual provides a useful discussion of the economic functions of the *corregidor* and other offices (folios 79–161): e.g., the authorization for royal officials to buy and sell on crown account, their broad regulatory powers over private commercial transactions, their authority to exact compulsory interest-free loans from the wealthy for financing public works, etc. Pedro de Valdivia, "Cartas de Don Pedro de Valdivia al Emperador Carlos V," *Colección de historiadores de Chile y documentos relativos a la historia nacional,* Santiago: Imprenta del Ferrocarril, 1861, Vol. I, pp. 24, 41, 53, sheds considerable light on royal ordinances and initiative in the settlement process.

29. The *municipios* were a rough equivalent of a combined town-country government as they exercised jurisdiction over the territory surrounding the towns. Relevant legal and administrative aspects of the state-directed, urban-based colonization pattern are found in Vol. 21, pp. 10–35, 61–89 of Don Angel de Atolaquirre y Duvale, *Gobernación espiritual y temporal de las Indias,* vols. 20–25 of *Colección de documentos inéditos relativos al descubrimiento, conquista, y organización de las antiguas posesiones españolas de ultramar.* Segunda serie, Madrid: Tipografía de Archivos, 1927–1932. Atolaquirre's work, published first around 1600, indicates, as does Paul Horgan in his *The Centuries of Santa Fé,* that the government could order people to go to new settlements, prohibit them from leaving, subsidize the establishment and subsequent maintenance of settlements, etc. See also José M. Ots Capdequí, *Estudios del derecho español en las Indias,* Bogotá: Editorial Minerva, S.A., 1940, pp. 8–16, 37, 86–94, 150–164, 406 ff., for the role of the state in colonization.

30. Interestingly, the urban planning decrees of the Spanish borrowed heavily from the Roman architect Vitruvius, whose work was used as a guide. D. Stanislawski, "Early Spanish Town Planning in the New World," *Geographical Review,* Vol. 37, No. 1 (January 1947), pp. 94–105.

31. This is also the contention of Julio Alemparte Robles, whose excellent and comprehensive study of the *cabildo* in Chile affords a vast amount of insight into the regulatory activity of municipal governments. Following the interpretation of the Spanish historian, Eduardo de Hinojosa (*Estudios sobre la historia del derecho español,* Madrid: Imprenta del Asilo de Huérfanos del Sagrado Corazón de Jesús, 1903, Chap. I), Alemparte traces the origins of the *cabildo's* municipal democracy to Germanic rather than Roman traditions in Hispanic culture, although other investigators of the subject have disputed this claim.

32. Oscar E. Reyes, *op. cit.,* Vol. I, pp. 105–197.

33. Given the prevailing transport costs, this alienation of the more favorably

situated lands was undoubtedly an important early factor in generating, through the process of economic rent, the sharp income differentials which have typified Latin American life ever since.

34. For an insight into the abuses and intragovernmental conflicts which arose in connection with this land distribution function, see Vol. IV, pp. 122, 324 of the collection *Gobernantes del Perú, Cartas y Papeles* ("Carta del Virrey Don Francisco de Toledo a Su Majestad," 1572, and *Ibid.*, 1574), Madrid: Colección de Publicaciones Históricas de la Biblioteca del Congreso Argentina 1921–1926; Fernando Montesinos, *Anales del Perú*, Madrid: Imprenta de Gabriel L. y del Horno, 1906, Vol. I, p. 119; and Emilio Romero, *Historia económica y financiera del Perú, antiguo Perú y vireinato*, Lima: 1937, p. 97.

35. Frederick Pike, "Aspects of Cabildo Economic Regulations in Spanish America under the Hapsburgs," *Inter-American Economic Affairs*, Vol. 13, No. 4 (Spring 1960), pp. 67–86. Pike's article, while mainly devoted to examining the way in which municipal government was used to consolidate the interests of the landed oligarchy vis à vis townsmen or burgher interests, is also useful for illustrating the range of regulatory activity carried on by the municipal councils. See also Julio Alemparte Robles, *op. cit.*, pp. 62–68, 93–104.

36. Frederick Pike, "The Cabildo and Colonial Loyalty to Hapsburg Rulers," *Journal of Inter-American Studies*, Vol. 2, No. 4 (October 1960), pp. 405–420.

37. Wilhelm Roscher, *The Spanish Colonial System*, New York: Henry Holt and Co., 1904

38. For an account of the inflation, see Earl J. Hamilton, *American Treasure and the Price Revolution in Spain, 1501–1650*, Cambridge: Harvard University Press, 1934, in which Hamilton depicts the clash between the expanding money supply and the rigidity of the surviving medieval trade organization, with its opportunities for monopoly power. In "The Decline of Spain," *The Economic History Review*, Vol. 8, No. 2 (May 1938), pp. 168–179, Hamilton attributes the decline also to the latifundian system of Spanish agriculture, the effects of the Mesta, the crushing burden of taxation, royal extravagance, costly wars, progressively inferior public administration, and the growth of the church. According to Hamilton, peninsular economic decline was mainly evident in the seventeenth century, in a process recounted at length in Pierre Chaunu, *Seville et l'Atlantique, 1504–1650*, Paris: A. Colin, 1955–1959, 8 vols. Other historians, however, have concluded that there was no significant agricultural and industrial progress in Spain even during the sixteenth century: e.g., Ramón Carande, *Carlos V y sus banqueros, la vida económica de España en una fase de su hegemonía, 1516–1556*, Madrid: Revista de Occidente, 1943.

39. According to Earl J. Hamilton, "American Treasure and Andalusian Prices," *Journal of Economic and Business History*, Vol. I, No. 1 (November 1928), pp. 1–35, the share of public bullion in total bullion imports was nearly 100 per cent up to 1536 and generally 20 to 30 per cent thereafter. But given the high taxation levels then prevailing in Spain, much of the balance was probably subsequently recovered for the treasury. According to Pierre Chaunu, the cumbersome political organization of the crown absorbed 50 per cent of the revenues from the Indies in the sixteenth century and 80 per cent in the eighteenth century. Pierre Chaunu, *Histoire de l'Amérique Latine*, Paris: Presses Universitaires de France, 1949.

40. On the costliness of the bureaucracy, see the report: *Memorial Los del Consejo Real de las Indias, por si, y por los Ministros inferiores que sirven en el dizen: Que a su instancia Su Majestad ha sido servida de nombrar una Junta, que determine en Justicia la pretension que tienen, que las Arcas Reales de aquellos Reynos . . . se les deve pagar enteramente todo lo que por razon de su Plaça y Oficios les pertenece . . .* Madrid: 1668.

41. According to Allan Christelow, "Great Britain and the Trades from Cadiz and Lisbon to Spanish America and Brazil, 1759–1783," *Hispanic American Historical Review*, Vol. XXVII, No. 1 (February 1947), pp. 2–29, French goods were dominant in

the fleets which sailed to Latin America until the eighteenth century, whereupon British goods gained the lead. C.H. Haring, in *Trade and Navigation Between Spain and the Indies in the Times of the Hapsburgs,* Cambridge: Harvard University Press, 1918, pp. 113, 122, 213–215, estimates that by the end of the seventeenth century 5/6 of the cargoes sent to the Americas were of non-Spanish origin. In the eighteenth century, perhaps as little as 1/20 of Spanish American imports were of Spanish origin, while Spanish shipping constituted only a little more than 1/10 of the vessels engaged in the American trade: M. Colmeiro, *Historia de la economía política en España,* Madrid: Librería de D. Angel Calleja, 1863, Vol. II, p. 418.

42. Earl J. Hamilton, "Spanish Mercantilism Before 1700," in *Facts and Factors in Economic History,* Cambridge: Harvard University Press, 1932, pp. 214–239. Though Spain encouraged American production of a variety of raw materials, it did not act decisively to preserve the home market for its colonial products, nor did it preserve the colonial markets for Spanish manufactures. Tariffs were mainly for revenue rather than protection, colonial shipbuilding was encouraged, and there were comparatively few restrictions on intercolonial trade except where injurious to Castilian or other interests or where conducive to smuggling. Spain also took a liberal policy towards colonial manufactures so long as these were mainly for local consumption and did not compete with Castilian manufacturers in an external market.

43. J.W. Horrocks, *A Short History of Mercantilism,* London: Methuen and Company, Ltd., 1924, p. 101.

44. There were substantial differences between Spanish mercantilist precepts and French and British norms, especially in respect of colonial industries. Bernardo Ward, for example, observed that while colonial agriculture and commerce had not met mercantilist standards of performance, colonial manufactures, which strict mercantilism would proscribe, were to be found all over. As Ward perceived, duties and restrictions on transoceanic trade had favored both illicit commerce and the growth of colonial industries. Bernardo Ward, *Proyecto económico, en que se proponen varias providencias dirigidas a promover los intereses de España, con los medios y fondos necessarios para su plantificación,* Madrid: Por la Viuda de Ibarra, Hijos, y Compañía, 1787 (Fourth Printing, written originally in 1762), pp. 229–234. Another mercantilist, Campillo, while acknowledging the presumed merits of French and British policies towards colonial industries, argued that Spain should encourage most colonial manufactures as a means of employing the Indians and incorporating them more effectively into the labor force. Most of the increased output would, he contended, be absorbed by the Indians' rising level of expenditures, for, using a rather modern notion of labor commitment, he felt that stimulating native demand for Spanish-type goods would enhance their willingness to work for wages. As Spain was lacking in industries, Campillo felt that rising colonial incomes would, if colonial industries were not fostered, only lead to heavier imports from other European powers—a line of reasoning which in some ways foreshadowed modern import-substitution industrialization arguments. Joseph del Campillo y Cosío, *Nuevo sistema de gobierno económico para la América,* Madrid: Imprenta de Benito Cano, 1789, pp. 112 ff.

45. Of special interest, since it anticipated an important modern policy problem, was the mercantilist view of the Indian problem. Both Campillo and Ward (e.g., Ward *op. cit.,* pp. 266–284) contended that a major objective of royal policy should be the integration of the indigenous population into the colonial economy, to which end both urged that the Indians be encouraged to adopt non-Indian consumption patterns. Both also felt that the existing tax level was contraproductive and that a lower rate of taxation would so stimulate the colonial economy as to provide greater revenues in the long run.

46. Eli F. Heckscher, *Mercantilism,* New York: The Macmillan Company, 1955, Vol. I, p. 344.

47. The Mexican treasury, for example, had to subsidize the settlements of the northern frontier as well as the governments of Cuba, the Philippines, Florida and Louisiana, and Venezuela. Chile was subsidized from Peru, while Cartagena received

fiscal support from the treasury at Quito.

48. Conde de Revilla Gigedo, *Instrucción reservada . . . a su sucesor en el mando . . . sobre el gobierno de este continente,* Mexico: Imprenta de la calle de las Escalerillas, a Cargo del C. Agustín Guiol., 1831 (written in 1794), p. 32.

49. In some areas, notably along the west coast, even ocean transport was, owing to the adverse sailing conditions created by prevailing winds and currents, quite difficult. *Ibid.,* p. 112; Alexander von Humboldt, *Political Essay on the Kingdom of New Spain,* London: Longman, Hurst, Rees, Orme, and Brown, 1811, Vol. IV, pp. 66 ff. Illustrative of the problems involved was a voyage made in 1698 between Panama and Acapulco. The voyage itself took 48 days and cost the lives of 21 of the crew; still other crew members were striken fatally with disease while ashore in the Mexican port. The subsequent overland trip from Acapulco to Mexico City required just under two weeks. G.F. Gemelli Careri, *A Voyage Round the World,* London: 1704.

50. A realistic contemporary awareness of transport obstacles to development is contained in the official report of Antonio de Ulloa and Jorge Juan y Santacilia, *Relación histórica del viage a la América meridional,* Madrid: Impressa de Orden del Rey Nuestro Señor por Antonio Marín, 1748, Vol. I, pp. 402–404.

51. A contemporary observation on the barriers to trade created by the tax system is found in Conde de Revilla Gigedo, *op. cit.,* pp. 106–107, but, as the viceroy further recognized (*ibid.,* p. 110), the trade taxes also created a shelter for the development of local manufacturing enterprises in the colonies.

52. For what is probably the most informative single study of the diversity of colonial manufactures, see Ricardo Cappa, *op. cit.,* Vol. VIII, "Industrias Mecánicas" (published 1892). Among the colonial manufactures were textiles (felts, cottons, velvets, woollens); shiprigging and ships; soap; furniture; glassware; shoes; wines (esp. in Peru, Chile, and Tucumán); carts, wagons, and saddles; leather chests; candles, lampwicks, and lamps; pottery; hats; basketry; foundries for bronze, copper, and iron products; bricks and tiles; tinsmiths, silversmiths, and goldsmiths; a variety of food products; and even shops for fabricating nails and sundry tools and implements. Puebla and Quito were especially important as manufacturing centers, but only Panama was practically without a complement of such activities. For a survey of the Ecuadorian industries, see Oscar E. Reyes, *op. cit.,* Vol. I, pp. 209–215, 246–247.

53. The stimulating effect of mining on agricultural development is noted in Alexander von Humboldt, *op. cit.,* Vol. II, pp. 283 ff.

54. Thomas Gage, a double religious renegade of English nationality who traveled extensively in Mexico and Guatemala between 1625 and 1637, was impressed, even at that early period, with the amenities of life available in the capital of New Spain. Thomas Gage, *The English-American, A New Survey of the West Indies, 1648,* London: George Routledge and Sons, Ltd., 1928, pp. 59–109. An almost contemporary French observer, S. de Champlain, was equally impressed with had been built in Mexico City. S. de Champlain, *Narrative of a Voyage to the West Indies and Mexico in the Years 1599–1602,* London: The Hakluyt Society, 1859, p. 24. For an eighteenth-century account of Lima, see Antonio de Ulloa and Jorge Juan y Santacilia, *op. cit.,* Vol. II, pp. 40–71, 139. Both Gage's book and the report of Ulloa and Juan contain a great deal of useful information on the production and trade patterns of the colonial economy—the latter as a report to the Spanish crown, the former to whet the English appetite for penetration of the Spanish possessions.

55. For these and other interesting observations, see Francisco de Miranda, *Diary, 1783–1784,* New York: The Hispanic Society of America, 1928.

56. The *consulados* were officially sanctioned merchant guilds, the chief ones in importance being the two at Mexico City and Lima. Others of somewhat lesser influence were established later in the colonial era in such places as Veracruz and Guadalajara in Mexico, Cartagena and Bogotá in Colombia, and Buenos Aires. Operating on the basis of privileged grants made in Madrid, the *consulados* were controlling factors in wholesale distribution but also were delegated public functions such as collection of sales taxes and the financing of public works. With establishment of the inten-

dant system in the late 1700's, however, a number of their public functions were rescind-
ed. For a comprehensive view of the functioning of the important *consulado* of Mexico
City, see R.S. Smith, "The Institution of the Consulado in New Spain," *Hispanic
American Historical Review,* Vol. 24, No. 1 (February 1944), pp. 61–83.

57. José M. Ots Capdequí, *Instituciones sociales de la América Española en el
período colonial,* La Plata, Argentina: Universidad de La Plata, 1934, pp. 62–69.

58. For one of the most comprehensive studies of the colonial administrative
apparatus, as it developed up to around 1700, see Ernst Schäfer, *El Consejo Real y
Supremo de las Indias,* Sevilla: Vol. I, 1935; Vol. II, 1947. The first volume deals
mainly with the Casa de Contratación and the Council of the Indies, while volume II
examines the overseas administrative organs. Also useful for its codification of the
legislation which defined the functions and powers of various parts of the administrative structure is the *Recopilación de leyes de los reynos de las Indias,* Madrid: Impre-
sora del Real y Supremo Consejo de las Indias, 1791, 3 vols.

59. Helpful to an understanding of the transoceanic trade system is the seventeenth-century work by José de Veitia Linaje, *Norte de la contratación de las Indias
occidentales,* Buenos Aires: Comisión Argentina de Fomento Interamericano, 1945
(published first in 1672).

60. Among the changes of this period were the creation of two additional viceroyalties (at Bogotá and Buenos Aires), an expansion of the number of sailings of registered ships and abolition of the fleet system, the relaxation of restrictions on immigration, the reduction of duties on colonial imports, and the abolition of duties on colonial
exports to Spain. In addition, more ports in Spain and the Americas were opened to trade,
the tax system was drastically simplified, private trading or chartered companies were
introduced, additional consulados were established, and the Casa de Contratación was
abolished (1790). Meanwhile, French ships had begun to trade with the colonies after 1701,
while in the Treaty of Utrecht of 1713 the British had gained the right to sell slaves to
the Americas (the slave *asiento* or concession) and to sell a limited volume of goods from
the slaving ships. The slave *asiento* carried with it the privilege of transacting the slave
business at any Atlantic port where there was a royal official available to certify the
number of slaves imported.

61. As a modern Spanish scholar has observed, the lack of a capitalistic tradition in the empire meant that practically all the initiative for economic reorganization
and rehabilitation had to come from the state and be sustained by government action
and investment. In the Bourbon reforms, aimed ultimately at improving the condition
of the treasury, the strategic importance of the fiscal system as an instrumentality of
economic growth was recognized. Guillermo Céspedes del Castillo, "Reorganización
de la Hacienda Virrenal Peruana en el Siglo XVIII," *Anuario de historia del derecho
español,* Madrid: Instituto Nacional de Estudios Jurídicos, Vol. 23, 1953, pp. 329–369.

62. As John Parry has put it (*op. cit.,* p. 72), "the important institutions there
[in the Indies], juridical, ecclesiastical, economic, and local, became converted into
one vast centralized civil service designed to enforce arbitrary legislation."

63. For an excellent study of viceregal powers, see Donald E. Smith, *The
Viceroy of New Spain,* Berkeley: University of California Press, 1913, esp. pp. 102–107,
127–128. As Smith noted (pp. 147 ff.), the viceroy was charged with considerable responsibility in a wide variety of economic development fields, though he exercised
this initiative within the context of a mass of minutely detailed decrees sent from Spain.
A good example of the various economic activities carried out by a progressive viceroy of
Mexico is found in Conde de Revilla Gigedo, *op. cit.,* pp. 32–47, 65–66, 73–83, 98–99,
and 172–174. The many economic functions of the viceregal office are also detailed in
Lillian E. Fisher, *Viceregal Administration in the Spanish American Colonies,* Berkeley:
University of California Press, 1926.

64. The economic functions of the *corregidor* are recounted in both Alonso de
Villadiego, *op. cit.,* and C.E. Castañeda, "The Corregidor in Spanish Colonial Administration," *Hispanic American Historical Review,* Vol. 9, No. 4 (November 1929),
pp. 446–470. Castañeda also gives useful insight into the abuse of official privileges

for personal gain. See also on this point: Juan de Aponte Figueroa, "Memorial que trata de la Reformación del Reino del Pirú," in *Colección de documentos inéditos para la historia de España,* Madrid: Imprenta de la Viuda de Calero, 1867, Vol. LI, pp. 524–526, and Antonio de Ulloa and Jorge Juan y Santacilia, *Noticias secretas de América,* London: R. Taylor, 1826, pp. 229–244.

65. Called by Schäfer the backbone of Spanish administration, the *audiencias* were important regulatory bodies. For details on the extent of their intervention in the economy, see Vol. I of Eusebio Beleña, compiler, *Recopilación sumaria de todos los autos acordados de la real audiencia y sala de crimen de esta Nueva España, y providencias de su superior gobierno,* Mexico: Con licencia por D. Felipe de Zúñiga, 1787, 2 vols.

66. Joaquín Maniau, *Compendio de la historia de la real hacienda de Nueva España,* Mexico: Secretaría de Industria y Comercio, 1914 (written in 1794); Fabian de Fonseca and Carlos de Urrutia, *Historia general de real hacienda,* Mexico: Vicente G. Torres, 1845–1853, 6 vols. See also Chap. 10 of H.I. Priestly, *José de Gálvez, Visitor-General of New Spain,* Berkeley: University of California Press, 1916, and J. Canga Arguelles, *Diccionario de hacienda para el uso de los encargados de la suprema dirección de ella,* London: Imprenta Española de M. Calero, 1826, 5 vols.

67. Julio Alemparte, *op. cit.,* p. 120.

68. It is interesting to note that the same considerations were manifested in the ecclesiastical arm of government in which most of the bishops were also *peninsulares.* The system, however, was made more comprehensive than the episcopate. By 1593, for example, the majority of friars in all orders in Peru were criollos, but over their opposition a device known as the *alternativa* was imposed in 1686. Under this arrangement, there was instituted a forced alternating election of *peninsulares* and criollos "to the main offices in the provinces irrespective of superior qualifications or superior numbers. The reason for selection, therefore, was primarily the place of birth." See Antonine Tibesar, O.F.M., "The Alternative: A Study in Spanish-Creole Relations in the Seventeenth Century," *The Americas,* Washington, D.C.: Vol. 11, No. 3 (January 1955), pp. 229–283. The quotation is from page 234. Fr. Tibesar believes that the *alternativa* may have contributed importantly to the growth of a Peruvian national consciousness and to the criollo desire for independence. Virtually all authorities are in agreement that this was the case regarding the privileged appointment of *peninsulares* to the top civil service offices.

69. H.I. Priestly, *op. cit.,* provides a great deal of information on the role of this office in colonial administration.

70. Frederick B. Pike, "The Municipality and the System of Checks and Balances in Spanish Colonial Administration," *The Americas,* Washington, D.C., Vol. 15, No. 2 (October 1958), pp. 139–158. This article also describes the degree to which the authority of local governments was overshadowed by the powers of the viceroys, the *audiencias,* and the governors and *corregidores.*

71. The previously cited reports by Antonio de Ulloa and Jorge Juan constitute examples of these, as does the previously cited work by von Humboldt. The *Noticias secretas* report of Ulloa and Juan was considered so revealing and damaging that it was not published by the Spanish government, although a copy was later smuggled out of the country and published in England. For a critical appraisal of its validity on some points, see Luis Merino, "The Relation Between the *Noticias Secretas* and the *Viaje a la América Meridional,*" *The Americas,* Washington, D.C.: Vol. 13, No. 2 (October 1956), pp. 111–125.

72. Note, for example, in Luis Rubio y Moreno, *op. cit.,* pp. 101–102, the *cédulas* on illicit trade and on pp. 235–236 the *cédulas* requiring the licensing of *obrajes* and *ingenios* (sugar mills). In the previously cited *Colección de documentos inéditos relativos al descubrimiento . . . ,* Vol. 21, pp. 130–348, and Vol. 22, pp. 7–84 are to be found numerous decrees regulating Indian affairs, while hundreds of regulations regarding economic life are to be found *ibid.,* Vol. 22, pp. 85–330, Vol. 24, pp. 6–315, and all of Vol. 25.

73. In addition to the previously cited *Recopilación* which was published in 1791, see M.J. de Ayala, *Notas a la recopilación de Indias,* Madrid: Ediciones Cultura Hispánica, 1945 (written in 1787), and V.M. Maurtua, *Antecedentes de la recopilación de Yndias,* Madrid: Imprenta de Bernardo Rodríguez, 1906.

74. Aside from the other sources cited in the text, this section draws heavily upon the evidence presented in: the *Recopilaciones;* Solórzano's *Política indiana;* M.A. Fuentes, editor, *Memorias de los vireyes que han gobernado el Perú,* Lima: Librería Central de Felipe Bailly, 1859, 6 vols.; *Instrucciones que los vireyes de Nueva España dejaron a sus sucesores,* Mexico: Imprenta de Ignacio Escalante, 1873, 2 vols.; Carlos Alberto Romero, ed., *Memoria del virrey del Perú, Marqués de Avilés,* Lima: Imprenta del Estado, 1901; Sebastián Lorente, ed., *Relaciones de los vireyes y audiencias que han gobernado el Perú,* Lima: Imprenta del Estado, 1867, vol. I; José Toribio Polo, *Memorias de los virreyes del Perú, Marqués de Mancera y Conde de Salvatierra,* Lima: Imprenta del Estado, 1899; Gonzalo Fernández de Oviedo y Valdés, *Historia general y natural de las Indias,* Madrid: Imprenta de la Real Academia de la Historia, 1851; Ministerio de Fomento (Spain), *Relaciones geográficas de Indias, Perú,* Madrid: Tipografía de M.G. Hernández e Hijos, 1881–1897, 4 vols.; Germán Latorre, ed., *Relaciones geográficas de Indias: La Hispano-América del Siglo XVI: Virreinato de Nueva España,* Sevilla: El Centro Oficial de Estudios Americanistas de Sevilla, 1920; Reginaldo de Lizárraga, *Descripción y población de las Indias,* Lima: Imprenta Americana, 1908; Agustín Rivera, *Principios críticos sobre el vireinato de la Nueva España,* San Juan de los Lagos, Mexico: Tipografía de José Martín Hermosillo, 1884–1889, Vols. I and III; Joseph Antonio de Villaseñor y Sánchez, *Teatro Americano,* Mexico. Con licencia en la Imprenta de la Viuda de D. Joseph Bernardo de Hogal, 1746; Gonzalo Gómez de Cervantes, *La vida económica y social de Nueva España al finalizar el siglo XVI,* Mexico: José Porrúa e Hijos, 1944.

75. See, for example, E. Arcila Farías, *op. cit.,* pp. 299, 304, 323 ff. for promotional measures employed in the colonization of Venezuela, while in Pedro M. Oliveira, *La política económica de la metrópoli,* Lima: Imprenta la Industria, 1905, pp. 29–30, 40 ff., is an account of the extensive involvement of government in Peruvian agriculture.

76. F.W. Blackmar, *Spanish Institutions of the Southwest,* Baltimore: The Johns Hopkins Press, 1891, p. 164, relates, in an illustrative case, how the governor provided each settler of San Jose, California, with a sum of money and food for the initial two years, provisions alone for the following three years, and livestock and agricultural implements. Title to the land was granted after five years conditional upon the settlers' having met certain requirements.

77. For a thorough study of the vital role of governmental and ecclesiastical entrepreneurship in developing a colonial silk industry in Mexico, as well as for a picture of the extensive regulatory framework within which that industry was conducted, see Woodrow W. Borah, *Silk Raising in Colonial Mexico,* Berkeley: University of California Press, 1943. Similarly enlightening, with regard to the sugar industry, are Fernando Ortiz Fernández, *Los primeros técnicos azucareros de América,* Havana: Asociación de Técnicos Azucareros de Cuba, 1955, and, especially, Fernando B. Sandoval, *La industria del azúcar en Nueva España,* Mexico: Instituto de Historia, Universidad Nacional Autómona de México, 1951. Still another interesting example of bureaucratic developmental entrepreneurship was the series of experiments conducted by royal officials in Mexico during the late eighteenth century to develop new uses for rubber (e.g., shipping containers and rubberized cloth). On the basis of these, the viceroy began to plan for a systematic cultivation of rubber trees and the establishment of rubber-using industries. S.K. Lowe and Maurice Ries, *Experiments with Rubber in Mexico, 1785–1798,* New Orleans: Tulane University, Middle American Research Institute, Philological and Documentary Studies, Vol. I, No. 3 (1944), pp. 43–113.

78. Ricardo Cappa, *op. cit.,* Vol. VIII, pp. 19–30, 158 ff., 163–195; J. Canga Argülles, *op. cit.,* Vol. III, pp. 190, 298. In 1805, for example, the government established an iron works in Mexico to utilize local ores. The venture was destroyed

during the War for Independence; Modesto Bargallo, *La minería y la metalurgía en la américa española durante la época colonial,* Mexico: Fondo de Cultura Económica, 1955, p. 355.

79. Frederick B. Pike, "Public Work and Social Welfare in Colonial Spanish American Towns," *The Americas,* Washington, D.C.: Vol. 13, No. 4 (April 1957), pp. 361–375. Also relevant is J. Preston Moore, *The Cabildo in Peru Under the Hapsburgs,* Durham, N.C.: Duke University Press, 1954. According to Alonso de Villadiego Vascuñana y Montoya, *op. cit.,* folios 135–137, royal officials were empowered not only to levy taxes for the support of public undertakings but also could levy compulsory interest-free loans on the rich. It was not unusual that the *consulados,* which received financial support from sharing in the taxes on trade, were charged with initiating and financing public works, while in Guatemala the *consulado* was also supposed to foster agricultural improvement. See, e.g., R.S. Smith, "Origins of the Consulado of Guatemala," *Hispanic American Historical Review,* Vol. 26, No. 2 (May 1946), pp. 150–161, and R.S. Smith, "The Institution of the Consulado in New Spain," *Hispanic American Historical Review,* Vol. 24, No. 1 (February 1944), pp. 61–83.

80. José A. Saco, *Historia de la esclavitud de los indios en el nuevo mundo,* Havana: Cultural, S. A., 1932, 2 vols.; José A. Saco, *Historia de la esclavitud de la raza africana en el nuevo mundo,* Havana: Cultural, S. A., 1938, 2 vols.

81. Silvio A. Zavala, *New Viewpoints on the Spanish Colonization of America,* Philadelphia: University of Pennsylvania Press, 1943, pp. 69–79, 93 ff. ; L.B. Simpson, *The Encomienda in New Spain,* Berkeley: University of California Press, 1950, p. 10; L.B. Simpson, *The Repartimiento System of Native Labor in New Spain and Guatemala,* Part III of *Studies in the Administration of the Indians in New Spain,* Ibero-Americana Series No. 13, Berkeley: University of California Press, 1938; John H. Rowe, "The Incas Under Spanish Colonial Institutions," *Hispanic American Historical Review,* Vol. 37, No. 2 (May 1957), pp. 170–179. A good description of the *mita* in Ecuador is to be found in Aquiles R. Pérez Tamayo, *Las mitas en la real audiencia de Quito,* Quito: Imprenta del Ministerio del Tesoro, 1947; while the Peruvian version of the institution is discussed in Jorge Basadre, "El Régimen de la Mita," in José M. Valega, *El virreinato del Perú,* Lima: Editorial Cultura Ecléctica, 1939.

82. In the eighteenth century the native population was again on the increase. Since by that time the growth of the latifundia had given large landowners control over the major agricultural resources and the lands available to the Indians for self-employment were increasingly marginal, conscript labor was no longer so necessary as a means of providing cheap labor in agriculture.

83. For a survey of viceregal ordinances controlling the use of labor in various fields, see Silvio A. Zavala, editor, *Ordenanzas del trabajo, siglos XVI y XVII,* Mexico: Editorial "Elede," S. A., 1947, pp. 29–72 (for agriculture and ranching), 83–122 (for mining), and 139–213 (for *obrajes*). Also in the same work is considerable information on the regulation of Negro labor, transport work, artisan labor, and the like.

84. For information on local trade controls, the following references are especially useful: Chester L. Guthrie, "Colonial Economy: Trade, Industry, and Labor in Seventeenth Century Mexico City," *Revista de Historia de América,* Mexico: Instituto Panamericano de Geografía e Historia, No. 7 (December 1939), pp. 103–134; W.H. Dusenberry, "The Regulation of Meat Supply in 16th Century Mexico City," *Hispanic American Historical Review,* Vol. 28, No. 1 (February 1948), pp. 38–52; R.L. Lee, "Grain Legislation in Colonial Mexico, 1575–1585," *Hispanic American Historical Review,* Vol. 27, No. 4 (November 1947), pp. 647–660; Arthur S. Aiton, "Early American Price-Fixing Legislation," *Michigan Law Review,* Vol. 25, No. 1 (November 1926), pp. 15–23; E. Arcila Farías, *op. cit.,* pp. 71 ff.; Julio Alemparte Robles, *op. cit.,* pp. 137–196, 221–230; *Gobernantes del Perú, cartas y papeles,* Madrid: Colección de Publicaciones Históricas de la Biblioteca del Congreso Argentino, 14 vols. 1921–1926, Vol. VIII, "Ordenanzas del Cuzco," pp. 36–142.

85. The *Actas de cabildo de la ciudad de México,* Mexico: Ignacio Bejarano, 1889–1900, Vol. XII, p. 15, for example, contains a proscription of forestalling in a

regulation which prohibited city dwellers from going to the countryside to purchase goods. The intention was, of course, to concentrate all sales in the public market. Julio Alemparte R., *op. cit.*, pp. 137—230, describes at length the pervasive scope of the system of market regulation, but notes that the rules were not always adhered to scrupulously. J.M. Ots Capdequí, in his "El Régimen Municipal Hispanoamericano del Período Colonial," *Revista de la Sección Hispanoamericana del Centro de Estudios Históricos,* Madrid: Año II, Nos. 3—4 (1937), p. 361, observes that on more than one occasion municipal regulatory power over mercantile transactions conflicted with special privileges conferred by the monarch on influential trading houses of Seville.

86. Some of these sumptuary restrictions are noted in the previously cited work by Alemparte, while the efforts (ultimately unsuccessful) of the government to combat conspicuous consumption in Lima are reported in Pedro M. Oliveira, *op. cit.*, pp. 147—151.

87. The *corregidores,* who were official collectors of tribute or the capitation tax from the Indians, were given exclusive rights to trade with the Indians of their district. While the intent was to protect the Indians from exploitation by private merchants, there is some evidence that the more corrupt *corregidores* sold the goods at prices higher than those officially set and pocketed the difference. Such were the opportunities of the post, that people paid the crown well to obtain appointments as *corregidores.* These and other deliquencies are discussed in Jorge Juan and Antonio de Ulloa's *Noticias secretas,* pp. 232—254. See also Richard Hawkins, *Observations of Sir Richard Hawkins in His Voyage into the South Sea in the Year 1593,* London: The Hakluyt Society, 1847, pp. 318 ff.

88. In 1592, for example, the *cabildo* of Mexico City, recognizing the increased price of wine in the city, asked the viceroy to refrain from issuing licenses for the shipment of wine out of the capital. *Actas de cabildo de la ciudad de Mexico,* Vol. XI, p. 16.

89. Manuel Carrera Stampa, *Los gremios mexicanos. La organización gremial en Nueva España, 1521—1861,* Mexico: Edición y Distribución Ibero Americana de Publicaciones, S. A., 1954, pp. 265—266.

90. In vol. XIII, pp. 113 ff., of the previously cited collection, *Gobernantes del Perú,* viceregal regulatory intervention is illustrated by the ordinances and decrees issued by Francisco de Toledo in Peru regarding the use of water and labor, mining practices, and the like. For relevant statutes in the royal code, see Libro IV, particularly Títulos 9 and 10 of the 1774 *Recopilación.* Also relevant is Alonso de Villadiego Vascuñana y Montoya, *op. cit.,* folios 116—122.

91. Aside from the legislative sources already mentioned, the following are useful in providing insights into the *obraje* system which, for at least a century or so, was based upon forced labor assignments, penal labor, and slave labor: Sebastián Lorente, *Historia del Perú bajo la dinastía austriaca, 1589—1700,* Paris: Imprenta de A.-E. Rochette, 1870, pp. 167—171; Emilio Romero, *Historia económica y financiera del Perú: antiguo Perú y virreynato,* Lima: Imprenta Torres Aguirre, 1937, pp. 138—140, 146 ff.; *ibid.,* pp. 154 ff., deals with artisan guild production in Peru.

92. Artisan manufacturing, although a part of the private sector, was so closely regulated by the guild system that in some respects it was but an extension of the public sector. Minutely detailed regulations governed master-apprentice relationships, techniques of production, prices, product quality, scale of output, and entry into the guild system. While, up to a point, the guilds were privileged groups, they were not independent organizations enjoying the right to administer themselves. Instead, they functioned under the tutelage of municipal authority and, as time went on, under royal authority whose inspectors saw to the enforcement of the ordinances promulgated by the administrative bureaucracy. Originally the guilds attempted to bar the entry of Indians and mestizos, but such practices were viewed with disfavor by the crown, which, along with the church, helped to incorporate these groups into the artisan sector. Some of the Indians, moreover, were permitted to practice their trades outside the guild system. One of the best studies of the matter is Manuel Carrera Stampa, *op. cit.,* while

the elaborateness of the ordinances under which the system functioned is detailed in Juan Francisco del Barrio Lorenzot, *Ordenanzas de gremios de la Nueva España,* Mexico: Secretaría de Gobernación, 1920.

93. M. Carrera Stampa, *op. cit.,* pp. 168–177, 264.

94. So contraproductive was the guild system that the eighteenth-century reformers (e.g., Ward, Campomanes, Jovellanos) urged the outright abolition of guilds.

95. Henry Bruman, "The Culture History of Mexican Vanilla," *Hispanic American Historical Review,* Vol. 28, No. 3 (August 1948), pp. 360–376. The early nineteenth-century decline of this export business appears to have been partly attributable to the deterioration in the quality of the harvested beans when royal regulations were removed.

96. R.S. Smith, "Statutes of the Guatemalan Indigo Growers' Society," *Hispanic American Historical Review,* Vol. 30, No. 3 (August 1950), pp. 336–345.

97. For information on the *fomento* or development measures applied to the mining industry, see: Fabián de Fonseca and Carlos de Urrutia, *Historia general de la real hacienda,* Mexico: Vicente G. Torres, 1845, Vol. I, pp. 1–44; and various reports in the *Instrucciones que los vireyes de Nueva España dejaron a sus sucesores,* Mexico: Imprenta de Ignacio Escalante, 1873, 2 vols. The excellent and comprehensive study by Modesto Bargalló, *La minería y la metalurgía en la américa española durante la época colonial,* Mexico: Fondo de Cultura Económica, 1955, also contains an informative discussion of state promotional and regulatory policies for the industry (pp. 83–101, 233 ff.)

98. Modesto Bargalló, *op. cit.,* p. 236.

99. Pedro Fermín de Vargas, *Pensamientos políticos y memorias sobre la población del nuevo reino de Granada,* Bogotá: Publicaciones del Banco de la República, 1953, pp. 58–59.

100. Luis Peñaloza, *Bancos de rescate y fomento minero,* La Paz: Banco Minero de Bolivia, 1943, p. 3. Conde de Revilla Gigedo, *op. cit.,* pp. 118–128, 248, 249.

101. For about twenty years following discovery of the Potosí silver veins in 1545, the silver content of the ores was so high that only primitive smelting furnaces were needed to refine them. Once the highest quality ores were depleted, however, a continuation of the prosperity of the center depended upon the introduction of hydraulically operated ore-grinding mills, an innovation which was difficult owing to the scarcity of water during the largely rainless season that extended from April to December. To remedy the situation, the viceroy (Francisco de Toledo) together with Spanish hydraulic engineers initiated a plan for constructing a complicated system of reservoirs, canals, and aqueducts to store the January to March rainfall and bring it to the new mills, employing the *mita* levy to construct and maintain the system. So large was the project that it required a half-century (1573–1621) for completion. W.E. Rudolph, "The Lakes of Potosí," *Geographical Review,* Vol. 26, No. 4 (October 1936), pp. 529–554.

102. See, for example, Ley XXVI, Título I, Libro VI of the *Recopilación* for the legislation establishing the system of state commissaries wherein foodstuffs and some clothing were sold to the native mine workers at prices below those prevailing in the market.

103. In Mexico, the recovery of the Indian population from its initial decline antedated the similar development in Peru, and with latifundism having preempted so much of the land available for agriculture and with debt peonage spreading in the rural sector, rising numbers of the growing Indian work force had to seek employment outside of agriculture. Consequently the dearth of remunerative employment alternatives served to direct a sufficient number of workers to the mines and thereby rendered the forced labor regime superfluous.

104. Pedro de Cieza de Leon, *Crónica del Perú,* Enrique de Vedia, *Historiadores Primitivos de Indias,* Vol. XXVI of Biblioteca de Autores Españoles Series, Madrid: Imprenta de M. Rivadeneyra, 1853, pp. 448–449.

105. Antonio Vásquez de Espinosa, *Compendium and Description of the West Indies,* Washington, D.C.: The Smithsonian Institution, 1942, pp. 623–625; John H.

Rowe, *op. cit.*, p. 171, reports that the *mitayo* wage generally was between a half and a third of the free-labor wage rate.

106. Alexander von Humboldt, *Political Essay . . .* , Vol. I, p. 170, Vol. III, pp. 231–246, 324. Also instructive on these points are: Walter Howe, *The Mining Guild of New Spain and its Tribunal General, 1770–1821*, Cambridge: Harvard University Press, 1949, and A.P. Whitaker, *The Huancavelica Mercury Mine*, Cambridge: Harvard University Press, 1941. All three of these works are also valuable references for governmental efforts to reform the mining industry.

107. See, for example, the contemporary account of Bartolomé Martínez y Vela, in his *Anales de la villa imperial de Potosí*, La Paz: Publicaciones del Ministerio de Educación, Bellas Artes, y Asuntos Indígenas, 1939, pp. 158–178, 411–413, which records the high level of ostentation at Potosí during the heyday of that mining center. The heavy consumption of costly imported luxury goods from Europe, Asia, and the Middle East reduced considerably the capital accumulation generated from the booming prosperity of Potosí—even though, since the center also drew in goods from various parts of South America, the description of the trade fair held there provides an interesting source of information on trade patterns in the empire. A brief description of the fair is also to be found in Pedro de Cieza de Leon, *op. cit.*

108. *Instrucciones que los vireyes de Nueva España dejaron a sus sucesores*, Vol. I, p. 265; Pedro M. Oliveira, *op. cit.*, pp. 76 ff.; M.A. Fuentes, ed., *Memorias de los vireyes que han gobernado el Perú*, Vol. VI, pp. 154–157; Carlos A. Romero, ed., *Memoria del virrey del Perú, Marques de Avilés*, p. 73. The foregoing are useful for both their insights into the shortcomings of the industry and their reports of the government's rehabilitation efforts.

109. The government's Huancavelica mercury mine in Peru, for example, had been leased to the local miner's guild as an operating group, though the state provided most of the working capital and controlled the marketing of the output. When the mine's output dropped (largely because of slipshod mining practices and the enormous number of casualties among the Indian workers), the government endeavored to raise productivity by sending in a technical mission to introduce more advanced practices. Unfortunately, however, the recommended improvements were resisted and finally thwarted by both the miners and certain corrupt elements in the bureaucracy who were linked with the miners in graft and mismanagement. A.P. Whitaker, *op. cit.*

110. While under private control, the tribunal board had voted itself handsome salaries and dissipated much of its financial reserves through gifts, loans, and a variety of irregular disbursements. W. Howe, *op. cit.*, is the definitive account of this experiment.

111. Lucas Alamán, *Historia de México*, Mexico: Editorial Jus, 1942, Vol. I, p. 140. Luis Peñaloza, *op. cit.*, pp. 4–6, 89; La Sociedad Académica de Amantes de Lima, *Mercurio Peruano*, Vol. 7, No. 215 (24 January 1793); Vol. 8, No. 242 (2 May 1793), and Vol. 8, No. 243 (5 May 1793); Carlos Alberto Romero, ed., *op. cit.*, pp. 72–73; Pedro M. Oliveira, *op. cit.*, pp. 76–78; and M.A. Fuentes, ed., *op. cit.*, Vol. IV, pp. 177, 181–184.

112. For good descriptions of intracolonial trade flows see A. von Humboldt, *op. cit.*; A. von Humboldt, *Personal Narrative of Travels to the Equinoctial Regions of the New Continent, During the Years 1799–1804*, London: Longman, Rees, Orme, Brown, and Green, 1829, 9 vols.; Antonio de Ulloa and Jorge Juan y Santacilia, *Relación Historica . . .* ; Woodrow W. Borah, *Early Colonial Trade and Navigation Between Mexico and Peru*, Berkeley: University of California Press, 1954; E. Arcila Farías, *Comercio entre México y Venezuela en los siglos XVI y XVII*, Mexico: Fondo de Cultura Económica, 1950.

113. E. Arcila Farías, *Comercio entre México y Venezuela . . .* , pp. 13–34, captures the essence of the system in a particularly lucid way.

114. Eventually, however, the American industry, which was principally in Mexico, lost out to the competition from Asian silks which were imported through the Philippines.

115. Fernando B. Sandoval, *op. cit.*, pp. 55 and 75.

116. The Venezuelan cacao industry had its inception largely in the growing demand of the Mexican market for the product. Tax concessions, along with other promotional measures, were employed to stimulate cultivation, and from 1620 on there was an active trade between the two countries in the product. During the seventeenth century, Spanish merchants and shippers vied with Venezuelan merchants for control of the trade, but a royal decree in 1784 settled the issue by reserving the traffic exclusively for the Venezuelans. A decade later, however, cacao prices in the Mexican market were depressed, owing to the clandestine introduction of large quantities of Ecuadoran cacao into Mexico via the Peruvian-Guatemalan wine trade which had been legalized in the 1680's. There then insued a struggle before the Council of the Indies, in which the powerful *consulado* of Lima argued for lifting the ban on Mexican imports of Ecuadoran cacao, while the merchants of Caracas argued for more stringent enforcement of the ban. The latter won, and the Council instructed the viceroys of Mexico and Peru to stop the Ecuadoran-Mexican trade. When, after several repetitions of the interdiction, the trade nevertheless continued, Venezuelan exporters had to settle for a favorable share in an import quota system. E. Arcila Farías, *Comercio entre México y Venezuela* . . . , pp. 92−95.

117. The Venezuelan group also won out in a contest with the Mexican consumer interest, for when, in the 1670's, the price of Venezuelan cacao rose in Mexico (the circumstance which had encouraged the imports from Ecuador), the viceroy of Mexico set a price ceiling on the imports. This the Venezuelan *cabildo* successfully contested before the crown, obtaining a ruling which directed all government functionaries in Mexico to refrain from setting a ceiling price on Venezuelan cacao.

118. When a natural catastrophe caused great damage to the Peruvian wheat industry, which had previously been producing an exportable surplus for shipment to Guayaquil and Panama, Chilean wheat began to enter South American markets in growing volume. During the eighteenth century, in an effort to revive Peruvian wheat production, colonial authorities intervened on both the supply and demand sides of the market by (a) requiring haciendas to devote a certain percentage of their acreage to wheat, (b) reducing mortgage interest payments on the haciendas cultivating wheat, and (c) setting up mixing quotas which obliged local grain merchants to sell Peruvian and Chilean wheat in a 50-50 proportion. Later the last mentioned of these regulations was revised to require that the merchants sell all the available Peruvian production before selling any of the grain imported from Chile. M.A. Fuentes, ed., *op. cit.*, Vol. IV, pp. 126−129. However, according to Pedro M. Oliveira, *op. cit.*, p. 55, neither the grain merchants nor the local growers complied strictly with these requirements.

119. John A. Rockwell, *A Compilation of Spanish and Mexican Law, in Relation to Mines, and Titles to Real Estate,* New York: John S. Voorhies, 1851, pp. 25−111, contains an English translation of the "Royal Ordinances for Direction, Regulation and Government of the Miners of New Spain, and of its Royal Tribunal General" which indicates the scope of central government intervention in the industry. It is of some amusement to note that the crown, aware of the unbusinesslike behavior of the miners, instructed judges to expostulate with the miners on the dangers of their profligate habits of consumption and gambling, and authorized the tribunal to appoint trustees to manage the affairs of incorrigible spendthrifts.

120. See, in addition to Rockwell, Modesto Bargalló, *op. cit.*, and Fabián de Fonseca and Carlos de Urrutia, *op. cit.*, Vol. I, pp. 52−108.

121. A. Whitaker, *op. cit.*, p. 6, notes that the tax on silver production was computed on the basis of mercury purchases rather than on reported output.

122. The features of this regulatory structure are described in Francisco Xavier de Gamboa, *Commentaries on the Mining Ordinances of Spain,* London: Longman, Rees, Orme, Brown, and Green, 1830, 2 vols.

123. A basic source of information concerning changes in the regulation of transatlantic trade, written by an official of the system, is Rafael Antúñez y Acevedo,

Memorias históricas sobre la legislación, y gobierno del comercio de los españoles con sus colonias en las Indias occidentales, Madrid: Imprenta de Sancha, 1797. The appendices of this work contain a number of the relevant decrees, as well as information on the size and frequency of the trade fleets.

124. W.L. Schurz, *The Manila Galleon,* New York: E.P. Dutton and Company, Inc., 1939.

125. V.L. Brown, "Contraband Trade: A Factor in the Decline of Spain's Empire in America," *Hispanic American Historical Review,* Vol. VIII, No. 2 (May 1928), pp. 178–189, gives a good picture of the link between the legal slave traffic and the accompanying large volume of smuggling. See also V.L. Brown, "The South Sea Company and Contraband Trade," *The American Historical Review,* Vol. 31, No. 4 (July 1926), pp. 662–678; and C.H. Haring, *Trade and Navigation Between Spain and the Indies,* Cambridge: Harvard University Press, 1918, pp. 111–122.

126. For descriptions of the Porto Bello fair, see Antonio de Ulloa y Jorge Juan y Santacilia, *Relación histórica . . . ,* pp. 109, 139–143; M. Colmeiro, *Historia de la economía política en España,* Madrid: Librería de D. Angel Calleja, 1863, Vol. II, p. 404; Thomas Gage, *op. cit.,* p. 446; and William Dampier, *A New Voyage Round the World, Describing particularly the Isthmus of America,* London: 1699, vol. I, pp. 184–185. See also the various títulos and leyes in Libro X of the *Recopilación.*

127. The *Recopilación* of 1756, Libro IV, tít. XVIII, ley 6 contains a *cédula* to this effect which was first promulgated in 1538 and reiterated in 1633. For descriptions of the goods sold at the fairs, see Rafael Antúñez y Acevedo, *op. cit.,* appendix XIV, pp. LVII–LXIII; Girolamo Benzoni, *History of the New World, 1572,* London: The Hakluyt Society, 1857, p. 116; and Joseph García de Prado, *Compendio general de las contribuciones, y gustos que ocasionan todos los efectos, frutos, caudales, y demás, que se trafican entre los reynos de Castilla, y América,* Cadiz: La Real de Marina y Real Audiencia de Contratación, 1762, pp. 44–67, 108–129.

128. During part of the early period, the depressed condition of the colonial economy may have accounted for the "insufficiency" of import demand, but later on, other circumstances undermined the fairs: the growth of "import substituting" colonial industries, the increased sailings of registered ships, and the growth of contraband trade.

129. W.L. Schurz, *op. cit.,* pp. 366–371. Schurz reports that nevertheless Chinese goods continued to be sold openly in Peru, while C.H. Haring, *Trade and Navigation . . . ,* p. 149, notes that a certain amount of illegal trade continued between Peru and Acapulco.

130. See J.P. Harrison, "The Evolution of the Colombian Tobacco Trade to 1875," *Hispanic American Historical Review,* Vol. 32, No. 2 (May 1952), pp. 163–174, for details on the way in which the state organized a successful tobacco industry in Colombia.

131. Pedro M. Oliveira, *op. cit.,* pp. 90–99.

132. Lucas Alamán, *op. cit.,* pp. 105–106, notes the cultivation of these crops in several parts of Mexico, while the Lima suburb of San Isidro contains a large olive grove which dates back to colonial days. Another example of this apparently contradictory treatment of the wine industry may be cited from Peruvian records. In 1601, the crown prohibited the use of Indian *repartimientos* for labor in the vineyards, ostensibly to inhibit the growth of an industry competitive with Spanish wine exports. The decree was repeated several times thereafter, suggesting that the prohibition had not been effective from the first. Pedro M. Oliveira, *op. cit.,* p. 36. Yet, later on the owners of vineyards were deemed eligible for participation in the land distribution process known as the *composición.* Sebastián Lorente, ed., *Relaciones de los vireyes . . . ,* Vol. II.

133. Pedro M. Oliveira, *op. cit.,* p. 92. The instructions received from Spain by Viceroy Toledo in Peru appeared to prohibit a textile industry, but in 1577 the same viceroy promulgated a set of ordinances conducive to the growth of this industry and explicitly stated the desirability of fostering its expansion. He even provided for the

assignment of Indians to the textile workshops.

134. One of the viceroys of Mexico, for example, even reported with evident pride, the varied assortment of manufacturing industries his jurisdiction contained. Conde de Revilla Gigedo, *op. cit.,* pp. 90–92. In a *cédula* of 1569, the basic royal view of colonial industries was made quite clear when the king, learning that a great many of the trained artisans who emigrated to the Americas were not practicing their trades there, ordered the expulsion of nonpracticing artisans. Pedro M. Oliveira, *op. cit.,* p. 91.

135. Antonio de Ulloa and Jorge Juan y Santacilia, *Noticias secretas,* pp. 196–224.

136. C.L. Guthrie, *op. cit.,* p. 114, charts the fluctuations in maize prices in seventeenth-century Mexico, indicating that the system was not impervious to the forces of supply and demand. In Gonzalo Gómez de Cervantes, *La vida económica y social de Nueva España al finalizar el siglo XVI,* Mexico: José Porrúa e Hijos, 1944, p. 100, there is a contemporary report of widespread violation of the rule requiring all sales to be made at the public *alhóndiga.*

137. M. Colmeiro, *op. cit.,* Vol. II, pp. 395–396.

138. Lucas Alamán, *op. cit.,* pp. 107–108, observes that most finer textiles were produced in colonial Mexico when wars cut off access to the customary European supply sources. When peace returned and imports resumed, American producers could seldom meet the competition of European goods in these lines. For most manufactured items, though, colonial producers were protected by (1) the inflated prices of Spanish-made goods, (2) the occasional restrictions placed by the crown on Spanish exports as an anti-inflation policy, (3) high maritime and overland transport costs, (4) the price-increasing cumulation of taxes on imported goods by the time they reached colonial markets beyond the trade entrepôts, and (5) the sporadic interruptions of transatlantic shipping. As was mentioned earlier, however, transport costs and taxes narrowed the regional markets for colonial manufactures, so that a proliferation of small-scale enterprises serving local markets was encouraged.

139. Bernardo de Ulloa, *Restablecimiento de las fábricas, y comercio español,* Madrid: Antonio Marín, 1740, contains a strong indictment of trade taxes.

140. When the *alcabala,* a sales tax which resembled the turnover tax since it was paid on each transfer, was introduced in 1575, it was figured at 2 per cent of the selling price in each transaction. Towards the end of the colonial period, however, it had risen to 8 per cent, although there were some exemptions (e.g., for Indians selling native crops, for the clergy, etc.). The tax was administered directly in some areas but elsewhere was farmed out to individuals, municipal governments (which imposed their own taxes in addition), or, as in the case of Mexico City, to the *consulado.* R.S. Smith, "Sales Taxes in New Spain, 1575–1770," *Hispanic American Historical Review,* Vol. 28, No. 1 (February 1948), pp. 2–37. Goods moving across the Atlantic were also subject to a variety of other duties: e.g., convoy charges, port taxes, and the like.

141. Gustav Schmoller, *The Mercantile System and Its Historical Significance,* New York: Peter Smith, 1931, p. 51. Something of this objective appeared in the later eighteenth-century Spanish reforms which did contain authentic elements of mercantilism. The object of discussion here is the premercantilistic era of some two and a half centuries in duration which preceded the reforms and which was much more decisive in setting the essential character of New World economic life.

142. This is certainly not to argue that other countries at the time completely subordinated political goals to the goal of economic power. Mercantilism, in fact, rested upon a double objective of state building and national-economy building, and the several nations practicing mercantilism achieved a varying success in reconciling the two goals. The matter in question is rather one of balance. In some of its incidentals, for example, the Spanish imperial system resembled the commercial practices of thirteenth and fourteenth century Venice. There too, economic and political power were united. Despite superficial resemblances, however, the Venetian case differed radically from

the Spanish case in the relative importance accorded the two sets of criteria. In the former, commercial interests were paramount; in the latter, they were distinctly subordinate. Part of the difference between Spanish policy and that of the northwest European powers may have originated in the differing historical sequence of institutional change in the two areas. In northwestern Europe, the rise of monarchies coincided with the commercial revolution, and kings and mercantile interests joined forces to disintegrate the structures of feudalism in order to effect a new social reintegration in the institution of the nation state. In Spain, as we have observed, the strengthening of the monarchy and the attenuation of feudalism antedated the commercial revolution.

143. The point at issue is, of course, a disputed one. Some of the justifications for the corvée may have been partially valid, for recent experience (e.g., the target worker phenomenon, high rates of absenteeism and turnover) would seem to reveal in some traditional societies the presence of cultural barriers to the commitment of native labor to wage employment. The evidence uncovered by Manning Nash in his study, *Machine Age Maya,* also suggests that large and continuing real wage differences may be necessary to overcome the lack of responsiveness of native labor to wage incentives. To the extent that this situation held true for colonial Spanish America, the state, by its compulsory labor policy, merely moved more directly than could a market mechanism to pull labor into the desired areas of employment (as desirability was determined by the state). On the other hand, in addition to the differential between the wages paid voluntary labor and the price fixed for involuntary recruits, there are other reasons for believing that the alleged inelasticity of the labor supply with respect to wages was a subterfuge to disguise the unwillingness of Spanish and criollo overlords to cover the costs of wage employment to the Indians. The latter had to take into account the high risks of disease mortality which attended closer association with the ladino populace, the strong probability of receiving abusive treatment and being defrauded in dealings with the Spanish settlers, and the difficulty of supporting family and village obligations while absent from the native community and therefore unable to till the fields assigned the native population for its subsistence. Moreover, it must certainly have been clear that removal from the structure of indigenous communities means a sacrifice of the meager but certain security arrangements provided in autochthonous society, while the alien non-Indian society, by its very nature, offered neither compensating security counterparts nor convincing opportunities for advancement to most of the Indians who might have contemplated the change.

144. An hereditary debt peonage was also recognized in the courts. In the seventeenth century, peonage became important in the Mexican viceroyalty; in the eighteenth century, in the Peruvian viceroyalty.

145. J.O. McLachlin, in *Trade and Peace With Old Spain, 1667–1750,* Cambridge: The University Press, 1940, indicates that of the goods shipped from England to Spain during this period a large portion was reexported to the American dominions. This was recognized clearly even at the time, as indicated by the eighteenth-century work by John Campbell, an English merchant, who likened Spain to a sieve and who wrote his book, in part, to demonstrate the gains to be had from an even greater economic penetration of the Spanish empire. John Campbell, *The Spanish Empire in America,* London: M. Cooper, 1747, Chap. 2, Book III. Campbell's study, which is a useful source of economic information on the colonial system, is also interesting for its veiled attack on the English mercantilistic policies. As Campbell discreetly put it (p. 292), "Besides, what we have to say of Spain, may possibly suit some other Nation; and there is great Pleasure in stating to the Public intricate and important Truths in such a Light, as may render them bearable. This is an Age in which Flattery and Calumny so much abound, that few Writers know how to mention our own Affairs in Terms acceptable to all Parties. But, with respect to the Spaniards, we may certainly say what we please, and be sure of an attentive Hearing."

146. R. Davis, in "English Foreign Trade, 1700–1774," *The Economic History Review,* 2nd Series, Vol. 15 (1961), has indicated how important was the Spanish

and American trade for the growth of British manufacturing exports during the first half of the eighteenth century.

147. Again, it must be remembered that politically inspired religious persecutions had also been a factor in arresting the development of the Spanish business and industrial structure. In this connection, it is interesting to contrast the Spanish approach to *limpieza de sangre* (ethnic and religious purity) with the religious toleration which "was the unanimous demand of all theoretical and practical economic politicians under mercantilism. On no other question was there such complete unanimity." Eli Heckscher, *op. cit.*, Vol. II, pp. 303–307.

148. *Ibid.*, Vol. I, p. 345.

149. See, for example, José Cepeda Adán, *En torno al concepto del estado en los reyes católicos,* Madrid: Consejo Superior de Investigaciones Científicas, Escuela de Historia Moderna, 1956.

150. The *patronato real,* granted in 1493 by the Holy See to the Spanish monarchs, conferred on the latter the right of patronage in filling ecclesiastical offices in the New World. Supplemented in 1501 by an agreement in which the pope granted in perpetuity to the crown the rights to collect the tithes in America, the pontifical concessions effectively placed the temporal government of the church under the monarchy, which even exercised the prerogative of approving papal bulls submitted for publication in the overseas possessions. Thereafter, the crown went still further by asserting its claim to the title of "Vicariate of the Indies," which, though not recignized by the Vatican, was nevertheless enforced de facto by the Spanish government. Efforts by the papacy to send papal nuncios to participate in the administration of church affairs in the New World were rebuffed, and the Congregation for the Propagation of the Faith (which was established in 1622) was prevented from sending delegates to the Americas. As an additional measure for interposing royal authority between the Vatican and the religious life of the Indies, the crown even limited by decrees the communications between the Holy See and the bishops. For a short statement of the relationships between the church and civil authority, see William J. Coleman, *Latin American Catholicism, A Self-Evaluation,* Maryknoll, New York: Maryknoll Publications, 1958, p. 6–14. A more extended study of the servitude of the church to the state is found in W. Eugene Shiels, *King and Church*, Chicago: Loyola University Press, 1961. See also, M.J. Ayala, *Notas a la Recopilación de Indias,* Madrid: Ediciones Cultura Hispánica, 1945 (written in 1787), Vol. I and Juan de Solórzano y Pereyra's *Política Indiana,* Vol. II, pp. 2–249, for the relevant provisions in Spanish law.

151. Octavio Paz, *op. cit.*, p. 92. "Thanks to religion, the colonial order is not a mere surface imposition of new historic forms, but a living organism." In Paz's rather poetic expression, the church opened up to the natives, their old cultural forms defeated, the possibilities of joining a living society.

152. These are contained in the *Recopilación* and also in Vol. I, pp. 59–171, of Solórzano's *Política Indiana.*

153. The Indians, for example, were exempted from the purview of the Inquisition.

154. Juan de Solórzano y Pereyra, *op. cit.,* Vol. I, pp. 184 ff.

155. F.W. Blackmar, *op. cit.,* pp. 80, 268–269, reports the success of the missionaries in California in introducing Indians who were still engaged in hunting and fishing to a sedentary pattern of living based on agriculture, animal husbandry, and new trades. Olives, grapes, and the growing of grain were all brought in by the missions, which, in fact, provided the large crops of grain necessary for general settlement since the colonists mainly devoted themselves to cattle and sheep ranching. Jorge Juan and Antonio de Ulloa, in their generally critical *Noticias secretas,* pp. 533 ff., found much that was praiseworthy in the educational activities of the Jesuits among the Indians and felt that by fostering better agricultural practices, the missionaries had done much to improve their lot. See also Oscar E. Reyes, *op. cit.,* Vol. II, pp. 548–549, on this point. Von Humboldt, in his *Political Essay . . . ,* Vol. III, p. 101, testified to the agricultural extension work of the clergy among the natives and remarked

that the church in the New World was not nearly so great a problem for economic development as it was in Spain.

156. J. García Icazbalceta, *Obras*, Mexico: Imprenta de V. Agüeros, 1896, Vol. II, pp. 427–434, contains an interesting description of a school established for the education of the daughters of leading Indians, while Jerome V. Jacobsen, *Educational Foundations of the Jesuits in Sixteenth Century New Spain*, Berkeley: University of California Press, 1938, pp. 43–51, describes the vocational training schools which provided the Indians (both children and adults) with skills as artists, stonecutters, tailors, shoemakers, sculptors, carpenters, and other trades people. As Jacobsen points out, even where religion was the main subject, the pupils were also exposed to the manners, customs, and concepts of Iberian culture. Constantino Bayle, in his *España y la educación popular en América*, Madrid: Editora Nacional, 1941, pp. 152 ff., reports on the general trade schools but notes, pp. 274–298, that the offspring of caciques were sometimes singled out for education at special schools in hopes that they would set a good example for other natives and help to spread European culture among their fellow Indians.

157. Though the confusion of *encomienda* grants with land grants is still frequently encountered in the literature, a great deal of painstaking research in recent decades has made it unmistakably clear that the two were quite distinct and separate. An *encomienda* was solely a grant of stipulated fiscal and other rights with respect to designated Indians, and in fact, the *encomenderos* were ordinarily prohibited from owning land within the boundaries of their *encomiendas*. With the New Laws of the mid-1500's, the practice of assigning private *encomiendas* was largely abandoned, and in subsequent decades to near the close of the colonial era the crown attempted with varying degrees of success to revoke existing *encomiendas*, or at the least to reduce their prerogatives. Apart from this early episode, which laid the basis for a small class of pensioners, the *encomiendas* were of little general significance and were not, as has been often suggested, the direct progenitors of the *hacienda* or large landed estate. The latter had other, more complicated origins, although, on occasion, *encomenderos* seem to have taken illegal advantage of their position and appropriated the land of their indigenous wards. Even as a category of free income, the *encomiendas* diminished in importance for two reasons: the government gradually reduced the schedule of payments and the demise of many Indians eroded the income base substantially. For details on the institution, see: Juan de Solórzana y Pereyra, *op. cit.*, Vol. I, pp. 224–432; Robert S. Chamberlain, *Castillian Backgrounds of the Repartimiento-Encomienda*, Washington, D.C.: Carnegie Institution of Washington, 1939 (Vol. 5, No. 25 of Series "Contributions to American Anthropology and History"); L.B. Simpson, *The Encomienda in New Spain*, Berkeley: University of California Press, 1950; Domingo Amunátegui Solar, *Las encomiendas de indígenas en Chile*, Santiago: Imprenta Cervantes, 1909–1910, 2 vols.; Silvio A. Zavala, *New Viewpoints on the Spanish Colonization of America*, Philadelphia: University of Pennsylvania Press, 1943, pp. 80–91; M.M. Lacas, "The Encomienda in Latin American History: A Reappraisal," *The Americas*, Vol. 8, No. 3 (January 1952), pp. 259–287.

158. In Vol. I, p. 81, of the *Instrucciones que los vireyes de Nueva España ...*, for example, a viceroy of Mexico complains of clerical exploitation of the Indians.

159. The same concern was evident in the steps taken by the crown to differentiate the *encomienda* arrangement from legal vassalage, for in that device the Indians owed no fealty to the *encomenderos* and jurisdiction of the natives was formally retained by the administrative hierarchy.

160. When the wars for independence came in the early nineteenth century, the Spanish monarchy and its ecclesiastical allies were able in more than a few instances to count on indigenous support.

161. Production taxes such as tithes were primarily applied to the new crops introduced by the Spaniards, but native crops were sometimes exempted from taxation. While a humanitarian or social-justice element seems to have been involved in the think-

ing behind this tax decision, it may unintentionally have operated as a disincentive tax to discourage Indians from shifting from nontaxed traditional cultivation to newer, taxable production.

162. José M.L. Mora, *Obras sueltas,* Paris: Librería de Rosa, 1837, Vol. I, p. 52, cites an illustrative case in which the bishop of Valladolid contributed heavily to the construction of bridges and roads and to the reconstruction of the municipal aqueduct.

163. See *ibid.* The bishop and church council of Valladolid exhausted the diocesan treasury in 1786 and 1790 by purchasing a large volume of maize which they sold at below cost to check profiteering by *hacendados* during periods of grain shortage.

164. For the most useful accounts of this aspect of the church's operations, see, C. Bayle, *op. cit.,* and Jerome Jacobsen, *op. cit.* See also E.G. Bourne, *Spain in America,* New York: Harper and Brothers, 1904, pp. 305—311; and Adolfo Garretón, *La instrucción primaria durante la dominación: española en el territorio que forma actualmente la república argentina,* Buenos Aires: Talleres Gráficos del Consejo Nacional de Educación, 1939.

165. For example, the first institution of higher learning, the College of Santa Cruz at Tlaltelolco (near Mexico City), was founded by Bishop Zumárraga, while it was also in Mexico that Bishop Quiroga devised an imaginative plan to set up schools to develop a complementary array of trades and crafts among the villages of his diocese in Michoacán. For insight into the pioneering educational efforts in Mexico, see J. García Icazbalceta, *op. cit.,* Vol. I ("Don Fray Juan Zumárraga, Primer Obispo y Arzobispo de México"), and other monographs in his collected works.

166. E.G. Bourne, *op. cit.,* p. 308. See also the impressions of colonial education recorded by von Humboldt in his *Travels . . . ,* Vol. III, p. 215.

167. See, e.g., Mariano Picón Salas, *De la conquista a la independencia, tres siglos de historia cultural hispanoamericana,* Mexico: Fondo de Cultura Económica, 1944, pp. 131—160. Picón Salas also notes in colonial intellectual life the strong element of mysticism and asceticism alluded to earlier. See also C. Bayle, *op. cit.,* pp. 138—298.

168. Irving A. Leonard, in a painstaking study of sixteenth-century colonial reading tastes (*Books of the Brave,* Cambridge: Harvard University Press, 1949) indicates that the religio-scholastic influence did not have a complete monopoly by any means. Though the Holy Office made intermittent efforts to control the reading matter imported into the New World, these attempts were generally quite perfunctory and on the whole ineffectual. Mostly concerned with heretical ideas, it also disapproved of "profane histories" and light literature. The former did not intrude much into the American possessions, but romances, fictional histories, adventures, and chivalric tales appear to have circulated rather widely. On occasion officials of the Inquisition aided this infraction, for a number of men were caught selling, for personal gain, the forbidden literature they had confiscated in performance of their public function. Nevertheless, these breaches of the educational system were of little value in providing skills for the development of the colonial economy.

169. Luis Alberto Sánchez, "The University in Latin America: The Colonial Period," *Americas,* Washington: Pan American Union, Vol. 13, No. 10 (October 1961), pp. 21—23.

170. Much of this type of educational experience has carried over into the present century in Latin America, which may account for the unfailing appeal of pure cerebration and the frequent elaboration of mental constructs untested by empirical procedures and divorced from the limits imposed by practical exigencies. A good many of the economic plans and programs announced in Latin America up to recent times, for example, appear to have been formulated *pour le sport,* as it were, with little or no concern for empirical verification or for the practical possibilities of their implementation. Their function, insofar as it is more than that of intellectual *divertissement,* seems to have been largely political and rather like that of the party platforms in North Amer-

ican political life. In addition, of course, the preparation of such plans has been a means of providing employment to influential intellectuals. So prevalent has been the practice of this disembodied sort of theorizing that a term for it has entered into the modern Spanish vocabulary: *Proyectismo.*

171. This spiritual or nonutilitarian ethos inherent in the education of the colonial period has nowhere received a clearer reaffirmation than in the "anti-Caliban, pro-Ariel" dialectic of José Rodó's influential *Ariel*, the widely acclaimed book which around 1900 set forth so cogently the value premises of traditional Hispanic culture.

172. The only time the Inquisition made significant attempts to put students and intellectuals on trial for reading banned books occurred between around 1790 and 1810 when, in reaction to the French Revolution, the Spanish crown reversed its previously more receptive attitude towards the intellectual ferment produced by the Enlightenment. The major objective of the Inquisition at that time was, of course, the suppression of the political theories which justified the overthrow of monarchies.

173. Picón Salas, *op. cit.*, p. 161. See, for example, Fr. José Gumilla's *El Orinoco Ilustrado* and Fr. Juan Ignacio Molina's *Compendio de la historia geográfica, natural y civil del reino de Chile y ensayo sobre la historia natural de Chile*, two of the important early works in this vein.

174. Of several nationalities—Spaniards such as Antonio de Ulloa and José Celestino Mutis, Germans such as Alexander von Humboldt and Thaddeus Haenke, and Frenchmen such as Bonpland, Frezier, and De la Condamine—these visitors brought with them the Enlightenment's concern with natural sciences and the new priority of empirically derived knowledge over inherited beliefs.

175. As Roland Hussey has observed, "Few of the high officials of Church and State sent to America in the last half century were reactionary men, and so many of them revealed modernism, and insistence on experimental science in their comments on education, that they must have belonged entirely to the Enlightenment." Arthur P. Whitaker, et. al., *Latin America and the Enlightenment*, New York: D. Appleton-Century Company, 1942, p. 29.

176. In large part motivated by a desire to acquire the wealth of the Jesuit's properties, the crown's attentiveness to the voices of critics of the Society was probably heightened by its knowledge that members of the order were debating, among other controversial philosophical topics, the conditions under which regicide was a legitimate political act.

177. The new republican governments claimed that legally they were the inheritors of the *patronato real*, but the Vatican took the occasion of the rupture in political continuity to attempt a recovery of its right to make clerical appointments without state control. While the issue was joined—over a rather lengthy period in some cases—the personnel deficit left by the exile of the Spanish clergy went unfilled.

178. Correspondingly, the social structure has also supported a dominant value system which appears to be in substantial conflict with the utilitarian values of modern technology. For an interesting and insightful essay on this point, see William S. Stokes, "The Drag of the Pensadores," in James W. Wiggins and Helmut Schoeck, editors, *Foreign Aid Reexamined: A Critical Appraisal*, Washington, D.C.: Public Affairs Press, 1958, pp. 56—89.

179. J.L. Mecham, *Church and State in Latin America*, Chapel Hill: University of North Carolina Press, 1934, pp. 45—50; Jorge Juan y Santacilia and Antonio de Ulloa, *Noticias secretas . . .*, pp. 523—525, wherein it is also noted that the bulk of the church's lands was rented out to others; Lucas Alamán, *Historia de Méjico*, Mexico: Editorial Jus, 1942, vol. I, pp. 70—72; Sebastián Lorente, *Historia del Perú bajo los Bourbones*, Lima: 1871, pp. 270—272.

180. Mariano Cuevas, in his *Historia de la iglesia en México*, Mexico: Imprenta del Asilo "Patricio Sanz, 1921—1922 (Vols. I and II), and El Paso: Editorial "Revista Católica," 1928 (Vols. III—V), Vol. V, pp. 284—308, notes the various sources of confusion which make many estimates of the church's wealth unreliable and exaggerated.

Some, for example, have cited as income that which was an estimate of capital worth. Others have failed to distinguish between productive capital such as land and unproductive capital such as temples and ornamentation. On occasion, estimates of church holdings have included funds and real assets actually belonging to guilds, while at other times writers have included as church property the total value of private estates which paid an annuity to the church as part of the bequest of the owner. Moreover, some of the secular clergy were from wealthy families and held property in their own right, most commonly deeding this, upon their death, back to their family instead of the church; yet these privately owned properties have also been counted as part of the church's domain by some writers. According to Cuevas, the estimates for Mexico made by von Humboldt, in his *Political Essay . . . ,* probably come fairly close to being accurate, as do the estimates made by Abad y Queipo. The estimate made by Bishop Manuel Abad y Queipo is found in vol. I, p. 101 of José M.L. Mora, *Obras sueltas,* which contains a number of the writings of this remarkably acute and judicious critic of the late colonial scene in Mexico.

181. At an early period, for example, Viceroy Mendoza was ordered to prevent land from falling into mortmain, and as early as 1573 there was issued a decree, one of several, forbidding religious orders to acquire more property. In 1796 the government imposed a special 15 per cent tax on any property sold to the church.

182. M. Cuevas, *op. cit.,* Vol. V, p. 302; Andrés Molina Enríquez, *Los grandes problemas nacionales,* Mexico: Imprenta de A. Carranza e Hijos, 1909, p. 33; Jorge Juan y Santacilia and Antonio de Ulloa, *Noticias secretas . . . ,* pp. 533 ff.. Rafael M. Baralt, in his *Resumen de la historia de Venezuela . . . hasta el año de 1797,* Paris: Desclée, De Brouwer, 1939, p. 366, reports that one of the Venezuelan bishops, in 1783, introduced large-scale coffee growing to that region and that he and other clerics were active in promoting the cultivation of coffee by private farmers.

183. José M.L. Mora, *op. cit.,* Vol. I, pp. 76—78.

184. *Ibid.,* pp. 80—85. It was not unknown, for that matter, for the church to permit its debtors to fall into arrears on interest payments for as much as two or three years. As Abad y Queipo noted, it was often the debtor's high propensity to consume (his maintenance of a standard of living "con el decoro que corresponde a su estado y condición") which prevented the repayment of principal. See also J.L. Mecham, *loc. cit.*

185. The practice continues to this day in some Latin American countries. In the Peruvian sierra, for example, most of the church's haciendas have long been operated under leasing arrangements by private individuals—generally quite inefficiently.

186. Fernando B. Sandoval, *op. cit.,* pp. 102—111, for instance, observes that religious orders, hospitals, and similar institutions had important sugar properties, some of which they operated directly and others which they leased out. Especially significant, at least in Mexico and Guatemala, were the large mills operated by the Jesuits, who had important sheep and cattle ranches and, in the missions of Paraguay, directed an entire regional economy. The produce from religious estates appears to have been sold in church-owned retail outlets with tax exemptions that were, however, gradually withdrawn throughout the colonial era.

187. M. Cuevas, *op. cit.,* Vol. V, p. 304.

188. The tithes which, it may be remembered, were legally collectable by the state did not all accrue to the church. Sometimes the crown took considerably more than the two-ninths to which it was entitled, and on other occasions it collected all the tithes and placed bishops on a straight salary. Rafael M. Baralt, *op. cit.,* pp. 313—314. For additional information on the tithe system, see Woodrow W. Borah, "The Collection of Tithes in the Bishopric of Oaxaca During the Sixteenth Century," *Hispanic American Historical Review,* Vol. 21, No. 3 (August 1941), pp. 386—409.

189. A good summary account of the sources of church income is contained in Helen Phipps, *Some Aspects of the Agrarian Question in Mexico,* Austin: University of Texas Press, Bulletin 2515, 12 April 1925, pp. 47—62. Among the commercial acti-

vities of the church were shops which sold, with partial tax exemption, the produce of church estates, the output of shops operated by religious institutions, and the tithes collected in kind. Undoubtedly it was this competition, together with the high value of certain pieces of church-owned real estate, which helps to explain the animosity expressed by a good many colonial subjects towards the church's involvement in temporal matters.

190. Fernando B. Sandoval, *op. cit.*, pp. 114–123; Alexander von Humboldt, *Political Essay . . . ,* Vol. III, pp. 99–101; José M.L. Mora, *op. cit.*, Vol. I, pp. 84–85.

191. When, for example, the crown attempted in 1804 to confiscate the charitable trusts (and ordered all persons in debt to these to pay the outstanding principal to the treasury), the Mining Tribunal of Mexico lodged a sharp protest with the king. In urging him to revoke the measure, the Tribunal pointed out that these trust funds were necessary to the economic life of the colony since they functioned as banks from which loans at low interest rates could be obtained for business. L.E. Fisher, *Champion of Reform, Abad y Queipo,* New York: Library Publishers, 1955, p. 45.

192. W.L. Schurz, *op. cit.*, p. 52; Fernando González Roa, *El aspecto agrario de la revolución mexicana,* Mexico: Poder Ejecutivo Federal, Talleres Gráficos, 1919, pp. 101–102. Sandoval notes, *loc. cit. supra,* that *avío* or crop production loans for the sugar industry were also, on occasion, made by the mayors (*alcaldes mayores*) of towns out of the capitation tax proceeds.

193. Lucas Alamán, *op. cit.*, pp. 134–136; Fernando González Roa, *op. cit.*, p. 102. When in 1804 the crown appropriated church funds invested in real estate, a number of families were reduced to financial ruin by the forced sales which were effected to liquidate the mortgages. In particular, the smaller holders were hard pressed to find substitute sources of financing and, thrown upon private moneylenders charging usurious rates, they often ended by losing their properties.

194. A 5 per cent rate of interest seems to have prevailed in sugar industry financing. Mecham notes, *loc. cit.,* that most clerical loans were put out on from 4 to 6 per cent.

195. The combination of repeated mortgage loans plus diversion of savings into consumption meant, of course, that eventually the hypothecated properties came to have a mortgage burden in excess of their valuation figured on the basis of their capitalized earnings. The disparity was probably one factor which inclined some of the criollo landowners to favor attacks on the church's temporal activities when independence came, for this was a means of wiping the slate clean of the accumulated evidence of past financial irresponsibility.

196. Bishop Abad y Queipo, for instance, observed that the productive efficiency of the haciendas was usually quite low and that their maintenance and expansion depended increasingly upon their ability to obtain low-cost loans from religious institutions. José M.L. Mora, *op. cit.*, Vol. I, pp. 87–88.

197. It is reported in Vol. I, p. 225, of the *Instrucciones que los vireyes de Nueva España dejaron a sus sucesores* that in the early eighteenth century there were only two private banking houses servicing the Mexican mining industry.

198. As Abad y Queipo pointed out near the end of the colonial period, Spanish capital and credit was still the basis for carrying on a sizable amount of economic activity in Mexico, there having been so little development of colonial financial intermediaries. José M.L. Mora, *op. cit.*, Vol. I, p. 92.

199. Until late in the colonial period, mutual aid societies were generally organized as religious confraternities which, in part, paralleled the guild structure, and it was these confraternities which held loanable funds in their treasuries. It is interesting to observe that towards the close of the colonial era the state encouraged the separation of these mutual aid funds from the confraternities in hopes that the secularized funds (known as *montepíos*) would become a means of providing credit for artisan producers to improve their economic standing, a system of popular industrial credit, as it were. Manuel Carrera Stampa, *op. cit.*, pp. 125–126.

200. In republican Chile, for example, the first banks of issue—Ossa y Cía, and Bazanilla, MacClure y Cía—were not established until several decades after independence was won, while not until 1855 was the first joint stock bank established (the Banco de Valparaíso which was organized by the merchants of that port). Guillermo Subercaseaux, *El sistema monetario i la organización bancaria de Chile,* Santiago: Imp. i Lit. Universo, 1920, pp. 121–124.

201. The significant withdrawal of capital by Spaniards leaving the area is discussed in Francisco López Camara, "Las Contradicciones de la Economía Mexicana después de la Revolución de Independencia," *Investigación Económica,* Mexico: Vol. 23, No. 1 (First Quarter 1963), pp. 218–219.

202. José M.L. Mora, *op. cit.,* Vol. I, pp. 413 ff. The domestic debt of the new regimes was also forced upon church organizations and, to a lesser extent, wealthy individuals.

NOTES FOR CHAPTER IV

1. Although the percentage of the total Latin American labor force in agriculture has been steadily declining for at least the past hundred years, it was around 65 per cent in 1925 and is at least 51 per cent today. Thus the population is still predominantly rural, even in such relatively advanced countries as Brazil and Mexico. In Argentina and Uruguay, where the agricultural labor force is less than 30 per cent of the total, this is largely due to their major agricultural activity being ranching, which is not labor intensive.

2. Except for Venezuela, Chile, and Bolivia, which are all primarily minerals exporters today, agricultural output is the mainstay of the Latin American export trade and hence the necessary springboard for financing the currently desired industrial development. Even for the three minerals exporting countries, conditions of productivity in domestic agriculture are of compelling interest for their effect on the composition of imports and thus on the amount of foreign exchange available for financing national development programs. Furthermore, since most of the present industrialization programs are based on protected national markets, the level of agricultural productivity and patterns of rural income distribution obviously relate directly to the size of these markets and to the range of feasible industrial development possibilities. In several of the countries today, agricultural supply inelasticities are also a major source of inflationary pressures which have adversely affected the general production in a number of ways.

3. In the discussion which follows, *latifundium* will be used generically to identify all large landholdings. Most of them during the colonial period could also be classified as haciendas, which, by current convention, implies a latifundium on which the production technology is of a traditional or primitive type, on which low levels of capitalization are typical, and on which resources tend to be used extensively rather then intensively. Despite the scale of ownership, the production organization of an hacienda is not necessarily on a large scale, and, characteristically, the orientation of the hacienda is only partially commercial. Its marketed output goes almost entirely to local or regional markets. A second type of latifundium, the plantation, is almost entirely commercial in its organization and is generally organized on a larger scale basis, with, at least in more recent times, a somewhat more advanced technology and higher levels of capitalization than the hacienda. Though part of the output of the plantation may be marketed domestically, most of it goes to export markets. Examples of plantation enterprise are, today, the sugar plantations of the Caribbean islands, the coffee *fincas* of Guatemala and the coffee *fazendas* of Brazil, the banana plantations of Central America, and the cattle *estancias* of the Argentine. Especially in colonial times, some latifundia were of an intermediate type, sharing features of both the plantation enterprise and the hacienda.

4. As mentioned in Chapter 3, honorific status was awarded as an incentive for mining activities, and successful merchants were also, at times, able to purchase aristocratic titles from the crown. Jorge Basadre, *Perú: problema y posibilidad,* Lima: Casa Editorial F. y E. Rosay, 1931, p. 108. In *Instrucciones que los vireyes de Nueva España dejaron a sus sucesores,* Mexico: Imprenta de Ingacio Escalante, 1873, Vol. I, p. 101, the viceroy of Mexico in 1673 noted that the colonial aristocracy was often involved in commerce.

5. The unitary social, administrative, and judicial organization of the traditional *hacienda* is well described in two recent articles. See Mario C. Vásquez, "Local Authority in a Peruvian Andean Hacienda," paper presented at the annual meeting of the American Anthropological Association, Philadelphia, 1961; and Thomas L. Norria, "Decision-Making Activity Sequences in an Hacienda Community," *Human Organization,* Vol. 12, No. 3 (Fall 1953), pp. 26–30, which deals with an hacienda community in Costa Rica.

6. Sebastián Lorente notes, for example, that by 1690–1700, latifundian expansion had already overrun a good many Peruvian Indian villages. Sebastián Lorente, *Historia del Perú bajo la dinastía austriaca, 1598–1700,* Paris: Imprenta de A.E. Rochette, 1870, p. 330. The equivalent trend in Colombia is remarked in Orlando Fals Borda, *El hombre y la tierra en Boyacá,* Bogotá: Ediciones Documentos Colombianos, 1957, pp. 82–91.

7. Emilio Romero reports that the Peruvian Indians began their noted historical involvement in lawsuits over land at least as early as the administration of viceroy Toledo in 1569. Emilio Romero, *Historia económica y financiera del Perú; antiguo Perú y virreynato,* Lima: Imprenta Torres Aguirre, 1937, p. 98.

8. As George Kubler puts it, "The Indians were constantly wandering back and forth between the *repartimiento* and the seat of their *audiencia* to secure legal papers, usually worthless, for which they were heavily charged by the swarms of parasite solicitors and scriveners who made their living in the Spanish cities from this occupation." An excellent account of the situation is the article from which the foregoing quotation was taken: George Kubler, "The Quechua in the Colonial World," in Julian Steward, ed., *Handbook of South American Indians,* Washington, D.C.: Smithsonian Institution, Bureau of American Ethnology, 1946, Vol. 2, pp. 331–410.

9. Under latifundian control, there was ordinarily little opportunity to develop functioning community structures in these villages. And in some instances, the villages thenselves were broken up and their inhabitants scattered over the hacienda in order to prevent the natives from pressing claims for community recognition in the courts, a recognition which under the Laws of the Indies would have made then eligible for an assignment of land.

10. For one of the finest single studies of latifundian growth, the reader should consult the recently translated work of François Chevalier, *Land and Society in Colonial Mexico; The Great Hacienda,* Berkeley: University of California Press, 1963.

11. In some cases, as in Peru and Bolivia, the hydraulic engineering achievements of the Indians had substantially enhanced the values provided as a free gift of nature so that a part of their attraction for the Spaniards derived from the preconquest capital accumulation activity.

12. Copper, which had been used by the Indians for copper and bronze tools, continued to be mined by the Spaniards, in limited quantities, in Mexico, Venezuela, and Chile. Tin, lead, and zinc were similarly mined in Mexico and Bolivia. But the export of these minerals to Europe was uneconomic, and the introduction by the Spaniards of superior iron implements and tools greatly reduced the colonial demand for copper and tin.

13. For example, Virginia tobacco competed with Spanish American exports, while the seventeenth-century penetration of the West Indies by the English, Dutch, and French, brought these areas into competition with such Spanish colonial exports as dyestuffs, tobacco, and, above all, sugar. Up through the first half of the seventeenth century, Brazil was the major supplier of sugar to the European markets. Apart from their advantageous inclusion in restricted trading areas, the Antillean and Brazilian competitors were also

more favorably situated with respect to locational factors. In view of the limited markets then available in Europe for products of this sort, this competition was especially significant as a brake on the development of Spanish American export agriculture. Even so, certain lines of export production which, by corresponding to regional comparative advantages, took on greatly increased importance during the nineteenth-century period of trade expansion got their start in these times.

14. Tallow came to be widely used for illumination in the households, the mines, and in ceremonial activities.

15. See, for example, Donald D. Brand, *Quiroga, A Mexican Municipio,* Washington, D.C.: U.S. Government Printing Office, 1951, p. 20, and Alexander von Humboldt, *Political Essay on the Kingdom of New Spain.* London: Longman, Hurst, Rees, Orme, and Brown, 1811, Vol. I, pp. 185–186.

16. Helen Phipps, *Some Aspects of the Agrarian Question in Mexico,* Austin: University of Texas Press, Bulletin #2515, 15 April 1925, pp. 21–28. For the legislation which attempted to safeguard Indian property rights, see Libros IV and VI of the *Recopilación.* Also informative are Anselmo de la Portilla, *España en México, cuestiones históricas y sociales,* Mexico: Imprenta de I. Escalante y Cía, 1871, pp. 66–71, and Andrés Molina Enríquez, *Los grandes problemas nacionales,* Mexico: Imprenta de A. Carranza e Hijos, 1909, pp. 57 ff. Portilla notes that the natives occasionally found ways to manipulate the protective legislation to enhance the size of their own properties.

17. In Mexico, the size of the Indian population appears to have sunk to its nadir around the middle of the seventeenth century, at which time it may have declined four-fifths or more from its level in 1519. From around 1650 on, there was a slow recovery and by 1793 the number of natives reached approximately 3.7 million, or approximately two and a half times its size in 1650. Peruvian sources have not yet been so well studied but a similar trend, somewhat delayed, occurred there as well, with the decline continuing into the early eighteenth century. Eventually, in South America, the population decline made the *mita* levies and capitation tax obligations (levied, like the Roman tributation tax on the *civitas,* on communities as a whole with insufficient allowance for changes in community size) so burdensome that a number of Indian rebellions occurred. The decline was not entirely a result of unavoidable contacts with disease, however, for as Jorge Juan and Antonio de Ulloa recognized at the time (*Noticias secretas de América,* London: R. Taylor, 1826, p. 321), the poverty of the Indians made then easy prey for disease. For two wellknown contemporary accounts of the ravages of epidemics, see José Bravo Ugarte, *Motolinía: carta al emperador,* Mexico: Editorial Jus, 1949, p. 36, which contains the letter of Fray Toribio de Motolinía to Charles V, and Fray Juan de Torquemada, *Monarquía indiana,* Mexico: S. Chávez Hayhoe, 1943, Vol. I, Book V, Chap. 22. To put these epidemics in perspective, it should be noted that when an Argentine boat docked at Tierra del Fuego in 1884, it brought an epidemic of measles which practically exterminated the native population within three years. E. Lucas Bridges, *Uttermost Part of the Earth,* London: Hodder and Stoughton, 1948

18. Anselmo de la Portilla, *op. cit.,* pp. 73–75; *Instrucciones que los vireyes de Nueva España . . . ,* pp. 59–60; Joaquín García Icazbalceta, ed., *Nueva colección de documentos para la historia de México,* Mexico: Antigua Librería de Andrade y Morales, sucesores, 1886, Vol. I, pp. 20–24; Mariano Cuevas, *Documentos inéditos del siglo XVI para la historia de México,* Mexico: Talleres del Museo Nacional de Arqueología, Historia, y Etnología, 1914, p. 202; Jorge Basadre, *op. cit.,* pp. 190–191; and Jorge Basadre, *Historia del derecho peruano,* Lima: Editorial Antena, 1937, p. 141.

19. Augustín Rivera, *Principios críticos sobre el vireinato de la Nueva España,* San Juan de los Lagos, Mexico: Tipografía de José Martín Hermosillo, 1884, Vol. I, p. 37; Woodrow W. Borah, *New Spain's Century of Depression,* Berkeley; University of California Press, 1951, p. 33.

20. Each *peonía* was about 20 acres in size, although some were given, later on, up to 5 *peonías.* The *caballerías* were about 105 acres in size; after the earliest period, some cavalry soldiers were given up to three such grants.

21. Mexico, Secretaría de Fomento, *Memoria presentada a S.M. el Emperador por el Ministro de Fomento, Luis Robles Pezuela,* Mexico: Imprenta de Andrade y Escalante, 1866, p. 113. Maximilian's minister of *fomento,* concerned with the extent of latifundism in Mexico during the 1860's, had a study made of land titles to check the size of the original grants. He discovered that, although no grantee had received more than one grant in excess of 100 square leagues, by the mid-nineteenth century some of the landowners held as many as eight or more haciendas, with some of the haciendas exceeding two hundred square leagues.

22. As one lasting consequence of this situation, which continued into post-colonial times, a great many landowners, even today, do not have clear title to their properties, and consequently it is often difficult for them, particularly the smaller ones, to obtain agricultural credit. See, for example, Orlando Fals Borda, *op. cit.,* pp. 51–64, and Orlando Fals Borda, *Peasant Society in the Colombian Andes: A Sociological Study of Saucío,* Gainesville: University of Florida Press, 1962, p. 172. The problem is also dealt with in *Factores sociales que inciden en el desarrollo económico de la hoya del río Subachoque,* Bogotá: Facultad de Sociología, Universidad Nacional de Colombia, 1963.

23. Woodrow W. Borah, *op. cit.,* p. 32. Borah observes that the reduction of the food surplus marketed by free native communities enhanced the value of the hacienda output. See also Oscar E. Reyes, *Breve historia general de Ecuador,* Quito: Editorial "Fray Jodoco Ricke," 1955, Vol. I, pp. 236 ff.

24. Many of the details of land grabbing were revealed in Jorge Juan and Antonio de Ulloa, *Noticias secretas . . . ,* Vol. I, pp. 295–299, 318–326.

25. Emilio Romero, *op. cit.,* pp. 97–99, 105–115.

26. Helen Phipps, *op. cit.,* pp. 30–33.

27. Legally, such concessions could be revoked if not used as intended.

28. Fernando B. Sandoval, *La industria del azúcar en Nueva España,* Mexico: Instituto de Historia, Universidad Nacional Autónoma de México, 1951, p. 134.

29. José M.L. Mora, *Obras sueltas,* Paris: Librería de Rosa, 1837, Vol. I, pp. 89–90.

30. The first *composición* was instituted in 1591, and others were held at irregular intervals thereafter. For details on the process, see: Joaquín Maniau, *Compendio de la historia de la real hacienda de Nueva España,* Mexico: Secretaría de Industria y Comercio, 1914 (written in 1794), p. 23; Eusebio Beleña, compiler, *Recopilación sumaria de todos los autos acordados de la real audiencia y sala de crimen de esta Nueva España, y providencias de su superior gobierno . . . ,* Mexico: con licencia por D. Felipe de Zúñiga, 1787, p. 233.

31. Emilio Romero, *op. cit.,* p. 99, observes that some of the lands registered through *composición* in Peru were those which belonged to natives who were away at work in the mines.

32. During the 1630's, the viceroy Conde de Chinchón suspended the *composición* procedure on the grounds that it cost more to administer the program than it returned in revenue and, because there were so many abuses in it, it was injurious to the Indians. Later officials, however, appear to have been less cautious in this regard.

33. D.D. Brand, *op. cit.,* p. 54.

34. T.R. Malthus, *Principles of Political Economy,* New York: Augustus M. Kelley, Inc., 1951, p. 342.

35. Julian H. Steward, "Perspectives on the Plantation," in Pan American Union, *Plantation Systems of the New World,* Social Science Monographs, VII, Washington, D.C.: 1959, p. 9. This particular bond persisted long after legal fetters were removed.

36. The Useful *Noticias secretas* of Juan and Ulloa constitutes a virtual catalogue of the contemporary practices by means of which the ties of the *campesino,* or rural inhabitant, with the estate were cemented into the bonds of debt peonage.

37. In the early seventeenth century, employers were vested with the responsi-

bility for collecting the capitation tax from their native workers, but advances for tax obligations eventually proved to be yet another means of keeping the Indians in debt to the large landowners.

38. Debt peonage was also utilized, albeit on a smaller scale, in colonial manufacturing workshops.

39. As if to demonstrate the aphoristic truth of *plus ça change, plus c'est la même chose,* a report issued in 1958 by the Food and Agriculture Organization and the Economic Commission for Latin America observed that, in Chile, large landlords "do not regard the land as a capital resource in the correct sense of the word. They do not expect from it an income representing a proper return on an investment, but rather one which will permit them to live at a certain level. As long as the income is adequate for this level, they will not invest in the land in order to raise its productivity." In 37 per cent of the estates surveyed in the provinces of Santiago and Valparaiso in central Chile, the landlords' apathy was believed to be a major factor in the defective production system. Chile has been one of the Latin American regions most exposed to influences which would ostensibly push the organization of agriculture in a much more modern and efficient direction. That the legacy of colonial times should show up so strongly in present-day Chile is therefore especially significant.

40. In this connection, it may be remarked that motivation and value systems do not enter the picture as independent variables but are, instead, functionally related to the total structure of the society in question. Until a number of the social parameters were shifted in Spanish America, owing chiefly to the local impact of exogenous forces, the kind of behavior described by such terms as the "Protestant ethic" and "achievement motivation" would have been not only anomalous but also largely meaningless or ineffective in the existing social context.

41. The backwardness of colonial agriculture was widely recognized by eighteenth-century visitors to Spanish America, and even by the more enlightened public officials and clergy working in the region. For a typical contemporary description and commentaries, see François R. J. De Pons, *Voyage à la partie orientale de la Terre-Firme, dans l'Amérique méridionale, fait pendant les anées 1801, 1802, 1803 et 1804,* Paris: l'Imprimerie de Fain et Compagnie, 1806, Vol. II, pp. 309—320; Pedro Fermín de Vargas, *Pensamientos políticos y memorias sobre la población del Nuevo Reino de Granada,* Bogotá: Publicaciones del Banco de la República, 1953, pp. 19—23; Bernardo Ward, *Proyecto económico . . . ,* Madrid: Por la Viuda de Ibarra, Hijos y Compañía, 1787 (4th printing), pp. 257 ff..

42. The casual grazing of livestock on unimproved pastures located on fertile valley bottom lands has been frequently remarked even today in many studies of Latin American agriculture.

43. A recent detailed study of the southern Peruvian economy, for example, revealed that rural workers were, on the average, actually working for only sixty to eighty days out of the year. A recent study of rural Colombia indicates that peasants are ordinarily gainfully employed about half of the time or less. While such studies have been made only in recent times, there is little reason to believe that the degree of labor use was superior over a century or more ago.

44. Doubtless the landowners' indifference to education reflected the fact that the primary labor need of the haciendas was simply for unskilled and semiskilled workers. But given the existence of a substantial body of protective legislation, it was probably just as well, from the *hacendados'* point of view, to keep the natives in ignorance so they would be less aware of the degree to which they had been defrauded of their formal rights under Spanish law.

45. Perhaps nowhere in colonial records are the deficiencies of economic organization more strikingly revealed than in the episode of the Paraguayan *reducciones,* the semi-theocratic mission enclave established by the Jesuits among the Guaraní Indians. All things considered (including the characteristics of the tribe, their low initial level

of development, and the resource base of the region), the material progress achieved under systematic Jesuit organization and management made the *reducciones* the most successful case of native development in the colonial period. Within a centrally directed communitarian structure, new crops and ranching were successfully introduced, artisan education and workshops were established, and a marketing organization was built up to dispose of the surplus in extraregional markets. The religious order therefore functioned as an agency of technical innovation, labor training, and marketing and production management—as well as an agency of capital accumulation, for expansion of the system appears to have taken place primarily on the basis of reinvested surplus. Eventually, however, the relatively high rural prosperity reached by the enterprise incited the cupidity of both the crown and the criollo settlers. Thereupon, in the 1760's, the experiment was terminated, and the assets were distributed among the royal exchequer and private settlers. Under the combined impact of criollo land usurpation and the venality of the civil officials who replaced the churchmen, the native communities disintegrated. The accumulated capital was dissipated, and the marketing organization was disrupted. The material well-being and security of the natives suffered such a setback that not until quite recent years have the Indians even approximated the conditions they enjoyed at the zenith of their earlier development.

46. Orlando Fals Borda, *El hombre y la tierra* . . . , pp. 120–137, contains a good description of the proliferation of minifundia units.

47. In this connection, it should be noted that the latifundian system was a significant factor in depriving Spanish America of a frontier in the North American sense. The extensiveness of the lands claimed by the haciendas was such that it pushed the frontier with unappropriated lands out so far that inaccessibility made it extremely difficult for settlers at the frontier to interact economically and socially with the more populated districts.

48. In a few areas, volcanic origins produced erosion-resistant soil structures, but these were exceptional cases.

49. Jacob Fried, from his studies of the backgrounds of migrants from Peruvian rural communities, has concluded that even indigenous subcultures frequently do not contain the integrative features that they are romantically supposed to possess, because of the breakdown of the traditional order under severe and chronic economic pressure. After examining many case histories, Fried stated that "the first striking conclusion resulting from [the] analysis . . . is that households are so jealously inner-directed that extended social obligations of any kind do not have any priority" and that ideal patterns are, usually, simply inoperative. Further, "there is a marked lack of actual social structural bonds that unite families that must rely on their own immediate resources for security. Interfamily strife based on jealous economic rivalry over land is common." Jacob Fried, "Acculturation and Mental Health Among Indian Migrants in Peru," Chap. 5 in Marvin K. Opler, ed., *Culture and Mental Health*, New York: The Macmillan Company, 1959, pp. 119–137.

50. "In the majority of [Latin American] countries, 'family' remains one of the strongest criteria not only for social position but for sharing wealth and power." Ralph Beals, "Social Stratification in Latin America," *American Journal of Sociology,* Vol. 58, No. 4 (January 1953), p. 328. In the same article, Beals also remarks the "powerful prejudice against manual work" which is associated with the system.

51. The characteristic Latin American village contrasts sharply with, say, the village of India, which has been described as "a living thing . . . a system" and a "well-defined entity . . . [having] an individual quality." See, for example, McKim Marriott, ed., *Village India: Studies in the Little Community,* Chicago: University of Chicago Press, 1955, p. 176, and Morris E. Opler, "The Extensions of an Indian Village," *Journal of Asian Studies,* Vol. 16, No. 1 (1956), p. 5.

52. Among other lasting consequences of the hierarchic system was the development of a deeply ingrained psychology of dependency: a widespread propensity to rely

upon higher authority to deal with problems and provide the major social solutions rather than coping with these directly through voluntary associations and collective action at subsidiary levels of social organization. The possible patterns of social action permitted by such a system contrast conspicuously with those described by D.W. Brogan in his *The American Character,* New York: Time Inc., Book Division, 1962. Observing the important integrative role in American social development played by voluntary associations such as labor unions, churches, and granges, Brogan notes also (pp. 33—34) that American towns, possessed of a true community of common purpose, were able to function in a significant way in opening up the West (and new sources of wealth and income). There, a spirit of local development was fostered by the cult of local improvement and the futuristic slant of the booster spirit which had their roots in a focus on material improvements and expectations of speculative pecuniary gains from windfall increases in the asset values of lands and businesses. While it became the butt of many jokes, local civic pride produced an interest in and even a preoccupation with building and a "conception of growth as everybody's business, everybody's interest."

53. See, for example, the views of Bishop Abad y Queipo which are presented in L.E. Fisher, *Champion of Reform, Manuel Abad y Queipo,* New York: Library Publishers, 1955, or pp. 33—34 of the report written in 1794 by Count Revilla Gigedo, the viceroy of Mexico, *Instrucción reservada . . . a su sucesor en el mando . . . sobre el govierno de este continente,* Mexico: Imprenta de la Calle de las Escalerillas, a Cargo del C. Agustín Guiol., 1831. As one might expect, von Humboldt was similarly cognizant of this point in his *Political Essay on the Kingdom of New Spain.*

54. The terms, "modern marketing apparatus" or "modern marketing structure," as used here, imply a system in which (a) the communication of market information is effected swiftly and comprehensively, (b) the standardization and grading of products is increasingly widespread, (c) the unit size of transactions increases to provide economies of scale, (d) physical distribution occurs with greater speed and geographical amplitude (with fewer losses in transit and more rapid inventory turnover), (e) the capital inputs increase relative to other factors (e.g., the construction of storage facilities to reduce the wastes of spoilage and to increase time utilities), (f) credit financing plays a larger role, (g) impersonal transactions predominate, and (h) there is development of more specialized firms for greater functional efficiency. The labor-intensive, atomistic, functionally diffused, and segmented marketing structure of colonial Spanish America moved little towards realizing any of these attributes, even though it could be argued that, for its economic setting, it was comparatively rational in its factor mix.

55. The most important South American mines, those in Bolivia, were located in a semi-arid region which had only limited agricultural potential. Consequently, the market pull of these centers stimulated agricultural development in more distant areas: e.g., northwest Argentina, Chile, and parts of Peru.

56. Ordinarily, of course, social mobility does not proceed by leaps from the bottom of the structure to the top, but rather by a gradual process of upward socio-economic movement. The colonial system, however, had "space" for only limited numbers of people on each level of the occupational structure, while the socio-economic "distance" between levels tended to be great. Both aspects, therefore, impeded the movement of significant numbers of people upwards and reinforced the concentration of wealth and income.

57. See, for example, Dan Stanislawski, *The Anatomy of Eleven Towns in Michoacán,* Austin: University of Texas Press, 1950.

58. Sergio Bagú, *Estructura social de la colonia,* Buenos Aires: Librería "El Ateneo" Editorial, 1952, pp. 87—90.

59. As the French sociologist, Jacques Lambert, has put it: "The tendency for social activity in the rural areas to be centred round the large estate has, in Latin America, greatly restricted the very important social function that a large number of small towns has generally fulfilled under other forms of social organization. In Europe,

for instance, for a very long time past few rural centres of population have been far from some small town and, where this has not been the case, the rural population has remained very backward. A wide variety of commercial or artisan activities were carried on in these small towns and this led to the formation of a middle class which still maintained very close links with the country. These small towns served as useful channels of contact between the truly urban society of the large towns and rural society; they made it possible for new ideas from the large centres to spread quickly throughout the rural districts. The existence of small towns meant that urban society was not divorced from rural society. Despite the swift changes taking place in urban society it was never far or for long removed from rural society . . . The small towns thus prevented the development, and above all the maintenance, of a dual society." Jacques Lambert, "Requirements for Rapid Economic and Social Development; The View of the Historian and Sociologist," in Egbert de Vries and José Medina Echavarría, editors, *Social Aspects of Economic Development in Latin America,* Paris: UNESCO, 1963, Vol. I, pp. 55—56. See also, *Ibid.,* pp. 57—58, 64—66, for insightful comments on social structure.

60. See, for example, Charles Wagley, *Amazon Town: A Study of Man in the Tropics,* New York: The Macmillan Company, 1958, for modern examples of instances in which persons of comparatively modest means have spent several weeks' or even months'.earnings to finance the fiestas required for status maintenance.

61. Demand patterns were stabilized by such factors as the generally slow rate of growth in population and incomes, by the force of convention and the fixed pattern of income distribution, and by the colonial isolation (geographical in origin, but politically reinforced) which inhibited the intrusion of external cultural influences. Thus, life styles and the array of taste preferences did not change much over centuries.

62. François de Pons, *op. cit.,* Vol. I, pp. 190—191, was struck by this aspect of colonial society and saw it as a considerable barrier to progress.

63. As Henry Hawkes, an Englishman who had lived in Mexico five years, related in 1572, the Indians "do worke so cheape that poore young men that go out of Spain to get their living are not set on worke; which is the occasion there are many idle people in the country. For the Indian will live all the weeke with less than one groat; which the Spanyard cannot do, nor any man els." Richard Hakluyt, comp., *The Principal Navigations, Voyages, Traffiques, and Discoveries of the English Nation,* Edinburgh: E. and G. Goldsmid, 1885—1890, Vol. XIV, p. 178.

64. Donald E. Smith, *The Viceroy of New Spain,* Berkeley: University of California Press, 1913, pp. 157 and 187, illustrates well how slow-moving the ponderous and complex administrative system was.

65. The contrasts between Anglo-American and Latin American jurisprudence are spelled out in a way especially relevant to this discussion in Phanor Eder, *A Comparative Survey of Anglo-American and Latin American Law,* New York: New York University Press, 1950, pp. 5—15, 21—27, 143—145. Whereas case law or judge-made law is the primary source of law in the Anglo-American system, the statute book is predominant in the Latin tradition. The former, according to Eder, grew out of the traditions and experience of the region and has tended to be more pragmatic, stable (in the long run), and circumstantially flexible (in the short run). In particular, the procedural flexibility of Anglo-American law stands in notable contrast to the rigid formalism of Iberian law. The latter, in turn, focuses on abstract reasoning and justice; doctrinal works of jurisconsults; pure legal logic, and the symmetry of institutions, with lawmakers laying down down the rules to govern human relations and conduct rather than leaving these to be worked out in court decisions on the basis of practice and a common sense adaptation to "grass roots" experience. Whereas Anglo-American law is formed "from below" and springs from the customs of the people, Iberian laws are, first and foremost, "acts of imposed authority" and reflect the concept of the unlimited power of the state over individual persons

66. The well-known *personalismo* value of Hispanic culture, therefore, has his-

torically connoted something more than a mere a priori regard for intrinsic individual worth, or *alma* (soul) as the Latin Americans usually express it. "Getting to know you, getting to know all about you" was, under the circumstances, very nearly prerequisite to the conduct of social activity.

67. The situation which existed approximates the "amoral familism" described by E.C. Banfield in his *The Moral Basis of a Backward Society,* Glencoe, Illinois: The Free Press, 1958. Suggestively, Banfield raises the possibility that the conditions he probes in the *mezzogiorno* may be prevalent in other Mediterranean culture areas.

68. It has accordingly been difficult to develop affectively neutral extrafamilial contracts of the sort required in modern economic organization since, under the circumstances, these have tended to become dichotomized into the *amigo-enemigo* categorization.

69. What nepotism and intraclass marriages could do for the strong, widespread resort to the institution of *compadrazgo* was also intended to accomplish for those less favorably situated in the social structure. A type of ritual kinship, *compadrazgo* social obligations were created through being godparents at baptism and sponsors at confirmation and were established on an interclass as well as an intraclass basis.

70. *Malicia* (a surpassing shrewdness), *engaño* (guilefulness), and *envidia* (a sentiment combining envy and jealousy with elements of the German *Schadenfreude*) all seem to have a high incidence of occurrence in ladino personalities.

71. As Ozzie Simmons has put it in his incisive analysis of the criollo outlook in Peru, most interpersonal networks (occupational, acquaintanceship, and even friendship and family) do not function as solidary relationships giving security and support but are, on the contrary, "subject to high levels of strain and conflict." Thus, the ladinos seem, on the whole, to have been "disposed to view people as potentially dangerous . . . . Everyone is presumed to be out for himself and unscrupulous in pursuing self-interest. There is a pervasive fear of theft and of being cheated." A fear of being victimized or deceived is, therefore, found in the principal economic relationships, and the initial expectation is that "most interaction episodes will result in outcomes somehow unfavorable or disadvantageous." Ozzie Simmons, "The Criollo Outlook in the Mestizo Culture of Peru," *American Anthropologist,* Vol. 57 (1955), pp. 107–117. The following references are also useful for a perspective on the apparently wide geographical incidence of these and related traits: Tomás Fillol, *Social Factors in Economic Development: The Argentine Case,* Cambridge: The M.I.T. Press, 1961; Thomas F. McGann, "The Argentine Crisis and Aspects of Argentine Social Character," paper read to the conference on Latin American History, San Francisco, December, 1965; Raúl Scalabrini Ortíz, *El hombre que está solo y espera,* Buenos Aires: Librerías Anaconda, 1932; John Gillin, "Ethos Components in Modern Latin American Culture," *American Anthropologist,* Vol. 57 (1955), pp. 488–500; John Gillin, "Some Signposts for Policy," in R.N. Adams, et al., *Social Change in Latin America Today,* New York: Harper and Brothers, 1960; John Fayerweather, *The Executive Overseas,* Syracuse: Syracuse University Press, 1959; F. Harbison and C. Myers, *Management in the Industrial World,* New York: McGraw-Hill Book Co., Inc., 1959, chapter on Chile; William F. Whyte and Allan R. Holmberg, "Human Problems of U.S. Enterprise in Latin America," special issue of *Human Organization,* Fall 1956; Daniel Cosío Villegas, *Change in Latin America; The Mexican and Cuban Revolutions,* Lincoln: University of Nebraska Press, 1961, esp. pp. 2 and 20; Octavio Paz, *El laberinto de la soledad,* Mexico: Fondo de Cultura Económica, 1959; Ancieto Aramoni, *Psicoanálisis de la dinámica de un pueblo,* Mexico: Universidad Nacional Autónoma de México, 1961; Francisco González Pineda, *El mexicano: su dinámica psicosocial,* Mexico: Editorial Pax México, 1959; Rogelio Díaz Guerrero, *Estudios de psicología del mexicano,* Mexico: Antigua Librería Robredo, 1961; W.H. Holtzman, "Cross-Cultural Research on Personality Development," *Human Development,* Vol. 8 (1965), pp. 81–82; George Foster, "Interpersonal Relations in Peasant Society," *Human Organization,* Vol. 19, No. 4 (Winter 1960–61), p. 175.

72. D.C. McClelland, *The Achieving Society,* Princeton: D. Van Nostrand Co., Inc., 1961. For a summary statement of the topic see also McClelland's article on the relations between achievement motivation and economic growth: "Business Drive and National Achievement," *Harvard Business Review,* July–August 1962, pp. 99–112. Research relevant to this motivational bias has been reported by William F. Whyte, "The Cultural Environment and Industrial Relations: The Case of Peru," Symposium lecture at the New York State School of Industrial and Labor Relations, 1 October 1962; by Bernard C. Rosen, "The Achievement Syndrome and Economic Growth in Brazil," *Social Forces,* Vol. 42, No. 3 (March 1964), pp. 341–354; and by John Gillin, "Ethos and Cultural Aspects of Personality," in Sol Tax, et al., *Heritage of Conquest, the Ethnology of Middle America,* Glencoe, Illinois: The Free Press, 1952, Chap. 9. The author is endebted to Prof. William Henry, psychologist at the University of Chicago, for making available his analyses of the motivational content of tests conducted in Colombia and Mexico by E.E. Hagen, James Abegglan, and Louis Schaw. Part of the Colombian data is referred to in E.E. Hagen, *On the Theory of Social Change,* Homewood, Illinois: The Dorsey Press, Inc., 1962. Considerable insight into ladino motivation was also provided the author by Prof. Arden King, anthropologist at Tulane University, in the course of a Tulane University field seminar in Guatemala during the summer of 1951. It should also be mentioned that references to achievement motivation are conspicuously absent in the psychological studies cited previously.

73. Manipulation of others and use of their toil, in other words, are much more highly prized than the manipulation of things for achievement in the McClelland sense.

74. Examples are legion in colonial economic history. In the Mexican silk industry for instance, profitability was often a function of royal subsidies, forced labor, monopolistic concessions and/or the firms' illegal exploitation of labor under protection from friends in political position; Woodrow W. Borah, *Silk Raising in Colonial Mexico,* Berkeley: University of California Press, 1943, pp. 21, 32–39. Similarly, the differential advantage given to *consulado* merchants by monopolistic privileges was considerable; R.S. Smith, "The Institution of the Consulado in New Spain," *Hispanic American Historical Review,* Vol. 24, No. 1 (February 1944), pp. 71–76, and Count of Revilla Gigedo, *op. cit.,* pp. 116–117. The use of public office for private enrichment seems to have been widespread among treasury officials, the *corregidores,* and others: see, e.g., Juan de Aponte Figueroa, "Memorial que Trata de la Reformación del Reino del Pirú," in *Colección de documentos inéditos para la historia de España,* Madrid: Imprenta de la Viuda de Calero, 1867, Vol. LI, pp. 523–531; John H. Rowe, "The Incas Under Spanish Colonial Institutions," *Hispanic American Historical Review,* Vol. 37, No. 2 (May 1957), pp. 161–170. A.P. Whitaker, in *The Huancavelica Mercury Mine,* Cambridge: Harvard University Press, 1941, documents the same phenomenon in the mining industry, where private interests were also, on a selective basis, the beneficiaries of public largesse conveyed through the implied subsidy of *mita* labor, differential taxes, subsidized supplies of mercury, and the like. Forced labor allocations were resorted to in Peru, for example, to permit the continued operation of mines which ore depletion had caused to become uneconomic; M.A. Fuentes, ed. *Memorias de los vireyes que han gobernado el Perú,* Lima: Librería Central de Felipe Bailly, 1859, Vol. I, p. 305; Vol. II, p. 224. In both agriculture and *obrajes* as well as in mining, coerced labor was a source of substantial individual profit; while in commerce, special trading licenses not only enhanced legal profits but were valuable as a source of contraband profits. Jorge Juan and Antonia de Ulloa, in *Noticias secretas . . . ,* pp. 201, 231–254, 266–299, illustrate a variety of such business methods. The whole matter of land acquisition, as previously indicated, had a great deal to do with this politico-legal basis of business growth.

75. The deprecation of labor was therefore more than a status-colored attitude and indicated popular awareness that the opportunities to get ahead lay elsewhere than in a diligent application to labor and thrift. The economic virtues were, in fact, negated by the environment. In this connection the passionate dedication to games of chance

and the strong belief in luck may have several implications. According to one investigation (John and Mavis Biesanz, *The People of Panama,* New York: Columbia University Press, 1955, p. 369), all of the poor families interviewed "invested" weekly in the lottery, spending in many instances more on it than on rent. The trait is a pervasive one in Latin America, and some have interpreted it as a desire to gain without work that which would ordinarily necessitate long sustained efforts. "The game, as a psychic reaction, is an escape from the submission to discipline and obligation," in the view of Ena Mouriño Hernández *(El Juego en Cuba,* Havana: Ucar, García y Cïa., 1947, pp. 20-23). This may well be true so far as it goes, but the propensity to gamble could also rest in part upon the reasonably plausible assumption that regular work simply does not pay off or pay off very well, in which case a stroke of fortune is for many the only real hope of getting ahead. It is interesting to note that a number of countries have utilized this gambling propensity to siphon off savings for public investment purposes, not only through regular lotteries but also through the sale of savings bonds to which a lottery feature is attached.

NOTES FOR CHAPTER V

1. Prior to the establishment of the Royal Printing Office in 1808-09, only one printing press, so far as is known, had been imported into Brazil. This was set up in Rio de Janeiro in 1747 but was suppressed shortly thereafter by the Portuguese government. Some seventeen or eighteen colleges offering instruction at a level below the university level had been founded by the Jesuits, but these were closed with the expulsion of the Society in 1759. The only university in the Portuguese empire was that at Coimbra in Portugal. See Fernando de Azevedo, *Brazilian Culture,* New York: The Macmillan Company, 1950, pp. 339-363, 370.

2. Dan Stanislawski, *The Individuality of Portugal, a Study in Historical-Political Geography,* Austin: The University of Texas Press, 1959, pp. 124-133.

3. From this time until the Napoleonic disturbances of the early nineteenth century, the chief interruption of Portuguese independence occurred in the "Spanish captivity" of 1580-1640. During the first part of this interlude of foreign rule, Portugal was left in a semi-autonomous status with most of its laws and administration unchanged.

4. This is according to Stanislawski. Alan K. Manchester in his *British Preeminence in Brazil, Its Rise and Decline: A Study in European Expansion,* Chapel Hill: The University of North Carolina Press, 1933, pp. 1-2, dates the first written trade treaty at 1353 and the first political alliance at 1373. For present purposes, of course, the slight discrepancy is immaterial. The treaties indicate the relatively cosmopolitan orientation of the Portuguese state and help to explain why Portugal did not develop the siege polity which was evolved in Spain.

5. *Ibid.,* pp. 2-5.

6. For studies dealing with this important commercial connection, see V. M. Shillington and A. B. Wallis Chapman, *The Commercial Relations of England and Portugal,* London: G. Routledge & Sons, Ltd., 1907; F. Mauro, *Le Portugal et l'Atlantique au XVIIe siècle (1570-1670),* Paris: École Pratique des Hautes Études, 1960; and J. de Macedo, *À situação econômica no tempo de Pombal,* Porto: Livraria Portugália, 1951.

7. *Ibid.,* p. 1. In consequence of these treaties, however, British power shielded the Portuguese from further predations by the Dutch.

8. At the time this was particularly valuable, since the staples of the sixteenth- and seventeenth-century exchange had been on the wane for some time. The British had established their own supply sources for many of the main goods they had formerly obtained from the Portuguese colonies, and Portugal had begun, with tariff protection, to develop its own textile industry. In the Methuen Treaty, both trade flows were amplified again. Portuguese wines were given preference in the British markets of Europe and North America, and Portugal abandoned its attempt to displace woollen imports. A rising volume and rather diversified pattern of interchange ensued. Apart from wines, Portugal supplied Britain with salt and provisioned the English ships heading for the

Thirteen Colonies. In turn, it imported (aside from English textiles) rice and pitch from North America, American corn for Madeira, and fish from Newfoundland. The foregoing treaty was critical for our purposes in that it served to preserve and strengthen an economic tie which was previously headed for eclipse. The tie was to mean much to Brazil in the eighteenth and nineteenth centuries.

9. See, e.g., Fernando de Azevedo, *op. cit.*, pp. 139-163, and Gilberto Freyre, *The Masters and the Slaves, A Study in the Development of Brazilian Civilization,* New York: Alfred A. Knopf, 1946, pp. 30-31, 80, 226-229. The Inquisition in Brazil was even more desultory in its activities than the Spanish American version, despite the presence there of a proportionately greater number of foreigners and others of religious inclinations which, from a Catholic point of view, were dubious. Not one *ato de fé* was held in Brazil, for example, although many of the clergy were aware of the presence of potentially diverse religious views; see Pedro Calmon, *Historia social do Brasil,* São Paulo: Companhia Editôra Nacional, 1941, Vol. I, pp. 26-29. This broader ideological tolerance was perhaps indicative of the more casual attitude taken by the Portuguese monarchy towards its American colonies. As a consequence of this policy, the state had less inducement to employ the church as an active second arm of government control.

10. Werner Sombart, *The Jews and Modern Capitalism,* Glencoe, Illinois: The Free Press, 1951, p. 33; Gilberto Freyre, *op. cit.,* pp. 231 ff.

11. Cecil Roth, *A History of the Marranos,* Philadelphia: The Jewish Publication Society of America, 1932, pp. 73, 76 ff.

12. Roberto C. Simonsen, *História econômica do Brasil, 1500-1820,* São Paulo: Companhia Editora Nacional, 1937, Vol. II, p. 184. Happily, the company turned out to be a good investment.

13. During the temporary unification of Spain and Portugal, some Marranos appear to have fled to Spanish America where their background could not easily be traced and where, correspondingly, inquisitorial detection was less likely.

14. Manuel Diégues Júnior, *População e açúcar no nordeste do Brasil,* Rio de Janeiro: Comissão Nacional de Alimentação, 1952, pp. 43 ff.

15. Arnold Wiznitzer, *Jews in Colonial Brazil,* New York: Columbia University Press, 1960. Despite the exile of many of the Brazilian *cristãos novos* after the Dutch intervention of 1624-1654, others remained (to judge from the records of the Holy Office) to assist in the later economic growth of the colony.

16. Fernando de Azevedo, *op. cit.*, pp. 115-136; Gilberto Freyre, *op. cit.,* various places throughout text. Ralph Beals, in his "Social Stratification in Latin America," *American Journal of Sociology,* Vol. 58, No. 4 (January 1953), p. 327, also remarks that in Brazil, in contrast to Spanish America, "conflict situations tend to be resolved with less overt violence." In this connection, it is intriguing to note Albert O. Hirschman's brief aside on a possible difference between the role of social conflict in in present-day Chilean and Brazilian inflations. "The Chilean situation," Hirschman observes, "appears to be weighted more heavily with the avoidance of agreement, with the maintenance of a militant stance on the part of all contending groups." In contrast, he adds, the Brazilian case may be attributable to avoidance of overt dissent. See Albert O. Hirschman, *Journeys Toward Progress, Studies of Economic Policy-Making in Latin America,* New York: The Twentieth Century Fund, 1963, p. 209. See also Emilio Willems, "Portuguese Culture in Brazil," *Proceedings of the International Colloquium on Luso-Brazilian Studies,* Nashville, Tennessee: Vanderbilt University Press, 1953, pp. 68-78.

17. The leniency with which the Portuguese treated the Dutch invaders following the recovery in 1654 of Brazilian territories seized by the Protestant Netherlands was an early example of this temperamental bent. See Charles R. Boxer, *The Dutch in Brazil, 1624-1654,* Oxford: The Clarendon Press, 1957, pp. 241-244.

18. Brazilian terms for race are both varied and variable, but generally speaking *mestiço* includes Negro-white as well as Indian-white mixtures. *Mameluco, caboclo,* and *caipira* also designated Indian-white mixtures, the latter two terms ordinarily connoting, in addition, a rural person of low socio-economic status with a primitive level of cultural and educational development. Gilberto Freyre's *The Masters and The Slaves* constitutes a sort of fascinating Brazilian Kinsey report in tracing the racial amalgam of the

country, although it seems, at times, to explain Brazilian social development on the basis of a Freudian theory of history.

19. Tax exemptions and exclusive trading privileges in certain goods were among the inducements offered by the crown.

20. The first *donatário,* for example, was Fernão de Noronha who, in a consortium organized along with other New Christians, established the first enterprise in northern Brazil for the exploitation of dyewood. Not long afterwards the group was among those which fostered the establishment of a colonial sugar industry.

21. Two works by Eulália M. Lahmeyer Lobo are particularly useful for indicating the contrasts with Spanish colonial administration: *Administração colonial Luso-Espanhola nas Américas,* Rio de Janeiro: Editôra Companhia Brasileira de Artes Gráficas, 1952, and *Processo administrativo Ibero-Americano,* Rio de Janeiro: Biblioteca do Exército Editôra, 1962.

22. For an especially informative study of the importance of local government in Portuguese colonial administration, see Charles R. Boxer, *Portuguese Society in the Tropics,* Madison: The University of Wisconsin Press, 1965.

23. See Roger Bastide, *Brésil, terre des contrastes,* Paris: Hachette, 1957, pp. 25 ff.

24. The *fazenda* was the landholding, while, strictly speaking, the *engenho* designated a primitive sort of sugar mill which was driven by water power or draught animals. In looser usage, however, the term *engenho* referred also to the sugar plantation surrounding the mill, since virtually all of the mills were part of plantations rather than independent or separate enterprises. From this more general usage, the term, *senhores de engenhos,* was employed to mean sugar plantation owners. Not all *fazendas,* however, were sugar estates. Some were large cattle ranching spreads, and later on the term came to be used to designate coffee and cacao plantations.

25. Even the *capitão-môr,* a military office which recruited and directed the local militia, was, more often than not, held by a prominent *fazendeiro* of the district.

26. While the Portuguese crown was not altogether insensitive to the doctrines preached by the church on the matter of Indian rights, it did not go to the lengths of the Spanish monarchs in implementing the ecclesiastically propounded natural law doctrines through protective legislation. A more practical and commercial compromise was reached with the settlers in 1611 when the crown authorized the enslavement of Indians captured in warfare or those who, in slavery, would be "protected" thereby against the predations of other aboriginals. Since the Brazilian tribes tended to be bellicose anyway, both among themselves and in resistance to the Portuguese, the agreement constituted the *de facto* extension of official sanction to the chief *paulista* enterprise.

27. Lewis Hanke, *Aristotle and the American Indians,* Chicago: H. Regnery Company, 1959, describes graphically the violent reactions provoked in Brazil when the Jesuits attempted to promulgate the papal bull of 1639 which forbade enslavement of the indigenous population.

28. The point is made in Freyre's *The Masters and the Slaves* and also in his *New World in the Tropics,* New York: Alfred A. Knopf, 1959, pp. 69-71. In such a subordinate office, the chaplain, who was often a kinsman of the owner, largely occupied himself with tutoring the offspring of the *senhor de engenho* and ministering to the routine religious needs of the *fazenda's* inhabitants.

29. According to Noel Deerr, *The History of Sugar,* London: Chapman, 1949-1950, Vol. II, p. 453, Dutch capital was heavily involved in developing the Brazilian sugar industry in the sixteenth century, not only through financing the marketing of the output but also in financing production and slave imports.

30. Although the aggregate annual rainfall in "good" years would appear to be adequate for crop production, it is unevenly distributed, being almost entirely concentrated in one part of the year. Furthermore, the rainfall in the sertão is highly variable from year to year and is not forthcoming at all during the irregularly recurring *secas* or droughts. Even in good years, the net utilizable precipitation is reduced by high temperatures, which make for a high rate of evaporation; over the centuries deforestation has also increased the amount of runoff.

31. Mills of two types were in use in colonial times. The *engenhos d'agua* were driven by water and had a milling capacity of about thirteen tons a day. The *trapiches* had about half the milling capacity of the water-powered mills and utilized animal power.

32. Alfredo Ellis Júnior, in his *A evolução da economia paulista e suas causas,* São Paulo: Companhia Editôra Nacional, 1937, pp. 34-35 ff., finds evidence that at an early period the *paulistas,* a goodly number of whom were descendents of the Sephardim, were unusually venturesome in their enterprises, since their backwater environment offered few easy opportunities for business success. The narrow coastal plain and the more distant location made São Paulo (or São Vicente, the original name of the territory) less suitable for cane cultivation than the northeastern sugar coast. Although a variety of crops could be grown and livestock was raised in the interior, there was little that could serve as a regional export. For this reason, the region's balance of payments could not support the importation of African slaves. In the absence of sufficient "foreign exchange" cover for African manpower imports, Indian slavery, which could be mobilized by internal resources (the local settlers living off the land on their expeditions) developed as an import substitute industry. In addition to providing for local slave requirements, the business gave São Paulo an exportable product which could be sold to the sugar coast to finance the southern region's rather modest imports.

33. Charles Boxer, *The Dutch in Brazil, 1624-1654,* p. 20. During the Dutch occupation there was a further, if temporary, liberalization of colonial trading privileges.

34. Roberto C. Simonsen, *op. cit.,* Vol. I, p. 129.

35. During the period of Spanish domination (1580-1640) the official policy was that the Portuguese and Spanish possessions should be separately administered For their part, the Portuguese colonials resisted Spanish penetration successfully, and anti-Spanish feeling was widespread. At the same time, the enterprising Portuguese (labeled, indiscriminately, Portuguese and Jews by the Spaniards) made considerable inroads into Spanish American traffic and were the occasion of numerous protests to the crown from the viceregal governments in Lima and Mexico City.

36. The Brazilian term is *derruba e queimada* or felling-and-burning.

37. Alan Manchester, *op. cit.,* p. 22.

38. Rival Latin American exporters — Ecuador, Colombia, and Venezuela — became important in the nineteenth-century world market, and African producers posed a still more serious threat later on, but Brazil has remained a leading factor in the world market for cacao until the present time.

39. The attitudinal conditioning provided by this protracted experience, which had its inception in early colonial times, produced a backward lower-class subculture that has persisted down to the present day, making it difficult to introduce programs to cope effectively with the problems of the northeastern interior.

40. The barriers to diversified regional growth produced by these conditions have carried over into the present-day problems of the Brazilian northeast. The lasting effects of the system are set forth with clarity in one of the finest brief socio-economic analyses that have been made for any Latin American country, Jacques Lambert's *Os dois Brasis,* Rio de Janeiro: Ministério de Educação e Cultura, 1959. A close runner up is the previously cited *Brésil, terre des contrastes* by Roger Bastide.

41. Indeed, because of deforestation, erosion, and soil mining, the boom probably left the region with higher real cost levels than it had at the beginning. Since the chief element in the ceteris paribus assumption — the state of the industrial arts — did in fact remain unchanged, the classical argument for diminishing returns was very likely a valid description of secular economic relationships on the Brazilian sugar coast.

42. See Roberto C. Simonsen, *op. cit.,* Vol. II, pp. 93-96, for a summary of the various estimates of production.

43. Basilio de Magalhães, *Expansão geográfica do Brasil colonial,* São Paulo: Companhia Editôra Nacional, 1935, pp. 70-171.

44. In this population movement out of the northeast, one sees an early example of the region's continuing later role as a reservoir of manpower for other areas of the country. In subsequent years it supplied labor for the coffee boom in southern Brazil, for the rubber boom of Amazonia, and more recently, inhabitants for the growing

industrial cities' slums.

45. See Manoel S. Cardozo, "The Brazilian Gold Rush," *Americas,* Washington: Vol. 3 (October 1946), pp. 137-160, and André João Antonil, *Cultura e opulencia do Brasil,* Bahia: Livraria Progresso Editôra, 1950.

46. Roger Bastide, *op. cit.,* p. 145 ff., contains a succinct overview of some of the sociological changes.

47. See, for example, V. Magalhães Godinho, "Flottes de sucre et Flottes de l'or, 1670-1770," *Annales, économies, sociétés, civilisations,* Vol. 5 (1950), pp. 184-197, and H. E. S. Fisher, "Anglo-Portuguese Trade, 1700-1770," *The Economic History Review,* second series, Vol. 16, No. 2 (1963), pp. 219-233.

48. João Pandiá Calógeras, *A History of Brazil,* Chapel Hill: University of North Carolina Press, 1939, pp. 42-43.

49. The effects of this growing interaction among regions were not always, however, beneficial to each of the regions involved. To some extent, the declining sugar economy was dislocated further by the impact of the mining boom which raised the prices of slaves, metals, cloth, cattle, and horses. Many of the freemen who worked in the plantation economy left for the mining centers, and so did a fair number of small farmers, whose exodus caused a shortage of food crops.

50. On a modest scale, some of the southern Brazilian wheat and flour was even exported to Argentina in the liberalized trading system of late colonial days, for until the iron plow was introduced in the nineteenth century the thick pampa grasses could not be cleared to permit the cultivation of grains.

51. The *paulistas* were resentful of the detachment of the mining area from their captaincy and also felt that recent immigrants received preferential treatment from the royal bureaucracy.

52. Roberto C. Simonsen, *op. cit.,* Vol. II, pp. 188-189. Apart from the concessions given the early *donatários,* only two other privileged commercial companies had been operative up to this time. One, the Companhia do Maranhão, was short lived (1678-1684) and nugatory as regards its constructive contribution to development. The other, the Companhia Geral do Commercio do Brasil, was established in 1649 and endured, with various modifications, until expropriated (with compensation) by the government in 1694, after which it operated as a state enterprise until 1720. During its existence, the company provided convoy services, for which it charged, and held a monopoly of the trade in oil, flour, wine, codfish, and brazil wood. *Ibid.,* pp. 184-187.

53. Antonio de Sousa Pedroso Carnaxide, *O Brasil no administração pombalina,* São Paulo: Companhia Editôra Nacional, 1940, pp. 92-93.

NOTES FOR CHAPTER VI

1. ECLA, *The Economic Development of Latin America and its Principal Problems,* Lake Success: United Nations Department of Economic Affairs, 1950.

2. In some ways, the term "reflex economy" seems to be preferable to the more generally employed term, "dependent economies." Economic interdependence being what it is in the mordern age (a function of international specialization and all the advantages thereof), the tendency to speak of the Latin American situation as that of dependence has often imparted an unjustifiable pejorative connotation, has masked the fruitful interdependence characteristic of highly productive national economies, and has probably played a role in motivating Latin American public opinion to acquiesce in, if not press for, policies ostensibly aimed at achieving an autarkic position. The term "reflex" does not call into question the facets of interdependence but rather, draws attention to the character of response and to the relative importance of movements responsive to external stimuli as contrasted with autonomously initiated or endogenously induced changes.

3. Interestingly, a hundred years later the post-World War II "remodernization" of European agriculture occasioned a Peruvian sequel in the form of the fishmeal boom.

4. See Nicolás García Samudio, *La independencia de hispanoamérica,* Mexico: Fondo de Cultura Económica, 1945, for a discussion of the great impact upon Latin American political thought of the U.S. Declaration of Independence and Constitution, and of the statements of U.S. revolutionary leaders.

5. In 1805 a royal decree called for the religious foundations to liquidate their mortgage holdings immediately and to transfer to the royal treasury for shipment to Spain the liquid capital resulting from this act. Given the preeminent role of religious communities in the system of colonial finance, the subsequent efforts to raise cash by recalling ecclesiastical loans and mortgages produced a violent antigovernment reaction on the part of the clergy as well as on the part of the landowners, merchants, and miners to whom the churchmen were creditors. See, for example, the interpretation of this measure offered in Enrique Lafuente Ferrari's *El Virrey Iturrigaray y los orígenes de la independencia de Méjico,* Madrid: Consejo Superior de Investigaciones Científicas, Instituto Gonzalo Fernández de Oviedo, 1941.

6. For discussions of the interesting *comunero* revolt, which anticipated several later political and social issues of importance in Colombia, see Jesús María Henao and Gerardo Arrubla, *Historia de Colombia,* Bogotá: Librería Colombiana, Camacho Roldán y Cía., 1936; José Manuel Groot, *Historia eclesiástica y civil de Nueva Granada, escrita sobre documentos auténticos,* Bogotá: M. Rivas y Cía., 1890, Vol. II; Germán Arciniegas, *Los comuneros,* Bogotá: Editorial ABC, 1939. The Túpac Amaru revolt was more restricted in compass, being almost entirely an expression of Indian interests, whereas the *comunero* rebellion included criollo and mestizo interests along with indigenous elements. The uprising led by Túpac Amaru is discussed in Daniel Valcarcel, *La rebelión de Túpac Amaru,* Mexico: Fondo de Cultura Económica, 1947.

7. Since the two priests, defrocked by a Hispanophile hierarchy, subsequently became national heroes, the literature relating to their movements is staggering in quantity. For what it reveals of the loss of ideological and institutional unity, however, it is germane to note that the Túpac Amaru rebellion in Peru, like the Hidalgo-Morelos insurrections, counted members of the clergy among its sympathizers.

8. See Luis Thayer Ojeda, *Elementos étnicos que han intervenido en la población de Chile,* Santiago: 1919, p. 59. Many of the Basques and Catalans also harbored separatist sentiments in Spain itself, it should be noted.

9. Herbert E. Priestley, *José de Gálvez, Visitor-General of New Spain, 1765-1771,* Berkeley: University of California Press, 1916.

10. For reports of the viceregal accomplishments in Nueva Granada, see José Antonio García y García, ed., *Relaciones de los vireyes del Nuevo Reino de Granada, ahora Estados Unidos de Venezuela, Estados Unidos de Colombia y Ecuador,* New York: Hallet and Breen, 1869.

11. To illustrate an interesting institutional contrast, it might be noted that as of the early seventeenth century the English kings had already chartered 34 international trading companies.

12. D. L. Molinari, *La representación de los hacendados de Mariano Moreno,* Buenos Aires: Universidad de Buenos Aires, Facultad de Ciencias Económicas, 1939, pp. 72-73, 78-79. On the other hand, the viceroys, who enriched themselves by selling trading licenses to foreigners, were in favor of freer trade policies *(ibid.,* p. 74). At the time several proposals were made to remedy the balance of payments deficit produced by freer trade by requiring that all or a part of the imports be paid for by exports of local goods *(ibid.,* pp. 153, 196-197).

13. Mexico (government), Secretaría de Gobernación, *La administración de Don Frey Antonio María de Bucareli y Ursúa, cuadragésimo sexto virrey de México,* Publicaciones del Archivo General de la Nación, XXX, Mexico: Talleres Gráficos de la Nación, 1936, 2 Vol., sheds light on some of these sectional conflicts, as does Vito Alessio Robles, ed., *Miguel Ramos Arizpe, discursos, memorias e informes,* Biblioteca del Estudiante Universitario, No. 36, Mexico: Universidad Nacional Autónoma de México, 1942, pp. 80-85. See also Lillian E. Fisher, *Background of the Revolution for Mexican Independence,* Boston: Christopher Publishing House, 1934, and Robert S. Smith,

"Shipping in the Port of Veracruz, 1790-1821," *Hispanic American Historical Review,* Vol. 23, No. 1 (February 1943).

14. For information on late colonial trade dislocations, see: Miron Burgin, *The Economic Aspects of Argentine Federalism, 1820-1852,* Cambridge: Harvard University Press, 1946, pp. 9-16, which examines particularly the undermining of the traditional economy of the interior of the Argentine; S. H. Wilcocke, *History of the Viceroyalty of Buenos Aires,* London: H. D. Symonds, 1807, pp. 529-533, which notes the decline in internal trade among Argentina, Paraguay, Bolivia, Peru, and Chile; Ricardo Levene, *A History of Argentina,* Chapel Hill: University of North Carolina Press, 1937, pp. 122 ff., which describes the adverse impact of imports on the colonial Argentine rice, wine, and manufacturing industries; M. S. Fuentes, ed., *Memorias de los vireyes que han gobernado el Perú,* Lima: Librería Central de Felipe Bailly, 1859, Vol. VI, pp. 80,81, 110, 121, 126, which records official awareness of the disruption of Lima's trade and the import-induced decline of manufacturing in Peru, along with a suggestion to restrict imports in the interest of raising employment levels; *ibid.,* Vol. III, p. 258, which contains an official's recognition of the trade shifts engendered in Peru by the opening of the port of Buenos Aires; *Mercurio Peruano,* Vol. 1, No. 1 (2 January 1791) and Vol. I, Nos. 23 and 31 (20 March 1791 and 17 April 1791) which contain information on Peruvian trade changes and manufacturing dislocation; *Instrucciones que los vireyes de Nueva España dejaron a sus sucesores,* Mexico: Imprenta de Ignacio Escalante, 1873, Vol. I, pp. 317-318, which comments on trade and industrial desplacement in Mexico; *Memoria del Virrey del Perú, Marqués de Avilés,* Lima: Imprenta del Estado, 1901, pp. 66-67, 91, which notes the decline in Peruvian commerce and the weakening of Peru's fiscal resources by creation of the viceroyalty in Buenos Aires; Pedro M. Oliveira, *La política económica de la metrópoli,* Lima: Imprenta la Industria, 1905, pp. 95-99, which notes that cheap European imports rather than royal legislation brought a shutdown of colonial industries; Eduardo Arcila Farías, *Comercio entre Venezuela y México en los siglos XVI y XVII,* Mexico: Fondo de Cultura Económica, 1950, pp. 15-33, which observes that trade liberalization ruptured the fundamental economic unity of the empire.

15. An American diplomat's account of the lurid political situation of Central America during this period contains much that is instructive for an understanding of the obstacles to economic development posed by civil turmoil. See John Lloyd Stephens, *Incidents of Travel in Central America, Chiapas, and Yucatán,* New Brunswick, New Jersey: Rutgers University Press, 1949. Stephens notes also the extremely primitive transport conditions which prevailed in the region in that day. See also G. A. Thompson, *Narrative of an Official Visit to Guatemala from Mexico,* London: John Murray, 1828; Henry Dunn, *Guatimala, or the United Provinces of Central America in 1827-8,* New York: G. and C. Carville, 1828; Ephraim G. Squier, *The States of Central America,* New York: Harpers, 1858; Arthur Morelet, *Travels in Central America, Including Accounts of Some Regions Unexplored since the Conquest,* London: Trübner, 1871; and Robert G. Dunlop, *Travels in Central America,* London: Longman, Brown, Green, and Longman, 1847—all of which are helpful for the insight they provide into the problems of doing business in a backward environment.

16. Among the geographically contiguous Central American countries, for example, few roads or railways were built to link together the production and market centers of the region. Thus the factor and product markets of the several nations developed quite independently of each other.

17. The harm done to the Ecuadoran economy by the conflicts of this period is mentioned in Oscar E. Reyes, *Breve historia general del Ecuador,* Quito: Editorial "Fray Jodoco Ricke," 1955-1956, Vol. I, pp. 223-224 (for late colonial times) and Vol. II, pp. 482-483 (for independence).

18. See Miron Burgin, *The Economic Aspects of Argentine Federalism, 1820-1852,* Cambridge: Harvard University Press, 1946.

19. After the nightmarish struggle, Paraguay passed into economic and political obscurity until its victory in the Chaco war with Bolivia in 1932-1935 temporarily brought it back into the news.

20. The second war against Chile resulted in a loss of the country's access to the sea and the territory which contained its increasingly valuable nitrate deposits.

21. In Venezuela, for example, there were at least 50 major rebellions from 1830 to 1900, and 13 times the central government was violently overthrown.

22. Robert Potash, *El Banco de Avío de México; el fomento de la industria, 1821-1846,* Mexico: Fondo de Cultura Económica, 1959, contains considerable useful information on Mexican policy developments during this early period, as does Agustín Cue Canovas, *La industria en México,* Mexico: Ediciones Centenario, 1959. One of the most interesting sources, however, is a two-volume biography of the man who was perhaps the most ardent early advocate of industrialization and who was himself a prominent textile manufacturer: Miguel A. Quintana, *Estevan de Antuñano, fundador de la industria textil en Puebla,* Mexico: Secretaría de Hacienda y Crédito Público (Boletín Bibliográfico División), 1957.

23. Basilio de Arrillaga, *Informe que dieron los señoras D. José Ruíz de la Bárcena, Comisario de Guerra Honorario, D. José Maria de Echabe y Teniente Coronel D. Gregorio Sáenz de Cicilia, Prior y Consules del Real Tribunal del Consulado de México, al Excmo. Sr. D. Juan Ruíz de Apodaca, Virey Gobernador y Capitán General de esta Nueva España, contestando a una Representación suscrita por doscientos veinte y nueve vecinos de Veracruz, que pretendieron se abriera aquel puerto al comercio con extrangeros amigos o neutrales contra el Dictamen de su Consulado, de su Junta de Gobierno y de otros muchos vecinos de la propia ciudad,* Mexico: Arizpe, 1818.

24. Luis Ospina Vásquez, *Industria y protección en Colombia, 1810-1930,* Medellín: Editoral San Francisco, 1955, pp. 85-194. Ospina Vásquez's invaluable book is thus far the classic economic history of Colombia. On page 119 and elsewhere in the cited section, there are, incidentally, a number of interesting early references to the remarkable economic agility and enterprise of the *antioqueños.*

25. Many of the liberals were well aware of the problems created by their cultural tradition but hoped that the panacea of education would reshape values and social psychology in a more modern direction, though education itself was slighted continuously in the allocation of public expenditures.

26. The prevalent attitude towards the Indians during the republican era is summed up in a statement by the philosopher Alejandro Deustúa, who was influential in the formation of Peruvian educational philosophy. Believing the Indians to be biologically incapable of development, Deustúa concluded that "the Indian is a machine and cannot be anything else" — quoted in Lewis Hanke, *Aristotle and the American Indians,* Chicago: H. Regnery Company, 1959, p. 105. See also the disdainful views of the Indians expressed by the Bolivian Alcides Arguedas, the Mexican Francisco Bulnes, and the Argentine Domingo Sarmiento, as reported in William Rex Crawford, *A Century of Latin American Thought,* Cambridge: Harvard University Press, 1961. In view of the prominence of the exponents of racist views and prejudices, it is perhaps understandable that governments felt morally and intellectually justified in their disregard of indigenous welfare.

27. See Andrés Molina Enríquez, *Los grandes problemas nacionales,* Mexico: Imprenta de A. Carranza e Hijos, 1909, pp. 88 ff., and Anselmo de la Portilla, *España en México, Cuestiones históricas y sociales,* Mexico: Imprenta de I. Escalante y Cía., 1871, p. 87, for observations on the changed legal status of Indians. Formerly exempt from military service, they were, under republican rule, often conscripted by various warring political factions. Further, various tax exemptions which the Indians enjoyed under colonial rule were removed, and thereafter, the natives were subject to arrest and abuse for tax delinquency.

28. Except in Brazil, Chile, and Costa Rica, the military dominated politics during most of the century. See Edwin Lieuwen, *Arms and Politics in Latin America,* New York: Frederick A. Praeger, Inc., 1960, Chaps. 1 and 2 for the best single treatment of this phenomenon.

29. *Ibid.,* p. 19.

30. *Ibid.,* p. 17.

31. For a thorough exposition of the fiscal disorder which prevailed in a typical case, see Walter F. McCaleb, *The Public Finances of Mexico,* New York: Harper and Brothers, Publishers, 1921, especially Chaps. 2-9. See also L. H. Jenks, *The Migration of British Capital to 1875,* New York: Alfred A. Knopf, 1927. pp. 109-115, for a short but informative account of the erratic state of public finance in Mexico up to the latter part of the nineteenth century.

32. Two useful studies of preindependence and postindependence foreign penetration are: J. B. Williams, "The Establishment of British Commerce with Argentina," *Hispanic American Historical Review,* Vol. 15, No. 1 (February 1935), pp. 43-64; and John Rydjord, *Foreign Interest in the Independence of New Spain,* Durham: Duke University Press, 1935. Something of the flavor of the thinking of the times is given in the translator's preface to Domingo Juarros, *A Statistical and Commercial History of the Kingdom of Guatemala,* London: George Cowie and Co., 1825, p. v: Spanish America will "probably, in a short time, open a most extensive field for the employment of British capital and British industry, and ultimately prove an inexhaustible source of advantage to the various branches of our manufactures and commerce."

33. See, for example, the discussion by José M. L. Mora in his *Obras sueltas,* Paris: Librería de Rosa, 1837, Vol. I, pp. 429 ff., of the substantial loans obtained by Mexico before 1833 through such London firms as B. A. Goldschmidt and Co., and Barclay, Herring, Richardson and Co.; L. H. Jenks, *op. cit.,* pp. 45-49, 53-59, 63-64, 70, discusses the sordid experience with the early revolutionary loans and suggests that the initial easy access of the new governments to the British capital market simply encouraged irresponsible behavior. Also informative of the misappropriations and chicane which characterized this period of public finance and external borrowing is the account of John Miers, *Travels in Chile and La Plata,* London: Baldwin, Cradock, and Joy, 1826, Vol. II, pp. 168-169, 203-204, 210-217. Miers reports that Chilean ministers in England used fraud and misrepresentation to float large loans in London, the proceeds of which were largely disbursed to government officials or otherwise wasted, and that, on the side, such ministers even participated in selling mining stocks of the blue-sky variety to a gullible investing public. According to Miers, *op. cit.,* Vol. II, pp. 166-167, British merchants resident in Chile lent considerable sums to the government and turned in the government bonds they received (together with those they purchased at a discount from others) at full value in payment of import duties. Because of the government's dependence on them, they were also able to engage openly in a great deal of smuggling activity. In the meantime (pp. 188-189) a rapid inflation had got under way in the 1820's.

34. The prostration of the Mexican mining industry during the early nineteenth-century is described in Modesto Bargalló, *La minería y la metalurgia en la América española durante la época colonial,* Mexico: Fondo de Cultura Económica, 1955, pp. 290, 355-366, who also takes note of various efforts by European entrepreneurs during the thirties and forties to establish new smelters. C. B. Merwin, *Three Years in Chile,* Columbus: Follett, Foster, and Co., 1861, p. 32, observes that as late as 1855 the silver mines near Iquique, Peru, were still flooded and unworked since the revolution for independence.

35. Luis Peñaloza, *Historia económica de Bolivia,* La Paz: privately printed, 1953-54, 2 Vols., provides an excellent picture of conditions in this early period. Bolivian mining, however, had already been declining before independence: S. H. Wilcocke, *History of the Viceroyalty of Buenos Aires,* London: H. D. Symonds, 1807, pp. 149 ff.

36. In addition to the previously cited work by Potash, a useful short account of the efforts of the Banco de Avío in Mexico to establish industries is found in Manuel Carrera Stampa, *Los gremios mexicanos: La organización gremial en Nueva España, 1521-1861,* Mexico: Edición y Distribución Ibero-Americana de Publicaciones, S. A., 1954, pp. 289-291. Established in 1830, the bank, which was funded by the government, imported machinery for a variety of industries and contracted with foreign technicians to teach and manage in the factories. It also lent money at low interest rates to private industrial firms to purchase at cost the machinery imported by the bank and to build and operate the plants for the machinery. In addition, useful promotional work was undertaken in agriculture by the bank. In 1842, however, the bank had to close its

doors, having failed because of (a) the narrowness of the markets for the new industries it established, (b) the exhaustion of state funds by payments to troops, and (c) the loss of part of the imported machinery during civil disturbances. Nevertheless, the enterprises it had launched often remained as a nucleus for mid-century industralization efforts. For an analysis of this, and related, experiments, see Henry G. Aubrey, "Deliberate Industrialization," *Social Research*, Vol. 16, No. 2 (June 1949), pp. 158-182. Aubrey presents convincing arguments for the general validity or appropriateness of the conservatives' interventionary approach to development in nineteenth-century Mexico, while indicating the nature of the contemporary obstacles to industrial development. Similar insight into the industrial development problems of the period is to be found in Howard F. Cline, "The 'Aurora Yucateca' and the Spirit of Enterprise in Yucatán, 1821-1847," *Hispanic American Historical Review*, Vol. 27, No. 1 (February 1947), pp. 30-60.

37. Apart from the general disruption of the financial system of colonial times, substantial capital flight appears to have accompanied the wars for independence in several regions, most notably Peru and Mexico. See, e.g., L. H. Jenks, *op. cit.*, p. 109, and R. A. Humphreys, ed., *British Consular Reports on the Trade and Politics of Latin America*, London: Royal Historical Society, 1940, pp. 114-115.

38. Disruption of the communications system and the breakdown of the rudimentary economic intelligence-gathering system of the bureaucracies and the *consulados* meant that reliable market information on prices, costs, and the like was extremely difficult to come by at a time when all of these items were becoming more variable because of the dissolution of the imperial system of economic controls.

39. For one of the numerous examples which could be cited to illustrate this point, see the vicissitudes of the river navigation company established in Colombia by a German businessman and those of other enterprises in the 1830's and 1840's as reported in R. L. Gilmore and J. P. Harrison, "Juan Bernardo Elbers and the Introduction of Steam Navigation on the Magdalena River," *Hispanic American Historical Review*, Vol. 28, No. 3 (August 1948), pp. 335-360. The article is also quite useful for its picture of the general environmental obstacles to business success during the first decades of independence in Colombia.

40. W. T. Easterbrook, "Uncertainty and Economic Change," *The Journal of Economic History*, Vol. 14, No. 4 (Fall 1954), pp. 346-360. Specific uncertainties refer, among other things, to the predictability of supply or cost factors and demand (or price and profit) factors. Primary uncertainties would include such things as possibilities of drastic changes in asset values and the distribution of assets through unforeseeable changes in government policy.

41. A particularly good résumé of the damage done by fighting and political division is found in Charles C. Griffin, "Economic and Social Aspects of the Era of Spanish American Independence," *Hispanic American Historical Review*, Vol. 29, No. 2 (May 1949), pp. 170-187. Griffin's article is also extremely useful as a guide to the literature on other aspects of economic dislocation during the period.

42. One of the most interesting cases concerns the Colombian tobacco industry, whose inception as a crown monopoly was one of the most successful instances of governmental entrepreneuring in the colonial age. Until 1850 the industry continued under governmental auspices and enjoyed considerable success in developing export markets for a quality output and in tying in with British commercial houses from which certain banking functions were obtained. For a while after the industry was turned over to private enterprise, it continued to ride the crest of the boom, but eventually the deficiencies of private organization led to decline and deterioration. J. P. Harrison, "The Evolution of the Colombian Tobacco Trade to 1875," *Hispanic American Historical Review*, Vol. 32, No. 2 (May 1952), pp. 163-174.

43. John Miers, *op. cit.*, Vol. II, pp. 168-169, 203-204, notes that even before 1826 the Chilean government, needing funds, had expropriated monastic estates and other church lands (and funds) and had distributed these among favorites and political insiders from the upper classes in payment of real or supposititious debts. In Colombia the church lands were lost to private latifundists in 1861 according to Orlando Fals-Borda, *El hombre y la tierra en Boyacá*, Bogotá: Ediciones Documentos Colombianos, 1957, p. 101.

44. See Eduardo Nieto Arteta, *Economía y cultura en la historia de Colombia,* Bogotá: Ediciones Librería Siglo XX, 1941, pp. 169-173; Luis Ospina Vásquez, *op. cit.,* pp. 189, 196-197; Orlando Fals-Borda, *op. cit.,* pp. 98 ff.

45. Emilio Romero, *Historia económica del Perú,* Buenos Aires: Editorial Sudamericana, 1949, pp. 275-281. The destruction of the indigenous communal properties of Peru is also noted in Jorge Basadre, *Perú: problema y posibilidad,* Lima: F. y E. Rosay, 1931, pp. 117-118, 190-191; and Luis E. Valcarcel, *Ruta cultural del Perú,* Mexico: Fondo de Cultura Económica, 1945, pp. 133, 138-139.

46. Luis Peñaloza, *Historia económica de Bolivia,* La Paz: privately printed, 1953, Vol. I, pp. 278-294.

47. N. L. Whetten, *Guatemala, The Land and the People,* New Haven: Yale University Press, 1961, p. 94, indicates the persistence of this pattern to the present day. Even many of the native freeholders, however, have such small parcels that they must hire out as part-time workers on the nearby large properties.

48. Since, with independence, the large landholders came into control of government, the ability to influence public policy added enormously to the " fringe benefits" which *hacendados* realized from latifundism. This, too, must be regarded as an "economy of scale" not available at all to the smaller landholding units. The existence of these supplementary values (i.e., ability to influence government, ability to hire labor monopsonistically, ability to rig local markets, etc.) for large properties tended to bid up the supply price of land to artificially high levels since its market value as an asset depended upon the imputable worth to the owner of these other latifundium-related functions. Thus, the influence of externalities on the land market deterred land acquisition by either the actual tenant operators or the growing number of landless natives.

49. The marketing apparatus was also, as mentioned earlier, appropriate to the conditions of supply flows, especially in much of agriculture and what remained of handicraft manufacturing: i.e., the frequent but irregular feeding of small quantities of output into the distribution system. It should also be kept in mind that the provincial distribution system of Latin America has always absorbed many part-time workers, which condition, given the amount of underemployment in agriculture and the limited employment alternatives available, does not seem to represent an unreasonable use of labor within the terms set by the whole system. In other words, lacking access to land and other cooperant factors (capital and management), underemployed units of agricultural labor power could be economically utilized in small scale trading where no land, little capital, and little refined managerial skill was required. If their returns from this activity were low, they might nevertheless have been higher than in existing alternatives and were, therefore, net returns in terms of the opportunity costs of labor.

50. Manuel Carrera Stampa, *op. cit.,* pp. 275-279, details the gradual abolition of the guild system in Mexico. In some cases, however, the guild system lingered on a bit longer, although in a very much weakened form. See, for example, Jorge Basadre, "La Riqueza Territorial y las Actividades Comerciales e Industriales en los Primeros Años de la República," *Mercurio Peruano,* Vol. 18, No. 15 (January 1928), p. 19.

51. Francisco R. Calderón, *Historia moderna de México: La república restaurada, La vida económica,* Mexico: Editorial Hermes, 1955, pp. 212-213. Calderón reports that most credit transactions in the early nineteenth century were handled through these commercial houses, but in addition there were innumerable smaller moneylending firms which sprang up to prey usuriously on the desperation of their clientele.

52. The Robertson brothers, who were merchants in Buenos Aires during the early 1800's, have left a valuable account of the business life of the times, including a description of the manner in which merchants financed production by advancing money *(habilitaciones)* to producers in exchange for a contract to purchase their output at a fixed price. John P. and William P. Robertson, *Letters on South America: Comprising Travels on the Banks of the Paraná and Río de la Plata,* London: J. Murray, 1843, Vol. I, p. 174.

53. John Miers, *op. cit.,* Vol. II, pp. 275-286, 287 ff., is especially instructive concerning contemporary problems in launching new business activities.

54. Luis Roque Gondra, *Historia económica de la República Argentina,* Buenos Aires: Editorial Sudamericana, 1943, p. 387.

55. Emilio Romero, *Historia económica del Perú,* Buenos Aires: Editorial Sudamericana, 1949, pp. 355-356.

56. R. Hawkins, *Observations of Sir Richard Hawkins in His Voyage into the South Sea in the Year 1593,* London: The Hakluyt Society, 1847, p. 157 (editorial note added for 1847 edition).

57. Luis López de Mesa, *De cómo se ha formado la nación colombiana,* Bogotá: Librería Colombiana, 1934, pp. 108-109.

58. Ramón Velóz, *Economía y finanzas de Venezuela desde 1830 hasta 1944,* Caracas: Impresores Unidos, 1945, pp. 26, 82.

59. Luis Peñaloza, *op. cit.,* Vol. II, pp. 111 ff.; López de Mesa, *op. cit.,* p. 108. Peñaloza notes that Colombian competition was felt keenly since the high market price established by the official control scheme had also encouraged a considerable expansion of output in Bolivia.

60. E. J. Pratt, "Anglo-American Commercial and Political Rivalry on the Plata, 1820-1830," *Hispanic American Historical Review,* Vol. 11, No. 3 (August 1931), pp. 302-335.

61. John Miers, *Travels in Chile and La Plata,* London: Baldwin, Cradock, and Joy, 1826, Vol. I, p. 164.

62. Maria G. Callcott, *Journal of a Residence in Chile During the Year 1822,* London: Longman, Hurst, Rees, Orme, Brown, and Green, 1824, p. 130. The stores were full of all kinds of European goods for the upper classes, though most of the population made everything except hats and shoes for themselves (*ibid.,* p. 125). Some German artisans (e.g., blacksmiths) were already present in Chile at this early date, as were English tailors, shoemakers, saddlers, and innkeepers (*ibid.,* p. 131). Other English immigrants had set up butcheries, were corning meat, and were making candles superior to those made by the customary local processes. See also: Basil Hall, *Extracts From a Journal Written on the Coasts of Chili, Peru, and Mexico in the Years 1820, 1821, 1822,* Edinburgh: Archibald Constable and Co., 1824, Vol. 2, p. 60 (for mention of foreign merchants in Santiago), p. 65 (for Lima), and pp. 184 ff. (for western Mexico). According to John Miers, *op. cit.,* Vol. II, pp. 239 ff., most of the foreign trade and wholesaling in Chile in the 1820's was in the hands of British commission houses.

63. J. F. Rippy, "French Investments in Mexico," *Inter-American Economic Affairs,* Vol. 2, No. 3 (Winter 1948), pp. 3-16, and Robert A. Potash, *El Banco de Avío de Mexico, El fomento de la industria, 1821-1846,* Mexico: Fondo de Cultura Económica, 1959, pp. 226-227. By 1865, aided, doubtless, by the intervention of Napoleon III, the French owned more than 400 industrial and mercantile establishments in Mexico.

64. Stanley J. Stein, *The Brazilian Cotton Manufacture; Textile Enterprise in an Underdeveloped Area, 1850-1950.* Cambridge: Harvard University Press, 1957.

65. J. F. Rippy, "Investments of Citizens of the United States in Latin America," *The Journal of Business of the University of Chicago,* Vol. 22, No. 1 (January 1949), pp. 17-29.

66. By 1865, for example, at least thirty (mostly British-owned) trade and commission houses were operating in Central America, gradually taking on banking functions to develop the local production of exportable items and even, when foreclosure procedures were necessary on outstanding loans, entering into production of these items. Charles Wilson, *Empire in Green and Gold,* New York: Holt, Rinehart, and Winston, Inc., 1947, p. 39. References to the various foreign merchants and other immigrant entrepreneurs in Central American mining and agriculture in 1840 are found throughout John L. Stephens, *op. cit.*

67. José M. L. Mora, for example, reports how the public debt of Mexico in 1833 had been financed to a large extent by forced loans extracted from the *consulados* of Veracruz and Mexico City, from various religious institutions, and to a lesser extent, from wealthy individuals. The dissipation of the proceeds and the decline in the value of the government bonds wiped out the capital reserves of these previously important sources of funds. J. M. L. Mora, *op. cit.,* Vol. I, pp. 413 ff.. Luis Ospina Vasquez, *op. cit.,* pp. 145-146, notes that during the 1830's in Colombia there was discussion of establishing a national bank but that nothing came of it; one bank, the Banco Colonial Británico was finally opened in Cartagena in 1839 but did not survive for long. Not

until 1871, with the establishment of the Banco de Bogotá, did a bank successfully survive in Colombia. As for interest rates, John Miers, *op. cit.,* Vol. II, p. 184, observes that already in 1824 Chilean interest rates ranged from 12-18 per cent, a level substantially higher than that which was charged by colonial lending institutions.

68. Both Callcott and Miers took note of the protracted litigation and high incidence of lawsuits in the early postcolonial period in Chile, in which respect a popular colonial custom continued unabated. M. G. Callcott, *op. cit.,* p. 236, and J. Miers, *op. cit.,* Vol. II, p. 242.

69. In this concatenation of conditions – the economic usefulness of state favors, the financial and other advantages of access to the machinery of government, the existence of several access routes (land ownership, partisan political manoeuver, military promotion and intervention) to the formal power structure – one finds the proximate origins of the multiple career pattern, a widely encountered phenomenon in Latin America. Individuals found, in other words, that there were distinct advantages in pursuing several careers more or less simultaneously: holding a putative "economic" occupation (e.g., as a landowner, financier, or merchant), involvement in the legal profession, activity in party politics and/or military endeavor, occupancy of a public post of an administrative or legislative nature, efforts as a political essayist, etc. Given the interpenetration of the different orders of social structure, very definite "economies of complementarity" could be realized by participation in several career lines, economies which gave greater returns and/or afforded more insurance against unexpected reverses than did intensive specialization in one field alone. The classic analysis of this phenomenon is Anthony Leeds, "Brazilian Careers and Social Structure: An Evolutionary Model and Case History," *American Anthropologist,* Vol. 66, No. 6, Part I (December 1964), pp. 1321-1347.

NOTES FOR CHAPTER VII

1. For this reason especially, Latin America is no exception to A. J. Youngson's observation that in most known cases success in the export sector has played an initiating role in the early stages of development. A. J. Youngson, *The Possibilities of Economic Progress,* Cambridge: The Cambridge University Press, 1959.

2. Figures for 1853-1873 are from Michael G. Mulhall, *The English in South America,* Buenos Aires: The "Standard" Office, 1878, p. 583; those for later years are from H. S. Ferns, *Britain and Argentina in the Nineteenth Century,* Oxford: The Clarendon Press, 1960, pp. 492-493.

3. Le Baron d'Anthouard, *Le progrès brésilien; la participation de la France,* Paris: Plon-Nourrit et Cie., 1911, pp. 68, 386, 392. So far as concerns the price of coffee, the chief export by far, the New York price had reached a high in 1890-1891, but had fallen to less than a third of the peak price by 1902-1903.

4. Figured in terms of constant pesos of the 1900-1901 value; *Estadísticas económicas del Porfiriato: comercio exterior de México, 1877-1911,* Mexico: El Colegio de México, 1960, p. 78.

5. Luis López de Mesa, *De cómo se ha formado la nación colombiana,* Bogotá: Librería Colombiana, 1934, p. 109. It is probable that these were 60-kilogram bags, so that the 1915 figure represented some 66,000,000 kilograms.

6. Ramón Velóz, *Economía y finanzas de Venezuela desde 1830 hasta 1944,* Caracas: Impresores Unidos, 1945, pp. 89, 170, 314.

7. Tomás Soley Güell, *Historia monetaria de Costa Rica,* San José: Imprenta Nacional, 1926, pp. 283-284.

8. Luis Peñaloza, *Historia económica de Bolivia,* La Paz: privately printed, 1953, Vol. I, pp. 213, 233-234.

9. For discussions of these investments, see Simon G. Hanson, *Economic Development in Latin America,* Washington: The Inter-American Affairs Press, 1950, Chap. 12; Cleona Lewis, *America's Stake in International Investments,* Washington: The Brookings Institution, 1938; J. F. Rippy, *British Investments in Latin America, 1822-1949,* Chaps. 3 and 4; Max Winkler, *Investments of United States Capital in Latin America,* Boston:

The World Peace Foundation, 1929; *International Capital Movements During the Inter-War Period,* United Nations, 1949, p. 2; H. Feis, *Europe, the World's Banker, 1870-1914,* New Haven: Yale University Press, 1930; *Foreign Capital in Latin America,* United Nations, Department of Economic and Social Affairs, 1955, Chap. 1. The estimates of investment magnitudes vary somewhat from study to study; Feis, for example, estimates the total of British investments in Latin America in 1913 as $3,682 million (p. 23), whereas Rippy and Winkler report figures closer to $5 billion (Winkler, p. 280, Rippy, p. 68). Unfortunately, the studies do not provide sufficient data to enable one to reconcile these discrepancies, but the difference is not important for present purposes.

  10. J. F. Rippy, *op. cit.,* pp. 23-25. During the sixties and seventies, however, some £70 million of the £123 million invested in public issues had gone into default, the largest defaulters being Peru (£33 million), Mexico (£23.5 million), Cost Rica (£3.8 million), Honduras (£3.2 million), Colombia (£2.1 million), and Ecuador (£1.8 million). L. H. Jenks, *The Migration of British Capital to 1875,* New York: Alfred A. Knopf, 1927, pp. 117-123, 195, and 270-291 *passim,* contains useful information on the terms of negotiation and the chicanery involved in these public loans. Of the £180 million total British investment in 1880, between £20 million and £30 million were liabilities carried over from the time of the wars for Spanish American independence and a further portion represented other past refunding operations.

  11. The foregoing distribution by categories of British investment summarizes the information presented in Chapter IV of Rippy's study of British overseas investments. The proportion that these represented of the total British overseas investment is noted in H. Feis, *op. cit.,* p. 21. For other information on the British participation in Latin American development, see: Alan K. Manchester, *British Preeminence in Brazil, Its Rise and Decline, A Study in European Expansion,* Chapel Hill: University of North Carolina Press, 1933; Alfred Tischendorf, *Great Britain and Mexico in the Era of Porfirio Díaz,* Durham, N. C.: Duke University Press, 1961; H. Feis, *op. cit.;* Henry S. Ferns, *Britain and Argentina in the Nineteenth Century,* Oxford: The Clarendon Press, 1960. Part III of Michael G. Mulhall, *The English in South America,* Buenos Aires: "Standard" Office, 1878, is quite informative for the early and middle decades of the century. Mulhall notes, p. 335, that the number of British residents in Buenos Aires province exceeded 30,000 by 1878.

  12. H. Feis, *op. cit.,* p. 51. Late Porfirian Mexico was especially attractive to the French, as there the expansion of French investments between 1900 and 1910 was very great — in the neighborhood of an eightfold increase. See J. F. Rippy, "French Investments in Mexico," *Inter-American Economic Affairs,* Vol. 2, No. 3 (Winter 1948), pp. 3-16.

  13. J. F. Rippy, "French Investments in Latin America," *Inter-American Economic Affairs,* Vol. 2, No. 3 (Winter 1948), pp. 52-71. For French economic activity in two of the major capital-receiving countries, there are particularly informative French studies: M. P. Arnaud, *L'Émigration et le commerce français au Mexique,* Paris: L. Boyer, Imprimeur, 1902, and Le Baron d'Anthouard, *Le progrès brésilien; la participation de la France,* Paris: Plon-Nourrit et Cie., Imprimeurs-Editeurs, 1911, especially Chap. 7.

  14. J. F. Rippy, "Investments of Citizens of the United States in Latin America," *The Journal of Business of the University of Chicago,* Vol. 22, No. 1 (January 1949), pp. 17-29, is the best short survey of these investments, but one should also consult the other references cited earlier for a more detailed exposition of trends.

  15. J. F. Rippy, "Notes on the Early Telephone Companies of Latin America," *Hispanic American Historical Review,* Vol. 26, No. 1 (February 1946), pp. 116-118. Also of significant interest for this period are J. F. Rippy, "Relations of the United States and Guatemala During the Epoch of Justo Rufino Barrios," *Hispanic American Historical Review,* Vol. 22, No. 4 (November 1942), pp. 595-605, which contains an account of North American railway companies and land companies in the opening up of Guatemala during the 1870's; J. F. Rippy, "Dawn of the Railway Era in Colombia," *Hispanic American Historical Review,* Vol. 23, No. 4 (November 1943), pp. 650-663; W. H. Gray, "Steamboat Transportation on the Orinoco," *Hispanic American Historical Review,* Vol. 25, No. 4 (November 1945), pp. 455-469; David M. Pletcher, *Rails, Mines,*

and Progress, Some American Promoters in Mexico, 1867-1911, Ithaca, New York:
Cornell University Press, 1958.

16. H. Feis, *op. cit.*, p. 74, places the total in 1914 at $900 million; according
to Rippy, the total in 1918 was $677 million − see J. F. Rippy, "German Investments
in Latin America," *The Journal of Business of the University of Chicago,* Vol. 21,
No. 2 (April 1948), pp. 63-73, J. F. Rippy, "German Investments in Argentina," *The
Journal of Business of the University of Chicago,* Vol. 21, No. 1 (January 1948), pp. 50-
54, provides a more detailed examination of German foreign investment activity in the
country in which Germans were most active, while J. F. Rippy, "German Investments
in Guatemala," *The Journal of Business of the University of Chicago,* Vol. 20, No. 4
(October 1947), pp. 212-219, surveys a smaller country in which German interests in
land, banking and insurance, and trading firms played a leading role in developing the
coffee production for which Germany was the chief customer. M. G. Mulhall, *Rio Grande
do Sul and Its German Colonies,* London: Longmans, Green, and Company, 1873, contains
some useful information on the Germanic settlement of southern Brazil, together with
quite a number of observations concerning British activity in the same area.

17. As late as the mid-1930's, it was estimated by the Guatemalan Central Coffee
Office that only 5 per cent of the value of coffee exports was handled by domestically
owned firms. Sixty-four per cent of the trade was carried on by German firms, 18 per
cent by United States firms, and 7 per cent by British firms. (Estimate cited by Chester
Lloyd Jones, *Guatemala, Past and Present,* Minneapolis: The University of Minnesota
Press, 1940, p. 208. Jones' scholarly study is, beyond question, the most useful source
of information on Guatemalan economic history and far surpasses any work available in
Spanish.)

18. The Gildemeister interests in Peru included also mining firms and a foreign
trade house.

19. Chapters 13 through 16 of Robert F. Foerster, *The Italian Immigration of Our
Times,* Cambridge: Harvard University Press, 1919, contain a comprehensive description of Italian activities in Argentina and Brazil.

20. See Luis Peñaloza, *op. cit.,* Vol. II, Chap. 80, for an account of the enterprise
launched by Simon Patiño, "The Tin King," a concern which reincorporated as a
Delaware corporation and came to include British and United States capital. For a brief
sketch of the development of the Grace company, established over a hundred years ago
in Peru by an astute Irish immigrant, see E. W. Burgess and F. H. Harbison, *Casa
Grace in Peru,* Washington, D.C.: National Planning Association, 1954. The Aramayo
group of mines, founded by Carlos V. Aramayo, a Bolivian, was later incorporated in
Switzerland with substantial capital participation by British and Swiss investors.

21. Not until the 1960's was through rail service available between Bogotá and
the coast.

22. The Mexican rubber plantations venture is described in Chap. 16 of J. F.
Rippy, *Latin America and the Industrial Age,* New York: G. P. Putnam's Sons, 1947
(2nd edition), an interesting source of vignettes about other foreign investments in the
region and which contains many possibly significant clues for further research employing economic analysis. The Costa Rican railway history, in which 19 years were required for connecting San José with the Caribbean port of Limón, is covered in résumé
in Chester Lloyd Jones, *Costa Rica and Civilization in the Caribbean,* pp. 85-91,
101-104; of greatest interest in the Costa Rican experience is its revelation of the
incredibly unsound financial practices pursued by the government and its European
investment banker co-conspirators.

23. The case of Bolivian mining presents something of an anomaly in that, while
small-scale foreign prospectors and entrepreneurs were active in Bolivia during the
late nineteenth century, two of the three largest tin mining companies were initiated by
Bolivians (albeit with foreign collaboration). In most instances in Latin America,
domestic turbulence seems to have placed national entrepreneurs at a disadvantage
vis-à-vis their foreign counterparts, who could draw resource support from the more
stable foreign scene and occasionally count on consular and other diplomatic intervention to grant them some measure of immunity from local strife. Bolivia was, however, one

of the most politically disturbed of all countries in Latin America. Conceivably, its domestic turmoil was so unappealing to the major foreign interests that such shrewd national entrepreneurs as Patiño and Aramayo were able to get a head start before would-be foreign competitors found it propitious to move in on a large scale.

24. See T. W. Hutchison, *Village and Plantation Life in Northeastern Brazil*, Seattle: University of Washington Press, 1957, for an account of this transformation.

25. M. Mulhall, *Rio Grande do Sul . . .*, p. 183.

26. During the latter half of the nineteenth century in Guatemala, for example, many export-oriented coffee *fincas* were established. Most of the largest were owned by foreign, especially German, immigrants. By 1914 it was estimated that nearly half of the country's coffee production came from properties owned by foreigners, with over one-third from the German-owned *fincas* alone. In that year, 1,657 Guatemalan owned *fincas* produced an average of 317 quintals of coffee; the 170 German-held *fincas* averaged over 2,100 quintals of coffee. *Memoria de la secretaría de fomento para 1914*, Guatemala: Tipografía Nacional, 1915, p. 7.

27. P. Walle, *Le Perou économique*, Paris: E. Guilmoto, Editeur, 1908, p. 183. On p. 159, Walle notes that most of the large littoral estates owned by Peruvians had employed foreign technicians, e.g., agronomists from France, England, Germany, and the United States. Sugar mill engineers from these countries and from the Netherlands were also prevalent. See also Thomas F. Sedgwick, *Relating to the Sugar Industry in Peru*, Trujillo, Peru: Imprenta Haya, Verjel y Cía, 1905, p. 4, and Chaps. 12 and 13 of Percy Martin, *Peru of the Twentieth Century*, London: Edward Arnold, 1911.

28. M. Mulhall, *Rio Grande do Sul . . .*, p. 182, cites a typical instance of this native adoption of foreign practices in describing his visit to an Uruguayan *estancia* which raised herds of Rambouillet sheep. Although foreign enterprise accounted for most of the innovations, there were some important exceptions. Successful expansion of the cotton culture of the Peruvian coast, for example, owed much to the experimentation conducted by an agriculturist from Ica, Fermín Tangüis. The premium grade variety of the fiber he developed has since been known by his name.

29. For example, the Buenos Aires stock exchange, known as the Bolsa de Comercio, was founded in 1854. See Chap. 9 of C. A. Tornquist, ed., *The Economic Development of the Argentine Republic in the Last Fifty Years*, Buenos Aires: Ernesto Tornquist and Co., Ltd., 1919, for information on its development by the First World War.

30. Jonathan V. Levin, *The Export Economies; Their Pattern of Development in Historical Perspective*, Cambridge: Harvard University Press, 1960, Part I. Levin's account of the partial transformation of Peru during the guano age illustrates a number of points relevant to this section of the chapter, especially the strategic role of foreign enterprise and of foreign finance of the export sector and the changing nature of domestic socio-economic structures.

31. M. Mulhall, *The English in South America*, p. 396. In association with other capitalists, Edwards later founded a bank in Bolivia and the Banco de San Juan in Argentina. Working with the North American promoter William Wheelwright, Edwards was also an important financial backer of the Copiapó rail line in Chile.

32. Luis Roque Gondra, *Historia económica de la República Argentina*, Buenos Aires: Editorial Sudamerica, 1943, pp. 447-448, and Paul B. Souweine, *L'Argentine au seuil de l'industrie*, Paris: Imprimerie des Etablissements Casterman, 1927, pp. 248, 282.

33. M. Arnaud, *op. cit.*, p. 131. French capital from abroad also came into Mexican banking during this period following liquidation of French interests in the Suez canal. During the 1880's there appears to have been a special movement of Spanish capital into Mexican banking.

34. T. Soley Güell, *op. cit.*, p. 49; *ibid.*, pp. 450-457, indicates the part played by foreign capital in others of the early, rather ephemeral, banking institutions.

35. P. Walle, *op. cit.*, pp. 79, 362-365.

36. M. P. Arnaud, *op. cit.*, pp. 67 ff., 93 ff.

37. M. Mulhall, *The English in South America*, Chaps. 34, 41, 42, and 43; R. Foerster, *op. cit.*, Chap. 14.

38. Stanley J. Stein, *The Brazilian Cotton Manufacture; Textile Enterprise in an Underdeveloped Area, 1850-1950,* Cambridge: Harvard University Press, 1957, p. 71. According to Stein, the non-British importers were aided by the arrival of the telegraph and by the growing practice of European manufacturers of establishing direct sales representatives in overseas markets. The market position of British trading firms was undercut because merchants in Brazil could, through these channels, bypass the local British importers and order directly from Europe. Furthermore, Portuguese firms were able to count on financial support from the homeland to a degree exceeded only by the British system of commercial finance, while Portuguese clerks in Brazilian banks and trading firms appear to have helped in furthering "the displacement of their entrenched British competitors."

39. R. Foerster, *op. cit.,* pp. 314-316.

40. To the extent that the capitalization of foreign-owned primary industries was built up out of reinvested earnings, it may be said that they contributed to the growth of Latin American productive capacity in essentially the same fashion; apart from the direct effect on local production abilities of imported machinery and technicians, these enterprises were also foreign-introduced vehicles for capital accumulation in Latin America.

41. The well-known Venezuelan firm of H. L. Boulton and Company, for example, dates back to a general trading agency established there in 1827 by English immigrants. Aside from serving as general agent for some 12 steamship lines, the company has holdings in breweries, cement, a ceramics factory, and a vegetable-oil processing plant, and established in 1942 the internal Venezuelan airline, Avensa. In the early 1960's the company joined with the Venezuelan government to form Viasa, an international airline, the late Henry Lord Boulton (Caracas-born and a Venezuelan citizen) serving as its first director.

42. The ambiguity which is encountered in properly identifying such firms as "national" or "foreign" derives chiefly from two sources: (a) the maintenance of ethnic identity by the proprietary families and (b) the dual citizenship which is often permitted in the legal systems of Europe and Latin America.

43. An early example of this, Thomas Armstrong (1800-1875) married into the wealthy criollo Villanueva family. For half a century, Armstrong contributed greatly to the economic development of Buenos Aires as proprietor of one of the most important commercial houses, as a director of the Provincial Bank, as a participant in the Central Argentine Railway Company and the Ensenada Port and Railway Company, and as a negotiator for the Buschenthal loan of 1862. M. Mulhall, *The English in South America,* pp. 417-419.

44. See, for example, the discussions of these *pensadores* in Harold Eugene Davis, *Latin American Social Thought,* Washington, D.C.: The [American] University Press, 1961, Chaps. 7-12, 14, 20, 21, and 23, and William Rex Crawford, *A Century of Latin American Thought,* Cambridge: Harvard University Press, 1961 (revised edition).

45. See the discussion of J. M. L. Mora in Leopoldo Zea, *El positivismo en México,* Mexico: Fondo de Cultura Económica, 1943, pp. 87-94, 124-125.

46. R. A. Potash, *op. cit.,* pp. 189-218, indicates, however, the extensive range of interventionist devices employed by the Mexican state to foster domestic industrialization alongside foreign investment in mining. Liberal political economy had not, in other words, been adopted altogether without modification.

47. Leopoldo Zea's study, *Apogeo y decadencia del positivismo en México,* Mexico: El Colegio de México, 1944, is one of the classic studies of the Mexican case, as is his previously cited *El positivismo en México.*

48. H. E. Davis, *op. cit.,* pp. 189, 188 (sentences quoted in reverse order of appearance in book). In some countries, the influence of positivism was so dominant that it carried over well into the twentieth century. See, e.g., Enrique Molina, "La filosofía en Chile en la primera mitad del siglo xx," in Universidad de Chile, Departamento de Estudios Generales, *Desarrollo de Chile en la primera mitad del siglo XX,* Santiago: Ediciones de la Universidad de Chile, 1953, pp. 445-453.

49. As Zea demonstrates in his *Apogeo y decadencia* . . . , especially pp. 23-42, positivism was offered as something of a synthesis, combining the liberals' aspirations for progress with the conservatives' more realistic regard for order. Development economics appears, in many respects, to be the present-day counterpart to positivism.

50. Zea, *El positivismo en México*, pp. 121-126, gives Gabina Barreda's early pronouncements on these points, while on pp. 171-177, the blatant apologia of later positivists such as Miguel Macedo are presented. Some, such as Manuel Ramos (pp. 179-184), resorted to the crude evolutionary views of social Darwinism to abjure social welfare measures to help the poor, who were deemed to be biologically inferior. Lastarria in Chile was similarly hostile to welfare legislation, as were many in other nations.

51. So excessive was the zeal for emulation of things foreign that later reaction often viewed the period as something of a sell-out of the national heritage. The Mexicans, with their characteristic facility in such matters, coined the term *malinchismo* to describe nineteenth-century governmental and intellectual leaders. *Malinchismo* is derived from Malinche, the name of the Indian woman who betrayed her people for the amatory and material favors of Hernán Cortés.

52. As Frederick Pike has noted, the cult of economic individualism was especially strong in Chile where Jean Gustave Courcelle-Seneuil was the chief theoretician of liberal economics. An avid partisan of free trade and *laissez faire*, Courcelle-Seneuil had great influence in the drafting of trade and monetary policy, both directly as advisor to the Minister of Finance and indirectly through his disciples, Zorababel Rodrigues, Marcial González, and Miguel Cruchaga Montt. Frederick B. Pike, *Chile and the United States, 1880-1902*, Notre Dame: The University of Notre Dame Press, 1963, pp. 9-10.

53. The great Chilean intellectual leader of early middle class radicalism, Letelier, was already veering from positivism towards socialism, but his call for an economically active state was nevertheless expressive of positivistic policy-in-practice elsewhere in Latin America. See his speech to the Radical party in 1896 which was reprinted in *Anales de la Universidad de Chile*, Año CXV, No. 105, (Primer Trimestre, 1957). As one of the "certified" Mexican positivistic *científicos* put it in 1905 (Augustín Aragón, "Un documento histórico," *Revista Positiva*, Mexico: Tip. Económica, Vol. 5, p. 238), "Now we are very far from that which constituted the ideals of the youth in our schools of some thirty years ago, since the sphere of government daily increases more and more and it is seen as utopian to want to bring about anything in the spiritual order without the powerful assistance of the state."

54. Because of this feature of positivist policy, the perspicacious Mexican economic historian, Daniel Cosío Villegas, has commented that liberalism did not achieve a complete victory anywhere in Latin America and that by the turn of the century, "there were signs of a return to a political organization similar to the one. . . received from Spain. . . a central political organization, somewhat authoritarian, in which initiative and *ultima ratio* rested with the state." Daniel Cosío Villegas, *Change in Latin America; The Mexican and Cuban Revolutions*, Lincoln: University of Nebraska Press, 1961, pp. 16-17.

55. The real property of hospitals, universities, colleges, etc., was also expropriated and sold in Mexico and Colombia, depriving these institutions of a significant portion of their revenue and causing them great harm — as was noted by Luis Ospina Vasquez, *op. cit.*, p. 234.

56. The classic study of the Colombian developments in this period is James J. Parsons, *Antioqueño Colonization in Western Colombia*, Ibero-Americana Series, No. 32, Berkeley: University of California Press, 1949. Portions of the eastern cordillera were also settled to a considerable extent in smaller-scale units, especially towards the north. In regions closer to the older population centers, however, e.g., in the department of Cundinamarca, the large landowning unit tended to predominate with the spread of coffee cultivation.

57. Soon after independence, the government of Costa Rica had given vigorous encouragement to coffee cultivation (introduced in the late 1700's) so that by 1829 it

was the most important single product in the country. Coffee production was exempted from payment of tithes and free title to lands of the public domain was ceded to those who put the lands in coffee plantings over a period of five years. (Chester Lloyd Jones, *Costa Rica and Civilization in the Caribbean,* Madison: University of Wisconsin Studies in the Social Sciences and History, No. 23, 1935, p. 58). A German merchant resident in San José is believed to have been the first to export coffee (in 1832 to Chile). Later on, British and German firms became the leaders in handling the marketing and shipping of the product.

58. London coffee merchants facilitated the growth of larger units of coffee production by advancing Costa Rican growers money on coffee futures, funds which were used to acquire the lands of small coffee farmers who had, owing to price swings, defaulted on production loans.

59. Actually, indigo production and export had been generally diminishing since the early 1790's, losing out to rival producers in Salvador, Venezuela, and elsewhere. On the other hand, cochineal, which had been an important export product in the seventeenth century, was reviving to the extent that in the early years of the republic it surpassed indigo exports in value. Thereafter it rose to a peak around mid-century, at which time it constituted almost the entirety of Guatemalan exports. The value of cochineal exports reached nearly $5 million in the 1851-55 period, according to Squier, *(op. cit.,* p. 528), but after displacement by chemical dyestuffs, exports diminished so rapidly that in 1884 only $406 of cochineal were sold abroad (William T. Brigham, *Guatemala, the Land of the Quetzal,* New York: Scribner's, 1887, p. 338).

60. In Costa Rica, the first important banana plantations were started by Minor C. Keith to provide freight traffic for the railway line he was constructing. Costa Rica was the first country of Central America to produce bananas for export, the initial shipments being made to New Orleans in 1878. There, as in others of the banana producing countries, the early period of industrial development included many small operators in the production stage. Though some of these remained and other small-scale growers entered from time to time, several factors contributed to the comparatively swift transition to large-scale enterprise. Economies of scale played a role, and because banana acreage in the region was subject to such natural catastrophes as blight and storms, the larger concerns, with acreage scattered over several regions and countries, enjoyed an overall security not available to the small producer, all of whose assets were located in one spot. Moreover, the marketing function was critical since the perishable nature of the product placed a high premium on synchronizing production and harvesting with shipping services and disposal of the product in the overseas market outlets. Thus, not only were those companies which controlled the expensive distribution facilities in a position to dominate all production stages of the industry, but also they were under considerable pressure to exercise this dominance in the form of vertical integration in order to obtain maximum coordination of all stages of the industry. Foreign firms located in the consuming centers had, of course, a marketing advantage (market contacts, knowledge of demand, etc.) that was not available to Latin American interests, added to which was the superior advantage of foreign concerns in acquiring the capital necessary to establish the expensive distributional facilities and to install superior production facilities.

61. The techniques of land distribution listed were the more or less official or publicly sanctioned measures. On the side, more land was added to the larger estates from smaller private holdings by foreclosures on mortgages (often used in Central America by the larger *fincas* as a means of acquiring smaller coffee holdings) and, as always, by simple force and robbery. One of the more imaginative land "entrepreneurs" of the day was a Mexican general sent to the state of Chihuahua in command of troops charged with the task of subduing Indians who were on the warpath and jeopardizing the safety of the ladino residents of the area. The general's family owed their status as the largest Mexican landholders in the state to his thoughtful foresight in delaying the army's entrance into Chihuahua until he had acquired at panic-sale prices a considerable number of properties from landowners fleeing south for their lives.

62. By the early twentieth century, various foreign observers were struck by the

undesirable economic and social consequences of the spread of latifundism. Noting the advances made in certain plantations along the Peruvian coast during the nineteenth century, a French commentator went on to add that, "Malheureusement, sur beaucoup de points de la Costa, mais surtout dans la Sierra et dans la Montaña, le plus grand nombre d'entre les hacendados emploie encore, en agriculture, les procédés de culture les plus rudimentaires, par routine ou par l'ignorance, si bien que les champs ne produisent pas les récoltes qu'ils devraient raisonnablement produire...En second lieu, la mauvaise division du sol: il y a trop et de trop grandes propriétés, cela limite la production, restreint la population et l'immigration; ces grandes propriétés restent souvent incultes, faute de capitaux ou d'initiative: des vallées entières de plusieurs centaines de milliers d'hectares appartiennent à une ou deux familles..." Paul Walle, *op. cit.* pp. 160-161; see also p. 177, *ibid.*.

63. Reproduced in C. L. Jones, *Guatemala, Past and Present*, p. 150. Chap. 12 of Jones' study of Guatemala gives a detailed account of the evolution of Guatemalan labor practices.

64. Article on mining labor in *Peru To-Day*, Vol. I, No. 7 (September 1909), p. 14. In Guatemala, the police were used to round up workers for a textile mill which was afflicted with a chronic problem of absenteeism. Manning Nash, *Machine Age Maya, The Industrialization of a Guatemalan Community*, Glencoe, Illinois: The Free Press, 1958, p. 14.

65. Around 80,000 of the imported coolies were employed in coastal agriculture, the balance going to the guano islands and to railway construction. The definitive study of this traffic in labor is Watt Stewart's *Chinese Bondage in Peru*, Durham, N.C.: Duke University Press, 1951.

66. Oscar Álvarez Andrews, *Historia del desarrollo industrial de Chile*, Santiago: Imp. y Lit. La Ilustración, 1936, p. 178.

67. According to a talk by John C. McClintock, vice-president of the United Fruit Company, reprinted in Dan Fenn, editor, *Management Guide to Overseas Operations*, New York: McGraw-Hill, 1957, pp. 33-40.

68. According to E. Romero, *Historia económica del Perú*, pp. 353-354, Peru had endeavored to promote domestic wheat and rice cultivation by a series of protectionist measures in the 1830's but with such unsatisfactory results that agricultural protectionism was soon abandoned.

69. H. S. Ferns, "Investment and Trade Between Britain and Argentina in the Nineteenth Century," *Economic History Review*, Second Series, Vol. 3 (1950), pp. 205-206; John C. Rayburn, "Rail Transportation in Venezuela," *Inter-American Economic Affairs*, Vol. 10, No. 4 (Spring 1957), p. 23.

70. O. Álvarez Andrews, *op. cit.*, p. 160.

71. J. S. Duncan, *Public and Private Operation of Railways in Brazil*, New York: Columbia University Press, 1932, pp. 22-23.

72. *Ibid.*, p. 26.

73. Owing to the financial support channeled into utility and railway concerns by public loan issues, the direct foreign investment in these fields seriously understates the actual external capital invested in infrastructure.

74. Jonathan Levin, *op. cit.*, Part I. The guano contract drawn up in 1841 gave the government 65 per cent of the profits, a portion which was revised in the following year to yield the government over 75 per cent of the profits.

75. After borrowing abroad to finance the government's operation of the mines, the Balmaceda administration decided to sell the industry to Chilean investors. When these proved unwilling to purchase the nitrate mines on a large scale, the government settled for increased state supervision of the industry.

76. See Servando Alzati, *Historia de la mexicanización de los ferrocarriles nacionales de México*, Mexico: La Empresa Editorial "Beatriz de Silva," 1946.

77. Julio C. Jobet, *Ensayo crítico del desarrollo económico-social de Chile*, Santiago: Editorial Universitaria, S. A., 1955, p. 68. Rising nitrate revenues permitted the Chilean government to suppress the taxes inherited from the days of colonialism.

78. Most of the locally financed insurance companies had collapsed during the

war with Chile. The 1895 legislation required the foreign company branches to maintain a minimum level of funds on deposit in Peru, following which action several foreign companies left the scene and local companies reappeared. The 1901 legislation shifted the business even more into national hands by requiring that all insurance reserves be invested in Peruvian mortgages, government securities, or other local assets.

79. This is, of course, excluding the earlier experiments in Mexico during the first half of the nineteenth century which were referred to in the preceding chapter.

80. Adolfo Dorfman, *Historia de la industria argentina*, Buenos Aires: Escuela de Estudios Argentinos, 1942, pp. 97-101. Under the administration of President Germán Riesco in Chile (1902-1906), the government began an even more frankly protectionist policy in the interest of promoting new industries and for the sulfuric acid and beet sugar industries went so far as to pay subventions for units of industrial output. Oscar Álvarez Andrews, *op. cit.*, pp. 185-186. In 1909, the administration of President Pedro Montt exempted from all import duties the equipment and machinery necessary for developing Chilean siderurgical industries.

81. The relatively free trade policy followed for a time occasioned much distress among the local machine construction industry which had grown up around mid-century. Developed largely by immigrant mechanics, this domestic capital-goods industry was able to offer sugar machinery to the Peruvian plantations with delivery schedules much more rapid than those of imported European and U. S.-manufactured equipment. Later on, improvements in maritime transport and international communications worked to the advantage of overseas suppliers, and the local industry entered a period of decline — with out, however, disappearing. For an interesting brief account of one firm in this field, see "Industrial Peru: Machinery Construction as Conducted by a Representative Establishment," *Peru To-Day*, Vol. 1, No. 9 (November 1909), pp. 25-28. The firm described, the Pieza Liza Foundry, had been established by Messrs. Stanton and White, later sold to a man from Manchester, and purchased in 1907 by Robert Reid, a Scottish mechanical engineer who had been working with railway companies in Peru.

82. It seems likely that some of these early firms may have received protection because of the influence possessed by their sponsors. One of the early cotton mills, for example, was established by an important foreign-owned commercial house in Lima; the pioneering Peruvian woollen mill was established on a small scale in 1888 by an Italian immigrant, Bartolomeo Boggio, but two years later was reorganized on a much more ample basis as the Santa Catalina Industrial Society with the participation, among others, of Dr. Mariano Prado y Ugarteche, a member of the Peruvian elite. Thereafter, "its progress was very marked." *Peru To-Day*, Vol. 3, No. 4 (June 1911), p. 44.

83. Percy F. Martin, *Peru of the Twentieth Century*, London: Edward Arnold, 1911, p. 255.

84. *Peru To-Day*, Vol. 4, No. 4 (July 1912), p. 196.

85. Stanley Stein, *op. cit.*, p. 81.

86. *Ibid.*, Chap. 7. As Stein observes, p. 88, falling exchange rates also assisted domestic manufacturers during this period.

87. United States Federal Trade Commission, *Report on Trade and Tariffs in Brazil, Uruguay, Argentina, Chile, Bolivia, and Peru*, Washington, D.C.: U.S. Government Printing Office, 1916, p. 57.

88. Le Baron d'Anthouard, *Le progrès brésilien; la participation de la France*, Paris: Plon-Nourrit et Cie., Imprimeurs-Editeurs, 1911, pp. 148-149.

89. Luis Ospina Vásquez, *op. cit.*, Chaps. 6 and 7.

90. *Ibid.*, p. 330.

91. George Wythe, *Industry in Latin America*, New York: Columbia University Press, 1949, p. 66.

92. Such influential Porfirian figures as Joaquín D. Cassasús and José Yves Limantour were both advocates of a moderate protectionism in the interests of furthering national industrial development. Jesús Silva Herzog, *El pensamiento económico en México*, Mexico: Fondo de Cultura Económica, 1947, pp. 100, 111.

93. M. P. Arnaud, *L'émigration et le commerce français au Méxique*, Paris: L. Boyer, Imprimeur, 1902. Arnaud observes that transport costs provided additional shelter for local industries, a factor which was certainly a consideration in the Colombian case, and that the devaluation of silver gave Mexican producers the advantage which Stein notes Brazilian manufacturers obtained from a falling exchange rate. Evolution of the Brazilian protective tariff seems, in retrospect, also to have been initially a side effect of gradual increases in revenue tariffs, and it is probable that a similar trend unwittingly accounted for the birth of protectionism elsewhere. A species of economic liberalism was dominant in Peru over much of the period, for example, but, as Romero notes, with the decline of the guano boom, the government of Peru sought to maintain its revenue base by levying increasingly high duties on imports and exports. Emilio Romero, "Perú," p. 310, in Luis Roque Gondra, *et al., Pensamiento económico latinoamericano*, Mexico: Fondo de Cultura Económica, 1945. Exemptions applied, primarily, only to sugar and cotton exports and to capital imports related to those industries, as well as to imports related to mining and rail development.

94. Alfred P. Tischendorf, *Great Britain and Mexico in the Era of Porfirio Diaz*, Durham, N. C.: Duke University Press, 1961, p. 133.

95. M. P. Arnaud, *op. cit.*, pp. 93-113. By 1883 French interests had come to hold a near monopoly of the wholesale and retail clothing trades in Mexico. In 1884 a group of the principal French houses formed a syndicate and contracted to purchase the total output of certain textile lines turned out by some of the local mills. To assure themselves a supply and a better bargaining position vis-à-vis the syndicate, various smaller French houses which felt unfavorably treated by the syndicate arrangement purchased their own textile mill. So successful, apparently, was this incursion into production, that some of these decided to branch out into other textile processes and in combination with the larger houses formed an investment consortium which, as the Compañía Industrial de Orizaba, acquired another existing mill nearby the first, modernized both older plants, and constructed new plants to form a factory complex employing well over 5,000 workers. Again nonparticipating French merchants were compelled to do likewise, and soon many trade houses had formed textile production corporations, purchased Spanish-owned plants, and re-equipped and otherwise renovated the production facilities thereof.

96. Access to the coal deposits of Coahuila was helped by virtue of the substantial stockholding interest in the enterprise held by the Madero family, owners of large tracts of land in the coal region and suppliers, also, of the presidential successor to Díaz.

97. M. P. Arnaud, *op. cit.*, pp. 114 ff.

NOTES FOR CHAPTER VIII

1. In this sense, imbalance is to economic progress what it is to ambulation, since the mechanics of walking involve consecutive forward falls or sequential states of disequilibria. Perhaps, in fact, balanced relationships are to be found only in the theoretical constructs of the stationary state or in very primitive societies in which the balance or equilibrium struck is essentially that of balanced stagnation.

2. The level of productivity prevailing in this and the colonial subsystem is suggested by a recent detailed study of an area dominated by the latifundia-minifundia complex. Although the region studied, southern Peru, includes about half of all agricultural workers in Peru and covers nearly half the land cultivated in the country and although 81 per cent of the economically active population of the region is employed in agriculture, the region manages to generate only about 18 per cent of total agricultural income. The lion's share of agricultural income is, instead, generated by the modern plantation agriculture which sells to export markets. According to the expert investigators, production on the coast could conservatively be doubled and highland production tripled through "the consistent application of known farm management and water

management techniques" and through the consolidation of minifundia and the division of the excessively large holdings into more efficient-sized economic units. Inter-American Cooperative Service of Southern Peru, *Southern Peru Regional Development Project*, Lima: 1959, Vol. XII *(Agriculture: Its Present Status and Future Prospects)*, pp. 1-3.

3. For an illustrative reference to the role of long-term mortgage credit in preserving latifundian structures, see Jean Borde and Mario Góngora, *Evolución de la propiedad rural en el Valle del Puangue*, Santiago: Editorial Universitaria, S. A., 1956, Vol. I, pp. 126-127.

4. It must be recognized that the capital requirements of the transport sector alone in such countries were almost overwhelming in magnitude. The Central Railway of Peru, for example, which serves the mining regions around Cerro de Pasco, rises almost steadily as it moves inland from the coastal terminal at Callao, crossing the Andes at an altitude of over 15,500 feet above sea level. Along its precipitous and rugged route are encountered 59 bridges, 19 switchbacks, and 66 tunnels. As another illustration of the effects of geography, in Bolivia, the mining regions were located in the barren highlands, far from fuel supplies, so that energy provision became a major item of cost.

5. For the same reason, foreign control in Chilean nitrates, originally brought about through shrewd financial maneuvers, was consolidated as time went on.

6. For a general discussion of several of the points mentioned in this section, see R. E. Baldwin, "Export Technology and Development from a Subsistence Level," *Economic Journal*, Vol. 73 (March 1963), pp. 80-92.

7. According to a recent study, Bolivian Indian workers acquired very little that was useful in the way of skills or discipline from mining employment, since they often regarded the employment as temporary. Many worked only for short periods, at wages so low as to provide no incentive to work hard or efficiently. See Francisco Sobrados Martín, *La influencia de la minería en las economías de Chile y Bolivia*, Madrid: Ediciones de Cultura Hispánica, 1953, p. 133. Richard N. Adams' well-known study of the Peruvian town of Muquiyauyo, however, credits mining employment with having had an important influence in reshaping the attitudes and skills endowment of that highland community; Richard N. Adams, *A Community in the Andes: Problems and Progress in Muquiyauyo*, Seattle: University of Washington Press, 1959, pp. 93-97. Among the new skills brought to Muquiyauyo by mining employment were knowledge of construction techniques and familiarity with various phases of mechanics and electricity. It seems likely that, in the majority of instances, employment in the minerals extraction industries has made some contribution in familiarizing natives with previously exotic mechanical skills. For that matter, in time Latin American nationals also gained some experience in mining engineering and geology.

8. In Bolivia, for example, the 1950 census revealed total employment in mining to be 43,441 − only about 3 per cent of the labor force. U.N., Economic Commission for Latin America, *Analysis and Projections of Economic Development, IV, The Economic Development of Bolivia*, Mexico: U.N. Department of Economic and Social Affairs, 1957, p. 9. For Latin America as a whole, only about 1 per cent of the labor force was employed in mining and other extractive industry as late as 1955. U.S. Department of Commerce, "Comparative Statistics on the American Republics," *World Trade Information Services*, Part 3, No. 58-3, Washington, D.C.: 1959.

9. Livestock ranching, while larger in scale than coffee growing, was also developed chiefly by domestic firms or firms initiated by resident immigrants. Colombia's pre-1914 growth, based mainly on growth in coffee production from 1880 on, was accomplished with relatively little foreign investment, although a modest beginning had been made by foreign enterprises in bananas and petroleum by that time. However, sustained by the debt-servicing possibilities of the rise in export earnings and attracted by investment opportunities (in bananas, petroleum, mining, government securities, and utilities), foreign capital poured into the country in the postwar period. A period of rapid growth ensued, the average annual increase in gross national product reaching 5.9 per cent in the 1925-1929 period. Around one-half of the new investment made during this time came from foreign sources, so that by 1930 foreign capital

represented one-eighth of the total national stock of capital. Economic Commission for Latin America, *Analysis and Projections of Economic Development*, III, *The Economic Development of Colombia*, New York: U.N. Department of Economic and Social Affairs, 1957, pp. 11, 29.

10. Even where most of an industry was probably in native hands, as in the case of Mexican sugar, it was not unusual for foreigners to be prominent in developing the export portion of the industry. While the large sugar plantations of Morelos, Michoacán, and Puebla were owned by Mexicans and sold their product chiefly in the domestic markets of the *mesa central*, British interests acquired large plantations in southern Vera Cruz and United States and French investors held sugar properties on the Isthmus of Tehuantepec and in the vicinity of Tampico. The foreign sugar companies were mostly in coastal regions and exported the bulk of their production. *Monthly Bulletin of the Bureau of American Republics*, Vol. 7, No. 5 (November 1899), p. 643; *ibid.*, Vol. 9, No. 3 (September 1901), pp. 35-36; and *ibid.*, Vol. 12, No. 2 (February 1902), p. 312.

11. In the previously cited study of Southern Peruvian agriculture, it was estimated that some 381,000 farm families received an average *cash* income of about 278 soles annually — approximately $11 in U.S. currency! Interamerican Cooperative Service of Southern Peru, *op. cit.*, p. 8.

12. Of the land factors employed in plantation agriculture and mining, a not inconsiderable amount was transferred to foreign ownership at modest cost, so that in these cases the income receipts for real property ownership constituted an external rather than a domestic claim against export sector earnings.

13. To refer again to Bolivia, which was perhaps the prime example of enclave development, the incomes of miners tended to be extremely low even after many decades of export sector development. Little discretionary income was possessed by workers, who mostly earned less than 55 cents (U.S. currency) a day in the early 1950's. Moreover, the significance of even this tiny income for local markets was diminished by the fact that mining companies (and some plantations) appear often to have supplied the limited demand of their workers with imported items sold in the *pulperías* or company stores; see Carter Goodrich, *The Economic Transformation of Bolivia*, Ithaca: New York State School of Industrial and Labor Relations, 1955, p. 8. Apropos of the social benefits derived from export booms, it is interesting to read in a twentieth-century commentary on the lot of the tin miners remarks which are strangely reminiscent of some of the chronicles of colonial days. A good deal of worker housing consisted of "miserable, dark, unhealthy, one-room hovels, unfit for human habitation. There is a widespread lack of even the most rudimentary sanitary facilities." Comisión Mixta Boliviana-Estadounidense del Trabajo, *Los problemas del trabajo en Bolivia*, Montreal: International Labour Office, 1943, pp. 8-9.

14. The research of Domingo Amunátegui has provided some interesting examples of the tremendous rise in land values in Chile during the nineteenth century. Part of the rise is attributable to the inflation which began with the introduction in 1878 of incovertible bank notes. In some instances, too, the rise in value was based upon the capitalization of productivity advances as there were, here and there, improvements effected in the breeding of livestock, and part of the wealth acquired in Tamaya copper and the Arqueros and Chañarcillo silver bonanzas went into financing the construction of irrigation systems. Still, productivity advances are far from accounting for the movement in values which in many instances increased the price of properties tenfold or even more. Near Santiago, for example, the *estancia* of Pudáhuel, which was bought for 14,622 pesos in 1771, was valued at 366,000 pesos in 1896, while the *estancia* of La Punta, which brought 95,535 pesos in a sale in 1776, was valued at 700,000 pesos in 1896. In Quillota, the value of Hacienda Las Palmas rose from 20,125 pesos to 220,000 pesos during a similar period. Domingo Amunátegui y Solar, *Estudios históricos*, Santiago: Ediciones de la Universidad de Chile, 1940, p. 67. The Chilean land appreciation described by Amunátegui was, however, picayune by contrast with some other cases. Feverish speculation in the Argentine of the 1880's brought a quadrupling of land values in the provinces of Entre Ríos and Santa Fé, over a sevenfold increase in those in the province of Córdoba, and a tenfold increase in Buenos Aires land values — all in the

1883-87 period! See *The Economist*, 5 May 1888, p. 570.

15. Ernesto Lobato López, *El crédito en México*, Mexico: Fondo de Cultura Económica, 1945, pp. 156-161.

16. Agustín Ross, *Chile, 1851-1910, Sixty Years of Monetary and Financial Questions and of Banking Problems*, Valparaíso: Imp. Inglesa Westcott and Co., 1910, pp. 37-38.

17. According to the testimony of Otto Kuhn of Kuhn, Loeb, and Company before the U.S. Senate Committee on Finance in January, 1932, there was keen competition among North American investment bankers to obtain South American securities and float them in the U.S. markets. Because of the handsome commissions and fees (running up to 7.5 per cent of the issues' face value) to be had from this business, representatives were sent down to Latin America to obtain loans to float. Other testimony before Senator Hiram Johnson's committee revealed that bond promoters who carried family names still prominent in Latin American life also received generous fees for such business as they could turn up. So lucrative was the process that investment bankers appear to have been actively pushing loans at times when U.S. Department of Commerce officials in Latin America were arguing (correctly, as it turned out) that the countries were already seriously overborrowed. U.S. Congress, Senate Committee on Finance, 72nd Congress, 1st session, *Hearings on Sale of Foreign Bonds or Securities in the United States*, Washington: U.S. Government Printing Office, 1932; Part II, pp. 343, 727; Part III, pp. 1275-76, 1300-09, 1311-18 ff.

18. *Peru To-Day*, Vol. 1, No. 5 (July 1909), p. 10. The penchant for inappropriate recruitment of public officials was condemned bitterly by contemporary Latin American essayists such as Manuel González Prada of Peru.

19. There were a very few exceptions to this practice, the short-lived Balmaceda administration in Chile (c. 1890) being, perhaps, the most notable. Among other things, President Balmaceda proposed that the nitrate revenues be used to finance special national development projects and that new internal taxes be levied to cover the ordinary costs of government administration. This proposal proved to be as controversial as several of the other parts of his program and was a factor in precipitating his overthrow.

20. The amplified volume of government spending multiplied the occasions for realizing gain through the peddling of influence and outright embezzlement. More than one prominent Peruvian family fortune, for example, dates from an ancestor who was lucky enough to hold a bureaucratic position during the freespending days when Henry Meiggs was promoting the Andean railways. Indeed, a most remarkable spirit of enterprise was sometimes displayed in the accumulation of fortunes. In one instance, an ancestor of a recent Peruvian president was dispatched to Europe with considerable funds for the purchase of arms needed for the war with Chile. The emissary must have been opposed to traffic in munitions, for neither he nor the arms nor the money came back. (Peru was not exceptional in this regard.)

21. F. García Calderón, *Latin America: Its Rise and Progress*, London: T. Fisher Unwin, Ltd., 1918, p. 381. Also see pp. 375-377, where the author laments that a proliferating bureaucracy constituted a primary problem by functioning as a vortex to draw native talent into it while the life of trade and industry was left to foreigners. The growth in the number of public offices during the guano boom, for example, is noted in Jorge Basadre, *Perú: problema y posibilidad*, Lima: F. y E. Rosay, 1931, p. 117.

22. *Ibid.*, p. 382. It is instructive that, writing in an era supposedly dominated by liberalism, García Calderón refers repeatedly to the heavy reliance of Latin Americans on the initiative of the state; e.g., see p. 378. The preference of Brazilians for government jobs was remarked by Agassiz in his well-known account of his travels in that country during the nineteenth century, while José M. L. Mora of Mexico advanced the theory that it was the lack of reasonable employment alternatives which attracted so many of his compatriots into public employment. See section two of Leopoldo Zea's *El positivismo en México;* Mexico: Fondo de Cultura Económica, 1943, for a discussion of this insight.

23. Great Britain, Parliament, House of Commons, Select Committee on Loans to Foreign States, *Report from the Select Committee on Loans to Foreign States,* London: 29 July 1875.

24. H. S. Ferns, *Britain and Argentina in the Nineteenth Century,* Oxford: Oxford University Press, 1960, pp. 410-415, 450-451.

25. Raúl Scalabrini Ortiz, *Historia de los ferrocarriles argentinos,* Buenos Aires: Editorial Devenir, 1958. The Argentine railway case was by no means the sole instance in which the interests of the external sector were implicated in questionable government practice. On the contrary, this involvement seems to have been quite general (though there is no evidence that development of domestic corruption necessarily awaited encouragement by foreigners and the export interests). In Bolivia, the tin-mining magnates are known to have manipulated the government by bribing officials and subsidizing candidates for office as a matter of course for years. See Charles W. Arnade, "Bolivia's Social Revolution, 1952-1959," *Journal of Inter-American Studies,* Vol. 1, No. 3 (July 1959), pp. 341-342, and Robert J. Alexander, *The Bolivian National Revolution,* New Brunswick: Rutgers University Press, 1958, p. 96. For a comprehensive study of international finance capitalism and its relation to Bolivia, see Margaret A. Marsh, *The Bankers in Bolivia,* New York: Vanguard Press, 1928, Chap. 6 especially.

26. U.S. Senate Committee on Finance, *op. cit.,* Part III, pp. 1277-1297, 1302-1305, 1611-1612. Though the firm claimed to be surprised in discovering (after the loan was negotiated) that the president's son was involved in the deal, they had paid his fee into an account he had apparently maintained with them for some time. According to the testimony of one member of the firm, it turned out that Peruvian government revenues were used in contravention of the terms of foreign loans, even to the point of paying interest on internal loans while neglecting to service external issues.

27. *Ibid.,* Part IV, pp. 1954-1955.

28. *Ibid.,* Part II, pp. 461-462.

29. House of Commons, Select Committee, *op. cit.,* p. XXXVIII.

30. *Ibid.,* p. V.

31. The bondholders were also given a first mortgage on the government-owned mahogany forests. When the prospects appeared dim for floating another loan in 1870, the government, just prior to issuing the prospectus, arranged for four shiploads of mahogany to be delivered to Bischoffscheim and Goldschmidt with appropriate publicity in the London *Times.* This the loan contractors sold to service the 1867 issue, the clear intent being to induce the public to believe that the hypothecated forests were being used as intended. As the Parliamentary investigating committee subsequently discovered, however, the cargoes (of inferior wood) had actually been bought on credit by the Honduran government from private shippers and were to be paid for from the proceeds of the bond issue the transaction was devised to promote! *Ibid.,* pp. X-XI ff.

32. U.S. Senate Committee on Finance, *op. cit.,* Part III, p. 1604.

33. House of Commons, Select Committee, *op. cit.,* pp. XI, XLIV-XLVI. For example, Baring Brothers intervened in the market to maintain the £100 Paraguayan bonds issued in 1871 at a £17.5 premium until all the bonds were sold (April, 1872) and the contracted £64 per bond was transferred to the sinking fund and interest reserve and to the issuing government. The complete artificiality of the situation was manifest when Baring Brothers cleared out of the market. Thereupon, the price fell more or less steadily. By October, 1872 the bonds had dropped to £80; by July, 1873, the price was £55. A year later, the hapless holders of the bonds saw the decline to £12.

34. The relativity of this statement must be emphasized. By the end of the period under discussion, Mexico had rail lines reaching from the center of the republic to the major points on its borders, but a closer look at this rail system reveals it to have been a multipart structure divided into fourteen companies, with no uniform gauge and poor or no interconnections between company lines. Not until 1898 was the Ley General de Ferrocarriles passed in an effort to give some semblance of order to the nation's railway industry; but by then it was too late, for the basic damage had been done. See Servando Alzati, *Historia de la mexicanización de los ferrocarriles nacionales de México.* Mexico: La Empresa Editorial "Beatriz de Silva," 1946.

35. Economic Commission for Latin America, *Analyses and Projections of Economic Development*, III, *The Economic Development of Colombia*, p. 343.

36. For additional information on development of the Argentine railways, see, besides the Scalabrini study, Ricardo M. Ortiz, *El ferrocarril en la economía argentina*, Buenos Aires: Editorial Argumentos, 1958, and Adolfo López Mayer, *Transporte en la Argentina*, Rosario: Editorial Rosario, 1946.

37. Even in the much smaller country of Venezuela, this lack of effective integration — a common condition over the continent — is a characteristic of the rail system. A railway shipment from the principal port of La Guaira to Barquisimeto, a provincial center of some importance, moves over lines of three different gauges.

38. Osvaldo Gordilho, *Os transportes no Brasil*, Rio de Janeiro: Ministerio da Viacão e Obras Publicas, 1956, p. 155.

39. João Baptiste Peixoto, *Produção, transporte e energia no Brasil*, Rio de Janeiro: Edificio do Ministerio da Guerra, 1957, p. 201.

40. See, e.g., V. Fuentes Díaz, *El problema ferrocarrilero de México*, Mexico; private edition, 1951.

41. A. B. Cuéllar, *La situación de los ferrocarriles nacionales de México*, Mexico: Universidad Nacional Autónoma de México, 1935, p. 90.

42. In Peru the national engineering school was inaugurated in 1876, but not until 1902 was the National School of Agriculture founded. Argentina's Instituto Agrícola was established in 1870 by the Sociedad Rural. The supply of such institutions for the region as a whole, however, was extremely deficient. For example, as recently as 1951, the Keenleyside Mission to Bolivia could observe that in that country — whose very existence, economically speaking, had depended on mining for several hundred years — there was a "dearth of technically trained Bolivian personnel" and that no facilities existed in the country for training competent mining engineers, metallurgists, or geologists! United Nations Technical Assistance Administration, *Report of the United Nations Mission of Technical Assistance to Bolivia*, New York: 1951, p. 48. Bolivia is an extreme case, but in 1957 there were still fewer than 200 agriculturists with master's degrees and fewer than 50 holding doctorates in the whole of Latin America, despite the tremendous importance of agriculture to the economic well-being of the region.

43. See the information taken from the Serviço's 1907-1909 report in "The Iron Ores of Brazil," *Bulletin of the Pan American Union*, No. 32 (April 1911), pp. 652-655.

44. Demetrio Díaz, *La educación en Brasil*, Madrid: Centro de Información y Sociología de la O.C.S.H.A. (Estudios Sociológicos de Latino-América), No. 5 (1961), pp. 17-19.

45. James Orton, *The Andes and the Amazon*, New York: Harper and Brothers, 1870, pp. 68-84.

46. *El Mercurio*, Santiago: 10 February 1916. It is especially significant that this was true even in Chile, which by most ways of reckoning was among the more progressive countries in the area. Among the many works which deal with the subject, see Amanda Labarca Hubertson, *Historia de la enseñanza en Chile*, Santiago: Imprenta Universitaria, 1939 and *ibid., Evolución de la segunda enseñanza*, Santiago: Talleres de la Editorial Nascimento, 1938. The relation of the educational structure to development requirements in Chile is thoughtfully discussed by Eduardo Hamuy in "Problemas de educación elemental y desarrollo económico," *Economía: Revista de la Facultad de Ciencias Económicas de la Universidad de Chile*, Santiago: Año XVIII, Nos. 60 and 61 (3°, 4° trimestres, 1958).

47. The land market was restricted by both of the major elements in the land tenure system, the minifundia no less than the latifundia. The study of southern Peru (Interamerican Cooperative Service of Southern Peru, *op. cit.*, p. 1) notes, for example, that land is rarely sold: "A cultural factor of fundamental importance to agriculture is that the population tends to look to the ownership of land, however small in quantity, as the only available guarantee of economic security and stability. For this reason, land holdings tend to be retained and subdivided, nearly always by inheritance, generation after generation until many individual holdings in the Sierra are now too small to provide even

marginal security, and economically active individuals are driven to seek sources of supplementary income by seasonal or temporary migration . . . nearly always returning, however, to the family farm as the base of operations." For problems in labor supply and labor commitment, see Manning Nash, "The Recruitment of Wage Labor and Development of New Skills," *The Annals of the American Academy of Political and Social Science,* Vol. 305 (May 1956).

48. Exact or even approximate statistical measurements of pre-1914 investment outlays in most of Latin America are not available, but there can be little doubt that enclave sector investment, and the other foreign investment which was supported ultimately by export earnings, constituted a very large portion of the total. In the Argentina of 1900-1914, for example, foreign investment represented nearly half of total capital formation. U.N., ECLA, *Analisis y proyecciones del desarrollo económico,* V, *El desarrollo económico de la Argentina,* Mexico: U.N. Department of Economic and Social Affairs, 1959, Vol. I, p. 71. According to this ECLA study, capital formation in Argentina reached extraordinary heights during the boom years of the early twentieth century, rising from 26 per cent of GNP in 1900-04 to 48 per cent in 1905-09 and 42 per cent in 1910-14! Foreign investment in critical areas of the economy represented 12 per cent, 18 per cent, and 21 per cent of GNP, respectively, in these intervals and undoubtedly constituted the necessary enabling investment for much of the accompanying domestic capital formation.

49. In Venezuela, for example, import duties provided between two-fifths and two-thirds of government tax receipts in the decade prior to the First World War; in Argentina, taxes on foreign trade (chiefly imports) contributed well over half of the government's tax revenues during the same period. Ramón Velóz, *Economía y finanzas de Venezuela desde 1830 hasta 1944,* Caracas: Impresores Unidos, 1945, pp. 273-311. Carlos A. Tornquist, ed., *The Economic Development of the Argentine Republic in the Last Fifty Years,* Buenos Aires: Ernesto Tornquist and Company, Ltd., 1919, pp. 289-292. In Chile the tax on nitrate exports was central to the public revenue structure.

50. For a meticulously detailed scholarly analysis of the problems created by this situation, see H. C. Wallich, *Monetary Problems of an Export Economy: The Cuban Experience, 1914-1947,* Cambridge: Harvard University Press, 1950.

51. Alfred Marshall, *Principles of Economics,* New York: The Macmillan Company, 1949, pp. 596-597.

52. For instance, the strong but selective overseas demand for resources in which Latin American countries enjoyed a comparative international advantage vs the much weaker domestic demand for a wider array of resources; the strong investment support (in key capital and organizational inputs) available from the international economy for developing the particular resources needed abroad vs. the limited supply of local capital and the poor economic organization available for developing alternative resources — the former demand antithesis pulled the economies toward monocultural specialization, while the latter supply antithesis pushed them toward developing only a limited portion of their total resource endowment. Other relevant aspects of the domestic economic scene would, of course, include the imperfections of capital and money markets, the poor communications network, the paucity of educational facilities, and the difficulty of recruiting labor from the subsistence sector and committing it to money-wage employment at the prevailing low wage level. The appeal of job opportunities in the money-wage market was further reduced by the instability of employment and the fluctuation of wage-goods prices, especially those of agricultural products, which varied considerably through time because little had been invested in domestic transport and storage facilities, and the marketable surplus, small to begin with, was greatly affected by weather variations. Both sources of wage-earner insecurity enhanced the value of the low but more certain level of security to be had in subsistence agriculture and eventually seem to have required the payment of a compensating wage premium for those who left the subsistence sector for employment in the money economy.

53. The chronic shortage of qualified, practicing agricultural technicians in Latin America is probably only partially attributable to the paucity of appropriate educational facilities. Given the lack of development and opportunity in agriculture, few rural people

have been interested in advanced agricultural training and able to move upward to become technicians to assist in the *tecnificación* of the sector. Urban people enjoyed the main access to education, but neither their value system nor their interests have disposed them to pursue agricultural specialties.

54. Two outstanding examples of the extent to which this channel functioned as a means of upward mobility were Porfirio Díaz and Mariano Melgarejo. The former was born into a poor mestizo family, but as a military officer he was astute enough to link his fortunes with the rising Liberal Party and ended his public career as the longest ruling "president" in Mexican history. The latter, a bastard son of an impoverished mother, became the political chieftain of Bolivia by virtue of his adeptness in gaining control of the army. Recent decades have, of course, presented a number of similar cases of this type of mobility: e.g., Batista of Cuba and Trujillo of the Dominican Republic.

55. As has been clearly indicated in such valuable studies as the Pan American Union's *Materiales para el estudio de la clase media en la América Latina* (Theo R. Cravenna, editor, Washington: Pan American Union, 1950-51, 6 Vols.), the most important economic base by far of the "old" (i.e., nineteenth and early twentieth centuries) middle class in Latin America was not in the fields of industry, finance, and trade but in bureaucratic employment and the liberal professions. The attitudes and class interests of the bourgeoisie have been strongly influenced by these occupational origins. Particularly does this show up when contrasted with the Anglo-American middle class, a group historically made up largely of upwardly mobile persons responding to the opportunities of economic activity in a market context.

56. T. Lynn Smith, *Current Social Trends and Problems in Latin America*, Gainesville: The University of Florida Press, 1957. The situation described by Smith provides, of course, a significant contrast to that obtaining in Anglo-America, where class differentials in reproduction rates have created something of a vacuum in the higher level positions of an expanding economy, to the benefit of upward mobility. As a compensating advantage, however, the "Mayflower game" – i.e., the claim to distinguishe ancestry – can be played convincingly by more members of the Latin American middle class than in the United States.

57. Harry W. Hutchinson in his *Village and Plantation Life in Northeastern Brazil*, Seattle: University of Washington Press, 1957, p. 132, notes that the extended family system constitutes an asset for the individual in the upper classes. "Because of the many positions in public life occupied by members of these extended families, the family is able to muster considerable pistolão ('pull') in many fields." Many factors contributed to the marked lack of probity in official life, among them the scarcity of reliable legitimate opportunities for gain, the lopsided distribution of power and the consequent absence of countervailing checks, and mass illiteracy and disenfranchisement which reduced public scrutiny of official conduct. Since, however, identification with the community and with extrafamilial groupings tended to be anemic, the primary sanctions felt by the individual were those connected with the loyalties and commitments prescribed by the institution of the extended family. The values of this affiliation, in other words, had priority over other competing attachments (to the nation, the community, or the work organization), and the claims of family linkage, transcending role identification, overrode other social claims. To a lesser extent, the same was true for the interpersonal loyalties established by ritual kinship and close friendship. Thus, nepotism, the distribution of public favors in other than an impartial manner, and the like were often a response to the primary loyalty structure (the web of familial obligations) which was legitimized by cultural tradition. When the existing cultural context is seen on its own actual terms, therefore, the label "corruption" is not altogether an accurate term to describe the sort of behavior which North Americans have deplored in Latin America.

58. In Mexico, for example, Benito Juárez, who was racially an Indian of lower-class birth, gained an education through the efforts of a sympathetic parish priest and in his career as lawyer-politician eventually reached the highest office in the land. In the twentieth century, the frequency of this route to social distinction has increased. The late Benito Nardone, one-time president of Uruguay, was born into an immigrant family in which the father was a longshoreman, and himself worked as a stevedore

before taking up journalism and politics. Similar examples could be drawn from other countries as well.

59. As to most such generalizations, there were exceptions. Simón Patiño, to name the conspicuous instance, was a business titan who emerged from the lower rungs of Bolivian society. Even so, political shrewdness was as much a factor in his success as economic astuteness.

60. In not a few cases, families whose wealth had been acquired through trade or trade and finance entered into the landed segment of society through land purchases or intermarriage.

61. The need for personalistic security hedges, discussed in an earlier chapter, continued to operate as a condition which confined the distribution of enterprise control to a closed circle of insiders. As a general rule, even among the elite class as a group the dissociative processes of competition, contravention, and conflict were too prevalent to permit ownership to be more widely distributed, for this would have required a degree of reliance on associative processes based on coordinate accommodation that was rarely feasible in the social milieu of the age. For the most part the only types of associative processes which were sufficiently reliable were those of an intrafamilial character, those consolidated by close friendship ties, and those of a superordinate-subordinate nature. Indeed, this particular patterning of the dynamics of social organization continues to the present day to influence the range of business organizational forms which are viable and accounts for the strong tradition of business secrecy which has been widely observed in Latin America.

62. Illustrative of the export-oriented activities of immigrant entrepreneurs are the British ranchers — Welshmen and Scots, primarily — who settled in the Argentine Patagonian territory and pioneered the development of sheep raising. Illustrative of the immigrant entrepreneurial activities directed toward the domestic market is the Cantel cotton mill established in Guatemala in 1876 by the Spanish firm of Sánchez and Sons. See the account of this firm given in Manning Nash, *Machine Age Maya: The Industrialization of a Guatemalan Community,* Glencoe, Illinois: The Free Press, 1958. Set up with twenty cotton spinning machines imported from England and directed initially by four English engineers, the Cantel firm was in the 1950's, still heavily dependent upon foreign technical guidance: English weaving and spining masters, and Belgian and Spanish engineers. Nash's excellent study of this firm, a protected industry which became the largest textile factory in Central America (producing nearly 70 per cent of the cotton goods purchased in Guatemala at the time the study was made), provides much insight into the problems of manufacturing development in a backward area.

63. For a fine study of the history of the leading institutions of this type, see David Joslin, *A Century of Banking in Latin America,* London: Oxford University Press, 1963, which deals with the Bank of London and South America.

64. Dudley M. Phelps, *Migration of Industry to South America,* New York: McGraw-Hill Book Company, Inc., 1936, pp. 11-13.

65. Examples of this relationship can be found among the German coffee exporters of Central America. In Peru the first of the Berckemeyer family to open a business was the son of the proprietor of an important commercial house in Hamburg, with which the Berckemeyer foreign trade concern in Lima maintained a close relationship for a number of years before it became identified as an essentially Peruvian business organization.

66. A careful scholar of the assimilation of immigrants has, in his studies of German immigrants in southern Brazil, suggested that the value orientation of these immigrants was a key ingredient in their economic success, even though this value orientation was in open conflict with the traditional value system of Brazil. Imbued with a strong desire for economic independence (which impelled them to establish, where possible, their own firms), a firm dedication to work, and a commitment to material advancement as their dominating concern, the German arrivals were motivated in a manner especially favorable to upward mobility. See Emilio Willems, *A aculturação dos alemães no Brasil,* São Paulo: Companhia Editôra Nacional, 1946, pp. 358-361, and Emilio Willems, *Assimilação e populações marginais no Brasil,* São Paulo: Companhia Editôra Nacional, 1940, pp. 252-268. A similar

motivational pattern was common among the Italian immigrants of the era, some of whom were unemployed industrial workers who migrated to the Americas when the unification of Italy drove the industries of the southern portion of the peninsula into a decline because of the competitive superiority of north Italian manufacturing. Contemporary accounts of the role of the Italian immigrants in Argentina's economic renaissance reported that "phenomenal is their [the Italian immigrants'] fever for work: all wish to get rich, and quickly. ... The railroad employee has his little foodshop, looking after it as he may, helped by his wife; the school teacher keeps the accounts of five or ten business houses; the shoemaker sells lottery tickets, runs an exchange, or a bootblacking establishment; the typesetter maintains a tailoring shop, administered by the women of his house." Quoted in Robert F. Foerster, *The Italian Immigration of Our Times,* Cambridge: Harvard University Press, 1919, p. 257. Nor was this feverish activity in vain. In 1893 an Italian consul could report that "the vendor of ices becomes, say, a liquor dealer, the fruit seller a restaurant or hotel keeper, the tailor a cloth merchant, the bricklayer a building contractor." *Ibid.,* p. 255.

67. E. Willems, *A aculturação . . .,* pp. 369 ff., observes that German Protestant immigrants were more successful on the whole than German Catholic immigrants in southern Brazil.

68. In Brazil the largest homegrown business and industrial empires seem not to have been the accomplishments of German Protestants but of others – e.g., the Italian Pignatari, Crespi, and Matarazzo families, the Syrian Maronite Jafet family, and the Klabin family of Baltic-Jewish origin.

69. This was true even in Paraguay during the latter half of the nineteenth century. See H. G. Warren, *Paraguay, an Informal History,* Norman: University of Oklahoma Press, 1949, for mention of the contribution made by immigrant entrepreneurs in this country which, because of its proximity to the bustling centers of expansion in Argentina and Uruguay, was able to build to some extent on the external economies provided by the commercial facilities established down river in Buenos Aires and Montevideo.

70. C. A. Tornquist, ed., *The Economic Development of the Argentine Republic in the Last Fifty Years,* Buenos Aires: Ernesto Tornquist and Co., Ltd., 1919, pp. 11-14, 40.

71. Ricardo M. Ortiz, *Historia económica de la Argentina,* Buenos Aires: Editorial Raigal, 1955, Vol. II, p. 226.

72. The percentage of the foreign-born in the total Argentine population was 29.9 per cent in 1895 and 28.7 per cent in 1914. By 1935, the foreign-born segment had declined to 20.3 per cent of the total, but 55.4 per cent of the industrial and commercial proprietors were still supplied by this group. Gino Germani, "La clase media en la Argentina con especial referencia a sus sectores urbanos," in T. Cravenna, ed., *Materiales para el estudio de la clase media en la América Latina,* Vol. I, p. 16. In 1914, according to Germani, native-born Argentines composed 50.8 per cent of the commercial white-collar employees, 54.5 per cent of the professional groups, and 82.2 per cent of the employees in public administration. Germani concludes (*ibid.,* p. 17) that historically the main avenue for advance into the middle class by the native-born has been the bureaucracy, while the chief upward mobility of foreigners has been through entrepreneuring. Sergio Bagú ("La clase media en la Argentina," in T. Cravenna, *ibid.,* Vol. I, pp. 49-51) offers a similar assessment of the differential social roles of the immigrants and natives in the Argentine, and the previously cited studies of the Germans in Brazil by Emilio Willems provide corroborating evidence for that country.

73. Wheelwright acquired monopoly rights for steam navigation along the Chilean, Peruvian, and Ecuadoran coasts but was unsuccessful in raising the capital investment necessary for the line from United States sources. English investors were more venturesome, however, and the funds which enabled Wheelwright's first sidewheelers to sail in 1840 were secured in England. Initial losses, which by 1844 had put the line £72,000 in the red, almost used up the investors' stake of £93,000, but by 1850 the fortunes of the company had improved to the extent that it was able to pay a 10 per cent dividend.

74. Brief sketches of the work of Waddington, Garland, Lambert, and Wheelwright are found in M. Mulhall, *The English in South America,* Buenos Aires: "Standard" Office, 1878.

75. Julio C. Jobet, *Ensayo crítico del desarrollo económico-social de Chile,* Santiago: Editorial Universitaria, S. A., 1955, pp. 70-71.

76. Francisco A. Encina, *Historia de Chile,* Santiago: Editorial Nascimento, 1951, Vol. XIX, p. 415.

77. Julio Vega, "La Clase Media en Chile," in T. Cravenna, ed., *op. cit.,* Vol. III, pp. 60-92.

78. The life of this amazing business adventurer is well told in Watt Stewart, *Henry Meiggs, Yankee Pizarro,* Durham, N.C.: Duke University Press, 1946.

79. For a useful account of the doings of these men (except Doheny) and others, see David M. Pletcher, *Rails, Mines, and Progress: Seven American Promoters in Mexico, 1867-1911,* Ithaca: Cornell University Press, 1958.

80. Foreign-owned firms, especially those located in the major cities and ports, could also bank on diplomatic protection from local vicissitudes, as the republican governments had to attempt to maintain good relations with actual and potential foreign lenders.

81. E. Willems, *A aculturação . . . ,* pp. 369-371, and *Assimilação e populações . . . ,* pp. 252 ff. A more recent wave of cooperative development in Brazil appears to be associated with the activities of the immigrant Japanese community.

82. R. Foerster, *op. cit.,* hints at this cohesion in various places, but a more concrete instance is provided in the early business career of the noted Argentine industrialist, Torcuato di Tella. For an account of di Tella and his enterprise (Sociedad Industrial Americana de Maquinarias), see Thomas C. Cochran and Ruben E. Reina, *Entrepreneurship in Argentine Culture,* Philadelphia: University of Pennsylvania Press, 1962. Although the matter has not been investigated, the ethnically based social associations, benevolent societies, and the like may well have reinforced the bonds of group cohesiveness, serving, in the economic order, as communications channels and as vehicles for establishing interpersonal relations useful in business transactions.

83. Special Basque societies were also generally established in the larger metropolitan areas of Spanish America, giving new arrivals the advantage of an established network of contacts.

84. Stanley Stein, *The Brazilian Cotton Manufacture: Textile Enterprise in an Undeveloped Area, 1850-1950,* Cambridge: Harvard University Press, 1957, p. 71.

85. R. Foerster, *op. cit.,* pp. 314-316.

86. M. Mulhall, *The English in South America,* Chaps. 34, and 41-43; Foerster, *op. cit.,* Chap. 14.

87. The Brazilian, Ireneo Evangelista de Souza, the Baron and Viscount Mauá, who was far and away the outstanding national entrepreneur in nineteenth-century Latin America, received his business training as an employee of an English firm.

88. David Joslin, *op. cit.,* pp. 17 and 19.

89. George Wythe, "The Rise of the Factory in Latin America," *Hispanic American Historical Review,* Vol. 25, No. 3 (August 1945), pp. 295-314. Also useful are Harry Franklin Jackson, "The Technological Development of Central America, 1823-1913," unpublished doctoral thesis at the University of Chicago, 1948, and M. B. Bowers, "The Dawn of Manufacturing in Peru," unpublished master of arts thesis at the University of Chicago, 1946. Adolfo Dorfman, *Historia de la industria argentina,* Buenos Aires: Escuela de Estudios Argentinos, 1942, pp. 102-115, contains a listing of early entrepreneurs and firms which demonstrates the preponderant role of immigrants in industrial development. In this connection, the membership of the first Consejo Directivo of the Chilean Sociedad de Fomento Fabril (established 1883) is also suggestive: Agustín Edwards Ross, Antonio Subercaseaux, Carlos Hillman, Guillermo Puelma Tupper, Julio Tiffou, Diego Mitchell, Federico Gabbler, Benjamín Velasco, Carlos Klein, Ernesto Muzard, Robert Lyon, Enrique Stuven, Salvador Izquierdo, Santiago Chrichton, Julio Bernstein, and Victor Riesco. O. Álvarez Andrews, *Historia de desarrollo industrial de Chile,* Santiago: Imp. y Lit. La Illustratión, 1936, p. 143.

90. Julio Vega, "La clase media en Chile," in T. Cravenna, ed., *op. cit.*, Vol. III, p. 80. See also: Jack B. Pfeiffer, "The Development of Manufacturing Industry in Chile, 1820-1940," unpublished doctoral thesis at the University of Chicago, 1947, and J. F. Rippy and Jack B. Pfeiffer, "Notes on the Dawn of Manufacturing in Chile," *Hispanic American Historical Review*, Vol. 27, No. 2 (May 1948), pp. 292-303.

91. *Peru To-Day*, Vol. 3, No. 4 (June 1911), p. 44. In this, as in other cases, the contribution of influential local investors may have extended beyond provision of capital to assistance in obtaining tariff protection and other favors.

92. M. G. Mulhall, *Rio Grande do Sul and Its German Colonies*, London: Longmans, Green, and Company, 1873, pp. 56-57, 71, reports on an early foundry in southern Brazil, established by the British Gardner brothers, which used British machinery, and imported British workers to train Brazilian apprentices in the craft. By the 1870's the firm was producing sawmills, brick-making machines, coffee mills, and other items for use on the *fazendas* in the interior. On the other side of the continent, one Richard Ashford established in 1872 a foundry and machine shop in Lima, the Fundición de Acho, which by 1911 had made machinery repairs for many of the larger companies in Peru and northern Chile and which was producing such equipment as soap presses, waterwheels, boilers and boiler settings, and grinding mills, pumps, and centrifugal separators for sugar works. *Peru To-Day*, Vol. 3, No. 2 (April 1911), p. 41. Potential customers were informed, it might be observed, that while water wheels were made in sizes up to twenty-six feet in diameter, there was "no one piece too heavy for a mule to carry."

93. The Germans of Southern Brazil were, of course, not the only ones to do this. Between 1893 and 1902, for example, nearly 8,000 European skilled workers were brought to Chile as immigrants by the Sociedad de Fomento Fabril, which maintained a recruiting center in Paris. O. Álvarez Andrews, *op. cit.*, p. 163.

94. E. Willems, *A aculturação . . .*, pp. 346-350.

95. The Italo-Argentine industrial magnate, Torcuato di Tella, himself a skilled technician (he invented a bread-kneading machine which was superior to imported models and received an engineering education in Italy), used his family connections in Italy to recruit the engineers and other skilled workers needed by his factory. T. Cochran and R. Reina, *op. cit.*, p. 55. In all probability others of the Italian firms in South America made a similar use of the international external economies provided by extended family networks.

96. The Backus and Johnston Company, sold later to a group of London investors, was also engaged in mining and the export-import trade.

97. Such was the case, for example, in the German firms discussed by Willems, in the di Tella enterprise in Argentina during its early life, and in the Brazilian cotton textile mills studied by Stein — though in the last mentioned of these there is an indication that sometimes the foreign technicians deliberately stalled in training local replacements.

98. José Soares Maciel Filho, "A economía da industria textil no Brasil," Rio de Janeiro: mimeographed, 1945, quoted in S. Stein, *op. cit.*, pp. 71-72; bracketed explanation added.

99. Among many other instances of mercantile-based industrial entrepreneuring in Peru, Duncan Fox and Co. established the largest of the early cotton textile mills (still in operation), Milne and Co. were leaders in flour milling, and Faustino G. Piaggio and Co. not only went into banking and the brewery business but also achieved great renown as developers of the Zorritos oil field. The firm Enrique Ferreyros y Cía. was started by Spanish immigrants as a family-operated export-import concern in the late nineteenth century, its successful growth being attributable mostly to the importation and sales of farm machinery and implements; over the course of three generations it branched out into such manufacturing lines as drugs, chemical fertilizers, and appliances.

100. T. Cochran and R. Reina, *op. cit.*, p. 39.

101. While still a rural merchant, Matarazzo first began to purchase hogs for lard distributors, soon going into the lard refinery business himself, where he innovated

the use of tin containers (wooden barrels had been the customary containers). The capital built up in this was turned into Matarazzo's flour and grain trade which, in turn, was the point of departure into flour mills, textile manufacturing (to produce flour bags), cottonseed oil mills, and the manufacture of soap and toilet products and the packing cases therefor. From thence it was but a step into such activities as sawmills, box factories, and metalworking plants for the production of tin containers and cooking-utensils.

102. Once import-substitution became a matter of deliberate national policy, the industrial empires established on a small scale in earlier decades enjoyed two further advantages. In the first place, they sometimes had influential connections among the makers of public policy and so could shape this to their advantage. In the second place, they were frequently able to acquire the local manufacturing rights for products of foreign origin.

NOTES FOR CHAPTER IX

1. None of the four, for example, was among 13 countries of the world which Paul Lamartine Yates has estimated achieved the highest percentage of increases in foreign trade (merchandise exports) between 1913 and 1953. From Latin America the list includes (in descending order of percentage gain): Venezuela (the highest percentage of all in Lamartine Yates' list), Colombia (the third ranking on the list), Honduras, El Salvador, Guatemala, and Peru. Argentina and Chile are among the 11 countries which have registered the least gain in foreign trade in the 1913-1953 period. Paul Lamartine Yates, *Forty Years of Foreign Trade: A Statistical Handbook with Special Reference to Primary Products and Under-Developed Countries,* London: George Allen and Unwin, Ltd., 1959, p. 160, 165. In both Colombia and Venezuela, the main period of foreign investment and rapid development came in the 1900's.

2. Economic Commission for Latin America, *Foreign Capital in Latin America,* New York: U.N. Department of Economic and Social Affairs, 1955, p. 6.

3. Of the 142,345 kilometers of railways in the Latin American republics by 1941, Argentina possessed 47,731 kilometers, Brazil had 34,204 kilometers, Mexico had 24,363 kilometers, and Chile had 9,112 kilometers. Next in order were Cuba with 4,941 kilometers and Peru with 4,448 kilometers. *Interamerican Statistical Yearbook,* Washington, D.C.: 1942. Comparatively little trackage has been built since 1940 except for some fairly important lines in Mexico and Colombia.

4. P. Lamartine Yates, *op. cit.,* p. 166.

5. Only Uruguay, whose economic evolution approximated that of the Argentine, moved as far in the direction of modern European modes of social organization. Indeed, Uruguay was to move ahead of Argentina in adopting progressive social policies during the early twentieth century.

6. The changeover was effected by upper-class groups and the military and was in no way a popular movement. While republican sentiments had been propagated by positivistic adherents, the decisive factors seem to have been the self-consciousness of the military as a power group and the disaffection of the landowning interests after the emperor had emancipated the slaves without indemnification to their former owners. The casual and rather unorthodox religious attitudes of the crown did nothing to win it the enthusiasm of the church, for whatever clerical backing might have been worth.

7. *Terra roxa* is the deep, porous, reddish soil which is almost ideally suited to coffee cultivation. The Paraíba Valley (also spelled Parahiba and Parahyba) is located west and southwest of Rio de Janeiro.

8. For example, the heavy costs of a predatory militarism were avoided throughout much of this period, whereas the social efficiency of the capital stock in nearly all other Latin American nations was substantially lowered by the burden of military expenditures which were both unproductive in themselves and contraproductive in their disruptive impact on the other sectors of the social order. Edwin Lieuwen has observed

that Brazil was unique in this regard. Edwin Lieuwen, *Arms and Politics in Latin America,* New York: Frederick A. Praeger, Inc., 1960, p. 17.

9. From the 1850's on, Brazil was supplying approximately half of the world production, and by the 1880's it was growing over half. J. F. Normano, *Brazil: A Study of Economic Types,* Chapel Hill: The University of North Carolina Press, 1935, p. 40. By mid-century, coffee was Brazil's leading export, accounting for some 40 per cent of the country's exports by value. In the previous 30 years, it had surpassed sugar and cotton in the export lists and indeed represented virtually the entire increase in Brazilian exports during the first half of the nineteenth century. Celso Furtado, *Formação econômica do Brasil,* Rio de Janeiro: Editôra Fundo de Cultura, 1961, p. 133.

10. *Ibid.,* pp. 163-164.

11. *Ibid.*

12. Agreements made with Great Britain in the late 1820's had called for the suppression of the traffic in slaves, but while the British navy interfered intermittently with the slave supply lanes it proved impossible to put an end to the importation until the 1850's. The slavery question is well presented in C. H. Haring, *Empire in Brazil: A New World Experiment with Monarchy,* Cambridge: Harvard University Press, 1958, Chap. 5.

13. Henry Koster, *Travels in Brazil,* London: Longman, Hurst, Rees, Orme, and Brown, 1816.

14. See José Wanderley de Araujo Pinho, *História de um engenho do Recôncovo, 1552-1944,* Rio de Janeiro: Livraria Editôra Zelio Valverde, 1946, p. 224, and Orlando Valverde, "O Nordeste da Mata Pernambucana (A região de Timbaúba)," *Boletim Carioca de Geografía,* Vol. 13 (1960), p. 26. The former account tells in considerable detail of the varying fortunes which befell the northeastern sugar industry in the nineteenth century: the stimulation produced by the Napoleonic wars, the devastation brought on by a cholera epidemic which decimated the labor force in 1855, a new stimulation produced by the U.S. Civil War, a sugar cane blight in the 1870's, and the disruption of the labor supply produced by emancipation.

15. A number of the states of the northeast attempted to forestall the crisis in the labor supply by prohibiting the exportation of slaves to the labor-hungry south, but such measures seem not to have been very effective. This, together with the loss of some labor upon abolition of slavery, probably induced the central and state governments to support the shift to more capital-intensive production functions in sugar milling.

16. Among the more useful works dealing with this topic are: Manoel Correia de Andrade, *A terra e o homen no Nordeste,* São Paulo: Editôra Brasiliense, 1963; Manuel Diegues Júnior, *O banquê nas Alagoas,* Rio de Janeiro: Edição do Instituto de Açucar e do Alcool, 1949, and *ibid., População de açucar no Nordeste do Brasil,* Rio de Janeiro: Commissão Nacional de Alimentação, 1954.

17. J. F. Normano, *op. cit.,* pp. 32-34. The record levels of exportation were reached in 1871-72.

18. Today Brazil ranks second only to Ghana, which overtook and surpassed Brazil in the twentieth century.

19. Jorge Amado's internationally famous *Gabriela, Clove and Cinnamon,* Greenwich, Connecticut: Fawcett Publications, Inc. (a Crest Book), 1964. In Amado's modern classic, one gains an insight into such matters as the conditions of land acquisition, the role of immigration and migration in the economy, and provincial political structure. For students of northeastern Brazil, incidentally, there is a wealth of insight to be gained from the literature of the region. Its poverty seems in fact to have been matched by the richness of the sociological perception which talented writers have brought to focus on the area's problems. Besides Amado, there are José Lins do Rego, Rachel de Queiroz, and Graciliano Ramos. The last mentioned of these has even provided a superb cross sectional analysis of the region in his three novels, *São Bernardo, Angustia,* and *Vidas seccas,* which deal, respectively, with the life of the *fazenda,* urban conditions, and conditions of existence in the drought-seared *sertão.*

20. In particular, the large-scale seasonal migration of field hands from the *sertões* operated to depress the wage level of the cacao districts.

21. The initial export of rubber from the region was made in 1827. In 1872 the Amazonian population reached 337,000. By 1906, it was 1.1 million. C. Prado Jr., *op. cit.*, p. 246.

22. José Eustacio Rivera's famous novel, *La vorágine,* depicts especially well the exploitation of the rubber gatherers by the middlemen of the trade.

23. The peak Brazilian exportation was reached in 1912 with 42,000 tons. The boom also spread to the Amazonian territories of Bolivia and Peru.

24. C. Prado, Jr., *op. cit.*, p. 245.

25. Even in these poorer areas, though, there were some changes. For example, the early cotton textile industry was, to a large extent, located in the northeast near its raw materials source.

26. The number of people — courtiers and functionaries and their families — amounted to 15,000, according to Roberto C. Simonsen, *História econômica do Brasil, 1500-1820,* São Paulo: Companhia Editôra Nacional, 1937, Vol. II, p. 239.

27. J. F. Normano, *op. cit.*, pp. 167-168.

28. R. C. Simonsen, *op. cit.*, pp. 265-273.

29. It could not be pretended for a moment, of course, that public sector resources were mobilized on anything like the scale adequate for development nor that those put into development were intelligently deployed to best effect. We have observed earlier, for example, that general education was ignored and that tiny enrollments typified the schools of higher learning. Moreover, the substantive content of much of the existing educational efforts was quite sterile. The court, while adding to local spending power, was certainly addicted to a sumptuous style of life which wasted enormous amounts of resources on socially unproductive outlays. For a judicious summary evaluation of the character of these social overhead outlays, see Fernando de Azevedo, *Brazilian Culture,* New York: The Macmillan Company, 1950, pp. 236-271, 371-407.

30. Royal efforts to develop an iron industry in Brazil had been made several times earlier, even during the late colonial era. By 1799, the crown had gone so far as to direct its governor in São Paulo to finance an iron works out of the royal treasury, operating it as a government enterprise. Between 1810 and 1820, the crown charged the German scientists Varnhagen and Eschwege with organizing iron works in São Paulo and Minas Gerais. The results were mostly rather mixed, but the efforts reflected a definite concern on the part of the state to develop local resources. R. C. Simonsen, *op. cit.*, pp. 319-327.

31. Nícia Vilela Luz, *A luta pela industrialização do Brasil, 1808 a 1930,* São Paulo: Difusão Europeía do Livro, 1961, p. 15.

32. C. Prado, Jr., *op. cit.*, p. 130.

33. *Ibid.,* p. 138-139. As a contemporary wag put it, "até caixões de defunto nos chegarão da Inglaterra já estofados e prontos para serem utilizados!"

34. Nícia Vilela Luz, *op. cit.*, pp. 18 ff.

35. *Ibid.,* pp. 19-21, 24. Somewhat later, duties were placed on raw materials for which local supply sources could theoretically be developed. This was intended as an additional developmental measure rather than a discouragement to new industries.

36. *Ibid.,* p. 29.

37. *Ibid.,* p. 35.

38. In a way, the efforts to modernize the northeastern sugar industry concentrated wealth rather than distributing it more widely for they fostered the rapid growth of large-scale ownership on an unprecedented scale in the region. Just prior to this, the declining fortunes of the industry and the end of slavery had begun to produce shifts in land use and the sale of estate properties. Undoubtedly had this process been allowed to continue it would have created a much more flexible agricultural structure in the region.

39. To illustrate the backward state of the Brazilian industry, it may be noted that Cuba had begun to switch to central processing of cane in the 1830's.

40. In 1875 the Brazilian Parliament had by law authorized the central government to guarantee the interest on foreign capital invested in rehabilitating the sugar industry.

Celso Furtado, *op. cit.*, p. 160. Furtado claims that in the next 10 years, 50 *usinas* were established with British investments. This allegation is questionable, both in terms of the numbers of *usinas* established in that interval and in terms of the nationality of the financing. Foreign capital may have been involved, but most of it appears not to have been equity capital. At least, foreign enterprise does not seem to have been a significant factor in the modern sugar industry of the northeast. The old class of *senhores de engenho* was displaced by the large *usina* corporations, but these were most often family corporations and, though the record is not altogether clear, were probably set up by wealthy mercantile families from the cities of the Northeast and, possibly, the South. These families, in turn, may have drawn upon foreign bank credit or had other recourse to foreign financing through their established commercial connections abroad.

41. With this change and a later legislative change permitting lenders to foreclose on mortgage loans in default, the way was open for the large-scale consolidation of landholdings around the new sugar centrals. Many of the older *engenho* units were absorbed by the *usina* corporations which had to extend their control directly (on their own lands) or indirectly (through rigid contractural obligations on independent suppliers) over the scheduling of cane planting and harvesting operations to maximize the use of the large fixed capital investment in processing facilities. Their monopsonistic position vis-à-vis independent suppliers permitted them eventually to accomplish what the traditional planters had originally feared: that is, to gain the upper hand in the bargain struck with independent suppliers and in so doing to pass on to them the downward fluctuations in sugar prices and to absorb them through purchase or foreclosure. In this trend toward larger-scale operations, the cane-carrying railway (which permitted the *usina* to draw upon a wider supply area than animal-drawn vehicles had previously allowed) was a major influence along with the new milling technology.

42. Harry Wm. Hutchinson, *Village and Plantation Life in Northeastern Brazil,* Seattle: University of Washington Press, 1957, p. 41. Also see Manuel Diegues, *População . . .*, pp. 112-113, 183.

43. John W. F. Rowe, *Studies in the Artificial Control of Raw Material Supplies, No. 3. Brazilian Coffee,* London: Executive Committee of the London and Cambridge Economic Service (London School of Economics), January, 1932, p. 8. Rowe's careful study is the definitive analysis of the various coffee control measures which were employed up to the 1930's. It indicates the widespread extent of miscreant activity and the disastrous political expediency to which these schemes gave rise.

44. Decree of 25 November 1808. R. C. Simonsen, *op. cit.*, Vol. II, p. 275.

45. *Ibid.*, p. 276. The Novo Friburgo colony was in the state of Rio de Janeiro. The first Swiss colony, however, may have been the one established at Leopoldina in the state of Bahia. In 1812, the crown had sponsored a new colony in the state of Espírito Santo, but the settlers were from the Azores and, therefore, Portuguese subjects.

46. A very useful review of imperial policy regarding colonization is contained in an official report made by the Baron of Paranapiacaba to the Minister of Agriculture in the 1870's. See João Cardoso de Menezes e Souza, *Theses sobre colonização no Brasil: projecto de solução a's questões sociais, que se prendem a este difficil problema,* Rio de Janeiro: Typographia Nacional, 1875.

47. The *fazendeiro*-linked efforts to bring in hands for the coffee industry led to such abusive treatment of the immigrants at times that foreign governments intervened both through diplomatic protests and by temporarily prohibiting emigration to Brazil.

48. Additional German colonies, as well as Swiss and Italian colonies were established from the 1840's on, particularly in the three southernmost states. Not all of these were successful. In some instances — for example, among German colonists in Espírito Santo state — the immigrants eventually degenerated to the primitive *caboclo* techniques, much to the horror of latter day German students of the subject (e.g., Leo Waibel, the noted geographer). Most, however, appear to have been viable enterprises and made an enormously valuable contribution to the agricultural progress of southern Brazil. For a record of these ventures, see Joaquim da Silva Rocha, *História da colonisação do Brasil,* 2 vols., Rio de Janeiro: Imprensa Nacional, 1918.

49. It appears that the immigrants were not altogether happy with their lot, and word to this effect got back to their homelands. Probably the preponderance of slave labor was still too great and the shortage of workers not yet great enough to provide a satisfactory income level for free labor.

50. Stanley Stein, *Vassouras, A Brazilian Coffee County, 1850-1900,* Cambridge: Harvard University Press, 1957, p. 29-30. Stein quotes a contemporary Brazilian economist to the effect that the domestic slave trade during the 1850's was such that the shortage of slave labor was not felt immediately after suspension of the international trade in slaves. This seems somewhat inconsistent, however, with the reported "rapid rise in slave prices after 1852." *Idem.* Also see *ibid.,* pp. 46-47, 65 ff., for references to the growing labor shortage of the 1850's. Slave prices nearly doubled in the 1852-1854 period.

51. As Celso Furtado has observed, there were conditions present which tended to concentrate income and wealth during both periods of coffee prosperity and periods of recession. During boom times, the relatively elastic supply of labor and land factors permitted higher prices to be translated into higher profits. During recessions, a policy of exchange devaluation permitted coffee growers to "socialize" a part of their losses. Milreis income, in other words, fell (if at all) by less than the export income expressed in terms of foreign currencies, while the consuming public at large absorbed the costs of higher prices on imports. Insofar as imported wage goods had a more inelastic demand than imported consumer superfluities, the real income of lower income groups may have been reduced relatively more than that of upper income groups who could postpone consumption of foreign-made luxury products, though local industry benefitted by the change in price relationships between domestic and imported manufactures. The coffee valorization programs of the twentieth century provided an additional channel for transferring income from the public at large to those engaged in coffee production. However, it is still probably safe to assume that the coffee economy, once it came to rely primarily upon the free labor market, produced a pattern of income distribution significantly broader than that which prevailed in the older parts of the country and, indeed, in most of Latin America except for Uruguay and the Argentine.

52. Richard M. Morse, *From Community to Metropolis; A Biography of São Paulo, Brazil,* Gainesville: University of Florida Press, 1958, p. 174. Also see *ibid.,* pp. 129-133, 172-177, 226-229. An especially interesting and perspicacious interpretation of the socio-economic implications of immigration in Brazil is found in Chap. 10 of Roger Bastide, *Brésil, terre des contrastes,* Paris: Librairie Hachette, 1957, pp. 229-259. Also see Chap. 3 of Jacques Lambert, *Os dois Brasís,* Rio de Janeiro: Centro Brasileiro de Pesquisas Educacionais, 1959. For studies of several of the more important industrial entrepreneurs, see: A. d'Atri, *L'Etat de São Paulo et le renouvellement économique de l'Europe,* Paris: Victor Allard, Chantelard, 1926; Antonio Piccarolo and Lino Finocchi, *O desenvolvimento industrial de S. Paulo atravez da primeira exposicão municipal,* São Paulo: Pocai, 1918.

53. S. J. Stein, *Vassouras...,* pp. 46 ff. This secondary impulse to commercialization of agriculture extended mainly to the three southernmost states of Brazil and to the eastern portions of Goias and Matto Grosso. In Goias, Matto Grosso, and Rio Grande do Sul, cattle ranching operations were developed to sell to the markets of the populous coffee economy. From the smaller and often immigrant-operated free holdings of the southern states came most of the wines, cereals, and other products used in the home market. Caio Prado Jr., *op. cit.,* p. 209.

54. S. J. Stein, *Vassouras...,* pp. 17-20, 81-84. Stein illustrates especially well the importance of the extended family as an institution for mobilizing capital, both for the early development of plantations and for financing later production and trade. Family links were also of some consequence in the conduct of marketing.

55. R. M. Morse, *op. cit.,* pp. 170 ff.

56. C. Prado, Jr., *op. cit.,* p. 214.

57. For example, the Baron of Piracicaba, whose wealth came largely from coffee *fazendas,* founded the first cotton-spinning and cotton-weaving factory in São Paulo. The Viscount of Paranaíba worked tirelessly in the promotion of immigration and in the

administration of the labor market in the same state. In the Paraíba coffee region, much of the crop financing was in the hands of the Teixeira Leite family, whose capital came from the large banking fortune the Baron of Itambê had accumulated in Minas Gerais and from the profits another family member earned in road construction contracts. Several of the important *fazendas* in that valley were the property of the Baron of Paty and the Baron of Bemposta. In a related field, some of the more successful private colonization companies were due to the enterprise of the Viscount of Indaiatuba while the first railway venture in Brazil, organized by the Baron of Mauá, numbered among its financial backers such persons as the Baron of Andarahy and the Viscount of Coudeixa.

58. Afonso Arinos de Melo Franco, *Síntese da história econômica do Brasil*, Salvador de Bahia: Progresso Livraria Editôra, 1958, p. 93.

59. C. Prado, Jr., *op. cit.*, p. 197; J. F. Normano, *op. cit.*, pp. 89 ff.; Nícia V. Luz, *op. cit.*, p. 29.

60. For useful biographies of this distinctive Brazilian, see: Lidia Besouchet, *Mauá y su época*, Buenos Aires: Ediciones "América Económica," 1940; the far more comprehensive but adulatory *Mauá* by Alberto de Faria, São Paulo: Companhia Editôra Nacional, 1946.

61. Norberto Piñero, *La moneda, el crédito y los bancos en la Argentina*, Buenos Aires: J. Menéndez, 1921. Also see A. S. J. Baster, *The International Banks*, London: P. S. King and Sons, Ltd., 1935, p. 129.

62. Heitor F. Lima, *Evolução industrial de São Paulo*, São Paulo: Livraria Martins Editôra, S.A., 1954, contains a survey of the industries in the state of São Paulo by 1901, together with brief sketches of such industrial pioneers as Coronel Rodovalho, the Jafet brothers, Francisco Matarazzo, and others. Also quite useful for pre-World War economic developments are: the Commissão d'Expansão Econômica's brochure, *Les progrés de São Paulo de 1887 à 1909*, Paris: Ailland et Cie., 1909; Carlos M. Delgado de Carvalho, *Un centre économique au Brésil; L'état de Minas en 1908*, Paris: Ailland et Cie., 1908; *ibid., Le Brésil méridional. Etude économique sur les états du sud: S. Paulo, Paraná, Santa-Catharina et Rio-Grande-do-Sul*, Paris: E. Desfossés Imprimeur, 1910; Centro Industrial do Brasil, *O Brasil: Suas requezas naturaes, suas industrias . . .*, Rio de Janeiro: Impressores M. Orosco e C., 1907; Emile Quoniam de Schompré, *La bourse de São Paulo*, São Paulo: Typ. Casa Garraux, 1911.

63. Jacques Lambert, *op. cit.*, Chaps. 5 and 8.

64. With the increase in population during the nineteenth century, the social impact of the drought became progressively more severe. By the 1870's, the government was finally moved to act on the problem. For a history of governmental efforts to cope with the drought problem, see A. O. Hirschman, *Journeys toward Progress: Studies of Economic Policy-Making in Latin America*, New York: Twentieth Century Fund, 1963.

65. A useful résumé of the history of developments in the Argentine economic center is to be found in W. S. Tower, "The Pampa of Argentina," *Geographical Review*, Vol. 5, No. 4 (April 1918), pp. 293-315.

66. See E. A. Coni, *Agricultura e industria coloniales (siglos XVI-XVIII)*, Buenos Aires: Librería Editorial "El Ateneo," 1941, for a comprehensive study of the colonial Argentine economy, though the work is more descriptive than analytical.

67. D. L. Molinari, *La representación de los hacendados de Mariano Moreno*, Buenos Aires: Facultad de Ciencias Económicas, Universidad de Buenos Aires, 1939, pp. 58-62.

68. Prior to this, the *asiento* shippers had regularly engaged in illicit trade, and the Luzo-Brazilians had assiduously cultivated the many opportunities for contraband traffic presented by the Spanish system.

69. See Alfredo Montoya, *Historia de los saladeros argentinos*, Buenos Aires: Editorial Raigal, 1956, and Horacio C. E. Giberti, *Historia económica de la ganadería argentina*, Buenos Aires: Editorial Raigal, 1954.

70. E. J. Pratt, "Anglo-American Commercial and Political Rivalry on the Plata, 1820-1830," *Hispanic American Historical Review*, Vol. 11, No. 3 (August 1931),

pp. 302-335, gives an excellent review of the early nineteenth-century foreign economic penetration of the Argentine.

71. Two particularly valuable contemporary accounts of conditions during that age are J. A. B. Beaumont, *Travels in Buenos Ayres and the Adjacent Provinces ...,* London: J. Ridgway, 1828, and Joseph Andrews, *Las provincias del norte en 1825,* Buenos Aires: Coni Hermanos, 1924, especially pp. 17-84. These are only two of a rather lengthy list of such accounts, however, as the Argentine seems to have given many a foreign traveler the inspiration to set his observations to paper. For a well written study of the development of Argentine foreign trade in this period, see Clifton B. Kroeber, *The Growth of the Shipping Industry in the Río de la Plata Region, 1794-1860,* Madison: The University of Wisconsin Press, 1957.

72. Woodbine Parish, *Buenos Ayres and the Provinces of the Río de la Plata,* London: J. Murray, 1838, p. 394. Parish was the British consul-general in Buenos Aires during the Rosas era. The later editions of his book cover developments up to the early 1850's.

73. For enlightening contemporary observations on the prominence of sheep ranching, see William McCann, *Two Thousand Miles' Ride Through the Argentine Provinces,* London: Smith, Elder, and Co., 1853, 2 vols., Vol. I, pp. 66 ff. Also see Herbert Gibson, *The History and Present State of the Sheep-Breeding in the Argentine Republic,* Edinburgh: Ravenscraft and Mills, 1893.

74. See Jacinto Oddone, *La burguesía terrateniente argentina,* Buenos Aires: 1936, pp. 47-83.

75. In addition to the previously cited work by Oddone, see Emilio A. Coni, *La verdad sobre la enfiteusis de Rivadavia,* Buenos Aires: Imprenta de la Universidad, 1927, for an account of the genesis of latifundism in the Argentine, and the much more comprehensive Miguel A. Cárcano, *Evolución histórica del régimen de la tierra pública, 1810-1916,* Buenos Aires: Librería Mandesky, 1915.

76. Indeed, as the Robertsons had discovered in the early days of the nation, many of the most important *estancieros* and caudillos were also engaged in mercantile activity and the occupation of merchant was one accorded high status. J. P. and W. P. Robertson, *Letters on South America,* London: J. Murray, 1843, Vol. I, p. 237. A most valuable review of the meat industry's development is found in Simon G. Hanson, *Argentine Meat and the British Market,* Stanford: Stanford University Press, 1938.

77. The best comprehensive account of Anglo-Argentine economic relations is contained in Henry S. Ferns, *Britain and Argentina in the Nineteenth Century,* Oxford: The Clarendon Press, 1960. Also useful, for the period of most intense interaction, are A. G. Ford, *The Gold Standard, 1880-1914; Britain and Argentina,* Oxford: The Clarendon Press, 1962, and Harold E. Peters, *The Foreign Debt of the Argentine Republic,* Baltimore: The Johns Hopkins Press, 1934.

78. As other, related indicators of transport development, it may be noted that between 1886 and 1908 the number of passengers carried annually rose from 6,458,674 to 47,150,384 while the tons of merchandise moved increased from 2,948,000 to 32,211,000. Alberto B. Martínez and Maurice Lewandowski, *The Argentine in the Twentieth Century,* New York: Charles Scribner's Sons, 1914, p. 94.

79. *Ibid.,* p. 101.

80. For a glimpse of regional responses, other than that of the pampeana area, see the short review by Eduardo Correas, *Historia económica de Mendoza,* Buenos Aires: Unión Industrial Argentina, Instituto de Estudios y Conferencias Industriales, 1945, and the slightly more useful work by Emilio J. Schleh, *La industria azucarera en su primer centenario, 1821-1921, consideraciones sobre su desarrollo y estado actual,* Buenos Aires: Establicimiento Gráfico Ferrári Hermanos, 1921. A rather more useful survey of regional developments was made in the early twentieth century by a talented young French economic geographer, Pierre Denis. See his *L'Argentine moderne,* Buenos Aires: Coni Frères, Imprimeurs-Editeurs, 1916.

81. Carlos F. Soares, *Economía y finanzas de la nación argentina, 1903-1916,* Buenos Aires: Talleres Gráficos Rodríguez Giles, 1916, Vol. I, pp. 140-153. Paul B. Souweine, in discussing this apparent contravention of the Mining Code (and of several opinions on the

subject handed down by distinguished legists), observes that state intervention in the petroleum field had numerous defenders and few opponents among the Argentines, who saw in this measure a means of averting foreign (and especially North American) control of this valuable national resource. There was some hope, also, that state exploitation of the resource would harness its utilization more effectively to national industrializa-. tion objectives. P. B. Souweine, *L'Argentine au seuil de l'industrie,* Paris: Imprimerie des Etablissements Casterman, 1927, pp. 108-121.

82. For a perceptive interpretation of Sarmiento's view of education, see Juan Mantovani, "La Tarea de Sarmiento y su Significación," *Universidades* (April-June 1961).

83. Prior to reaching the presidency, Sarmiento, as Director of Schools for Buenos Aires, began the development of education at the provincial level. During the six years of his administration, the number of public schools doubled (to 1,645) and several institutes of higher education (e.g., normal schools, a school of mining, a naval academy, a military academy, a school of exact sciences) were established.

84. José Ingenieros, *La evolución de las ideas argentinas,* Buenos Aires: Talleres Gráficos Argentinos de L. J. Rosso y Cía., 1918-1920, 2 Vols., contains considerable information on educational developments during the period in question.

85. Of the many studies of Argentine colonization and immigration, the following are especially useful: Juan A. Alsina, *La inmigración europea en la República Argentina,* Buenos Aires: (3rd ed.) Imprenta Calle México 1422, 1898; Antonio Gómez Langenheim, *Colonización en la República Argentina,* Buenos Aires: M. Biedma é Hijo, 1906; Roberto Schopflocher, *Historia de la colonización agrícola en Argentina,* Buenos Aires: Editorial Raigal, 1955; Carl C. Taylor, *Rural Life in Argentina,* Baton Rouge: Louisiana State University Press, 1948; and Mark Jefferson, *Peopling the Argentine Pampa,* New York: American Geographical Society, 1926. Taylor's study is particularly worthwhile as it documents the economically undesirable aspects of Argentine latifundism.

86. Quite early in the twentieth century, the system of large holdings was identified in one study as the "Chief obstacle to the peopling of the country," quoted in A. B. Martinez and M. Lewandowski, *op. cit.,* pp. 117, 121, 128-130. Martínez and Lewandowski also condemned the latifundia system of Argentina as a brake on agricultural development. Similarly condemnatory of Argentine latifundism was the thoughtful work by Paul B. Souweine, *op. cit.,* pp. 63-79.

87. Federico Pinedo, *Siglo y medio de economía argentina,* México: Centro de Estudios Monetarios Latinoamericanos, 1961, p. 67.

88. Rapid population growth was a major feature of the late nineteenth-and early twentieth-century period. According to estimates reproduced in A. B. Martinez and M. Lewandowski, *op. cit.,* p. 213, the population grew as follows: 1,882,615 (1870), 3,377,780 (1890), and 5,712,489 (1908). By the 1914 census the national population reached 7,884,900. Ricardo M. Ortiz, *Historia económica de la Argentina, 1850-1930,* Buenos Aires: Editorial Raigal, 1955, Vol. II, pp. 154-158.

89. J. A. Alsina, *op. cit.,* 0. 45. Also see P. B. Souweine, *op. cit.,* p. 8-63, for a useful summary of immigration policy and immigrant contributions to Argentine, economic development. Also useful in depicting the entrepreneurial role of immigrants in Argentine development is Manual Chueco, *Los pioneros de la industria argentina,* Buenos Aires: Imprenta de la Nación, 1886.

90. In 1916, the Radical Party won the presidency. Social structural changes in this critical period have been examined in a way meaningful to the economist in Chaps. 7 and 8 of Gino Germani, *Política y sociedad en una época de transición,* Buenos Aires: Editorial Paidos, 1962. One notes (p. 196), for example, that by 1914 over 30 per cent of the Argentine population could be classified more or less as middle or upper class, while another 18 per cent was made up of artisans and other self-employed persons.

91. A. B. Martínez and M. Lewandowski, *op. cit.,* pp. 262 ff. For more comprehensive studies of banking developments, see P. B. Souweine, *op. cit.,* pp. 241-282, and Norberto Piñero, *op. cit.,* and "Los Bancos en la Confederación," *Anales de la Facultad de Derecho y Ciencias Sociales de la Universidad Nacional de Buenos Aires,* Vol. XX (1919), pp. 5-22. Also see Ricardo M. Ortíz, *op. cit.,* Vol. I, pp. 143-153, and Vol. II, pp. 298-299; and Nicolás

Casarino, *El Banco de la Provincia de Buenos Aires en su primer centenario, 1822-1922,* Buenos Aires: Peuser, 1922.

92. The 33 foreign insurance companies, however, had a capitalization of 46,642,897 pesos as contrasted with the 27,413,373 pesos capitalization of the 52 national firms. Carlos F. Soares, *op. cit.,* Vol. I, p. 176.

93. A. B. Martínez and M. Lewandowski, *op. cit.,* pp. 278 ff. It is interesting to note that of the £ 72.5 million nominal capitalization of the companies launched via the Bourse in 1905-1908, some £ 14.5 million went to industrial and mining enterprises; £ 11 million to railways and tramways; £ 1.3 million to telephone and telegraph companies; £ 9.1 million to land companies, colonization concerns, and agricultural and ranching companies; £ 6.8 million to mercantile enterprises; £ 13.6 million to insurance companies; £ 4 million to mortgage companies and real estate companies; and £ 9.9 million to commercial and savings banks.

94. The portion of gross national product devoted to capital formation reached 25.9 per cent in 1900-04, 48.2 per cent in 1905-09, and 42.2 per cent in 1910-14. The amount contributed by foreign investment ranged between 30 per cent and 47 per cent of the total invested. See the estimates of this investment, and the distribution thereof, in Vol. I of the Economic Commission for Latin America study, *Analisis y proyecciones del desarrollo económico. V. El desarrollo económico de la Argentina,* Mexico: U. N. Department of Economic and Social Affairs, 1959.

95. Ricardo M. Ortiz, *op. cit.,* Vol. II, pp. 198-212; A. B. Martínez and M. Lewandowski, *op. cit.,* pp. 187-207, 235-260; C. A. Tornquist, ed., *The Economic Development of the Argentine Republic in the Last Fifty Years,* Buenos Aires: Ernesto Tornquist y Cía., 1919.

96. Adolfo Dorfman, *Evolución industrial argentina,* Buenos Aires: Editorial Losada, S.A., 1942, p. 9. More helpful for the early period of industrialization is Adolfo Dorfman, *Historia de la industria argentina,* Buenos Aires: Escuela de Estudios Argentinos, 1942.

97. The Argentines, like the Brazilians and Chileans, had even evolved to the point that they had made foreign investments of their own in other Latin American countries. The largest foreign enterprise is Paraguay, for example, was a ranching-colonization-quebracho operation which was launched in 1886 by Carlos Casado, a prominent Argentine landowner who was active in banking and colonization projects.

98. The classic study of Chilean agricultural organization is George McCutchen McBride, *Chile: Land and Society,* New York: American Geographical Society, 1936. McBride is especially thorough in his treatment of the hacienda or *fundo* system and the conditions of the *inquilino.* Valuable for its detailed historical examination of land tenure in a typical central Chilean valley is Jean Borde and Mario Góngora, *Evolución de la propiedad rural en el Valle del Puangue,* Santiago: Editorial Universitaria, S.A., 1956, 2 Vols.. Borde's and Góngora's study reveals the fundamental stability of the large estates as landholding units for a 300 year period that ended in the closing decades of the nineteenth century. McBride's research also takes cognizance of latter-day tendencies toward subdivision, especially through inheritance. A useful study specifically oriented toward the institution of *inquilinaje* is Mario Góngora, *Orígen de los "inquilinos" de Chile Central,* Santiago: Editorial Universitaria, S.A., 1960.

99. Luis Thayer Ojeda, *Elementos étnicos que han intervenido en la población de Chile,* Santiago: Imprenta la Ilustracion, 1919. Even before the colonial regime came to an end, the Chilean aristocracy had begun to take on a certain bourgeois cast. See Sergio Bagú, *Estructura social de la colonia,* Buenos Aires: Librería "El Ateneo" Editorial, 1952, p. 95. In the early republican years, John Miers observed that while foreign commerce and wholesaling were in the hands of British and other foreign commission houses, the internal distribution system was largely carried on by criollo merchants, of whom a goodly number came from landowning families. John Miers, *Travels in Chile and La Plata,* London: Baldwin, Cradock, and Joy, 1826, Vol. II, p. 240.

100. A good discussion of Chilean mining development in the eighteenth and nineteenth centuries is contained in Julio Ruíz Bourgeois, "La Minería en la Vida de Chile," in Humberto Fuenzalida et al., *Chile: geografía, educación, literatura,*

legislación, economía, minería, Buenos Aires: Editorial Losada, S.A., 1946, pp. 275-343.

101. See Basil Hall, *Extracts from a Journal Written on the Coasts of Chile, Peru, and Mexico in the Years 1820, 1821, 1822,* Edinburgh: Archibald Constable and Company, 1824, Vol. I, pp. 25-26, 87, and Vol. II, p. 60.

102. Julio C. Jobet, *Ensayo crítico del desarrollo económico-social de Chile,* Santiago: Editorial Universitaria, S.A., 1955, p. 42.

103. Roberto Hernández, *Juan Godoy, o el descubrimiento de Chañarcillo,* Valparaíso: Imprenta Victoria, 1932, 2 Vols. Also see the references to the progress of silver mining in Oscar Álvarez Andrews, *Historia del desarrollo industrial de Chile,* Santiago: Imprenta y Lit. la Ilustración, 1936.

104. See Roberto Hernández, *El salitre: resumen histórico desde su descubrimiento y explotación,* Valparaíso: Fisher Hermanos, 1930, and Miguel Cruchaga Montt, *Salitre y guano,* Madrid: Editorial Reus, S.A., 1929.

105. Useful information on economic development in this early period is also to be found in Daniel Martner, *Estudio de política comercial chilena e historia económica nacional,* Santiago: Imprenta Universitaria, 1923.

106. Less of the rising revenues were dissipated on internal armed conflicts, although as one writer delicately expressed it, "It may be said of Chile generally that money voted for improvements is not always spent without leakage upon the object for which it was raised." Francis J. G. Maitland, *Chile: Its Land and People: The History, Natural Features, Development and Industrial Resources of a Great South American Republic,* London: Francis Griffiths, 1914, p. 178.

107. See, for example, Benjamín Vicuña Mackenna, *The First Britons in Valparaíso (1817-1827),* Valparaíso: Imprenta Gordon, Henderson y Cía., 1884, and Henry Sewell Gana, *British Capital and Chilean Industries,* Santiago: Imprenta Cervantes, 1887. Also useful is Oscar Álvarez Andrews, *op. cit.*

108. Such was the tenor of a report by Nicolás Palacios, *Colonización chilena: reparos y remedios,* Valparaíso: Imprenta Alemana, 1904. A half-century earlier, a government report on the new German colonies described their initial accomplishments in glowing terms: Vicente Pérez Rosales, *Memoria sobre emigración, inmigración y colonización,* Santiago: Imprenta Julio Balin, 1854. Also see the official report issued a few years later: Joaquín Villarino, *Estudio sobre la colonización y emigración europea en Chile,* Santiago: Imprenta Nacional, 1867.

109. A description of the financial organization of the mining business and of the role of the capitalists known as *habilitadores* is found in Basil Hall, *op. cit.,* Vol. II, pp. 49-62. Captain Hall notes that English (and some North American) merchants also entered the field of mining finance, taking business away from the Chilean *habilitadores* because of the very high profit margins demanded by these latter. A distinctly Marxian but not altogether useless view of this early capitalist development is to be found on pp. 47-145 of Marcelo Segall, *Desarrollo del capitalismo en Chile,* Santiago: Editorial del Pacífico, 1953.

110. Julio C. Jobet, *op. cit.,* pp. 58-59.

111. The first bank established was the Banco de Chile de Arcos y Cía. in 1849, but it lasted only a very short while. For a discussion of early banking developments, see Ramón E. Santelicas, *Los bancos chilenos,* Santiago: Imprenta y Encuadernación "Barcelona," 1893, and Guillermo Subercaseaux, *El sistema monetario i la organización bancaria de Chile,* Santiago: Sociedad Imprenta i Litográfica Universo, 1920, Chaps. 14-16, 19.

112. Large landowners, apparently, borrowed a great deal from this institution to expand their properties, counting on inflation to lower the real value of their debt obligation. By the end of the century, most of the larger agricultural properties were heavily mortgaged — as was the case in Mexico and elsewhere. J. Borde and M. Góngora, *op. cit.,* p. 127.

113. Luis Escobar Cerda, *Aspectos de nuestra organización financiera en relación con el progreso de la economía nacional; El mercado de valores,* Santiago: Editorial Universitaria, 1954, pp. 38-39. By 1880, the Valparaíso bourse had sold

shares to its membership, but formal incorporation came later.

114. Some indication of the larger implications of the conflict is given in V. G. Kiernan's judicious article, "Foreign Interests in the War of the Pacific," *The Hispanic American Historical Review*, Vol. 35, No. 1 (February 1955), pp. 14-36.

115. The survey, reported in the pages of *El Mercurio*, a daily newspaper of Valparaíso, in a May 1882, issue, is quoted in the very useful study, "La Constitución de 1925 y las nuevas tendencias político-sociales," by Julio Heise González which was published in the no. 80, fourth trimester, issue of *Anales de la Universidad de Chile*, 1950; see especially pp. 126-154. In English, there is an excellent historical presentation of social structural changes in Frederick B. Pike, "Aspects of Class Relations in Chile, 1850-1960," *The Hispanic American Historical Review*, Vol. 43, No. 1 (February 1963), pp. 14-33. Professor Pike's article contains material which appears also in his longer study of Chilean political life, *Chile and the United States, 1880-1962*, Notre Dame: University of Notre Dame Press, 1963 — a book which is much more comprehensive than its title might suggest and which is, in fact, one of the most insightful and informative books ever written about Chile.

116. J. Heise González, *op. cit.*, p. 154; J. Borde and M. Góngora, *op. cit.*, p. 140. For an analysis of this social structure in more recent times, see Dale L. Johnson, "Industrialization, Social Mobility, and Class Formation in Chile," *Studies in Comparative International Development*, Vol. 3, No. 7 (1967-1968). Johnson concludes that Chile, in spite of its past, has a relatively rigid social structure.

117. The nineteenth-century copper boom was based upon high grade ores which could be profitably exploited by prevailing Chilean mining techniques with comparatively slight modification and improvement. These ores were gradually depleted, however, and during the 1870's and 1880's, the large copper mines of the western United States were opened up to exploitation. African producers also entered the scene later, so that whereas Chile had supplied 61 per cent of the world's copper in 1869, it supplied only a little over 4 per cent in the early years of the twentieth century. With the growth of the electrical industry after 1880, global demand increased sharply, and with superior technological and financial backing, companies from the advanced countries (first France and then the United States) came in after 1900 to develop the extensive lower grade Chilean copper deposits. North American capital began to develop the famous El Teniente mine in 1911, for example, and a couple of years later the exploitation of Chuquicamata began.

118. In an influential book on the contemporary Chilean crisis, the distinguished Chilean economist, Jorge Ahumada, singled out this socio-political constriction as a principal block to renewed progress. See Jorge Ahumada Corvalán, *En vez de la miseria*, Santiago: Editorial del Pacífico, S.A., 1958, pp. 19-20, 53. Also see the damaging indictment in Ernest Feder, "Feudalism and Agricultural Development: The Role of Controlled Credit in Chile's Agriculture," *Land Economics*, Vol. 36, No. 1 (February 1960). Also relevant to the point are two doctoral dissertations on Chilean agriculture: Thomas F. Carroll, "Agricultural Development in Chile," Unpublished doctoral dissertation, Cornell University, 1951, and Glen Ellis Martin, *La división de la tierra en Chile central*, Santiago: Editorial Nascimento, 1960. The works dealing with Chile's incompletely transformed social structure are legion in number.

119. Pedro L. Gonzáles and Miguel Soto Núñez, eds., *Album gráfico e histórico de la Sociedad de Fomento Fabril y de la industria nacional*, Santiago: S. F. F., 1926, Chap. 1.

120. O. Álvarez Andrews, *op. cit.*, p. 95.

121. The great Argentine promoter of education, Domingo Sarmiento, worked for a while in the new Chilean school system during a period of exile. Primary schools, organized with North American assistance, were established in the cities and institutions of engineering, medicine, and a normal school were also established. In 1842 the National University of Chile was founded. Although the total Chilean effort was probably less substantial than that carried through later in the century in the Argentine, it was nevertheless much more consequential than the educational programs of any other Spanish American country at the time or, for that matter, most other Spanish

American countries even into the twentieth century.

122. To indicate the constructive role of immigrants, it may be noted that the two main foundry and metal-working enterprises were the Lever-and-Murphy and the Balfour-and-Lyon Companies.

123. Balmaceda remains an especially controversial historical figure down to the present day. Among the many volumes written about the era, a representative Marxian interpretation is that given by Hernán Ramírez Necochea in *Balmaceda y la contrarrevolución de 1891,* Santiago: Editorial Universitaria, S.A., 1958. A reasonably objective, non-Marxian assessment is contained in José Miguel Yrarrázaval Larraín, *El Presidente Balmaceda,* Santiago: Editorial Nascimento, 1940, 2 Vols.

124. J. Fred Rippy, "Economic Enterprises of the 'Nitrate King' and His Associates in Chile," *Pacific Historical Review,* Vol. 17, No. 4 (November 1948), pp. 457-465.

125. J. C. Jobet, *op. cit.,* pp. 84 ff., 117, makes the claim that Chilean companies operated only about 16 per cent of the industry by 1897, but Jorge González von Marées, citing figures from the Central Statistical Office, claims that over half the capital was Chilean in the early 1900's. See Jorge González von Marées, *El problema obrero en Chile* (tesis de prueba), Santiago: Imprenta Universidad, 1923, p. 67. One capable historian, J. R. Brown, has found that as early as 1890 English companies alone accounted for 60 per cent of the output, so it would seem that foreign ownership was quite conspicuous even though influential Chilean capitalists were also engaged in nitrate production. See J. R. Brown, "Nitrate Crises, Combinations, and the Chilean Government in the Nitrate Age," *The Hispanic American Historical Review,* Vol. 43, No. 2 (May 1963), p. 234. Additional support for the alienation viewpoint is found in Aníbal Pinto Santa-Cruz, *Chile, un caso del desarrollo frustrado,* Santiago: Editorial Universitaria, S.A., 1959, pp. 52 ff., and Francisco A. Encina, *Historia de Chile,* Santiago: Editorial Nascimento, 1951, Vol. XIX, Chap. 14.

126. J. R. Brown's fine article cited above documents the developing conflict between national and foreign interests in the nitrate field. Chilean nitrate producers later came to feel that the cartelization of nitrates was an essential device for preserving the share of the national companies in the industry.

127. By "nationalizing" inflation, the government offended those wealthy private interests which had formerly benefited by presiding over the inflation-generating process. The continuation of inflationary finance, however, was injurious to middle class interests and probably was an additional factor in undermining the power of the Balmaceda regime.

128. The urban population rose from 27 per cent of the total in 1875 to upwards of 40 per cent in 1902. *Memoria presentada al Supremo Gobierno por la Comisión Central del Censo,* Santiago: 1910, p. 1262.

129. See Alberto Hurtado Cruchaga, *Sindicalismo (historia, teoría y práctica),* Santiago: Editorial del Pacífico, 1950; Moisés Poblete Troncoso, *La organización sindical en Chile y otros problemas sociales,* Santiago: Imprenta R. Brías, 1926; *ibid., El movimiento obrero latinoamericano,* Mexico: Fondo de Cultura Económica, 1946. For a Marxian view, see Hernán Ramírez Necochea, *Historia del movimiento obrero en Chile (siglo XIX),* Santiago: Talleres Gráficos Lautaro, 1956.

130. Alejandro Venegas, *Sinceridad: Chile íntimo en 1910,* Santiago: Imprenta Universitaria, 1910. Venegas wrote under the nom de plume of Dr. J. Valdés Cange in order to escape persecution for his devastating critique. A schoolteacher, he included in his book an especially damning attack on the contraproductive values and uneconomic skills instilled in young *chilenos* by the national educational system. Two years before Venegas' work appeared, the extremely influential novel, *Casa grande,* had come from the pen of an upper-class writer, Luis Orrego Luca, as a scathing indictment of the conspicuous consumption and general disutility of the Chilean determining classes.

131. See Pedro Aguirre Cerda, *El problema agrario,* Paris: Imprimerie Française, 1929; Luis Correa Vergara, *Agricultura chilena,* Santiago: Imprenta Nascimento, 1938, 2 Vols.; Leonicio Chaparro Ruminot, "Régimen de la Tierra (Las Instituciones Campesinas Chilenas: Inquilinaje y Aparcería)," *Revista Occidente,* (Santiago: Talleres Gráficos de

la Nación, 1950) Nos. 62 and 63, pp. 17-29; Carlos Keller R., *Revolución en la agricultura,* Santiago: Editorial Zig-Zag, 1956; Nicolas Kaldor, "El crecimiento económico y el problema de la inflación," *El Trimestre Económico,* January-March 1960, pp. 92-121. Earlier accounts which are useful are Lauro Barros, *Ensayo sobre las condiciones de las clases rurales de Chile,* Santiago: Imprenta Agrícola, 1875; Ramón Domínguez, *Nuestro sistema de inquilinaje* (tesis de prueba), Santiago: Imprenta del Correo, 1867; and Marcial González, *Condición de los trabajadores rurales en Chile,* Santiago: Imprenta la República, 1876.

132. Frank Fetter's previously cited work is the classic study of Chilean inflation, but over the years the perception of the relation between political struggle and inflation has been sharpened. See Carl Iversen et al., *Informe de la Misión Económica de las Naciones Unidas para Chile, 1949-1950,* New York: U.N. Technical Assistance Administration, 1951. Tom E. Davis, "Eight Decades of Inflation in Chile, 1879-1959, a Political Interpretation," *The Journal of Political Economy,* Vol. 71, No. 4 (August 1963), pp. 389-397. David Felix, "Structural Imbalances, Social Conflict and Inflation," *Economic Development and Cultural Change,* Vol. 8, No. 2 (January 1960), pp. 113-147. A highly sophisticated analysis of the problem is contained in the chapter on Chile in A. O. Hirschman's *Journeys Toward Progress.*

133. By 1900 the Laguna District regularly produced around 90 per cent of the total national cotton crop. For informative contemporary accounts of this development, see Percy F. Martin, *Mexico of the Twentieth Century,* London: E. Arnold, 1907, and W. A. Graham Clark, *Cotton Goods in Latin America, Part I,* Washington: U.S. Department of Commerce, 1909. See also Francisco Quintanas A., "Regiones Algodoneras de México," *México Agrícola,* Vol. 7, No. 76 (June 1960).

134. For a useful summary of the minerals development of this period, see L. de Launay, "Mines et Industries Minières," in *Le Méxique au début du XXe siècle,* Paris: Librarie Ch. Delagrave, 1902, Vol. I.

135. George McCutcheon McBride, *The Land Systems of Mexico,* New York: The American Geographical Society, 1923, p. 71. Also see Mariano Cuevas, *Historia de la iglesia en México,* El Paso: Editorial "Revista Católica," 1928, Vol. V, p. 302. The vast scale on which the state redistributed property during this period − properties of religious institutions, of villages, and of the public domain − makes those characterizations of the economic policy of the era which see it as a case of laissez-faire seem odd indeed.

136. For a brief period in 1880-1884, Manuel González, a Díaz-backed candidate, held office, but in 1884 Díaz himself resumed the position of chief executive, not to relinquish it until forced out by the onset of the Mexican Revolution.

137. The article, by one Mr. Lummis, was quoted approvingly on pages 6-7 in another of the typical public relations publications of the times, *Facts and Figures about Mexico, and Her Great Railroad, the Mexican Central,* which was distributed on a complimentary basis in 1900 by the Mexican Central Railway Company (3d ed., published in Mexico City by the company). The flavor of this latter work is anything but subtle − down to the quotation of Tennyson's "The old order changeth, yielding place to new (sic)" on the title page. The booklet is, however, useful in identifying the chief economic activity in various regions of the country and is representative of the many works of its genre which were distributed from Latin America in that era. Gullible writers and public relations experts were not the only persons to hold to such hyperbolic and sanguine views. No less a person than Cecil Rhodes, who lost funds in one of the early Mexican petroleum companies, was moved to state that "Mexico is the treasure house from which will come the gold, silver, copper and precious stones that will build the empire of tomorrow, and make the future cities of the world veritable Jerusalems." Title page quotation from P. Harvey Middleton, *Industrial Mexico, 1919 Facts and Figures,* New York: Dodd, Mead and Company, 1919.

138. The *rurales* were rural police employed by Díaz to keep the peace in the countryside.

139. For a perhaps excessively favorable judgment on these advances, see Walter F. McCaleb, *The Public Finances of Mexico,* New York: Harper and Brothers Publishers,

1921, pp. 143-192. Also see pp. 435-515 of Pablo Macedo, *La evolución mercantil, comunicaciones y obras públicas, la hacienda pública,* Mexico: J. Ballescá y Cía. Editores, 1905.

140. Pablo Macedo, *op. cit.,* pp. 267-273.

141. Francisco R. Calderón, *Historia moderna de México, la república restaurada: la vida económica,* Mexico: Editorial Hermes, 1955, pp. 105-114.

142. Alfred Picard, "Industrie, Commerce et Navigation," in *Le Mexique au début du XXe siècle,* Vol. I, p. 340-341; F. Calderón, *op. cit.,* pp. 99-102.

143. The federal and state capitals came close to doubling in size between 1876 and 1910, while many northern mining and transport centers grew even more markedly. Moisés González Navarro, *Historia moderna de México, el porfiriato: la vida social,* Mexico: Editorial Hermes, 1957, pp. 20-24.

144. L. de Launay, *op. cit.,* pp. 268-270, 320.

145. As early as 1865 the Mexican government had issued a permit to a Spaniard for the exploitation of deposits of asphaltum and free-flowing oil in Tamaulipas; but while this activity met with limited success, several later exploratory efforts on the Gulf Coast failed to produce much in the way of positive results. Real development of the nation's oil industry may be said to have started in 1900 when E. L. Doheny and C. A. Canfield formed the Mexican Petroleum Company. P. H. Middleton, *op. cit.,* pp. 48-52.

146. El Colegio de México, *Estadísticas económics del porfiriato. Comercio exterior de México (1877-1911),* Mexico: Fondo de Cultura Económica, 1960, pp. 75, 78, 152-153.

147. *Ibid.,* pp. 45-59.

148. A. Picard, *op. cit.,* p. 22.

149. In the early 1880's, the note issue functions of the Monte de Piedad were terminated because abuse of the privilege had brought the institution to ruin. In 1884 the Banco Nacional was formed from a merger of the Banco Nacional Mexicano and the Banco Mercantil, Agrícola e Hipotecario.

150. A useful study of early Mexican banking is Walter F. McCaleb, *Present and Past Banking in Mexico,* New York: Harper and Brothers Publishers, 1920.

151. See, for example, the relevant sections in the *Memoria de Hacienda, 1907-08,* Secretaría de Hacienda, Mexico: Talleres Gráficos, 1908.

152. The government did increase the national investment in education during the Díaz era and supported the modernization of such professional institutions as the Schools of Jurisprudence, Medicine, Engineering, and Fine Arts. Normal schools were opened for both men and women, and the program of the National School of Commerce, in which a growing number of students were enrolled, was strengthened. Oddly, in view of the importance of the agricultural sector, the School of Agriculture seems to have been the least favored (by students) of these various institutions for specialized education; around the turn of the century, its student body numbered only about 50. The situation undoubtedly reflected the fact that nearly all of the progress made in increasing the number of primary and secondary schools was confined to the towns and cities, while very little (and, in most cases, nothing) was done to increase the access of the rural populace to opportunities for primary and secondary education (and, hence, higher education). Urban-reared school children seldom opted for training for agricultural careers, which, in any case, were not likely to be either very numerous or very promising because of the organizational structure of the agricultural sector. For two useful accounts of educational developments, see the section on education by E. A. Chávez in Justo Sierra, ed., *México, su evolución social,* 3 Vols., Mexico: J. Ballescá y Cía., 1900-1902, and Moisés González Navarro, *op. cit.,* pp. 564-675.

153. For a perceptive discussion of this issue, see Moisés González Navarro, *op. cit.,* pp. 153-184. Some idea of the extent of the preferential treatment accorded foreigners is seen in the 1910 incident in which Enrique Creel, the minister of foreign affairs and son of a Kentuckian who had married into one of the wealthiest families of northern Mexico, suppressed the Catholic daily *El País* and the *Diario del Hogar for* publishing anti-American articles which had provoked an official protest by the United

States Ambassador. Ernest Gruening, *Mexico and Its Heritage,* New York: Appleton-Century Crofts, Inc., 1928, p. 560.

154. E. D. Trowbridge, *Mexico Today and Tomorrow,* New York: The Macmillan Company, 1919, pp. 119-120.

155. Two aphoristic expressions of the times — "Poor Mexico, so far from God and so close to the United States" and "Poor Mexico, mother to foreigners and stepmother to Mexicans" — tell us as much about the subjective (and negative) assessment by Mexicans of their situation as about the objective reality itself. The animosity directed toward *yanqui* penetration was by no means confined to its presumed economic and social consequences. Fueling the resentment was the nascent, and largely middle-class, reaction against the prevailing *malinchismo* in cultural norms. José Vasconcelos, in his interesting *Breve historia de México* (Mexico: Ediciones Botas, 1950), illustrates the degree of rancor harbored by some of the outstanding young intellectuals toward the cultural imperialism of the United States.

156. See Helen Phipps, "Some Aspects of the Agrarian Question in Mexico: A Historical Study," *University of Texas Bulletin* No. 2515, Austin: University of Texas, 15 April 1925, pp. 112-130.

157. Moisés González Navarro, *op. cit.,* pp. 134-153; Francisco Calderón, *op. cit.,* pp. 61-79.

158. *Ibid.,* pp. 187-216.

159. *Ibid.,* pp. 143-147, 218.

160. *Ibid.,* pp. 265-273. The first Catholic conference on rural problems was held in 1903. By the close of 1910, there had been at least five others of some importance, an incidence of occurrence which is reflective of the growing concern over rural deprivation. Some of the conferences' recommendations were of a decidely moralistic bent, but others, as indicated, were closer to the point of the problems. It is particularly interesting to note that on several of these occasions the capitalistic system was indicted for its dehumanized character.

161. *Ibid.,* pp. 280-297.

162. A *campesino* congress was held in 1877, and thereafter a number of *ligas campesinas* were formed. Their efforts and existence were, however, ephemeral. Victor Alba, *Historia del movimiento obrero en América Latina,* Mexico: Libreros Mexicanos Unidos, 1964, p. 441.

163. Victor Alba, *Le mouvement ouvrier en Amérique Latine,* Paris: Les Editions Ouvrières, 1953, p. 109; Moisés González Navarro, *op. cit.,* pp. 344-368. The Gran Círculo at first supported Porfirio Díaz through its newspaper *El Socialista,* in the belief that Díaz would continue the liberalizing work of Juárez.

164. Moisés González Navarro, *op. cit.,* pp. 298-344. Approximately 250 strikes occurred during the Porfirian era.

165. Manuel González Ramírez, *La huelga de Cananea,* Mexico: Fondo de Cultura Económica, 1957. In the strike, the usual work issues were made more intense by a charge of discriminatory treatment against Mexican workers by the foreign-owned mining concern. United States intervention in the dispute was also a disquieting element from a Mexican point of view.

166. The petroleum strike, like the earlier one at Cananea, pitted Mexican workers against foreign employers. In the first episode, the Porfirian government sided with the foreigners and put down the strike with repressive measures. In the petroleum strike, the foreign companies defied first the workers organization, then the labor courts, and ultimately the Supreme Court of Mexico. The answer of the government, now a Revolutionary one, was expropriation. During the crisis which attended the confrontation, various feuding sectors of the Mexican body politic rallied to the support of the government in an unprecedented display of national solidarity.

NOTES FOR CHAPTER X

1. Symposium on the transformation of peasant societies co-sponsored by the

American Political Association and the American Association for the Advancement of Science, Montreal, 26 December 1964. Dobyn's observation is as relevant in explaining the economic preeminence of immigrant entrepreneurs in Latin America and in accounting for the characteristic middleman domination of consumers and small producers (rural and urban) as it is to explaining the maintenance of upper class domination of economic life in an environment in which communications systems are neither widespread and well developed nor easily available to the public and where access to the means of acquiring skills is severely restricted.

2. Francisco A. Encina, *Nuestra inferioridad económica, sus causas, sus consecuencias,* Santiago: Imprenta Universitaria, 1912. While Encina placed much of the blame on the Chilean educational system and Chilean behavioral traits (Chap. 4, especially), he also lamented foreign domination of national economic life, particularly in mining and commerce.

3. Santiago Marín Vicuña, *Los ferrocarriles de Chile,* Santiago: Imprenta Cervantes, 1916, pp. 125-127.

4. J. R. Brown, "Nitrate Crises, Combinations, and the Chilean Government in the Nitrate Age," *The Hispanic American Historical Review,* Vol. 43, No. 2 (May 1963), pp. 230-246. The language used has a strikingly modern ring. The national wealth was seen in imminent danger of being converted into a "foreign factory." The "high-handed and insolent conduct of certain of the capitalists, who control the Nitrate industry from their board rooms in London" was singled out for "violent attack." Charges were raised that national concerns were being squeezed out, that workers were being thrown into unemployment, that foreigners were reaping high profits, and that the public treasury was suffering because of policies designed to enhance foreign interests.

5. Oscar Alvarez Andrews, *Historia del desarrollo industrial de Chile,* Santiago: Imp. y Lit. La Ilustración, 1936, p. 143. Francisco A. Encina, *Historia de Chile,* Santiago: Editorial Nascimento, 1951, Vol. XIX, p. 411.

6. H. S. Ferns, *Britain and Argentina in the Nineteenth Century,* Oxford: The Clarendon Press, 1960, pp. 377, 462.

7. Adolfo Dorfman, *Historia de la industria Argentina,* Buenos Aires: Escuela de Estudios Argentinos, 1942, pp. 97-101.

8. *Ibid.,* pp. 117-120.

9. See Luis Ospina Vásquez, *Industria y protección en Colombia, 1810-1930,* Medellín: Editorial San Francisco, 1955, Chaps. 6 and 7 for a discussion of the growing Colombian interest in induced industrialization.

10. Nicia Vilela Luz, *A luta pela industrialização do Brasil (1808 a 1930),* São Paulo: Difusão Europeía do Livro, 1961, pp. 52-54.

11. *Ibid.,* pp. 20, 28.

12. In this the viscount seems rather clearly to have had in mind a concept similar to that expressed in the late Erich W. Zimmermann's memorably phrased statement that the industrial revolution produced an "emancipation of man from the limits of the organic."

13. Luis Nogueira de Paula, "Brasil", in Luis Roque Gondra et al., *El pensamiento económico latinoamericano,* Mexico: Fondo de Cultura Económica, 1945, p. 91. See also Stanley J. Stein, *The Brazilian Cotton Manufacture; Textile Enterprise in an Underdeveloped Area, 1850-1950,* Cambridge: Harvard University Press, 1957, Chap. 7.

14. Victor Paz Estenssoro, "Bolivia", in Luis Roque Gondra et al., *op. cit.,* pp. 47-51.

15. A. F. Cesarino, Jr., *Direito Social Brasileiro,* São Paulo: Ed. Freitas Bastos, 1963, Vol. I, p. 236. An informative analysis of the origins and consequences of this legislative decree is found in J. V. Freitas Marcondes, *First Brazilian Legislation Relating to Rural Labor Unions, A Sociological Study,* Latin American Monographs Series No. 20, Gainesville: University of Florida Press, June 1962.

16. Even today, it is not uncommon for the workers of a large foreign enterprise to personalize the foreign corporation as an "hacendado", a manner of speaking which suggests that in popular usage the meaning of the word is large-scale absentee ownership.

17. Somewhat later, Colombia received a substantial indemnification payment from the United States which, along with heavy United States investment in Colombian public securities and certain industries (bananas, petroleum, mining), made the decade of the 1920's an era of rapid economic expansion in that country.

18. A. B. Martinez and M. Lewandowski, *The Argentine in the Twentieth Century,* New York: Charles Scribner's Sons, 1914, p. 22.

19. Other relevant considerations which led to the establishment of branch assembly plants were the lower freight charges and duties applicable to component parts as compared with finished products, while the branch assembly plants also enabled manufacturers to take advantage of lower labor cost in the labor-intensive assembly operations. One of the earliest of these assembly plants was that established by the Pullman Company in Rio de Janeiro in 1913 for the assembly of railway equipment.

20. Both the prevailing fiscal systems and the relations of production in the agricultural sector, the latter in combination with the institution of absentee ownership, tended to siphon off such income increases as were generated in the rural and provincial areas, transferring this purchasing power in concentrated form to the principal urban centers.

21. The southern Brazilian foundry mentioned by Mulhall in *Rio Grande do Sul . . .,* pp. 56-57, was engaged in this sort of production as were a number of the late nineteenth-century ironworks in Antioquia and elsewhere in Colombia (L. Ospina Vásquez, *op. cit.,* pp. 311, 342). Ospina Vásquez also cites *(Ibid.,* pp. 316-317) the example of the ironworks which manufactured rails for Colombian railways during the years 1880-1897 before operations had to be suspended because of disruptions born of the civil war in that country.

22. S. Stein, *op. cit.,* p. 39, mentions this in connection with the Brazilian cotton textile plants, while L. Ospina Vásquez, *op. cit.,* pp. 340-341, relates an interesting case in which a Colombian entrepreneur from Medellín ordered (in 1903) machinery from England to set up a plant similar to those he had studied in Mexico. Some modification of the machinery was necessary to permit its shipment over the rough transport routes into Medellín, but despite this modification, the transport was so difficult that when the equipment arrived, an extensive repair operation which amounted to virtually rebuilding it had to be undertaken before actual installation could be effected. This was probably an extreme case, but quite widely it was essential for producers to have near at hand the facilities for fabricating such components as they needed for repair.

23. *Peru To-Day,* Vol. 3, No. 9 (November-December 1911), p. 55.

24. Adolfo Dorfman, *op. cit.,* pp. 117-120. In the Chile of 1910, some 60 foundries were in operation according to O. Alvarez Andrews, *op. cit.,* p. 191.

25. In this regard, for instance, it is significant that of the 200 Argentine manufacturers of farm implements and other agricultural machinery which displayed their products at the first Exhibition of Argentine Agricultural Machinery in March 1965, most of the firms were the outgrowth of pioneering establishments which began around the middle of the nineteenth century as tool shops designing and building machinery suited to Argentine agricultural conditions.

26. The following studies are especially helpful in understanding the conditions which have influenced the rise of labor in Latin America: Moisés Poblete Troncoso, *El movimiento obrero latinoamericano,* Mexico: Fondo de Cultura Económica, 1946; Robert J. Alexander, *Labor Relations in Argentina, Brazil, and Chile,* New York: McGraw-Hill Book Company, 1962; Miles E. Galvin, *Unionism in Latin America,* Ithaca: New York State School of Industrial and Labor Relations, Bulletin 45, October, 1962; and John J. Crowley, Jr., "Labor and Political Parties in Latin America: Three examples," Madison: University of Wisconsin unpublished paper, 1960. Worthy of special mention is the extremely incisive study by James L. Payne, *Labor and Politics in Peru: The System of Political Bargaining,* New Haven: Yale University Press, 1965.

27. In these cases, it is at least arguable that government intervention did not necessarily do violence to the factor returns distribution which would correspond to a model of pure competition, for the pressures exerted on behalf of native labor may merely have served to offset the oligopsonistic (or, in some cases, monopsonistic) position of

export-sector employers and to compensate for imperfections in the labor market which ordinarily may have worked more to the disadvantage of laborers than to that of employers. Indeed, it is theoretically conceivable that, in the absence of government intervention, an element of exploitation may sometimes have been involved in the employment of local factors of production since an oligopsonistic or monopsonistic employer would be able to pay factor returns (wages) below the marginal revenue product of labor.

28. It has been essentially this kind of political environment that has permitted a modest success for what A. O. Hirschman has called "reform mongering" in his book *Journeys Toward Progress*. It is interesting to note, however, that middle-class power has generally been accommodated even more than working-class power in the twentieth-century regimes. In a number of countries social welfare schemes provide more ample benefits for *empleados* (white-collar workers) than for *obreros* (blue-collar workers). Indeed, in the prevalent custom of providing special social security systems for different professions and industries so that social benefits are distributed on a privileged basis, there is strong evidence of the effects of differential political responsiveness.

29. Brazil was not the only Latin American country affected adversely by this development although it was the chief loser. Mexico, Peru, and Bolivia were also hurt to some extent.

30. V. D. Wickizer, *The World Coffee Economy with Special Reference to Control Schemes*, Palo Alto: Stanford University Food Research Institute, 1943, p. 248-249.

31. For an analysis of the harm done by protective policies in sugar, see R. H. Snape, "Some Effects of Protection in the World Sugar Insustry," *Economica*, London: Vol. 30, No. 117 New Series (February 1963), pp. 63-73.

32. The problem, a continuing one, has been the source of policy friction. In June 1960, for example, the director of the Banco Nacional de México, Rodrigo Gómez, denounced international credit agencies for injuring the Latin American economies by helping new areas produce agricultural products already in oversupply. Later the same month, the Brazilian ambassador to Washington, Walther Moreira Salles, accused the World Bank of accelerating the development of African countries at the expense of Latin America by financing the expansion of African coffee and cotton crops in competition with Latin American producers.

33. The rubber producing areas of southeast Asia, for example, were more accessible by cheap ocean transport and had more abundant labor resources as well. Somewhat the same advantages held for tin producers in southeast Asia, who also enjoyed the advantage of working with placer deposits rather than the lode deposits which are typical of the Bolivian industry. Compared with the ores of southeast Asia, Bolivian tin ores are complex, low-grade, and difficult to treat; in addition, because of the location of the mines in the high sierra, applicable transport costs are high. For two revealing studies of Bolivian tin, see H. P. Milstead "Bolivia as a Source of Tin," *Economic Geography*, Vol. 23, No. 3 (July 1947), pp. 355 ff., and P. R. Greiss, "The Bolivian Tin Industry," *Economic Geography*, Vol. 27, No. 3 (July 1951), pp. 238 ff.

34. United States Tariff Commission, *Chemical Nitrogen*, Report No. 114, Washington, D.C.: 1937, p. 60. See also R. H. Whitbeck, "Chilean Nitrate and the Nitrogen Revolution", *Economic Geography*, Vol. 7, No. 3 (July 1931), pp. 273 ff. Apart from the extraction of nitrogen from the air, an increasing amount was also being produced as a by-product of other industries. The same influence adversely affected the fortunes of silver exporters, as improved smelting techniques enabled larger amounts of silver to be extracted as a by-product of other minerals processing operations.

35. The demise of these firms was also hastened by declining banana yields which were attributable to the leaching of the soil on cleared lands by heavy rains on the Caribbean side of Middle America.

36. The move to the dry Pacific coast was not without several offsetting advantages which may have held operating costs down despite the need to employ irrigation: (1) there was less leaching of the soil, (2) roads were more easily built and maintained, (3) control of malaria and other tropical diseases was facilitated, (4) fewer labor hours were lost because of rain, and (5) the control of sigatoka was easier. On the other hand,

the geographical shift in production necessitated further outlays on railway lines, port facilities, and other installations associated with banana production and exportation.

37. Pan American Union, Division of Economic Research, *The Foreign Trade of Latin America Since 1913*, Washington: Pan American Union, 1952.

38. Simon G. Hanson, *Argentine Meat and the British Market*, Palo Alto: Stanford University Press, 1938.

39. B. C. Swerling, *International Control of Sugar, 1918-1941*, Palo Alto: Stanford University Food Research Institute, Commodity Policy Studies No. 7, 1949.

40. For useful studies of capital movements in the post-1914 period, see United Nations, Department of Economic and Social Affairs, *Foreign Capital in Latin America*, New York: United Nations, 1955, and Raymond E. Mikesell, *Foreign Investments in Latin America*, Washington: Pan American Union, 1955.

41. For a reasonably typical statement of the new attitude towards foreign investment, see Eduardo Arcila Farías, *El capital extranjero*, Caracas: 1950, the appendix of which surveys contemporary controls exercised over foreign capital in the major Latin American countries. Arcila Farías, like many others, proposed that production facilities geared to the domestic market should be reserved, in the main, for domestic investors and that the participation of foreign capital in these fields should be closely regulated by public authorities. The 1949 annual report of the Banco Central de Venezuela, for example, expressed views similar to those of Arcila Farías as official policy.

42. Interestingly, this argument against the rootlessness of foreign capital appeared fairly early on the Latin American scene. In a report prepared for the Uruguayan congress in 1888, an economist of that country asked,"(What) can we expect as a commercial nation, when a great part of our business elements are not native, and commercial capital is always uncertain? Commercial capital goes as it comes, as a result of any chance fluctuation: never takes root; is always moving, capricious; tomorrow it will turn its back on what it eagerly seeks today.... The making of a nation and of economic independence depends on domestic industry, that is to say, on the proportional development of productive forces for the employment of the national labor force, and on permanent capital investments." Quotation translated and reproduced in Pedro C. M. Teichert, *Economic Policy Revolution and Industrialization in Latin America*, Oxford, Mississippi: University of Mississippi, Bureau of Business Research, 1959, p. 51.

43. The validity of this particular line of reasoning is open to question on several counts, but be that as it may, it has become a commonly accepted assumption in contemporary Latin American policy discussion.

44. Much the same sort of reasoning has been employed in connection with other policies of the period. The social controls applied to foreign investment activities, for example, have tended to favor manufacturing investments on the grounds that these contribute more widely to domestic growth through the transmission of more skills to the labor force, through their backward and forward linkages with other firms in the domestic sector, and through their contribution to the development of local marketing systems.

45. United Nations Economic Commission for Latin America, *Analisis y proyecciones..., El desarrollo económico de la Argentina*, Vol. II, pp. 159-160.

46. G. Palm, *Industrialização e economia natural*, Rio de Janeiro: Instituto Superior de Estudos Brasileiros, 1957, pp. 66-67.

47. Oscar Alvarez Andrews, *op. cit.*, pp. 188-193. Although the exact comparability of the figures given for the two dates is doubtful, the general direction of the trend suggested seems correct.

NOTES FOR CHAPTER XI

1. For a useful account of Peruvian experience in "decontrolling" the economy after the mid-1940's, see Manuel Fuentes Irurozqui, *Una experiencia interesante en el*

Perú; del intervencionismo a la libertad económica, Madrid: Ediciones Cultura Hispánica, 1952. From 1949 on, it was the declared policy of the Peruvian government to encourage private enterprise and foreign investment. An excellent review of these policies, and their results, is found in Shane Hunt, *The Economic Development of Peru,* Homewood, Illinois: Richard D. Irwin, Inc., (forthcoming).

2. The main outlines of the corrective policies which were partially implemented during this period (1956-1958) are to be found in three reports prepared for the Argentine government by Raúl Prebisch, then executive secretary of the United Nations Economic Commission for Latin America and formerly the chief organizer and first director-general of the Argentine central bank. See Raúl Prebisch, *The Economic State of Argentina,* London: Bank of London and South America, Ltd., 1955; *Ibid., Plan for Economic Restoration,* London: Bank of London and South America, Ltd., 1956; and *Ibid., Sound Money or Runaway Inflation,* London: Bank of London and South America, Ltd., 1956. The economic doctrine propounded in these reports, incidentally, varies in several respects, at least in point of emphasis, from that implicit in most of the E.C.L.A. work during the 1950's. While the Prebisch Report (as the three documents were collectively known) hewed fairly closely to the lines of economic orthodoxy, the E.C.L.A. doctrine of development generally strengthened the influence of more nationalistically or internally oriented policies.

3. In passing, it might also be said that there is a degree of affinity between this general point of view and those who, particularly during the 1950's, saw the development of Puerto Rico as a possible prototype for Latin America. Among the aspects of Puerto Rican experience which were held up for emulation were the island economy's effective public administration, its tax structure, its success in programing and carrying out public investment programs in a context of monetary stability, and its program of industrial promotion based upon "export" industries and "foreign" investment. Of the several worthwhile studies of this experience, see in particular William H. Stead, *Fomento – The Economic Development of Puerto Rico,* Washington, D.C.: National Planning Association, Planning Pamphlet No. 103, 1958, and Earl P. Hanson, *Puerto Rico: Ally for Progress,* Princeton: D. Van Nostrand Company, Inc., 1962.

4. For examples of the way in which foreign investment is supported as a means of increasing the supply not only of capital but of managerial and technical capabilities as well, see IBRD, *The Basis of a Development Program for Colombia,* Washington, D.C.: 1950, p. 406; IBRD, *The Economic Development of Guatemala,* Baltimore: The Johns Hopkins Press, 1951, pp. 96-97; IBRD, *The Economic Development of Nicaragua,* Baltimore: The Johns Hopkins Press, 1953, pp. 122-125; Combined Mexican Working Party, *The Economic Development of Mexico,* Baltimore: The Johns Hopkins Press, 1953, p. 81-82. The report on Guatemala also, on pp. 128, 130-131, urged that national legislation be changed to permit oil development by foreign capital since "no national interests, either private or public, have shown themselves willing or able to initiate effective oil development." A similar open door policy for foreign investment in petroleum was urged upon Argentina during the mid-1950's.

5. In this connection it is germane to remark the notably poor performance of most Latin American exports during the postwar period, even when compared with other underdeveloped regions, none of which, as a whole, encountered particularly more favorable price trends than Latin America during this period. In both commodities whose prices were falling and those whose prices were rising, the growth of Latin American exports tended to lag appreciably behind the rate of expansion in global trading. According to studies compiled by the research division of the Chase Manhattan Bank, the value of Latin American exports grew by only 27 per cent between 1948 and 1960 (only 8 per cent, if Venezuelan exports are excluded). During the same interval, the corresponding increases for other areas were: the Middle East, 70 per cent; Africa, 80 per cent; and Asia, 109 per cent. *Latin American Business Highlights,* New York: The Chase Manhattan Bank, Vol. 11, No. 2 (Second Quarter 1961), pp. 18-22.

6. Aside from the possible tendency of such schemes to reduce the pressure for efficient resource use, it has also been argued that the transfer of additional resources to Latin America through aid programs rather than through commodity price support

arrangements permits some degree of outside control to be exercised over the use of the resources so transferred – an insurance against an unproductive dissipation of these external resources. On the other hand, Latin Americans have frequently found the aid route less palatable than the trade route for precisely the reason that it does permit outside control over resource use, as well as for the reason that foreign aid appropriations might well be more unstable from year to year than commodity control agreements in their provision of external resources. To the extent that the latter Latin American contention is valid, the commodity stabilization route for effecting international transfers of resources would facilitate development planning by stabilizing one of the main planning parameters, that of foreign exchange availabilities.

Latin American spokesmen have also argued that the trade route is preferable to the aid route in that it introduces the external resources into the economy through the private export sector where, it is said, there are already available the institutions (corporations, banks, etc.) and the accumulated investing and production experience needed to put the resources to work effectively. In view of the problems which have frequently been encountered in the organization of the Latin American public sector (which would be the more likely recipient of aid-transferred resources), this contention can certainly not be dismissed lightly. Yet, as the marginal propensity to consume tends to be rather high in most of Latin America, it may well be that a given volume of internationally transferred resources could more completely be channeled directly into capital accumulation via the aid route than it could via the trade route where only a fraction of the volume would flow into the domestic savings and investment stream.

7. See Frank Tamagna, *La banca central en América Latina*, Mexico: Centro de Estudios Monetarios Latinoamericanos, 1963, pp. 63-86, for a summary of these developments. See also Robert Trifflin, "Central Banking and Monetary Management in Latin America," in S. E. Harris, ed., *Economic Problems of Latin America*, New York, McGraw-Hill Book Company, Inc., 1944, pp. 93-116.

8. Aside from a large number of unpublished memoranda, reports, and advisory commission recommendations, the following published works are among the more notable examples of the studies issued by these groups: IBRD, *The Basis of a Development Program for Colombia;* IBRD, *Report on Cuba,* Baltimore: The Johns Hopkins Press, 1951; IBRD, *The Economic Development of Guatemala;* IBRD and FAO, *The Agricultural Development of Uruguay,* Washington, D.C.: 1951; IBRD, *The Economic Development of Nicaragua;* Combined Mexican Working Party, *The Economic Development of Mexico;* IBRD, *The Agricultural Development of Colombia,* Washington, D.C.: 1956; IBRD and FAO, *The Economic Development of Venezuela,* Baltimore: The Johns Hopkins Press, 1961; H. C. Wallich and J. H. Adler, *Public Finance in a Developing Country,* Cambridge: Harvard University Press, 1951; J. H. Adler et al., *Public Finance and Economic Development in Guatemala,* Palo Alto: Stanford University Press, 1952; Joint Brazil-United States Economic Development Commission, *The Development of Brazil,* Washington, D.C.: Institute of Inter-American Affairs, 1954; *ibid.,Brazilian Technical Studies,* Washington, D.C.: Institute of Inter-American Affairs, 1955; Carl S. Shoup et. al., *The Fiscal System of Venezuela,* Baltimore: The Johns Hopkins Press, 1959; Milton C. Taylor et al., *Fiscal Survey of Colombia,* Baltimore: The Johns Hopkins Press, 1965.

9. In this position, the voice of the foreigner has occasionally been echoed by certain domestic interest groups, particularly those most directly linked with the export sector and the older, more established industries. Such has been the case, for example, in Peru, Mexico, and Argentina, in each of which there is a noticeable division of opinion regarding proper industrial policy. In the last two of these countries, the split in thinking between old groups and new groups has even been institutionalized into separate associations of industrialists, the new groups generally favoring a more interventionist role for government. In Peru, the difference in views is manifested more clearly in the press, with the *La Prensa* newspaper generally acting as spokesman for the economic liberals while the *El Comercio* newspaper and such magazines as *Oiga* and *Caretas* put forward the more interventionist viewpoint.

10. While low import duties have ordinarily been favored in the interests of promoting economic efficiency, there has been a more general disposition to accept high duties on luxury imports as a supplement to progressive direct taxation in curtailing conspicuous consumption. It should be mentioned that the IBRD report on Venezuela adopts a relatively more flexible attitude towards national industrialization policies than was present in most of the earlier country studies. See, for example, the treatment of the new government-owned steel plant and the general discussion of manufacturing development in IBRD, *The Economic Development of Venezuela*, pp. 59, 269 ff. Even in this report, however, the mission's acceptance of public industrial ventures was highly qualified. For the record, it should be kept in mind that as early as the 1940-1944 period the U.S. government had made loans (through the Export-Import Bank) to Latin American governmental development authorities for the purpose of establishing and expanding basic industrial enterprises.

11. *Ibid.*

12. IBRD, *The Economic Development of Guatemala*, pp. 54-59, 126-173.

13. IBRD, *The Basis of a Development Program for Colombia*. The subsequently established government iron and steel mill at Paz del Río was analyzed and held to be uneconomic.

14. While the attention to banking reforms has been mainly expressed through conferences and missions of central banking technicians and in the work of the Centro de Estudios Monetarios Latinoamericanos, it has also come up for consideration in the World Bank's country studies. See, for example, IBRD, *The Basis of a Development Program for Colombia*, pp. 567-576.

15. By calling these "enabling" sectors, it is meant that these generate external economies which enable or facilitate the development of other industries.

16. Recurrent references to this situation are to be found, for example, throughout the World Bank's report, *The Economic Development of Venezuela*, and the same is true of the other studies, though perhaps the *Report on Cuba* contains the most severe indictment in this regard. See also IBRD, *The Agricultural Development of Colombia*, pp. 43-44, 147-206; IBRD, *The Economic Development of Nicaragua*, pp. 85-98; IBRD and FAO, *The Agricultural Development of Peru*, Part I, pp. 13-22, Part II, pp. 314 ff.; IBRD, *The Basis of a Development Program for Colombia*, pp. 22 ff., 104-106, 119, 341-349, 584-592, and Appendix A; IBRD, *The Economic Development of Guatemala*, pp. 212, 244-249, 262-264; Combined Mexican Working Party, *The Economic Development of Mexico*, pp. 97-98.

17. IBRD, *Report on Cuba*, p. 459. See also *ibid.*, pp. 9-12, 67, 266, 405, 453.

18. For a brief report on the subject, see Public Administration Clearing House, *Public Administration in Latin America*, Washington, D.C.: Pan American Union, 1955. For the last half of the decade of the 1950's the United States foreign economic assistance program put well over a million dollars into the effort to modernize Latin American public administration.

19. In addition to cases of such preferential tax treatment for land-based enterprises, the difficulty of establishing with certainty the taxable net income of rural enterprises has in most countries tended to influence investor preference towards the acquisition of rural holdings and has afforded a means of escaping taxes on other income sources. Further, even where land taxation has been employed, the effects of inflation, combined with initial underevaluation, infrequent reassessment, and the practical difficulties of enforcement have generally resulted in a ludicrously small land-tax burden. Informative references to these sorts of problems are to be found in several of the papers contained in Harvard Law School, International Program on Taxation, *Conference on Agricultural Taxation and Economic Development*, Cambridge: Harvard University Press, 1954.

20. "Local initiative is given little chance, and the public is accustomed to expect the central government to do everything. Paradoxically, however, it has learned to expect very little from Habana." IBRD, *Report on Cuba*, p. 465. The same source notes also that the 1940 Constitution stated that local governments could not borrow money without getting approval of such loans from the Tribunal of Accounts of the

central government. Yet, ten years later the Tribunal had still not been established. For a view of the situation in another country, see Carr L. Donald, "The Politics of Local Government Finance in Brazil," *Inter-American Economic Affairs*, Vol. 13, No. 1 (Summer 1959), pp. 21-37.

21. "The Growth and Decline of Import Substitution in Brazil," *Economic Bulletin for Latin America*, United Nations: Vol. 9, No. 1 (March 1964), pp. 53-56.

22. In addition to the cited studies by Taylor, Shoup, Adler et al., see IBRD, *The Basis of a Development Program for Colombia*, pp. 255-286, 550-566; and IBRD, *The Economic Development of Nicaragua*, pp. 77-83, 318-389, for a review of taxation and government spending problems.

23. Arthur D. Little, Inc., *Industrial Development in Argentina*, Cambridge, Massachusetts: 1961, p. 54.

24. See IBRD, *The Basis of a Development Program for Colombia*, pp. 241-253, and IBRD and FAO, *The Agricultural Development of Peru*, Part II, pp. 240 ff., for typical discussions of these points. To indicate the importance attached to human resource development, it may be noted that the World Bank missions slated health and education to receive important shares (well over 10 per cent in each case) in the programmed investment schedules of the countries with which they have worked. Approximately a quarter of the project obligations of the International Cooperation Administration in the 1955-60 period were for the fields of health, sanitation, and education, a proportion which placed human resources development second only to the projects in agriculture and natural resources development in the technical assistance program. In this, as in the field of public administration, other support was provided by agencies of the United Nations.

The long-term logic of the emphasis on technical assistance programs rests upon the assumption that such programs exert a strong influence on a nation's capacity to absorb capital effectively; for this reason, they are inseparable from the other components of the external assistance effort and prepare the way for larger programs of loans and grants.

25. Highway construction had also received some emphasis (as in Brazil, Argentina, and Colombia) in the 1920's and 1930's, but the efforts were far from sufficient. Brazil, for example, built some 280,000 kilometers of roads by 1945, but of these only about 3,000 kilometers were paved. Elsewhere, the situation was almost uniformly bad. As late as the early thirties, for example, there was no coastal highway linking together the most economically active regions of Peru. For characteristic handling of the transport problem in development, see IBRD, *The Economic Development of Nicaragua*, pp. 64-73, 192-249; IBRD, *The Basis of a Development Program for Colombia*, pp. 100-167, 440-491; and Joint Brazil-United States Economic Development Commission, *The Development of Brazil*, pp. 32-35, 83-153. Additional insight into the situation described by the last mentioned of these reports is easily come by as in Brazil there has been a considerable amount of expressed concern with the transport problem. See, in this connection, such works as Osvaldo Gordilho, *Os transportes no Brasil*, Rio de Janeiro: Ministério da Viação e Obras Públicas, 1956; Helio Vianna, *História da viação brasileira*, Rio de Janeiro: Ministério da Guerra, 1949; and Paulo de Assis Ribeiro, *Estrutura, economia e política dos transportes*, Rio de Janeiro: Instituto Nacional do Livro, 1956. An excellent background to the report of the World Bank's mission to Colombia is to be found in Donald S. Barnhart, "Colombian Transportation Problems and Policies, 1923-1948," University of Chicago, Unpublished doctoral thesis, 1953.

26. Conversely, some of the limited improvements which were effected in the transport system have provided striking testimony to the gains which could be realized from additional investment in this sector. It has been estimated, for example, that with the opening of the new Presidente Dutra highway between Rio de Janeiro and São Paulo, freight rates on this vital route dropped 50 per cent because of a 23 per cent fuel saving, a 53 per cent oil saving, a two-thirds decrease in tire wear, a two-thirds decrease in vehicular maintenance costs, and the greater rapidity with which goods could be moved between the two points. Paulo de Assis Ribeiro, *op. cit.*, p. 87. In Bolivia the opening of the new highway between La Paz and Cochabamba cut travel

time during the rainy season from several weeks to fifteen hours and made possible the virtual elimination of costly rice imports. The one paved highway of any length in Bolivia, however, remains that (now in deteriorating condition) between Cochabamba and Santa Cruz.

27. *Ibid.*, p. 196. According to Ribeiro, operating inefficiency has caused the Brazilian railway system to generate a growing deficit since at least 1945. Some lines have failed even to cover operating costs, much less these plus a portion of their capital costs.

28. Pan American Union, *Financing Economic Development in Latin America*, Washington, D.C.: 1958, p. 152. Loans for electric power and water development ranked second in importance, accounting for about 20 per cent of the Exim Bank's loans to Latin America (again, excluding balance of payments loans).

29. IBRD, *Fourteenth Annual Report*, 1958-59, Washington, D.C.: 1959, p. 11. The volume of financing actually granted transport and communications projects does not contradict the top priority accorded this item in the World Bank missions's reports, as the institution operates mainly to cover the external financial requirements of development projects. Since many of the recommended transport projects include highway construction programs for which domestic resources are available, the direct and indirect external requirements (and, hence, the role of World Bank financing) are correspondingly lowered. For most of the countries, the external requirements implied by electric power projects are proportionately larger. A further factor which has tended to reduce the portion of foreign lending directed into transport development has stemmed from the difficulties encountered in implementing recommendations for the rehabilitation of railway systems. On this score, bureaucratic rigidities have retarded the pace of reforms which would make specific loan projects feasible.

30. Mexican railway lines have been extended in both a southerly direction (especially to connect the Yucatan peninsula and intervening points with the economic center of the nation) and in the northwestern parts of the country where flourishing regions have developed in recent times. The large post-1945 railway project in Colombia involved providing through rail service between Bogotá and the Caribbean coast, which line also served to integrate a number of hitherto disconnected regional lines into a national rail system.

31. The general preference for highway transport may also relate to the difficulties many Latin American countries have experienced in putting their railway lines on a satisfactory working basis, an operational consideration which tends to shift the economic advantage to highway transport by raising the capital-output ratio in railways.

32. A number of the cited reports allude to the conditions which at present hamper the movement of merchandise through Latin American ports. In this connection, see also the Working and Reference Documents Issued by the General Secretariat of the Organization of American States in conjunction with the Second Inter-American Port and Harbor Conference held at Cartagena, Colombia, in 1962, especially Documents 5 and 23 (OAS Official Records, OEA/Ser.K/X.2.1).

33. IBRD, *The Basis of a Development Program for Colombia*, pp. 208-214, 436, 514-522; IBRD, *The Economic Development of Nicaragua*, pp. 60-63, 174-184; IBRD, *The Economic Development of Guatemala*, pp. 218-243; IBRD, *The Economic Development of Venezuela*, pp. 281-300. See also D. F. Cavers and J. R. Nelson, *Electric Power Regulation in Latin America*, Baltimore: The Johns Hopkins Press, 1959, for a thorough discussion of the institutional constrictions (outmoded regulatory systems) which have contributed to the chronic power shortages in Latin America.

34. D. F. Cavers and J. R. Nelson, *op. cit.*, p. 8.

35. IBRD, *Eleventh Annual Report*, 1955-56, Washington, D.C.: 1956, pp. 8-9.

36. See, for example, IBRD, *The Basis of a Development Program for Colombia*, pp. 360 ff.; IBRD, *The Economic Development of Guatemala*, p. 91, also pp. 22-90; IBRD and FAO, *The Agricultural Development of Peru*, Part I, pp. 1-3; IBRD, *The Economic Development of Nicaragua*, p. 29, also pp. 30-54, 292-304.

37. The World Bank's report on Nicaragua, for instance, recommends a diversification into commercial cattle ranching (for local needs and for export), dairying, oil palm cultivation, hog raising, citrus fruits, cacao, and various types of vegetable production.

38. For typical references to these matters, see IBRD, *The Basis of a Development Program for Colombia*, pp. 389-391, 393-397, 399; IBRD, *The Economic Development of Guatemala*, pp. 31-32, 35, 42-45, 54-56, 61-67; IBRD, *The Economic Development of Nicaragua*, pp. 29, 31, 45-46. The Joint IBRD – FAO reports on Peru and Uruguay are even more detailed, as is the IBRD report on *The Agricultural Development of Colombia*.

39. Through the end of the 1950's, only about 7 per cent of the Export-Import Bank's lending activity in Latin America (excluding balance-of-payments loans) was for financing agricultural equipment, while only around 10 per cent of the World Bank's loans to Latin America had gone to finance various agricultural activities (farm mechanization, irrigation and flood control). This is not, however, altogether inconsistent with the leading position accorded agricultural modernization by the expert advisors whose views are herein under consideration. For one thing, the need for external financial assistance probably tends to be relatively lower in programs of agricultural improvement than in such sectors as transport and power development, and, for another, actual recourse to external financing ordinarily, if it is to be effective, awaits certain prior minimum changes in organization and the human agents of production (e.g., the creation of research and extension service facilities, farmer education, the installation of new financial mechanisms for handling rural credit) which have, in practice, been rather slow to materialize. As this preparatory phase necessarily entails a great deal of help of the sort which falls under the category of technical assistance rather than bank financing, it is significant that the largest single share of the United States' technical assistance program in Latin America went, through the end of the 1950's, into the field of agriculture and natural resources development. For an incisive study of this work, see Arthur T. Mosher, *Technical Co-operation in Latin American Agriculture*, Chicago: The University of Chicago Press, 1956. Additional U. S. assistance to Latin American agricultural development was channeled through the FAO and the Inter-American Institute of Agricultural Sciences which was established in 1941 at Turrialba, Costa Rica.

40. See IBRD, *The Agricultural Development of Colombia*, pp. 8, 40, 42-43, 64, and 104-5; IBRD and FAO, *The Agricultural Development of Peru*, Part II, pp. 148-157; IBRD, *The Economic Development of Guatemala*, p. 26; IBRD, *The Economic Development of Nicaragua*, p. 310; and IBRD, *The Basis of a Development Program for Colombia*, pp. 383-387, for discussions of the land tenure problem as an obstacle to development.

41. During the same decade, the Food and Agriculture Organization of the United Nations, which had collaborated with the World Bank on a number of Latin American studies, sponsored two major conferences which took as their focus the backwardness of Latin American institutional organization in agriculture. The first of the conferences was held at Campinas, Brazil, in 1953; the second, at Montevideo, Uruguay, in late 1959. At a more general level, interest in land reform had also been stimulated by a United Nations report issued in 1951, *Land Reform: Defects in Agrarian Structure as Obstacles to Economic Development*, and by two follow-up reports, both entitled *Progress in Land Reform*, issued in 1954 and 1956.

42. For the endorsement of cooperatives, see IBRD, *Report on Cuba*, pp. 610-611; IBRD, *The Basis of a Development Program for Colombia*, p. 83-84; IBRD, *The Economic Development of Guatemala*, p. 58; IBRD and FAO, *The Agricultural Development of Peru*, pp. 163-164. The last mentioned of these references endorses the use of cooperatives, land taxation, and land redistribution as means of changing contraproductive land tenure patterns. For an assessment of the problems and potentialities of cooperative organization in the light of Latin American experience with this form of organization, see Cooperative Credit League of the United States, *Socio-Economic Development of Cooperatives in Latin America*, San Juan, Puerto Rico: Inter-American Cooperative Development Committee, 1963.

43. IBRD, *The Basis of a Development Program for Colombia*, p. 384; IBRD, *The Agricultural Development of Colombia*, p. 65.

44. IBRD, *The Basis of a Development Program for Colombia*, p. 392.

45. IBRD, *The Basis of a Development Program for Colombia*, pp. 384-387;

IBRD, *The Agricultural Development of Colombia,* pp. 7-8, 65; IBRD and FAO, *The Agricultural Development of Peru,* Part II, p. 164.

46. For a description of this notable experiment, see Camilo Torres Restrepo and Berta Corredor, *Las escuelas radiofónicas de Sutatenza-Colombia,* Bogotá: Centro de Investigaciones Sociales, 1961.

47. Leon A. Mears, "Private Foreign Investment and Economic Development: Venezuela, Saudi Arabia, and Puerto Rico," *Inter-American Economic Affairs,* Washington, D.C.: Vol. 7, No. 1 (Summer 1953), pp. 3-19; see also Edwin Lieuwen, *Petroleum in Venezuela; a History,* Berkeley: University of California Press, 1954.

48. Arthur D. Little, Inc., *A Program for the Industrial and Regional Development of Peru,* Cambridge, Massachusetts: 1960, p. XV.

49. The IBRD study of Nicaragua was only slightly more helpful in this regard.

NOTES FOR CHAPTER XII

1. By the time of the Chapultepec Conference of February 1945, the policy views of Latin America had begun to give shape to a distinct regional bloc in inter-American relations. For example, in drawing up the Economic Charter of the Americas, the Latin American delegates to that conference insisted, against U.S. opposition, that their countries should have the recognized right to retain tariff protection, to establish state enterprises, to use import controls, and to restrict the scope of foreign capital.

2. For a succinct and sympathetic account of this development, see Eastin Nelson, "A Revolution in Economic Policy: An Hypothesis of Social Dynamics in Latin America," *The Southwestern Social Science Quarterly,* December 1953, pp. 3-16. A less sympathetic but quite suggestive treatment of the subject from a conservative point of view is found in Eudocio Ravines, *América latina, un continente en erupción,* Buenos Aires: Editorial Claridad, S.A., 1956. Also see Robert J. Alexander, "The Latin American Aprista Parties," *The Political Quarterly,* Vol. 20, No. 3 (July-September 1949), pp. 236-247.

3. For the now classic presentation of the ECLA position, see United Nations Economic Commission for Latin America, *The Economic Development of Latin America and Its Principal Problems,* United Nations: 1950, and United Nations Economic Commission for Latin America, *Economic Survey of Latin America,* 1949, United Nations: 1950, pp. 1-88. A third important statement of this position is to be found in Raúl Prébisch, "Commercial Policy in the Underdeveloped Countries," *American Economic Review, Papers and Proceedings,* Menasha: Vol. 49, No. 2 (May 1959), pp. 251-273. For critical appraisals of the ECLA or Prébisch thesis, particularly its terms of trade interpretation, see the following articles: William H. Fink, "Trends in Latin America's Capacity to Import and the Gains from Trade," *Inter-American Economic Affairs,* Washington, D.C.: Vol. 9, No. 1 (Summer 1955), pp. 61-77; Benjamin A. Rogge, "Economic Development in Latin America: The Prébisch Thesis," *Inter-American Economic Affairs,* Washington, D.C.: Vol. 9, No. 4 (Spring 1956), pp. 24-49; P. T. Ellsworth, "The Terms of Trade between Primary Producing and Industrial Countries," *Inter-American Economic Affairs,* Washington, D.C.: Vol. 10, No. 1 (Summer 1956), pp. 47-65. An excellent, and comprehensive, critique of the ECLA theory has been made by M. June Flanders, in "Prebisch on Protectionism: An Evaluation," Lafayette, Ind.: Purdue University, Institute for Quantitative Research in Economics and Management, Institute Paper No. 43, May 1963.

4. In the preoccupation with disparities in growth rates, it may be questioned whether adequate consideration has been given the matter of absolute differences in the size of the respective import demands of the center and the periphery. Still other questions may be raised concerning the validity of the assumption.

5. Additional reasons for preferring public loans to private foreign investments were presented by the distinguished Cuban economist, Felipe Pazos, in his article "Inversiones públicas versus inversiones privadas extranjeras en las regiones

subdesarrolladas," which appeared in the *Revista Bimestre Cubana,* La Habana: Vol. 75, segundo semestre (July-December 1958), pp. 216-248, an article which elaborates on theme developed a few years previously by ECLA. For the ECLA statement, see United Nations Economic Commission for Latin America, *La cooperación internacional en la política de desarrollo latinoamericano,* United Nations: 1954. According to the point of view expressed in these works, it is cheaper in the long run for an underdeveloped country to finance its development by means of loans which can be liquidated than by foreign equity investments which create a charge of indefinite duration and possibly growing magnitude against the recipient country's balance of payments.

6. During recent years, the inflation analysis of traditional economic theory has come to be labeled the "monetarist" theory while the analysis of the Latin American neo-orthodox group has been called the "structuralist" theory. For a convenient introduction to this tangled controversy, see the essays by Roberto de Oliveira Campos, David Felix, and Joseph Grunwald, in A. O. Hirschman, ed., *Latin American Issues,* New York: The Twentieth Century Fund, 1961, pp. 69-123.

7. It is this view which has suggested that the neo-orthodox structuralists are inclined to accept the costs of inflation as a more or less unavoidable cost of rapid development. On the other hand, as Raúl Prébisch has pointed out recently, such is not an altogether accurate reading of the structuralist doctrine. Raúl Prébisch, "Economic Development or Monetary Stability: The False Dilemma," *Economic Bulletin for Latin America,* United Nations: Vol. 6, No. 1 (March 1961), pp. 1-25.

8. For some interesting illustrations of how exchange control has been used to influence foreign investment, see pp. 31-33 of José Garrido Torres and Denio Nogueira, *Joint International Business Ventures in Brazil,* Country Study 11 in the Joint International Business Ventures Research Project, New York: Columbia University Law School, 1959.

9. Frank Brandenburg, *The Development of Latin American Private Enterprise,* Washington: National Planning Association, May 1964, pp. 51-66. Brandenburg's statistics, however, must be read carefully, for in Venezuela and Chile he has excluded a large portion of the private sector: i.e., the extractive enterprises which are, after all, an essential part of the total economic picture.

10. The most noteworthy efforts to improve the leadership capacity of the public sector have come through bilateral and multilateral technical-assistance programs, the training facilities for public functionaries offered by the Economic Development Institute of the World Bank, the vigorous training programs conducted by the ECLA secretariat from around 1953 on, and the recently (1963) established Latin American Institute for Economic and Social Planning which gives basic instruction at its headquarters in Santiago, Chile, and shorter-term intensive courses in other countries.

11. The quantity of modern Latin American writing in dispraise of liberal economics and in support of an expansion of state economic action is large, but a few citations may be taken as representative examples of this literature. In *La redención de la clase media* (Bogotá: Editorial ABC, 1936, esp. pp. 121-126, 157-159), J. M. Quintana Pereyra issued what can only be called a clarion call to the Colombian middle class to take up political action on behalf of President López' New Deal type of program, urging them to use the "Poder Público" or active state intervention to attain their objectives and national economic growth. A few years later, another Colombian writer, Antonio García, argued that only by means of aggressive intervention along a broad front could national life be reoriented to modern exigencies and the national economy be restructured to defend the interests of society. These latter, he observed, were not automatically defended under a regime of economic liberalism because "el automatismo no rige las relaciones sociales." Antonio García, "La Crisis de la Libertad Económica" (Vol. 6, No. 12, 20 June 1943, pp. 39-42) and "La Autarquía y el Orden Nacional" (Vol. 6, No. 13, 5 July 1943, pp. 13-17) *Anales de Economía y Estadística,* Bogotá: Contraloría General de la República. Somewhat the same theme was put forward in the same year by one of the more conservative Peruvian economists, Rómulo A. Ferrero, who saw state intervention in national economic life

as a "definitive and permanent fact with which one would have to reckon in the future" because it was "required for the solution of great socio-economic problems." R. A. Ferrero, "Perspectivas Económicas de la Post-Guerra," *Mercurio Peruano*, Lima: Año XVIII. Eduardo Larrea likewise saw a collectivistic planned economy as the only feasible postwar form of economic organization. Eduardo Larrea S., "Problemas de la Post-Guerra," *América;* Habana: Asociación de Escritores y Artistas Americanos, Vol. 22, Nos. 1, 2, and 3 (April-June 1944) pp. 19-21. For a thoughtful discussion of basic concepts in which the writer, one of Latin America's most distinguished legal philosophers, maintains that the state should project the exigencies of social justice upon economic relationships, see Luis Recaséns Siches, *Human Life, Society and Law: Fundamentals of the Philosophy of the Law,* Cambridge: Harvard University Press, 1948, esp. pp. 199-230, 320-334.

12. Two particularly helpful studies covering the Brazilian case are H. W. Spiegel, *The Brazilian Economy*, Philadelphia: The Blakiston Company, 1949, and Werner Baer, *Industrialization and Economic Development in Brazil*, Homewood, Ill.: Richard D. Irwin, Inc., 1965.

13. The Act of 1875 as well as the earlier tariff schedule introduced in 1866, which was similar in intent but more limited in scope, were argued as means of providing alternative employment for the workers being shifted out of agriculture.

14. Among the studies of the modern period, the following may be cited as especially useful: Simon G. Hanson, *Utopia in Uruguay*, New York: Oxford University Press, 1938; George Pendle, *Uruguay*, London: Oxford University Press, 1957; Russel H. Fitzgibbon, *Uruguay: Portrait of a Democracy*, New Brunswick: Rutgers University Press, 1954; Milton Vanger, *José Batlle y Ordóñez of Uruguay*, Cambridge: Harvard University Press, 1963. Also see: Eugenio Gómez, *Los grandes problemas de la economía nacional*, Montevideo: Editorial "America," 1945; Julio Martinez Lamas, *Riqueza y pobreza del Uruguay*, Montevideo: Tipografía Atlántida, 1946.

15. Freire Sanquinetti, "Social Legislation in Uruguay," *International Labor Review*, No. 59 (March 1959), p. 277. Lax administration, the generosity of the social benefits provided, excessive bureaucratization, and various abuses have, over the years, made the welfare system a source of inflationary pressure and other problems in Uruguay.

16. The Rural Development Section of the Mortgage Bank has established several colonies, providing them with technical assistance and with supplies (which it also sells to others) produced on the Bank's seed farms, tree nurseries, stud animal centers and so forth. In connection with its rural development program, the Bank operates grain elevators, a port facility, and schools and organizes cooperative associations.

17. The slogan devised to win approval for governmental ownership of the electric-power industry was indicative of Batlle's economic creed and of the view which has been much decried by foreign development advisers, as noted earlier — "Buena luz y barata, aunque el Estado no gane; buena luz y barata aunque el Estado pierde. ("Good and cheap lighting, even if the state makes no profits; good and cheap lightning even if the state incurs losses.") Quoted in Simon Hanson, *op. cit.,* p. 45.

18. As will become evident in the discussions of Argentina and Chile, the petroleum industry has commonly been singled out as a field for state participation. In all three of these countries, government enterprises control or even monopolize important segments of the industry. Since 1938 the petroleum industry in Mexico has been almost entirely in the hands of the government's company, Petróleos Mexicanos (Pemex). In Brazil, oil exploration and development began in 1938 as a government undertaking (the National Petroleum Council), and in 1953 a state corporation (Petroleos Brasileiros, or Petrobras) was created to continue this work as well as to operate refineries, import petroleum products, and develop a petrochemical and fertilizer industry (although private companies were also permitted to import, refine, and distribute petroleum products). In Bolivia the Yacimientos Petrolíferos Fiscales Bolivianos was set up in 1937 to take over the concessions of the Standard Oil Company and to produce, refine, and distribute petroleum products; some private activity has continued

since that time, however. In several other countries, government concerns have also operated alongside private firms: e.g., the Peruvian Empresa Petrolera Fiscal (created in the 1948 reorganization of an earlier entity), the Empresa Colombiana de Petróleos (established 1951), and the Corporación Venezolana de Petróleo (1960).

19. The policy adopted in this tariff act has since become the general practice in Latin America, for by placing tariffs on finished goods but not on raw materials, it was hoped to give local manufacturers an advantage over foreign producers.

20. Historically, most Latin American tariffs had been specific duties. As part of the readjustment to twentieth century foreign trade disturbances, however, a majority of the countries, Uruguay included, began to adopt combinations of ad valorem and specific duties. At the same time — especially in Argentina, Brazil, and Venezuela but to a lesser degree also in Uruguay, Chile, Peru, Colombia, Costa Rica, and Guatemala — the executive power was given a broad latitude in changing tariff rate structures. In addition, several countries have adopted multiple-column tariff schedules: e.g., Argentina in 1905, and Colombia, Costa Rica, Cuba, Ecuador, El Salvador, Guatemala, Haiti, and Uruguay from 1931 on. A multiple-column tariff schedule was instituted by Chile in 1945.

21. In 1931, Uruguay and six other countries (Argentina, Bolivia, Brazil, Chile, Colombia, and Nicaragua) adopted exchange-control systems. From 1932 through 1934, six other countries followed suit (Costa Rica, Ecuador, Paraguay, Mexico, Honduras, and Venezuela). Peru did not adopt them until 1945. In addition, multiple exchange rates were incorporated into the exchange control systems during the 1930's in Argentina, Brazil, Chile, Colombia, and Uruguay, and employed more widely still in the 1940's. Mexico and Honduras subsequently dropped their exchange control systems, but from 1948 on, increasing reliance was placed by Mexico on an import-licensing system which eventually became its primary means of restricting imports. By the end of the 1940's, exchange control systems (and multiple rates, save in the case of Peru) were still in effect in all of the South American countries and, in addition, in Costa Rica and Nicaragua. Moreover, all twelve of the countries which retained exchange controls had also followed the Chilean example, introduced in 1932, of supplementing exchange controls with quantitative import-licensing restrictions, in connection with which a variety of quota systems (i.e., global quotas, product quotas, tariff quotas) were used. On an occasional basis, some of the countries have imposed outright embargoes on certain categories of imports. Finally, at least eight countries (Argentina, Brazil, Chile, Peru, Venezuela, Ecuador, Uruguay, and Nicaragua) have, at one time or another, used exchange controls to restrict certain categories of exports in order to control local supplies.

22. The net result, however, was to depress exports, for the domestic woollen goods were unable to meet the price and quality standards prevailing in export markets.

23. Government intervention in dairying, fishing, and meat processing was aimed at, among other things, the objective of holding prices down for the benefit of urban consumers. Later, a number of countries experimented with both price controls and subsidies in order to avert price increases in the staples of food consumption. To this end, several countries also moved even further, especially during the 1930's and 1940's, by creating state trading enterprises which have attempted to manipulate prices through domestic purchases and sales as well as through imports. The precedents for such measures were, of course, firmly grounded in Hispanic tradition.

In some instances, the state trading enterprises have been granted monopoly rights for certain imports. In most cases, such enterprises have also been authorized to operate warehouses, food-processing plants (such as grain elevators, rice-drying facilities, and meat-packing plants), and the like. Typical of these institutions are: the Chilean Instituto Nacional de Comercio (superseded in 1960 by the Empresa de Comercio Agrícola), the Instituto Nacional de Abastecimientos of Colombia, the Distribuidora Nacional of Ecuador, the Comissão Federal de Abastecimento e Preços of Brazil, and the Compañía Exportadora e Importadora Mexicana, S.A.

Aside from their obvious political uses in buying the favor of urban consumers, such market control agencies have also represented an attempt by public authorities to build new institutional structures which could compensate for the recognized imperfections in domestic market organization and the production rigidities of the agricultural sector. Often, however, their subsidized sales have contributed to domestic inflation (via the government deficit) and have generated disincentives for domestic agricultural producers.

24. Among the many works which deal with Argentine policy developments, the following are especially helpful: Ysabel F. Rennie, *The Argentine Republic,* New York: The Macmillan Company, 1945; Felix Weil, *Argentine Riddle,* New York: The John Day Company, 1944; Leonard T. Richmond, *Argentina's Third Position,* Buenos Aires: Acme Agency, 1949; George I. Blanksten, *Peron's Argentina,* Chicago: University of Chicago Press, 1953; Robert J. Alexander, *The Peron Era,* New York: Columbia University Press, 1951; Manuel Zymelman, "Economic History of Argentina (1933-1952)," Cambridge, Mass.: Massachusetts Institute of Technology, unpublished doctoral dissertation, 1958; and John Frikart, "Effects of the Peron Regime on the Argentine Economy," Boulder, Col.: University of Colorado, unpublished doctoral dissertation, 1959. There is also, of course, a considerable amount of literature in Spanish on the subject, but a great deal of it is polemical. For two general historical works which provide useful background, see: Thomas F. McGann, *Argentina: The Divided Land,* Princeton: D. Van Nostrand, Inc., 1966, and James R. Scobie, *Argentina: A City and a Nation,* New York: Oxford University Press, 1964.

25. The National Grain Board turned out to be the predecessor agency of the IAPI agency established by Perón. After the creation of IAPI, the grain board continued to function as the control agency for the domestic trade in grains, as did the other regulatory boards in their respective fields.

26. While these concessions did assist Argentine development by increasing foreign investors' confidence in the country and while the Roca-Runciman agreement helped further by safeguarding a share for Argentine exports in the British market, the cost of these benefits involved a number of pernicious concessions. Among other things the Roca-Runciman pact forced Argentina (1) to insure that Argentine packing houses would not have over 15 per cent of the Argentine packing business (the balance being reserved for the large Anglo-American concerns), (2) to enact a transport coordination law taking over bus lines which were competing with British-owned railways, (3) to stop building highways in competition with British rail routes, limiting new construction to the building of feeder roads for the rail lines (a provision subsequently disregarded in practice), and (4) to give Britain a favorable rate of exchange with the peso and use this together with exchange controls and import quotas to give preference to British goods to the detriment of imports from the United States. As many of the new manufacturers had been buying their heavy machinery in the United States, the effect of this last concession was to displace the position of the United States as the chief supplier of Argentine imports and to restore British sellers to the number one spot. In return for renegotiating the agreement three years later, the British compelled the Argentine government (1) to confiscate the domestically owned micro-buses which had been competing with the Anglo-Argentine tram company (whose service was notoriously poor), (2) to forego taxes on the company in exchange for shares in a new street railway monopoly, and (3) to guarantee a 7 per cent rate of return on the capitalization of the new company, into which the full capitalization of the preexisting enterprise was incorporated, although subsequent investigations revealed the stock to have been highly watered.

27. The Secretariat of Labor was also empowered to declare individual strikes legal or illegal, a sanction which gave the regime yet another means of dealing with recalcitrant unions.

28. The CGT, formed in 1930, was small and quite weak until Perón began to use it as his primary labor instrument; afterward it grew rapidly as a consequence both of affiliating new unions and of the sharp increase of unionization among workers.

29. These two government banks dated from the latter part of the nineteenth century, as did the Chilean Mortgage Credit Institute. All three institutions were engaged from an early date in lending to rural firms, a practice which suggests that even

dominant traditional interests, who were on other issues inclined to favor a more minimalist role for the state, were not doctrinaire in their advocacy of economic liberalism — at least when intervention might be employed to structure the money market in favor of an influential rural clientele. In this connection it is worth noting that, even before a more generalized intervention was adopted to respond to the needs of other groups, government banking had, in several cases, begun with the formation of lending institutions which in practice have dealt mainly with the more prosperous property owners. Other examples of this development are to be found in the Banco Agrícola y Pecuario of Venezuela (established 1928), the Banco Agrícola of Peru (established 1931), the Banco Hipotecario de El Salvador (established 1934), and the Banco Hipotecario of Nicaragua (established in the late 1930's). Since mortgage lending is also one of the oldest and most well established types of financing in Latin America, dating back into early colonial times, it is perhaps understandable that state banking should have begun in this area rather than in financial fields where fewer guidelines were available.

30. The 1940's brought a flurry of interest in cooperatives in several parts of Latin America. In 1942 legislation was passed encouraging their formation in Mexico, Colombia, and Peru. During the year following, national congresses of cooperatives were convened in Uruguay, Colombia, Mexico, and Argentina, while other countries (Venezuela and Ecuador) also enacted laws to foster cooperative development. Governmental loans were given as special assistance to agricultural cooperatives in both Paraguay and El Salvador during this time.

31. Even during the post-Perón period, it is interesting to note that the ACIEL groups and CGE groups have generally held divergent opinions regarding appropriate public policy, the latter adhering to a more interventionist stand and maintaining a more accommodating attitude toward the CGT. As the well-known studies of Mosk and Brandenburg have indicated, a not altogether dissimilar division exists among organized business groups in Mexico.

32. While a good many Latin American countries have a significant governmental stake in railways and a number have also developed airlines as state companies or mixed enterprises, direct intervention in shipping has not been quite so widespread. Among the other examples which might be cited are the Paraguayan State Merchant Fleet or Flota Mercante del Estado (founded in 1945 to lower rates and curb foreign domination of the vital river traffic), the Compañía Anónima Venezolana de Navegación (established in 1917, handling coastal, river, and some ocean shipping), the Corporación Peruana de Vapores (established 1944 for both coastal and ocean transport services), the Colombian Compañía Nacional de Navegación (established to operate in both coastwise shipping and the main river traffic), the Lloyd Brasileiro (a coastal shipping company taken over by the government in 1937 and thereafter expanded to include river and ocean shipping), and the Serviço de Navegação da Amazônia (a river shipping line organized through expropriation of a private company in 1940). The Flota Mercante Grancolombiana was originally established in 1946 as a jointly owned merchant marine of Venezuela, Colombia, and Ecuador for handling the international shipping of these countries. In 1953, Venezuela withdrew from participation, leaving the other two nations as the joint-owners (Colombia 80 per cent, Ecuador 20 per cent). Chile, as will be later noted, has a government-operated coastal shipping line, while the Mexican state oil company operates a fleet of tankers (as do most of the government oil enterprises).

33. In 1954 the Investment Institute became a saving and investment agency, accepting deposits for investment with a governmental guarantee of safety of principal and of a minimum three per cent return.

34. In the early forties Mexico and Brazil had both built government steel mills, the former at Monclova and the latter at Volta Redonda. From the mid-forties, Chile was developing its government steel mill at Huachipato, while Peru was doing the same at Chimbote. Argentina was, therefore, the fifth country to begin public investment in steel. Colombia was next with its governmental coal and steel complex at

Paz del Río-Belencito, while Venezuela has more recently begun the same sort of public investment.

35. United Nations Economic Commission for Latin America, *Analisis y proyecciones del desarrollo económico:* V. *El desarrollo económico de la Argentina,* Mexico: U.N. Department of Economic and Social Affairs, 1959, Vol. III, p. 5.

36. Dirección Nacional de Estadística y Censos, *Censo Industrial,* 1939, 1946, 1954.

37. U.N., ECLA, *op. cit.,* Vol. II, p. 161.

38. U.N., ECLA, *Economic Survey of Latin America,* 1956, New York: U.N. Department of Economic and Social Affairs, 1957, p. 127. The Argentine manufacturing production index for the 1945-1955 period is given as follows: 1945 = 77, 1946 = 86, 1947 = 100, 1948 = 101, 1949 = 97, 1950 = 100, 1951 = 103, 1952 = 95, 1953 = 93, 1954 = 101, 1955 = 111.

39. Under the terms of the law, guarantees were extended to permit annual remittances of earnings up to the amount of 8 per cent of the registered capital investment (following an initial two-year period). Repatriation of capital was allowed after a ten-year period.

40. Among the studies of Chilean developments in the modern period, the following are particularly helpful: P. T. Ellsworth, *Chile: An Economy in Transition,* New York: The Macmillan Company, 1945; Herman Finer, *The Chilean Development Corporation,* Montreal: International Labor Office, 1947; Kalman Silvert, "The Chilean Development Corporation," Philadelphia: University of Pennsylvania, unpublished doctoral dissertation, 1948; and J. R. Stevenson, *The Chilean Popular Front,* Philadelphia: The University of Pennsylvania Press, 1942. In Spanish, see Instituto de Economía de la Universidad de Chile, *Desarrollo económico de Chile, 1940-1956,* Santiago: Editoral Universitaria, 1956; United Nations Economic Commission for Latin America, *Antecedentes sobre el desarrollo de la enconomía chilena, 1925-1952,* Santiago: Editorial del Pacífico, S.A., 1954; Carl Hudeczek, *Economía chilena, rumbos y metas,* Santiago: Editorial del Pacífico, S.A., 1956; A. Labarca Hubertson, ed., *Desarrollo de Chile en la primera mitad del siglo XX,* Santiago: Editorial Universitaria, 1951, Vol. I.

41. In view of what has been said regarding governmental control of the labor movement in Peronist Argentina, it should be noted that in Chile, as in Uruguay and several other countries, the labor movement was not converted into a mere arm of the political party holding office. Nevertheless, there, as in Peru, Brazil, and elsewhere, the pervasive scope of the labor legislation enacted over the years – particularly in its detailed regulation of internal union affairs and settlement procedures – bears witness to the culturally engrained suspicion of autonomous groups. The high percentage of decree laws in the legislation relating to labor has been indicative of the close involvement of the executive branch of government in determining industrial relations. Moreover, in the Chilean legislation (as well as that of Peru and several other countries) class distinction was institutionalized in the form of differential benefits for *empleados* (white-collar workers) and *obreros* (blue-collar workers). All three of these features were, of course, paramount characteristics of the traditional Hispanic approach to social organization.

42. Some of the Latin American legislation in this matter has attempted to specify the percentage of company payrolls which should go to nationals of the country; other versions have set as the target a proportion of the total employees of the firms. In some laws, the two criteria are combined. Exceptions have generally been allowed, however, in cases of managerial and technical personnel where qualified nationals are presumably not available.

43. In 1953 a National Social Security Investment Corporation was set up to plan the investment program for the many funds, but met with little success in carrying out its coordinating task. Such overall supervision as has existed has come from the Caja de Seguro Obligatorio, which was set up to administer the 1924 laws, and the Superintencency of Social Security in the Ministry of Public Health and Social Insurance.

44. The Mortgage Credit Institute had been created to issue special bonds for the purpose of making loans on mortgages, with preference for loans for developing

agricultural production and construction. The National Savings Bank had been established as an amalgamation of several small savings institutions which were created between 1901 and 1910. In 1931, it absorbed also the first of the savings institutes, the Caja de Ahorros de Santiago, which had been established in 1884. The only institution legally authorized to accept savings deposits (except for the Santiago Savings Institute and the Government Pawn Shop opened in 1921), the National Savings Bank was permitted to invest up to 50 per cent of its reserves in first-class securities listed on the two major stock exchanges of the country (Santiago and Valparaíso), a restriction which, while sound from the standpoint of protecting the Bank's reserves, ruled out the possibility of its being used as a significant provider of developmental finance. The monopoly of savings accounts granted the government institution is not incidentally, unique to Chile. Nicaragua has done the same, while in Colombia, bo cause of restrictions placed on private banking institutions, over 80 per cent of the savings deposits in the nation are held by the Caja Colombiana de Ahorros which was established by the government in 1932.

45. By the late 1950's, the Government Pawnshop was handling some 85 per cent of the legal pawnbrokering activity in Chile. A similar institution, the Caja Nacional de Crédito Popular, was organized by the government of Nicaragua as a pawnbroker for small loans and as the only bank authorized to receive savings deposits from the Nicaraguan public. In Brazil, pawnbroking is theoretically a monopoly of the federally operated savings banks *(caixas econômicas)* which handle a large portion of middle class savings and make personal loans. The oldest governmental pawnshop, however, is the Monte de Piedad of Mexico, which was established in late colonial times and which also functions today as a savings bank.

46. That is, firms with 75 per cent or more of the payroll going to Chileans and with at least 79 per cent of their stock owned by Chileans or by foreigners resident in Chile for more than five years. The intent was that lending would be channeled particularly toward smaller enterprises which had little or no access to regular private lending institutions.

47. For more information on the reasoning employed in creating these institutions, see Guillermo Gandarillas M., *Legislación sobre fomento de las industrias minero, agrícola, y fabril,* Santiago: Imprenta Nascimento, 1929. The Nitrate Development Institute's activities were soon superseded by other government intervention in that industry.

48. Over the next three decades, the Colonization Institute applied its activities to only a little more than a million acres, benefiting less than four thousand settlers. Of these, a good number appear to have been persons with some background of official employment. Very few of Chile's *rotos* and *inquilinos* were ever touched by the Institute's operations.

49. On June 30, 1958, the Chilean State Bank was made the sole depository for the peso funds of the central government and most of its autonomous agencies and, as such, the main banking and financial agent of these latter. The Bank can also, by virtue of the original charge given the *cajas* which compose it, operate enterprises financed through its investments and loans. It is empowered to make loans of up to ten years' maturity in the agricultural and industrial fields and to operate a regular commercial banking business as well. Over 50 per cent of its credits have been channeled into agriculture, at interest rates somewhat lower than those available from commercial banks. There is some evidence, however, that the larger agricultural enterprises have been the ones who have mainly benefited from this preferential treatment. On this point, see Ernest Feder, "Feudalism and Agricultural Development: The Role of Controlled Credit in Chile's Agriculture," *Land Economics*, Madison, Wis.: Vol. 36, No. 1 (February 1960), pp. 92-108.

50. In this respect, the *cajas* differed from, say, the previously mentioned Institute of Industrial Chemistry in Uruguay, which was more a case of a gradually increasing direct involvement by a governmental agency in production activity. The nearest historical antecedent of the *cajas* was the Banco de Avío of early republican Mexico.

51. Some idea of the subsequent proliferation of state-operated, sectorally oriented banks may be gained from the following quite partial listing. *Brazil:* the Banco do Brasil's Carteira de Crédito Agrícola e Industrial (1936), Banco de Crédito da Borracha (in 1940's, for crude rubber), Banco do Estado de Rio de Janeiro (1950, for rural credit); *Colombia:* Banco Agrícola Hipotecario (1924), Caja de Crédito Agrario, Industrial y Minero (1931, mainly for agriculture), Banco Popular (1950, for small-scale and artisan industries); *El Salvador:* Federación de Cajas de Crédito (1943, system of government-supported cooperative banks, chiefly for farmers); *Guatemala:* Banco Nacional Agrario (1953); *Paraguay:* Crédito Agrícola de Habilitación (1951); *Peru:* Banco Agrícola (1931), Banco Industrial (1937), Banco Minero (1941); *Venezuela:* Banco Agrícola y Pecuario (1928), Banco Industrial (1938). In addition to the sector financing institutions, a number of countries have set up state banks to operate in the housing and construction field: e.g., *Colombia:* Instituto de Crédito Territorial (1939), Banco Hipotecario Popular (1954); *Costa Rica:* Instituto Nacional de Vivienda y Urbanismo (1954); *Venezuela:* Banco Obrero (1928).

52. The Institute was also authorized to sell or lease all sorts of supplies and equipment to miners and to buy shares in mining, smelting, and mining supply companies. In the course of its business, it even acquired some mines which it operated on its own account.

53. Long before this time, it should be remembered, the state had begun to operate public enterprises. Telegraph services had been acquired by default in 1855 when the private company which had initiated telegraph service (one of William Wheelwright's undertakings) went under. Thereafter the State Telegraph Service was operated as a department of the postoffice, in the European fashion. Also from an early date, the government was a major investor in and operator of railway lines. With expansion of this interest through the years, including during the more conservative Alessandri administration of the 1930's, by the middle of the present century the government came to own somewhat over 80 per cent of the total national railway mileage. Until 1943 the Chilean State Railways operated a coastal shipping service, but in that year the shipping line was separated from the railway administration and placed under the newly created State Shipping Company (Empresa Marítima del Estado). Urban transit lines in Santiago, Valparaíso, Concepción, and Antofagasta have been government-owned for many years as well.

54. A law of 1932 which permitted the state to monopolize petroleum imports was not exercised, but in 1934 a Chilean petroleum company (Compañia de Petróleos de Chile) was formed with governmental encouragement to participate along with foreign companies in the importation of petroleum products.

55. For its 50 per cent interest in the capitalization and profits of COSACH, the government contributed a large amount of publicly owned nitrate reserves, abolished the nitrate export tax, and limited the future income tax liability of the combine to 6 per cent. In some respects, the venture into nitrates constituted a precedent for the copper industry reforms sponsored by the Frei administration in 1965-1966.

56. Although actual production is carried on by private enterprise, production quotas are set by COVENSA. Another branch of the domestic fertilizer industry, the guano trade, is, however, a public monopoly administered by the Sociedad Chilena de Fertilizantes, a subsidiary of the Chilean Development Corporation.

57. A detailed presentation and discussion of the legislation relating to economic controls is to be found in Oscar Aramayo, *Legislación económica,* Santiago: Editorial Jurídica de Chile, 1953.

58. For a description of the Chilean exchange control system and an assessment of its consequences, see Eric N. Baklanoff, "Model for Economic Stagnation: The Chilean Experience with Multiple Exchange Rates," *Inter-American Economic Affairs,* Vol. 13, No. 1 (Summer 1959), pp. 58-82.

59. Computed from figures in the *Economic Survey of Latin America, 1949,* New York: United Nations, Department of Economic Affairs, 1951, p. 287.

60. The forerunners of such controls were, it may be recalled, an established part of Spanish law during colonial times.

61. Further stimulation of the construction industry came with the establishment in 1936 of the Public Housing Institute (Caja de Habitación Popular) and with the previously mentioned 1935 change authorizing social security funds to be invested in low-cost housing projects and mortgages.

62. As certain categories of copper-company transactions were required by law to take place at an officially determined exchange rate, the difference between this rate and the higher free-market rate accrued to the Treasury as a form of indirect taxation. Venezuela has also applied this type of indirect tax to its petroleum export industry.

63. This Chilean approach to taxation of the minerals export sector was in marked contrast to the policy employed by Peru where, after 1952, the copper industry was given the benefit of a new mining code which, in its tax aspects, provided strong encouragement for an expansion of investment and production in the minerals industries. See Stanley K. Hamilton, "Factors Influencing Investment in the Peruvian Mining Industry and Effects of this Investment on the Peruvian Economy," Madison: University of Wisconsin, unpublished doctoral dissertation, 1967. In Chile, production remained more or less stable between 1947 and 1952, increasing by 35 per cent between 1952 and 1959. In Peru, production grew by 40 per cent between 1947 and 1952, and by 70 per cent between 1952 and 1959. Nevertheless, since taxation has been the principal means by which the domestic economy shares in the copper-export sector, the Chilean economy benefited proportionately more from copper exports in the 1947-1959 period than did the Peruvian economy, notwithstanding the much greater increase in aggregate output registered in the latter. Pedro Mendive, "Tax Incentives in Latin America," *Economic Bulletin for Latin America,* United Nations: Vol. 9, No. 1 (March 1964), p. 112.

64. The private associations represented include the National Agricultural Society, the National Mining Society, the Society for Manufacturing Development, the Chilean Engineering Association, the Confederation of Chilean Workers, and the Chilean Chambers of Commerce. As in most other Latin American countries, such private associations enjoy a semipublic or quasi-official character. Consequently, their inclusion in the governing boards of autonomous state agencies is a common practice throughout the region. In Colombia, for example, a number of development programs for agriculture have even been channeled through such associations as the National Federation of Colombian Coffee Growers, the Colombian Livestock Association, the National Cotton Institute, the Rice Growers' Institute, etc. Similarly, a mixed enterprise known as the Paraguayan Meat Corporation (established 1944) controls much of the meat industry in that country.

65. Prepared for the agricultural development of the Maule-Nuble-Concepción region, the Plan Chillán was jointly sponsored by the Chilean Ministry of Agriculture and the U.S. International Cooperation Administration. The elements of this relatively successful program included: agricultural research and extension, the establishment of a national agricultural training center, soil conservation, road construction, rural hygiene, forestry experiments, water development, farm mechanization, animal husbandry, and the establishment of a private nonprofit corporation (the Instituto Agrícola de Asistencia Técnica) supported by the Ministry of Agriculture and the powerful National Agricultural Society for the purpose of improving farm management.

66. In this last-mentioned capacity, CORFO has arranged for loans from both the U.S. Export-Import Bank and the IBRD, in addition to negotiating credit from other foreign financial institutions.

67. Given the breadth of functions assigned such institutions, it is obvious that no precise line of distinction can be drawn between the state banks set up for financing particular sectors and the general development authorities (both regional and national). The latter have also performed investment and commercial banking functions and have, in some cases, been actually organized as banks while in other cases they have been established as autonomous or semiautonomous agencies having banking departments. In all cases, however, they, like the sectoral banks, should be thought of as para-financial institutions, with planning and entrepreneurial functions that go considerably beyond what is conventional in, say, North American banking practice.

Among the varied institutions which function in this general development capacity, the following are representative: *Brazil:* Banco de Crédito da Amazônia (1950, a reorganization of the earlier Rubber Bank), Banco Nacional do Desenvolvimento Econômico (1952), Banco do Nordeste do Brasil (1954), Banco do Desenvolvimento do Extremo Sul (1962), Superintendência do Desenvolvimento do Nordeste (1960); *Bolivia:* Corporación Boliviana de Fomento (1943); *Colombia:* Instituto de Fomento Municipal (1940, for local public works), Instituto de Fomento Industrial (1940, merged in 1957 into the new Corporación Nacional de Fomento); *Ecuador:* Banco Nacional de Fomento (1944), the center of a system of provincial development banks; *El Salvador:* Instituto Salvadoreño de Fomento de la Producción (1955); *Guatemala:* Instituto de Fomento de la Producción (1949); *Honduras:* Banco Nacional de Fomento (1950); *Mexico:* Nacional Financiera (after the 1941 reorganization); *Nicaragua:* Instituto Nacional de Fomento (1953); *Paraguay:* Banco de Paraguay (1952); *Venezuela:* Corporación Venezolana de Fomento (1946).

A number of countries have also set up regional authorities for integrated river-basin development, somewhat after the TVA model: *Brazil:* Gomissão do Vale do São Francisco (1949); *Colombia:* Corporación del Valle del Cauca (1954), Corporación para el Valle del Magdalena (1960); *Mexico:* Comisión del Papaloapan (1947), Comisión del Tepalcatepec (1947), Comisión del Río Fuerte (1951), Comisión del Grijalva (1953); *Peru:* Corporación Peruana del Santa (1943); *Venezuela:* Corporación Venezolana de Guayana (1960).

It should also be kept in mind that a large number of ministries, commissions, institutes, colonization entities, and decentralized agencies of various sorts are deeply involved in the development field, and often in a way very similar to the work of the foregoing. It need hardly be added that the accomplishments of the entire lot of development institutions have been quite uneven.

68. In 21 of these, the CORFO share of stock ownership was 80 per cent or greater.

69. In spite of CORFO support for electric power development, the extent of industrialization produced a rate of increase in demand which has tended to outstrip the expansion of supply. In no small part this is attributable to the combination of inflation and unrealistically controlled rates, which has seriously deterred new investment for expansion of the privately owned public service enterprises.

70. The agricultural equipment and machinery company has both financed the importation and domestic sale of agricultural machinery and encouraged the domestic production thereof. In addition, it has assisted buyers in setting up equipment and machinery cooperatives and has established repair shops as an important auxiliary service.

71. The forty years between 1920 and 1960 cover the life history of the Chilean case, even though from the mid-1950's on there was a partial drawing back from the policy stance of the prior years: namely, in the simplification of the exchange structure, the removal of a number of the interventionist controls over the agricultural sector, an attempted return to more conventional monetary and fiscal policies (as part of an effort to dampen the rate of inflation), and a more favorable policy in regard to the nitrate and copper export industries.

72. An important explanatory factor in this situation appears to be the social security system which, through heavy charges against both the public and private employers of labor (especially white-collar workers) exacted substantial resources that might otherwise have been invested. These, in turn, were returned to the economy in two main ways: as benefit payments which enhanced the flow of consumption spending and as financing for residential construction. See Tom E. Davis, "Dualism, Stagnation, and Inequality: The Impact of Pension Legislation in the Chilean Labor Market," *Industrial and Labor Relations Review,* Vol. 17, No. 3 (April 1963), pp. 380-398.

73. In Chile, as in several other Latin American countries, the social-security system is structured so as to provide more generous benefits for white-collar workers than for blue-collar workers. Two-thirds of the white-collar workers in Chile are,

incidentally, employees of the state.

74. As in the Peronist regime of Argentina, the trade union movement was utilized as the principal popular arm of the governing party; but in Brazil the dependence of labor on official party organization and government support as well as the degree of government control exercised over labor were probably even greater than in the Argentine though the consolidation of this relationship was effected in a more subtle manner, with much less recourse to strong arm tactics.

75. Agricultural modernization has also been notably in evidence in some sections of southern Brazil, but it appears that much of the increase in agricultural output of recent times has been attributable to an expansion of the acreage in production and the absolute growth of the rural labor force rather than to widespread gains in productivity.

76. The combined populations of Guatemala, El Salvador, Nicaragua, Honduras, and Costa Rica amount to only about eleven or twelve million people, most of them quite poor, even by Latin American standards, while in Guatemala, the most populous of the five countries, a sizable bloc of the population consists of indigenous folk who live on or beyond the fringes of modern economic life.

77. For a good summary account of the development of Central American economic integration, see Joseph Pincus, *The Central American Common Market,* Washington, D.C.: U.S. Department of State, Agency for International Development, Regional Office for Central America and Panama Affairs, 1962. Also see U.N., ECLA, *La integración económica de Centroamérica,* United Nations, Department of Economic and Social Affairs: 1956, for a comprehensive statement of the rationale of the project. A short review of the program is contained in W. R. Gigax, "The Central American Common Market," *Inter-American Economic Affairs,* Vol. 16, No. 2 (Autumn 1962), pp. 59-77.

78. U.S. Department of Commerce, *International Commerce,* Washington, D.C.: Vol. 71, No. 36 (6 September 1965), pp. 7-10. Among the new foreign investments and joint enterprises established on the base of the common market have been tire and tube plants, insecticide and fertilizer plants, caustic soda plants, shirt and other garment manufacturers, pharmaceuticals, detergent factories, a flat glass plant, manufactured metals such as steel building-frames and tanks, paper and paper products, food products, electric storage battery plants, nickel mining and processing facilities, paints and varnishes, cotton and jute-bag plants, light bulbs, radio and television assembly facilities.

79. Occasionally Denmark, New Zealand, and Australia have been cited as instances of countries which are primarily agricultural, but have attained high income levels without resorting to deliberate industrialization. Yet, because it overlooks the interpenetration of the agricultural and industrial sectors within the European culture area, the contention would not seem to be very germane to the situation of many underdeveloped agricultural economies.

80. A particularly serious source of difficulty in this regard was the widespread resort to multiple exchange-rate systems, for in view of the great relative importance of foreign trade to the total pattern of domestic activity in most Latin American economies, the consequences for the pricing of imports and exports have meant, in effect, the mixing or scrambling of the signals and indicators which foreign trade could provide for the domestic allocation of resources.

81. Even in Chile, where political life has been more orderly than in most of the other countries, the 1965 congressional elections which gave the Christian Democratic Party a majority in the lower house represented a landmark in political development. For the first time, a single party succeeded in attaining a majority position. Previously, as in other countries, the exigencies of shifting coalitions had done much to hinder development of consistent policies which could be applied for any substantial length of time.

82. The efficacy of public policy must also be judged in the light of the widespread and deeply engrained tradition of evasion of the law and even, on occasion, open defiance of the law by powerful groups adversely affected by various public

policies. When, for example, in 1964 the Chilean government imprisoned a person for tax evasion, this was the first instance of such action in modern Latin American history.

83. The case is much less certain, however, if one considers the possible public investment options in infrastructure; but since in the short run there have been encountered substantial difficulties in shifting resources from the private sector to the public sector, the opportunity-cost argument might be justifiable in rearranging resource use within the private sector.

84. In this, domestic industrialization was a more powerful agent of change than conventional foreign investments, for the latter being often land-based (i.e., export-oriented plantation agriculture or mining) and utilizing cheap undifferentiated labor, tended to fit into the traditional pattern of society much more than has industry. That nineteenth-century foreign investment evolved its own specialized set of auxiliary institutions which were geared in the main to serving the export, extractive sector rather than the domestic economy at large was also a probable factor in minimizing the disturbance of local power arrangements. Only slowly did the impact of enclaves affect the domestic alignments of social groups, at least as compared with twentieth-century industrialization.

85. Both of these financing institutions had lent a large portion of their credit resources to projects in Latin American countries, as did other international lending agencies, and the chief restriction against still larger lending activity appears to have been the lack of sound projects rather than any insufficiency of loan capital. For this reason the United States was not receptive until the late 1950's to Latin American proposals for creating a special regional bank for Latin America (an idea which had first been considered around 1940 but which had been dropped with the outbreak of World War II).

86. An especially lucid analysis of the discriminatory treatment of agriculture is found in the essay by Markos Mamalakis in Markos Mamalakis and Clark Reynolds, *Essays on the Chilean Economy,* Homewood, Ill.: Richard D. Irwin, Inc., 1965.

87. For all its deficiencies, the Bolivian revolution has, by changing the rural pattern of income distribution in a more egalitarian direction, produced a notable diversification of the occupational structure in provincial towns and cities, giving an impetus both to artisan employment in such traditional lines as hats and clothing and to new trades such as bicycle servicing.

88. The experience in this regard would appear to confirm the intervening opportunity hypothesis which, in a somewhat different statement, has been employed to account for the large-scale exodus of rural Negroes from the southern United States to the principal northern cities.

89. The migration of the poor to the primate cities has also strengthened investor preference for urban rental properties, since the migrants, being unable to purchase shelter outright and likewise unable to obtain low-cost, long-term loans for home construction or purchase, must perforce either seek out lands on which to settle as squatters or else rent substandard accommodations at what are relatively high rents (a phenomenon which is, of course, familiar in the United States).

90. While the direction of industrial evolution implied the need for a substantial rise in the savings and investment ratios in national income, concurrent inflationary pressures encouraged domestic capital flights and discouraged voluntary savings, thereby adding to the difficulty of maintaining capital formation rates at requisite levels.

91. While indirect export taxation (either explicit, as through customs levies, or concealed, as in multiple exchange rates) has been employed as a substitute for direct taxation for reasons of administrative convenience, the result has been different from a general system of direct taxation of business income in that the tax burden falls mainly on only certain categories of income-producing activities — i.e., the export industries which operate in competitive overseas markets — and thus constitutes a disincentive to investment in these lines relative to other alternatives (such as the more lightly taxed producers selling to the domestic market).

92. The lengthy gestation periods of some of the infrastructure projects have, of

course, created a lag between the injection through investment expenditures of new purchasing power into the economy and the subsequent increase in real output. With the high propensity to consume that commonly prevails, the result has often been a further stimulus to inflation which, with controlled exchange rates, has tended to impair export expansion.

93. In this connection, the appeals for international commodity price support schemes would appear to represent an effort to shift the burden of support for exporting interests to foreign consumers.

94. The chaotic situation in Ecuador affords a particularly revealing insight into the cumbersome nature of contemporary tax systems. There, most revenue has been raised by indirect taxes, with several distinct taxes applicable to a substantial number of commodities. Moreover, a considerable resort was had, until recently, to earmarked taxes, since over the years, the government, in the course of expanding its functions, has established several hundred special agencies outside the regular administrative apparatus and has allocated certain taxes to these independent entities as their patrimony for carrying out their particular functions. Few of the agencies, however, were equipped to collect these tax revenues; so parallel to their creation there came into being a system of tax farming, the agencies' auctioning off to private groups (including the families and associates of agency directors) the right to collect the assigned taxes. There is reason to believe that, not uncommonly, the auction price of the tax-farming privilege returned to the agencies less than half of the revenue collected, the tax farmers pocketing the major share. In any case the dispersion of the tax system has left the central government with as little as a half or less of the total tax revenue collected. When in 1964 the central government attempted direct collection of these special taxes and moved to subject the autonomous agencies to central budgetary and administrative control, it ran into conflict with the powerful independent agencies of Guayaquil, the nation's chief port. After an incipient revolt and a goodly number of arrests, a compromise was reached permitting the central government to collect taxes and exercise general budgetary control but not administrative control.

95. As recently as the early 1960's, for example, a survey of some of the largest landholders in central Chile revealed that for the sample group as a whole consumption expenditures accounted for 83.6 per cent of disposable income. Yet even this high figure was misleading because in one of the sample cases (that of a prosperous immigrant) consumption was only 11 per cent of disposable income. Eliminating this exceptional case, the mean value of the consumption function was 94.2 per cent, while the median level of consumption was 99 per cent of disposable income! See Marvin J. Sternberg, "Chilean Land Tenure and Land Reform," Berkeley: University of California, unpublished doctoral thesis in agricultural economics, 1962, pp. 74-84.

96. The failures of conventional banking along this line have been revealed by recent innovations in the field of credit unions and popular savings-and-loan associations, both of which suggest strongly that the savings function may well be institution-elastic as well as elastic with respect to income.

97. It has not been unusual that little improvement in the situation followed the creation of government banks. In Chile, as in many other countries, the state bank for agriculture benefited mainly those who were already the beneficiaries of private banking credit, while the Peruvian state industrial bank for years was forced to operate with very small resources.

98. This feature of the system has, it should be recognized, doubly distorted the capital allocation process. In the first place, the presence of monopoly power has meant that relative profitability has not necessarily reflected relative efficiency. In the second place, the availability of investable funds to particular users of those funds has had no necessary correspondence to their capacity to use them to increase real output. Yet, as was noted in an earlier chapter, in the absence of reliable, impersonal transactional controls, there has been an understandable reluctance on the part of the holders of investable funds to channel them through the market to others who might use them. The consequent preference for keeping such funds under personal scrutiny — e.g., through reinvestment in the same or some closely associated line of production — has clearly

inhibited the inter-firm, inter-industry, and inter-sectoral movement of capital.

99. Typical in this regard is the case of Colombia where approximately half the population is rural. According to recent estimates, less than 1 per cent of Colombian students attend a university and fewer still actually graduate. To enter a university, it is necessary first to have been graduated from a preparatory school and there only about a thousand of these in the entire country. Moreover, over 30 per cent of them are located in Botogá while over 80 per cent of the preparatory schools are located in either the national capital or departmental capitals. Seldom, then, do people in the rural areas or provincial towns get to attend the preporatory schools unless they have had the requisite previous schooling and can afford to attend as boarding students. Rarely is either of these conditions met, as poverty precludes the latter while the available evidence seems to indicate that the majority of rural children who do attend school do so for no more than two or three years.

100. For a typical observation concerning the effects of educational policy on industrialization, namely, the shortage of foremen and competent skilled laborers, see W. D. Galbraith, *Colombia: A General Survey,* London: Oxford University Press, 1953, pp. 111-112.

101. It is possibly for the reverse of this reason that the general availability of education in Uruguay has been greater than in most other countries of Latin America. With its broader distribution of income, the consequent greater correspondence between the distribution of costs and the distribution of benefits has made for a much stronger social incentive to invest in public education. At the same time, however, the advanced degree of urbanization in Uruguay facilitated the program, while the influence of heavy European immigration undoubtedly fortified popular demands for educational services.

102. See also the examples of inefficient management cited in William Glade, "Social Backwardness, Social Reform, and Productivity in Latin America," *Inter-American Economic Affairs,* Vol. 15, No. 3 (Winter 1961), and ECLA, *Labour Productivity of the Cotton Textile Industry in Five Latin-American Countries,* New York: United Nations, Department of Economic and Social Affairs, 1951.

103. Indeed, for this reason (i.e., to absorb inefficiencies) as well as to lower the real burden of accumulated fixed overhead charges, it seems likely that private businesses have at times viewed inflation with some favor. Moreover, given the insufficiency of primary deposits as a source of loanable funds, the use of bank credit creation as a means of raising capital in lieu of placing securities on the stock exchanges has tended, by expanding the money supply, to foster inflation, while at the same time it has, by its effect on the position of business borrowers, given the business community the debtor's interest in currency depreciation.

104. Differential enforcement of labor-law provisions is a notorious feature of the Latin American scene, although governments have generally tended to enforce the provisions forthrightly in the case of foreign concerns as a means of establishing more control over external sector relationships without offending any part of the domestic constituency.

105. The same circumstances, of course, often had the effect of divorcing labor returns in selected industries from productivity levels and in so doing distorted the allocational pattern in the deployment of labor resources, creating privileged high-wage groups in the midst of extensive unemployment and underemployment. Moreover, the legalistic approach to labor relations, oblivious of the economic and social implications of the case, has produced a variety of social and labor programs which are ill-designed to provide incentives for productivity.

For example, since under some systems the discharging of workers after a certain term of employment involves a considerable number of formalities, the practice has been to discharge automatically most workers before the legally fixed period of employment security has elapsed. In other instances, the obligation to provide maternity benefits at company expense has hindered the employment demand for women. Where the legal provisions are such that unionization is authorized only in plants over a certain minimum size, there is some evidence that manufacturers have reacted by scattering their operations among several plants, each nominally established as a separate entity and each under the legally fixed minimum size — a situation which, of course, inhibits the rationalization and coordination of production processes and tends to increase overhead costs.

106. A masterly résumé of the Argentine political predicament is to be found in James W. Rowe, "Argentina's Durable Peronists: A Twentieth Anniversary Note," *American Universities Field Staff Reports Service,* East Coast South America Series, Vol. 12, No. 2 (April 1966).

107. Roberto de Oliveira Campos, "Inflation and Balanced Growth," in H. S. Ellis and H. C. Wallich, eds., *Economic Development for Latin America,* New York: St. Martin's Press, 1961, pp. 82-103. For a recent summary of thinking on the subject of inflation in Latin America, see Werner Baer and Isaac Kerstenetzky, eds. *Inflation and Growth in Latin America,* Homewood, Ill.: Richard D. Irwin, Inc., 1964, especially the papers presented by Seers, Grunwald, and Felix. One of the most comprehensive analyses of the problem is Denis Lambert, *Les inflations sud-américaines, inflation de sous-développement et inflation de croissance,* Paris: Institut des Hautes Etudes de L'Amérique Latine, 1959, while also of great value is Ronald A. Krieger, "Inflation Propagation in Argentina: A Short-Run Dynamic Analysis," unpublished doctoral thesis in economics, Madison: University of Wisconsin, 1965.

108. The following ECLA studies are representative of this new trend in thinking, which grew directly out of the logic of the case for import substitution industrialization: *Study of Inter-Latin American Trade and Its Prospects: Southern Zone of Latin America,* United Nations: 1953; *Study of Inter-Latin American Trade,* United Nations: 1956; *Inter-Latin American Trade · Current Problems,* United Nations: 1957, *Some Problems of the Latin American Regional Market,* Santiago de Chile: 1958; *Consultations on Trade Policy; Summary Record of Meetings Held at the ECLA Headquarters,* Santiago de Chile: 1958; *The Latin American Common Market,* United Nations: 1959. Also see the joint ECLA — FAO publications: *The Role of Agricultural Products in a Regional Market,* Santiago de Chile: 1959, and *The Role of Agriculture in the Latin American Common Market and Free-Trade Area Arrangements,* Santiago de Chile: 1961.

109. While LAFTA participation might theoretically mitigate inflationary pressures, it is at least as likely, considering the social sources of inflation in Latin America, that inflation will restrict participation in LAFTA.

110. Article 23 of the Treaty of Montevideo. Further special concessions were provided the poorer countries, while countries in general were authorized to slow down liberalization if an import deficit should develop (or to accelerate liberalization if an export surplus should develop) — an approach which carries interesting implications for the rewards for efficiency and the penalties for inefficiency. Moreover, even wider escape clauses were provided for agricultural items.

The emphasis on reciprocity, which ran strongly throughout the LAFTA negotiations, appears mainly to be concerned with reciprocity in results rather than reciprocity in opportunities, an aspect which restricts the gains to be realized by those participating members which move ahead more rapidly in developing efficient industries, in adopting more realistic exchange rates, and the like. The escape clauses, for example, would require adjustments to be made when, as a result of such developments (or say, inflation in other member countries), the more progressive members should succeed in developing LAFTA export surpluses. It may be added, of course, that the Treaty's emphasis on maintaining an equilibrium of trade within the area seems inappropriate for a scheme which operates on the basis of a system of convertible currencies.

111. Certain tariff concessions were to be determined by each country independently, creating the so-called National Schedules of Concessions, which, accordingly, would vary in composition from country to country. Other concessions, which were to be made on a collective basis, would constitute a Common Schedule. Since, however, the countries remained free to vary their duties on imports from nonmember countries, concessions granted at any particular stage of the scheme's evolution would not necessarily provide an adequate measure of the degree of preference accorded intra-LAFTA trade at a later date. Moreover, the treaty permits concessions to take the form of either a reduction of the duties applied to intra-LAFTA trade or an increase in the duties

applied to trade with nonmember nations. Complicating the problem further, particular tariff cuts granted on the National Schedules may later be withdrawn and replaced by an equivalent concession on some other product.

　　While every country is obliged to eliminate, by the end of the period, charges on goods added to the Common Schedule, whether or not it had previously imported such goods from another LAFTA member, the rate at which the tariffs on commodities in the Common Schedule were to be reduced throughout the period was not determined.

　　112. For a brief discussion of some of the complications introduced by divergent fiscal and monetary policies, see Raul Branco, "Brazilian Finances and Their Implication for Economic Integration," *Inter-American Economic Affairs,* Vol. 19, No. 2 (Autumn 1965), pp. 87-97.

　　113. Helpful for an insight into current proposals for a reform of LAFTA are: Raúl Prébisch, *Towards a Dynamic Development Policy for Latin America,* United Nations: 1964; "Declaración Conjunta de los Presidentes de Brasil y Chile," *Comercio Exterior* (Mexico), Vol. 13, No. 5 (May 1963), pp. 316-317; Victor L. Urquidi, *Free Trade and Economic Integration in Latin America,* Berkeley: University of California Press, 1962; Miguel S. Wionczek, ed., *Integración de América Latina, experiencias y perspectivas,* Mexico: Fondo de Cultura Económica, 1964; and José Antonio Mayobre et al., *Hacia la integración acelerada de América Latina,* Mexico: Fondo de Cultura Económica, 1965.

　　114. The nine countries which have been participating are Argentina, Brazil, Chile, Colombia, Ecuador, Mexico, Paraguay, Peru, and Uruguay.

　　115. Within the past two years, for example, there has been a notable growth of industrial complementarity agreements coming out of the industrial sectoral meetings sponsored by LAFTA and attended by Latin American entrepreneurs.

　　116. Bolivia, which was originally a party to the treaty negotiations, withdrew for fear that it would not benefit much from the integration scheme.

　　117. S. S. Dell, *Problemas de un mercado común en América Latina,* Mexico: Centro de Estudios Monetarios Latinoamericanos, 1959, p. 160.

　　118. See also the exposition of other problems in mobilizing broad support for LAFTA which are discussed in the thoughtful work by Miguel S. Wionczek, *Latin American Free Trade Association,* New York: Carnegie Endowment for International Peace, 1965, pp. 52-62.

　　119. Ernest Feder, "Some Reflections on Latin America's Common Market," *The American Journal of Economics and Sociology,* Vol. 20, No. 4 (July 1961), p. 437. Feder deserves special credit for being one of the first analysts to call attention to concerns which have since spread rather widely among the more articulate reform-minded groups in Latin America.

NOTES FOR CHAPTER XIII

　　1. Useful for a survey of conditions in prerevolutionary Cuba are IBRD, *Report on Cuba,* Washington, D.C., 1950; Lowry Nelson, *Rural Cuba,* Minneapolis: University of Minnesota Press, 1950; and Henry C. Wallich, *Monetary Problems of an Export Economy,* Cambridge: Harvard University Press, 1950. For an early evaluation of revolutionary consequences, see Dudley Seers et al., *Cuba: The Economic and Social Revolution,* Chapel Hill: University of North Carolina Press, 1964.

　　2. An enthusiastic view of the Bolivian scene is presented in Robert Alexander, *The Bolivian National Revolution,* New Brunswick, N. J.: Rutgers University Press, 1958. For insight into more recent developments in that country, the author is indebted to the Land Tenure Center of the University of Wisconsin, which has sponsored a number of studies of contemporary Bolivian conditions.

　　3. United Nations, Technical Assistance Administration, *Report of the United Nations Mission of Technical Assistance to Bolivia,* United Nations: 1951, pp. 45-49.

4. *Ibid.*, pp. 89-109; Comisión Mixta Boliviana – Estadounidense del Trabajo, *Los problemas del trabajo en Bolivia,* Montreal: ILO, 1943.

5. For an introduction into the Peruvian version of these ideas, see Victor Raúl Haya de la Torre, *Treinta años de aprismo,* Mexico: Fondo de Cultura Económica, 1956, and Jesús Véliz Lizárraga, *Principios fundamentales del aprismo,* Lima: Instituto de Estudios Apristas, 1956.

6. Daniel Cosío Villegas, *Change in Latin America: The Mexican and Cuban Revolutions,* Lincoln: University of Nebraska Press, 1961, p. 25.

7. Much of the material which follows draws heavily upon research published previously in William Glade, *Las empresas gubernamentales descentralizadas,* Mexico: Problemas Agrícolas e Industriales de México, Vol. 11, No. 1, 1959; and William Glade, "Revolution and Economic Development: A Mexican Reprise," in W. Glade and Charles W. Anderson, *The Political Economy of Mexico,* Madison: The University of Wisconsin Press, 1963. In addition to the references cited in those works, see also: Raymond Vernon, editor, *Public Policy and Private Enterprise in Mexico,* Cambridge: Harvard University Press, 1964, for particularly informative essays by Miguel Wionczek, David Shelton, Calvin Blair, and Rafael Izquierdo; and Frank Brandenburg, *The Making of Modern Mexico,* Englewood Cliffs, New Jersey: Prentice-Hall, Inc., 1964, which is helpful for its insight into the behind-the-scenes working of the political system and its presentation of the private sector's organization and points of view.

As the Brandenburg study indicates, the directing groups in the Mexican Revolution have not been exempt from internal dissent and factionalism, particularly up to the Cárdenas period of the thirties. Nevertheless, dissention within the so-called Revolutionary family was in large measure counterbalanced by an at least equal degree of internal division among the opposition. For a well-documented view of this generally less appreciated aspect of Mexican development, see J. W. Wilkie, "The Meaning of the Cristero Religious War Against the Mexican Revolution," *Journal of Church and State,* Vol. 8, No. 2 (Spring 1966), pp. 214-233.

8. Besides the sources cited in the preceding note, the reader should consult the valuable study by Charles W. Anderson, "Bankers as Revolutionaries: Politics and Development Banking in Mexico," in W. Glade and C. W. Anderson, *op. cit.,* which deals with the growth of development banking as an aspect of the exercise of political authority and the use of credit as a political sanction. The importance of governmental institutions, especially the nonmonetary intermediaries, in effecting both a rapid quantitative change in the financial sector's assets and qualitative changes in the distribution of those assets during the early years of the development effort is strongly suggested by the research of Robert L. Bennett in his excellent work, *The Financial Sector and Economic Development: The Mexican Case,* Baltimore: The Johns Hopkins Press, 1965.

9. Interestingly, as early as 1925, the government of Calles had begun to urge a policy of management-labor cooperation as a means of restoring strength to the national economy, and in the same year, the important Federation of Labor Syndicates of the Federal District, an affiliate of C.R.O.M. (then the principal labor confederation), supported the policy on the grounds that it would reduce the high cost of manufacturing and encourage the entrance of foreign capital. *The United States Department of State Records Relating to the Internal Affairs of Mexico: 1910 to 1929* (microfilm), 812.504/696.

10. For an interesting study of Nacional Financiera's role and an examination of the question regarding the degree to which that institution's backing has been essential to the success of individual industrial firms, see Robert T. Aubey, *Nacional Financiera and Mexican Industry,* Los Angeles: University of California, Latin American Center, 1966. One of the especially critical areas of governmental industrial promotion has been the iron and steel industry, a detailed analysis of which is found in William E. Cole, *Steel and Economic Growth in Mexico,* Austin: The University of Texas Press, 1967.

11. At times, U.S. policy, such as domestic crop support practices, helped the development of Mexican exports (e.g., cotton) by bolstering world market prices. Moreover, the comparative ease of smuggling goods across the northern frontier may have

helped in restraining Mexican industrial development from some of the excesses which have characterized protected infant industries in others of the Latin American countries. A comprehensive analysis of Mexican export policy is to be found in William O. Freithaler, *Mexico's Foreign Trade and Economic Development,* New York: Frederick A. Praeger, 1968.

12. Robert Bennett, *op. cit.,* pp. 112-118.

13. Dwight S. Brothers and Leopoldo Solís M., *Mexican Financial Development,* Austin: The University of Texas Press, 1966, p. 48. Additional insight into the evolution of crucial financial institutions is provided in Raymond W. Goldsmith, *The Financial Development of Mexico,* Paris: Organization for Economic Cooperation and Development, 1966.

14. A superbly written recent study of this evolution is Robert J. Shafer, *Mexico: Mutual Adjustment Planning,* Syracuse: Syracuse University Press, 1966. Shafer's work also provides a judiciously balanced appraisal of a number of the more prominent development policy issues in Mexico.

15. The concept of a "mobilization system" a structure which Mexico has had but which most other Latin American countries have yet to develop effectively, is one of the many useful contributions to development analysis contained in David E. Apter, *The Politics of Modernization,* Chicago: University of Chicago Press, 1965.

16. It is very much to the point to observe that the Revolutionary constitution of 1917, by departing from the individualistic conceptual framework of earlier constitutions, set up what amounted to a loose plan for institution building and socio-economic integration. In it the intermediary social groupings and corporate interests which had remained beyond the scope of earlier constitutions were explicitly recognized as composing the basis and fabric of society, and the state was assigned a tutelary role in guiding the formation of such interests. For a useful discussion of the changed juridical relationships between individuals and the state under the new constitutional dispensation, see Alberto Trueba Urbina, *Qué es una constitución político-social?,* Mexico: Librería Herrero Editorial, 1954. Also helpful is Carlos Roman Celis, *El estado administrativo como forma política del mundo moderno,* Mexico: Universidad Nacional Autónoma de México, Facultad de Derecho, 1956.

17. Inasmuch as the land reform affected rural, but not urban properties, a number of the wealthy landowning families from Porfirian and earlier times retained a portion of their economic base but thenceforth were obliged to repair their fortunes through participation in the development of the urban sector of the economy. An example is provided in the Sánchez-Navarro family which, in post-revolutionary times, has made its way in the brewery industry of Mexico City as well as in various other financial and commercial pursuits.

18. George F. Kneller, *The Education of the Mexican Nation,* New York: Columbia University Press, 1951. As a consequence of efforts to implement the Revolutionary slogan, *educar es redimir,* the exposure to forces of cultural change has been vastly increased. Although the aggregate expenditure on education has increased. the per capita expenditure has not risen very rapidly, and it is probable that the country has "underinvested" in this field. Even so, a generally favorable judgment is made regarding Mexico's educational policy in Charles N. Myers, *Education and National Development in Mexico,* Princeton: Princeton University Press, 1965.

19. Additional evidence of the comparative stability of the system is provided by the relatively low rate of inflation which has accompanied the transformation of the Mexican economy in recent years – a phenomenon attributable as much to the reduction in interclass and intersectoral conflicts as to the efficiency of the fiscal system and the supply elasticity of the production sector. It might also be noted that the extent of mass loyalty gained through agrarian reform, labor and social legislation, and other measures has enabled the country to save considerably on its military expenditures. For information on federal expenditure patterns, see the extraordinarily useful study by James W. Wilkie, *The Mexican Revolution: Federal Expenditure and Social Change since 1910,* Berkeley: The University of California Press, 1967. Wilkie's study is supplemented by Secretaría de la Presidencia, Dirección de

Inversiones Públicas, *México: inversión pública federal, 1925-1963,* Mexico: 1964.

20. The possible losses of foreign capital should not, however, be exaggerated. At the time, international capital movements were declining anyhow because of conditions in the metropolitan economies, while foreign investment in certain sectors (e.g., manufacturing) related to internal Mexican development was actually increasing.

21. In effect, the range of interventionary policies tended (for domestic investment processes) to reduce the influence of uncontrollable exogenous variables relative to the more controllable endogenous variables. The higher level of national capital formation also, of course, provided an enhanced capability for directing supporting capital outlays into a greater variety of development possibilities.

22. By upgrading the quality and increasing the quantity of such resources as skilled labor and management, the policies of the Revolutionary governments increased the adaptive capacity of the economy; for once a growth momentum had been built up, it became easier to shift resources about than it was in earlier stages when inexperienced management and unskilled labor predominated and when foreign capital figured more prominently. For a summary view of the extent of labor mobility which has occurred, see Laura Randall, "Labor Migration and Mexican Economic Development," *Social and Economic Studies,* Vol. 11, No. 1 (March 1962), pp. 73-81.

23. Ralph L. Beals, "Some Value Changes in Modern Mexico," in Robert A. Manners, ed., *Process and Pattern in Culture,* Chicago: Aldine Publishing Company, 1964, pp. 326-336, indicates the spread of modern values in Mexico: e.g., the greater value assigned to instrumental education, the faith in science and reason, the higher value placed on initiative and enterprise, and the reduced inclination to accept authority unquestioningly. The new range of socially valued occupations and the facility of social mobility were also remarked by Beals. Significantly, by the late 1950's, the number of students pursuing technical and scientific curricula in higher education exceeded the number in humanities, law, and the arts. Frederick Harbison and Charles A. Myers, *Education, Manpower, and Economic Growth,* New York: McGraw-Hill Book Company 1964, p. 47.

24. See the brief and incisive treatment of these aspects of socialization in Manning Nash, "Social Prerequisites to Economic Growth in Latin America and Southeast Asia," *Economic Development and Cultural Change,* Vol. 12, No. 3 (April 1964), pp. 225-242.

25. In interviews with corporate officials from a number of large U. S. companies having interests in Mexico and other Latin American countries, the view was frequently expressed that, although official Mexican technicians often take a more rigorous or "tougher" position regarding the "defense of national interests" in their dealings with foreign investors, their greater economic competence and sophistication and their ability to manage national economic affairs successfully make Mexico a more attractive investment site than many countries which are overtly more receptive to foreign capital.

26. Charles E. Lindblom, *The Intelligence of Democracy,* New York: The Free Press, 1965.

27. It is relevant to note, in this connection, that the as yet unpublished research by Richard U. Miller on the Mexican industrial relations system appears to indicate a growing importance of the collective bargaining process in the resolution of industrial disputes. While the Mexican labor movement is still not without its political aspects, it has grown less politicized in its instrumental operations, and political activity has tended to recede to a more ceremonial position. To a degree which is impressive when contrasted with the more immature labor-management relations in the general run of Latin American countries, the Mexican system has been able to begin to realize some of the benefits of the "industrial goodwill" of which John R. Commons wrote. For a thoughtful view of the Chilean system for managing industrial conflict, which is more typical of the general state of affairs in Latin America, see James O. Morris, "Consensus, Ideology, and Labor Relations," *Journal of Inter-American Studies,* Vol. 7, No. 3 (July 1965), pp. 301-315.

28. A particularly useful compilation of statistical time series and other information on Mexican economic growth is Nacional Financiera, *La economía mexicana en cifras,*

Mexico: 1965. Also helpful is the collection of essays by Enrique Pérez López and others, *Mexico's Recent Economic Growth: the Mexican View,* Austin: The University of Texas Press, 1967.

29. Additional assistance had been forthcoming through the FAO, the ILO, the IMF, the OAS, and other international agencies.

30. An illuminating portrayal of the social conditions prevailing at the time of the Act of Bogotá is contained in ECLA, "Social Development of Latin America in the Post-War Period," Santiago: ECLA (mimeographed report), 15 April 1964.

31. Although it has sometimes been alleged that the policies formulated in this period, and continued in the Alliance for Progress, were conducive to statism and inimical to private enterprise, a study of the policy documents themselves and of such reports as are available on the actual deliberations of the conferences, does not seem to support the contention. More accurately, it may be said that the dominant themes which informed the policy framework were fairly sophisticated in recognizing that private enterprise is a form of organization which is contingent upon other aspects of the institutional milieu. Its viability is, therefore, conditioned by the context in which it functions. The new policies, in essence, aimed at institutional reforms (necessarily involving a great deal of governmental action) which would create an environment in which private initiative could play a more constructive role than it had in the past.

32. During the period in which the Alliance was being set up, for example, the United States negotiators agreed to participate in the coffee scheme, indicated interest in joining a similar agreement on tin, and consented, in principle, to lend support to establishing a multimillion dollar fund for stabilizing export earnings. In addition, U.S. officials promised to intercede for Latin America in Europe to try to prevent discrimination against Latin American exports.

33. Among the aspects of rural development contemplated were tax policies affecting land use, land reclamation and resettlement projects, the improvement of agricultural marketing and supervised credit systems, the expansion of agricultural research and extension systems, farm-to-market road building programs, and land redistribution programs.

34. The necessity for redistributing already appropriated lands was admitted in an oblique recognition that the magnitude of nineteenth-century land transfers was such that the resettlement of farmers on the public domain was only a partial answer to the agrarian problem. On the one hand, the evidence was unchallengeable that a great deal of the occupied land was being exploited in a socially inefficient manner; on the other, the lands which remained in the public domain were often marginal or submarginal (either for natural or locational reasons or because of the scarcity of capital for extensive land clearing, road construction, and the other elements of colonization schemes). The Alliance also called for the integration of the indigenous population into national life, another feature of Mexican experience.

35. The proposal for reducing military spending was initiated by Chile and Costa Rica on the grounds that the United States armed forces, in effect, shielded the hemisphere and made local military establishments redundant.

36. Concurrently, the United States indicated its intention of increasing the surplus food shipments to Latin America.

37. The overall target was a 2.5 per cent annual increase in per capita income, with a broader distribution of the national income and a rise in the savings rate. Among the other ten-year targets were: facilities for six years of free and compulsory schooling for all children, an adult education program to "alphabetize" some fifty million adult illiterates, a 50 per cent reduction in the child mortality rate and the eradication of malaria, and the provision of potable water and sanitation systems for 70 per cent of the urban and 50 per cent of the rural population.

38. In a somewhat ambiguous context, it was suggested that the less developed countries would receive preferential treatment in the allocation of U.S. government funds.

39. One section of the Punta del Este Declaration urged mutual aid among the

Latin American nations, wherever possible, and in recent times (e.g., the development consortium organized to assist Ecuador) the Inter-American Development Bank has occasionally been able to secure the participation of Latin American countries in group efforts for others of the Alliance members.

40. The Council was also to assist in improving country plans.

41. Argentina, Brazil, Chile, and Mexico led the opposition on the grounds that (a) the proposed review board constituted an infringement of their sovereignty, (b) each country should have the right to determine its own needs, and (c) individual countries should not be denied the right to engage in direct bilateral negotiations with foreign lending institutions.

42. In Guatemala, Honduras, Nicaragua, Panama, and Paraguay, for example, the success in increasing the value of exports was considerably greater than in the region as a whole.

43. According to the IMF, *International Financial Statistics* and the U.N., *Demographic Yearbook*, from which the Latin American statistics were derived, the per capita capacity to import almost doubled between 1948 and 1963 for the Middle Eastern countries, while the corresponding change for Asia (excluding Japan) was approximately a 40 per cent rise.

44. ECLA, *The Latin American Economy in 1965; Excerpt from a Survey*, United Nations: 1966, p. 5.

45. It could be questioned, of course, whether the initial target rate of growth set in the Punta del Este conference was sufficient to ameliorate the problem of disguised and overt unemployment.

46. Albert Waterston, *Development Planning, Lessons of Experience*, Baltimore: The Johns Hopkins Press, 1965, p. 100.

47. With a fair degree of regularity, for example, the organized trade union movements of the hemisphere have remarked their exclusion from significant participation in the formation of public policy. The public information aspect, recommended as an important feature in development strategy as early as the IBRD country report on Nicaragua, might have performed at least four useful functions: (1) that of diffusing knowledge on prospective investment and job opportunities, (2) that of detecting the felt needs of the population and incorporating these into the development program, (3) that of mobilizing popular support for politically difficult reforms, and (4) that of feeding back field reactions to the planning agencies to guide the modification of development programs.

48. For the most recent and thorough study of the agricultural situation, the reader should consult the series of studies made by the Inter-American Committee on Agricultural Development.

49. For an especially valuable contribution to the understanding of agricultural modernization and its implications for factor use in an underdeveloped setting, see Morton Paglin, "'Surplus' Agricultural Labor and Economic Development," *American Economic Review*, Vol. 55, No. 4 (September 1965), pp. 815-834. Much of the analysis which Paglin develops for the Indian case seems equally applicable to many parts of Latin America.

50. Walter Krause, *The United States and Latin America: The Alliance for Progress Program*, Austin: The University of Texas, Bureau of Business Research, 1963, pp. 17, 23, 33.

51. *Ibid.*, p. 9. Later on (on p. 19), agrarian reform, labor legislation, and fiscal reform were also added to the so-called reform-redistribution-welfare category, although initially they were identified in the study as "economic" goals. The confusion, of course, results from the attempt to make rather artificial distinctions in programs which are inherently multidimensional. While, for example, an improved industrial relations system and a strengthened trade union movement relate to productivity objectives, they also relate to socialization objectives by diffusing material progress and nonmaterial welfare elements more widely.

52. S. H. Frankel, *The Economic Impact on Under-developed Societies*, Oxford: Basil Blackwell, 1953, pp. 18-19.

53. For its insight into a similar area of economic relationships, another especially

creative experiment in institutional innovation merits mention. Following the suggestion of the late Jorge Ahumada, the Banco del Estado of Chile began a program to encourage popular savings by setting up branch offices in low-income districts where the established private commercial banks had reckoned that there was little or no ability to save. More or less concurrently, the government had approached domestic bicycle manufacturers to encourage the production of economy-model bicycles. The manufacturers expressed little interest, however, in the belief (unsubstantiated by any market research) that there was no market for such vehicles. To elicit production of the bicycles, the Banco del Estado then placed a large order for the bicycles and assumed the full risks of marketing them, while at the same time it announced that depositors maintaining a certain balance in their savings accounts at the new branches would be eligible to buy the bicycles. Savings increased to unanticipated levels, while the successful sale of the bicycles demonstrated to private "enterprise" the existence of a segment of the vehicle market they had customarily ignored.

Index

16-19
23 ✓
25 ✓
9 5 ✓
97
105-07
110
129
134
139
145
153
155
158
167
170
173
175
184
245
268
286
317
365
381
363
414
443
448

105
109
111
114
115
135
139
339
350
356
360